LORD GREY

1764–1845

LORD GREY

1764–1845

E. A. Smith

CLARENDON PRESS · OXFORD

1990

Oxford University Press, Walton Street, Oxford OX2 6DP

Oxford New York Toronto
Delhi Bombay Calcutta Madras Karachi
Petaling Jaya Singapore Hong Kong Tokyo
Nairobi Dar es Salaam Cape Town
Melbourne Auckland
and associated companies in
Berlin Ibadan

Oxford is a trade mark of Oxford University Press

Published in the United States
by Oxford University Press, New York

British Library Cataloguing in Publication Data
Smith, E. A.
Lord Grey, 1764–1845.
1. Great Britain. Grey, Charles, Earl, 1764–1845
I. Title 941.07′092′4
ISBN 0–19–820163–X

Library of Congress Cataloging in Publication Data
Smith, E. A.
Lord Grey, 1764–1845 / E. A. Smith.
Includes bibliographical references
1. Grey, Charles Grey, Earl, 1764–1845.
2. Great Britain—Politics and government—1800–1837.
3. Great Britain—Politics and
government—1789–1820.
4. Prime ministers—Great Britain—Biography.
I. Title.
DA536.G84S65   1990   941.07′5′092—dc20   [B]
ISBN 0 19–820163–X

Printed in Great Britain
by Butler & Tanner Ltd,
Frome and London

For Virginia

Preface

This is the first biography of Charles, second Earl Grey, since G. M. Trevelyan's study published in 1920. Like its predecessor, it is largely based on the papers of Grey and his family which are now preserved in the Department of Palaeography and Diplomatic of the University of Durham, but it also draws on all the major collections of contemporary papers, in print or in manuscript, which have come to light since Trevelyan's day. Grey is almost the only major British politician of the later eighteenth and early nineteenth centuries, and the only Prime Minister except for the relatively minor figure of the Duke of Portland, who has not hitherto been the subject of a scholarly biography. This neglect may partly be due to the virtual absence of family papers and personal correspondence for the period before 1801, which makes it difficult to assess the development of his character in his childhood and youth, but it may also be the consequence of a tendency to see his career in the light of his role in the passing of the 'Great Reform Act' of 1832, and perhaps to take Grey too readily at his own word in seeing his political life before 1830 as a failure. Yet he was 66 years of age when he became Prime Minister, and the previous 44 years during which he had served in Parliament, and for a very short time in office, were more than merely a preparation for his role as 'Lord Grey of the Reform Bill'. I hope that in this biography I have shown that his political career was of broader significance than has previously been recognized, and I have tried also to suggest that its vicissitudes were related to his complex and often troubled personality. Grey was not an easy man to deal with. He could be abrasive, selfish, and opportunistic in politics, and in private life both a genial host, devoted family man, and yet something of a libertine. He was, however, a man with a deep sense of political rectitude and unquestionable integrity. It is these contradictions that make him an interesting subject.

During the many years that it has taken to write this book I have incurred many debts to the kindness of others. First of all, I am most grateful to Mr J. E. Fagg and his successor Dr J. M. Fewster, the archivists in charge of the Grey papers at Durham, for their unfailing interest and helpfulness, and to their assistants for their exceptionally efficient service during many pleasant visits to Durham. My thanks are also due to the Research Board of the University of Reading for generous assistance with the cost of travel, subsistence, and photocopying of documents during the whole period of my research.

I am indebted to the owners and custodians of the following manuscript collections for their helpfulness and their kind permission to use and to quote from these sources: Althorp MSS (then at Althorp, now in the British Library); Anglesey MSS, Northern Ireland Record Office; Bowood MSS, Bowood; Chatsworth MSS, Chatsworth; Cochrane MSS, National Library of Scotland;

Creevey MSS, Northumberland Record Office: microfilm at University College, London; Croker MSS, Duke University Library, North Carolina; Ellice MSS, National Library of Scotland; Fitzwilliam MSS, Northamptonshire Record Office and Sheffield City Library; Harewood MSS, Leeds City Libraries; Hatherton MSS, Staffordshire Record Office; Hickleton MSS, Garrowby; Holland MSS, Duke University Library; Minto MSS, National Library of Scotland; Newcastle MSS, Nottingham University Library; Ponsonby MSS, University of Durham; Ridley MSS, Northumberland Record Office; Lord John Russell MSS, Duke University Library; Stair MSS, National Library of Scotland; Sutherland MSS, Staffordshire Record Office; Swinburne MSS, Northumberland Record Office; Tankerville MSS, Northumberland Record Office; Tierney MSS, Hampshire Record Office; Wharncliffe MSS, Sheffield City Library; Whitbread MSS, Bedfordshire Record Office; Wyvill MSS, North Yorkshire Record Office; and the following collections in the British Library, British Museum, London: Auckland MSS; Charles James Fox MSS; Holland House MSS; Dropmore MSS; Lauderdale MSS; Melbourne MSS; Wellesley MSS; Willoughby-Gordon MSS; Sir Robert Wilson MSS; Windham MSS.

I have not listed individually the many collections of published printed sources and secondary works from which I have taken information. I trust that the authors and editors of these works will accept the appearance of their titles in the footnotes as an acknowledgement of my gratitude. The full titles and bibliographical details of all printed works are given on their first appearance in the footnotes; on subsequent citation they are abbreviated to save space. A list of abbreviations used in citing certain standard works is given below.

I am most grateful to Professor I. R. Christie, Professor N. Gash, and Dr P. J. Jupp for reading parts of the typescript of this work at various times, and for their helpful comments and suggestions. For what I have written, however, I remain solely responsible.

My late wife, Dr Anne Pallister, read those parts of my manuscript which I had completed before her untimely death, and her wisdom and scholarship contributed greatly to it. Sadly, she did not live to see it completed.

Finally, I thank my wife Virginia for encouraging and helping me to finish this book and for suggesting many improvements.

E.A.S.

Dove Cottage, Westcott, Dorking
April, 1989

Contents

List of Plates   x

List of Abbreviations   xi

Introduction   1

I. 1764–1807

1. Political Apprenticeship, 1764–1792   7
2. The Commitment to Reform, 1792–1802   36
3. The Road to Leadership, 1802–1807   83

II. 1807–1845

4. The Lessons of Experience, 1807–1815   135
5. Whigs out of Place, 1810–1830   190
6. Prime Minister, 1830–1834   254
7. Return to Howick, 1834–1845   308

Epilogue   323
Index   329

List of Plates

between pp. 164 and 165

1. Grey addressing the House of Lords during the 'trial' of Queen Caroline, 1820. (National Portrait Gallery, London.)

2. Grey, *c*.1828. (National Portrait Gallery, London.)

3. 'A Parliamentary Group'.

4. Sketch of Grey, 1834. (National Portrait Gallery, London.)

Abbreviations

The following abbreviations have been used throughout this book to indicate the sources mentioned:

Printed sources:

BLT: *The Life and Times of Henry Lord Brougham, written by himself.* 3 vols. 1871.

CGPW: *Correspondence of George, Prince of Wales, 1770–1812*, ed. A. Aspinall, 8 vols. 1963–71.

Eng. Hist. Docs: *English Historical Documents*, gen. ed. D. C. Douglas, 12 vols. 1953–77.

HHD: *The Holland House Diaries, 1831–1840*, ed. A. D. Kriegel, 1977.

HMC: *Historical Manuscripts Commission*, printed reports on the MSS of J. B. Fortescue, Esq. (*Fortescue MSS*), 10 vols. 1892–1927, and of R. R. Hastings, Esq. (*Hastings MSS*), 4 vols. 1928–47.

LCGIII: *Later Correspondence of George III*, ed. A. Aspinall, 5 vols. Cambridge, 1962–70.

Parl. Hist: *The Parliamentary History of England from the earliest period to the year 1803* ... ed. W. Cobbett, 36 vols. 1806–20.

Parl. Deb: *The Parliamentary Debates from the year 1803 to the present time*, ed. T. C. Hansard, 41 vols. 1812–20.

Hansard: *The Parliamentary Debates* ... New Series. 25 vols. 1820–30, and *Hansard's Parliamentary Debates*, 3rd Ser. 1830 ff.

Unless otherwise stated, the place of publication of all printed works is London.

Manuscript sources:

BL Add. MS: Manuscript from the British Library, Additional MSS collection.
G.: Grey MSS, Durham.

Introduction

Monday, 15 September 1834 was a bright, crisp, autumn morning in the city of Edinburgh. From an early hour thousands of citizens and visitors had been pouring on to the streets, jostling for places along the processional route from the eastern entrance to the city, through Leith walk and to the Lord Provost's house at Newington. The upper windows of shops and houses were crowded with spectators, while men and boys clambered on to the leads to find a vantage point. Nothing like it had been seen since the visit of George IV twelve years before. Bands played and banners floated in the breeze as the members of the Edinburgh and Leith trades formed up in full livery and marched to the assembly point in Newington. Among the thirty-three banners of the trades others appeared, specially made for the occasion. Their inscriptions proclaimed 'Our gratitude brings us, in spite of all stratagems, to do honour to the Friend of the People', and exclaimed 'O! Happy Day!' and 'Welcome the Champion of Reform'. A body of fifty or so gentlemen, farmers, and others on horseback rode out of the city to meet a procession of carriages, which they escorted back through the streets at a hand-gallop, slowing to a walk as the crowds pressed round to greet the hero of the day. In the leading carriage, drawn by four grey horses, sat an elderly but slim, erect, and handsome figure, raising his hat to the people and smiling at the attractive, dark-haired woman beside him as she waved to the crowd. The sound of the bells of the city churches ebbed and flowed among the cheers of the people, pressing closer to the carriage. Charles, second Earl Grey, and his Countess were the centre of a public triumph to pay tribute to a life spent, as acclaimed in the speeches of the day and evening, in unremitting dedication to the liberties of the people and crowned by the Great Reform Act.

From Newington the procession took nearly two hours to reach the Waterloo Hotel where the dignitaries dismounted. After changing into their ceremonial robes the Lord Provost, Magistrates, and Council of the City processed into a large room thronged with noblemen, gentlemen, and ladies to present the Freedom of the City in a gold box crowned by the city's arms within a wreath of thistles and ornamented by views of the Castle, Holyrood House, the High School, and other local scenes. A short speech by the Lord Provost mentioned Grey's lifelong dedication to 'the cause of civil and religious liberty', his consistent opposition to the slave-trade, the Test and Corporation Acts, and the Catholic disabilities, but above all his achievement during four years of ministerial office in ending slavery in the British Empire and carrying into effect reform 'in the Church and in every department of the State'. A deputation of the city trades followed with an address, succeeded by similar presentations from Aberdeen, Glasgow, and nearly seventy other towns. After a suitable reply, during which the great statesman was for some time overcome by his emotions, the meeting dispersed and Lord Grey continued on to his hotel, the crowd again pressing close in Princes Street and shaking the hands which he held out from the carriage.

The evening was taken up by a great dinner in a specially prepared pavilion on Calton Hill. Sixteen pillars supported a sloping roof rising from canvas-lined side walls 18 feet high to a central cupola 33 feet above the ground, borne by four columns coloured to represent porphyry and entwined with spirals of laurel wreaths picked out in gold. At each end of the pavilion, 113 feet long, stood platforms raised 3 feet above the floor, above which the arms of Grey and of Scotland faced each other from opposite sides. A ladies' gallery was built over one end, and a corner was railed off for a band who played throughout the dinner. The great crystal chandelier from the Theatre Royal was hung in the centre of the pavilion and, together with four others at the corners, provided a blaze of light equivalent, it was said, to nearly 2,000 wax candles. Counting the 240 ladies in the gallery, it was computed that 2,768 persons were present at this splendid occasion.

Earl Grey, supported by an assemblage of Scottish and English noblemen, gentlemen and dignitaries, entered the pavilion at six o'clock, and the dinner proceeded until the removal of the cloths and the loyal toasts: after which the chairman for the evening, Lord Rosebery, proposed amongst mounting applause the health of the principal guest as a man of 'exalted character ... great talents ... unimpeached and inflexible integrity ... rare political consistency' who had been chiefly responsible by his 'sound advice ... counsel ... perseverance and ... ability' for the crowning glory of his career, the achievement of parliamentary reform. Grey's reply, interrupted by frequent and long bursts of cheering, was appropriate to the occasion:

I desire no better remembrance to posterity, or any other inscription on my tomb, than that I have assisted in restoring to the people of England and Scotland their fair, just, and necessary representation in Parliament ... Let us proceed, then, on the same principles on which Parliamentary reform was founded—namely, in strengthening and preserving all the settled institutions of the State—on the principles of preserving, and effectually improving, according to the increased intelligence of the people, and the necessities of the times, the constitution of the country: and in doing this, I need not say to a meeting so intelligent as the present, that they should abstain from pressing all extreme and violent changes. [He concluded by speaking of] the great truth, that, for the sake of liberty itself, the peace and good order of society must be preserved—the authority of the law must be restored—and that the power which, for the good of the subject, must belong to the Government, should be supported.

Despite these caveats, enthusiasm for the principle of reform was unbounded, and its association with the name of Charles Grey was sealed. As *The Times* remarked a few days later, 'His fame lies, and will long live, in the hearts of Englishmen. His monument is based on the rights of his countrymen.... He makes himself the symbol of his cause.' The *Courier* commented: 'No public individual has ever had so great a claim to the gratitude of his country ... as Earl

Grey.' The verdict has passed into history. Grey's name is inseparable from the events of 1831–2 and the cause of liberal, constitutional reform. As his previous biographer immortalized him in the title of his work, he is 'Lord Grey of the Reform Bill'.[1]

Nearly 70 years have passed since Trevelyan's biography was published, and in those 70 years the supremacy of the old values of liberal England has waned. In every generation, the verdicts of history must be questioned and re-assessed. In many ways, the Reform Act now seems an unexpected climax to Grey's 44 years of political activity, and its purposes seem remote from those once attributed to it by nineteenth-century liberals. It is now interpreted in relation to the immediate circumstances of its time, to the aims and interests of the government which introduced it, and, not least, to the character and personality of Grey himself. It was not so much the outcome of a lifetime's commitment to liberty or liberal principles, as the result of political accident and party interest. Grey became a Whig by accident, and a reformer by miscalculation. He was not a man attracted by ideology, though he had a deep sense of public duty and a lively awareness of the true needs of the country in the circumstances of 1830–2, as he had done in the period of the French Revolution after 1789. On both occasions, he was attracted to parliamentary reform as the practical solution to a national crisis. It was as a remedy for the defects of the constitution, not as a response to new ideas and principles, that Grey saw reform. His object was to preserve, not to innovate; to ensure the continuance of aristocratic dominance and the traditional institutions of Monarchy, Church, and Parliament, and not to subject them to the control of democracy. Reform was essentially a conservative solution to the problem of social and political change. Grey's principles and attitudes as well as his temperament were profoundly aristocratic, and it was as the servant of the English aristocracy and its tradition of paternalistic governance that he sought to guide the nation through the dangers of popular unrest and social upheaval. Grey deserved, and still deserves, his country's gratitude for ensuring that the transition from eighteenth-century aristocracy to later nineteenth- and twentieth-century democracy was a peaceful one, and that the British preference remains one for gradual and organic, rather than sudden and sweeping, change; but he achieved it by ensuring that the new was blended with the old, and that the fundamentals of the constitution remained, as they still remain, connected to a historic past which gives them roots in tradition and continuity of experience.

[1] G. M. Trevelyan, *Lord Grey of the Reform Bill* (1920, 2nd edn. 1929). For descriptions of the Edinburgh celebrations to honour Lord Grey, see *The Grey Festival: being a narrative of the proceedings connected with the dinner given to Earl Grey, at Edinburgh, on Monday 15 September 1834* ... (Edinburgh, 1834); the *Edinburgh Weekly Journal*, 17 Sept. 1834; the *Newcastle Journal*, 20 Sept. 1834. Grey wrote to Lord Holland on 27 Sept. that 'My reception ... exceeded everything I could have imagined and was indeed most gratifying': Grey MSS, Durham.

Part I

1764–1807

1 Political Apprenticeship, 1764–1792

Charles Grey was born on 13 March 1764, at Fallodon. The Greys were a long-established and well-connected Northumberland family of moderate estate, amounting in 1883 to 17,599 acres. Though small in comparison with the Duke of Northumberland's 186,000 acres, their property gave them a substantial place in the county. They traced their ancestry back to the fourteenth century. The principal family home for the past hundred years was Howick, originally a peel tower near the rocks and windswept coast between Alnmouth and Dunstanburgh. In 1764 Howick was occupied by Sir Henry Grey, second holder of a baronetcy conferred in 1746 for loyalty to the Hanoverian cause against the Jacobite rising of '45. Grey's father, Sir Charles, was Sir Henry's younger brother and lived at Fallodon, the second family home, which he inherited from his mother Hannah, daughter and heiress of Thomas Wood of Fallodon. In 1762 he married Elizabeth, daughter of George Grey of Southwick, Co. Durham. Their first child was a son, named Henry, who died three months after the birth of their second child, Charles, in 1764. As Sir Henry remained a bachelor, this son became heir to both Howick and Fallodon, though he always from childhood preferred Howick and Fallodon was, in the event, inherited by his next brother Henry George, and subsequently by another brother named George, who became the ancestor of the nineteenth-century Greys of Fallodon.

Charles Grey's relations with his parents were occasionally difficult. He was an intelligent boy, but nervous and inclined to be stubborn. His father was a distinguished soldier, one of the few British generals to make a reputation in the American War of Independence and in the West Indies in the 1790s. No doubt Sir Henry was more easy-going than his brother who as a professional soldier was inclined to demand obedience and discipline—qualities which his son Charles was later to require from his own sons, though he was also to develop a more relaxed relationship with all his children than was usually the case in aristocratic families of the time. In any case, Charles came to look upon Howick as his natural home, and even before he inherited it in 1808, he and his wife had occupied it at Sir Henry's request in 1801. His father was distressed by Charles's rejection of Fallodon, as Charles was angry when his father solicited a peerage from Addington in 1801 without consulting him, so consigning him in the near future to the House of Lords which he came to detest. Visiting his father in 1802, Charles remarked that he was in a most uncomfortable state to all his family, but particularly to me who am considered as in a great degree the cause of it on account of what has passed about Fallodon.... He professes himself to be hurt and disappointed, as if in return for repeated marks of kindness I had refused to gratify him in a moderate and reasonable request, but refuses to enter into any explanation on the subject.... He appears in the lowest spirits and seldom speaks but to aggravate his own complaints, and to declare that he feels himself daily declining.

Grey was to inherit nothing from his parents. Fallodon passed to his younger brother and Grey's mother who died in 1822 left her personal estate to her daughters Elizabeth and Hannah.[1] Grey's inheritance came from Sir Henry, who died in 1808, and who had financed his nephew's European tour and his first election to the House of Commons in 1786.

Little is known of Charles's schooldays. He was sent to a school at Marylebone at the age of six, but he was lonely and unhappy there and suffered from a series of illnesses that may have had a nervous origin. Trevelyan tells the story of his being sent on one occasion to a nurse at Tyburn who lived across the street from the gallows and who, on the first day he was well enough to go out of doors, took him to watch an execution. The sight struck deep into his memory and even in old age he would wake from nightmares of this harrowing experience. Three years later, he went up to Eton, where he remained for eight years until 1781. He later looked back on his schooldays without affection, and was in the habit of declaring that Eton taught him nothing of value. He told Miss Ord in 1792 that it was the best of the public schools, but 'none of them are as good as they ought to be', and he was to have his own sons educated elsewhere. According to a later gossip, at Eton Grey was 'reckoned clever' but he was not a particularly co-operative pupil and he criticized the formal nature of the curriculum in which he found little to interest him. His headmaster, the great Dr Heath, later remarked that Grey 'was what he now is, able in his exercises, impetuous, overbearing, &c ...'; though Grey did later say that to Dr Heath 'I owe all that I have of good.'[2]

Eton, however, moulded Grey in one way, as it did many other of the great political figures of the age. It introduced him to boys who were to become his distinguished contemporaries and in some cases, friends, and to a circle of acquaintances which he could never have found in the remote north. Richard Wellesley, the later Marquess and elder brother of the Duke of Wellington, became a close friend, as did Samuel Whitbread, later to be his brother-in-law and fellow Whig politician. Another was William Lambton, father of 'Radical Jack', first Earl of Durham, who was to marry Grey's eldest daughter and serve under him in the Cabinet of 1830. Like many such men, Grey found Eton a nursery for public life, a training for political responsibility and for parliamentary oratory, which was to provide his particular road to distinction. He was a lively and boisterous companion

[1] Grey to Whitbread [27 Apr. 1802], Whitbread MSS 876; Creevey to Miss Ord, 3 May 1834, *The Creevey Papers*, ed. Sir H. Maxwell (1903), ii. 273.

[2] Trevelyan, *Lord Grey*, 4; Grey to Miss Ord, 8 Nov. 1792, J. Gore, *Creevey's Life and Times* (1934), 8; J. Farington, *The Farington Diary*, i. (1922), 179.

and may also, like many contemporaries, have found at Eton an introduction to the less respectable *demi-monde* of gambling and sexual adventure into which he plunged when he began his political career in London at the end of the decade.

Eton was followed by Cambridge, where at Trinity he continued to associate with Lambton, and with Whitbread who went up to St John's, next door. Here academic study seems to have played no more of a part in his life than at Eton. He wrote to a friend in 1782 that he liked Cambridge 'very much' but 'I think the study too confined, if a man is not a mathematician he is nobody ... though whatever mode is most agreeable to a young man he is at perfect liberty to pursue.' However, Cambridge seems not to have provided him with any intellectual tastes or accomplishments beyond the commonplace of the time. After three years he left, again following the practice of young gentlemen without taking a degree, since he seems not to have been destined for any professional career. He set out on a European tour, rather less grand than many since the family finances would not stretch so far, but spending some time attached to the suite of the liberal Duke of Cumberland. Again there is almost no information about his experiences. Only one letter survives, recounting a visit to Verona which evidently did not much impress him. He saw two Veroneses, but declared that the pleasure he derived from them came from their 'faithful representation of nature in her true colours' and that he had 'no pretensions to taste, or to the knowledge necessary to be a conoisseur'. He dismissed academic controversy over the precise age of the amphitheatre, professing satisfaction merely with 'knowing that it is a work of the ancients, without troubling myself to enquire in what year or by what hand the first stone was laid'. On this prosaic note the young statesman abandoned the cultural experiences of Italy for the political arena of London.[3]

Grey was not present at the birth of his own political career. He was still travelling in Europe when an unexpected vacancy occurred in the representation of Northumberland, soon after his twenty-second birthday. His uncle Sir Henry at once set about securing his nephew's nomination as one who would follow in his own footsteps and who would be agreeable to the local county squires as a quiet backbencher of conservative instincts. The family tradition was, indeed, on the ministerial rather than the opposition side. Grey's father, as a professional soldier, was inclined both by his sense of duty and by the need of advancement in his profession to support the government of the day, irrespective of its political complexion. Sir Henry had been member for the county between 1754 and 1768 but had filled the role of backbench country gentleman to such perfection that on one occasion he was turned away at the door of the Commons by a doorkeeper who did not recognize him. He had supported the Shelburne group of Whigs during the American War period and he continued to approve of Shelburne's successor, the younger William Pitt. His nephew followed this line, on the evidence at least of the only surviving letter from his youth which makes any reference to politics: he wrote in 1782 that the combined Rockingham and Shelburne

[3] Grey to Ellison, 25 Jan. 1782, G. 14.

administration displayed 'such a combination of abilities, property and importance . . . [as] Englishmen never before could boast'. This, however, hardly amounts
to evidence of lifelong liberal views. The election address drawn up for him in
1786 avoided any political commitment and referred in conventional terms only
to his diffidence at standing forward at so young an age for such an eminent
distinction, and declared that 'I think it not now necessary to make any parade of
principles', and that he stood on terms of 'absolute independence only'.

Nevertheless, the young Grey was too ardent and spirited to accept the passive
role of a backbench country gentleman. Unlike his uncle he was no elderly
backwoodsman from the far north, but an intelligent and sophisticated young man.
He threw himself with enthusiasm not only into the political arena but into the
most brilliant and exciting social circles to which he could gain entry: both
inclinations led him into the society of Fox, Sheridan, and Devonshire House. It
was these influences that quickly began to shape his temperament. Within a year,
perhaps two at most, Grey had become what he was to remain for the rest of his
life: a disciple of Fox's brand of liberal, populist yet basically conservative
Whiggism, an advocate of 'civil and religious liberty all over the world', yet a
political realist ever ready to temper idealism with expediency, a pragmatist who
never lost sight of reputation and consistency, at once ardent and cautious, idealistic
and calculating.[4]

In the beginnings of his career, it was the society rather than the politics of
later-eighteenth century Whiggery that attracted him. The Whig party into which
Grey was quickly drawn was as much a network of family relationships and
social intercourse as it was a political entity. The events of the immediate post-
American War period had revived the 'rage of party' which had been characteristic
of English political life over half a century before. Once again political connection
reflected deep divisions in the social circles from which the political class was
recruited. Bitter personal animosities were engendered by the rivalry of the major
political leaders in 1782, the formation of the Fox–North coalition in 1783, and
the establishment of Pitt's administration in 1784. Pitt, once the rising young hope
of the reformers against the influence of the Crown, appeared to have given up
his liberal principles for the sake of office—an office he held only by the support
of the King, the court and the men who in later years would have been labelled
'Tories': their support was conditional upon his accepting the former role of Lord
North as the King's Minister. Gestures such as his attempt to introduce a
parliamentary reform bill in 1785 were empty in the face of the knowledge that in
this case neither his Cabinet colleagues nor his normal parliamentary supporters
would countenance it, and that the King would not order the placemen to vote in
its favour.

From the Whig point of view, Pitt was an apostate, not merely from the cause
of parliamentary reform—which Fox, too, had deserted in return for North's

---

[4] to Ellison, 31 Mar. 1782, ibid. For Sir Henry Grey see L. B. Namier and J. Brooke, *The House of
Commons, 1754–90* (1964), i. 384 and ii. 552–3. For Grey's election address, G. 62.

political alliance in 1783—but from the whole canon of Whig principles, involving the subordination of the King to ministers possessing the confidence of Parliament and the people, and the conduct of public affairs by men not chosen solely on account of royal favour but designated by their weight and influence in society at large. It is easy enough, in a more democratic age, to point to the inconsistencies in this creed and to interpret Whig constitutionalism as mere window-dressing for the selfish demand by a group of irresponsible aristocrats for a monopoly of power in the state. But from behind the self-interest and wounded pride of the Whig families there was already emerging a view of the constitution based upon a genuine, if idiosyncratic, feeling for the liberties of the subject and a conviction that those liberties were best preserved and protected by a government that depended upon the consensus of men of property, education, and wealth, whose position designated them as the natural leaders of society. Whig principles were aristocratic principles, but the principles of a responsible and outward-looking aristocracy, whose authority was conditional upon the acceptance of obligations and the performance of duties towards those in subordinate positions.

At its best, later-eighteenth century Whiggism was the political expression of a paternalistic and liberal view of society. It was essentially a *laissez-faire* creed, which saw government as a minimal force, a necessary evil for the restraint of men's anti-social passions rather than as the mainspring of a system of laws and regulations compelling the obedience of the subject to those in power. The operation of natural forces deriving from existing social and economic circumstances was to be as far as possible unchecked by political intervention. Reform was thus not the central watchword of Whig principles, except in so far as it meant the correction of distortions in this natural fabric. The essential requisite was the protection of the liberty of the individual, within the limits of his capabilities and his social and economic position, to order his own affairs without hindrance from others.[5]

The young Charles Grey's gravitation to the Whig party and its principles was natural enough in these terms. Throughout his life his manner, bearing, and attitudes were aristocratic in the broadest sense. Though he soon came to adopt the cause of reform, he did so in order to diminish the personal influence of the Crown and the political influence of its nominees, to strengthen the natural leadership of the aristocracy, and to reconcile the intelligent and responsible classes in society to the existing order of things. This was the Whig tradition he came to understand through his early association with Fox and his friends.

Fox's circle was the most brilliant in later-eighteenth century London. Its central figure was the lovely Georgiana, Duchess of Devonshire, married to a dull and unexciting husband but herself mercurial, fascinating, and highly-strung. At Devonshire House itself, or at the country villa at Chiswick, the grandees of Whig

[5] E. A. Smith, *Whig Principles and Party Politics: Earl Fitzwilliam and the Whig Party* (Manchester, 1975), *passim*; A. D. Kriegel, 'Liberty and Whiggery in early 19th-century England', *Journal of Modern History*, 52 (June 1980), 253-78.

society and their hangers-on gathered after parliamentary debates to discuss the politics of the day, or at levées, balls, card parties, and assemblies to while away the tedium of residence in London during the parliamentary session. The Prince of Wales was a long-standing *habitué* and intimate friend of Georgiana, whom he made his confidante and reluctant ally in his pursuit of the chaste Mrs Fitzherbert. Fox and Sheridan were constantly there, Fox holding court amidst his admirers and Sheridan, one of the wittiest men of the age, pursuing his political ambition to become the Prince's leading adviser. It was a glittering society, though looked upon by outsiders as the haunt of immorality and intrigue. Georgiana's character was probably unjustly maligned. Her flirtations were in general harmless, though she was certainly careless enough of her reputation for her to be warned several times by her mother, Lady Spencer, to observe the proprieties of the time. She had, after all, little enough cause to be faithful to her incommunicative and morose husband, who loved his dogs more than people and made his wife share his affections with Lady Elizabeth Foster in a notorious *ménage-à-trois*. But she seems never to have fallen deeply in love until the arrival of Grey. At thirty, she was seven years older than Grey, who was fascinated by her lively spirits and perhaps eager to demonstrate by a notable conquest his arrival in the most fashionable set in London. His courtship was a stormy and demanding one. His nature always demanded that he should dominate and he was never content with second place. The consequence was a number of angry scenes which even the curtain of discretion round the affairs of Devonshire House could not always hide. When the phlegmatic Duke began to show signs of irritation at his wife's 'open flirtation with that young puppy Grey', Sheridan and Lady Elizabeth Foster had to intervene to placate him and to urge Grey to be more discreet. He unhappily confessed to Lady Melbourne that 'indeed I never meant to plague her, but I believe I am born to be a plague to everybody.'[6] For the present Georgiana remained faithful to the Duke, though attracted to Grey, until the birth of a son to inherit her husband's title freed her, as Lady Melbourne suggested, from the obligation to be faithful to him.[7] After the arrival of the future sixth Duke in 1790 she no longer resisted Grey's importunity, seeking with him the affection so rarely displayed by her husband.

In May 1791 she went to Bath to look after her sister Harriet, who was seriously ill, and shortly after her arrival she discovered that she was pregnant. The secret soon leaked out, possibly, it was suspected, because Grey had been indiscreet during a drinking bout, and Georgiana's mother received an anonymous letter. In October the Duke stormed down to Bath to confront his wife and there was a violent scene. Georgiana retired to bed with a headache while the Duke walked up and down, fuming in silence. Though he had had two children by Lady Elizabeth Foster in 1785 and 1788 and had taken them into his household, with Georgiana's agreement, there could be no question of his accepting another man's

---

[6] *Georgiana*, ed. Lord Bessborough (1955), 4–5; M. Villiers, *The Grand Whiggery* (1939), 81–2, 105; A. Calder-Marshall, *The Two Duchesses* (1978), esp. 69–71, 82–7, 111–15, 122.

[7] Ibid. 25.

child. Grey had no desire that he should. He begged Georgiana to leave the Duke
and live with him, but the Duke made it plain that in that case she would never
see their children again. It was a choice she could not bear to make, and Grey was
told that their relationship must come to an end. To make doubly sure, and to
avoid a public scandal, the Duke insisted that she should go abroad to have the
child.[8]

Nothing else will do [wrote Harriet], neither prayers nor entreaties nor representations will
alter him, he says there is no choice between this, or public entire separation at home....
My poor sister is quite ill.... When I see all the vexation and unhappiness that surrounds
me, I almost wish myself at the bottom of the sea ... only that I believe I am of use to my
sister.

An elaborate deception was hatched by the Devonshire ladies. Harriet's doctor
was persuaded to certify that she must spend the winter in the south of France
and it was announced that Georgiana was to go with her. They were to leave
immediately from Bath, for the Duke vindictively refused even to allow her to say
goodbye to her children. Arrangements were made for a secret correspondence
with Grey during the exile. He was to be rather thinly disguised as 'Mr Black', a
pretended friend of Harriet, and Georgiana's letters to him were to be sent to
Lady Melbourne who would pass them on. In November the sisters set off for
Southampton and Le Havre, accompanied by Lady Spencer, Georgiana's mother,
and Lady Elizabeth Foster, who agreed to travel with them at Georgiana's insistence. At least the Duke would not live with his mistress while his wife was abroad,
small consolation as it was for the separation from Grey and her children. The
party made its way to the south of France, Georgiana's misery only thinly disguised
by her attempts to appear cheerful at the inevitable assembles they attended on
the way.[9]

Grey's letters did not relieve her spirits. He was deeply hurt by her refusal to
put him before her children and his tone was reproachful and unfeeling. 'He was
very cruel,' Georgiana wrote from Paris, 'but very deserving of pity too—and I
have in leaving him for ever, left my heart and soul, but it is over now—Heaven
bless him ... and he has one consolation that I have given him up to my children
only.' From Lyons a week later she wrote:

I am not very well; and Black has again been very cruel, and my letters from him yesterday
have given me a head which is not gone. Why will people be harsh at such a distance—
however he is quite in the right, *de ne pas se gêner.*...

Grey's letters were all destroyed at a later date, but it is clear from Georgiana's
and Harriet's correspondence with Lady Melbourne that the pain of separation
and the bitterness of rejection were too acute for him to show the kindness and

[8] Harriet to Lady Melbourne [1791], [11 Oct. 1791] and [24 Oct.], BL Add. MS 45911 fos. 15–16
and 45548 fos. 36–9.
[9] Calder-Marshall, *The Two Duchesses*, 111–12.

affection that Georgiana needed and that she expressed for him. He seemed to Harriet to be cruel and unfeeling, and she never forgave him. She wrote in 1795:[10]

He is a brute, a beast, and I have no patience with him, there is a want of feeling and consideration for her that make me quite mad with him.

On 20 February at Aix-en-Provence Georgiana gave birth to a daughter who was given the name Eliza Courtney, the surname of Georgiana's aunt before her marriage and Georgiana's alias in her correspondence with 'Black'. They did not return to England until 1793, the delay being imposed in the hope that Georgiana would recover from her attachment, and on their arrival the child was taken to Fallodon, where as a final irony she was brought up by Grey's parents as their own child, so that in the eyes of the world she was Grey's sister rather than his daughter. Her mother saw her rarely, and corresponded with her as a family friend. For long periods the only news she had of her daughter by the only man she ever loved came in whispered conversations with Grey during supper parties and assemblies in London or through common friends.

Her relationship with Grey never returned to its old intensity, though he continued to come to Devonshire House with his political colleagues and Lady Holland described him in 1793 as a 'a fractious and exigeant lover'. The Duke kept too close an eye on his wife to permit intimacy, and in any case Grey realized that there was no future in the relationship. He could not be expected to pine for ever in a hopeless cause. His attentions turned elsewhere, and in the autumn of 1794 he became engaged to Mary Ponsonby and they married in November. By yet another irony, Mary was second cousin to Harriet's husband, Viscount Duncannon, later third Earl of Bessborough, and related through her mother to the Cavendishes. Either from thoughtlessness or as a final punishment for Georgiana's desertion, Grey did not tell her beforehand of his engagement—a last proof, in Harriet's mind, of his cruel character. Nor did Mary know until later of Eliza's parentage. Gossip had it that the Duke took his final revenge by telling her on her wedding-day, but there is no evidence to support the story. Mary nevertheless became a faithful and devoted wife who succeeded in making her fretful husband happy. Their fifteen children and the close family life which they built at Howick after 1801 testify to the success of the marriage and provided Grey with the domestic happiness which he needed to counter the frustrations of his political career.[11]

Georgiana soon established an affectionate friendship with Mary which lasted for the rest of her life. She wrote in 1797 of her love and friendship for all the family, declaring that she felt almost like a grandmother to the eldest daughter Louisa; in 1801 she told Grey that he and Mary were her best friends. Grey, however, was wary of gossip, and warned her in 1803 that when they met in public

---

[10] Georgiana to Lady Melbourne 20 [Nov.] and 10 [Dec. 1791], BL Add. MS 45911 fos. 24–5 and 45548 fo. 10; Harriet to Lady Melbourne Jan. [1795], ibid. 45911 fos. 40–1.

[11] *Journal of Elizabeth, Lady Holland*, ed. Lord Ilchester (1908), i. 98 [1 Dec. 1793].

'I beg there may be no particular conversation between us ... the subject is immaterial if we are seen in a long whisper together.' Yet the break from Grey left a gap in her life which was never filled. The long history of illness which led to her death in 1806 at the age of 49 began shortly after Grey's marriage. Blinding headaches and a disease in one eye gave her constant pain, and two operations disfigured her former beauty. 'Scarcely has she a vestige of those charms which once attracted all hearts', wrote Lady Holland. 'Her figure is corpulent, her complexion worse, one eye gone, and her neck immense. How frail is the tenure of beauty.' Her last meeting with Grey was at a brilliant supper party at Devonshire House for the incoming Talents Ministers in 1806: shortly afterwards Georgiana suffered her last illness, in which she endured 'long and dreadful pains' before the final lethargy in which she said at last that 'she did not mind it'. Her unhappy private life had been hidden behind a facade of gaiety and a round of balls, parties, and the gaming tables: perhaps the reckless way in which she threw herself into the role of Whig hostess reflected the despair of her separation from the only man she ever really loved. Her death closed a chapter in Grey's life with personal tragedy.[12]

THE HOUSE OF COMMONS, 1786–1788

Grey's establishment as a leading member of the brilliant circle of Whig politicians in the House of Commons was as rapid as his advance in society. He was attracted to Fox and his set by their scintillating company and friendship; he was no less welcome to them for his parliamentary talents. From the very first, he shone as an orator in the House of Commons. It was to be his most remarkable gift in public life. All those who, throughout his life, commented on his political achievements mentioned his powers of oratory as amongst the foremost of his time. In the age of Pitt, Fox, Burke, Sheridan, and later Canning, a high reputation for parliamentary speaking was not easily gained. It was the classical age of public oratory, when the leading debaters in the Commons were expected to speak for two or three hours at a stretch; their speeches were reported at great length in the newspapers to be read with avidity by large numbers of the public. Speeches were expected to be orderly and methodical in arrangement, but eloquent and impassioned in delivery, garnished (in moderation) with classical tags and allusions according to the prevalent taste, and accompanied by appropriate gestures.[1]

Grey's style was less flamboyant than the theatricality of Sheridan or the

---

[12] Georgiana to Mary Grey [1797] and to Grey [1801], Hickleton MSS A.1.4.11/9 and 14; Grey to Georgiana [1803], *Private Correspondence of Lord Granville Leveson-Gower*, ed. Castalia, Countess Granville (1916), i. 422–3; Calder-Marshall, *The Two Duchesses*, 125, 127, 146. Mary wrote to Georgiana's son, the sixth Duke, in 1832 enclosing a portrait of his mother which she had given to her before her marriage: 'I value it more than anything I possess', she wrote: Chatsworth MSS 2512.

[1] A. Aspinall, 'The Reporting and Publishing of the House of Commons Debates, 1771–1834', *Essays presented to Sir Lewis Namier*, ed. R. Pares and A. J. P. Taylor (1956), 227–57.

passionate declamation of Burke. He modelled himself on Fox, whose speeches were, or seemed, less contrived, more impromptu, and more closely argued than those of his associates. Like Fox, Grey excelled in replying to a debate, answering his opponents' arguments in methodical order and convincing by reason rather than by mere eloquence. James Grant, the early-nineteenth century parliamentary journalist, observed in 1836 that Grey's facility in reply was the fruit of conscientious study beforehand both of the subject of debate and of his opponents' likely tactics, which enabled him to anticipate their arguments. No man surpassed him, in Grant's long experience as a reporter in both Houses, in this respect. Yet his set speeches were often no less brilliant. Grant thought them clear, sound, well illustrated, elegant in style, and closely reasoned, though sometimes lacking in animation. He was, Grant observed, 'dignified in his manner as well as in his mind ... No-one ever yet glanced his eye at the noble Earl without being that instant struck with the dignity of his appearance', and with his 'deep-seated habitual gravity, and a profoundly thoughtful air ... When he began his speech he usually did so in so low a tone as to be hardly audible 12 or 14 yards distant', but his voice gradually became louder and audible throughout the chamber. 'His voice was soft and pleasant, and his articulation clear'; he eschewed flamboyance of style or gesture and relied upon the clarity and forcefulness of his reasoning for his effect.

His usual practice was to join his hands, and then allow them to repose on his person for 8 or 10 minutes. He would then separate them and after suffering them to hang loose by his side, would put both to his back, where he would again join them, and continue in that attitude for another 8 or 10 minutes.

'He seldom stood many seconds on the same spot', but would step up and down the centre of the chamber, looking not directly at his audience but on the floor or the nearby benches. 'His language was beautifully correct, without being what is called elegant.' His manner in the House was one of aristocratic reserve; he sat at the end of the front bench, with his back to his colleagues so that no one would converse with him and he could give full attention to the debate. He was courteous to his opponents, never descended to personalities and had great command of his temper.

Grant never witnessed Grey's youthful intemperance, but others support his impressions. Wellington remarked that his oratory in the Commons had been 'quite perfect' and Holland said of him in 1832: 'Lord Grey's judgement and execution exceed those of the greatest orators or statesmen I have known. He is more perspicuous, clear, and methodical than Mr. Fox, more conciliatory and just than Mr. Pitt, and more circumspect and cautious than Mr. Canning, yet as full of spirit, life, and energy as any of them.' As Creevey—not yet the admirer of Grey he was later to become—wrote of his speech on the Bill of Pains and Penalties on behalf of Queen Caroline in 1820, 'There is nothing approaching this damned fellow in the kingdom, when he mounts his best horse.' His resignation speech in 1834, Creevey thought 'the most beautiful speech ever delivered by man'.[2]

Applause greeted Grey's very first venture in the House of Commons, on 21 February 1787. The debate was on the Commercial Treaty with France, negotiated by Pitt's government in the previous year and hailed by the Minister's supporters as well as by the leading manufacturing interests of the country as a great triumph for British diplomacy. Grey showed none of the hesitancy felt by most new members in facing a critical audience so soon after his arrival in the House. He was determined to make an impact at the very first opportunity, and not only chose for his début a major debate on a leading national question, but flung himself without hesitation into the battle by rising first to catch the Speaker's eye. Nor was his maiden speech the usual deferential exercise expected of a young member on his first appearance. He did not hesitate to condemn the Treaty in the strongest terms, and despite his lack of political connection with the opposition, he denounced the measure in language which might have suggested that he was their leading spokesman. He anticipated Fox's own argument that the Treaty would prejudice the interests of the merchant navy and expressed the opposition's long-standing Francophobia by declaring that the French remained our natural enemies, and that they planned to accomplish Britain's economic ruin by subtler means than those that had failed to defeat us by force of arms. The central argument of the speech hardly held water: the Treaty was justly regarded as highly advantageous to British commercial and industrial interests, but as a parliamentary performance it was highly praised. Sir Gilbert Elliot wrote that the speech was 'excessively good indeed, and such as has given everybody the highest opinion both of his abilities and his character', while Henry Addington from the ministerial side remarked that the speech was received 'with an éclat which has not been equalled within my recollection ... in ... figure, voice, elocution, and manner, he is not surpassed by any one member of the House'.[3]

It was an astonishing début, and whether it was intended or not, it seemed to indicate a bid to recruit himself to the opposition. He ended his speech by declaring that he opposed the Treaty 'not from any want of personal attachment or respect for H.M., as he should always be one of the first and most eager to approach the throne with sentiments of true loyalty and veneration', nor from 'any personal prejudice against him [Pitt], or any party view whatever'. Yet the tone of the speech was hardly so impartial. Addington concluded his praise by remarking that 'I grieve to say that he was last night in the ranks of opposition, from whence there is no chance of his being detached.' Pitt certainly viewed him as a personal

[2] J. Grant, *Random Recollections of the House of Lords from 1830 to 1836*, 2nd edn. 1836, 259–81; *HHD*, 156; *Creevey Papers*, i. 286, 336, ii. 282. Lady Holland thought Grey's oratory was 'more pleasing and agreeable than forcible and deep': *Journal* (1798), i. 171. For Grey's posture in the House of Lords, see plate 3, 'A Parliamentary Group', by 'HB' (1832).

[3] *Parl. Hist.* xxvi. 471–81; *Life and Letters of Sir Gilbert Elliot*, ed. Lady Minto (1874), i. 130; G. Pellew, *Life and Correspondence of the Rt. Hon. Henry Addington* (1847), i. 45–6.

opponent from this time onwards. Grey's subsequent conduct hardly belied this assessment.[4]

Two months later, his second recorded intervention in debate was in defence of the opposition's motion on the Prince of Wales's debts, when he attacked Pitt for making mysterious hints about circumstances that might be exposed if a full inquiry into the Prince's affairs was undertaken.[5] Grey was already established as one of the Prince's circle, and knew full well what these mysterious circumstances were. In 1785 the Prince had married Mrs Fitzherbert, a Roman Catholic widow. The marriage was not only illegal under the Royal Marriage Act, but under the Act of Settlement it would have thrown the Prince out of the line of succession to the Crown. In April 1787 the House of Commons was asked to help relieve the Prince of his enormous debts and during the discussion hints were dropped about possible disclosure of the marriage. To save himself from the consequences, the Prince asked Fox to deny the fact of the marriage in the House of Commons. Fox's compliance saved a constitutional crisis but embarrassed Mrs Fitzherbert, who was openly living with the Prince. The Prince turned to Grey, hoping to use him to extricate himself, and asked him to make a statement in the House that would 'take off the effect of Fox's declaration' and satisfy Mrs Fitzherbert, while leaving the House and the public satisfied as to the Prince's position and conduct. Grey later recollected, as Grenville recorded, that

the Prince was in such disorder and agony of mind as he scarcely ever saw any other person in. That he was in tears walking about the room and beating his head against the walls. That he then told Grey *that the truth was a marriage had taken place between him and Mrs Fitzherbert*— ... a marriage twice solemnised—once according to the forms of the Church of Rome (Mrs Fitzherbert being a Papist) and once according to the Church of England. That the Prince then said that it was *absolutely necessary* that the denial given to this fact by Fox and Grey should be contradicted ...[6]

Even so young and inexperienced a politician as Grey could hardly lend himself to such a crazy scheme, and he had the courage to tell the Prince so outright. Grey later remarked that 'from this time his favour at Carlton House had declined', not only because of his refusal to perjure himself for the Prince's sake, but also because he told Fox of the Prince's admission. Fox, also disgusted by the Prince's duplicity, withdrew from Carlton House society and politics along with the majority of the Whig party—a breach patched up only by the advent of the Regency crisis in 1788 but never fully healed. It was clear to the Whig leaders that full identification of the party with the Prince's interests could only be on terms degrading to their political and personal honour. Their conviction of his utter selfishness and lack of political principle remained a barrier henceforward to

[4] Lady Holland later wrote that Grey gravitated to opposition after this speech because of Pitt's manner towards him and Fox's contrasting encouragement: *Journal*, i. 100.

[5] *Parl. Hist.* xxvi. 1073.

[6] *Memorials & Correspondence of Charles James Fox*, ed. Lord John Russell (1853), ii. 287–90; *CGPW*, i. 174; Memorandum of a conversation between Lords Grey and Grenville about the Prince of Wales and Mrs Fitzherbert, 28 Apr. 1814, BL Add. MS 58949, fos. 116–21.

any close and lasting confidence between them, and laid the foundation for Grey's refusal in 1812 to commit himself to the Prince's support without substantial political guarantees.

Grey's third parliamentary appearance in his first session was equally embarrassing. On 15 May he moved for a committee of enquiry into alleged abuses in the Post Office. This arose from the misfortunes of his relative and neighbour in Northumberland, Lord Tankerville, who had been dismissed by Pitt from the office of Joint Postmaster-General after he had accused certain officials in the Post Office of corrupt practices and malversation of public money. Tankerville demanded an enquiry, and tried to embroil both Grey and the opposition in the affair. Grey was understandably reluctant to become involved, for Tankerville had a hasty temper and it was by no means certain that his accusations could be substantiated. It seemed more of a personal squabble than a genuine public question. Grey consulted Fox and Sheridan, who joined him in attempting to deter Tankerville from further public action, agreeing with Grey that it would do his reputation no good at this stage in his career to be involved in such a scrape. As he wrote to Tankerville, 'I cannot help ... feeling awkwardly when I consider that such a reflection might be thrown upon me for taking too forward a part in a matter of this nature.' Tankerville, however, insisted upon a public vindication of his conduct, leaving Grey with no alternative but to raise the question in the House.

Grey therefore tried to ground his motion on public rather than private concern, and went out of his way to disavow any party views: but he lost his temper when Pitt imputed party motives to him and was on the verge of issuing a challenge to the Prime Minister when Sheridan intervened to soothe his temper. Grey was reproved by the Speaker for his 'tone of defiance' and a fortnight later, when the report of the committee was presented, Pitt followed up the attack by remarking that

he could not but observe upon the singularity of the hon. gentleman's conduct, who began his political career in an early part of the session, by an opposition (a reluctant one, as he had himself said) to a particular measure of government, and who had accompanied that opposition with professions of great personal regard and respect for him, and of a desire, as far as he could do it consistently with his duty as a member of Parliament, to give his general support to administration, and had particularly disclaimed the character and imputation of being what was called a party man ... Notwithstanding those professions of a reluctance to oppose Government, of respect to administration, and of disclaiming the character of a party man, he could not but say that he thought the present a wanton attack on Government, and that it was conducted in a manner highly personal and disrespectful to him, and besides favoured very much of the utmost asperity of party.

Fox sprang to Grey's defence, referring to him as 'his hon. friend' and in reply to Pitt's strictures on Grey as a party man, declared 'that the hon. gentleman was not of that description, but he hoped by degrees he might become a party man', which he asserted to be an honourable term. Grey concluded the debate by remarking sourly to Pitt that 'if on any future occasion a compliment to the right hon. gentleman should suggest itself to his mind, he would studiously suppress it, to avoid the risk of being afterwards charged with insincerity.'[7]

Grey's first parliamentary session closed, therefore, on an unfortunate note. He had distinguished himself in his maiden speech, but admiration for his gifts was tempered by his descent into personal altercations with Pitt, which labelled him as a brash, ambitious, and hot-tempered young man. The dispersal of the House of Commons in the early summer of 1787 must have come as a relief to his friends as well as to his temper.

His first session had nevertheless been decisive for Grey's political future. Despite his professions of impartiality, his political conduct had drawn him where his social connections also placed him, into close consultation and co-operation with Fox and his circle. The following two years consolidated his association with the opposition and saw his emergence as one of their chief parliamentary spokesmen and one of their leading prospects for future office. His own ambition pointed in the same way—so much so that some of his new colleagues soon expressed jealousy and anxiety that he seemed too pushing, too impatient, and too self-regarding to serve the apprenticeship expected of younger men before they aspired to the higher ranks of politics. Perhaps the example of the younger Pitt, in this respect if in no other, commended itself to another young man who thought his talents prominent enough to deserve only the higher offices of state. Lady Holland described Grey at this time as 'a man of violent temper and unbounded ambition' and asserted that he was drawn into Whig circles by 'fashion ... all the beauty and wit of London ... and the seduction of Devonshire House'. Comparing him with Pitt in 1793, she remarked that 'they both considered their abilities so transcendant, that they seemed to despise experience, and treated their elders with contempt and sarcasm.'[8]

Grey certainly lacked neither the ambition nor the self-confidence of his rival, though unlike Pitt, who had shown no hesitation in supplanting Shelburne as leader of his party, Grey always swore that he would never be other than a follower and subordinate of Fox. But apart from Fox, there was no man in the Whig party whom Grey considered his superior in claims or in worth. Fox was to live another 19 years, and Grey's loyalty to him never wavered for an instant; but neither did his mounting conviction and assurance that he alone was worthy of the succession. His inheritance of the party leadership in 1806 was foreshadowed in his own mind almost from the moment of his first full commitment to the Whigs.

The year 1787 presented another opportunity for Grey to confirm his political stance. Burke's crusade for the purification of Indian administration, undertaken since 1782, had for two years past been focused on the impeachment for high

---

[7] Grey to Tankerville [c. 6 May 1787] and 10 May, Tankerville to Grey 10 May, Fox to Tankerville 10 May, Tankerville MSS, Northumberland Record Office; *Parl. Hist.* xxvi. 1172–82, 1191–4, 1197–9.

[8] Lady Holland, *Journal*, i. 100–1.

crimes and misdemeanours of Warren Hastings, who returned from the Governor-Generalship of Bengal in 1785. The campaign had been eagerly taken up by the Whig opposition as an issue which might pay substantial political dividends, counteract the reputation for political dishonesty which the coalition of 1783 had fastened upon them, and embarrass the relationship between the King, an enthusiastic supporter of Hastings, and his ministers—of whom Dundas in particular was believed to be fearful of Hastings's influence at Court, and Pitt sensitive to the imputation of shielding corruption.

During the parliamentary sessions of 1785 and 1786 the various charges were brought forward in turn by the leading opposition speakers and, with the exception of the first charge, voted as items of impeachment, with the support of Pitt, Dundas, and their ally and political conscience, Wilberforce. By the spring of 1787, the charges were complete and the House agreed to appoint a committee to draw up the formal articles of impeachment. Grey, who had arrived in the House too late to be involved in the preliminary debates on the charges, was now brought into the hunt and named as the last of the twenty members of the committee. In his first session, his association with the Whig party was recognized by this nomination. In December 1787, the committee was replaced by a committee of managers, the House having approved the articles of impeachment, and again Grey was one of the twenty. He was given the duty of seconding Fox, who was to move the first charge, that concerning Hastings's conduct towards Cheyt Singh, the Rajah of Benares. Thus when the great 'crisis of Imperial conscience' opened in February, 1788 before the assembled House of Lords and a crowded and fashionable audience crammed into Westminster Hall, Grey was the third speaker to begin the long seven years' labour. Burke opened the proceedings with a great speech lasting four days, in which the alleged enormities of Hastings's rule were contrasted with the principles of justice and humanity: the fifth day was Fox's, opening the first of the series of individual charges; and Grey rose on 25 February to second his friend. He spoke to the charges relating to Hastings's conduct after the expulsion of Cheyt Singh from Benares, particularly the plunder of Bidjey Guv and the changes made by Hastings in the government of Benares—contrasting the former state of the province under the native prince, when 'the fields were cultivated, the villages full of inhabitants, the country a garden, and the ayots happy' with its condition under Hastings's 'most cruel and vexatious oppression', when 'famine and misery stalked hand in hand, through uncultivated fields and deserted villages'. His conclusion rose to those heights of oratory expected by contemporary taste. If, he declared, he had been led into extreme language or emotion, it was because 'I pant for truth'; and he concluded:

I have, alas! taken a task that is above my strength, and have been forced to follow, *multa gemens longo intervallo*, after abilities such as no strength, I know, can keep up with. However, thank God, I have tried to do my duty; and the best of men can do no more ... and after all, it is not genius—it is not oratory—it is not the charm of unexpected throws of language, nor the rapt gaze after new sublimity in ideas—No, my Lords, it is nature—

it is truth—it is from duties well done—from privileges well asserted—from the steady maintenance of every thing right, and from the strong impeachment of all who are wrong, that we can satisfy the claims of existence and responsibility—decorate ourselves with the only ennobling quality, worth—and transmit the remembrance of ourselves, and the very name of our country, with common honour to our children.

The speech, delivered to a smaller audience than that which had crowded the hall to hear Burke and Fox, was nevertheless much praised.

Mr. Grey was nearly two hours in delivering his speech [wrote Debrett's reporter]; his manner was suited to the occasion; he was fervid, graceful, and impressive. He was well collected, without arrogance; free in his expression, without any rattle of volubility; firm in his sentiments, with scarcely any disgusting obduracy to the defendant. Mr. Grey spoke like a man in earnest. He did not philosophize, agitate, and edify, so powerfully as Mr. Burke; but he showed some reading, and some abstract reflection. He not only declaimed, but his speech had, what is less attainable by so young a man, much good arrangement and lucid order.

Gilbert Elliot was charmed by the speech, which he described as 'a very great performance indeed ... he has acquired a fund of reputation to last his life', while Georgiana described it as 'the finest of speeches ... beautiful is the common expression for the language'. Though his oratory always cost him dearly in nervous energy and anxiety beforehand, and doubts and fears of his performance afterwards, Grey's reputation as a speaker was now securely established.[9]

Grey soon lost enthusiasm for the Hastings impeachment. Later in life, his long championship of the causes of Catholic emancipation and parliamentary reform was to show that he did not lack steadfastness of character and patience in the face of discouragement; but as a young man he was impatient for quick results. He also shared the growing feeling of many of his colleagues that the trial was unlikely to yield the political dividends expected from it, and would tire the public as well as the party, diverting their energies from more promising efforts to overturn the ministry. Barely a year after his success in seconding the Benares charge, Grey was dragging his feet unwillingly to Westminster Hall and, when asked by Burke to second Burgoyne in the prosecution of the 12th and 13th articles, showed evident unwillingness to give any more time to the business. Both Grey and Sheridan suggested that the remaining articles ought to be abandoned in the interests of a quick conclusion to the whole trial, and persuaded Fox to take the same view.

Burke was distressed at Grey's lack of zeal, and even more so at the possibility of his withdrawal, 'not only because the interest of this prosecution must be materially affected by the loss of so much admirable eloquence, but that the general cause must always suffer by whatever tends to keep back the display of the splendid

---

[9] P. J. Marshall, *The Impeachment of Warren Hastings* (Oxford, 1965), 1–60, 180; *History of the Trial of Warren Hastings, Esq.* (1796), p. xii, and 17–21; E. A. Bond, *Speeches of the Managers and Counsel on the Trial of Warren Hastings* (1859), i. 265–307; *Elliot*, i. 196; Georgiana to Lady Elizabeth Foster [25 Feb. 1788], Chatsworth MSS.

talents that support it'. Greatly as he would be disappointed at Grey's withdrawal, Burke wrote, 'I should recommend to those who are zealous in our cause to please him at any rate or by any sacrifice.' In the event, Burke's persistence won the day. Fox and Grey decided to stop the impeachment in May 1789, but failed to arrive at Westminster Hall in time to move an adjournment before the sitting resumed, and the trial continued to drag its weary length along for another six years. Grey later accepted the role of seconding Burke on the presents charge, and he took part in the presentation of evidence on the Nundcomar and Oudh charges in 1789. In May 1794 he made the closing speech for the prosecution on the Benares charge. But his enthusiasm had waned and it was a sorry contrast to the vivid elegance of his opening speech seven years before, 'dry and uninteresting to the greatest part of the auditory' as the reporter remarked, and his attempted defence of Philip Francis 'completely failed'.[10]

The unenthusiastic tone of the report mirrored the prevailing weariness with what had become a tiresome and long-drawn-out affair. The excitement of 1787 had long ago evaporated, and even among the original managers only Burke really cared by 1794 whether Hastings was condemned or not. The conclusion of the trial and the expected acquittal was to the remnant of the Whig opposition in 1795 a relief from a burden which had never gained them the political advantages they had hoped for. Grey's sense of political reality was vindicated at the last, though Burke's weightier stature and deeper sense of moral principle had carried the party unwillingly after him.

Even before the crises of the Regency in 1788–9 and the reform question in 1792, the rift that these later crises were to open in the Whig party was already evident in the spring of 1788, as Burke strove to lift the party's eyes from the tactics of expediency to the principles of ethical justice. In the debate that was to split the party, Grey's part was already foreshadowed by his attitude to the Hastings impeachment. Fox clearly consulted him and was probably swayed more by his opinion than by anyone else. Grey had already established himself as Fox's closest colleague and subordinate.

AMBITION FRUSTRATED, 1788–1791

By the autumn of 1788, Grey's place in the Whig party and in Whig society seemed established. A constant *habitué* of Devonshire House and of Brooks's Club, a prominent member of Fox's circle of intimate young friends, and a regular attender at the debates in the House of Commons, he impressed all who met him as 'a very clever, spirited, and pleasant man, and extremely ripe indeed for his

---

[10] Marshall, *The Impeachment of Warren Hastings*, 78–9; W. Sichel, *Life of Sheridan* (1909), ii. 404; Burke to J. Burgoyne, 4 May 1788, and to Sheridan [30 Mar. 1789], *Correspondence of Edmund Burke* v. ed. H. Furber (1965), 395–6, 458; *Fox*, ii. 355–9; *History of the Trial*, ii. 39–44, 58, v. 110; Holland, *Memoirs of the Whig Party during my Time* (1852), i. 9.

age'.[1] The man who could both captivate the beautiful Georgiana and win the lasting affection of Fox was not deficient in personal charm, and though he also seemed proud, vain, and ambitious, his solid talents were generally admitted. He had now to consolidate his position and to assert his right to a leading place in the party hierarchy. He was to do so at a critical time for his party and his country. Grey and the Whigs were now to pass through the fires of the Regency crisis and the French Revolution and its aftermath in England. Together, these events shattered the party's unity and led to the formation of a new alignment in British politics that laid the foundation for the political divisions of the next hundred years. The illness of one king and the deposition and execution of another were the events that set in motion these far-reaching changes.

George III's first prolonged attack of mental derangement occurred in the autumn of 1788.[2] Pitt's administration had now successfully established its control, assisted by the economic recovery from the effects of the American War of Independence. The rapid growth of prosperity had blunted the edge of political strife, and Pitt's financial policies, together with his success in ending British isolation in Europe by the Triple Alliance of 1787 and his commercial treaty with France in 1786, had gained him widespread political support. Even his failure to persuade the King, his colleagues, and the House of Commons to redeem his pledges to the parliamentary reformers in 1785 was not held against him; the revival of prosperity had helped to damp down the agitation for reform to a few negligible embers.

Pitt's government had its failures and its weaknesses in the 1780s. His attempt to solve the problem of Anglo-Irish commercial relations had to be abandoned in face of the irreconcilable differences of interest on the two sides of St George's Channel. Politically, he had failed to make any substantial inroads into the numbers of the opposition in Parliament, which had even increased its strength since 1784 by gaining a few by-election seats;[3] and his own Cabinet was over-much dependent on his own brilliance as an administrator and Parliamentary orator. The government had too much the air of a one-man band to be secure against an opposition apparently brimming with parliamentary talent. Only the staunch support of George III held it safe, and even that support was more the consequence of the King's hatred and personal detestation of Fox than of his affection for Pitt himself, whom he respected for his talents and clung to as his refuge but for whom he never felt the warm regard he gave to men like North before 1782 or Addington after 1801. The collapse of the King's support would kick the prop from under Pitt's Cabinet, and George's sudden lapse into what seemed at best almost incurable insanity, at worst a possibly fatal illness, shattered the security of the political fabric. On 5 November 1788—by inauspicious coincidence the centenary of the

[1] Sir Gilbert Elliot to his wife, 12 Jan. 1788, *Elliot*, i. 188–9.
[2] For the Regency crisis see J. Derry, *The Regency Crisis and the Whigs, 1788–9* (1963); and I. Macalpine and R. Hunter, *George III and the Mad Business* (1969), 1–107.
[3] F. O'Gorman, *The Whig Party and the French Revolution* (1967), 247.

arrival of William of Orange in Torbay—the King's steadily worsening health reached a state of utter derangement. He was clearly incapable of performing his royal functions, and possibly at the point of death.

The news came as a tonic to the Foxites. George III's personal hatred of Fox was not in itself reciprocated by the Whig leader, but as a symbol of all that English Whiggism had been taught to detest he had no equal since the days of James II. Without George III's backing, Pitt was vulnerable; with the favour and support of his heir, the Prince of Wales, the Whigs would be triumphant. The leaders of the party—in Fox's absence, on holiday in Italy—hurried to make up the breach that had divided them from the Prince for the past 18 months. The Duke of Portland, the titular and much respected leader of the party, hastened to renew contact with Carlton House, now dominated by the influence of Sheridan and of understrappers like Jack Payne, who had not ostracized the Prince like the more respectable men in the party. An express messenger was despatched to bring Fox back from Italy, but until his return the advantage lay with the Prince and his cronies.

Their first move was an ominous one for the Whig leaders. Apparently on Sheridan's initiative, approaches were made to Thurlow, the Lord Chancellor, on the understanding that he would retain his office in the Prince's new administration. This pre-empted one of the most important posts, which in a full Whig administration was understood to be destined for Lord Loughborough, an ambitious Scots lawyer who had come over with North in 1783. Other posts were also provisionally allocated. To counteract these schemes and the alarming influence of Sheridan, Portland reconciled himself to the Prince and offered to 'forget a transaction in which my zeal for your glory, though sincere, was perhaps intemperate'. In the full expectation of the Prince's being invested with his father's authority as Regent, discussions began on the structure of a new administration. Fox returned to join the discussions on 24 November, but his hurried journey of more than a thousand miles over eighteenth-century roads in nine days left him weak and debilitated, and unable to assert a strong authority. The result was a degree of confusion and acrimony amongst the Whig leaders.[4]

The crisis proved to be a testing time for Grey as well as for the party in general. Georgiana later wrote that he 'gave proof of his talents, integrity and attachment to Mr. Fox and also of the imprudent warmth and eagerness that afterwards was the means of his being so shamefully misrepresented and misunderstood', while Sheridan exposed both the extent of his own talents and 'the dangers of his character'. The political crisis in the party was to a considerable extent the outcome of the clash between these two ambitious and able men which began within a month of the King's derangement. By the beginning of December, Grey's position in the expected new administration was under discussion. There is no doubt that Grey's ambition was to be Chancellor of the Exchequer. Lord John Cavendish, who had held the post in 1782 and 1783, was generally considered as

[4] *CGPW*, i. 364–6, 353, 390–1 and n.

having a prior claim, but he was undecided whether to accept it. The Prince, on Sheridan's advice, took matters into his own hands and, without consulting Fox, with whom Grey himself had not yet had an opportunity to discuss the question, spoke to Grey at Carlton House on 2 December. He put his arm round Grey's shoulder and declared that 'you must have something indeed', and mentioned to him a Lordship of the Treasury—a much inferior post, though one usually considered appropriate for a man of Grey's age and service. Grey's embarrassment was acute; he replied that he wished for nothing. Lady Elizabeth Foster told the story in her journal:

'Oh yes', replied the Prince, 'you must indeed, don't be so diffident, you are a young man of talents, and should be encouraged—come to me some morning and we will talk about it.' Grey kept bowing, ready to sink all the time, and refusing all places that could be offered him. 'Sheridan', said the Prince, 'Grey should not be so diffident'. 'Sir', replied Sheridan, 'it may be diffidence, or it may be ambition'. 'Oh', said the Prince, 'perhaps he don't think this good enough, come to me Grey and we will talk it over'.

Sheridan, wrote Lady Elizabeth, repeated the conversation 'with infinite humour' at Grey's discomfiture. Grey rushed off the next day to speak to Fox about his pretensions, and had a long conversation in the evening with the Prince at Brooks's. He was determined, if he could not have the Exchequer, to be Secretary at War and, wrote Georgiana, not to be subordinate to any 'but Fox, Cavendish or Sheridan himself—certainly not to those Norfolks, Windhams and Pelhams'. He was still sore and angry at Sheridan's conduct, and reacted violently when Sheridan tried to convince him that the Lordship of the Treasury was not beneath his acceptance. Georgiana wrote on the 4th that Grey was 'a little mortified' but determined to refuse the office, and on the 5th that the feud with Sheridan was 'worse than ever'. On the 7th, however, Lady Elizabeth reported that the quarrel was made up and Grey agreed to take 'what his friend advises him'. It left him in a bad temper nevertheless, and on the following day he quarrelled angrily with another of Fox's friends, Richard Fitzpatrick, over Sheridan's influence with the Prince, Fitzpatrick having taken exception to Grey's remark that Sheridan ought not to be trusted.[5]

The crisis was affecting everyone's nerves, and the tactical errors which the Whigs were to make in handling the Regency question in Parliament no doubt derived to a large extent from their increasing tendency to fall out amongst themselves. Well into late January, by which time the political initiative had passed to Pitt and the government's Regency Bill was making its way successfully through Parliament despite violent Whig opposition, the party was still torn by internal

[5] Duchess of Devonshire's Diary, Chatsworth MSS, partly printed in Sichel, *Sheridan*, ii. App. iii; preface (1802), 400, 406, 411, 413; Lady E. Foster's Journal, Chatsworth MSS. Elliot wrote on 5 Dec. that Grey 'is a great favourite, and is admitted to all the Prince's most private or Cabinet councils. We are rather afraid of his premature ambition running foul of the established heads of the party one day and doing mischief': Minto MSS, incorrectly printed in *Elliot*, i. 244. In Fox's list of proposed Cabinet places, sent to Portland on 21 Jan., Cavendish was named as Chancellor of the Exchequer and Grey as Vice-President of the Board of Trade: Trevelyan, *Lord Grey*, 21; *Fox*, iv. 284.

jealousies and quarrels. They had lost their early confidence and were beginning to talk gloomily of being unable to form a lasting administration. Evidence poured in, in the shape of addresses and resolutions of public meetings, of Pitt's popularity and support in the country. It was even suggested that the Whigs would be uncertain of securing a majority in the Commons by a dissolution after taking office.[6]

The mishandling of the parliamentary proceedings on the King's illness and the question of Regency arrangements was the Whigs' worst mistake at this period. Committed as they were to the Prince—or, rather, as they hoped he was to them—their best interests would have been served by his adoption as Regent in the shortest possible time. Pitt's early decision to propose a parliamentary settlement involving restricted powers for a Regent during the King's lifetime caught them neatly in a dilemma. If they accepted the government's scheme, which involved restricting the Regent's power over the King's real or personal property and household, and depriving him of any power to grant peerages or offices, in reversion or otherwise, other than during pleasure, they might still look forward to an early enjoyment of power. Even Pitt dared not propose restricting the Regent's authority to appoint and dismiss his own servants or to dissolve parliament to provide them with a majority. As Sheridan pointed out, once in office and with a majority in the Commons, they might be able to remove the remaining political restrictions, though the refusal of the prerogative of making peers and the lack of control of Household appointments might prejudice their chances of pushing such a measure through the Lords. The question was whether it was worth accepting the restricted Regency, and denying their more eminent followers the peerages and other patronage they would normally expect to acquire, in order to achieve office, or risk a long battle during which the King's recovery might deny them office altogether. In the latter case, they would either have to present acceptable constitutional arguments against a parliamentary regulation of the Regency and in favour of the Prince's acquisition of his father's full prerogatives by hereditary right and in his father's lifetime, or they would have to defeat the government's proposals clause by clause and so leave the Prince with unrestricted powers acquired on Parliament's authority.

Foolishly, they attempted both. Fox, in a speech which contemporaries and historians have generally condemned as thoughtless and needlessly provocative, declared outright that Parliament had no standing in the matter, and that the Prince became Regent by hereditary right at the moment of his father's incapacity, which was equivalent to a demise of the Crown. All that was necessary was for a joint Address of the two Houses to the Prince to ask him to take up these powers. The alternative proposed by the government of a parliamentary statute was, he pointed out, constitutionally impossible, since the purpose of the statute was to supply the missing legislative power of the royal assent; but until the Bill received the royal assent it could not itself be a law. The dilemma could be resolved in no

[6] *Journal & Correspondence of William, Lord Auckland*, ed. Bishop of Bath and Wells (1861), ii. 267.

other way than by the recognition of the Prince's existing authority. The scheme later proposed by Pitt to overcome this objection, of the affixing of the great seal to the Bill in token of the royal assent by the Lord Chancellor on the authority of the two Houses, was scorned by the opposition under the nickname of 'the Phantom'. Constitutionally there was something to be said for the opposition's contention: but in political terms it was disastrous. Englishmen in the centenary year of the Glorious Revolution were too readily reminded of the anathema of Stuart divine-right principles, and Fox's doctrine was immediately likened to that of the monarchist Sir Robert Filmer. Pitt was presented with an advantage he immediately seized and never lost. Whatever the legal rights or wrongs of the case, Fox and the Whigs were branded once again, as in 1783, as a faction of unscrupulous politicians who were ready to give up their vaunted 'Whig' principles for the sake of personal advancement. The House of Commons responded to Pitt's arguments, and the majority in the first division stayed firmly on his side, giving him a decided tactical advantage in the following weeks' debates.[7]

Having failed to establish the Prince of Wales's right to the Regency without parliamentary intervention, the Whigs made a second blunder in deciding to fight the Regency restrictions clause by clause in both Houses. They thus not only exposed their weakness, failing to gain sufficient support to win a single division, but also prolonged by several weeks the moment when the Bill would pass into law. Fate cheated them at the last when the King's recovery was announced in late February, a few days before the Bill was due to reach its final stage in the Lords.

Defeat demoralized the Whigs, and exacerbated the personal quarrels amongst them as each blamed the other for the mistakes which had robbed them of victory. Grey was one of those who had doubts about the party's tactics from the beginning. Both the Devonshire House ladies noted in their diaries that Sheridan and Grey were, as Georgiana wrote, 'in their hearts' against Fox's declaration of the Prince's right, but resolved to go through with it in Fox's support. Grey tried to make the best of a bad case in the House, partly by trying to turn the attack on Pitt by accusing him of attempting 'to make a republican government out of a limited monarchy' and of showing disrespect to the Prince of Wales; and in his last speech on the Regency Bill on 12 February he returned to the original issue and claimed that 'no right whatever to exercise the royal authority, independent of the authority of Parliament' had ever been asserted by the Whigs, but that Fox's declaration had been merely a personal opinion that such a right existed. His attempts at a more statesmanlike approach to the Regency question were, however, spoilt by the recurrence of his touchiness and bad temper when baited from the government benches during the committee stage. Particularly embarrassing was the attempt

---

[7] Sichel, *Sheridan*, ii. 418 (19 Dec.); *Parl. Hist.* xxvii. 707. The legal argument behind the opposition's case was probably drafted by Loughborough: *CGPW*, i. 370–1; *Fox*, ii. 291–9. Georgiana wrote on 10 Dec. that Fox's speech had done the opposition much harm with the independent members in the Commons: Sichel, *Sheridan*, ii. 414.

by John Rolle, the Prince's old adversary in this matter, to raise again the question of the Prince's supposed marriage. Finally Grey, taunted by references to a newspaper article on the rumours, was led into an indiscreet denial of what he knew to be true. He declared that Fox's denial of the marriage in 1787 had been 'strictly true'—no doubt salving his conscience by mental reservations about the distinction between a legal marriage and a *de facto* marriage. There were times when Grey seemed to rival even Burke, whose parliamentary performances were beginning to alarm his friends by his lack of discretion and control. Though Grey's set speeches in the Commons were praised by his friends, he had not yet acquired a reputation for restraint and statesmanship in the heat of debate, and this fact no doubt hampered his attempt to claim a high position in a Whig administration if one should be formed.[8]

The King's recovery, however, postponed that occasion to a still more remote future than had seemed likely even before the crisis began. The only consolation that Grey could find was that, despite the widespread public support of Pitt's strategy throughout the country, his own constituents in Northumberland had voted him an address of thanks for his conduct in Parliament. It was something to know that his seat was unlikely to be at risk as the result of his alignment with the opposition, but it was a poor consolation for the loss of the chance of office which his ambition craved.[9]

The Regency crisis therefore left the Whig party not only more unpopular than ever in the country but also more deeply divided by internal feuds and recriminations.[10] Burke in particular resented the way in which his colleagues had plunged after Fox on the Prince's right, and their neglect of his own attempt to construct a reasonable constitutional basis for their opposition to Pitt's scheme. Together with the party's growing reluctance to persist with the Hastings impeachment, the Regency episode helped to convince Burke that he had lost his former influence—indeed, that he was looked upon as a nuisance by his colleagues. He began to consider the party as insensitive to all questions of principle, and concerned only with political advantage. The onset of the issues arising from the French Revolution was seen to confirm him in that view and to lead inexorably to his breach with the Foxite group to which Grey belonged.

Even in that group, however, all was not unity and friendship. Grey had not forgiven Sheridan for his attitude towards his claims to office, and in June 1789 they had another violent quarrel. It began, Lady Elizabeth Foster recorded, about politics, and ended with Grey angrily shouting that

---

[8] Ibid. (11 Dec.); Lady Elizabeth Foster's Journal, 11 and 18 Dec.; *Parl. Hist.* xxvii. 1014–17, 1096, 1104, 1110–12, 1166, 1191–3, 1258; Trevelyan, *Lord Grey*, 22.

[9] Lady Elizabeth Foster's Journal, 23 Jan.

[10] Fox was hissed by the crowd when he attended the thanksgiving service for the King's recovery in St Paul's (ibid). Georgiana later wrote that the Regency crisis sowed 'those seeds of disunion in the opposition party which have since so fatally for itself and for the country operated against it': Sichel, *Sheridan*, 400.

if he [Sheridan] quitted the party there would not be half a vote to follow him. Sheridan said that if he had not had a contempt for his character before this would have given it him. They almost gave each other the lie, and had not Mr. Fitzpatrick and others interfered who resented the shame to the party thus to fall out amongst themselves, it must have ended in a duel.[11]

Relations between the two remained stormy for a considerable time, Sheridan suspecting Grey of trying to usurp the position of the key figure in the party next to Fox and its chief link with Carlton House, Grey equally regarding Sheridan as the major obstacle to his own advancement. However, personal rivalry did not preclude political co-operation, and on many of the issues of the 1790s the two were to differ more on tactics than on strategy. Sheridan's opportunism and hot temper made him at times seem even readier to go to extreme lengths than Grey, whose earlier rashness was beginning to be tempered by his growing concern over the dangers of radicalism. But both opposed Pitt's repressive policies in the 1790s and both had a genuine concern for the Whig tradition of liberty, which led them into common action despite their temperamental difficulties. In the end their political friendship proved stronger than their clashes of personality.

The following three years were a period of consolidation for Grey's influence and reputation as a leading member of the Whig party in the Commons. He remained under the shadow of Fox, supporting him particularly in the field which Fox always preferred, that of foreign affairs. This too was an important ground of inter-party conflict. Traditionally, Whigs and Tories since the reign of Charles II had favoured opposed systems of foreign alliances and policies. In the 1780s, the Whig party advocated the maintenance of traditional anti-French hostility. Fox as Foreign Secretary in 1782 had been prepared to recognize American independence as a preliminary to peace negotiations, in the hope of splitting the Franco-American alliance and continuing the European and colonial war against the Bourbon powers. The Whigs opposed the French Commercial Treaty of 1786 largely because they did not believe that the old enmity of France was more than disguised by it, and it was significant that it was Grey's opposition to the Treaty that had first brought him into political alliance with them. The Whigs were also supporters of a northern policy, and alliance with Catherine of Russia in particular. When, therefore, in 1790 and 1791 Pitt's government became embroiled in conflict, first with Spain on the west coast of North America, and then with Russia over the Black Sea port of Ochakov, the Whigs mounted a full scale parliamentary and propaganda campaign against both those policies. In the first case, the government was attacked for its rashness in over-reacting to the threat of Spanish territorial claims in America; in the second, it was censured for its over-belligerent attitude towards Russia in an area which, it was claimed, was of little importance to Britain.[12]

[11] Journal, 5 June 1789.
[12] For British foreign policy in this period see J. Holland Rose, *Pitt and National Revival* (1911), 562–632; P. Langford, *The Eighteenth Century* (Modern British Foreign Policy series) (1976), 189–205; and J. Ehrman, *The Younger Pitt*, i. (1969) 552–71, and ii. 3–41.

The Spanish crisis arose over disputed claims to territorial rights at Nootka Sound on the west coast of Vancouver Island. Two Spanish naval vessels arrived at Nootka in May 1789 and proceeded to occupy the British settlement and seize their trading-ships and their crews, allegedly ill-treating them and causing the suicide of one petty officer. The Spanish envoy in London then demanded the recognition of Spanish sovereignty over the area, the withdrawal of British traders and settlers, and their punishment for infringing Spanish rights. In February 1790 the Cabinet responded with a denial of the Spanish claims and a threat of war unless restitution was made for British losses. At the beginning of May naval mobilization began and war seemed inevitable. Parliament unhesitatingly voted a credit of £1 million, and diplomatic pressure was put on Spain by British interference in South America and by calling on the support of our Triple Alliance partners, Prussia and the Netherlands. In the autumn Pitt decided to force the issue to a conclusion by sending an ultimatum to Madrid. The Spanish goverment gave way and agreed to a Convention, which restored the buildings and territory seized from the British and recognized British rights to trade along the whole north-west American coast.

The episode established the foundations of a future British Empire on the west coast of Canada, but the prevailing ignorance of the strategic and economic importance of the area made that seem of little account to contemporary Englishmen. What was apparent was that Pitt had taken the country to the verge of what might have become a European war, involving France and Russia on the side of Spain, with the support of Holland and Prussia for Britain. The Whigs were alarmed at this prospect. The establishment of a liberal and constitutional regime in France after 1789 had modified Whig hostility towards the old enemy, and the opposition's policy of friendship with Catherine the Great was threatened by the possibility of war against Russia and Denmark. The Whigs therefore adopted the line that the warlike preparations of Pitt's government were rash and unnecessary, that their object was trivial, and that the dangers were great: and when the Convention was signed it was represented not as a diplomatic triumph but as a vague and unsatisfactory document which settled nothing and contained the seeds of future conflict.

The opposition's case, however, was a weak one. Despite the slight economic importance at present of the Nootka Sound area, wars overseas against the old Bourbon enemy in pursuit of commercial advantage were still popular, and the mood of the country was jingoistic. The opposition had to be careful not to seem unpatriotic in face of this general mood of aggressive economic nationalism. They focused their campaign therefore, not on the policy of resisting Spanish aggression in itself, but upon the way in which the government had handled the crisis.[13] They were, in fact, groping for a policy on Nootka Sound, and it is difficult to resist the view that they were opposing for the sake of opposition rather than because they

[13] W. L. Cook, *Flood Tide of Empire: Spain in the Pacific North West, 1543–1819* (1973), 213–14.

had any constructive alternative to offer. The tone of Grey's leading speeches both in May and in December 1790 was intensely political: though on 6 May both he and Fox had supported the government in its warlike preparations, on the 12th he moved for papers to be laid before the House as the basis of a parliamentary enquiry into the government's conduct and policy. He inferred that the country had been brought to the brink of war by rash incompetence, and contrasted Pitt's recent speech on the Budget, which held out the prospect of a long period of European peace, with the present posture of the government in preparing for war. Either Pitt had deceived the House in making that speech, or he was guilty of neglect in not responding quickly enough to the development of the Spanish threat. In reply to the debate, however, Grey was more evasive, declaring that his motion was purely one of enquiry and not of censure, and that the opposition were not objecting to the possibility of Britain's going to war under any circumstances to protect her interests, but questioning whether the objective in this case justified the expense. He concluded with a panegyric on Fox for his 'most perfect disinterestedness' in a life of public service. It was a good example of an opposition trying to make bricks with very little straw, and the motion was defeated by the administration's usual majority.[14]

In December, Grey renewed the contest by moving for papers concerning the Convention, and by leading the subsequent debate on it. Nothing new or damaging to the government emerged, nor was much public interest stirred up. Grey's speech was chiefly remarkable for an attack on Grenville, who had recently left the Speaker's Chair to become a member of the House of Lords as Home Secretary. Grey asked ironically whether he had been promoted for 'his long and laborious services in the Chair' as all Pitt's peers had been 'raised for their eminent and distinguished services'. The weary reporter merely recorded that he pursued 'this strain of irony to some length' before his motion was rejected by 134 to 258. The Convention was approved, despite a further speech from Grey, on 14 December by 123 to 247.[15]

The 'Russian armament' of the following year provided the opposition with a much more promising opportunity, on which they succeeded in doing what they had signally failed to achieve in 1790—arousing a strong public opposition to the government and forcing it to a humiliating change of policy. It was their greatest triumph over Pitt in all the years of his administration, and its repercussions significantly affected the course of domestic politics in the following three years.

The Ochakov crisis developed out of Britain's attempt to block Russian penetration to the Mediterranean Sea. Pitt's foreign policy was directed towards arranging a solution of the conflicts in central and eastern Europe which involved Russia, Poland, Austria, and Turkey. Russian ambitions were directed towards southward expansion, while Joseph II of Austria also hoped to acquire territories on the western side of the Black Sea. The Russian annexation of the Crimea in

---

[14] *Parl. Hist.* xxviii. 779, 794–7.
[15] Ibid. 949–53, 977–8, 1003. Grenville had been elected Speaker only in Jan. 1789.

1783 was followed by a joint Austro-Russian plan to strip Turkey of much of her Balkan empire. The Turks responded by declaring a pre-emptive war on Russia in the summer of 1787. The Austrians joined the war in the following February, but the intervention of Gustavus III of Sweden in the Baltic forced the Russians to switch their main forces to the north. Britain wished to preserve the existing balance of power in northern Europe, and supported Prussia in attempting to prevent Russian aggrandizement in that area. In December 1788, however, the Russians resumed the offensive in the Black Sea and occupied the Turkish outpost at Ochakov.

The British government was temporarily paralysed by the Regency crisis, and Catherine the Great renewed her contacts with the Whig opposition in London, hoping to secure the alliance of the prospective Whig administration and neutralize the diplomatic threat to her expansionist ambitions. Compliments were exchanged between the Russian Empress and the Whig leaders, including the presentation to her of a bust of Fox, and the Russian Ambassador in London, Count Woronzov, encouraged the opposition and supplied them with information and arguments. The scene was set for both an international and an internal party conflict. Once the threat to his position at home was over, Pitt attempted to energize the Triple Alliance to contain Russian expansionism in northern, central, and south-eastern Europe. In February 1791 the British and Prussian governments sent an ultimatum demanding the withdrawal of the Russian forces from Ochakov.

Pitt overplayed his hand. The country was not yet accustomed to what was to become Britain's traditional Near-Eastern policy of Russian containment. Russia was believed by most British politicians to be, in Fox's words, 'a power whom we could neither attack, nor be attacked by'. Nor was the hitherto unheard-of port of Ochakov generally regarded as a place of sufficient importance, in whatever hands it was held, to justify Britain's going to the lengths of war. It was not easy to see what British interests were involved; and in the Cabinet itself there were doubts and hesitations. While Pitt and his Foreign Secretary, the Duke of Leeds, favoured a belligerent policy, half the Cabinet was doubtful. The newspapers generally adopted a hostile tone towards the government's policy, and the opposition seized gratefully an unprecedented opportunity to exploit the internal divisions in the Cabinet and to capture the support of public opinion.[16]

Fox set the strategy of the opposition's campaign on 29 March 1791. In a statesmanlike review of British foreign policy and its objectives, he reminded the House that his party had supported the Triple Alliance and, in the Nootka Sound crisis, had criticized the government not for its policy but merely for its weakness in carrying it out. He pointed out that Russia had been strengthening her position in the Black Sea area for twenty years, with no protests from Britain even at the time of the annexation of the Crimea: where now was the threat to the balance of power which was alleged as the reason for British involvement? The British

[16] *Speeches of the Rt. Hon. C. J. Fox in the House of Commons* (1815), iv. 198–9; D. B. Horn, *Britain and Europe in the eighteenth century* (Oxford, 1967), 225–6, 228.

government had been inconsistent, obstinate, and unrealistic; the itch to interfere in the internal affairs of other states—notably France—was further evidence of a dangerous tendency in the present government to pursue policies of senseless aggrandizement. He urged that 'an alliance with Russia was the most natural and advantageous that we could enter into', and implied that Pitt was seeking to identify British interests with those of Austria and Prussia, the two powers most prominent in the European reaction against the liberalization of the government in France.[17]

As the debate proceeded, it became apparent that Pitt's support in the Commons was diminishing, and on 12 April Grey rose to press home the advantage with a series of resolutions opposing the 'Russian armament'. He seconded Fox's contention that 'the only just cause of war originated in the principle of self-defence'; this principle was to be invoked only to claim a right withheld, to provide for the future safety of the kingdom, or to repel an unjust attack on ourselves or an ally. The present conflict fell under none of these heads, and indeed the government's policies ran counter to British interests in that our valuable trade with Russia was put at risk. He then moved on to the attack on a more constitutional point, declaring that Pitt's policies in many fields provided evidence of an increasing tendency to ride roughshod over Parliament and public opinion merely in pursuit of power. Referring to a constant theme of Pitt's speeches since January 1784, that the House of Commons owed a degree of confidence to the ministry of the day unless the government was found to have committed an error of policy or administration, he denounced

those doctrines of confidence which were every day carried to a great extent, and which converted the House of Commons into what was little better than the Parlement of Paris before the late revolution. If this doctrine of confidence was still extended, that House would soon serve no other purpose but merely to approve and register the edicts of the King's Ministers.

Grey concluded by a firm declaration of his party alignment:

He declared it was his glory to announce, that he had attached himself by principle to his right hon. friend (Mr. Fox), and to a set of men ... who deserved the praises of their countrymen, for resisting, on all occasions, every principle that was unconstitutional.

And he declared that it was the essence of Whig principles that the prerogative of the Crown should be exercised on behalf of the good and safety of the people.[18]

Grey's resolutions were lost by a vote of 173 to 253, a vote encouraging enough for the opposition to continue the contest. A new motion was presented by William Baker on 15 April, on which occasion Fox digressed to utter his famous panegyric on the new French constitution and Burke was prevented by his friends from rising in anger to answer him. The Ochakov affair was assuming implications for the domestic party struggle as well as for British foreign policy: but the

[17] *Parl. Hist.* xxix. 61–70.
[18] Ibid. 164–7.

opposition's attempt to extend their success to a general attack on the government's competence was bound to break down in face of the reluctance of Pitt's supporters and of the neutrals to go beyond a withdrawal of support on the one issue. It may be that Fox and Grey, in raising the wider question of the government's attitude towards the constitution, were seeking to avoid the charge of factious opposition and attempting to put their objections to Pitt's foreign policy into an effective framework of political principle; it is clear, however, that in so doing they were bound to dilute the support they would otherwise have received on the particular question. Fox's inability to restrain his enthusiasm for French constitutionalism was a further blow to their prospects of launching a successful campaign against the government in general from the base of foreign policy. So, despite their success in forcing Pitt to withdraw his ultimatum and recognize the Russian possession of Ochakov, and despite the subsequent resignation of the Duke of Leeds who, to his credit, refused to reverse the policy he had advocated, the Whigs drew no concrete advantage from the Ochakov affair. It was clear that the old prejudices against Fox and his friends remained in force and, in particular, that the Whig party itself was unable to form a united front on domestic and constitutional questions while the shadow of events in France still lay over the political scene. It was the French Revolution and its consequences which now dominated British politics: and it was with these issues that Grey's political future was to be concerned.[19]

[19] Ibid. 218–49; J. Derry, *Charles James Fox* (1972), 283–4.

2 The Commitment to Reform, 1792–1802

Grey's reactions to the news of the fall of the Bastille in the summer of 1789 are not on record, but it is reasonable to suppose that he echoed Fox's enthusiasm for the dawning of a more liberal era in France and all over Europe. His natural inclination was to side with Fox's section of the party, though his attitude was in general more calculating in terms of party advantage than Fox's generous impulsiveness. His more thrusting personal ambition focused upon the opportunities which the events of 1789 and afterwards provided for the Whigs to emerge as the champions of popular causes. There was no future, as he realized, in their drifting towards Pitt and ending up as a subordinate group in Pitt's empire. The alternative was to present a distinctive image to the public, to take advantage of the increasing conservatism of Pitt's ministry, and to offer responsible leadership to liberal and enlightened opinion in the country.

Grey assumed in the early 1790s the political attitude which was to characterize the greater part of his life. He realized that the fundamentals of the eighteenth-century balanced constitution and of aristocratic dominance were coming increasingly under threat from new forces in society and he argued that Pitt's tactics of repression would merely inflame the situation further. He proposed that judicious conciliation would persuade the public to look for leadership towards the liberal section of the existing governing class. The Reform Bills of 1831–2 were based upon the same principles as those which led to the formation of the Society of the Friends of the People in 1792. Neither was designed to advance the cause of radical change, or to lead Britain to democracy. Both were intended to restrain and disarm the latent violence of class conflict. Perhaps above all, they were meant to preserve Whig hegemony in an era when purely aristocratic and landed wealth were being increasingly challenged by new men and new ideas. Grey's career for forty years and more after 1792 was dedicated to these purposes.

The issue did not arise in this extreme form until the spring of 1792, but the crisis began in 1790. Burke was beginning to express alarm at the revolutionary implications of the doctrine of the Rights of Man—implications which he believed to be as ominous for Britain as for France herself. The renewed activity of the Dissenters from 1787 onwards in agitating for the repeal of the Test and Corporation Acts, which threatened the Anglican monopoly of offices and authority, and the celebrations of the centenary of the English Revolution, which drew attention to the alleged corruption of the constitution since 1689, demonstrated the awakening of reform sentiment in England.[1] The Whigs had from the first taken

---

[1] See H. T. Dickinson, *Liberty and Property* (1977), 195–231; and C. Bonwick, *English Radicals and*

an ambivalent attitude towards these movements. Though Fox had responded favourably to the Dissenters' cause, the Duke of Portland and the other conservative and aristocratic leaders of the party had held aloof. Burke's attitude towards the Dissenters became more hostile when he found many of their leaders in the forefront of those who welcomed events in France, and when they endorsed the radical reform programme at home. During the winter of 1789–90 Burke came to identify the English reformers with the supporters of radical social and political change on the French model, implying the abolition of aristocratic rank and privilege and the re-ordering of society on democratic principles.[2] By the beginning of 1790 he was beginning to order his thoughts into the context of his pamphlet *Reflections on the Revolution in France*, to be published in November 1790. His purpose now was to warn Englishmen against the dangers of remodelling their ancient constitution on abstract philosophical principles, neglecting the wisdom of ages and the cohesive strength of precedent and tradition.

Burke was also a party politician, who saw it as his duty not only to warn his colleagues against subversive influences but to act with resolution against all those who might introduce them into his party. In particular he distrusted Sheridan, whose conduct since the Regency crisis he regarded as motivated by mere personal ambition. He feared, too, that Fox was too easily influenced by his friends and too ready to adopt popular courses without adequate consideration. Still smarting from the neglect with which the Foxites had treated his advice on the Regency, he was determined to destroy Sheridan's influence in the party on the issue of the French Revolution. He was therefore on the lookout for any signs of an endorsement by Fox of radical principles, and he professed to find it in Fox's remarks, in a debate on the army estimates in February 1790, that standing armies were no longer to be so feared, the French having shown that soldiers could also be citizens. Burke took this as a text upon which to condemn

cabals he thought were forming in England to make alterations under the idea of reforms in our constitution, and looking at Mr Sheridan gave it to be understood that he was the person, and that if C. Fox gave in to these maxims, much as he loved and admired him ... that still he should desert him.

Sheridan he would break with 'for ever'.

Fox rose in astonishment and distress to disavow any differences of principle from Burke, whom he praised on the verge of tears, but Sheridan took the bait, 'rose in a fury' and 'abused Burke very much'. Burke then declared, to ministerial cheers and delight, that all connection between himself and Sheridan was at an end. Sheridan's bad temper rarely lasted for long, and, discovering that his violent language was disapproved of by the party leaders, he tried to make up the quarrel: but misunderstanding followed misunderstanding and despite the Duke of

the American Revolution (Durham, NC, 1977), 216–19. For Whig attitudes see O'Gorman, *The Whig Party*, 32–69; and my *Whig Principles*, 117–42. For the Dissenters see U. Henriques, *Religious Toleration in England, 1787–1833* (1961), 54–135; and A. Goodwin, *The Friends of Liberty* (1979), 65–98.

  [2] *Burke Correspondence*, v. 469–71, vi. 82–5, 100–4, 125–30.

Portland's mediation the breach remained. The consequences, wrote William Elliot, might well be 'essentially injurious to the party'. It was a prophecy which soon came true.[3]

Grey's sympathies appear to have been with Sheridan, whom he considered unjustly attacked by Burke. At the same time, however, Burke's draft of his pamphlet on the Revolution was being passed round the leading members of the party and his sentiments were being generally approved. Only his former close ally and confidant Philip Francis astonished him by the violence and personal asperity of his criticisms. If, however, Burke drew comfort from the party leaders' general approval of his pamphlet, he was distressed by their equally apparent unwillingness to act on his advice and disavow those who continued, with Fox and Sheridan, to praise the French Revolution and to consort with the English reformers. The lines of division were beginning to be drawn on which the party would split, effectively in 1792, and formally in 1794. The crucial question, as Fox wrote to his close friend and the deputy party leader Lord Fitzwilliam in May 1792, was not whether the party as a body, or individuals within it, approved or disapproved of events in France, but whether the party was to maintain its distinctive identity as the only respectable body pledged to the principle of liberty. On this reasoning, it was clear that Fox's stand was taken. It was equally certain that Grey would follow him, but there were times when Grey's enthusiasm overrode those bounds of prudence and political calculation to which Fox was trying to keep in the following months. From this circumstance arose what an older, wiser, and infinitely more experienced Grey was to call in the year of his death 'all the mess of the "Friends of the People" '.[4]

The political background to the establishment of the Friends of the People may be found in the efforts made after 1789 by the younger and more active members of the Whig party to recover from the disasters of the Regency crisis. The events of 1788–9 had re-established Pitt's popularity in the country and linked it closely to a new affection for the unfortunate George III. Despite the personal weaknesses of Pitt's Cabinet, his administration now rested upon two strong props: the favour of the King and the support of many of the public. The Whigs could not hope to remove the first, at least until the Prince of Wales should succeed to the throne, but they could hack away at the other. If they were to hope for anything during George III's lifetime, they needed to identify themselves with public interests and popular causes, and they needed to revive the campaign of the American War period to reduce the 'influence of the Crown' in order to allow those popular interests greater weight in the electoral system. Some progress had been made in and after 1782, when certain categories of public servants and men under government influence had been debarred from voting in elections or sitting in the

---

[3] 5 Feb. 1790: *Parl. Hist.* xxviii. 330; Lady Elizabeth Foster's Journal, 15 Feb. 1790; *Elliot*, i. 349–54 (23 Feb.).

[4] Ibid. 365–7; *Burke Correspondence*, vi. 85–92; Smith, *Whig Principles*, 134–6; General C. Grey, *Life and Opinions of Charles, second Earl Grey* (1861), 11.

Commons, and when the resources of the Civil List for political influence had been placed within some (though not as yet fully effective) bounds. The Whigs as a party had not hitherto, however, envisaged electoral reform as an instrument in this process. The aristocratic heads and supporters of the party had too much to lose themselves by a widespread abolition of close constituencies, and many among them found it impossible to overcome their distaste on principle for structural reform of the old political system. Rockingham had laid it down in 1780 that priority should be given to removing temptation from the paths of 'men when chosen into Parliament' rather than to reform of the way in which they got there, and this had remained the view of Burke, Portland, Fitzwilliam, and other party notables.[5]

However, Fox and a few others had committed themselves further. In 1780 Fox had tried to take over the Westminster Association for Parliamentary Reform, mainly in order to convert it into an organization to support Whig electoral interests in the Westminster constituency, but he had failed to prevent its committee from being dominated by a radical group which had published a far-reaching parliamentary reform programme. Many reformers, however, distrusted Fox's party as too aristocratic and, like Christopher Wyvill's Yorkshire Association, gave their support in 1784 to Pitt. Fox, meanwhile, had secretly agreed in 1783 to drop reform in order to win the alliance of Lord North and his followers. The Whigs after 1783 were a less liberal body than they had appeared to be under Rockingham. Fox never explicitly repudiated his earlier commitment to reform, but in 1792 he admitted to Fitzwilliam that 'I am more bound by former declarations and consistency than by any strong opinion I entertain in its favour.' Pitt's loss of interest in the question after 1785 had begun to arouse suspicions among reformers of his apostasy, but they were not yet ready to transfer their hopes and allegiance to the Whigs. When in March 1790 Henry Flood, an Irish member, renewed the question in Parliament with the first motion on the subject since 1785, Fox temporized, declaring that his opinions on the subject were unchanged, but that he considered it a 'sleeping question' on which the public at large was not yet ready for a measure.[6]

During the next twelve months, public agitation for reform developed rapidly. Popular societies and associations were founded in many of the manufacturing districts, and produced manifestos and addresses demanding constitutional reform, as yet by peaceful and legitimate methods. Many of those who energized or encouraged these movements and helped to draw up their propaganda were old reformers, men of status and substance in society, like the already veteran reformer Major John Cartwright, while others like Wyvill and Dr Joseph Priestley also represented an element of continuity with the American War period and the

---

[5] Smith, *Whig Principles*, 56–84, 104–5, 135; E. A. Reitan, 'The civil list in 18th-century politics', *Hist. Journal* ix. no. 3 (1966), 318–37; J. Norris, *Shelburne and Reform* (1963), 170–98; Rockingham to P. Milnes, 28 Feb. 1780, *Eng. Hist. Docs.* x. ed. D. B. Horn and M. Ransome (1957), 215–17.

[6] I. R. Christie, *Wilkes, Wyvill and Reform* (1962), *passim*; *Fox*, ii. 37–8; *Parl. Hist.* xxviii. 471.

respectable Dissenters of the 1780s. But the economic changes following indu-strialization, and their social consequences, were beginning to add another dimen-sion to the movement which made it seem more threatening to the old social structure. Intelligent artisans and craftsmen from the industries of Sheffield, Nottingham, Leicester, and Norwich were beginning to take an interest in politics and provided a rapidly expanding market for political literature of a more radical kind than that which had appealed to the gentlemen reformers of Cartwright's Society for Constitutional Information. Thomas Paine's *Rights of Man* was read at public meetings and republished in thousands of cheap copies; its language and style, vivid and immediately comprehensible to the ordinary man, captured the first mass audience for political argument and convinced many among the govern-ing class of the imminence of popular revolution, the overthrow of the monarchy, the levelling of social distinctions, and the confiscation of private property. By the spring of 1792 the mass meetings, petitions, and organized societies of reformers had created a mood of alarmist reaction in which any profession of support for reform, of however moderate an extent, was becoming indistinguishable from sedition, social revolution, and even high treason.[7]

It was in such a climate of opinion that the Whig grandees grew more susceptible to the alarmism of Burke, and began to move the party towards a profession of general support for the 'cause of order' and, in practical terms, for Pitt's admin-istration and its measures against popular agitation. It was partly to prevent this from happening that Sheridan, Grey, and the rest of the more partisan Whigs resolved to reaffirm the more liberal tradition of their party. They recognized the real danger of a polarization of opinion, which would force all men of moderately liberal views to choose between revolution and repression. Their solution was for the Whigs to claim the centre ground, repudiating both Paineite radicalism and reactionary conservatism. The Friends of the People was a Society formed pri-marily to save the Whig party from Burkean extremism and to further its political objective of destroying Pitt's administration, but at the same time to provide a check to the wilder radicalism of Paine and the popular societies.

The Society was formed at a dinner given by Lord Porchester, a middle-aged opposition peer, on 11 April 1792. It was not a gathering of irresponsible young men. Porchester was 51 years old, and neither Philip Francis, 52, nor Sheridan, 41, was in the first bloom of youth. Other attenders besides Grey, now 27, were Lords Lauderdale and Buchan, two Scots peers, Thomas Erskine, William Henry Lambton, and Samuel Whitbread. The average age of these 9 was 39. Only Grey and Lambton were under 30. They were a 'younger' element in the party only in comparative terms. The full list of members eventually contained 147 names, 28 of them members of Parliament and three peers. Also included in the Society were

---

[7] For the reform movements of the 1790s see Goodwin, *The Friends of Liberty*; G. S. Veitch, *The Genesis of Parliamentary Reform* (1913); J. Cannon, *Parliamentary Reform, 1640–1832* (Cambridge, 1973); P. A. Brown, *The French Revolution in English History* (1918); G. A. Williams, *Artisans and Sansculottes* (1968); E. P. Thompson, *The Making of the English Working Class* (1968).

'outsiders' such as Cartwright himself, Thomas Brand Hollis, another prominent radical member of the Society for Constitutional Information, Sir John Swinburne of Northumberland, Grey's close friend since early youth, James Mackintosh, one of the more extreme writers against Burke's *Reflections*, George Tierney, James Losh, a radical attorney from Northumberland, Jeremiah Batley, a friend of Wyvill, and Lord Edward Fitzgerald. The committee consisted of twelve members, including Grey, Whitbread, Francis, Sheridan, Lambton, and Mackintosh. Grey was the first signatory, and was regarded as the leading spirit of the Society. Holland later wrote that it was 'the impetuosity of Mr. Grey, wrought upon by the restless activity of Lord Lauderdale, and the ambition of some of his younger friends, *viz* Mr. Whitbread, Mr. Lambton and Mr. Tierney' which led to the foundation of the Society. Others, observing with alarm Grey's close friendship with Fox, believed that his influence might draw him into the scheme. Fox's old friend James Hare expressed concern lest he would allow himself, as he was too liable to do, 'to be led, and perhaps act against his own judgement'.[8]

Fox, however, was embarrassed by the formation of the Society. In so far as he had a clear strategy at that moment, it was to try to maintain a middle position between the extremes of Burke and Windham on the one hand, and Sheridan and Lauderdale, the most enthusiastic supporters of the French Revolution, on the other. He regarded the crisis as a temporary one, which would go away if the party did nothing rash. As he wrote to Fitzwilliam in March 1792, 'I never can allow that while we agree about what is and ought to be the constitution of our own country, it can be of any importance how far we do so about what passes in France.' His aim therefore was to avoid an outright commitment to either wing of the party, in the hope that both would eventually rally to the centre. The Friends of the People did not at once destroy Fox's strategy but they made his task infinitely more difficult. The foundation of the Society, together with Grey's declared intention to move in the Commons for parliamentary reform at the end of April, forced Fox to take a stand. Either he must disavow men who were his friends, and who, though acting without his advice, had done what they thought was in the best interests of the party, or he must come out in support of reform and blow the fragile unity of the party sky high. In this respect the Friends of the People precipitated the crisis which destroyed the Whig party in 1794.[9]

Though the Friends of the People failed in their primary objectives of preventing a movement of the leading Whigs towards Pitt, and of guiding and controlling the popular reform societies in the country, from Grey's point of view the Society raised him into greater public prominence and put him in touch with many of the

---

[8] A list of members of the Friends of the People in Cartwright's papers gives 101 names, another in Wyvill's papers lists 137, but omits 10 listed by Cartwright and adds 12 non-resident members: F. D. Cartwright, *Life and Correspondence of Major Cartwright* (1826), ii. 346–7; and C. Wyvill, *Political Papers* (York 1794–1802), iii. app. 129–31; Holland, *Memoirs*, 13; L. G. Mitchell, *C. J. Fox and the Disintegration of the Whig Party, 1782–1794* (Oxford, 1971), 178.

[9] Fox to Fitzwilliam, 15 Mar. 1792, Fitzwilliam MSS, quoted in Smith, *Whig Principles*, 135; O'Gorman, *The Whig Party*, 83–4; sup. n. 4.

local leaders of reform. The question was now firmly linked with his name. The experience helped greatly to mature him as a politician. The sober and responsible attitude which he recommended to others was mirrored in an increasingly responsible tone in his own letters and speeches. It was from this period, Lord Holland declared, that Grey's eloquence acquired 'that tone of earnestness and decision, which has ever been its characteristic excellence, and raised his reputation to a pitch which it had long deserved.... From this period he was only the second to Mr. Fox in the estimation of the party and of the country.'[10]

Grey used this position to set out, in both private and public correspondence, the moderate creed of the Friends. In September he was approached for advice by the reform societies at Norwich who sent him a letter of thanks for his support of reform and enclosed a fraternal letter for the committee of the Friends of the People. Grey, in reply, pledged 'my sincerity and zeal' in the cause, added words of advice, recommending 'moderation in both your views and in your language' to guard against those who represented every type of reform 'as tending to subvert the constitution', and agreed to continue to correspond with them 'so long as your proceedings shall be temperately and wisely conducted', and directed towards 'such a reform as will correct the abuses, without impairing the forms or violating the principles of the constitution'.

Another letter of thanks came from 'the Friends of the Constitution of the People' at Glasgow. A group of Scottish reformers in Edinburgh asked in July 1792 for his help in preparing a Bill to reform the particularly unrepresentative Scottish electoral system, and though a letter from one of their delegates in November contained the rather ominous boast that 'Farmers, ploughmen, peasants, manufacturers, artificers, shopkeepers, sailors, merchants, are all employed in studying and reasoning on the nature of society and government', the writer went on to assure Grey that there was no real risk of popular insurrection unless the government took up an uncompromising stance against reform. For the present, he wrote, the movement was in the hands of 'the middle order of citizens, neither very rich or very poor; certainly not in the least like rabble', who had applauded recommendations of constitutional conduct and warnings against all disturbances.

Grey's prominence also attracted the approval of the reformers and Dissenters who formed a considerable part of the population around Newcastle in his own constituency of Northumberland. He was voted thanks by a meeting of Unitarians in Newcastle for his support for their petition against the Act of 1698 which penalized anti-Trinitarians, and a meeting of Dissenting ministers at Morpeth resolved that, though a public address of thanks to Grey at that juncture would probably do him more harm than good, they owed him as individuals 'every possible token of respect and gratitude'. Their spokesman assured Grey that he had written to all the most eminent Dissenting ministers in the county requesting them to influence their congregations in his favour. Throughout 1793 and 1794,

[10] Holland, *Memoirs*, 31–2.

Grey was in touch with moderate and respectable reformers in the north-east and elsewhere, all apparently regarding him as their leading advocate in Parliament and in the Whig party, seeking his advice about possible petitions for reform and, after January 1793, for peace.[11]

The Society's declaration and rules were carefully framed. Their objectives were defined as 'to restore the freedom of election, and a more equal representation of the people in Parliament' and 'to secure to the people a more frequent exercise of their right of electing their representatives', in order to correct abuses arising from 'a neglect of the acknowledged principles of the Constitution' and to secure 'those subordinate objects of reform, which they deem to be essential to the liberties of the people, and to the good government of the kingdom'. The constitution of the Society provided for the election of new members by ballot at their meetings, and the payment of a subscription of two and a half guineas per annum, and empowered the committee of twelve to conduct correspondence with 'all individuals or societies, desirous of promoting the cause of parliamentary reform', enjoining the committee to conduct such correspondence in conformity with the principles of the declaration which was to be signed by every member.

At its first full meeting on 26 April the Society approved an *Address to the People of Great Britain* in which the authority of an assorted company of Locke, Blackstone, the first Earl of Chatham, Sir George Savile, the Duke of Richmond, the Marquess of Lansdowne, Pitt, and Fox was claimed for the principles they espoused, to show that 'we are not aiming at reforms unthought of by wise virtuous men ... and that we cannot be accused or suspected of factious purposes, or dangerous designs ...'. The Address asserted that 'the reforms we have in view are not innovations. Our intention is not to change, but to restore; not to displace, but to reinstate the constitution upon its true principles, and original grounds.' It declared, in bold capitals, that there was no resemblance between the cases of Britain and France and that 'WE UTTERLY DISCLAIM THE NECESSITY OF RESORTING TO SIMILAR REMEDIES' to those of the French Revolutionaries. The Address concluded with a resolution that Grey should give notice that he would move for reform early in the next parliamentary session.[12]

He did so to a crowded House of Commons on 30 April. His speech was short, moderate, and conciliatory. He declared the necessity of preserving the constitution by timely reforms, which would allay the complaints of the public and restore the tranquillity of the nation. He disavowed all intention of promoting public disturbance, and assured the House that neither he nor his colleagues in the Society were pledged to any detailed and specific scheme which they were determined to force upon the House: 'he would not be connected with any set of men, who could act on terms so narrow-minded and illiberal.'

---

[11] Letters of 24 Sept. and 7 Nov. 1792; Col. N. Mcleod MP to Grey, July 1792, and other correspondence, G. 46.

[12] Wyvill, *Political Papers*, iii. app. 128–9 and 132–44, v. pp. xxi–xxiii, 30 May 1795.

The House, however, was waiting to hear what Fox would say. He had already assured Tom Pelham in private of his apprehensions about the Friends of the People and their divisive effect on the party, but he could not bring himself to speak against them in public. This was not only because of his feelings of friendship and sympathy towards them, and what he later referred to as his dislike of discouraging 'the young ones', but also because the Friends had made it more difficult for him to do so without appearing himself to be an apostate towards reform. If the Friends had been merely a small group of members of the party, Fox could have dealt with the threat they represented by private pressure: but with over a hundred members from outside Parliament in their ranks, the Friends were a public body over whom Fox could exert little direct influence and many of whom would be ready to denounce him if he went back on his former pledges. The debate caught Fox in a trap from which there was no easy escape. Despite his attempt to stress his disapproval of both Burke and Paine, his support of Grey's motion was decisive. George III was not the only man who could not see 'any substantial difference in their being joined in debate by Mr. Fox and his not being a member of that Society'. Even Gilbert Elliot, who had been trying in his own fashion to help maintain party unity, regarded it as the breaking point: although Fox had not signed the Association, he wrote to his wife on 1 May, 'he might just as well have signed it as made the speech he did yesterday'; and he foretold that the consequence would be, 'if not certainly to divide and break up our party, at least to expose it to very great danger of being separated, and drive Fox still further than ever from any hope of reconciling to him the moderate and prudent part of the country'. Though 'we all profess to desire not to break on this ground, ... whether it can be avoided time will show.'[13]

The Society was certainly encouraged by Fox's support, but the more moderate members recognized the danger of becoming too closely associated with popular radicalism. It was vital to conciliate the centre of the party, by exerting a firmer control over the non-parliamentary members of the Society. At the end of April a letter was received from Major Cartwright as Chairman of the Society for Constitutional Information in which he remarked that the MPs among the Friends of the People might expect the public to doubt their sincerity, since if they were to 'prove faithfully instrumental in effecting a substantial reform', it would be the first time that the nation's trust would not have been betrayed by their elected representatives. He further assserted that 'the long lost rights of representation are rights, Sir, which, in truth, are not to be recovered but by the exertions and unanimity of the people themselves' and said that the mission of the Friends should be that of 'calling forth the energies of the nation ... casting from it with disdain all aristocratic reserves, and fairly and honestly contending for the people's rights in their full extent'. The letter continued with an approving reference to the Society for Constitutional Information's 'Declaration of Rights' and its

[13] *Parl. Hist.* xxix. 1300–1, 1335–6; T. Pelham to Lady Webster, 29 Apr. 1792, BL Add. MS 51705 fo.11; Grey. *Life and Opinions*, 10–11; *LCGIII*, i. (1962), 591, 1 May 1792; *Elliot*, ii. 17–18.

programme of 'a substantial reform of Parliament', and ended with the pious hope that the MPs among the Friends would be the first to be able to 'sacrifice both prejudice and unwarranted power at the altar of freedom'.

The Friends drew up a sharp reply, which disavowed any commitment to 'the Rights of the People in their full extent' to which Cartwright had referred, drew attention to the S.C.I.'s publication of resolutions from the Manchester Constitutional Society praising Paine's work, and remarked tartly that 'your letter appears to us to be written with a view to create distrust of our designs; to insinuate doubts of our sincerity, and to excite an early suspicion of our principles in the minds of the people.' All intercourse with the S.C.I. was declared to be at an end. A month later, Grey, as chairman for the day, signed a reply to a much more deferential letter from the Sheffield Constitutional Society, approving 'the firm and virtuous tone' of the letter, and advising the Society to adhere to moderate and constitutional principles and language. 'It is indeed', the letter concluded, 'only with Societies who express the same moderation of principles, and adopt the same wariness of language, that this Society can entertain any correspondence, or promise any co-operation.'[14]

The necessity of such firm declarations was underlined on 4 June, when five MPs resigned from the Friends in protest against Cartwright's continued membership.[15] Others, however, were determined to press ahead. George Tierney, one of the leading activists in this group, set to work to prepare a state of the representation which was intended to provide detailed evidence of abuses and inadequacies of the system as a backing for Grey's intended motion. His efforts to assemble a small conclave of the leading members in the autumn of 1792 were hindered, however, by Sheridan's preoccupation with the Prince of Wales's affairs and by Grey's reluctance to attend a suggested meeting at Bath in October, where, as Tierney wrote, 'five or six of us might have got together without being suspected of any scheme in so doing, and where we might have spent as many hours of the day as we chose in close divan without comment or observation'. He wrote reproachfully, 'I really acquit every individual of the Society of any intentional neglect of our interests. But what I lament is that we do not seem to be aware of the very critical situation in which we stand.' He warned Grey that events in France

have made one party desperate and the other drunk; many are become wild republicans who a few months back were moderate reformers, and numbers who six weeks ago were contented with plain old fashioned Toryism have now worked themselves up into such

[14] Wyvill, *Political Papers*, iii. app. 149–53, 168–9. S. Shore to Wyvill, 11 May, ibid. v. 46. Fitzwilliam expressed concern at Grey's letter as 'approving the sentiments and principles of the Sheffield Society and admitting them to be the same as those of the Friends of the People'. He thought that the popular societies would become much more formidable 'when they were to be headed by a new Association, formed of some of the first men in the kingdom in point of rank, ability, and activity': to Revd H. Zouch, 5 June 1792, Fitzwilliam MSS, Sheffield.

[15] Wyvill, *Political Papers*, iii. app. 169–71. The five were Lord John Russell, William Baker, J. C. Curwen, Dudley North, and J. Courtenay.

apprehensions for the fate of royalty as to be incapable of distinguishing between reform and treason, and to threaten death and destruction to all who differ from them.'

He appealed for decisive action before it was too late.[16]

Grey, however, was even becoming anxious whether he should go ahead with his intended motion at all. The news from France of the September massacres and the defeat of Brunswick's army of invasion had frightened many away from reform. A group of leading Friends, meeting at the beginning of November, unanimously advised him to persist, but to move for a committee of enquiry rather than to propose a detailed and specific plan of reform, in order to conciliate as far as possible the middling groups in the House.[17] On Erskine's suggestion it was agreed that Tierney should draw up a form of petition, containing the main principles of their Declaration and Address, for circulation to various local centres for signatures. Thus Grey's motion would be supported by a show of public opinion from many different areas of the country, and the uniformity of the petitions would obviate the usual criticism of their opponents, that there was no general agreement amongst reformers as to the evils or the measures they referred to. The committee was also to meet at an early date 'to let the world know that we are still alive and in health', and there would be a general meeting early in January to receive the reports on the state of the representation in England and in Scotland.

The major question facing the Friends was, however, their status in the party rather than their slight prospects of success with a parliamentary reform motion. Here too the decision was to press ahead and to follow the same strategy of attempting to commit the main section of the party to reform. It was decided to propose a motion for parliamentary reform to the party's main public body, the Whig Club, where the liberal wing of the party was more strongly represented. Tierney was confident that it would be passed by a majority of two to one, but accepted that it would 'be the cause of many divisions' in the party at large, and even that it might push the 'great Dukes' into open alliance with Pitt: so much the better, he remarked, for they were already so in secret.[18]

Grey's response was more cautious. In particular, he advised consulting Fox about the proposal. Erskine invited Fox to dinner and disclosed the plan, to be met by what Tierney said he had expected, a reply 'that he wished to know nothing of the matter'. As to reform itself, Fox was ready to give it his strong support provided he knew exactly what was to be proposed. Tierney replied that no specific plan had yet been drawn up, but that 'we should esteem it a very particular favour if Fox would give us his ideas, as I was convinced the majority of our Society were above all things anxious to act cordially with him.' He advised Grey to talk to Fox immediately on the question, and warn him that the radicals in the country were turning against him and that he was 'losing ground every

[16] Wyvill, Political Papers, 189–269; Tierney to Grey, 29 Oct. 1792, G. 55.
[17] The group consisted of Francis, Piggot, Erskine, Rous, and Tierney.
[18] Tierney to Grey, 4 Nov., ibid.

hour' in his Westminster constituency. Unless Fox came out openly into the lead on the reform question he would lose his public influence altogether. As Tierney wrote, matters had reached the stage when 'either Fox must ruin the cabal at Burlington House, or that cabal will ruin him.'

Fox's embarrassments with the Friends of the People were not yet over; but the events of December 1792 and January 1793 forced him to break more decisively than hitherto with the aristocratic wing of the party and in effect left him with nowhere else to go than into closer alliance with the radicals. When Grey's motion was eventually reached, in May 1793, the political situation was very different from that of the summer and autumn of 1792. The split in the party had effectively taken place, not in the end over the simple question of reform, but on the whole complex group of issues connected with events in Europe and, in particular, the outbreak of war in January 1793. After that, Fox resumed the position for which the reformers had cast him unavailingly in the spring of 1792, as leader of a more liberal, though greatly reduced, party seeking to keep alive the flame of constitutional liberty and reform.

Grey's motion on 6 May 1793 was heralded by the presentation of a number of petitions for reform, including one from the Sheffield Constitutional Society, the extremely radical tone and numerous popular membership of which were now the cause of much concern, particularly to Fitzwilliam whose residence at Wentworth was a short distance away. The Sheffield petition declared that the Commons were 'not the real, fair, and independent representatives of the whole people of Great Britain' and that they represented only 'a partial interest'. The subsequent debate focused more on the question whether the petition should be rejected as disrespectful to the House than on the merits of the question itself: but it was significant that those speakers who were to support Grey's motion four days later argued for bringing up the petition, even though some of them declared their opposition to the radical reform it proposed. Francis, Grey, Lambton, Fox, Sheridan, and Whitbread all spoke for receiving the petition, and pointed out, in Grey's reported words, that 'the people had a right to petition for a reform of the representation in Parliament' and that it could not reasonably be argued that 'the House of Commons was, at this moment, in a just sense of the word, a proper representation of the people'. Grey further remarked that there had been a time when Pitt himself had expressed the same sentiments. Lambton and Sheridan also pointed out that if the language of the petition was rough and unpolished, that was because it was drawn up by men of a lower station in life, who nevertheless had a right to be heard; and Fox entered into a lengthy argument, bolstered by precedents, to prove that the petition was not disrespectful, observing that no petition for reform of Parliament could be expected not to say 'that the House was not pure, or that it was corrupt, or that it did not fully represent the people'.[19] Fox's speech left no doubt as to where his sympathies now lay. He referred to the 'many and unanimous declarations of attachment to the constitution echoed from

[19] Smith, *Whig Principles*, 129–38; *Parl. Hist.* xxx. 775–86. The petition was rejected by 29 to 108.

every part of the kingdom' as a proof that there was no danger of subversion; but he also declared at the outset of his speech that 'there was not in the kingdom a more steady or decided enemy to general and universal representation, than himself'.

After these preliminaries, it was clear that Grey's motion on 6 May would have the support of Fox as well as of the other Friends of the People in the House. The chamber was full for the debate,[20] which began with the reading of the Society's lengthy petition, summarizing the main findings of the Report of the Committee on the Representation published in February. Grey's speech was one of his more notable ones, not only because of the widespread political interest in the topic, but also on account of his careful, moderate and statesmanlike presentation of the case for reform. His tone was defensive; he was more concerned to meet the objections which he expected from the opponents of reform and to dissociate himself from radical extremism than to urge any positive measure. The speech attempted to prevent damage to the party and to establish respectable and con-stitutional grounds for a moderate reform in order to avert something worse. Admitting that since April 1792 the circumstances of the country had greatly changed, and the 'prejudices against all reform and innovation' had considerably increased, he argued that the example of France should no longer be regarded as relevant to the question: 'for it was impossible that any set of men, who had not actually lost their senses, should ever propose the French revolution as a model for imitation'. The question should be considered not in the context of events in France, but in the light of its true domestic and constitutional importance, and not under the argument of 'the danger of the times' which he anticipated would be the principal objection to it. Indeed, he contended, it was always argued against reform, that in time of peace and prosperity it was unnecessary, and that in time of war and adversity it was dangerous. Thus no reform would ever be achieved. It was essential, on the contrary, to look at the abuses which had crept into the representative system, and to restore public confidence in the present constitution by reforming them. For this argument he quoted the support of precedents from 1733, 1745, 1758, and 1782–5, when proposals for reform—in the last case from Pitt himself—had been blocked by the argument of the 'danger of the times'. Now, however, the dangers came not from the excesses of reformers but from the extension of the prerogative and the restrictions on the liberty of the subject enacted by the repressive legislation of December 1792.

Grey then set out the principles which lay behind his advocacy of reform. He rested his argument, he said, 'not on natural right, but upon what was in itself the best system of government, and most conducive to the happiness of the country'. The present constitution had not been established at any one moment, but had grown gradually out of the needs of the times. One of the basic principles

---

[20] Smith, *Whig Principles*, 787–925. William Adam tried to reassure the ever-watchful Fitzwilliam that Fox's support of Grey's motion was 'unconnected with the Society of the Friends of the People, and the result of a formerly pledged opinion in Parliament': 31 Oct. 1793, Fitzwilliam MSS, Northampton.

established at the Revolution of 1688, however, was the freedom of elections to the House of Commons, another, that 'a man ought not to be governed by laws, in the framing of which he had not a voice, either in person or by his representative, and that he ought not to be made to pay any tax to which he should not have consented in the same way'; and finally, that Parliaments should be of short duration. Contrasting these principles with the present state of the representation, could it be said that they still prevailed? On the contrary, the power of the Crown and of the House of Lords had increased, both in themselves and in respect of their influence over the Commons: Pitt alone had added 30 peers who nominated or indirectly influenced the return of a total of 40 MPs. The growth of influence and the inadequacy of the representation he claimed were together responsible for the evils of the American War: and though it had been suggested that Pitt's retreat in the Ochakov crisis had shown that the House of Commons still spoke the sense of the people, he maintained that the crisis would never have arisen had that in fact been the case. The House, in short, was not a true representative of the people and was

too much influenced by passion, prejudice, or interest. . . . No government could be lasting or free which was not founded on virtue, and on that independence of mind and conduct among the people which created energy, and led to everything that was noble and generous, and that alone could conduce to the strength and safety of the state.

Grey concluded by declaring that he wished to refer the petition of the Friends of the People to a committee, and not to propose himself any particular scheme. Thus the House itself would determine what was proper to be done.

The speech was a good parliamentary performance. It was forceful, methodical, and strongly argued: it relied upon both principle and historical precedents: and Grey not only put forward arguments in favour of his proposal, but tried to answer in anticipation the principal contentions which might be used against it. However, parliamentary speeches rarely change strongly held attitudes, and Grey was followed by R. B. Jenkinson, a determined opponent of all reform, Thomas Powys, representing the conservative country gentlemen, and William Windham, author of the famous speech against Flood's motion of 1790 in which he had warned against repairing the roof of one's house in the hurricane season. All stressed the virtues of the present system in the balanced representation of interests rather than simply of the numerical majority. Jenkinson put forward the famous defence of the close boroughs as an avenue for talent to make its way into the House, and declared that, while public opinion ought to have weight in its deliberations, it should not override the consideration of other interests. He argued that it was not necessarily true that members for 'counties and populous places' were more often on the side of opposition, nor that those for close boroughs were usually found supporting government; and that on the acid test, whether the government was just, equitable, and generally acceptable to the people as a whole, the present constitution was adequate to the needs of the nation. He claimed to have proved that even the admitted theoretical defects of the system were 'necessary to the constitution, and that any attempt to reform them might prove dangerous to its very existence'. Powys too praised the present 'happy frame of our government' and raised the smear of the French example. Windham spoke heatedly against democratic principles and put forward the 'open door' argument that Peel was to use against Grey's Reform Bill 38 years later—if the door was opened, who would be able to shut it?

After these speakers against the proposal, Erskine seconded Grey at length, until the House agreed to adjourn to the next day. Then, amongst others, Francis made a long speech in answer to Windham and Jenkinson, to be answered at even greater length by Lord Mornington, later Marquess Wellesley, a close friend of Grey at Eton but now on the opposite side in politics. Mornington made much of the baneful influence of French philosophy in general and of Rousseau in particular. Whitbread followed with a defence of the Friends of the People and their 'truly constitutional' principles, claiming that they had 'not been wholly unsuccessful' in countering the pernicious activities of the loyalist associations in limiting the freedom of the press. Finally, late in the evening, Pitt, Sheridan, and Fox wound up the debate. Pitt explained his opposition to reform at the present juncture on the grounds that it would encourage the supporters of the French Revolution. The Friends of the People had attempted to present reform as a safeguard against such men; but the events of the past months had shown how unsuccessful they had been. More and more societies had been founded, 'affiliated with the Jacobin clubs in France, and . . . for the purpose of spreading Jacobin principles'. These societies had taken up the question of parliamentary reform merely as the first stage in a campaign to overthrow the constitution; thus the issue before the House was not merely that of reform: 'it is the same question which is now at issue with the whole of Europe, who are contending for the cause of order, of justice, of humanity, of religion, in opposition to anarchy, to injustice, to cruelty, to infidelity.' The British constitution, however, provided in practice all the benefits of liberty and stability; 'The question is, then, whether you will abide by your constitution, or hazard a change, with all that dreadful train of consequences with which we have seen it attended in a neighbouring kingdom.'

As Sheridan remarked in reply, it was a speech of great power and great art, and though it was hardly necessary for the purposes of simply defeating Grey's motion, for the result was a foregone conclusion from the start, it hammered home the nails which Grey had tried to prevent being driven, the assertions that reform was tantamount to revolution and that, in the present circumstances, all reform was equally dangerous. Fox's closing speech was partly a debating reply to Pitt, repeating the charge of inconsistency on the question he had once supported, arguing against the view that the times were too dangerous for reform to be contemplated, and denying that French principles or examples were relevant to the question. It was also a defence of his own position, a review of the inadequacies of the representation, and a statement of the legitimacy of reform.

The debate closed in the early hours of the morning. The reformers were defeated by the crushing majority of 282 against only 41. More discouraging perhaps than the smallness of the minority vote was the demonstration that some 300 members of the House were prepared to sit out such a long debate and listen to so many repetitious arguments on a question on which few could have come prepared to modify their existing opinions. It was not merely a sign that the cause of reform was, for the foreseeable future, a hopeless one: it was a blow from which the Whig opposition was not to recover for many years. Grey's strategy of using reform as a popular issue on which to reconstitute a powerful Whig party lay in ruins, and it was a lesson he never forgot. Though, like Fox, he never wavered for the rest of his life in his commitment to the necessity of moderate constitutional reform, he never again tried to force it on the Whig party. In November 1793 he confessed to his friend and supporter in Northumberland, Thomas Bigge, that 'I almost begin to despair' and that the prospect was that 'the People, maddened by excessive injury and roused to a feeling of their own strength, will not stop within the limits of moderate reformation.'[21] But the reform question was one which involved the unity of the party as well as the state of public opinion, and for the future it was the former which prevailed in his mind. He remained almost morbidly sensitive, even in 1819 and 1820, when for a time the conditions of 1792–3 seemed to be re-established, of the need to conciliate and carry with the party the conservative and aristocratic elements whose predecessors had deserted him in 1792 and 1793. Not until the party was established in actual control of the government in November 1830 did Grey allow reform to be made a party question; but then he dealt with it in the spirit of 1792, and presented it to the King, Parliament, party, and country as a question that must be settled by extensive changes but within the solid framework of the existing constitution.

THE FRIEND OF LIBERTY, 1792–1797

The humiliating defeat of Grey's first motion for parliamentary reform reflected the changing climate of opinion in the years 1792 and 1793. A rapid tide of events eroded the base of liberal sentiment on which the Friends of the People had tried to stand. As the policy of domestic repression got under way, in Europe the dream of the universal brotherhood of nations was shattered by the sound of war. By May 1793 the Friends were not only regarded as foolish political speculators, but were represented by the loyalists as a fifth column to support French invasion. The issue of domestic reform became entangled with that of Anglo-French relations, and Pitt and his colleagues took advantage of the foreign crisis to split the Whig party along the line of division which the Friends of the People had opened up. It is significant that Pitt's first overt intervention in the party's internal

[21] 6 Nov. 1793, G. 7.

troubles came only a few weeks after the foundation of the Society. It was expertly calculated to maximize Fox's embarrassment and to play upon the fears of the leadership that he would be drawn into radical courses.

The Prime Minister's strategy was two-pronged. On the one hand, he proposed in Parliament issues which would stimulate the fears of the aristocratic Whigs, while on the other he dangled the temptation of a possible coalition and the conferment of offices and honours upon them. The first move was attempted in the middle of May 1792, when Pitt informed Portland that the government had it in mind to issue a proclamation urging the magistrates to take action against the flood of 'seditious' literature now pouring from the presses and to be vigilant against any signs of popular tumult. He desired 'an unreserved communication ... on that one point' and offered, not only to consult the Duke and his friends on the wording of the proclamation, but to allow them to attend the meeting of the Privy Council which would order it. He further offered to make any colleagues whom the Duke wished to bring to the meeting Privy Councillors if they were not already so. The proclamation would then be laid before Parliament and the two Houses would have the opportunity to vote Addresses condemning radical agitation. Pitt rubbed home the message by assuring Portland 'that he had undoubted information of many foreigners who are employed to raise sedition in England, and that money is sent over from France to assist in this attempt'.[1]

It was too obvious a trap even for Portland, who in any case immediately consulted Fox and was promptly told that 'he saw no danger to warrant any unusual measure'. The offer of attendance at the Privy Council was declined, but the Whig leaders did propose some verbal changes in the draft of the proclamation, designed to make it less objectionable to the reformers in the party. A party meeting was called on the eve of the parliamentary debate. It was attended, wrote Elliot, by 'reformers and anti-reformers; that is, of Grey and his party, and the duke of Portland and us who are against these irregular measures'. The object was to try to avert 'personal asperity' in the debate by reaching some kind of general agreement. Grey in particular, however, was not to be easily suppressed. He spoke at length in the Commons on 25 May against the proclamation as 'an insidious measure, and adopted with no other view than to separate those who had been long connected'; and he went on to attack Pitt personally as the author of discord:

If there ever was a man in that House, who delighted more in these sinister practices than the right hon. gentleman, he had never heard of him—he whose whole political life was a tissue of inconsistencies; of assertion and retractation—he who never proposed a measure without intending to delude his hearers; who promised every thing and performed nothing; who never kept his word with the public; who studied all the arts of captivating popularity, without ever intending to deserve it; who was a complete public apostate from the first step of his political life down to the present moment; whose political malignity was now to be crowned by an endeavour to separate the dearest ...

[1] 14 May 1792: *Elliot*, ii. 23–4.

Here he was interrupted by loud cries of 'Order' and, from his own friends, of 'Go on, Go on!' and he resumed his speech to declare that Pitt's 'whole conduct was an uninterrupted series of contemptuous disdain of the dearest rights and privileges of the people, [and] whose uniform practice was calculated to destroy the best privilege of that House . . .'. He contested the necessity of the proclamation on the grounds that 'there ought to be a perfect liberty for the circulation of all opinions upon public affairs', and that if any writers or publishers overstepped the bounds of the law the government already possessed the power to deal with them. The proclamation, however, would itself 'create a general alarm' amongst the public and turn respectable magistrates into spies and informers. 'It was as surprising as it was odious, that such a proclamation should issue from the sovereign of a free people.'

Turning to the specific question of reform, Grey defended those 'gentlemen whose object was a temperate reform' from the slander that they saw any similarity between the condition of England and that of France. He went on to recall Pitt's own past as a reformer, reading out the resolutions of the meeting at the Thatched House Tavern on 16 May 1782 to show that the Friends of the People, in calling for petitions from the people and demanding a parliamentary committee to investigate the representative system, had done no more than the Prime Minister and his friends had proposed ten years earlier. Pitt's present arguments 'ill accorded with his former professions, or with those of his illustrious father, with whom a parliamentary reform was a darling object'. Yet it was now 'deemed fit to issue a proclamation to warn the public against the conduct of men with such honourable intentions' in order merely to sow suspicion in the minds of the public towards them. In reality, 'there was not one man of honour in the kingdom, who knew anything of them, who was not satisfied they were in reality what they called themselves, "the Friends of the People".' The proclamation was defamatory towards the Society, and intended to divide the Whig party. Grey closed with a reference to his attachment to Fox, that might have been considered an attempt to claim his support for the Society: he described him as

a man who, although placed in a situation exceedingly delicate, between friends of a different opinion, and for whom he had an equal degree of affection, yet, even here, had manifested an elevation of soul, a dignity of deportment, a nobility of principle, a consistency of conduct, that cast a lustre on his unrivalled talents, and ornamented his virtues.

He then moved an amendment to the proposed address, regretting the proclamation as unnecessary and liable to excite 'groundless jealousies and alarms in the minds of his majesty's faithful and loving people'. The amendment concluded with a reference to the Birmingham riots of the previous year, suggesting that the government might be better employed in seeking out and punishing those responsible for organizing them and those magistrates who had failed in their duty of suppressing them—a clear allusion to the Loyalist Associations and 'Church and

King' Clubs who were suspected to have been at work to set the mob upon the Dissenters and reformers in many parts of the country.[2]

The amendment was lost without a division. The debate did not lead to an immediate split in the party, but it convinced Elliot that the differences in it were wide and fundamental and that the breach was incurable; he now suspected 'there is also in *some* such a design of setting up a new *head* and a separate interest in the party, instead of the duke of Portland, that I think it very unlikely that a total and open rupture should be avoided.'[3]

The end of the parliamentary session shortly after the debate on the proclamation did not lead to a slackening of the political tension. Pitt now brought into operation the second prong of his strategy, by opening negotiations for a more general union and holding out the possibility of four Cabinet offices. The Whig leaders received the offer with reserve and a degree of scepticism: both Fox and Fitzwilliam advised Portland that it was 'utterly inadmissible' and Fox stuck to the line he had taken on the proclamation, that it was merely another political device to split the opposition. Though a section of the leadership, urged on by Burke, Loughborough, and Malmesbury, was prepared to undertake exploratory discussions in the hope of raising the terms of the offer, it soon became clear that Pitt was thinking in terms of picking off individuals to strengthen his ministry rather than of a full coalition of parties. Fox's stipulation that any junction must be on equal terms in respect of both offices and patronage was designed to demonstrate that point. On Pitt's side, it was clear that he would not be prepared to step down in favour of a 'neutral' Prime Minister to allow Fox to be placed in a position of equality with himself, even if the King would allow such an arrangement. On the other hand, it made Fox seem the major obstacle to a union of parties in the interests of national order and security. The result was to force him into a closer relationship with Grey and the reformers. During the summer, while Burke continued to work upon Portland and Fitzwilliam, Fox grew more angry at this attempt to force him into a commitment which would split the party.[4]

In the meantime, the European crisis deepened. The retreat of Brunswick's army after Valmy, the September massacres in Paris, and the deposition of Louis XVI moved the Whig leaders into an interventionist position. Fitzwilliam, who had hitherto used his moderating influence to prevent a division, was disturbed by the growing intransigence of Fox's stand against intervention in French affairs. Portland now thought Fox's opinions disturbingly radical: in November he found him 'hostile to what he calls the cause of kings', pleased at the failure of Brunswick's

---

[2] *Elliot*, ii. 23-4 and 30-1; *Parl. Hist.* xxix. 1480-9. For Grey's speech on the Birmingham riots on 21 May see ibid. 1456-64. He accused the magistrates of openly encouraging the rioters.

[3] *Elliot*, ii. 33-4.

[4] Portland to Loughborough, 25 May and reply, Portland MSS Pwf 9220. For the negotiations see O'Gorman, *The Whig Party*, 90-7; Mitchell, *C. J. Fox and the Disintegration of the Whig Party*, 183-9; Smith, *Whig Principles*, 142-5; Malmesbury, *Diaries and Correspondence of James Harris, first Earl of Malmesbury* (1845), ii. 418-36.

expedition, and 'insensible to the effect of the power of France', so that he remained unmoved by

the danger to which this country is exposed by the inundation of levelling doctrines and the support they derive from the success of French arms.... I fear I observed symptoms of no very strong indisposition to submit to the experiment of a new and possibly a republican form of government.

Burke joined in, warning Fitzwilliam that Fox was openly declaring his support for a French republic, Catholic emancipation, the repeal of the Test Act, Scottish burgh reform, and carrying on 'a regular opposition ... as usual'. In face of hardening attitudes on both sides of the party the middle ground hitherto occupied by the leadership began to collapse.[5]

Fox and Grey were now as one in their attitude towards the drift of events. Fox's days of trimming were over. At a meeting of the Whig Club on 4 December he joined in toasts to 'the friends of liberty all over the world' and declared that 'the rights of the people' were the only true foundation of legitimate government. It was the last straw for his aristocratic friends. Fox, however, blamed them, and not Grey, Sheridan, or the Friends of the People. The provocation had come from 'those on the aristocratic side' who had set themselves 'to pervert the duke of Portland, Fitzwilliam, Windham, etc.'. Grey's support of parliamentary reform he now regarded, not as an untimely provocation, but as a legitimate reversion to the attitude of Fox himself, Lord John Cavendish, and even Pitt ten years ago.[6]

Pitt completed the destruction of the Whig party with his proclamation on 1st December calling out the militia on the pretext of an imminent insurrection in the country. For some weeks the Home Office had been deluged with alarming reports of disaffection throughout the country, and especially in London. Hitherto, the ministers had been sceptical of the danger to public order and political stability, but the decrees of the French National Convention of 16 and 19 November, proclaiming the opening of the River Scheldt and offering 'fraternity and assistance to all people who wished to recover their liberty' opened up new fears of internal subversion and external conflict. The tone of the reported speeches at meetings of the radical societies was alarming, and as winter approached a deterioration in food supplies and employment aroused fears that popular discontents might be exploited by foreign emissaries and domestic agitators. Evidence of actual treasonable activities was thin, but the government felt obliged to take precautions. The militia was called out in ten counties during November, and regular troops were moved into London to protect the Tower, the Bank, and the centres of government. Pitt's proclamation calling out the militia in general on 1 December also enabled him to recall Parliament, to propose further measures to protect

[5] Portland to Fitzwilliam, 30 Nov. Fitzwilliam MSS, Northampton; Burke to Fitzwilliam, 29 Nov., *Burke*, vii. 306–18.

[6] Mitchell, *Holland House*, 201; Fox to Adair, 26 and 29 Nov. 1792, *Fox*, iii. 257, 259. Fox wrote (29 Nov.) that 'Grey &c had good reason to be surprised at so violent a storm arising from his undertaking what ... so many of us had done before him': ibid. 260.

national security. It is probably true that the reaction was unnecessarily extreme. The Foxites, however, viewed Pitt's action merely as an attempt to take advantage of their disharmony and to frighten the aristocratic leaders away from the liberal section of the party. Thus, when the Whig peers met at Burlington House on the eve of the session on 11 December, and were agreeing not to oppose Pitt's Address, Fox burst in with a copy of the King's Speech 'and with an oath declared that there was no address at this moment Pitt could frame he would not propose an amendment to and divide the House upon'. The meeting broke up in disorder and on the following day both Fox and Grey spoke and voted against the Address, in company with forty-eight of the party.[7]

Grey's speech was uncompromising. The danger the country faced, he declared, came not from the few republicans and levellers, but from the alarmist measures of the government. The 'writings of a certain tendency' of which they complained were circulating merely 'in consequence of the very means which had been taken to suppress them', but their seditious effects upon the minds of the people 'he completely denied'. He repeated Fox's offence at the Whig Club by declaring

He was not a friend to Paine's doctrines, but he was not to be deterred by a name from acknowledging that he considered the rights of man as the foundation of every government, and those who stood out against those rights as conspirators against the people.

The ministers' claim of imminent insurrection was 'a political device' and did not reflect the true state of the country: while Brunswick's retreat from France 'he, along with his right hon. friend, and every friend of freedom, considered a matter of joy and exultation'. Two days later, Fox proposed the sending of a British minister to Paris and the recognition of the French Republic, and again Grey seconded the motion with a forthright declaration of his political position:[8]

If the enthusiasm of any man for my right hon. friend who made the motion be abated, mine, if possible, is increased. The state of the country calls upon him to stand in the gap and defend the constitution. He has said he will do so; and while I have power of body or mind he shall not stand alone. A firm band of admiring friends not the less respectable nor the less likely to prevail from the present disproportion of their number, will faithfully stand by him, against all the calumnies of those who betray while they affect to defend the constitution.

Grey had set the theme of Whig politics on the French Revolutionary war, and he did not swerve from it during the next nine years. In a succession of speeches between mid-December 1792 and the end of the session in June 1793, he stood forward as the champion of Fox and liberty. He counter-attacked the ministry's campaign against seditious literature by calling for the prosecution of the Crown and Anchor Association for its pamphlet 'One Pennyworth of Truth, from Thomas Bull to his Brother John', blaming it for arousing the Birmingham mob in 1791;

[7] C. Emsley, 'The London "Insurrection" of December 1792: Fact or Fantasy', *Journal of British Studies* xvii (1978), 66–86; *Malmesbury*, ii. 440–6; Smith, *Whig Principles*, 150–1.

[8] *Parl. Hist.* xxx. 41–2.

he opposed the Aliens Bill, objecting to the extensive discretionary powers it granted to ministers, enabling them to act against individuals on mere suspicion; he supported Fox's resolutions against war with France on 18 February, and three days later himself moved an Address to restore peace with France, 'to court the distinction of being recorded as one of those who had, with every possible exertion, opposed those impolitic measures, whereby we had been plunged into a war, which was likely to be so ruinous and calamitous to this country'; and on 22 March he opposed the Traitorous Correspondence Bill as a libel on the loyal people of England. He ended the session with a silent vote on 17 June for Fox's motion for peace.[9]

In all these debates, the size of the minority remained below 50; the Foxite group which was to be the sole remnant of the Whig party through the Revolutionary War was now formed, and Grey had established his position in it as second only to Fox himself. Its watchword remained the cry of 'civil and religious liberty all over the world'. It endorsed the view that the war was an unjust war against liberty, in England as well as in France, and not a defensive war against foreign aggression. It gave continuing support to the cause of constitutional reform, attempting still to steer between the rocks of repression and revolution, and it opposed the penal sentences imposed in 1793 on the Scottish reformers and their associates in the British Convention at Edinburgh. Thomas Fysshe Palmer, sentenced to seven years transportation for taking part in the reform movement, wrote to Grey in October 1793 as 'an obscure individual crushed by the tyrannical hand of government' and a few months later to thank him for his unavailing efforts to have the sentence altered or at least to make its terms more humane.[10] But the tide of opinion was moving against the reformers. Pitt's government echoed the deep-seated fears of the propertied classes that popular agitation was directed from abroad and aimed at the subversion of the social order and the redistribution of wealth. Successive measures limited the freedom of publication and of public meeting, and the expression of liberal opinions became dangerous to the personal safety of any who spoke or wrote in favour of reform.

Fox and Grey were both men devoted to the established social and political system, and their anger at Pitt's tactics was understandable. Believing that his aim was to split the Whig party and to discredit the Foxite remnant by linking it with subversion and disloyalty, they contested his measures as unnecessary, provocative, and politically-motivated. They asserted that the dangers to liberty arose more from the extensive and increasing influence of the Crown and the extremism of the loyalist movement than from any revolutionary disaffection in the country. Above all, they stood for the political integrity of the Whig party. It has often been said that the continuing existence in Parliament of Fox's small but devoted

---

[9] Ibid. 128–30, 206–11, 440–1, 454–9, 607–8, 1024. Grey wrote however to Mrs Ord on 24 Jan. 1793 of Louis XVI's execution, 'Bad as I am thought, I cannot express the horror I feel at this atrocity': *Creevey Papers*, i. 1.

[10] Palmer to Grey, 29 Oct. 1793, and 8 Jan. 1794, G. 46.

band preserved the liberal tradition during the years of repression. That may be so, but Fox and Grey were more concerned to maintain an independent political base from which the struggle against Pitt might be resumed in better times. They recognized that those times might be far away. Fox wrote wearily to Lord Holland on 9 March 1794 that

it seemed some way as if I had the world to begin anew, and if I could have done it with honour, what I should best have liked would have been to retire from politics altogether, but this could not be done, and therefore there remains nothing but to get together the remains of our party, and begin, like Sisyphus, to roll up the stone again.[11]

By the summer of 1794 the aristocratic leaders of the party had deserted opposition, and in July they entered into formal coalition with the government and occupied six Cabinet posts. They carried with them the bulk of the party membership in both Houses, leaving Fox with around fifty supporters in the Commons and a handful in the Lords. If weak in numbers, however, the new opposition, in Fox's view, was not so 'in argument, nor I think in credit'. In the Lords, Bedford, described by Fox as 'one of the main pillars of the party', was assisted by Lauderdale, Guilford, Albemarle, and Derby. In the Commons there were Sheridan and Whitbread as well as Grey, who seized the opportunity to distinguish himself as second only to Fox. His temper was now under better control and his experience with the Friends of the People had taught him caution and responsibility. Fox declared that Grey was 'the person the most improved' on the Whig side during the 1793–4 session and he now became Fox's closest and most trusted friend and adviser. His political apprenticeship was over.[12]

The summer of 1794 was one of wider political crisis. The coalition between Pitt and the Portland group was preceded—or, as Fox and Grey believed, stimulated—by the government's decision to act against the popular reform societies. Twelve of the radical leaders, including Thomas Hardy, John Horne Tooke, and John Thelwall, were arrested in May on charges of high treason and brought to trial in the autumn. There was no certainty that it would stop there. John Cartwright wrote that

a system of proscription and terror like that of Robespierre has been for some time growing

---

[11] Fox's assertion that the 'insurrections and rebellions' which the government professed to be guarding against '*never did exist* but in the imagination of *a set of men who raise such reports* that they may the more easily depress the cause of freedom' is now contested by some historians who believe in the existence of a 'revolutionary underground' in the 1790s and early 1800s, but there is no reason to suppose that at the time the Whigs were not sincere in believing that the government was scaremongering: *The celebrated speech of . . . Fox, with the proceedings of the meeting at the Shakespeare Tavern . . . 10 October 1800*, quoted by J. A. Hone, 'Radicalism in London, 1796–1802', in J. Stevenson (ed.), *London in the Age of Reform* (Oxford, 1977), 79–101; J. L. Baxter and F. K. Donnelly, 'Sheffield and the English revolutionary tradition, 1791–1820', *International Review of Social History* xx. (1975), 398–423.
[12] Fox to Holland, 9 Mar. & 5 Oct. 1794, *Fox*, iii. 64–8, 88–92.

in this country, and had these trials been otherwise decided than they had been, it would have been completed and written in innocent and virtuous blood.

Grey attended Hardy's trial at the Old Bailey and wrote to Mary from his seat on the Bench

with a judge at my elbow, who I am not quite sure does not think I ought rather to be in Mr Hardy's place at the bar. . . . If this man is hanged, there is no safety for any man—innocence no longer affords protection to a person obnoxious to those in power, and I do not know how soon it may come to my turn.

The acquittals of all the defendants who were brought to trial, and the release of the rest, were hailed with joy in London and probably with a good deal of relief by Grey and his colleagues.[13]

The acquittals freed the Whigs from the fear of further suppression and the trials did no more than temporarily interrupt the party's campaign, whose recurrent theme was the defence of constitutional liberty. In February and March 1794 Grey had spoken against the enlistment of foreign subjects into the armed forces and the disembarkation of Hessian troops in the south of England, on the ground that the constitution required the assent of Parliament to the landing of foreign troops in the kingdom; in the following week he joined Fox and other colleagues in attacking the plan to raise Volunteer corps for internal defence, arguing that the financing of the corps by private subscriptions was a violation of Parliament's exclusive right to grant supply for public purposes. He declared, however, that he was sincerely attached to the British constitution and asserted that 'he would rather live under the most despotic monarchy, nay, even under that of the king of Prussia, or the empress of Russia, than under the present government of France'.

In April, opposing the foreign enlistment bill, he again stressed his horror at the present state of France, though he attributed it to a combination of the after-effects of her 'ancient despotism' and of the hostile activites of the Allied Powers. Whether Britain would be influenced by the French example, he declared, depended on whether timely reforms were adopted in this country; but 'such was the overbearing influence of the present system, that he was inclined to relinquish all further efforts and retire from public life, where the only effect of his exertion was personal odium and disapprobation.' He remained in his place, however, to oppose the suspension of Habeas Corpus in May 1794, declaring that though he was not a member of the London Corresponding Society or the Society for Constitutional Information, and though he disapproved of some of their plans and admitted that there might be among them 'men of desperate fortunes and sinister purposes', nevertheless they were legal associations professing legal aims and working by legal means. He supported Sheridan's motion to repeal the suspension in January 1795, and opposed the Treasonable Practices Bill and Seditious Meet-

---

[13] Cartwright to Mrs Cartwright, Sunday [Nov. 1794], *Cartwright*, i. 210; Grey to Mary, Thursday [Oct. 1794], G. 31. For the best account of Pitt's repressive measures see Goodwin, *The Friends of Liberty*, 263–358.

ings Bill at the end of the year, both on the grounds that the disaffection which ministers declared was prevalent in the country was due not to the influence of the societies but to the corruption and folly of the government. The Prime Minister himself remained a primary target. In May 1794 he attacked Pitt's

haughtiness as the overflowing of an arrogant mind, swelled with the too long enjoyment of an ill-gotten power. He admired the Right Hon. Gentleman's abilities, he had never denied them; but talents, however transcendant, when unsupported by honour or honesty, should never meet respect from him.

Grey's personal vendetta against Pitt so coloured his speeches in this period that Wilberforce alleged, in the debates of November 1795, that 'personality to the Minister, and not the good of his country, swayed him.' Attacks of this kind had been part of the opposition's armoury since December 1783, but Grey's were especially vehement. The personal rivalry he had conceived for Pitt at the outset of his career was still a strong element in his opposition.[14]

Peace with France was the second main arm of the Whig programme in these years. Grey along with Fox, Sheridan, and nearly all the steady Foxites supported Wilberforce's amendment to the Address, seeking a peace negotiation, on 30 December 1794, and on 26 January 1795 Grey himself moved a declaration that, although an immediate negotiation was not feasible, the form of the French government should not be regarded as an insuperable bar to it. Grey here asserted what was to be a consistent element in Whig thinking on foreign affairs in and after the Napoleonic wars, that intervention in the domestic government of another country, though not excluded in principle, could be justified only in extreme circumstances. He again supported Wilberforce's amendment for peace on 27 May 1795, and renewed his own motion for peace in February 1796.[15]

One of the the principal arguments against the war was that it imposed intolerable financial burdens on the nation, so promoting that distress which in turn led to popular disaffection. Financial questions were therefore another staple of the opposition's parliamentary campaign. They attacked the ministry's proposals for an establishment for the Prince and Princess of Wales in April and May 1795, when Grey, sharing the disgust of his colleagues at the Prince's desertion of the Whigs since 1792, contrasted his extravagance with 'the cries of the starving poor' and declared that

the dignity of the Prince of Wales would be best maintained by his showing a feeling heart for the poor, and an unwillingness to add to their distresses. . . . He was afraid of proceeding, lest he should be betrayed into anything that might have the appearance of disrespect towards that august personage.

His language might recommend him to the popular radicals but it was hardly

---

[14] *Parl. Hist.* xxx. 1363–7, xxxi. 1–5, 89, 94–5, 215, 233, 386–7, 512–13, 531–4, 1130, 1189–91, xxxii. 298–303, 386, 469; Farington, *Diary*, i. 111 (24 Nov.).

[15] *Parl. Hist.* xxxi. 1061, 1193–1204, xxxii. 715–20; *Debrett's Parl. Register* xli. 425–6.

calculated to endear him at Carlton House, though he moderated it in the subsequent proceedings on the Bill.

The theme of governmental wastefulness and the consequent burdens placed on the country was pursued, however, in Grey's motion on the State of the Nation on 10 March 1796, when he alleged that the expense of the war had failed to produce any favourable result or benefit; and he linked the financial with the constitutional argument by pointing out that the stringent enforcement of the assessed taxes, which formed an increasingly important part of the war budget, was oppressive to the people and, by increasing the summary powers of the magistrates, established 'the agency of a vile herd of informers' and lessened the rights of the subject to trial by jury. Grey also took the lead on a number of other financial questions, perhaps still mindful of his former ambition to become Chancellor of the Exchequer: he opposed the legacy duty, charged ministers with misappropriation of public expenditure, and spoke against the Budget in 1796. In the early weeks of 1797 he was appointed a member of the committee on the suspension of cash payments by the Bank of England. He was in a minority in the committee in opposing the suspension, and spoke in the House against the Bank Restriction Bill in March. Two months later, he charged Pitt with financial misconduct leading to the Bank crisis, making a particular point of Pitt's sanctioning a loan to the Austrian Emperor without parliamentary authority.

Finally, Grey supported other liberal causes in Parliament during these years. He spoke in March 1796 in favour of Curwen's Bill to repeal the Game Laws, which he described as 'vexatious and tyrannical institutions', he condemned the penal laws against the Irish Catholics in 1797, and he voted for the abolition of the slave-trade in March 1796. In all the opposition's major debates his name appears, often as a speaker, almost invariably in the division lists. During the lean years of opposition he was one of the most effective of the speakers against Pitt and his policies.[16]

Reform was only a part of this strategy. The Friends of the People could do little but stand by during the months of repression in 1794, though they were not cowed into total silence. On 9 April they approved a public address declaring their constancy in pursuit of reform, though admitting that the moment was unsuitable for renewing an application to Parliament. On 31 May a further declaration attempted to justify the Society's conduct during its two years' existence. It argued that the increasing discontent of the people was to be attributed to the government's repressive and unsympathetic attitude, and that the removal of discontent was more likely to be achieved by timely concession than by 'coercive laws'. The confidence and affection of the nation would be restored to the established constitution only by 'a substantial reform in the Representation of the People', irrespective of events in France which were irrelevant to the issue. In calling themselves 'The Friends of the People', the Society asserted that they

[16] *Parl. Hist.* xxxi. 1466–7, 1475–80, xxxii. 94–9, 113, 902–11, 1033, 1062–72, 1264–5, 1280–2, 1555–6, xxxiii. 58, 541–54.

sought to serve the interests not of any one section of the nation but 'the People in its amplest, happiest, and most harmonious sense ... united and inseparable in their mutual interests and relations'.[17]

In private, the language of the Society's members was less confident. A division was developing between those who wished to present a programme which would appeal to respectable support in the country, and the more radical, who wanted to work with the popular societies and were willing to adopt universal suffrage. Most of those who had seen it as primarily a bid to capture the party leadership and to maintain the party's distinctive image as a constitutional opposition were cowed into silence or resignation from the Society by the treason trials of 1794. Those who remained had to decide how much further they were now prepared to go along the road towards a national movement based on popular sentiment. Some of the moderates shied away from the implications of such a strategy. Wyvill, who had never joined the Society though he sympathized with its objectives, urged his friends amongst its members to stick 'to moderate principles' lest they be represented as 'hostile to the constitution, and tending to throw the country into confusion'. He warned them that the Society's plans must be moderate enough to win the approval of 'my old associates in Yorkshire' and suggested the model of Pitt's scheme in 1785, which had proposed the setting up of a fund to buy out the close boroughs and so induce voluntary disfranchisement rather than offend those who feared the confiscation of existing electoral rights.[18]

Wyvill's other proposals included the transfer of a number of seats to London and the counties, the enfranchisement of Sheffield, Birmingham, Manchester, and Leeds, the addition of further members for Scotland, the extension of the franchise to 40s. copyholders in the counties and householders paying taxes in the boroughs, the restriction of polling to one day, annual parliaments, and the payment of salaries to MPs. Such a plan, he argued, would satisfy the respectable supporters of reform and might not be too offensive to those who stood to lose by a more radical scheme. In particular he warned against universal (manhood) suffrage and the replacement of the borough constituencies by electoral districts of approximately equal numerical size, two of the major planks in the radical programme. Cartwright, however, pressed for universal suffrage and annual parliaments as 'the only ground on which you can ever hope to call forth sufficient energy for saving your country' and the only proposals which would satisfy the demand for the 'rights of men'. Grey rebuffed Cartwright's advances, declaring that although no one held the rights of men in greater esteem, those rights

do not consist in universal representation or in any particular form of government. Government being formed for the protection and security of rights, whatever mode is best calculated to produce that end, whether it be universal or a more limited system of representation, is that to which the people have a *right*.

[17] *Parl. Hist.* xxxii. 845, xxxiii. 16–19, xxxii. 902.
[18] Wyvill, *Political Papers*, v. pp. ix–xiv.

Householder suffrage would be adequate to that purpose and it would be dangerous to go further. In the circumstances of later 1794 and early 1795 he even doubted the wisdom of continuing the campaign at all, when public opinion was agitated by the possibility of French invasion after the defeat of the Duke of York's expedition to the Netherlands. A meeting of the Friends in January 1795 accordingly resolved to suspend all activity for the time being.[19]

Others in the Society, however, were eager to continue the agitation on more radical grounds. During and in the weeks following the treason trials Philip Francis and William Smith MP, the spokesman of the Dissenters, worked out a programme of reforms which was submitted to a meeting of the Society in May 1795 and adopted in a declaration published afterwards. The declaration argued for householder rather than universal suffrage, but it also put forward a scheme for the replacement of the existing constituencies by a system of electoral districts which it was hoped would attract popular support. The public climate was beginning to look more favourable in the summer of 1795, as enthusiasm for the war cooled in face of the social and economic distress which it was helping to produce. That summer also brought the first of a series of bad harvests which increased political tensions for the remainder of the decade.[20]

Many thousands attended an open meeting called by the London Corresponding Society in St George's Fields in June to demand universal suffrage and annual parliaments, and an even bigger gathering in Copenhagen Fields in October approved a 'Remonstrance to the King' which addressed the sovereign in terms of thinly-veiled insult. It was shortly followed by an attack on the royal procession to open Parliament, which provoked the government into introducing the 'Two Bills' to put severe restrictions on public meetings and to extend the law of treason to written or spoken words calculated to incite hatred or contempt of the King, constitution, or government. The Bills provided an opportunity for co-operation between the liberal Whigs, who saw them as a threat to established liberty, and the radicals, who were the main target of governmental attack. Both groups worked to stimulate protest meetings, petitions, and addresses against the Bills, although the L.C.S. and its allies were still pledged to universal suffrage and the societies refused to support the Whig Club's proposed National Association to work for the repeal of the Acts after they were passed at the end of the year.[21]

Some at least of the radicals were prepared to drop the extremism of Thomas Paine and to co-operate with the Whigs for reform by constitutional methods. Foremost among these was the Revd John Horne Tooke, once a Wilkite, a prominent member of the Society for Constitutional Information, and since 1792

---

[19] *Autobiography of Francis Place*, ed. M. Thale (Cambridge, 1972), 139–40; Wyvill to S. Shore, 17 Mar. and 7 Apr. 1794; to T. B. Hollis, 13 and 24 Mar.; to Francis, 20 Dec.; Hollis to Wyvill, 7 Apr., Resolutions, 29 Nov., Wyvill, *Political Papers*, v. 232–53, pp. xiv–xvii; Cartwright to Grey, 1 Mar. 1794, G. 46; and Grey to Cartwright, 8 Mar., Trevelyan, *Lord Grey*, 94.

[20] Francis to Wyvill, 20 Jan. 1795, Wyvill, *Political Papers*, v. 279 and correspondence ibid. 233–78. Wyvill disapproved of the adoption of electoral districts: to Shore, 26 June 1795, ibid. 299–301.

[21] Smith, *Whig Principles*, 219–20.

a leading spirit in the L.C.S. Tooke's radicalism had symbolized to Fitzwilliam and other conservative Whigs in 1792 the worst dangers of reform, and he had been one of those brought to trial in the autumn of 1794, when he had called Pitt himself as a witness for the defence and questioned him on his former support for the cause. In 1796, Tooke was beginning to seek an alliance with the Whigs. At the general election of that year, Fox's radical city friend Harvey Christian Combe was returned for London, and George Tierney stood as the popular candidate at Southwark, depicted in loyalist propaganda as Tooke's puppet. Tooke himself came forward at Westminster. He stood independently of Fox, but he let it be known that he was prepared to work with the Whigs and his election address expressed hopes of 'union among all friends to freedom'. Fox responded cautiously but wrote to his nephew Lord Holland of the need to 'go further towards agreeing with the democratic or popular party'.[22]

The Whigs certainly shared certain common objectives with the radicals, opposing the French war, Pitt's repressive policies, and Portland's severe administration at the Home Office, and advocating some degree of reform to appease popular disaffection. They wished, however, to separate themselves clearly from any revolutionary or treasonable activities. Their political objective was the destruction of Pitt's administration and its replacement by one of their own, which would negotiate a peace and restore constitutional liberties. They aimed to make themselves an acceptable alternative government in the eyes of moderate as well as the more responsible radical opinion. They were fully aware of the dangers of too close an association with men of suspect principles, and Grey at least was aware that there was no sufficiently comprehensive radical body to provide a power-base in the country. In the circumstances, he thought it essential to draw a line between opposition to the government's policies and support of radical ideology, designed to overturn the political and social establishment. This was a line which he had followed consistently since 1792, both in the strategy of the Friends of the People and in his correspondence with his friends in the North, particularly with Thomas Bigge, a country gentleman from the Newcastle district who represented the moderate reformers in that area. In March 1795, for example, Grey wrote that 'the high prerogative doctrines of the Government on one side, and the violence of those on the other, whose conduct I do not commend, but whose temper I cannot much wonder at, seem to threaten an alarming crisis.' Though he encouraged a scheme in the summer of 1795 for a county meeting in Northumberland to petition against the war, he advised Bigge that it would be prudent to omit any censure of ministers or any mention of reform in order to attract the widest possible support. Even this limited measure had its political hazards. Grey's father strongly advised him against becoming involved in the scheme on the grounds that it would endanger his support in the forthcoming election, and it was ominous that the Duke of Northumberland also opposed it. Grey accordingly hesitated, and plans

[22] J. A. Hone, *For the Cause of Truth*, (Oxford, 1982) 26–34. Fox to Holland, Wed., 1796, *Fox*, iii. 135–6.

for the meeting were shelved, to be hastily revived in November when the 'Two Bills' were published.[23]

The object was now to support the opposition campaign for public meetings throughout the country. If the Bills were to pass, Grey wrote, 'there is an end of everything like freedom in this constitution'. With the Duke's support on this occasion Northumberland was one of the few counties to petition Parliament and to vote an Address to the Throne, which Grey presented at the beginning of December. On the passing of the Bills, the Whig Club proposed the setting up of a National Association to work for their repeal, and drew up a form of declaration to be adopted by local societies throughout the kingom. Grey forwarded the proposal to Bigge, but confessed himself not sanguine: he doubted whether the Association would attract enough support when by signing the declaration people would in effect expose themselves to possible retaliation or intimidation. Grey thought that the opposition would do better to concentrate on agitating for peace and attacking the government with motions for enquiry into the failure of military expeditions and the spending of public money. He feared that in other respects the nation was in a state of 'almost incurable apathy' and confessed that though he had given notice of another motion for peace he did not expect to gain another single vote or any external support.

By the end of the session he was utterly despondent, writing to Sir John Swinburne in Northumberland on 25 March to say that he did not know what more could be done 'to animate a people stupidly blind to their own destruction'. 'I for one', he added, 'have done at least as much as under all the discouragements which I have met with could well be expected.' He professed himself indifferent whether he was to be re-elected for the county, and declared his determination

not to spend any money which I cannot afford, to retire if I cannot come in on independent grounds, and therefore not to shrink from a full and open explanation of my principles and opinions to any who may require it.

Grey was re-elected without opposition for the county, but he did not look forward to resuming his duties in the House. He despaired, he wrote in August, of any useful activity there or in the country, and announced his intention of remaining at Howick for the whole of the new session. He soon realized, however, that his absence might diminish the leading position he was trying to establish in the party and that the distance of Howick from London 'prevents my taking part in whatever exertions can be made'. He returned to town in January 1797.[24]

The suspension of cash payments by the Bank of England inaugurated a year of crisis at home and abroad. In these circumstances, Grey proposed a grand

[23] Grey to Bigge, 21 Mar., 20 Aug., 1, 5, 15 Sept. 1795, G. 7; Bigge to Swinburne, 9 Sept., Swinburne MSS, Northumberland Record Office, 614/9.

[24] Grey to Bigge, 11, 28 Nov., 3 Dec. 1795, 1 Jan., 6 Feb. 1796, G. 7; Bigge to Swinburne [Nov. 1795], Swinburne MSS 614/13. For the Northumberland Address and Resolutions see Wyvill, *Political Papers*, v. pp. xxiv–vii. For the Yorkshire and Durham meetings see ibid., pp. xxvii–xlvi. Grey to Swinburne, n.d., 13 Jan. and 25 Mar. [1796], Swinburne MSS 614/32, 29, 31. Grey's election address [May 1796], and Grey to Bigge, 26 Aug. and 9 Oct. [1796], G. 7.

gesture of defiance and disgust against Pitt's policies. He proposed that after throwing all their energies into 'some great motion' attacking 'the whole mis-conduct of administration [and] the calamities it has produced', and proposing 'a total change both of the present Ministers and the system on which they have acted', if the House remained unresponsive the Whigs should secede from Par-liament, 'with a declaration of the motives which have influenced our conduct, and of the principles to which we hold ourselves pledged'. The opposition, Grey averred, had no wish to turn out the ministers merely for the sake of occupying their places—'a man must be strangely ambitious, who merely for the sake of office, would wish in the present state of things to enter upon the task of Government'—and if a change did take place, Grey himself would not be induced to take office without 'a pledge and promise' to carry reform. 'In this determination I know I agree with Fox.'[25]

The opposition was not yet quite ready for so extreme a step, but Grey persisted, writing in March that he still longed for 'that period when I may be enabled to quit with honour'. Eventually, and after considerable argument, it was decided that the 'great motion' on which secession or continuance in active opposition should depend was to be a further attempt to persuade the House in favour of reform. Grey again took up the leading role and on 26 May 1797 he proposed his second reform motion. He based it on the Friends' scheme of 1795 as the most radical measure that he was willing to accept, and he presented it in strikingly moderate language. The proposal went far beyond what Grey was to believe sufficient in 1832. An increase in the number of county representatives and the admission of copyholders and long leaseholders to the county franchise were moderate enough. The radical aspect of the measure lay in the substitution of electoral districts, each returning one representative, in place of the existing system of two-member constituencies, together with a uniform householder franchise in the borough districts. Grey, however, disclaimed any theoretical basis of political or natural rights and established his arguments on the ground that the scheme would enable the Commons to fulfil its proper constitutional role as the effective guardian of the public purse. It was not the inequality of the representative system that was the major fault, but the inadequacy of the representation of those who bore the burden of taxation. The House was thus unable to act as an effective check on the executive in the public interest. Grey's arguments showed that he still viewed reform within the limits of traditional Whig principles. The House of Commons was not seen as the voice of the people so much as an instrument to maintain the traditional balance of the constitution, acting on the people's behalf but independently of popular pressures.[26]

---

[25] Grey to Bigge, 23 Feb. 1797, ibid.

[26] Grey to Swinburne, 9 Mar. [1797], Swinburne MSS 614/28. A memorandum in the Prince of Wales's papers asserted that the Whigs, including Fox, Grey, and Bedford, were having second thoughts about the proposed reform motion and that the proposal was condemned by the Cavendishes, Norfolk, Sheridan, and several others: CGPW, iii. 341–3. Parl. Hist. xxxiii. 644–53. Hone, Cause

This moderation may have gained votes in the House, for the size of the minority rose to 91, the opposition's most successful division since 1792. The majority numbered 256, however, showing that the cause of reform was hopeless for the foreseeable future, and the L.C.S. denounced Grey's scheme because of its limited extension of the suffrage. The outcome was that the Whigs and the popular radicals drifted apart once more. The defeat of Grey's motion now led to the Foxite secession from the House as a demonstration of the hopelessness of opposition to an all-powerful administration. It was, however, a selfish and, as many of the radicals believed, irresponsible act which deprived the reformers and liberal opinion of a parliamentary platform for over three years. Cartwright continued to deplore it and many of the Whigs themselves felt uncomfortable about it. Holland recorded that at the party meeting which resolved on the secession— his first attendance at such a meeting—Lord Guilford, Richard Fitzpatrick, and Tierney opposed the step, the last arguing that the only honourable alternative to attendance was resignation from the House. Lansdowne made the forthright comment that 'Secession means rebellion, or it is nonsense.' The meeting was so divided that it was not possible to make the secession the formal act of the party; it was from the beginning a decision for each individual, and many accepted it only from loyalty to Fox, who allowed his better judgement to be overridden by the intemperance of Grey, Bedford, and Lauderdale and by his own weariness with the struggle. Tierney remained a regular attender, and Sheridan was occasionally present during the next three years. Grey soon went through torments of conscience because of his role as the initiator of the measure: Holland recorded that Grey was already disturbed by the awareness that 'much of the obloquy cast on the party [since 1792] was founded on measures of which he had been the author', and as the secession went on Grey became himself its major victim. Trapped by his loyalty to Fox, who retreated into the pleasures of indolence at Chertsey, Grey dared not return to the House while Fox stayed away. Once again Grey's influence had been decisive for the conduct and policy of the party, and once again he became convinced that he was responsible for a serious misjudgement which harmed the Whigs in the eyes of the public and condemned him to political impotence. Grey's mood for the next three years was one of despondency and irritation with himself which even the delights of family life at Howick could not dispel for long.[27]

of Truth, 86. Grey's speech was not one of his best: Veitch describes it as 'a bad one, tortuous in thought and clumsy in expression': *Genesis of Parliamentary Reform*, 332.

[27] Holland, *Memoirs*, i. 31, 84, 88–91; Lady Holland, *Journal*, i. 215. Grey wrote to Bigge on 3 June that he did not regret giving up 'exertions which only subjected us to daily insult, without producing any benefit to the country': G. 7.

THE RETURN TO OPPOSITION, 1797–1802

After eleven years in the House of Commons Grey was established as second only to Fox in the ranks of Whig opposition. His talent for public speaking, his diligence in attending debates on all major questions, and his support of liberal causes had given him a high reputation. His personal qualities, however, were more in doubt. Hasty and impulsive in action, impatient of contradiction, quarrelsome in face of opposition and too overtly ambitious, he was inclined to alternating extremes of enthusiasm and despondency. His temperament was a commanding one and he never took easily to criticism or to co-operation with others. A naturally imperious disposition was allied to a tendency to sullen dejection in the face of failure or discouragement. The often-repeated wish to withdraw into political seclusion and to give up public life masked an underlying resentment against checks to his ambition; but the ambition remained, and quickly brought him back to the treadmill he had come to detest.

Yet there was never a serious doubt as to his political principles. Though he shared the concern of men of property for the maintenance of the established order of society, he was convinced that a policy of repression against political radicalism would produce the very revolution it was designed to avert. The unity, loyalty and good feeling of the nation was only to be secured by judicious and timely concessions to popular feeling when that feeling was expressed by responsible and respectable elements in society. His support for moderate parliamentary reform at home and for the removal of religious discrimination in Ireland became the cornerstones of his political career during the 1790s and they remained his objectives for the rest of his active life.

Grey's advocacy of the secession had been determined and persistent, but he soon realized that it could not be permanent. Almost as soon as the secession took effect, therefore, Grey was seeking for ways and means to bring it to an end. If the party was to sustain its claim to be the champion of reformist causes, it could do so only through parliamentary action and eventual success in achieving office; but these required a degree of unity and enthusiasm sadly lacking in the dispirited and quarrelsome state of the party. The task of the next five years was to restore it to an ordered, disciplined and coherent opposition. That it took so long was partly due to Grey's own continuing doubts and mistrust, both of himself and of many of his colleagues; but the responsibility also lay with Fox, whose natural indolence made him resist all attempts to bring him back into full political activity.

Grey's loyalty to Fox was deep and unwavering, and it had been confirmed by Fox's equal demonstration of loyalty to Grey both in 1792 and in 1797. Grey would do nothing that would cast doubt upon his commitment to Fox's leadership, and when Fox repeatedly attempted to thrust his position on Grey and to encourage him to grasp it, the result was only to increase the dilemma Grey had created for himself in 1797. Fox and Grey together must share the responsibility for what Lord John Russell called that 'rash, ill-judged, and ever to be lamented measure' of secession, and for the failure to bring it to an end sooner than they did. Fox afterwards confessed that he had always doubted its wisdom, but that having taken the decision 'I think it far best to adhere to it'. His reluctance to reappear in public life was reinforced by his newly-found domestic happiness after his marriage in 1795, and by his enthusiasm for his new project of a Whiggish history of England in the time of the Glorious Revolution. These combined to keep him in seclusion at St Anne's Hill with his books and the nightingales to await the 'euthanasia' of the constitution once predicted by David Hume and now frequently alluded to in his letters, inclined more to literary criticism and advice than to politics, to his favourite young nephew.[1]

Grey's resolution was tested at the very outset of the secession, in May and June 1797, when proposals emerged for the setting up of a new 'third party' independent of both Pitt and Fox. Grey refused to have anything to do with it, even though Sheridan urged, 'upon grounds not altogether without plausibility' as Grey remarked, the benefits of setting up a broadly based administration to include 'a great part of Fox's friends, with his concurrence and support'. Fox offered to stand aside to facilitate the arrangement and on 24 May sought an interview with the King to declare his willingness, as Grey put it, to 'sacrifice himself for the public interest'. Grey, Bedford, and Guilford were particularly mentioned for Cabinet offices. Grey's response, however, was '*a decisive and peremptory* refusal', on the ground that such a coalition, including Moira as the Prince of Wales's friend, and a number of politically lightweight figures such as the Duke of Northumberland, Sir William Pulteney, and Sir John Sinclair, would be weak and ineffective against the opposition of Pitt and the machinations of the Court and would be forced 'to maintain the present system of corruption and abuse to the last extremity ... without a possibility of doing anything effectual for the people'.[2]

Grey's attitude was not the sole reason for the scheme's collapse, for the new 'party' possessed neither unity of principle nor weight of talent, and it certainly failed to impress George III. Grey realized, as French Laurence, Burke's disciple and Fitzwilliam's confidant, remarked, that 'The government of this country must be in the hands either of Mr Pitt or Mr Fox', though he would not have agreed with Laurence's gloomy prognostication that 'between the specious treachery of the one, and the undisguised violence of the other, nothing apparently but the

---

[1] Lord John Russell to Tierney, 26 Nov. [1801], Tierney MSS 60. Lady Holland wrote of Grey's 'most awkward situation', wishing to end the secession but aware that his return would appear 'most deceitful ... to have gotten Mr Fox pledged to absence, and then become a leader', though she acquitted him of the accusation: *Journal*, i. 215. Fox to Grey, 5 Oct. 1801, BL Add. MS 47565, fo.46; *Fox*, iii *passim*. On Fox's *History of the early part of the reign of James II* see J. R. Dinwiddy, 'Charles James Fox as Historian', *Hist. Journal* xii. no. 1, 1969, 23–34.

[2] Sichel, *Sheridan*, ii. 281. Lady Holland reported that the King had been deliberately prejudiced against Grey because of reform: *Journal*, i. 180. Grey to Bigge, 15 June 1797, G. 7/10. On the 'Third Party' scheme see *LCGIII*, ii. (1963), pp. xxiii–xxix. The scheme was the occasion for a reconciliation between Grey and the Prince of Wales, who had not spoken since Grey's refusal to make a statement about the Prince's marriage to Mrs Fitzherbert: Lady Holland, *Journal*, i. 178.

merciful interposition of Him, who brings good out of evil by his own mysterious ways, can save us'. Grey was realistic enough to know that his future was still bound up with Fox and that no other alliance would serve his prospects.[3]

A similar reserve marked Grey's reception of overtures from the ambitious new Whig recruit, George Tierney, a close associate in the Friends of the People and newly returned to the Commons as the popular candidate at Southwark. The secession, taking place only a few months after Tierney's return to the House, seemed likely to deprive him of his chance of distinction and he refused to accept so premature a termination of his career. He tried to persuade Grey to attend with him, but to no avail. As Grey wrote to Whitbread, he was willing to give Tierney credit for 'perfectly fair and honourable motives' and recognized that as he had never assented to the secession, which had always been a matter for individuals and not a formal party commitment, he was entitled to attend if he chose. As he feelingly remarked,

It is hard for men who like business and bustle, and who have no dislike to the good things attending them, to see persons of no greater pretensions than themselves daily advancing in honour and profit, whilst for the sacrifices they make they do not receive the smallest thanks from the public.

However, he feared that Tierney's attendance would harm the party by producing 'a still further diminution of the small band which was leagued against corruption', while those who remained absent would be 'neglected and forgotten'. The unity of the Whigs was still his first consideration, but his manner and conversation failed to hide his inner dissatisfaction: Lady Holland noted his irritability and discontent at the check to his ambition.[4]

As the year 1797 drew to a close, Grey took what consolation he could from his life at Howick. One side of his nature craved the life of a retired country gentleman, riding by day through the wild Northumbrian countryside or along the rugged cliffs of Craster and Dunstanburgh, lounging in the evenings by the fireside and reading to his wife from Scott or Spenser, or playing cribbage to the accompaniment of 'the hollow wintry wind howling through the passages of this great ... house'. For the rest of his life, the company and happiness of his wife and family took precedence over political obligations. It was to be almost legendary that he could never be brought to London but for the most urgent political transactions.

To resign his seat and end his political career, however, was impossible for a man who hungered for public distinction as much as he. Though Grey recognized more than once that resignation was ultimately the only honourable course, there were always reasons to be found for not giving up the House. He frequently qualified his absence by declaring that he would always attend for any discussion which affected the interests of his constituents, and when in November 1797 there

---

[3] French Laurence to Fitzwilliam, 26 Oct. 1796, Fitzwilliam MSS, Sheffield.

[4] Lady Holland, *Journal*, i. 171; Grey to Whitbread, 16 Oct. 1797, Whitbread MSS 1/866. Tierney had entered the House as member for Colchester in 1789 but he lost this seat in 1790. He won Southwark after petitioning against his opponent in 1796.

was a move to call a meeting of freeholders of Northumberland 'to consider what is proper to be done in the present unrepresented state of the county', he offered to go and to declare his willingness to give up his seat if his constituents so wished. It was a relief, however, when the proposal came to nothing. To vacate his seat for the county would have been political suicide, for he would be unlikely ever to get it back, especially as he was not rich enough to finance a contest. Nor could he or his family afford to buy a seat elsewhere.[5]

His father, too, would have been deeply offended by his resignation, for Grey's membership of the Commons provided some protection against attacks on Sir Charles's military conduct such as that of 1795, when his activities as military commander in the West Indies were investigated by the War Office after protests from British and American merchants about the exaction of excessive prize-money from the conquered French islands. As Grey wrote to Thomas Bigge in December 1798,

... when one takes a single wrong step, there is no line to be pursued which does not lead to some kind of embarrassment. A total secession, without resigning my seat, I must acknowledge to be wrong and so long as it is out of my power (on account of private reasons which have not escaped you) to resign my seat ... there is no mode of conduct I can adopt which in my own opinion would be perfectly right.

The dilemma was ever present and it was no consolation to know that it was of his own making.[6]

Nevertheless, Grey was soon to resume political activity. Two causes claimed his support. The first was parliamentary reform, the second the Irish question. During 1797 there was a temporary revival of public agitation by the reformers, stimulated by the unpopularity of the war and of Pitt's new taxes. In the spring of 1797 Wyvill had attempted to rouse Yorkshire and Northumberland to petition 'for peace, and for a redress of grievances'. Wyvill suspended his plans when Pitt's peace negotiations opened in the summer, but he revived them in the autumn when the negotiations were over and when the new taxes were beginning to bite. He proposed a preparatory meeting of Yorkshire gentlemen and wrote to enlist Grey's support in Northumberland. John Cartwright too urged that Grey should once again take the lead at Westminster: 'from his seat in the House of Commons

---

[5] Grey to Whitbread, 5, 24 Nov. and 31 Dec. [1797], Whitbread MSS 1/867, 869–70.

[6] It was alleged that in 1794 Sir Charles Grey and his naval co-commander Jervis had exacted excessive booty from the conquered islands, harming American as well as French citizens and prejudicing the interests of British West India merchants, who petitioned for the condemnation of Grey and Jervis in 1795. The commanders demanded a public enquiry to clear them from suspicion. Grey, Fox, and Sheridan, supported by Dundas, defended them in the Commons and the House exonerated them in May 1795. Despite this vindication, Sir Charles Grey was never given another overseas command but was appointed commander-in-chief of the southern English military district: *Parl. Hist.* xxxii. 54–74; J. M. Fewster, 'Prize money and the British expedition to the West Indies of 1793–4', *Journal of Imperial and Commonwealth History* xii. (1983), 1–28; Grey to Bigge, 30 Dec. 1798, G. 7/10.

he may speak to the millions', he wrote. 'The secession is to me a grievous mortification.'[7]

Grey did not speak in the House for reform but he came to London in early January 1798 to try to promote the movement, and urged his friends to write to their contacts in the country to stir up the public. The mood, however, was apathetic. Middlesex, the hoped-for centre of a national agitation, failed to move, and in February the Yorkshire reformers decided to defer all activity and wait for 'better times'. Grey was convinced that 'till a general and determined spirit of resistance ... against the whole system of the present Ministers, arises in the country it is in vain to hope for good.' He attended a meeting in London at the beginning of March which agreed to suspend the plan; his suggestion of a public, non-party declaration of support for a moderate course of action was dropped. Nothing was left but 'silence and sorrow' in face of the government's vigorous repression of all reforming activity.[8] He announced to Bigge in December 1798 his intention of being present at 'the most material measures' of the session, but he added that he would not take an active part unless requested by his constituents. Since Fox confirmed his resolve to stay away, even if it left him as 'the sole seceder', Grey could do little. He came up for the debate on the Address, though without speaking or voting, and he voted against the Income Tax Bill. He made no speech, however, until the debate in the next session on the Irish Union Bill.[9]

It was the Irish question which brought Grey back into regular attendance in the winter of 1798–9. He confessed to Holland that he felt 'a little uncomfortable' in appearing without Fox, but the Irish question was one he could not ignore.[10] The Foxites had begun to take up the old Whig cause of Ireland in 1795, when Fitzwilliam's recall from the Viceroyalty created a political crisis inside the new coalition administration. The opposition hoped to reclaim Fitzwilliam now that he had fallen out with Pitt and they also hoped to institute a joint Anglo-Irish opposition with Grattan and the Ponsonbys, who had tried to use Fitzwilliam to win concessions for the Catholics and power for themselves, and whose adoption of parliamentary reform had created another bond with the Foxites.

Grey's marriage to Lady Fitzwilliam's niece had allied him to the powerful Ponsonby clan. He wrote to his mother-in-law Lady Ponsonby in July 1798 that with regard to Ireland, 'if there is anything to be done on this side by a party without numbers or power ... you may depend upon it there is nothing that I will leave unattempted.' His speech in defence of Fitzwilliam's Irish Viceroyalty in May 1795 marked the beginning of his public attachment to the Catholic cause

[7] Wyvill, *Political Papers*, iv. 344–75; Wyvill to Grey, 29 Jan. 1798, Wyvill MSS 251; Cartwright to Wyvill, 10 Dec. 1797, Wyvill, *Political Papers*, iv. 379.

[8] Grey to Whitbread, 31 Dec. 1797, Whitbread MSS 1/870; letters from Grey to Bigge, 11 Oct. 1797 to 5 Mar. 1798, G. 7/10; *CGPW*, iii. 433 n.1; Grey to Mary [21–23 May 1798], G. 27.

[9] Grey to Bigge, 14 and 30 Dec. 1798, G. 7/10; Fox to Holland, 21 Oct. 1798, *Fox*, iii. 146; *Parl. Hist.* xxxiv. 109.

[10] Grey to Holland [1799], G. 35. Fox was consulted in April 1800 about the line to be taken on the Union Bill but he declared that 'nothing can persuade me to attend': Grey to Fitzpatrick [20 Feb. 1800], G. 14/10; Fox to Fitzpatrick, 3 Apr., *Fox*, iii. 295.

and in June 1798 he voted for Cavendish's motion on the state of Ireland. In February 1799 he broke his long silence at Westminster in the first debate on the Union Bill. He spoke both on behalf of a more liberal policy towards Ireland and, in particular, for the end of religious discrimination. He declared that a Union should be 'a union, not of Parliaments, but of hearts, affections, and interests', warning that a forced Union would ultimately be repudiated by the Irish people. In the next session he voted for the amendment to the Address on 3 February 1800, and he took the leading role in opposition to the Union in the debates which followed.[11]

By the spring of 1800 the second Union Bill had been forced through the Dublin Parliament, which had voted for its own extinction after an intense campaign by the Irish administration involving much corrupt bargaining with leading Protestant interests and veiled promises of some unspecified measure of emancipation to gain the support of the Catholics. The Irish Commons had also received many petitions from counties and boroughs in favour of the Union, which provided a spurious appearance of consent by the Irish people themselves. When the Bill was introduced at Westminster, it was on these aspects of its passage in Dublin that Grey concentrated his opposition.

He spoke first against Pitt's resolutions on 21 April which set out the main proposals. He declared the 'strongest and most insuperable objections' both to the principles and to the provisions of the Bill, foremost amongst which was the opposition of the majority of the Irish nation. He denied Pitt's contention that the Addresses and petitions in favour of the Bill represented five-sevenths of the Irish people, pointing out that 27 counties and almost all the respectable towns, including the city of Dublin, had petitioned against it: these provided a total of over 700,000 signatures against a mere 3,000 who had signed the pro-Union Addresses. It was not the few Jacobins and fanatics who opposed the Bill, but the most respectable people of every class. Two thirds of the Irish county members and almost all the representatives of the towns which would retain their parliamentary representation after the Union had voted against it; of the 162 Irish MPs who voted for the Bill, 116 were placemen or British army officers, upon whom all the arts of patronage and influence had been employed. 'We have no right to discuss this question', he stated, 'unless it be proved to us that the passing of these resolutions will be acceptable to the great body of the Irish nation.'

Grey then proceeded to refute the main arguments for the measure, denying the force of any parallel with the Scottish Union of 1707 and pointing out that the Westminster Parliament would be able to tax the Irish for the support of the much greater British national debt. Nor would the Union itself unite the affections of Ireland to Britain; the only way to win those was to 'adopt liberal measures',

---

[11] Grey to Lady Ponsonby, 11 July 1798, G. 48; *Parl. Hist.* xxxi. 1556–7, xxxiv. 330–1, 336–45. Lady Elizabeth Foster recorded that Grey's speech in Feb. 1799 was 'one of the best speeches' against the Union: Journal. Grey's vote in June 1798 was concerted with the Prince of Wales and Fox: Lady Holland, *Journal*, i. 190–1.

for the grievances of Ireland arose from the tyranny of British government. As for the Catholic question, he denied that concession would be dangerous without a Union, quoting the history of Ireland since 1782 and in particular that of Fitz-william's Viceroyalty to show that the leading Irish Catholics were men whose loyalty could be trusted. The Irish had been driven to rebellion only by 'a system of tyranny, cruelty and barbarity' which followed Fitzwilliam's recall. Until the Catholic disabilities were removed 'no progress will be made [towards] securing the public tranquillity, or in promoting the extension of commerce or of wealth'.

Finally, Grey pointed out the constitutional dangers for the whole United Kingdom of admitting 100 extra members to the House of Commons who 'will rarely be adverse to the measures of any administration' and would greatly increase the influence of the Crown. They would be the ministers' 'constant and unalterable supporters'. The principal issue, however, was the necessity of the full and free consent of the Irish people: 'Why do we inveigh against the violence of the French for compelling into their connection countries to whom they leave no room for free deliberation?' The principle of the independence of nations applied to the Irish as much as to any people in Europe and, like Chatham in the case of the Americans, Grey rejoiced that the Irish had resisted the tyranny of British policy.[12]

Four days later Grey attacked on another front with a motion to consider 'the most effectual means of providing for, and securing the independence of Parliament'. This motion enabled him to link the Union question with par-liamentary reform for, although he declared that it was not at present his intention to make 'any separate and distinct motion' on that subject, it was proper to consider the general principles of parliamentary representation in the context of the proposals for providing Ireland with members at Westminster. He hoped also to reassert that the principles on which he was an advocate of reform were far removed from those purely theoretical grounds insinuated by its enemies, and to distinguish his standpoint clearly from that of the radicals:[13]

The only reason why I ever urged the House to adopt a parliamentary reform was because it appeared to me a necessary remedy for an actual existing grievance. No man can subscribe more cordially than I do to the maxim, that in government practical good is infinitely preferable to speculative perfection.

Though the subject of the debate was the future representation of Ireland, Grey took the opportunity to set out his general views on reform. Firstly, he declared that there were certain basic principles behind any system of representation. One of these must be that representation must have some relationship to population: 'Its object is to obtain such a composition of the representative body as will qualify the members of it to be the organ and to speak the sense of the people.' No one could deny that in this respect the passage of time had produced anomalies in the system; to purge these anomalies was not to innovate, but 'to reverence ancient

---

[12] G. C. Bolton, *The Passing of the Irish Act of Union* (Oxford, 1966), esp. 126–84; *Parl. Hist.* xxxv. 57–72. Grey's motion was lost by 30 to 236.

[13] Ibid. 88–102. Fox praised it as 'an extraordinary good speech': to Grey, n.d. 1800, *Fox*, iii. 311.

institutions' by restoring their former character. True, before 1688 the representation of particular communities was to some extent at the discretion of the Crown, but in general it was the practice to summon representatives from 'those towns which were considered best fitted, from their population, for the exercise of such a right'.

The second argument concerned the reverence men felt for the Revolution of 1688: 'It is pleaded as an invincible bar to any improvement proposed in favour of the people.' No one could have a greater admiration than he for the constitution as fixed at the Revolution: 'A better system of practical liberty was never enjoyed by any people, than was then established for the happiness and glory of the British nation.' But it would be absurd to say either that no further improvement was possible, or that time and circumstances had not eroded the liberties enjoyed in 1689. In particular, there had been a great increase in the influence of the Crown 'beyond the regulated portion assigned by ... our ancestors, and which either has been, or threatens to become, injurious to ... liberty and to the prosperity of the empire'. The increase of revenue, of civil and military establishments, and of the empire in India, had notoriously increased Crown influence without any countervailing increase in the liberties of the subject or the power of Parliament. Since 1782 the progress of that influence had greatly accelerated from the increase in the national debt, the 'monstrous increase of naval and military establishments, ... the restrictions on popular rights', and the refusal of the House and the government to heed the expressed wishes of the people, for example in opposition to the war. Reform should be viewed not as a dangerous experiment in democracy, but as the only means to strengthen the existing constitution and confirm the principles which lay behind its establishment after 1688:

Convinced that freedom is the only sure basis on which the stability of government can be founded, I still feel myself disposed to move a general reform of parliament, as the best means of maintaining the constitution in its purity and vigour ... Hating innovations, however, I consider it my duty to promote reform. It is by timely reform alone that the danger of great crisis and of violent innovation is prevented.

Grey then returned to the subject of the extra 100 members proposed at Westminster for Ireland. He objected to the principle of increasing the size of the House at all, since he considered '558 a number as great as would be consistent with order'. He proposed, therefore, the disfranchisement of some of 'the most decayed' existing British constituencies and the reduction of the Irish quota to 85, to leave the total membership unchanged. Thus the Union would result in the achievement of some moderate degree of parliamentary reform in both kingdoms.

Grey's motion was of course defeated, by 34 votes to 176: and his final intervention in this year's Union debates, to reduce the number of Irish members allowed to hold places from 20 to 10, was also rejected. He neither spoke nor voted on any other question during the session. Yet his two major speeches on the Union heralded his return to full opposition, and his reassertion of his commitment to reform made it clear that he did so on the same grounds as in 1792 and 1797. When he arrived at Westminster at the end of 1800 for the next session, though he proposed at first not to draw up a formal amendment to the Address on the grounds that it would be 'rather too formal a declaration of active opposition', he was ready to admit that secession was 'no longer defensible upon any ground either of principle or prudence'.[14]

His return did not, however, bring about a harmonious reunion of the Whig party. Grey was still too prone to act independently, and too disinclined to treat his colleagues with consideration. Despite his declared intention not to move an amendment he decided at the last moment to do so; but he had not informed his friends, and when Sheridan caught the Speaker's eye first he opened the debate with a declaration that, in view of the need for unanimity in a time of severe popular hardship, he would not oppose the Address. Grey then launched into a full-scale attack on the 'weakness and folly' of the government, asserting that their continued refusal to seek an end to the war was the real cause of the country's troubles, and concluding by moving his amendment. The opposition was thrown into disarray, and Sheridan wrote after the debate to remonstrate; had Grey even hinted at his intentions beforehand, Sheridan would not have said what he did. The letter ended on a conciliatory note, Sheridan assuring Grey that the incident 'did not leave a moment's unkind feeling' on his mind, though 'I thought myself the aggrieved person.' He even welcomed Grey's return to the House

as well on public grounds as because I truly think that activity of exertion in a sphere your talents are peculiarly calculated for, and the interest that application of them creates in your mind are as essential to your own happiness as the character and lead you ought to hold in the country. I will not deal in professions but whether I shall be diligent or idle you will always find me fair and sincere in supporting the cause and principles which I am sure are your objects as a public man.[15]

Despite these conciliatory words, the incident left no doubt that an oppposition headed by Grey and Sheridan would not be a harmonious one, and that Fox's return was necessary to make it so. Fox, however, found in it further reasons for holding aloof from the Commons: 'These things cannot be helped,' Fox wrote, 'but they are additional reasons to make me satisfied with secession as far as relates to myself.' Tierney and Sheridan were also at loggerheads, and once again Fox was inclined to blame Sheridan, who 'will never do anything quite wrong in politics but whether he will ever go on very steadily and straightforward I doubt'.[16]

Pitt's resignation at the beginning of February 1801 made it necessary for Fox to consider returning to Parliament, but he confessed that he thought differently 'every five minutes' about resuming the leadership. He still hoped to persuade Grey to step into his shoes, and to reconcile his friends to the idea rather than to

---

[14] Grey to Holland, 7 Nov. [1800], BL Add. MS 51544, fo.66.
[15] *Parl. Hist.* xxxv. 531–6; Sheridan to Grey [Nov. 1800], G. 52.
[16] Fox to Grey [25 Nov. 1800], G. 27.

take up the post himself.[17] Fitzwilliam was now preparing to return to Fox's side, influenced by the growing unpopularity of the war in the West Riding as its economic effects began to become damaging to the formerly prosperous woollen trade. Fox suggested that Grey, as Fitzwilliam's nephew by marriage, should try to recruit him to Wyvill's renewed scheme for a county meeting to petition for peace and the removal of ministers. Grey warned Wyvill that Fitzwilliam would fight shy of any proposal for parliamentary reform and would find it difficult to trust himself to those who were its avowed champions. Fox hoped that he might 'gradually make up his mind to it' and urged Fitzwilliam not to be too scrupulous about acting with men of differing views on the question; he repeated that he would have no more to do with public affairs and that nothing would induce him to resume the party leadership: 'I think if ever good is to be done Grey and the duke of Bedford are the men to do it.'[18]

Fitzwilliam could not yet bring himself to co-operate with his old enemy Wyvill, but he was prepared to work in friendly harmony with Grey, and in February 1801 he adopted and moved in the Lords an amendment to the Address which Grey had prepared for him. Fox professed his 'pleasure to see all those I love in open and declared opposition to this most detestable government', but his colleagues were not yet ready to accept Grey as his successor. Though Grey took the lead at the opening of the new session, it was only a matter of time before Fox returned to his old position in the House.[19]

The political atmosphere was now one of crisis and uncertainty, and strong leadership was necessary if the opposition was to exploit it. Pitt's attempt to persuade George III to crown the Irish Union with the repeal of the penal laws against the Catholics failed to move the King's stubborn conscience, and at the beginning of February the Prime Minister resigned.[20] The appointment of Addington as his successor and with his blessing seemed to Fox a mere 'juggle'; but the refusal of several of Pitt's colleagues in the old administration to continue in office meant a more extensive change than perhaps had been intended, and left the new ministry dangerously short of talent and experience. In the middle of the handover of office, the King suffered a relapse into mental derangement, during which time Pitt let it be known secretly to the Court that he would not press the Catholic question upon him when he recovered. Fox knew nothing of the declaration, but he was suspicious of Pitt's sincerity and thought his return to office a mere question of time and opportunity. The Whigs tried to force Pitt to declare his hand in public, and on 25 March Grey demanded to know what pledges

[17] Fox to Fitzpatrick, 3 Feb. 1801 and to Lauderdale, 19 Feb., *Fox*, iii. 319–20, 325–8.

[18] Fox to Grey [7 Nov.] 1800; Sunday, 1800; and 1800: *Fox*, iii. 305, 306–9, 314; Wyvill to Grey, 7 Jan. 1801, Wyvill MSS 250; Grey to Wyvill, 12 Jan. 1801, G. 60; Wyvill, *Political Papers*, vi. pt. ii, 67–70; Fitzwilliam to Lady Fitzwilliam [2 Feb. 1801] and to Laurence [Jan. 1801], Fox to Fitzwilliam, 1 Feb. 1801, Fitzwilliam MSS, Northampton. The proposed Yorkshire meeting was abandoned when Pitt resigned in Feb. 1801.

[19] Fox to Fitzwilliam, 1 Feb. 1801, ibid.

[20] On the reasons for Pitt's resignation see R. E. Willis, 'William Pitt's resignation in 1801', *Bulletin of the Institute of Historical Research*, xliv. no. 110 (1971), 239–57.

had been given to the Irish Catholics, and whether emancipation had been blocked by a royal veto. Otherwise, he hinted, Pitt was guilty of deceiving the Catholics— 'one of the greatest crimes of which any minister ever stood convicted'.[21]

Pitt was equal to the occasion. He had handed out a severe drubbing to Grey a fortnight earlier on the Irish Martial Law Bill, when Grey had again taunted him with desertion of his old pledges to the reformers. In reply, Pitt had drawn a distinction between the support of reform in times of peace and harmony and its agitation in co-operation with men who 'professed that object to conceal deeper and more dangerous views'. Grey complained after the debate that his friends had not intervened to save him from Pitt's mauling: 'I never was present at a debate which left upon my mind so strong a feeling of disgust, and I am more anxious than ever to quit politics', he wrote on the next morning. His apprehensiveness on 25 March was the more understandable. He wrote to Mary on the eve of the debate that he was 'very nervous ... and as usual deprived of sleep by it, so that instead of being in full strength as I ought to be, I shall be all to pieces'. It was the first full muster of the opposition since 1797, and with Fox's support, speaking as he said 'as a new member', the minority topped 100 for the first time since the Ochakov debates in 1791. Pitt, however, avoided the trap Grey had tried to set for him, denying that the House had any right to enquire into the reasons for his resignation and refusing to commit himself on the Catholic question for the future. It was clear that there was little hope of political co-operation with the outgoing Prime Minister against his successor and that the old personal hostility between Pitt and Grey was as deep as ever. The Whigs turned to other tactics, hoping either to negotiate a junction with Addington that would admit them to a substantial share of offices, or, if that were not feasible, to explore the possibilities of a new and powerful opposition in alliance with Fitzwilliam and the followers of Lord Grenville, formerly Pitt's Foreign Secretary, whose disgust at the peace terms was soon to make them implacable enemies of the new ministry.[22]

Fox's earliest preference was for the former solution, thinking that 'the new men may be better ... than the old' and preferring to support peace with France rather than ally with men who were still resolute enemies of any settlement with the regicide republic. He even expressed surprise that Grey had not already been approached with an invitation to join the Cabinet. The new Prime Minister too saw the Whigs as a more promising source of strength than Pitt, Grenville, or Canning who would be likely to make harsher terms for their support. The opening of peace negotiations at Amiens removed a major obstacle to a junction between Addington and Fox's friends, if they could be persuaded to take office without their leader, who was still subject to the King's veto and still unpopular with the country gentlemen because of his 'unpatriotic' record on the war. Addington therefore made cautious and secretive overtures to Tierney, whose quarrel with

[21] Fox to Fitzpatrick, 3 Feb. 1801, *Fox*, iii. 320; *Parl. Hist.* xxxv. 1051–70.

[22] Ibid. 1022–4, 12 Mar. 1801; Grey to Mary [13 and 24 Mar. 1801], G. 27; *Parl. Hist.* xxxv. 1128–69.

Fox over secession was public knowledge and whose attendance in Parliament since 1797 seemed to indicate a willingness to take part. Tierney was acting in close concert with Moira, leader of the Prince's friends, and hoped to secure Cabinet places for him and Grey and an office for himself. On 16th October Tierney and Addington met on horseback in the Park, by arrangement through Bragge, Addington's brother-in-law, and two days later they held a further secret meeting on Wimbledon Common. The conversations were promising enough for Tierney to approach Grey, professing a wish to be considered 'amongst the first of your friends' and with 'a thorough disposition to give you the most unreserved confidence'. He suggested a meeting halfway between London and Howick to discuss the details of the proposals.[23]

Grey disapproved of Tierney's actions and threw cold water on the whole idea of a junction with Addington. He had written in February 1801 that he considered the ministry to be formed 'avowedly on the same principles' as Pitt's, and to differ 'only in carrying to greater length ... the principle of intolerance and persecution'. He had already declared his unwillingness to come to town before Christmas or even until the debate on the preliminaries of peace in the New Year, and he now refused to be a party to Tierney's clandestine negotiations without Fox's knowledge or participation. He was disposed to tread cautiously until he knew more about the ministry's future domestic policies. Tierney declared his conviction that the peace would quickly lead to the restoration of the Habeas Corpus Act and the repeal of Pitt's other repressive legislation against political opinions; but Grey was not disposed to take Tierney's word for Addington's good intentions, and demanded some public demonstration of them. When a direct approach was made to Grey in November by Lord St Vincent, formerly Sir John Jervis, First Lord of the Admiralty and a friend of Grey's father, he replied with an immediate refusal, though he was careful to place his objections on public and not personal grounds: he sought not 'personal power or patronage' but 'a real security for myself and a certain indication to the public that the Government is to be conducted on different principles from those which have prevailed of late years'. This could be achieved either by the admission of a considerable number of Whigs to the Cabinet or by the adoption of 'some great and leading measures which would speak for themselves' as 'an unequivocal proof of a change of system'; and there must at least be a change of men and a reversal of policy in Ireland. Grey did not believe in fact that Addington was willing, or would be allowed by the Court to comply with such terms, and he cautioned Tierney against joining an administration whose measures were as yet undeclared and might prove embarrassing to him. Though Tierney did not give up hope of an eventual alliance, he assured Grey in January 1802 that he had had no more conferences with Addington and did not intend to seek any. His object, he wrote in February, was 'to keep the

---

[23] Fox to Grey, Wed. [Feb. 1801], *Fox*, iii. 323–4; P. Ziegler, *Addington* (1965), 132–3; Tierney to Moira [Nov. 1801], Tierney MSS 52c.

door open and to avoid being pressed too much to walk in'. He nevertheless complained to Whitbread of Grey's intransigence:[24]

As to Grey, does he or does he not mean to look to high station in this country? If he does not, instead of coming forward upon Mr Fox's retirement, he had surely better accompany him in his retreat. If he does, can he show me any reasonable prospect of forming an administration of his own? I am sure he will not pretend to it. He must then look to a junction with some man with whom he has not hitherto been in the habit of acting, and I should, in that case, be glad to know to what quarter he can turn where fewer difficulties present themselves than stand in the way between him and Mr A.

Grey however was too sensitive to accusations that he coveted Fox's place as leader of the Whigs and that he might desert opposition without a pledge from the ministry on parliamentary reform. Lady Holland was already inclined to condemn his conduct in listening to overtures from Addington and it was necessary to make his position clear. Though Laurence told Fitzwilliam that the negotiations had been broken off on the Whig demand for the repeal of the Treason and Sedition Acts, the newspapers were still reporting rumours of a Whig junction with the government in February 1802, Grey being named as President of the Board of Control, Moira Secretary of State, and Bedford President of the Council, with Portland going to Ireland as Viceroy, and Tierney becoming Secretary to the Treasury. Suspicions were encouraged by an intemperate speech by Sheridan at the Whig Club dinner in January, when he referred to

those persons who, thrown by accident in the outset of life into situations for which they are not fitted, become Friends of the People for a time, and afterwards, finding their mistake, desert the popular cause.

Sheridan almost certainly intended to refer to Tierney but as he was drunk at the time his meaning was not altogether clear. Grey, in his sensitive mood, took the allusion to be to himself and was deeply resentful. He was all the more determined to avoid any conduct that could possibly be interpreted as a desertion of his commitment to reform. Wyvill wrote to Fox on 14 January that he attributed Grey's 'honourable conduct' in refusing office to Addington's unwillingness to accept his condition of a 'mild reform'. Fox assured Wyvill of his 'perfect confidence that Grey never will or ever can, either on the subject of reform, or any other, act otherwise than is consistent with his own honour and the good of his country'. Fox nevertheless asked Grey to confirm that all negotiation with Addington was at an end, and was hurt in turn by Grey's irritable response in which he accused Fox of suspicion of his actions.[25]

[24] Grey to Wyvill, 11 Feb. 1801, Wyvill MSS 251/9; Tierney to Grey [19 Oct. 1801], 22 Oct. [Jan. 1802, and Feb. 1802], G. 55; Grey to Tierney, 16 Oct. and 28 Dec. 1801, Tierney MSS 33. On Tierney's negotiations see H. K. Olphin, *George Tierney* (1934), 74–8. Tierney to Whitbread, Friday [16 Oct. 1801], Whitbread MSS 2408.

[25] Lady Holland, *Journal*, ii. 147; Laurence to Fitzwilliam [29 Jan. 1802], Fitzwilliam MSS; *Worcester Journal*, 4 Feb. 1802. Addington had offered via Tierney three Cabinet places for Grey, Bedford, and Moira and a prospective undertaking to make Erskine Chief Justice of Common Pleas

Tierney, meanwhile, had not given up hope of drawing Grey into his schemes. On 10 February he met Lord St Vincent at Grey's father's house to discuss the state of political affairs. St Vincent agreed that the administration must be strengthened in view of the state of Europe and of the King's precarious health, and, Tierney wrote to Grey,

Everything will play into your hands ... The time is not very distant when terms will be offered to you which you will find it difficult to reject ... It is next to impossible that the present Administration, constituted as it now is, should stand.

Tierney's continued resentment against Fox, however, alienated Grey, who was unwilling to place himself in the position of a deserter from his party and principles for the sake of office and who suspected that Tierney was about to do so. His terms for taking office remained high. As he wrote to Mary twelve months later, he would not negotiate 'on any ground but that of having a majority in the Cabinet, Fox being one'. On these conditions, as he realized, his prospects were remote, and he determined to attend as little as possible in the new session. It was not until March that he was persuaded to appear at Westminster, and even then, as he announced to Whitbread, 'I had rather be anywhere than here', and he declared he would 'as much as possible abstain of [sic] all political connections of every kind'. He now believed that Pitt and the Grenvilles would be reconciled and that they would together drive Addington from office, leaving the Whigs still in opposition. He was accordingly disinclined to any vigorous exertion, to the extent that even Fox was irritated by his lethargy and tartly remarked that if he was not willing to put some enthusiasm into the opposition to the government's measures he would have done better to stay in Northumberland. He even read him a lesson on the subject:[26]

Pray above all things, my dear Grey, do not fancy that it is possible for you to be present ... and not to do your very utmost. I know it is very disagreeable to be told such a thing, as it seems to be setting one such a task; but there are occasions when this must not be minded.

Grey's mood remained one of depression and disillusionment. The pessimism which was always near to the surface of his character, together with his reluctance to leave Howick, made him an unwilling actor in the political events of the next few years. The roles of 1797–1801 were reversed; now it was Fox who burned

when the post should become vacant: Tierney to Moira, [Nov. 1801], Tierney MSS; *Morning Post*, 20 Jan. 1802. Tierney wrote that Sheridan's speech was partly levelled at him but 'part I think at other people'—to Grey, Sat. [Jan. 1802], G. 55. Fox tried to persuade Grey that Sheridan meant only to refer to Tierney (*Fox*, iii. 355) but Grey wrote 'full of wrath' against Sheridan to Lauderdale: Tierney to Grey, Feb. 1802, G. 55; Wyvill to Fox, 14 Jan. 1802, Fox to Wyvill, 20 Jan., Wyvill, *Political Papers*, vi. pt. ii, 145–7; Fox to Grey, 20, 31 Jan. and 21 Feb. 1802, *Fox*, iii. 351–3, 354–9; Grey to Whitbread, 31 Jan., G. 59.

[26] Tierney to Grey, 11 and 19 Feb. 1802, G. 55; Grey to Mary, 23 Apr. 1803, G. 27; Grey to Whitbread, [26 Mar. 1802], Whitbread MSS WbI/1875; Fox to Lauderdale, 26 Mar. and 26 Nov. 1802, to Grey, May 1802, *Fox*, iii. 366, 370, 373.

with zeal for active and vigorous opposition to 'make our party, weak and disbanded as it is, of some consequence, and enable us to [do] a real good service to the country', while Grey dragged his feet unwillingly to Westminster and hankered after domestic seclusion in the country as a relief from the cares of public life.

3 The Road to Leadership, 1802–1807

The Whig party's return to Parliament did not establish a united and harmonious opposition to Addington's new government. The Whigs remained divided on several important issues and co-operation with other political groups outside the ministry was not easy. A whole range of new problems had to be tackled, both internal and external, threatening to widen existing differences within and among the parties. Grey found himself at odds with some of his former colleagues and unsure of the direction he and his party ought to take. The change in his personal and domestic circumstances since his marriage, the births of his first children, and his establishment at Howick in 1801 also contributed to the tensions and frustrations to which his volatile personality always subjected him. His ambitions were still high, but moods of self-doubt and repugnance for the apparently pointless political struggle after the experience of the past ten years became more and more frequent.

Most crushing of all the blows he had to endure in this period of his life was his father's acceptance, at his own solicitation, of a peerage from Addington in June 1801. Grey compained bitterly that he had not been consulted beforehand, particularly since his father, at the age of 72, was unlikely to enjoy the distinction for long. Grey now expected his early removal from the Commons, where the whole of his political life and reputation had been built, to the Upper House where his oratorical gifts would be muffled by the deadening atmosphere. Fox's attempt to console him with the remark that 'the constitution of the country is declining so rapidly, that the House of Commons has in great measure ceased, and will shortly cease entirely to be a place of much importance', had a hollow ring. The Commons was still the great theatre of British political life, the focus of all the major public issues of the day, and, in the present state of the Whig party, the place where strong leadership was most essential to it. Grey could not but contrast his approaching fate with that of Pitt and Fox who, as younger sons of peers, were able to remain in the Commons, while the death in infancy of his own first brother had destined him for the Lords. It was another reason for the mood of despondency that seemed rarely to leave him during the next few years and which contributed to a notorious reluctance to come to town from Howick and play an active role in party affairs. Mary's state of health, her successive pregnancies, or, in 1803–4, the fear of leaving her and the children in danger from French raids on the coast, provided a series of excuses for staying in Northumberland when Fox needed him in London. Fox was to complain in December 1804 that it was as difficult to fetch Grey from Northumberland as his nephew Lord Holland from Spain, though

Grey admitted that he was idling his time away at Howick doing 'literally nothing'. Even when he consented to come to town he arrived grumbling about the inconvenience, threatening to resign his seat at the end of the session, and so out of spirits that he irritated his friends and cast a gloom over their deliberations. Even speaking in the House had become an ordeal to him. His former self-assurance had given way to a nervous tension that incapacitated him before a major speech and gave him sleepless nights. In May 1803 he referred to his constant 'debating nervousness' and described the Commons as 'this odious place'.[1]

Yet Fox had come to rely on Grey's talent and judgement, and now marked him as his natural successor and chief adviser. In April 1801 he remarked to Lauderdale that Grey was 'certainly improved, not only in speaking (in which he is very greatly so) but I think in everything'. He confided in and trusted Grey, and felt that Grey shared his point of view and sympathies as few others did. Fox was disappointed, therefore, at Grey's lack of enthusiasm for the renewed political prospects which he felt lay before the Whig party after 1802. Fox was a man who valued friendship above all other things in life, but the loyalty he gave to his friends exposed him all too often to their conflicting advice and sapped his confidence in his own judgement. On his own, he was apt to blunder impulsively into untenable positions, to blurt out extreme opinions which were a later embarrassment to himself and his party. He needed a strong-minded counsellor and supporter in these years when, as he recognized, the party needed to work out and follow through a coherent political strategy. Fox appealed to Grey frequently for advice. In March 1803 he wrote:

I wish your presence, not because I wish you to follow my line, or to agree in my opinion, but because I wish you to take one yourself, and to help me with your opinion; whatever that line and opinion may be, I will implicitly follow it.

And again, in October,

Now let me repeat to you, my dear Grey, how very desirous I am that you should decide, and how certain I am that I shall think your decision, whatever it may be, right: whereas, if I am forced to decide myself, whatever I decide I am sure to think wrong.

Fox knew that his own years in the leadership of the Whig party were numbered, and by 1802 he was beginning the slow decline in health that ended in his death four years later. He realized too that George III's personal hostility to him was the major obstacle to the Whigs' admittance to office, and hoped by standing aside to make it easier for them to achieve it. Yet the survival of the Whig party as a distinct and powerful entity was first in Fox's thoughts, and he became acutely conscious in the years following 1801 of the dangers of its fragmentation or absorption by one or more of the other groups which had now been formed. The search for his own successor was therefore never far from his thoughts, and Grey

---

[1] Fox to Grey, n.d., and 17 Dec. 1803, *Fox*, iii. 340–1, 442–5; Grey to Fox, 3, 14 Aug., 26 Oct. 1803, 25 Nov. 1804, G. 16; to Whitbread, 16 Oct., Whitbread MSS 1/887; to Mary, [19] and 25 May 1803, 28 Feb. 1804, G. 27; Fox to Holland, 12 Dec. 1804, *Fox*, iv. 66.

remained the obvious choice. The death of the fifth Duke of Bedford in 1802 at the early age of 36 removed the only other major contender in the eyes of most of the party. Lauderdale, Bedford's successor in the Lords, was too unstable and lightweight, and, like Grey, a difficult man to bring to town, in this case from his Scottish estates. In the Commons, Grey stood head and shoulders above all his colleagues. All that was needed was the courage to grasp the role he was so clearly marked out to fill. As Fox wrote to him in 1803:[2]

If our *reliquiae* could be kept together, if it were ony the Russells and Cavendishes and a few more, with you at the head of them, not only would it give me great satisfaction, but it might be a foundation for better things at some future period.

Grey, however, hesitated as he had done during the secession. It had not been forgotten that as a young man, he had been accused of arrogance and excessive ambition. The Prince of Wales talked to Mrs Creevey in 1805 of 'his bad temper and his early presumption in over-rating his talents' at the time of the Regency crisis. As Grey approached middle age he was wary of making the same mistake again. He assured Fox in 1803:

I can take *no line of my own*, except as an individual. I *cannot* take upon myself any lead or direction, even if it were offered to me under much more favourable circumstances than any that are likely to occur ... I say this in the sincerity of my heart.

His terms for taking office remained what they had been since 1794: he could do so only 'on such terms as should prove to the world that ... the whole power of the Government was Fox's'. Nor was he confident that he would be any more acceptable to the King than his friend, because of his commitment to parliamentary reform. He wrote in May 1803:

It is not only my connection with Fox that stands in the way of my admission, but my own character and principles must form an effectual bar to me under the present circumstances and probably for ever.... The whole situation of public affairs presents on every side so many unpleasant circumstances, with so little temptation to any honourable ambition that my disposition to withdraw myself from it entirely increases every hour.

So, although Fox repeated his view that Grey would be the best possible candidate for the premiership, Grey refused to budge from the opinion that 'there is only one man who ought to be there, and whom alone I really believe the unbiased voice of England and Europe would place there.'[3]

Grey therefore set his own limitations on his political advancement as long as Fox lived. In the meantime, his hope was to work with Fox into a political position which would be to the best advantage of the party. At the outset of this

[2] Fox to Lauderdale, 1 Apr. 1801, BL Add. MS 47564, fo. 95; Derry, *Charles James Fox*, 391; Fox to Grey, 12 Mar., 19 Oct. 1803, *Fox*, iii. 397–400, 427–32, 20 Nov. 1802, BL Add. MS 47565, fos. 62–4. Fox told Wyvill in 1804 that 'when young, he owned, he might look with some degree of ambition to share with others in governing the country; but that was over with him. He was fond of his place in the country, fond of reading, and loved to be quiet': Wyvill MSS 164/2.

[3] Mrs Creevey to Thomas Creevey, 29 Nov. [1805], *Creevey Papers*, i. 72; Grey to Fox, 15 Mar. 1803 and 18 Feb. 1804, G. 16, to Mary, [3 May], G. 27.

period, immediately after the Peace of Amiens, that task was made difficult by an apparent difference of view over the French question. During the previous war, there had been no disagreement between them. They had opposed it throughout as an unjustified campaign against liberty all over Europe, and condemned without reservation its consequences on the liberties and prosperity of the British people. Fox, however, carried his detestation of Pitt's government and policies beyond the limits set by Grey's more cautious appreciation of British national interests. In October 1801 Fox made a provocative speech to the Westminster electors at the Shakespeare Tavern to celebrate the twenty-first anniversary of his election, in which he publicly welcomed Britain's defeat at the hands of the French. His words dismayed all his friends. Lord Bute, a friend of Moira and the Prince of Wales, deplored 'the strange revolutionary speech pronounced by Mr. Fox at the alehouse' and Moira was angry that Fox had spoken without consulting his colleagues. Grey too was alarmed by Fox's tone, and not mollified by his assurance that the speech was intended more as 'the most decided condemnation' of ministers than as approval of Britain's disgrace. Fox admitted that the speech was 'indiscreet', but remarked that 'you know that of late I have not considered much for myself what in a political view may or may not be judicious'[4] and added,

for the truth is, I am gone something further in hate to the English Government than perhaps you and the rest of my friends are, and certainly further than can with prudence be avowed. The triumph of the French Government over the English does in fact afford me a degree of pleasure which it is very difficult to disguise.

Grey not only thought this language politically indiscreet, but felt himself unable to ignore, as he thought Fox did, the changed nature of Anglo-French relations since the advent of Bonaparte to power. Though he joined Fox in welcoming the peace treaty, he did so only on the grounds that Britain's financial exhaustion made it inevitable, and he later confessed himself inclined to alter his earlier opinion on the grounds that subsequent events demonstrated French ambition to control the whole of Europe. In December 1802 he cautioned Fox against public approbation of the French government's actions since the peace, and declared that he doubted whether 'two countries situated as France and England are with respect to each other can long remain ... without coming to blows'. He agreed that the peace should be preserved as long as possible, but only 'with honour', and he considered the eventual renewal of war as 'too certain'. He thought the Whigs would have no alternative but to support a defensive war against French aggression, and he pointed to French actions in respect of Malta, Italy, and Switzerland as proof. The late war had turned, since Bonaparte's accession to power, into a war for revolutionary principles—almost as Burke and his friends had declared it to be from the outset—and Bonaparte himself now

---

[4] Bute to Tierney, 16 Oct. 1801, Tierney MSS 13a; Tierney to Grey, 22 Oct., G. 55; Fox to Grey, 12 and 22 Oct., *Fox*, iii. 345–50. For Fox's speech see *The Speech of the Hon. C. J. Fox ... at the Shakespeare Tavern on 10th October, 1801* (London, J. S. Jordan, 1801).

appeared as 'the child and champion of jacobinism', a creed which, even as a fervent advocate of reform at home, Grey had taken pains always to condemn.[5]

Grey's disagreement with Fox over the French question added to his reluctance to appear in Parliament at the end of 1802, for fear of being compelled to make these differences public. He told Whitbread in the New Year that he was determined not to leave Howick if he could avoid it, and added that 'I regret more and more that I gave up my own judgement, and consented to come again into Parliament' at the 1802 election. Mary's pregnancy gave him the excuse he needed to resist Fox's urgings to appear at Westminster until the crisis loomed in March, 1803. He had told Whitbread the previous autumn that if war were renewed, he would be 'much inclined to give it an active and decided support'. When Fox summoned him to town for the debates on the drift towards war in March, he wrote that he received the news with 'the feeling of a man who is all at once informed of some event that threatens the probable ruin of his family and children', and assured Fox that he regarded the renewal of war as 'absolute madness', but, he added, 'short of a complete necessity'. That necessity had, in his view, arrived. Britain had refused to evacuate Malta as required by the Treaty of Amiens, on the grounds that French actions in other parts of Europe and Bonaparte's designs on Egypt made it necessary to retain the island as a counterpoise to increased French power since the peace. Relations between the two countries accordingly deteriorated, and in early March a royal message to Parliament announced that preparations for an invasion of Britain had been observed in the Channel ports. Negotiations dragged on fruitlessly for two months and were ended by a British declaration of war on 18 May.[6]

The outbreak of war added a new urgency to the political scene in London. Since Pitt's resignation the political world had been turned upside-down by new alignments and party groupings, which opened up new possibilities for the Whigs. Ever since the formation of the party under Rockingham in 1766 the Whigs had attempted to promote a distinctive image as the guardians of popular rights and interests against the personal influence of the Crown, which they regarded as the 'true source of every evil' in politics since the accession of George III.[7] In practice, however, they were never strong enough to overcome the royal disinclination to employ them in government without an alliance with some other group. In 1782 they had joined Shelburne, and in 1783 North. On both occasions they had had to sacrifice some of their policies in order to gain the support of their allies. In 1782 Shelburne had blocked their programme of unconditional independence for America in order to continue the war against France and Spain. In 1783 North

---

[5] *Parl. Hist.* xxxvi 623–33 (7 May 1802); Grey to Fox, 5 Dec. 1802, G. 16.

[6] Grey to Whitbread, 28 Oct. 1802, 9 Jan. 1803, Whitbread MSS 1/882–3. He remarked that in his election address 'all that I meant to say, was that I did not care whether they chose me or not; and to avoid giving any expectation of an active attendance' (11 July 1802, ibid.). For an account of the nomination meeting, see *Newcastle Chronicle*, 24 July 1802. Fox to Grey, 12 Mar. 1803, *Fox*, iii 397–400, Grey to Fox, 15 Mar., G. 16.

[7] Fitzwilliam to W. Chaloner, 9 Mar. 1780, Wyvill, *Political Papers*, iv. 127.

had insisted on a moratorium on further reform, which enabled Pitt to swing public opinion against the 'infamous coalition'. Though Pitt sacrificed the support of the reformers after 1792, Grey's attempt to recapture their allegiance for the Whigs had split the party and left the Foxites as a mere rump, with no prospect of office as a major partner in any conceivable administration. Pitt's resignation in 1801 split his previous following into three parts, those still attached to Pitt and Dundas, the friends of Addington, and the adherents of Grenville and Windham who deplored Addington's peace treaty but differed from Pitt over the Catholic question. The Whig party made a fourth at the table, but it was not clear by the end of 1802 who were to be partners in the new deal. The major questions to be decided upon were foreign policy and Catholic emancipation, but the lines of division crossed each other. Pitt and Addington in effect agreed upon the inexpediency of the Catholic claims, whereas Fox, Grey, and Grenville were for conciliation; but Fox and Addington were closer in their wish to attain and preserve peace for Europe than either was to the warlike Grenvilles. Addington's overtures to the Whigs in 1801 had been rejected both because he offered too few offices in the Cabinet and on account of their differences on religious and domestic policy. Fox needed to make up his mind whether his prospects were better with Addington or with Grenville; but while Pitt remained the joker in the pack, it was uncertain whether Addington or Grenville would prefer him to Fox, whose major card, the Prince of Wales, was no stronger than a knave. As Britain drifted towards the most desperate war in her history until the twentieth century, the parties in London jockeyed for advantage, their inability to find a common ground largely responsible for the weakness of the war effort in the early years after 1803.

Addington's government, formed in derision in 1801, was generally believed to be incapable of fighting the war with energy or success, but its position was secure so long as the King gave it his backing and the other parties failed to combine against it. The attitude of the Whigs was crucial. So long as it seemed possible to preserve peace, Fox favoured co-operation with Addington rather than alliance with the Grenvilles and alarmists such as Windham, who had never wavered in their conviction that the French Republic must be destroyed if Britain were to be secure at home and in Europe. Fox suggested in November 1802 that Grey should make terms with Addington to preserve peace. Grey, however, believed that Addington was not so desperate as to concede the only terms on which he would agree to a junction—a substantial number of Cabinet offices for the Whigs, and Fox's inclusion. He was also convinced of Addington's total incompetence, and deeply affronted and embarrassed by his father's support of the government, in which his close friend St Vincent was a member of the Cabinet. His disgust and alarm were the greater to find Sheridan in the summer of 1803 still working to swing Carlton House behind Addington. Fox had also come to suspect Sheridan and his 'vanity and folly' and he too was alarmed at the prospect of the Whigs' absorption into Addington's party. He countered by trying to reconcile the Prince to Grey's claims. 'I am now in high favour and Fox is the man he swears by' reported Grey after a 'sad drinking dinner' with the Prince at Norfolk House on 3 May.[8]

Nevertheless, Grey still considered the Prince unreliable—he quoted Thurlow's former remark about him as 'the worst anchoring ground in Europe'—and counselled caution in Fox's dealings with him. Finally, at a conference at Lord Moira's on 20 October, Fox brought matters to a head by suggesting that Sheridan should go to Addington to discover on what terms a junction might be arranged—a step which horrified Grey, though Fox assured him that it was done only to prove the futility of any such plans. Grey hastened to assure his friends in Northumberland that Sheridan's conduct was 'entirely without the sanction or concurrence of either Fox or myself' and that he was 'courting popularity at the expense of all sense and honesty'. He himself had rejected overtures from Addington via Tierney in the early summer, when it was suggested that he might succeed Lord Pelham at the Home Office, and again in the autumn when Moira called at Howick to discuss possible arrangements. 'The folly and falsehood of the present men are my detestation', he assured Whitbread, 'and nothing could bring me to give my consent to any junction with them but on such terms as should prove to the world that ... the whole power of the Government was Fox's.' Such terms were clearly not to be had, even if Addington were *in extremis*, and the negotiations petered out.[9]

Grey, meanwhile, was using all his influence to persuade Fox that the best hope of the Whigs lay in a junction with the Grenvilles who were committed to the Catholic question and with whom it would be possible to co-operate in a party. His attempts to tone down Fox's language on the peace since 1802 had been partly undertaken in the hope of drawing him and the Grenvilles together. He feared, however, that Grenville would not easily be weaned from his dependence on Pitt, whom the Grenvilles saw as the only pilot capable of weathering the new storm, and he recognized that the Grenvilles' uncompromising attitude to France made them unpopular. He therefore advocated a cautious policy of moving towards the alliance, hoping that either an arrangement could be formed to include Pitt as well as the Grenvilles, or that if Pitt ruled out such an extensive coalition Grenville would reconcile himself to the Whigs. His first task, however, was to convince Fox, both to support the war with energy and to look upon the Grenvilles with favour. He wrote to him in March, 1803:

... there never was a time which requires so much the sacrifice of all private resentment, and the remembrance of all past injuries for the sake of the public defence ... I do think

---

[8] Fox to Grey, 29 Nov. 1802 and 27 Nov. 1803, *Fox*, iii. 373–7, 433–7; Grey to Mary [23 Apr.], [5] and 25 May 1803, G. 27. 'Unsatisfactory as the situation of us all is in politics,' Grey wrote to Fox on 10 Apr. 1804, 'you must allow mine to be rather the most unpleasant from my father's voting every day for this rascally administration': G.16.

[9] Grey to Fox, 30 Aug. 1803, ibid.; to T. Bigge, 20 Nov. 1803, G.7/10. Bigge told W. Benton (2 Oct.) that Grey refused because 'he is steady to Mr Fox and to an opposite system of government in Ireland', and Wyvill recorded his gratification: 'It stamps his character with honour, I hope, never to be defaced': Wyvill MSS 160/10. Grey to Whitbread, 27 Nov. 1803, Whitbread MSS 1/888.

it would be right for us in the common danger which threatens us to avoid as much as we can all reference to past disputes ... and without any violence of manner towards them I should be inclined in the event of war ... to join with those who call for an Administration which might afford a better hope to the country.

He professed himself 'nearly indifferent as to the different parties', but thought:

There is a vigour and ability on the side of the Grenvilles, and a principle which while you are acting with them would make them more to be depended on, which appears to me to be wanting in all the others.

He concluded, '*You and I both have political duties to perform*' and assured Fox that if he would take an active part 'you shall not want all the assistance I can give you.' As he wrote to Whitbread seven months later, the great objective was to form 'a strong union ... against the Court' to get rid of an administration 'which under circumstances of such extraordinary danger at once disables and disgraces us'. He was even prepared to co-operate with Pitt, if Pitt could be trusted, though he was always suspicious of Pitt's motives and sincerity. The old enmity ran too deep to be easily overcome.[10]

Pitt might be tested, and the prospects of a Grenville alliance fostered, by the revival of the Catholic question in the House of Commons. This was the major issue on which the old and new oppositions, as the Whigs and Grenvilles were now respectively known, were heartily at one, and since as yet even Grenville was unaware of Pitt's secret assurances that he would not raise emancipation again during the King's lifetime, they hoped to draw Pitt into the open with them. Grey felt the question so promising that he even volunteered to leave Howick in December, 1803 to move it himself: 'It is the question which *I* should like better to move than any other' he told Fox, and it would flush out Pitt, whom he suspected of intending 'to return to the nominal enjoyment of power by the favour of the Court and the patronage of the Doctor'. A union with the Grenvilles, as Fox recognized, would also be the only hope of forming a party strong enough to force emancipation on the King.[11]

Grenville was even more determined on the Catholic question, and pressed the Irish Whig leaders Grattan and George Ponsonby to promote a petition for relief from the Irish Catholics, though it was thought advisable to defer its presentation until March to allow a fuller attendance of Irish members. In the meantime, a closer understanding was achieved on general opposition. At the end of January

[10] Buckingham wrote on 26 Sept. 1802 that Fox's opposition to war with France made co-operation impossible, but he also pointed out on 1 Nov. that the peace and the Catholic question made an alliance with Addington equally impracticable: HMC, *Fortescue MSS*, vii. 111, 117–22. Grenville to Buckingham, 20 Oct. and – Nov. 1802, *Memoirs of the Court and Cabinets of George III*, ed. Buckingham (1855), iii. 211–15; Grey to Fox, 15 Mar. 1803, G. 16; to Whitbread, 16 Oct. 1803, Whitbread MSS 1/887. On Grenville's attitude see P. Jupp, *Lord Grenville* (Oxford, 1985), 327–30.

[11] Grey to Fox, 24 Dec. 1803, G. 16. Fox calculated in June 1803 that the Grenvilles and Foxites together could muster 105 votes in the Commons against 58 Pittites, and that the ministerial party numbered about 300: to Holland, 6 June, BL Add. MS 47675, fos. 46–9. 'The Doctor' was the nickname of Addington, whose father had been a physician.

Fox reported a direct approach from the Grenvilles 'to join with us in a systematic opposition, for the purpose of removing the Ministry, and substituting one on the broadest possible basis'. Grenville's previous approach to Pitt in similar terms had been rebuffed: it seemed as though he was now prepared to throw in his lot unreservedly with the Whigs. Grey, however, now counselled caution. He repeated his view that the Grenville alliance was the only feasible one, and admitted that Grenville's conduct had been 'direct and open', but he feared that their opposition derived only from 'personal disappointment' and not from principle. The result would be to make the new alliance unpopular, as appearing merely factious, and also to make it more difficult for the Foxites to follow their distinctive policies, on which, apart from the Catholic question, there was no agreement with their allies. The parallel with 1783, when the Foxites had joined North to overthrow Shelburne but had paid a heavy price in public estimation when they had had to drop reform from their programme, was too close to be comfortable. It was indeed even worse than in 1783, for as Grey suspected the Grenvilles had turned to the Whigs only after failing to reunite with Pitt, their first preference, and he feared that their hard-line attitude on the war would create future problems for a coalition government, if they attempted to negotiate a peace treaty. Grey therefore pronounced his opinion that only if the Grenvilles were reasonable about a future negotiated peace and if they could give assurances of strong numbers in Parliament, should the offer be accepted; but then only for a trial period and without indefinite commitment. He feared that the union 'tho' formidable in talents and not contemptible in numbers, would ... make only what at best would be called a strong opposition' requiring 'great activity and unremitting perseverance' over a long period to make it successful, and he doubted whether he or Fox had sufficient inclination for such a course.[12]

The project for a union with the Grenvilles and a number of their supporters who had previously acted with the Whigs before 1794 began to bear fruit in the winter of 1803–4. The path was, however, a stony and difficult one. Wyvill was anxious at the news of Fox's conversations with the Grenvilles, particularly since reform had not been mentioned and their agreement was limited to foreign affairs and the Catholic question. He was reassured by Fox himself, who declared 'he was growing old and indolent, and power was now no material object to him', and that he was not intending to rush into any arrangement. Grey, however, pressed for decision, even if that meant accepting Pitt as well as the Grenvilles as partners in a new administration. Lady Bessborough reported at the end of 1803 that he was 'all for junction', though characteristically 'despairing of the possibility, and the old story no good to be done—all the underlings of old opposition loud against

---

[12] Grey to Fox, 7, 13 Jan., 2 Feb. 1804, G. 16; Fox to Grey, 29 Jan., *Fox*, iii. 449–52. Grenville approached Fox through his elder brother Thomas, Fox's old friend, in Jan. 1804. They agreed on foreign policy and on the need to negotiate a peace which would give Europe time to recover and to form a barrier against further French aggression. In subsequent meetings they also came to an agreement on the Catholic question. St A. St John to W. Smith, 22 Feb., Wyvill MSS 161/1; *Fortescue MSS*, vii. 211–14. Fox to Lauderdale, 24 Feb., BL Add. MS 47564, fos. 197–8.

it'. He suggested to Whitbread in April 1804 that the old problem of precedence between Pitt and Fox might be resolved by appointing Fitzwilliam nominal Premier as First Lord of the Treasury, but he added: 'I confess I think of office with a feeling approaching to horror, particularly in such times and with such connections as we must have.' Wyvill too was afraid that Fox might be pushed into an unpopular coalition 'by partizans, of whom not a few are anxious to get into power, without much solicitude either to preserve his consistency or their own'.[13]

The political crisis reached a new pitch of intensity in the spring of 1804, when George III relapsed into another attack of his illness. Grey hurried to town to counter the influence of Sheridan and Moira at Carlton House, and at an interview with the Prince in March he was given a pledge that no government would be formed without Fox. As for a junction with Addington, however, Grey declared his total repugnance and refusal to co-operate in it. Moira ended by persuading the Prince that he should form 'an extensive plan of government' including 'the propriety of his embracing with cordiality the support and connection of Mr. Pitt and Lord Melville'. In the meantime, the opposition in Parliament attempted to force a full disclosure of the King's state of health. Grey joined in the debates, but wrote that 'I feel very much the want of habit and of exercise in debate, which is absolutely necessary to give that readiness without which nothing can be done, and which I unfortunately do not naturally possess', and he complained of 'my unfitness for a pursuit which I detest, which interferes with my private comfort, and which I only sigh for an opportunity of abandoning decidedly and for ever'. During the opposition's conferences on tactics in March, accordingly, his voice was raised on the side of caution. He advised Fox not to play Pitt's game for him by forcing Addington out, only to let in Pitt as his successor either under the Prince or under George III when he recovered. The final party conference on 10 March resolved to delay a decision, so releasing Grey to return to Mary in time for the birth on 15 March of his second son Charles, the future general, royal equerry, and first biographer of his father.[14]

George's recovery did not save Addington, pressed as he now was on all sides. Pitt had turned against his financial policies and was convinced of his incapacity to manage the war, Grenville and his party were implacably hostile, and the Whigs were ready for the kill. Grey returned to London in April, assuring his wife on his way to town that 'I never felt less heart, the contest does not animate me, and I hardly wish for success', but he warned her that if all turned out as the Whigs hoped he would soon be in office and she must make up her mind to join him. On 16 April the followers of Pitt, Grenville, and Fox joined in voting against the

[13] Wyvill to Fox, 27 Apr. 1804, and memorandum of conversation with Fox, 29 Apr., Wyvill MSS 164/1 and 2; *Leveson-Gower*, i. 441–2; Grey to Whitbread, 11 Apr. 1804, Whitbread MSS 1/923; Wyvill to W. Smith, 4 Apr., Wyvill MSS 161/8. J. B. Fenwick told Wyvill on 28 Jan. that Grey considered a junction with Pitt 'the only thing which can save the country', ibid. 163/10.

[14] Creevey to Dr Currie, 2 Apr. 1804, *Creevey Papers*, i. 25–6; Melville to Pitt, 6 Apr., BL Add. MS 40102 fo. 133; *CGPW*, iv. 531–2 n; Grey to Mary, 28 Feb. [9] and [10] Mar., G. 27.

Irish Militia Bill and the government's majority fell to 21. Pitt drew up a tentative scheme for a united administration including Grey, Fox, and Fitzwilliam, but as Grey feared he failed to press it on the King. Grey thought the most probable outcome would be a government formed without the Foxites, and so it turned out to be. When Addington resigned it was Pitt who was summoned by the King, and, when George refused to have Fox in the ministry, he immediately agreed to form one without the Whigs or the Grenvilles if they would not serve without Fox. Grey heard the news direct when Fox returned from his conference with Grenville, who had just seen Pitt, on 7 May, and his reaction was immediate and predictable: 'no earthly consideration should make me accept office without Fox. How unceasing the persecution of him is; how honourable to himself; how disgraceful in all those who concur in and submit to it.' And he added, characteristically, 'As far as concerns myself, I am not sorry for this for I had really and unaffectedly something like a horror of office.' Fox was again ready to sacrifice himself and stand aside to allow his friends to take office, but it was Grey who prevented any such plan. 'I put an absolute veto on it, and we are all excluded' he wrote.[15]

So yet another set of new political alignments was formed. The Grenvilles, who as Grey allowed 'have behaved in the most honourable way', refused to serve unless Fox and his friends were given office, and Pitt was forced back on his own resources, 'eking out his government with Roses and Dundases' while the other major parties coalesced against him. At first Grey was disposed to allow that Pitt had done the best he could and acted not unfairly, but in the end the episode confirmed his low opinion of Pitt's character—'nothing can exceed my contempt for the meanness of his conduct ... I should be sorry to think that either Fox or I, if placed in the same situation, could have acted as he has done.'[16]

Pitt paid the price of a government 'formed on the principle of exclusion' in the weakness of his Cabinet, fuller even than usual of nonentities, and in the hazardous state of his majority in the House of Commons. The opposition's numbers, wrote Grey, 'in ordinary times ... would have been decisive'. In mid-June they mustered 223 in the lobby against a ministerial division of 265. The *Morning Herald*, a non-partisan newspaper, remarked that the opposition 'combines an extent of property, and talents, unknown before in the political world'. But even this failed to rouse Grey's enthusiasm. As the prospects of office brightened—or, rather, darkened—his spirits sank lower at the thought of confinement in London. He had told Whitbread in April that

[15] Grey to Mary [29 Apr.], 7 and 8 May, ibid.; Grey to Fox, 22 Apr., G. 16. Fox brought him up by assuring him that 'your attendance [is] of the greatest consequence' and that there was 'a very good chance' of defeating Addington: 13 Apr., *Fox*, iii. 461–3. Lord Stanhope, *Pitt* (1862), iv. 148, 176–7; Jupp, *Grenville*, 320–6. Grenville's refusal to serve without Fox is in *Court & Cabinets of George III*, iii. 252–3; see also Stanhope, *Pitt*, iv. pp. viii–xii.

[16] Grenville to Buckingham, 21 May, ibid. 355; Grey to Mary [8] and [14] May, G. 27. For Pitt's government see A. D. Harvey, *Britain in the early nineteenth century* (1978), 151–2. Canning deplored 'the miserable colleagues whom he has thought fit to associate to himself': 25 Feb., *Leveson-Gower*, ii. 28–32.

My total despair of any political good, deprives me of all energy. A constitutional languor contributes to the same effect. I feel quite unequal to any great exertion, and dread being placed in a situation, that may require it.

It took all Fox's persuasion at the end of the year to drag him unwillingly as ever from Howick for the 1805 session: only by reading him a lesson on his duty to his friends and his country did he succeed in bringing him to town, accompanied by Mary and the four eldest children but again threatening that he would resign at the end of the session. 'You cannot easily conceive what it costs me', he assured Fox, and he once more confessed his despair of any good to be done in either foreign or home affairs. Fox handled him skilfully, humouring his ill-temper and conciliating him by offering him the choice of subject on which to speak. Grey chose the question of the opening of hostilities with Spain, and made his first major speech for some time on that subject on 11 February. His motion of censure won 106 votes, a small enough division but an encouraging one in that it included both the leading Foxites and the Windham, Laurence, and Elliot group of Burkean disciples. As the various elements in opposition became more closely fused together, Fox's optimism grew. He wrote to Holland in March that 'even our enemies cannot deny that we are a respectable opposition, & few will now dispute Pitt's being a contemptible Minister.'[17]

The great crisis of the session broke in March with the publication of the tenth report of the Commissioners of Naval Enquiry, set up by Addington's government to look into alleged abuses in the administration of the naval department during Pitt's first administration. This report implicated Dundas, now Lord Melville and First Lord of the Admiralty, in certain financial irregularities in the navy pay office. The opposition gathered for a full-scale attack on Pitt's closest lieutenant, believing, as Fox wrote, that it would 'hurt him beyond measure'. In early April Whitbread moved that Melville should be censured by the Commons, and, though Lord Grenville disapproved of the personal tone of the question, his friends joined the Whigs in supporting it. The crushing blow for Pitt was the defection of Wilberforce, the conscience of the House, and the 'Saints', which it was said swayed forty votes against Melville. In the early hours of 9 April the House divided equally, 216 on each side; the Speaker sat ashen faced for ten minutes before giving his casting vote against the government. Melville resigned on the same day.[18]

The opposition was now in full cry against the government, which was not only weakened by the loss of one of its most experienced members but also damaged in the eyes of middle-class public opinion which looked increasingly askance at the corrupt activities of politicians and was deeply influenced by the moral

[17] Grey to Mary, 9 and 16 June, G. 27; to Whitbread, 22 Apr., Whitbread MSS 1/893; to Fox, 13 Jan., G. 16; Fox to Grey, 17 Dec. 1804 and 7 Jan. 1805; to Holland, 19 Mar., *Fox*, iv. 69–75; Harvey, *Britain in early nineteenth century*, 152–3; *Parl. Deb.* iii. 385–400.

[18] Ibid. iv. 255–371; Harvey, *Britain in early nineteenth century*, 156. Dundas was Treasurer of the Navy at the time of the offences alleged against Alexander Trotter, one of the clerks in the office.

leadership of men like the 'Saints'. A two fold campaign began against the administration, the opposition in Parliament demanding exemplary punishment for all those implicated in the scandal, and public meetings in many leading towns and counties assembling to vote petitions urging parliamentary enquiry 'to vindicate the sullied honour of government'.[19] The country reformers, with Wyvill and Cartwright in the lead, resumed their campaigns to stir up the public and energize the politicians. Grey seized the opportunity to resume his old stance as the parliamentary spokesman of liberal opinion and at a conference at Whitbread's house at Southill joined in plans to promote county meetings all over the country. He urged his friends in Northumberland, through his main contact Sir John Swinburne, to organize a meeting there and set about recruiting the Duke of Northumberland's support. Grey however prudently abstained from signing the requisition as 'my own conduct must come under the consideration of the meeting'.[20]

This was partly due to the differences between himself and his Tory colleague in the county representation, Thomas Beaumont, a steady supporter of the ministry, which were bound to come under discussion, but it may also have reflected Grey's embarrassment about his father's political position. Lord Grey was implicated, through his friend St Vincent, in the attack on Melville, and in the debate on the tenth report Canning chose to refer to the circumstances of 1795, when Grey's and St Vincent's conduct in the West Indies had been defended by Dundas. It was a poor return, he declared, to be now 'hunted down' by Grey and his friends on a not dissimilar charge. Grey rose to deny any personal bitterness in his conduct, and pointed out that in 1795 his father and Jervis had not shirked, but had demanded an enquiry to clear their reputations; furthermore, it was Dundas who had employed them in the expedition to the West Indies and it was natural that he should defend them. He had done so not as a personal favour, now to be returned, but as a just recognition of their distinguished services. Canning's words were merely 'calculated to raise unpleasant feelings'; he continued by supporting Whitbread's demand that Melville should give up all the valuable offices he held and not be allowed to escape merely by resigning the Admiralty.

Grey told Georgiana that 'he was hurt and surprised beyond measure' at Canning's speech, for he had been trying to establish better relations with Canning in the past few months and had even had long discussions with him in March on the Melville affair. Grey had purposely remained silent in the first debate on the tenth report, partly out of delicacy because of his father's case in 1795, but though he averred that 'he never rose more unwillingly in his life to answer anyone', he could not ignore 'so tender a point as anything concerning his father'. Canning

---

[19] Lady Bessborough wrote that the affair could not be stopped for it had passed out of the opposition's hands and 'the city people have taken it up': *Leveson-Gower*, ii. 59. For the Southwark petition, 11 May, see *Political Register*, vii. 696.

[20] Grey declared his disappointment at the smallness of the attendance at the meeting but his pleasure at its respectability: to Swinburne, 10 Apr. and 1 May, Swinburne MSS; *Parl. Deb.* iv. 341–5 (10 Apr.).

too regretted afterwards that he had been so impulsive and tried to claim that his target had been Whitbread, Grey's brother-in-law, and not Grey himself. It was more likely, however, that Canning's anger was aroused by the suspicion that St Vincent was behind the attack on Melville, for the original enquiry had been set up by him when First Lord of the Admiralty in Addington's Cabinet. Lady Bessborough feared that the episode would ruin the prospects of an understanding between Canning and the Whigs and that Canning's rashness would 'set the whole op. in a flame'.[21]

If, however, the prospects for that particular alliance were endangered, it was Pitt's government that was most damaged by the Melville case. Addington, now as Lord Sidmouth a member of the Cabinet, decided to use the eposide for his own ends and demanded that his influence be increased by the giving of Melville's vacated office to one of his own followers. When Pitt instead appointed the octogenarian Sir Charles Middleton, Sidmouth took deep offence and at the end of June he resigned in a flurry of resentment. Sidmouth's resignation came too late to be of immediate benefit to the opposition. As Fox complained, had he gone in April it would have destroyed Pitt there and then. Now Pitt had been given a respite and the opportunity to recover his position by an approach to Grenville. Even without Grenville, however, Fox thought Pitt would survive, 'weak and contemptible' though his ministry now was; the likelihood of an acceptable approach to the Foxites to join the government seemed as remote as ever.[22]

The re-emergence of the Catholic question in the midst of the Melville episode did nothing to improve their chances. When the Irish Catholics petitioned for relief in March, they applied to Fox to present their petition, Pitt having refused to do so. The opportunity to demonstrate the opposition's unity on the question was prejudiced, however, by the Prince of Wales's attitude. Mrs Fitzherbert was involved in a suit by Lord Henry Seymour for the return of his daughter, whom Mrs Fitzherbert had adopted, on the grounds that as a Catholic she was not a suitable foster parent. The Prince feared that adverse public reaction to the Catholic petition would prejudice her case, and urged Windham and Thomas Grenville to stop or postpone the petition. Grey was also in favour of delay. He was aware that Fox and Grenville had agreed that a refusal by the King to accept emancipation should not of itself be a necessary bar to their accepting office, and he did not wish to arouse the King's prejudices anew at this crucial moment. He also suspected, as was to be proved correct, that the Prince, now under the anti-Catholic influence of Lady Jersey, was moving closer to his father's opinions on the question: the Catholic issue was no longer one that could promote the opposition's political interests and it should be handled with caution. Fox, Lord Grenville, and the Irish Whigs, however, were for pressing on; their hopes were dashed when the debate produced a vote of only 124 for the petition against 336, the low number

[21] *Leveson-Gower*, ii. 9–10, 18–19, 43, 55, 56, 57, 60.
[22] Fox to O'Bryen, 7 July 1805, *Fox*, iv. 87.

of the minority being affected by the absence of many of the Carlton House party and the Duke of Northumberland's friends.[23]

Grey was disappointed that, on this as other questions, the opposition had failed to sustain the political momentum built up by the Melville case. He attempted to revive their flagging energies by taking up the question of a possible peace negotiation. The King's Speech at the opening of the Session had disclosed that an overture had been received from the French, but that Britain would make no response until she had consulted her allies. After Pitt had several times refused to make any further statement Grey introduced a motion on 'the state of public affairs' on 20 June. It was his most important speech for some time. Reviewing the whole position of the country, financial, naval and military, and domestic, and the state of Ireland, he asserted that in view of the heavy financial burdens borne by the people and the lack of progress in building up forces comparable, even at sea, to those of the enemy, it could not be said that any of the objectives for which war had been resumed were in sight of achievement. Napoleon, meanwhile, had gone from strength to strength. Not only was he now Emperor of the French, but King of Italy, virtual ruler of Portugal, Switzerland, and the Low Countries, allied with Spain, and in occupation of Hanover. Only British naval superiority in the Channel had prevented an invasion of these islands, but the threat remained, keeping the nation in a state of alarm and exposed to great expense. Ireland, meanwhile, though relatively peaceful under the conciliatory government of Lord Hardwicke, remained 'our weakness' instead of being, as she ought, 'one of the chief instruments of our greatness'—which she could only become when the full emancipation of her Catholic population was achieved. Britain now stood almost alone against the might of France's European dominion. In such circumstances 'war ought not to be pursued, if peace on fair and honourable terms can be obtained', and he called on the government to give the House some assurance of a rational prospect of success, or to explain why peace on such terms could not be had. Such a peace, he declared, was preferable to a merely defensive war which seemed to be the only alternative; but, he concluded, in terms which were doubtless designed to please his Grenville allies, if France refused fair and moderate conditions for peace then indeed the nation must fight on, accepting every sacrifice rather than submit to French domination.[24]

The speech marked Grey's re-emergence as one of the most eloquent of the opposition's orators, and though his motion was lost by 110 to 261, with Canning and Pitt speaking against it, the debate helped to consolidate the opposition's unity on foreign affairs. Windham and Fox made the major supporting speeches, signifying the agreement of both wings of opposition on the desirability of peace, but the necessity of continuing the war if honourable terms could not be attained. This delicate middle ground between Fox's advocacy of peace and Grenville's

---

[23] Buckingham to Grenville [Apr. 1805], *Fortescue MSS*, xi. 268; Fox to Grenville, 20 Apr. 1804, to Grey 19 Apr., *Fox*, iv. 45–8; *Parl. Deb.* iv. 824–1060 (13–14 May).

[24] Ibid. v. 12, 192, 451, 490–506; Grey to Swinburne, 1 May, Swinburne MSS.

support of war against French aggression sustained for a time both sides of the coalition and energized their efforts during the summer recess to replace the present government by a broader based union. When Grey departed for Howick at the end of June, he left Fox full authority to speak for him in the negotiations, making only one condition for his entry into office, that Pitt should cease to be Prime Minister. Fox was optimistic about the prospects, for Pitt could hardly survive another session with Sidmouth's party in opposition, but he warned Grey that, though his own preference was for Grey himself as Premier, 'perhaps it would be expected that the nominal head should be a person less marked than you or I.' Grey agreed and stipulated that there were only two offices he would refuse to take: the War Department, so long as the Duke of York remained Commander-in-Chief (it was the Duke who had refused his father another active command since 1795) and the Chancellorship of the Exchequer, which 'nothing could induce me to undertake ... but your feeling it to be absolutely necessary,' since 'my dislike of the business of finance is only equalled by my ignorance of it'. For the rest of the ministry, he urged that 'personal dislikes and predilictions' ought not to weigh at such a time, though due regard should be paid to policies and principles.[25]

Pitt was thinking along similar lines, and attempted to persuade the King to abandon the 'principle of exclusion' which had been insisted on when he took office, so as to admit Fox, Grey, Grenville, and perhaps Moira and Spencer to the Cabinet. Any decision was delayed, however, by the King's convalescence at Weymouth, and it was in an atmosphere of increasing suspicion of his motives that Pitt eventually went to see him in September, only to have his proposals firmly rebuffed. Grey expected no other outcome. Georgiana had written before Pitt's visit to say that in London nothing was expected to come of it, and both Whigs and Grenvilles feared that Pitt would try to drive a wedge between them on foreign affairs in order to survive alone.[26]

Differences were opening up between the Foxites and their allies on this question. Though Grey admitted the necessity of 'a great and powerful co-operation on the continent' if French military power were to be destroyed, he and Fox deplored Pitt's policy of giving large subsidies to powers whose military performance was ineffective and whose participation in the war was apparently limited to their own political objectives. Grenville, however, was unwillng to condemn a system to which he had been a party as Foreign Secretary under Pitt, and objected to Fox's proposal for an all-out attack on Pitt's strategy. At the same time the return of Grenville's old and close friend Marquess Wellesley from India seemed likely to draw him away from the Foxites into an alternative alliance half-

[25] Fox to Grey, 6 July, Grey to Fox 7 July, *Fox*, iv. 83–4, 90–1, Grey to Fox 10 July, G. 16; to Whitbread, 15 July, G. 59. The Exchequer without the First Lordship of the Treasury was at that time reckoned one of the less important Cabinet offices: *CGPW*, v. 315 n.1.

[26] T. Grenville to Lord Grenville, 18 July and 20 Sept., *Fortescue MSS*, vii. 296–7, 302–4; Harvey, *Britain in early nineteenth century*, 166; Grey to Fox, 22 Sept., G. 16; Grenville to Buckingham, 3 Oct., T. Grenville to Buckingham, 22 Oct., *Court & Cabinets of George III*, iii. 439–40, 442–4.

way at least towards the administration. Windham feared, as he wrote to Grey in December, that the new session would open up the old party divisions, and that the opposition would 'have to move, I think, in somewhat separate columns, not less than three probably, but ... terminating I trust in the same point'. Grey feared that the columns would be 'separate armies' and might well end in disarray, with some of them at least deserting to the enemy.[27]

Grenville's disapproval of 'hostile confederacies' based on factious or personal hostility and his apparent inability still to commit himself wholeheartedly against Pitt gave plausibility to Grey's pessimism. As the time for the new session in January approached, therefore, Grey expressed his fear that the Whigs and the Grenvilles would drift apart and that Pitt would be able to survive as he had done in 1784. He promised to come up for the debates, but in his usual mood of reluctance. The disaster of Austerlitz in December 1805, when Napoleon crushed the main Allied forces on the Continent, convinced him of the folly of organizing future European confederacies, but he recognized that his attitude would not be shared by the Grenville group and he was full of foreboding about the political prospects. Grenville too was dispirited by the collapse of his hopes of bringing about a genuine broad-based ministry of all parties, and disposed to blame Whig factiousness as much as Pitt's 'great misconduct' for their failure. He feared that an outright opposition such as Fox was proposing would 'tear the country to pieces' and, if the result were a new administration formed by himself and Fox its members would 'differ on the leading question of our whole policy' at the first Cabinet meeting. He attributed all the country's problems to the factiousness of parties and refused to 'lend myself as an instrument to inflame all those passions'.[28]

The prospects for the new parliamentary session seemed dark, therefore, when the politicians began to assemble at Westminster in January. The situation was suddenly and dramatically altered by the collapse of Pitt's health; his old stomach complaint had flared up in December and he had gone to Bath to try to recover his strength on the 7th, but on his return a month later it was evident that he was dying. Grey expressed his disbelief in Pitt's illness, and Fox even suggested that it was a political stratagem to delay or disarm the coming confrontation; Pitt's death on the early morning of 23 January took the political world by surprise and shattered the spirits of his friends.

It was the end of a long and, so it had seemed, imperishable era in politics. Even Fox was shocked by the news, and said 'that it felt as if there was something missing in the world—a chasm, a blank that cannot be supplied'. Lady Bessborough reported that Grey was deeply upset—'In short', she wrote, '... to judge by the appearance of people, it would be imagined opposition had lost a dearer friend than Ministers.' Though Fox could not bring himself to deny the propriety of

[27] Ibid. 457–8; Grey to Fox, 5 Jan. 1805, G. 16; Grey, *Life and Opinions*, 103–4; Windham to Grey, 9 Dec., G. 60/5; Grey's reply 13 Dec., BL Add. MS 37847, fo. 240.
[28] Grey to Fox, 5 Jan. 1806, G. 16; to Creevey, 29 Dec. 1805, *Creevey Papers*, i. 45; Grenville to Buckingham, 7 Jan. 1806, *Court & Cabinets of George III*, iv. 9–10.

half a lifetime's bitter opposition to Pitt and his politics by supporting a parliamentary motion for a state funeral, he and Grey showed more generosity of
spirit in approving the proposal for the payment of Pitt's debts, and in private
expressed their real sorrow at the loss of his talents, however misguidedly they
thought they had been applied. But the political game had to continue: the question
now was what government would replace one which had depended almost entirely
on those talents. The remnant of the old Cabinet was clearly incapable of continuing without Pitt, and Hawkesbury sensibly declined the King's offer of the
Premiership. Grenville was the obvious next choice: but what kind of ministry he
would form was as yet unknown, and whether Grey would at last achieve the high
office his career had promised by no means certain. The path to the 'Ministry of
all the Talents' was almost trodden out: the next few days were to determine
where it would end.[29]

THE SUCCESSION TO FOX, 1806–1807

Grey's presence in the Cabinet of the new ministry, named the 'Ministry of all
the Talents',[1] was assured on 27 January 1806, when the King accepted, without
objection, Grenville's stipulation that Fox must be included in the arrangements.
Fox at first proposed Grey for the Treasury, since Grenville held the sinecure of
Auditor of the Exchequer, an office incompatible with the Treasury for it would
have put the First Lord formally in the position of being able to audit his own
accounts. Grenville, however, insisted on the premier office, to Fox's mortification:
'there has always been something in the manner of receiving my proposal of Grey
for the Treasury that I do not like', he complained. Lord Grenville's position was
regularized by a special Act of Parliament, but the incident soured relations
between the Grenville group and the more radical Whigs such as Whitbread, who
regarded the Grenvilles as major beneficiaries of the hated patronage system. Fox
stipulated for a more generous share of Cabinet places in return for conceding 'the
enormous point that the Treasury should be in your hands'; in the end, the Foxites
secured five Cabinet offices. Erskine became Lord Chancellor, Lord Henry Petty
Chancellor of the Exchequer, and Fitzwilliam Lord President of the Council. Fox
took the Foreign Office, leaving Grey and Lord Spencer to choose between the
Admiralty and the Home Office. Spencer expressed a preference for the latter,
the less burdensome of the two posts, and Grey reluctantly took on the Admiralty,
perhaps the most strenuous office in a wartime Cabinet. Spencer and Windham
were the sole representatives of Grenville's party apart from the Prime Minister
himself, but as both were formerly Portland Whigs the Grenvillite element in the

[29] Grey to Creevey, 13 Jan. *Creevey Papers*, i. 74; Lady Bessborough to G. Leveson-Gower, 23 Jan.
Leveson-Gower, ii. 162. Georgiana wrote on 22 Jan. that Grey and Fox 'have shown more feeling than
many of his [Pitt's] quondam friends': Chatsworth MSS; *Parl. Deb.* vi. 41–72, 137–8.
[1] The phrase was Canning's: *Parl. Deb.* vi. 463–5, 17 Mar. 1806.

Cabinet was minimal. In addition, the Foxite Duke of Bedford was sent as Lord-Lieutenant to Ireland, with William Elliot, another Grenvillite who had been a Portland Whig before 1794, as Chief Secretary. To complete the Cabinet, Sidmouth became Lord Privy Seal, and his friend Lord Ellenborough sat in the Cabinet as Lord Chief Justice. Their inclusion was objectionable to many Whigs, but it left the Pittites alone in opposition and, since Sidmouth was personally congenial to the King, it blocked one possible rival channel to the Court—or, as Fox put it, it 'stopped up all the earths'. Ellenborough's inclusion raised a constitutional difficulty, for it could be said that it violated the principle of the separation of executive and judiciary, but it was necessary to give Sidmouth adequate representation when his first choice, Lord Buckinghamshire, was vetoed by Fox and Grenville because of his anti-Catholic attitude. The opposition, however, raised the question in Parliament and the ministers had a difficult task to justify Ellenborough's appointment. Grey later remarked that there was nothing he so deeply regretted in all the acts of the administration.[2]

The struggle over Cabinet offices was as nothing compared to the battle over the lower posts in the government. The three parties had long tails of needy dependants and the Whigs in particular after twenty-three years of opposition had many supporters to gratify. Both Fox and Grenville, as Sidmouth reported, 'were nearly inundated by the pretensions and claims which poured in from their respective connections' and driven almost to distraction by what Grenville described as the 'inconceivable difficulties' of the position. Fox fought for several friends without success. Grenville refused his proposal of Lauderdale for the Cabinet, and Tierney and Philip Francis were also excluded. Another victim was Whitbread. He coveted the Secretaryship at War, a post which Fox had reserved for his old friend Richard Fitzpatrick. Grey suggested that Whitbread should be given a peerage in compensation, but his brother-in-law refused to be pushed out of the House of Commons and indignantly declared that he wished for no appointment whatever. Grey, perhaps insensitively, took him at his word, only to discover too late what his true wishes were. Though he assured Whitbread of his distress, even writing that, had he realized the depth of his feelings, he would have refused office himself rather than consent to his exclusion, the incident contributed to the breach that opened up between the two men over the peace negotiations later in the year.[3]

The ministerial arrangements were completed and the new ministers were sworn in on 5 February, the King being reported as 'particularly gracious' to Grey. The

[2] Fox to T. Grenville, 28 Jan. 1806, BL Add. MS 41856, fos. 196–8; J. J. Sack, *The Grenvillites, 1801–29* (1979), 85–91; G. Pellew, *Life of Sidmouth* (1847) ii. 413–23; *Memoirs of Sir Philip Francis*, ed. J. Parkes and H. Merivale (1867), ii. 457; *Fortescue MSS*, viii. p. i; Harvey, *Britain in early nineteenth century*, 170–5; Jupp, *Grenville*, 346–7; Holland, *Memoirs*, i. 209–10; *Parl. Deb.* vi. 253–84 (Lords), 286–342 (Commons).

[3] Harvey, *Britain in early nineteenth century*, 171; Sidmouth to Bragge-Bathurst, 31 Jan. 1806, Sidmouth MSS; Grenville to Windham, 29 Jan., BL Add. MS 37847, fo. 5; Whitbread to Grey, 7 Feb. 1806, Grey to Whitbread [Feb.], G. 59; Grey, *Life and Opinions*, 107–9.

Whigs had again to pay a price for coming into office in alliance with parties who did not share their reformist opinions. Though practical necessity dictated their sharing power with Grenville and Sidmouth, some of their followers resented what they considered to be the dereliction of principle involved. Particularly ominous for Grey was the attitude of the Duke of Northumberland, who protested that he could not be expected to give his hearty support to a ministry largely composed of men of whose policies he had disapproved for seventeen years. Northumberland's closeness to the Prince of Wales and his influence in Grey's own constituency cast a shadow over Grey's political future. The reformers in the country and their friends in the Whig party, Whitbread especially, were concerned that the new government could not be a reforming administration. Fox and Grey were personally pledged to reform, but they could not be expected to present it as a government measure when they sat in Cabinet with Grenville, Sidmouth, Spencer, and Fitzwilliam and were flanked on the Treasury Bench by their supporters.[4]

The reform question, indeed, became an embarrassment to the new ministers. Shortly before Pitt's death the ever-watchful Major Cartwright began another attempt to organize public meetings for reform, and in particular arranged a county meeting in Middlesex to call upon Grey to renew 'as soon as he shall find it convenient, his virtuous efforts towards obtaining for the people a sufficient representation in Parliament'. The Foxites were willing to endorse the proposal while still in opposition, and Wyvill was authorized by Fox to tell Cartwright that the scheme 'will be very far from not according with the wishes of Mr Fox and his confidential friends'. In order not to alarm their new allies, the leading Whigs would not appear in person at the meeting, so that it would appear 'the spontaneous zeal of those classes of men, uninfluenced by Great Men', but it was to be 'distinctly understood, that Mr Fox does not dissuade or discourage the holding of such meetings'. Indeed, Fox suggested only that the meeting be postponed until February in order that the attendance might be as full as possible.[5]

By the beginning of that month, however, Pitt was dead and the Foxites were about to take office. They accordingly went into reverse and Cartwright discovered, to his dismay, that Fox's friends were now talking of opposing the scheme. He asked for a meeting with Fox on 5 February to clarify the position, and was told that the Whigs now wished the plan to be postponed indefinitely. In deference to their wishes, the meeting was held only to thank the King for the change of ministers. Wyvill was again called in to soothe Cartwright's feelings, assuring him that it was to be expected that 'a more favourable opportunity than the present will occur in the course of the next twelve months' and that there might well be 'a change of political circumstances and consequently of opinions' during that period. In fact the Talents were to do nothing for reform, apart from the introduction of

[4] Georgiana to Hartington [6 Feb.], Chatsworth MSS 1853; Northumberland to MacMahon, 6 Feb., *CGPW*, iv. 327.
[5] Cartwright to James Perry, 5 Jan. 1806, Wyvill to Cartwright, 18 Jan., BL Add. MS 51468, fos. 91–3, 98–9.

a Bill by Tierney to strengthen the laws against bribery and treating at elections; even this was defeated, Fox opposing it on the grounds that, by classifying the payment to voters of travelling expenses to the poll as 'treating', it would diminish the number who would go to vote. Grey's effort to salvage something from the wreck by a Bill to allow postal voting failed to make any progress. So, despite the change of ministers, the prospects for reform remained bleak. The Melville scandal had begun to draw attention once again to the prevalence of corruption in public life, but the Talents' failure to act on reform seemed to suggest that Grey had lost his enthusiasm for the question. The new generation of radicals that now began to emerge came to look either, like Cartwright, to the spontaneous efforts of the people 'out of doors' or, if they hoped for support from the politicians, to Whitbread, Folkestone, Burdett and other back-benchers who seemed less inhibited by the lure of office.[6]

Apart from this issue, however, the Ministry of all the Talents was not disunited on major questions. Old differences over the French wars were less marked after 1803, and limited to the expediency of a negotiated peace rather than concerned with the principle of the war. On the Catholic question too, all parties were disposed to move cautiously in view of the King's state of health and the mood of public opinion. Grenville's hope that they would be able 'to administer the affairs of this country, *without retrospect* to former differences' was in general fulfilled.[7] That this was so is not remarkable. Eighteenth- and early nineteenth-century governments were rarely, if ever, formed on a distinctive programme of policies. They were composed from a relatively small and fairly homogeneous class of men who shared most opinions in common and were rarely pledged to specific measures. They were formed at the initiative of the King and their policies had to be acceptable in general to him, and not to the opinions of a large and fickle electorate. General elections were not held in order to determine the composition or the policies of governments. In the House of Commons the 'party of the crown' still looked to the King rather than to ministers and thus exerted a moderating influence on party programmes. In any case, it was not considered that governments should concern themselves with economic or social matters unless they affected the public finances or the preservation of law and order. 'Administrations' were simply that and no more: they existed to administer the laws, preserve and protect the existing interests and property of the country, carry on foreign relations, and supervise the execution of the various departments into which government was divided. Only at the political margins did real differences of approach or principle operate to produce disagreement inside the political class.

---

[6] Cartwright to Fox, 4 Feb., ibid. fo. 106; Wyvill to Cartwright, 26, 29 Jan., 6 Feb., *Cartwright*, i. 336–8; *Parl. Deb.* vi. 371–80, 505–21, 955–7, vii. 571–4. For Cartwright's disenchantment with the Whigs after 1807 see his letter to W. Smith, 13 June 1808, *Cartwright*, i. 357–8.

[7] Grenville to Windham, 4 June, BL Add. MS 37847, fos. 67–9; Fox to Grenville, 20 Apr. 1804, *Fox*, iv. 46. On the previous day Fox wrote to Grey that 'you and I have often agreed' that even if the ministry were united on emancipation, 'some consideration, at least as far as delay went, might be had of the king's prejudices, especially in his present state': ibid. 44–5.

On the personal level, relations between the ministry's leaders were soon on a cordial footing. Lady Elizabeth Foster exclaimed in July that relations between Fox and Grenville were 'quite perfect' and that it was impossible to tell whether either was serving under the other: 'I really believe their great and good minds despise the form.' Grey, too, soon struck up a *rapport* with Grenville, based on respect for his personal character and gratitude for his loyalty to Fox. Though very different in outward personality—'ice and fire', as Sheridan's biographer described them—their opinions were not dissimilar and they found themselves often agreeing on political tactics and circumstances. Their qualities supplemented rather than jarred against each other, and 1806 marked the beginning of a long and harmonious political relationship, though they were never intimate enough to develop deep bonds of affection. Grenville's famous reserve of manner was rarely penetrated by others, and they had few interests in common. Grenville was a classical scholar of much repute, and something of a recluse in private life: Grey's interests were less intellectual. Whereas Grenville's reluctance to engage in the cut and thrust of opposition politics after 1807 could be ascribed to the counter-attraction of scholarly pursuits, Grey's absences from Westminster in the period of their co-leadership of the opposition derived more from his tendency to intellectual idleness, his love of leisure and the attractions of family life at Howick.[8]

Auckland remarked at the outset that 'the character and permanency of the new government must depend eventually on the wisdom of its measures, and on the providential results of those measures.' The principal questions on which they had to take decisions were the long-drawn-out problem of military recruitment and the management of the war or the negotiation of the peace still dear to Fox's heart. On the former, Windham set about implementing the reforms he had been advocating for the past three years, replacing the inefficient Volunteer system of internal defence by an 'army of reserve' recruited on a more permanent basis, and in addition attempting to introduce schemes for shorter-term recruitment for the regular army and to improve pay and conditions. The scheme was disliked by the King and by Sidmouth, who resented what seemed to be a condemnation of his policy upon the Volunteers, and it aroused the bitter opposition of Pitt's old friends who regarded it as a slight on their former leader's memory. Windham's incompetence both as an administrator and as a parliamentary spokesman created enormous difficulties for the ministry, and the plan had a rough parliamentary passage. Something was done, however, to increase the pay of the army, and Grey at the Admiralty introduced similar improvements for the navy, whose rates of pay for officers had not been changed since Queen Anne's time and where conditions of service for the seamen had long been notoriously brutal and wretched. Some slight improvements had been wrung from Pitt's government by the mutineers of 1797, but the general state of pay and service left much to be desired.[9]

---

[8] *The Two Duchesses*, ed. Vere Foster (1898), 285–6; Sichel, *Sheridan*, ii. 323; Jupp, *Grenville*, 355.
[9] Auckland to Grenville, 1 Feb. 1806, *Fortescue MSS*, viii. 5; *Parl. Deb.* vi. 652–722, 961–1109, vii. 1–923 *passim*.

Grey brought his proposals before the Commons at the end of April, suggesting an addition of 2s. per month for ordinary seamen, 4s. for able seamen, 5s. for petty officers, whose numbers were also to be increased, and more substantial rises for commissioned officers, ranging from 1s. a day for Lieutenants to 10s. for Admirals of the Fleet. The total cost of the increases would amount to nearly £300,000 per annum. In addition, it was proposed to raise the allowances to navy pensioners and to improve conditions at Greenwich Hospital by appropriating larger sums from prize monies and the droits of Admiralty. Grey's measure was welcomed by the navy, despite the inequality of the increases for officers and other ranks, and it established rates of pay which lasted until the end of the war; but it was no more than a palliative for what remained a generally unattractive way of life and the lot of the men who did so much to save British honour and to contribute to her final victory remained hard and bitter throughout the war. Romilly asserted that Grey disapproved of the severe punishments common in the navy, but nothing effective was done to mitigate them. Nevertheless, Grey's conduct of his duties at the Admiralty impressed his colleagues. Ellenborough wrote in July 1806 that his 'discharge of his duties in the naval department is deserving of the highest praise'. He did nothing to alter the notorious way in which patronage was handled in the navy, and if anything exploited the considerable opportunities of his office in the conventional way to reward and to promote friends and relatives. His brother George (whose wife was Whitbread's sister), a captain in the navy, was appointed to the office of Superintendent of Portsmouth Dockyard. When challenged in the Commons, Grey retorted that his naval appointments were made only with a view to the efficiency of the service, and that his brother 'was fully qualified for the office'. A second brother, Henry George, was promoted in the army during the summer of 1806 and at Grey's request was allowed the local rank of Lieutenant-General, rather to Windham's disgust. Grey never shrank from any opportunity to promote the interests of his relatives, but every government of the period naturally sought to distribute patronage in favour of its own members and their dependants, and failure to oblige men of influence in this way might be politically damaging. The Duke of Northumberland's annoyance at the supposed neglect of his friends was to culminate in Grey's loss of his seat for Northumberland in 1807.[10]

The major piece of patronage acquired by the Grey family in 1806 was the earldom conferred on Grey's father in April 1806. Although he might have had claims of his own on the ministry, for he had supported Sidmouth in the past, the promotion was clearly designed for his son. Since Grey was destined for the House of Lords in any case, he wished for the earldom, but he had sufficient delicacy to refrain from asking for it himself. Fox, however, was in no doubt as to his views,

---

[10] Ibid. 908–14, vii. 679. M. Lewis, *A Social History of the Navy, 1793–1815* (1960), 293–315; Romilly, *Memoirs*, ii. 140; Ellenborough to Sidmouth, 30 July 1806, Pellew, *Sidmouth*, ii. 432; Grey to Windham, 11 July 1806, BL Add. MS 37847, fo. 253; Windham to Grenville, 28 Feb. 1807, *Fortescue MSS*, ix. 63.

and pressed it on Grenville. Sheridan joined in, though not with Grey's knowledge or connivance, and attempted to take the credit for enlisting the support of the Prince of Wales, claiming that he had persuaded the Prince to overcome his dislike of Grey. Sheridan, by his own account, told the Prince that 'if anything were to happen to Fox and me, both as his minister and private friend, he would look nowhere for anyone to be put in competition with Grey.' The Prince, wrote Sheridan, adopted the idea 'most cheerfully' and declared he would propose it warmly to Grey at Devonshire House. Whether Sheridan's meddling had any influence or not, Grey, as the son of an earl, adopted the courtesy title of Lord Howick, by which he was known until he inherited the peerage in November 1807. Since, however, he was known by that title for only a year and a half, he will continue to be referred to as Grey in these pages.[11]

Grey's importance in the Cabinet increased as Fox's fatal illness took hold in the spring and summer of 1806. Yet his position as Fox's successor still had to be fought for. Lord Holland, Fox's favourite nephew, was regarded by many as the true representative of his uncle's principles, and on his deathbed Fox had designated him for his office. Fox's death on 13 September was not only a deep personal sorrow to Grey, but a threat to his political future. As Grey's son was later to write, 'by none was his loss more keenly felt and bitterly deplored', and there followed a struggle amongst the factions in the ministry which reopened old rivalries and almost led to its dissolution. Buckingham, ever alert for his family's interests, told Grenville in July that there was no other person in the Whig party to whom he ought to defer as he had done to Fox, and urged that their brother Thomas should succeed to the Foreign Office to balance the greater weight which Grey would have as leader of the Commons. The Whigs, however, would have resented the loss of that important department to a Grenville, especially in the middle of a peace negotiation for which they suspected that their political allies had no enthusiasm. Even Thomas Grenville himself wished Grey to have the office, fearing that if it went to a Grenville the more extreme Foxites would 'run riot'. Some of the Foxites, however, wished to see Holland take his uncle's department, suspecting that Grey would be less dedicated to peace than Fox would have been. In setting his course towards the Foreign Office, therefore, Grey had to surmount possible objections from both wings of the coalition.[12]

The first obstacle was Lord Holland and his support from the Prince. After a preliminary but inconclusive conversation with Grenville on the day after Fox's death, Grey wrote to the Prince the next day. He did not mention the Foreign Office directly but declared his intention that 'whatever arrangements may be

---

[11] Fox to Grenville, 5 Mar. 1806, ibid. viii. 48; Sheridan to Mrs Sheridan, n.d., W. Fraser Rae, *Sheridan* (1896), 255–6; *CGPW*, v. 413 n. 3; Grey to Whitbread [Feb. 1806], G. 59/2.

[12] Grey, *Life and Opinions*, 111–5; Farington, *Diary*, iv. 32. Grey paid tribute to Fox in the Commons on 5 Jan. 1807 as 'that loved friend and instructor without whose guidance and support I have no confidence in my own strength': *Parl. Deb.* viii. 305. Buckingham to Grenville, 23 and 27 July, 11 Sept. 1806, *Fortescue MSS*, viii. 241–2, 248, 316; T. Grenville to Buckingham, 21 July, *Court & Cabinets of George III*, iv. 52.

made ... will be in strict conformity to what we may believe Mr. Fox himself, if living, would have wished' and added that 'nothing could be more distressing to me than any doubt of Your Royal Highness's approbation in any step I may venture to take.' He concluded by assuring the Prince of his 'true attachment and devotion'. The Prince replied from Knowsley, where he was staying on a northern tour, that his preference would be for no other change in the ministry but the appointment of Holland as Foreign Secretary, sugaring the pill by a disingenuous reference to what he called 'the regard and estimation with which I have viewed your talents and the friendship which has always subsisted between us'. On the 19th, however, and before the Prince's reply had arrived in London, Grey was writing again to say that it had been decided that it was essential that he should lead the Commons, and that the position was incompatible with the Admiralty because of the heavy work-load of that office. He asserted that he would personally have preferred Holland to have the seals, but admitted that the Foreign Office would be the post 'most pleasant to me'; and he concluded that 'if this arrangement cannot be made I am afraid there is no alternative left but that of declaring at once to the king that we are unable to meet the present crisis.' Holland accordingly advised the Prince to acquiesce. The Grenvilles, however, were determined to exact a price. They demanded that, in return for Grey's promotion, Thomas Grenville should take over the Home Department and Spencer return to the Admiralty. The difficulty then arose that, under the Civil List Act, only two Secretaries of State at any one time could sit in the lower House. Unless Windham could be persuaded to go to the Lords, the arrangement would not be feasible. Lord Grenville therefore made it a condition of Grey's taking the foreign seals that he should join them in pressing Windham to take a peerage. Grey did so with extreme reluctance, and only when Grenville threatened that his refusal would either put an end to the administration or force him to take in a substantial number of Pittites. Windham was obdurate: he saw no reason why he should be kicked upstairs for other people's convenience and refused point blank to agree.[13]

Grey broke the deadlock and secured his own position by a master-stroke. He drew up a scheme cleverly designed to put pressure on all concerned, suggesting three possible solutions. The first was to give Thomas Grenville the Admiralty, leaving Spencer at the Home Office and himself at the Foreign Office. The second was to retain the Admiralty himself with the lead in the Commons, giving Holland the Foreign and Tom Grenville the Home seals; this was open to the objections that Grenville mistrusted Holland as too liberal for the Foreign Office, and that, as was generally agreed, the lead of the Commons could not practicably be combined with so burdensome an office as the Admiralty. The third suggestion was the one designed to bring everyone to his senses: Grey would take a peerage,

[13] CGPW, v. 432–3, 439–41, 441–4, 447; Grenville to Grey, 18 Sept., Fortescue MSS, viii. 337–8; Grey to Whitbread, 20 Sept., G. 59; Holland to Grey, 19 Sept., Holland, Memoirs, ii. 59–60. For the negotiations with Windham see BL Add. MS 39847, fos. 119–26 and Fortescue MSS, viii. 319–20, 340–5.

and go to the Lords as Lord President or Privy Seal, and the leadership of the Commons would be conferred on the inexperienced George Ponsonby. Grey professed his own inclination towards the last course, as merely anticipating by a short interval his inevitable departure from the lower House, and he remarked that 'my wish is to make all personal considerations subservient to the general interest of the Government.'[14]

Grey's letter opened Grenville's eyes to reality. The prospect of George Ponsonby leading the Commons, and Grey virtually retiring from active participation in the government, amounted to 'so great a misfortune that no idea can be entertained of it'. If the Grenvilles would not have Ponsonby as leader of the Commons, nor would the Whigs accept Thomas Grenville or Windham in that position, and Grey's friends also rushed to dissuade him from giving it up. Even Whitbread, who was still being difficult about his ambition to be Secretary at War, placed his concern at the possible increase of the Grenvilles' strength before his anxiety about Grey as Fox's successor. He urged Grey to take the Foreign Office if only to save the country from a new Grenville–Pittite alliance. Sidmouth also threw his not inconsiderable weight behind Grey, being anxious to avert the spectre of Canning joining the Cabinet. In the end, therefore, Grey was placed in Fox's old office and the leadership of the Commons by the almost unanimous desire of all his colleagues and friends. He had worked upon their fears with great skill, and at the same time impressed them—Sidmouth especially—with his modesty and public spirit in offering to sacrifice himself for the general good. Though he responded to Grenville's invitation to take the Foreign Office with a further assurance that he wished he could have been 'exempted ... from a responsibility that terrifies me', he added that he 'said this for the last time' and that 'I will do my best'.[15]

The Cabinet reshuffle was therefore not extensive. Spencer stayed where he was, room was found for Holland by Fitzwilliam's remaining in the Cabinet without portfolio and giving up the Lord Presidency to Sidmouth, whose Privy Seal was taken over by Holland, and Thomas Grenville reluctantly accepted the Admiralty. The balance of forces was little changed, at least on the surface. Perhaps the most significant of these changes in the long run was Sidmouth's move to the Presidency, an office which gave him closer and more frequent contact with the King and so enabled him to warn George III on the Catholic Bill in the spring of 1807. But for the time being Grey had succeeded in preventing a crisis within the administration as well as in strengthening his own political position. Finally, the successful resolution of these problems left Canning out of the ministry. Grenville had for some time had him in mind as Grey's eventual successor in the Commons. Grey declared himself not unfavourable if Canning would come in alone: but Canning pitched his terms too high by demanding places for four more

[14] Grey to Grenville, 20 Sept., ibid. 345–7.
[15] Grenville to Grey, 21 Sept., G. 21/2/46; Whitbread to Grey, 9 Sept., G. 59; Grey to Grenville, 21 Sept., *Fortescue MSS*, viii. 349.

of Pitt's old friends, and there was no room for so large a number. Negotiations with Canning continued at intervals until the final collapse of the Talents, but perhaps more to keep the opposition in disarray than with any serious hope of his accession. In the end, Canning's decision to throw in his lot with the anti-Catholic Portland government in 1807 gained him Grey's office, but lost him what was left of Grey's goodwill. Grey considered Canning's action a base desertion of his pro-Catholic sympathies, and for the rest of their lives refused to contemplate any co-operation with him on the grounds of his lack of principle and over-riding ambition for office. The events of 1807 were to cast a long shadow twenty years later, when Grey's refusal to countenance a Whig–Canningite coalition on grounds of both public principle and personal dislike preserved the Whig party from absorption into Canning's following.[16]

If Grey's succession to Fox was managed without splitting the Grenville alliance, it weakened the connection between the official Whig party and Carlton House. The Prince accepted as graciously as he was able Grey's succession to the Foreign Office, Grey writing to assure him that it was satisfactory to all Fox's friends. No doubt the Prince applied to himself as well as to Grey his admonition that

this is a strange world we live in, and nothing can be done in it without a little temper and a little policy. We must do the best we can, and because we cannot have everything our own way, we must not therefore instantly throw up the whole game.

His dislike of Grey was not, however, diminished by the episode, and with the loss of Fox and his continuing dependence on Sheridan the Prince's attachment to the Whigs continued to weaken—a process that was to be accelerated by his disapproval of the Catholic Bill and his annoyance over the ministry's conduct of the 'delicate investigation' into his wife's affairs in the coming winter. The Prince had been strangely apathetic during the reconstruction of the ministry, declaring his indifference to politics since Fox's death and showing signs of detachment from his old connections which were ominous for their future prospects.

If this alliance was weakening, however, Grey's association with Grenville was greatly strengthened. Grenville's firmness had established Grey in the position he coveted, and he was suitably grateful. 'Everything he has done,' Grey remarked, 'and every view he has taken of this melancholy subject, has been entirely in that fair and liberal spirit in which the union between him and Mr. Fox was originally formed. Nothing indeed could have been in every respect more cordial and more open than the whole of his conduct.' This cordiality between the two major figures in the administration was essential to its continued existence, and it survived the ministry's collapse in 1807 to become the cornerstone of the Whig–Grenville alliance for the next ten years.[17]

---

[16] For the negotiations with Canning see ibid. 387–91 and ix. 440–1; Revd C. Moss to J. King, 31 July, BL Dropmore MSS Ser. 2, B7 (i). For the Cabinet reshuffle see Jupp, *Grenville*, 376–9.

[17] *CGPW*, v. 454–5, 458–9. Sheridan was 'very mortified': J. Whishaw to H. Brougham, 19 Sept. 1806, *Life & Times of Henry Lord Brougham written by himself* (1871) [*BLT*], i. 373; Fitzwilliam to

Grey was now established as Fox's successor at the head of the Whig party. Despite the reservations of some of its members about his lack of that personal warmth that had drawn them to Fox, few doubted his ability for the post. Shortly before Fox's death William Smith, for many years the spokesman of radical dissent in the Commons, had written to urge him to grasp the opportunity:[18]

I yet confidently feel that you are the only man in the kingdom to whom it will be yielded— and that you may be able to assume it, if you shall so please. But you must then make up your mind to sacrifice to popularity no more than you have ever hitherto done. You will not suspect me of meaning a sacrifice of honour or principle—but somewhat more of leisure, perhaps even also of business, a good deal probably of taste and disposition. And this, permit me to say, you ought to do—the country will have a right to demand of you this effort ... I repeat that in the present state of the Party, I see no one but you who would be accepted as its leader, and for you to be so, I firmly believe depends chiefly on yourself.... You have a right to propose to yourself as your object, the being at the head both of the Party and the Government. I hope you do so, and will attain it in spite of all the desponding fancies which may rise in your mind ...

Grey's succession to the leadership of the Commons was considered incontestable even by such diverse characters as Sheridan and Buckingham. No one, however, could replace Fox entirely. The deep personal affections of his friends had been Fox's greatest strength as a political leader, and these Grey lacked. His abilities commanded respect, but the memory of his too overt ambition as a young man, his impatience, and his tendency to irritability under pressure gave an impression of egotism which contrasted with the easy-going openness of Fox. Colonel MacMahon, the Prince's secretary, told Northumberland that there was 'a general want of personal attachment' to Grey in the House, and added that he himself thought him 'most odious'. Another observer, J. W. Ward, wrote in April 1807 after some months of experience of Grey as leader of the House, that though his manner was always most agreeable towards his friends and those he liked, it 'was not much calculated to captivate and hold together country gentlemen and weak brethren', while T. W. Coke, a firm Whig stalwart, admitted that though he was 'the first man on his side of the House' he was not popular on the back-benches because he was too 'hot and irritable'. Some thought, therefore, that Fox's death would shatter the Whig party. Francis Horner wrote that there was 'no man of acknowledged and commanding talents left to supply his place', and Canning asserted that without Fox the Treasury Bench would be 'absolutely at our mercy'. Even Lady Elizabeth Foster bemoaned that since Fox's death 'we have nothing left but secondary characters', though her son Augustus reproached her for so describing Grey and Grenville, and within a few months she was sufficiently impressed by Grey's performance to give him the supreme accolade of 'a true Foxite'. As leader of the House, Grey showed again the qualities which

Holland, 24 Sept., BL Add. MS 51593, fo. 26, to Grenville, 24 Sept. and 6 Nov., *Fortescue MSS*, viii. 356, 427; Grey, *Life and Opinions*, 126.

[18] W. Smith to Grey, 2 July 1806, G. 52.

had made his parliamentary reputation. Wellington remarked to Creevey several years later that 'as leader of the House of Commons Grey's manner and speaking were quite perfect', and as the only man on the Treasury Bench capable of taking on Canning his gifts were to be much in demand. Towards the end of the ministry, Erskine assured him that 'You have in a very short time raised a great reputation as I always foresaw you would when you had the lead and management of the House of Commons.'[19]

In his departmental office, Grey showed a firmness and realism that soon contrasted with the vacillations of Grenville and the over-idealistic attitudes of some of his Whig colleagues. He considered himself as continuing the policies of Fox, whose enthusiasm for a negotiated peace had begun to wane in face of French intransigence even before his illness incapacitated him. By 1805, Fox had become convinced that Napoleon's imperialism was a greater threat to Britain and to Europe than the ambitions of the absolutist central powers. He had moved towards a 'continental' policy, hoping to resurrect Pitt's alliances with Austria and Prussia and to further British influence in the Mediterranean. He made it a condition of the negotiations that Sicily be retained in friendly hands as a British naval base. It was chiefly on this issue that the negotiations began to break down in the summer of 1806, Napoleon insisting that the island be kept by his brother Joseph in Naples. Grenville, too, wavered on the Sicilian question, being willing to consider an exchange with Sardinia by the King of Naples. It was an ominous portent of future divisions in the Cabinet on foreign strategy. Grey adopted what he believed to be Fox's line, and when the negotiations finally collapsed in the autumn he expressed satisfaction: he told Holland that though he still wished for peace on honourable terms, he did not think it attainable at present, though he added that 'perhaps you may think I am myself too warlike'. Holland assured him that he did not, and accepted that the Cabinet had not abandoned Fox's policy. Whitbread, however, accused Grey of giving in to the Grenvilles and deserting Whig principles. Grey's speech on the breakdown of the negotiations was considered too Grenvillian in tone, and Whitbread went so far as to move a resolution of censure in the exact words which Grey had used against Pitt's failure to make peace in the 1790s. Brougham observed that Whitbread's speech was personal towards Grey, and though it remained as Grey remarked, 'a solitary opinion', it marked a widening of the breach between them.[20]

The episode strengthened Grey's alliance with Grenville at the expense of some of his Whig support. As Grenville's second-in-command, Grey contributed qualities which Grenville lacked. He was more adept at dealing with the King,

[19] *CGPW*, vi. 19 (25 Oct. 1806); *Letters to 'Ivy' from the first Earl of Dudley*, ed. S. H. Romilly (1905), 49; Farington, *Diary*, iv. 144; *Memoirs of Francis Horner*, ed. L. Horner (Edinburgh, 2nd. edn. 1849), 180–1; Canning to Mrs Canning, 16 June 1806, Harewood MSS; *The Two Duchesses* (ed. Vere Foster), 289–91, 303; *Creevey Papers*, i. 286 (1817–18); Erskine to Grey, 15 Mar. 1807, G. 14/2.

[20] Grey to Holland, 28 Sept. 1806, BL Add. MS 51550, fos. 14–15; Holland to Grey, 28 Sept., ibid. 51544, fos. 78–91; Holland, *Memoirs*, ii. 78; Brougham to Rosslyn, 1 Dec. 1806 (misdated 1807), *BLT*, i. 390–5; Holland, *Memoirs*, ii. 76; Grey to R. Adair, 13 Jan. 1807, G. 1/3.

whom Grenville treated brusquely and with little consideration: Grey took George III's views into account in his foreign policy and tried to keep within bounds which the King would approve. Grey also established a rapport with Sidmouth, whom Grenville tactlessly offended by his repeated attempts to win over Canning as a future replacement in the leadership of the Commons when Grey's father died. Sidmouth reciprocated by supporting Grey's policies in Cabinet, until his own change of mind over the South American strategy and the onset of the Catholic crisis caused a rift between them. In the coming months it was often Grey who supplied the leadership of the ministry that Grenville was too remote and uncertain to grasp with success.

Foreign affairs were the source of some of the major problems with which the Talents Ministry had to deal in the months after Fox's death. Though in January 1807 Grey felt confident enough to assure Robert Adair, Fox's emissary at Vienna, that 'the government is strong and united, and I believe the public never was more unanimous in opinion than it is on the subject of the war', their differences over strategy were mainly responsible for the breakup of the government even before the Catholic crisis three months later. The failure of the peace negotiations left unresolved the question as to how the war was to be carried on in face of Napoleon's European dominance. In the search for a coherent strategy, the Cabinet was divided between those who, like Grey, favoured the 'European' principle of attempting to win the war on the Continent with the support of European allies, and those who wished to concentrate on overseas expeditions in various parts of the globe in the hope of countering Napoleon's economic blockade and forcing the French to terms by building up spheres of influence elsewhere. Across the Atlantic, the naval and commercial power of the United States seemed to be leading to a possible collision with British imperialist ambitions and economic interests, while French intervention in Spain and Portugal opened the question of the future of their South American colonies as potential markets for British trade. In these spheres, Grey and Holland, representing the Foxite tradition in the Cabinet, found themselves at odds with the Prime Minister and other colleagues. The Whigs had a long tradition of admiration for the American republic, coupled with a lively fear of the damage it might inflict as an enemy to British naval and colonial power. Their attitude therefore was a conciliatory one. The Americans resented the British claim to a right of search of neutral vessels for 'contraband' trade with France, and the practice of impressment of British seamen from American ships into the navy. In October 1806 they passed a non-importation act against British goods as a reprisal. Grey and Holland worked for a compromise on these issues but after the end of the peace negotiations in Paris the Cabinet's attitude hardened and Holland's proposals were rejected. Napoleon's Berlin decrees of November intensified the problem. On 22 December the Cabinet agreed that US ships might carry goods to enemy ports but only if they originated from or were shipped via American harbours. American carrying trade between enemy ports was to remain liable to search and seizure. The American government however refused the compromise and Anglo-American relations remained in disarray.[21]

On the European Continent the Whigs had been traditionally suspicious of the absolutist powers and of Pitt's policies of subsidizing Prussia, Austria, and other European allies in the 1790s. Holland, as the leading representative of Foxite liberalism, distrusted collaboration with absolutist regimes and showed signs of wishing to promote opposition movements especially in the Iberian peninsula. Windham, as ever, favoured the contrary line, believing still that the war would have to be fought sooner or later on French soil and that aid should be given to the internal opponents of Bonapartism and jacobinism to restore the old monarchy. Sidmouth was inclined to agree. Grenville, as Prime Minister, failed to balance these various forces or to compel their resolution into a single coherent strategy. The Talents' foreign policy remained one of shifts and expedients and uncertain direction.

The supporters of the 'European' view in the Cabinet won the first victory in September 1806, when it was agreed to approach Prussia for a renewal of the alliance against France. The King, however, was concerned primarily for the restitution of Hanover, now occupied by Prussian troops, and Grey, while professing a willingness to consider renewing subsidies to Prussia and even to Austria to bring them back into full-scale operations, laid it down that there could be no Prussian alliance unless there was an immediate and unconditional evacuation of Hanover. He declared his lack of faith in Prussia's good intentions, which aligned him with Holland, Lauderdale, and other Foxites. Nevertheless, Grey believed fundamentally in the 'European' viewpoint, and even when the news of Prussia's defeat by the French at Jena arrived at the end of October, he continued to advocate concentration on a new continental offensive. His Grenville allies however vacillated. In the summer of 1806 Sir Home Popham, commander of an expedition to the Cape of Good Hope, had carried out a successful, though unauthorized, attack on Buenos Aires. Hopes were aroused in Britain of extensive conquests in South America and a consequent new outlet for British trade. Although Grenville's first reaction to Popham's success was to express his 'great reluctance to the embarking in South American projects because I knew it was much easier to get into them than out again', he allowed himself to be swept along by the enthusiasm of the merchants and the City. It was decided to reinforce the South American theatre, and in October further troops were sent to Chile and Grenville toyed with the idea of an expedition to Mexico. Apart from the possible commercial gains, Grenville argued that France would come to terms in Europe rather than see Britain conquer the whole of South America, an outcome he was optimistic enough to forecast. It was also hoped that Spain and Portugal might thus be induced to join Britain and declare war on France.[22]

---

[21] Holland, *Memoirs*, ii. 98–103. For Grenville's foreign policy see Jupp, *Grenville*, 391–4.
[22] Grey to Grenville, 3 Oct. 1806, *Fortescue MSS*, viii. 371–2; Adair to Fox, 19 Sept., Grey to

The plan was controversial however, and Grenville admitted that there was 'some want of clearness on the subject' in the Cabinet. Sidmouth joined Grey in opposing diversions from the European theatre, while Holland, whose travels in Spain had made him an enthusiast for the Spanish liberals, deplored the use of British forces on mere plundering expeditions for the benefit of British merchants. Grey agreed. He was unwilling to divert substantial forces to South America at the expense of Europe, even when the normally irresistible bait of giving his brother the command of the expedition was dangled before him. As Holland remarked, 'in conformity with ... the true spirit of his direct, bold and honourable character' he urged the recall of Popham's troops for disposal in Europe, where he hoped to energize the Spanish and Portuguese governments against Napoleon. He also proposed an expedition to seize the Portuguese navy if that power refused to join Britain, and laid plans for an offensive in the Mediterranean. Troops were to be sent to Alexandria to secure the eastern Mediterranean and protect Greece and to promote an attack on Sicily to help the Austrians. Reinforcements were to be sent to Naples, and an expedition was mounted against Constantinople to force the Turks to allow Russia access to the Mediterranean. So the 'soft underbelly' of French-dominated Europe would beome the major British target, as it was to be Churchill's in 1942. Unfortunately, the execution of these projects was less successful. The Constantinople expedition was a total failure, largely because of Thomas Grenville's bungling at the Admiralty and also because the commander, Sir John Duckworth, disobeyed his orders. Canning later admitted that Grey's instructions had been 'clear and reasonable, though so ill-observed and executed', but the collapse of the expedition helped to discredit the Talents' foreign policy still further.[23]

The ministry was groping for a strategy. Grenville occupied himself with complicated schemes for shuffling miscellaneous forces around the globe, while Holland pressed for concentration on Spain and Portugal and suggested that pressure be put on the King of Naples to introduce a more liberal regime in Sicily. Windham and Grenville, however, objected to the idea of stirring up insurrectionary movements in these areas even against the French. In the New World too the ministers failed to commit themselves to a consistent approach. A rising in Caracas led by General Miranda during the summer of 1806 had attracted British support, but once again the commander on the spot, Admiral Cochrane, exceeded his cautious instructions and Grey sent him a severe reprimand in July for unauthorized intervention in South American affairs. This rising was accordingly crushed in November. In December the Spaniards recaptured Buenos Aires; but far from putting an end to the Cabinet's South American ambitions, this event only intensified the argument for further intervention. Sidmouth,

Adair, 7 Oct., G.1/3; *Adair*, 162–9; Holland, *Memoirs*, ii. 82; Cabinet minute, 14 Nov., George III to Grey and reply, 15 Nov., *LCGIII*, iv. 487–8; Grenville to Lauderdale, 22 Sept., to Grey, 29 Sept., *Fortescue MSS*, viii. 352, 366–8.

[23] Grenville to Lauderdale, 1 Oct.; Grey to Grenville, 30 July, 7 Aug. 1806, ibid., 368–9, 250, 259–60; Holland, *Memoirs*, ii. 109–17, L. G. Mitchell, *Holland House* (1980), 217–39; *LCGIII*, iv. 488–9.

convinced that Prussia's defeat had closed Europe as an accessible theatre for British efforts, and believing that Windham's reforms had failed to build up a sufficient army for continental operations, switched his support from the European to the South American policy. A series of Cabinet meetings in January and February intensified the split. A stormy meeting on 7 January failed to agree on the principle of an Old or a New World strategy and a month later Grey and Holland found themselves the only supporters of concentration on Europe, while Thomas Grenville and Sidmouth advocated another attempt on Buenos Aires, and Moira, to Grenville's horror, proposed fomenting a revolution in South America. Though the Foxites were outnumbered, Grey, as the responsible minister, refused to accept the majority vote and insisted on recording his dissent in writing in the minute intended for the King. The Cabinet consequently adjourned to the following day, when Grey made a forceful plea against diversions from Europe and in favour of a large expedition to northern Europe to assist Russia and to encourage Austria and Sweden. He argued that to concentrate British efforts in America would be a breach of faith with our European allies, but only Holland was convinced. Grey therefore gave way, against his better judgement, and drafted instructions to the South American commanders to attack Buenos Aires.[24]

Though Grey had done his best to rescue something from the ruins of the peace negotiations, the results were merely disagreement and disarray. Grey always argued that the Buenos Aires expedition was one of which he had never approved and which had been forced upon him by circumstances and by his Cabinet colleagues. He was not surprised, therefore, at its ultimate failure. The collapse of the Talents' foreign policy should be more directly laid at the Prime Minister's door, for Grenville vacillated, did not back up his Foreign Secretary as he should have done, and failed to offer decisive leadership at the crucial moments. As the Talents Ministry moved towards its final catastrophe over the Catholic question in the spring of 1807, its internal divisions on foreign affairs contributed to the air of failure and discord in which it finally came to an end.[25]

THE END OF THE TALENTS, 1806–1807

Fox's death weakened the ministry in more respects than in foreign policy. His presence had smoothed relations with the Prince of Wales, whose restiveness over his marriage was becoming intense. He wished to be free of his estranged wife and became obsessed with reports of her supposed immoral conduct which were made

[24] Grenville to Buckingham, 31 Oct., Windham to Grenville, 2 Nov., *Fortescue MSS*, viii. 415–16, 418–20; Grey to Cochrane, 3 June, 17 July 1806, Cochrane MSS, N.L.S.; Sidmouth to Bragge-Bathurst, 2 Dec., to Hiley Addington, 3 Dec., Pellew, *Sidmouth*, ii. 441–3; the Cabinet meetings are recorded by Holland, *Memoirs*, ii. 114–15, and by Windham, *Diary*, 467–8.
[25] General Charles Grey's assertion in *Life and Opinions*, 138 that the failures and disagreements of the ministry in foreign affairs did not contribute to its breaking-up cannot be sustained.

public in the summer of 1806. Grey told Holland in December that the business was 'without any comparison, the most disagreeable of any in which any government was ever engaged. It cannot end well for us, in any way.'[1] It presented the opposition with an opportunity to capitalize on the Princess's popular appeal as a woman deeply wronged by a husband who was morally at least no better than she was, while the government was under intense pressure from the Prince to rid him of a wife whom he detested, on evidence that was highly questionable. Failure to comply with the Prince's wishes would hardly be less damaging politically than to have to face the public outcry against injustice to his wife.

A Commission of Investigation of four senior ministers was set up in the summer to report on charges made against the Princess that she had borne an illegitimate child. It reported in July that, while there was no firm evidence to substantiate that allegation, it appeared that the Princess's conduct was open to 'very unfavourable interpretations'. In reply Perceval and Eldon, for the opposition, drew up a defence of her conduct that amounted to a public manifesto against her husband. The prospect of its publication threw the Prince into a frenzy, and he urged the Cabinet to clear his reputation by condemning his wife. Two long and difficult Cabinet meetings produced a compromise suggested jointly by Grey and Grenville, that the facts warranted no proceedings against the Princess, but that the King should himself decide whether to receive her again at Court. The King, however, demanded more positive advice, and on 25 January there was another long meeting. Grey suggested that the King should allow the Princess to appear at Court but should warn her about her general conduct. The Prince was enraged. He had written in November to Moira, threatening that he would 'have no further concern with this government which . . . have failed in their solemn engagement to me who have been their sheet anchor' and authorizing him to show his letter to 'my friend Lord Howick'. By early December the Prince's friend the Duke of Northumberland was writing of his grievances against Grey and Grenville and threatening to sever his connection with them, adding that Grey had too 'closely connected himself with Lord Grenville' for his liking. Northumberland's desertion was virtually complete by March 1807, when the Prince wrote to Moira that after the 'delicate investigation' into his wife's conduct he had resolved to 'cease to be a party man'. The loss of the Prince's goodwill was complete.[2]

One of the major questions to come before Parliament in the session of 1807 was the Bill to abolish the slave-trade in the British Empire. It had been taken up by Wilberforce and the 'Saints' in the later 1780s, but despite disclosures of the cruelty of the trade, economic interests in the West Indies and Britain had successfully resisted abolition, while the abolitionists had also suffered from their association in the eyes of the loyalists with political radicalism and the general

---

[1] [29 Dec. 1806], BL Add. MS 51550, fos. 45–7.

[2] Cabinet minutes, 23 Dec. (with Holland's notes on the discussions) and 25 Jan., *CGPW*, vi. 104–10, 125–6; Windham, *Diary*, 465, 467; Prince of Wales to Moira, 7 Nov. 1806, 30 Mar. 1807; Northumberland to MacMahon, 5, 16, and 26 Dec. 1806, *CGPW*, vi. 40–3, 95, 101, 111, 156; Northumberland to Grenville, 17 and 22 Oct., BL Add. MS 58992, fos. 77, 81.

horror at the massacre of white settlers by freed slaves in San Domingo. Fox told Holland that abolition of the slave-trade and peace with France were the two objects dearest to his heart, while Grenville favoured abolition as a cause which Pitt had supported. Others, however, opposed it on grounds of national interest. Windham and Sidmouth believed that unilateral abolition of the British trade would merely hand it over to foreign countries, and argued that regulation of the trade by Britain to alleviate the atrocious conditions of the 'middle passage' would better serve humanitarian purposes.[3]

Grenville and Grey however were determined to achieve abolition, as a tribute to Fox's memory as well as on humanitarian grounds. The main credit must be Grenville's but Grey piloted the Bill through the Commons, declaring that 'the measure was of such importance in itself, and he felt so much more deeply interested in it, than in any other measure that had been brought forward since he had a share in the administration of public affairs'. In his speech he collected together all the arguments for abolition on economic, moral, and humanitarian grounds, declaring that the trade 'was contrary to the fundamental principles of Christianity', and also that abolition would positively benefit rather than injure the interests of planters and merchants alike—an argument backed by an array of statistics to prove that the diminished resources now devoted to the trade would be easily absorbed by the expansion of commerce in other branches. He also claimed that natural increase and the milder treatment of the slaves that could be expected after the abolition of the trade would amply supply the foreseeable demand for negro labour on the plantations. He looked forward to the possibility of the ultimate abolition of slavery itself, a measure which was to be eventually achieved under his own Premiership in 1833. He ended by calling on the names of Pitt and Fox and asking the House 'to pay tribute to their memories' by passing the Bill.[4]

Grey's speech was typical of his set performances in that he chose to concentrate, not on abstract principles but on the arguments which might be advanced by the opponents of the measure. The stress on the 'sound policy' of abolition might have been carried too far to be wholly convincing, in that it was somewhat disingenuous to assert that the planters would be better off without slave labour, but it was important to refute the economic arguments which had so often blocked previous Bills. It might be true, as one historian of abolition has asserted, that Grey misjudged the readiness of the House to respond to the moral argument against the trade—as shown by the division of 283 against only 16, and the ovation given to Wilberforce at the end of the debate. Nevertheless, Grey was aware that Sidmouth's followers and Windham, from his own side of the House, were opposed to the Bill, and it was important to counter their objections. In the event, that opposition did not materialize and it may be due to Grey's tactics that the Bill had so smooth a passage. In the longer term, however, the Abolition Bill did

---

[3] Holland, *Memoirs*, i. 250.
[4] *Parl. Deb.* viii. 946–56, 23 Feb. 1807.

weaken the cohesion of the ministry by driving Sidmouth further into isolation from his colleagues. How important that was the Catholic Relief Bill was soon to show.[5]

Ireland was the cause of the Talents' fall, as it had destroyed Pitt's government in 1801. The administration had been formed without any precise commitment to the Irish Catholics, for though Fox, Grey, and Grenville were all pledged to emancipation they had agreed that it would be inexpedient to force it on the King at the outset. They were soon to reap the consequences of that omission. The appointment of the Duke of Bedford as Lord-Lieutenant with instructions to be as conciliatory as possible towards Irish claims, soon proved to be insufficient to maintain peace and order in that troubled country, more bitterly divided than ever since the atrocities of 1798. Efforts were made to stave off another petition for emancipation in the first weeks of the new administration. James Ryan, a Dublin banker and one of the Catholic leaders, informed Fox in January 1806 of their intention to renew their petition. He warned of 'the futility of doing things by halves' and declared that only full emancipation would reconcile Ireland to the British connection. He hinted, however, that a lesser concession might create an atmosphere of goodwill in the interim: 'the unfortunate disasters on the continent have diffused a Universal desire throughout our body to be put on a footing which will render them qualified in every part of the British Empire to perform their duty to their sovereign and their country.' The Irish Relief Act of 1793 had allowed Catholics to hold army commissions below the rank of general on the staff, but the Act of Union had omitted to extend this right to other parts of the British dominions. The anomaly thus arose that a Catholic officer became liable to penalties if his regiment were posted overseas, so that the raising of additional forces in Ireland was of little value to the war effort. In July, Grey attempted a survey of the number of troops available for overseas operations. He calculated that the forces at the government's disposal totalled 167,966, including 46,063 stationed in Ireland. Of the remainder, some 7,000 were embarked for Sicily and for Buenos Aires, and a further 6,000 were earmarked for the Mediterranean. If 7,000 more were to be sent to Brazil, and 1,500 each to Madeira and Tenerife, there would be 100,000 left, assuming the recruitment of an additional 1,000 in the meantime. Most of these detachments however would be from the regular infantry, which would leave only 25,000 of these troops still uncommitted; this was too small a number and must be augmented by other recruitment. Grey concluded that 'the best step for that purpose would undoubtedly be the raising of Irish regiments by the assistance of the Catholics.' Both on grounds of national defence and of Irish conciliation, therefore, the plan to extend Catholic service beyond Ireland seemed to recommend itself. Governments can rarely resist schemes which appear to solve two difficulties at once; unfortunately two half-measures seldom make one whole, but as the Cabinet's attention was very properly

[5] R. Anstey, *The Atlantic Slave Trade and British Abolition, 1760–1810* (1975), 376–82, 389–90, 397–9.

concentrated on the necessities of the war, a step which promised a partial solution of the Irish question—at least for a time—had many attractions.[6]

The urgency of the war and preoccupation with the reconstruction of the ministry and the general election in the autumn of 1806 meant that nothing was done before the end of the year. Meanwhile, disorders between Catholics and Orangemen increased in Ireland. The government attempted to hold the balance evenly between the two, but they had reckoned without the Ponsonbys' political ambitions. Bedford complained in November that they were pestering him for official support to their interests in Cork city and county, where there had been Orange riots at the recent elections, and for exclusive use of his patronage against their rivals the Beresfords at the head of the Protestant interest. He pointed out that his instructions from the Cabinet were to deal impartially between the two factions; the result was that each complained of preference to the other. Grey had warned Lord Ponsonby in October that the government had decided not to take sides between 'two inveterate parties', but his relationship to his wife's family and his need to conciliate the Ponsonbys as a channel to influence the Catholics made him change his tune in November. He now urged Bedford to give preference in his patronage arrangements to 'old friends' and in December he told the Lord-Lieutenant that the Orangemen were 'a sanguinary and bigoted faction' whose power, sooner or later, would be exerted against the present government. He admitted that 'the general policy of conciliation ... was the principle on which this government was formed' in both countries, since the Beresfords were the long-standing protégés of Buckingham and the Grenvilles, but he declared himself against any co-operation with 'a name so terribly distinguished in the history of Irish persecution' and said that if he had been consulted he would have advised against it. The next three months were to bring home yet again the relevance of Irish politics to the security of governments at Westminster.[7]

Grey's role in the crisis was a central one. Spencer, who as Home Secretary was responsible for communications with Dublin, fell ill and was absent from London during the crucial period. Grey, as the other principal Secretary of State, therefore took over the correspondence with the Irish Lord-Lieutenant. His relationship with the Ponsonbys also made him the main channel for the attempt to influence and moderate the demands of the Catholic party, so that the various threads of the affair now passed mainly through his hands. Throughout the crisis, he was one of the few ministers who tried to follow a consistent policy, and he was particularly concerned to maintain a reputation for honourable dealing with both the King and with the Irish.

By the end of 1806, the Talents' policy of general conciliation without actual concession was running into difficulties. In December, the Catholic Committee in

[6] Ryan to Fox, 7 Jan. 1806, BL Add. MS 51468, fos. 94–7; Grey to Grenville, 8 Aug. and enc. dated 1 July, ibid. 58946, fos. 109–12.
[7] Bedford to Grey, 25 Nov. 1806; Grey to Lord Ponsonby [Oct. 1806], and to Bedford, 11 Nov., 4 Dec., Grey, *Life and Opinions*, 161–3, G. 6/17.

Dublin decided to renew their petition for emancipation. The leadership was now in the hands of a new middle-class group under John Keogh, who were less amenable than the former aristocratic section under Lord Fingall to management from London. When no mention was made of emancipation in the King's Speech on 13 December they decided to act. Bedford had written in November to urge attention to Ireland where there had been another outbreak of agrarian disorder by the 'Threshers'. George Ponsonby warned Grey on 4 December that since the breakdown of the French negotiations there was talk of a union of both Catholics and Protestants to welcome a French invasion and drive out the British. The government again tried to delay the crisis. Bedford was instructed to use every effort to prevent the Catholic petition, and Grey used Ponsonby as a channel for a warning that any attempt to force the government to take up the question would only lead to its fall and replacement by one committed to the Protestant system. Fitzwilliam, remembering the experience of 1795, proved a sound if gloomy prophet:[8]

One administration after another has lost the confidence of Ireland, and ours I fear will do so too; we shall do nothing till the hour of necessity is come, then what we shall do, will be done too late for any advantageous effect.

The Cabinet decided to press ahead with the scheme to extend the service of Catholic officers beyond Ireland in the hope that this 'unsolicited boon' would conciliate the gentry and forestall the petition. On 10 January Grey asked Ponsonby whether it would be sufficient to do so. Even this limited measure, however, proved too difficult to accomplish. Elliot, the Irish Chief Secretary, warned that the Catholics would not be satisfied with the mere extension of the limited rights of 1793 to the rest of the Empire, and that they wanted to be able to serve in the highest ranks of the army. He thought that the appointment of some Catholic officers to field rank would encourage recruitment. He met a Catholic delegation in Dublin on 17 and 22 January, and persuaded them to postpone their meeting, fixed for 7 February, to allow time for consultation with London; Keogh refused, however, to postpone the petitioning meeting indefinitely and under this pressure Bedford urged the removal of all restrictions on service and promotion in the army, membership of corporations, and appointments as sheriffs, and called for a decision without further delay. The Cabinet met on 9 February and decided that there was already no bar to Catholic membership of corporations and that the right to serve as sheriffs would be too controversial, but agreed to proceed with the military plan. Even this decision was shrouded in ambiguity. Sidmouth and Ellenborough agreed to it on the understanding that it extended only to the limits of service imposed in 1793, that is not to the rank of general on the staff. In fact, however, the proposal as submitted to the King would have allowed both Catholics and Protestant Dissenters to hold any rank in the army and it was also extended

---

[8] Bedford to Grey, 25 Nov. 1806, 22 Feb. 1807, ibid.; Ponsonby to Grey, 4 Dec., G. 47/11; Grenville to Bedford, 29 Dec. and n.d., *Fortescue MSS*, viii. 486–8, 491–2; Grey to G. Ponsonby, 31 Dec., G. 47/11; to Holland, 22 Dec., BL Add. MS 51544, fos. 90–1; Fitzwilliam to Grey, 12 Dec., G. 14/11.

to the navy. Nevertheless, the minute stressed that the scheme did not differ in principle from the 1793 act. The King's first reaction was to refuse, but, under Sidmouth's persuasion, he finally gave a grudging assent on 12 February, declaring that he would accept nothing further.[9]

The stage was set for the tragic farce of mutual deception and misunderstanding which was to ruin the Talents. Though some historians have scoffed at their measure as a 'pitiful expedient' and indeed the ministers themselves attempted to play down its importance, there is no doubt, as Speaker Abbot realized, that it contained a substantial principle. The pro-Catholic ministers could see no other way of smuggling it past George III's conscience than to pretend that it was merely designed to rectify the anomaly in the Act of Union; their hope was that it could be presented to Ireland as a substantial measure while their own 'Protestant' faction and the King would accept it as a trivial one.[10]

No one was deceived. The Catholic Committee resolved on 9 February that they would press ahead with a petition for full emancipation, and even though Elliot assured them a week later that the government intended to allow Catholics to hold commissions in any rank, further Catholic meetings on the 17th and 24th agreed on and adopted a petition. The ministers and their friends in Ireland made valiant efforts to avert its presentation. Lord Ponsonby worked on Fingall and the moderates in the hope that the influence of the Catholic lords and country gentry would prevail over that of Keogh who, he warned Grey, 'rules the mob'. Grattan was also brought in to persuade Keogh that the government was favourable towards the Catholics, but unable to act because of the King's prejudices, while Grey reminded Ponsonby that British public opinion was generally hostile and that Perceval and the opposition were attempting to 'raise a flame' and to arouse 'such a spirit of illiberality and bigotry, as would have been worthy of the darkest ages of superstition and intolerance'. He pressed Ponsonby to continue his efforts to keep the Irish quiet until public opinion could be softened in Great Britain. To Bedford, Grey declared the impossibility of buying off the petition by any substantial concession short of emancipation. The King's attitude to the initial proposal made it clear that nothing more than the mere extension of the 1793 act beyond Ireland could be gained; for the Catholics to insist on presenting the petition would achieve only the embarrassment, and possibly the dissolution of the government. The only hope was that the more respectable Catholics would see reason; otherwise, he hinted, the ministers pledged to the Catholic cause would be compelled to resign. He warned George Ponsonby too that the Catholics' demand for concessions beyond what the King had now agreed to would wreck the administration, and would be 'productive of nothing but mischief' to the interests of the Catholics themselves. He argued that the petition must be stopped

[9] Grey to G. Ponsonby, 10 Jan. 1807, G. 47/11; W. Elliot to Grenville, 18 Jan., 10 Feb.; Bedford to Spencer, 4 Feb., Cabinet minutes and corresp., 9–12 Feb., *Fortescue MSS*, ix. 20–2, 31–4, 100–11; Holland, *Memoirs*, ii. 173–88; Pellew, *Sidmouth*, ii. 452–3; Colchester, *Diary*, ii. 93.

[10] M. Roberts, *The Whig Party, 1807–12* (2nd ed. 1965), 34; A. Fremantle, *England in the 19th century* (1930), ii. 184–5; Colchester, *Diary*, ii. 95.

without conditions; and if Keogh, whom he blamed for the Catholics' intransigence, would not agree, efforts should be made to divide the Catholic body and isolate the extremists from the moderates. He concluded that in any case it would be very unlikely that he himself would be able to remain in the government.[11]

Grey's attempt to restrain the Catholics failed. The Dublin militants were not amenable to Ponsonby's influence. In any case, the political crisis in England made the Catholic petition irrelevant. The Irish press reported Elliot's assurances about the scope of the intended military scheme on 20 February, which forced Grey to announce it on the same day in the Commons, in the form of a new clause in the Mutiny Bill. On 1 March Sidmouth called on Speaker Abbot to say that his support had always been limited to the extension of the 1793 Act beyond Ireland, but that the Cabinet appeared likely to resolve that the scheme 'should be carried into effect in its largest sense'. On the next day the Cabinet decided for the wider proposal. Grenville, however, 'declined to be the person who should state the subject again to the King or ask his consent upon it'. Sidmouth warned him that he was to see the King on the 4th and that, while he should not volunteer his opinion, he would state it to the King if he was asked. On the next day Abbot told Grey that he was bound to oppose the measure in committee, and on the 4th he wrote to the Vice-Chancellor of Oxford University of his 'strong objections, . . . both in principle and form', declaring his hope 'that the friends to the Protestant constitution of our monarchy will resist it to the utmost'.[12]

Sidmouth's move to alert Abbot and the King may have been influenced by Grenville's foolishness in renewing at this moment his approaches to Canning, fearing Grey's imminent removal to the Lords. Sidmouth's detestation of Canning remained absolute, but his anti-Catholic attitude was constant, undisguised, and well known to his Cabinet colleagues. If the King had a conscientious objection to Catholic emancipation in any form, Sidmouth shared it on grounds both of principle and of attachment to his sovereign. They made a formidable combination.

At this stage the government hit a procedural snag. The proposed new clause in the Mutiny Bill had, by a standing order of 1772, to go through a committee of the whole House since it affected the religious establishment. The ministers therefore decided, without consulting Sidmouth, Ellenborough, or the Lord Chancellor, to substitute a new Bill specifically extending the 1793 Act to allow promotion to general and to include the navy. Grey drew up a draft despatch to Bedford giving full details of the proposal, telling Bedford that it was written 'for the purpose of attracting the King's attention to the *extent* of the measure now proposed', and sent it to the King for approval. It was returned without comment, which Grey assumed meant that he did not object. He was soon disillusioned. On the 4th the King gave audiences to Grey and afterwards to Grenville. The first interview was stormy. According to Canning, the King declared his total opposition

[11] Lord Ponsonby to Grey [25], 26, 28 Feb. 1807, G. 48/1; Grey to Ponsonby, 5 Mar., Grey, *Life and Opinions*, 147–9; Grey to Bedford, 18 Feb., G. 6/17; to G. Ponsonby, 18 Feb., G. 47/11.
[12] Colchester, *Diary*, ii. 92–6; Pellew, *Sidmouth*, ii. 458–9.

to the Bill, and said that Grey left 'very cavalierly'. Grey's account was somewhat different. He wrote that the King began by saying that he understood the Bill was no more extensive than the 1793 Act. Grey expressed his astonishment at this misapprehension, particularly since the King had, presumably, read his despatch to Bedford which clearly set out the new scheme. He explained to him

the difference, with the reasons of it, and ended by expressing my hope that, upon the whole, this change would not produce any further objection from him. He [the King] said he was sorry for it, he was no Catholic, that, if his opinion was asked, he must say that he disapproved of it, that he had consented to its being brought into Parliament and nothing more. I left him with general expressions of regret for the difference of our opinions, but certainly under an impression that he had not withdrawn the reluctant consent which he had originally given.

On the way out Grey told the waiting Grenville that the King had agreed to the Bill's being proposed in Parliament. Consequently Grenville did not mention the matter during his interview. Either he was in no heart for a row with the King, or, more likely, he simply believed that the King had given way under pressure, as he had done previously over Windham's army reforms and the 1806 dissolution, when his objections had been overruled. It was a fatal mistake. George III was now prepared to be as unscrupulous with his ministers as he believed them to be with him. Holland drew the parallel with 1783, when he had allowed Fox to introduce the India Bill under a similar misapprehension in order to create the opportunity to dismiss his ministers.[13]

Grey's version of his audience is unlikely to have been inaccurate, so far as the King's literal words were concerned. Holland recorded that Grey, 'whose clear understanding is not very liable to mistakes, and whose honest nature is quite incapable of misrepresentation or subterfuge', stated clearly afterwards that the King had agreed to the measure being laid before Parliament and expressed no reservations as to its extent. In the context of early-nineteenth century politics, that could only mean that Grey honestly believed that he was free to present it to the House as an official government Bill, which would involve calling upon the placemen and courtiers to support it. At that stage also he could not have known that the King was taking the step, of doubtful constitutional propriety at least, of contacting the opposition and concerting with them a plan to overthrow the ministry; if he had done so he was a sufficiently experienced and skilful politician to realize that further explanations, or the modification of the Bill, were necessary to avert such a constitutional crisis. Nor did Grey as yet realize that Sidmouth was involved in the intrigue. The consequences of such a rupture within the Cabinet, in the full knowledge that public opinion was likely to be against the ministry, would so plainly have been disastrous that Grey cannot be accused of

---

[13] Grey to Bedford, 3 Mar., and Grenville's note, *Fortescue MSS*, ix. 115–16; Canning to Mrs Canning, 11 Mar., Harewood MSS; Grey to Fitzwilliam, 17 Mar., Fitzwilliam MSS; Holland, Memoirs, ii. 190–1, 194; Grey to Bedford, 6 Mar., G. 6/17. See also General C. Grey to C. Wood, 5 Dec. 1858, Hickleton MSS A.4.64.56.

deliberate deception or provocation of the monarch. He simply assumed that the King, being unable to find an alternative government to protect him from the Catholic Bill, had relieved his natural feelings by giving him an uncomfortable half hour in the closet, but that he would allow the Bill to pass. It was a serious miscalculation.

The decision to press ahead with the Bill opened up the division between Sidmouth and his colleagues, and the breach was widened by Grenville's almost incredible tactlessness and want of imagination in choosing this moment to disclose to Sidmouth his latest negotiations with Canning. If Sidmouth had had any scruples about his conduct they now disappeared. He protested to Grenville about Canning, and in his routine audience with the King on 8 March disclosed his opposition to the Bill and quite probably discussed ways and means of defeating it. Three days later the King opened negotiations through secret channels with Portland and the opposition. Grenville saw George III that evening and was deeply disturbed by the King's manner; on the following day Sidmouth told Grey of the King's attitude. Grey at once postponed the second reading of the Catholic Bill and he and Grenville sought audiences at Buckingham House.[14]

The Grenville brothers, Grey, Petty, and Holland met in a state of shock and concern on the evening of the 12th, the day before the audiences. They decided that they would offer to modify the Bill to bring it back within the limits the King was prepared to accept. When Grey saw the King privately on the following day, however, it became apparent that it was too late, and he left the closet believing that the ministry must collapse. 'There has been some mismanagement on both sides of the water,' he wrote to Ponsonby on the 17th, 'and the truth is we have got into a scrape, out of which I do not see any very good way of extricating ourselves.' Though Holland declared that there had been an 'honest' misunderstanding with the King, there can be no doubt that the hope of recovering their position was gone.

It remained to be decided what the best course of action was. Cabinets on the 14th and 15th, to which Sidmouth and Ellenborough were not invited, broke up without agreement. Grey, Holland, and Windham were for pressing on with the Bill, to force the King to secure its Parliamentary defeat by unconstitutional means such as those used in 1783 and to dismiss them. Thomas Grenville, Moira, and Petty argued for dropping the Bill and trying to stay in office. Fitzwilliam, Spencer, and Erskine were unable to attend. Grenville gave his casting vote for dropping the Bill, but the meeting agreed to declare to the King that they felt at liberty to propose such future measures as they might deem necessary. Grey accepted the decision but with grave misgivings and torments of conscience. 'My opinion yielded to that of others', he told Fitzwilliam. The decision as to resignation 'was left so much personally to me, that I could not venture to incur the responsibility of

[14] Pellew, *Sidmouth*, ii. 461, Colchester, *Diary*, ii. 96–7; Grenville to George III, 12 Mar., *Fortescue MSS*, ix. 72; Grey to George III, 12 Mar., *LCGIII*, iv. 524; Sidmouth to Grenville, 11 Mar., BL Add. MS 58928, fo. 161.

dissolving the Government'. He informed Bedford on the 19th that he was decisively influenced by the opinions of others, including Grattan, that resignation would mean the appointment of an administration 'founded on principles of exclusion'. But his mind was not easy. 'From the time I had consented to it', he wrote, 'I never had a happy moment.' He realized that both dropping the Bill and resignation would constitute a breach of faith with the Irish Catholics and the Irish administration; in either event, the ministry was likely to collapse and it only remained to find the honourable way out.[15]

The King provided it. In reply to the ministers' declaration that they reserved the right to propose a similar measure in future, he demanded a written pledge individually from each one that they would not propose 'in any case, any further concessions to the Catholics'. 'To this', wrote Grey to Fitzwilliam, 'there can of course be only one answer ... and the government must be considered as broke up.' He told Bedford of his 'relief' at the King's demand: 'We now stand upon better ground than if we had gone out on the original question.' Even Grenville now accepted that 'this is a pledge which as honest men we cannot give', while Fitzwilliam, whose blunt honesty was never in doubt, offered stout support: 'Circumstanced as things are,' he wrote to Grey, 'I am most sincerely happy, that the result is to be the dissolution of the administration. Consistent with their characters and principles, it must be so, there can be no other honourable conclusion.' Spencer too wrote to say that he favoured resignation, and would have voted for it if he had attended the Cabinet on the 14th. Grenville recognized that the decision was inevitable. As Grey had hoped, his Irish friends endorsed it. Ponsonby wrote that if they had submitted to the King the ministers would 'be considered as *enemies* by the Catholics. No man (myself excepted) will believe you were ever sincere towards them ... your only power is your character.'[16]

The King's demand for the pledge not only cleared Grey's conscience and provided the ministry with an honourable retreat, but it also embarrassed his prospective ministers. A formal invitation to Hawkesbury and Eldon to set about forming a new administration was considered at Portland's residence, Burlington House, on the 19th, but the mood was uncertain: any new government would have to take responsibility for the King's action in face of possible constitutional objections in Parliament, and the attitude of many members in both Houses could not be foretold. Sidmouth, too, could no longer be counted on. Canning broke off his negotiations with Grenville and decided to throw in his lot with his successors—

[15] Grenville to Bedford, 13 Mar., *Fortescue MSS*, ix. 80–2; Grey and Grenville to the Prince of Wales, 2 Feb. 1811, ibid. 116–18; Grey to Ponsonby, 17 Mar., G. 48/1; Holland to Bedford, 13 Mar., BL Add. MS 51661, fo. 71; Colchester, *Diary*, ii. 103; Holland, *Memoirs*, ii. 200–1; *Court & Cabinets of George III*, iv. 136–40; Pellew, *Sidmouth*, ii. 463; Grey to Erskine, 17 Mar., G. 14/2; T. Grenville to Spencer, 13 Mar., Althorp MSS; Grey to Fitzwilliam, 17 Mar., Fitzwilliam MSS; to Bedford, 19 Mar., G. 6/17.
[16] Grey to Fitzwilliam and to Bedford, ibid.; Erskine to Grey, 15 Mar. and reply, 17 Mar., G. 14/2; Grenville to Earl Fortescue, 18 Mar., Earl Fortescue MSS, at Barnstaple; Fitzwilliam to Grey, 18 Mar., G. 14/11; Grenville to Spencer, 17 Mar., Althorp MSS; G. Ponsonby to Grey, 16 Mar., G. 48/1.

a step which barred Sidmouth from any new Cabinet, since Canning was as equally determined not to serve with him as Sidmouth was with Canning. Sidmouth therefore approached Grey, the only member of the Cabinet for whom he retained much respect. The momentary hope of a return of the Talents to office was illusory, however. The crucial question was the mood of the public. A new ministry would presumably take an immediate dissolution of Parliament, and by raising the cry of 'no Popery', a slogan so long acceptable to the British people, ride into office as Pitt had done in 1784 on a wave of popular sentiment. Sniffing the 'Protestant wind', Perceval and Portland agreed to undertake the task. On the 23rd Grey was authorized to state to the House that a new administration was being formed, and on the 25th the Talents handed over the seals of office, the Duke of Portland now assuming the headship of the Treasury which he had given up, in almost precisely similar circumstances, in December 1783.[17]

The Whigs, back in the familiar role of opposition, resolved to fight again the constitutional battle of 1784. Grey was happier than he had been for a month. 'We stand perhaps better with the public, than if we had gone out on what I still think would in principle have been the plainer ground, the original question', he wrote to George Ponsonby. He looked forward with optimism to the prospect of 'a triumphant majority in the House of Commons'. Before the resignation, Grey had suggested a resolution to the House referring to the King's demand and asking who was responsible for advising him to make it—a strong measure, since it seems most likely that the King acted on this occasion without any advice whatever. Others, however, were cautious. When Grey asked Auckland's advice, that elder statesman, who as William Eden had been closely involved with the events of 1783, remarked that it would not do to suggest to the public that they were 'seeking to hold the Throne in thraldom' or that they were 'turned out for Popery'. The only safe ground was to object to their having been required 'to accede to a proposition impossible to be acceded to without personal dishonour and public criminality'. Grenville too was reluctant to force the issue: the question, he warned Grey, was 'full of difficulties' and he added

I feel great repugnance to any course of very active opposition—having been most un-affectedly disinclined to take upon me the task in which I have been engaged, and feeling so much pleasure in an honourable release, I could not easily bring myself to struggle much to get my chains on again.

He repeated that vigorous opposition would contradict 'the whole course of my public life' and pointed out that it would do no good with the country to force the King to continue with a government against his wishes, nor would it be easy to carry on such a government or for it to deal with the Catholic question. 'The fault of all oppositions that I have seen in this country', he declared, 'has been that . . .

---

[17] E. A. Smith, 'The Duke of Portland' in *The Prime Ministers*, ed. H. van Thal, i. (1974) 207–8; Malmesbury, *Diary*, iv. 359–81; Pellew, *Sidmouth*, ii. 443; Grey, *Life and Opinions*, 168–9; Canning to Mrs Canning, 14 Mar., Harewood MSS.

the eagerness of those who were least qualified to decide has always run away with the judgement of those who are supposed to direct.'[18]

It was with the Foxites that the political initiative therefore lay. Grey and his friends resolved to press their case in Parliament, where Tierney calculated that they would have 240 certain votes against only 150 supporters of the new ministry. Grey set to work to get the Irish members to attend with the help of George Ponsonby: 'everything depends up on it', he wrote, and he was optimistic enough to ask what the attitude of the Catholics would be if the Talents were to force their way back into office. He also tried to arrange for the Prince's support, but he was unsuccessful in both attempts. The Irish did not come, and despite Grey's assurance that if the Prince could be 'kept steady by any reasonable sacrifices I should fully concur in . . . making them', the influence of Lady Hertford and Lord Yarmouth against the Catholic cause was stronger. Only Erskine of the Prince's friends voted for the opposition in the Lords. Grey's sole success was to win the vote of Granville Leveson-Gower despite his connection with Canning. In the meantime the ministry's efforts bore heavier fruit. Anti-Catholic opinion was stirred up in the country by newspaper articles and by addresses from Cambridge, Oxford, and Dublin Universities, preparing the ground for a general election and putting pressure on MPs who might fear for their seats. When Thomas Brand moved the opposition's censure on 9 April it was defeated by 226 to 258, a result attributable to the absence of the 'Saints' and of most of the Irish members, in addition to the hesitancy of nearly a hundred of the new members elected in 1806 as supporters of the Talents. Grey was present at the debate but unable to take part because of a violent headache: he could scarcely listen to the speeches. A similar motion in the Lords was lost on the 13th by 90 to 171, and Lyttelton's motion in the Commons two days later regretting the change of administration was defeated by 198 to 244. On the 25th the King agreed to the dissolution.[19]

The collapse of the Talents' administration was mainly the result of its fundamental weaknesses. It never overcame its original division into three factions. The Whigs and the Grenvilles had managed on the whole to work together because of Grenville's personal rapport with Fox and then Grey, and because on matters of religious and foreign policy these leaders were broadly in agreement, despite dissent from their respective extremists on both sides. Sidmouth's adherence was weakened by the slave-trade abolition and by Grenville's flirtation with Canning as well as by his feelings over the principle of the Catholic Bill and the tactics

[18] Grey to G. Ponsonby, 27 Mar., G. 47/11; Colchester, *Diary*, ii. 104; Grey to Auckland, 22 Mar., BL Add. MS 34457, fos. 262–3; Auckland to Grey, 23 Mar., G. 5/5; Grenville to Grey, 20, 23 Mar., G. 21/2. Bathurst warned Grenville on 10 Mar. that 'every moderate man must, and does deprecate such a struggle [with the King]. The country is not in a situation to bear it, and it would lose much more by such a battle than you could possibly gain by such a victory': BL Add. MS 58944, fo. 152.

[19] Tierney to Grey, 11, 18 May, G. 55; to Grenville, 19 May, BL Dropmore MSS, Ser. 2, B7 (i). Grey told Auckland that the party hoped to divide 220, 'not including the Sidmouths': BL Add. MS 34457, fos. 262–3; Grey to G. Ponsonby, 28 Mar., 24 Apr., G. 47/11. Grey estimated an opposition vote of 250 on the second division. *Parl. Deb.* ix. 284–349, 350–423, 432–75. Holland, *Memoirs*, ii. 220–1.

used to introduce it. Grey was one of the few colleagues in the Cabinet who built up a successful working and personal relationship with him and who gained his respect, cemented no doubt by their common opinion of Canning, but even that alliance was weakened when Sidmouth deserted Grey's 'European' strategy and threw his support behind the advocates of South American diversions. At the end, it was Sidmouth whom Grey blamed for breaking up the administration though, as he told Fitzwilliam, he did not believe that he had acted dishonourably. In truth, Fox's death was the crucial blow to the Talents for no one else possessed his flair for conciliating difficult colleagues and threading a way through differences of opinion and policy.

Grey learnt several lessons for the future from his brief experience in office. Despite the heavy pressures under which he had to work at the Admiralty and in the Foreign Office, he seems to have performed his duties efficiently and to have enjoyed doing so. There is no trace in his letters of this period of the despondency characteristic of his correspondence in opposition, and the vigour with which he reacted to the crisis over the King's resistance to the Catholic Bill suggests a new confidence in himself and his abilities. Holland wrote that Grey's 'perspicuous statements and manly character' gave him 'fresh ascendancy in the Commons' from this time. He did not endorse Grenville's reluctance to engage in a renewed parliamentary struggle against the Court and he acted energetically to keep the Whigs together in a cause which he believed was honourable and constitutional. Yet he resented the way in which he thought he had been forced by others to walk into the King's trap on an issue on which public opinion was hostile. He declared to Ponsonby that he had been pushed by the Irish Catholics into a premature action which could only result in the defeat of their hopes;

their hasty proceedings ... and above all the speech of Keogh, have not only produced the dissolution of the Administration, but have indisposed the mind of the public towards them, to a degree that will not easily be recovered.... I yielded to the opinions of others, more particularly to that of Grattan, and to the fear of re-establishing an Orange Government in Ireland.

The incident stayed in Grey's mind for the rest of his life. He was convinced that the original mistake of the Talents was not to insist on Catholic relief as a condition of their appointment in 1806, when the King would have been unable to find an alternative to them; three years later he declared to Grenville that he was determined in future 'not to take office unless the power of *immediately* proposing measures for the conciliation of Ireland be conceded to us'. Though, as his son wrote in 1861, this determination 'resulted in his exclusion from office for upwards of three and twenty years', it was one he never wavered from. Catholic emancipation, rather than parliamentary reform, blocked his return to the Cabinet until 1830.[20]

[20] Ibid. 221; Grey to Lord Ponsonby, 19 Mar. 1807, G. 48/1; to Grenville, 3 Nov. 1809, *Fortescue MSS*, ix. 362–4, Grey, *Life and Opinions*, 165.

On reform, Grey learnt a different lesson. The fact that the Talents had resigned over their refusal to desert the Catholics made it essential, in Grey's view, that they should continue to be publicly pledged to their interests. Reform, however, had not been involved in the fall of the ministry, nor had it ever been discussed in the Cabinet. It must therefore, remain an 'open' question as long as the Grenville alliance continued. Grey felt very keenly the accusation of the radicals that his failure to move for reform while in office marked his apostasy from the question. He argued that since it would be impossible for him to form an administration with Grenville on a pledge to reform, its supporters should accept that a government of a generally liberal character was all that could be hoped for in the foreseeable future. He laid down his views as follows:

It is in vain that you carry on a Government in the true spirit of all those measures, that you are moderate, forbearing and liberal; if you do not force their literal execution, if you enter into any compromise with those whom you have formerly opposed, in a word if you do not make it utterly impossible to form an Administration in which you can take any share, you will be branded as an apostate. . . . The lesson that I have learned therefore is to pledge myself to as little as possible whilst in opposition, and when in Government, if ever it should be my lot to be again in that situation, to do as much as I can.

Grey took the view that although reformist opinion should be encouraged to look to the Whigs for ultimate support, the radicals should admit the necessity to work gradually towards it; in the meantime, it should not stand in the way of the Whigs' coming into office and conducting the government in a generally liberal spirit. The radicals' refusal to accept that position was to plague Grey's reputation and relationship with them for the next 23 years.[21]

One further consequence of the Talents ministry remained to be worked out in the year 1807. The new government under Portland immediately asked the King for a dissolution, despite the short period since the last election, and the Commons was dismissed on 27 April. Grey's position in Northumberland was immediately menaced by the Duke's desertion from the Foxite camp. His return had been uncontested in the county since his first election in 1786, but now the Duke put up his own son, Lord Percy, as a third candidate. The election of 1807 was marked everywhere by the cry of 'No Popery' raised by Perceval in his constituency at Northampton and adopted by the supporters of the new administration throughout the country. Grenville wrote angrily in mid-April of their 'profligate . . . attempt to excite in this country a spirit of religious dissent at a time when we have so much need of showing ourselves as a united people'. He castigated the new administration as 'a Government formed by a court intrigue, and resting for its support on a hypocritical attempt to excite a popular clamour in favour of religious interests which no man of sense can believe in any danger'. Nevertheless, the prejudices of the people were easily aroused. On his arrival at Alnwick from

---

[21] Grey to Holland, 19 Mar. 1811, G. 35; Francis to Grey, 22 May 1797, G. 46.

London on 10 May, Grey found the cry of the crowd to be against him, and in addition discovered that the shipowners of Shields had been agitated against his interest as a result of the American Intercourse Bill, which they conceived to be harmful to their trade. Three days later, after canvassing Alnwick, Morpeth, and district, he expressed his forebodings of defeat. He was particularly mortified that 'the name of Lord Percy far outweighs all my parliamentary exertion during twenty years'. He was incensed at what he considered the Duke's 'duplicity, treachery and meanness', for when the dissolution was first announced Northumberland had assured him in London of his wish to see 'the county not disturbed', while on the same day sending his agents to begin his son's canvass.

The ten days' start which Percy's agents had gained proved decisive and Grey decided not to spend his uncle's money to fight a contest when his father's age and health made it unlikely that he would remain in the Commons for many months. So, despite a superior show of hands at the nomination meeting on the 15th, and despite the favour of the crowd at Alnwick, where 'nothing was heard but my name in the streets, and those who had got drunk with Lord Percy and Beaumont's ale, did nothing but cry "Howick for ever"',' he withdrew from the contest without going to the poll. His retiring speech, wrote one observer, 'harrowed one's very soul, and roused alternately all one's passions—of admiration for him, of hatred for his vile betrayers and of contempt for the miserable wretches who were opposed to him. The multitude were affected to the greatest possible degree of enthusiasm.' Grey himself affected relief at his release from a burdensome duty. 'I shall now have plenty of time', he remarked characteristically to Mary, 'for they will not send me to the House of Commons any more, and I shall be able to stay with dear Mama and you as much as I like; to go to Howick when I please and not be obliged to come away before I chuse it.' Another cause for thankfulness was that he would no longer have to put up with the Duke's tantrums in local society or in London. 'All communication between him and me must be at an end', he avowed, 'and I never will set my foot again within the walls of the Castle in which he lives.' He rejoiced to Holland that 'what he has done will relieve me from the necessity of listening to his lies and his small talk on Saturday, his damned dinner at Alnwick Castle for the remainder of my life.'[22]

Grey's parliamentary career was not interrupted, however, for despite his reluctance to return to Westminster his friends were quick to ensure his election elsewhere. Lauderdale and Grenville approached the Duke of Argyll, Lord Rosslyn, and Lady Stafford for a Scottish seat, but Lord Thanet, an old friend, acted immediately to return Grey for Appleby, and Bedford also offered Tavistock. Until Grey was seated, Holland declared, it would be 'useless to think of our conduct on the opening of Parliament which must be regulated in a great measure by the circumstance of his being present or not'. Thomas Grenville too admitted

[22] Grenville to Minto, 16 Apr. 1807, Minto MSS, N.L.S. 11139; Grey to Mary [10], 12, 13, 15, 17, 19, 22 May, G. 27; to Lauderdale, 15 May, BL Dropmore MSS Ser. 2, B7 (i); to Grenville, 17 May, ibid., Grey, *Life and Opinions*, 171.

that the opposition would have been in 'a most helpless state' without Grey to lead them. Grey described Thanet as having acted 'in the handsomest manner'and declared that he would never forget his obligation to him, for despite his professed desire to remain at leisure Grey was soon looking forward to renewing the attack in the Commons on the new ministers whose conduct he so deeply resented.[23]

The parliamentary session after the general election was a very short one, and it was Grey's last in the House of Commons. Grenville counted upon over 200 supporters in the new House and Grey was generally acclaimed as the leader of those forces. When the House assembled for the debate on the Address at the end of June he spoke first in the debate, accusing the ministry of exerting an influence in the elections 'such as they ought to have been ashamed of' and declaring their raising of religious animosities as 'criminal'. He denied that the Talents had attempted to 'force the conscience of the king' and declared that the use of the coronation oath to bar any religious changes was absurd: there had been no wish 'to undermine the Protestant establishment of the country'. He even called upon Pitt's name in his support:

Although he should belie the whole of his political life, if he were to consider Mr. Pitt as the extraordinary statesman which he had been represented to have been by the hon. gentleman, he was yet aware that he possessed great qualities and splendid talents.

And he quoted Pitt, Fox, and Burke as 'three men, whose talents, whose wisdom, and whose experience, were as great, or perhaps greater, than those of any triumvirate that ever existed'. He asserted that the present ministers had declared an unconstitutional doctrine, that the King could act without any responsible adviser, that they had interfered with the freedom of elections by using the King's name, and had endangered the throne itself by encouraging the notion that the King could appeal to the people for support. A further section of his speech defended the previous ministry's foreign policy and military system, advocated conciliation of Ireland, and declared that though he would oppose none of the new government's measures which appeared to be of service to the country, he would be an enemy to a ministry founded on court intrigue, internally divided, and led by a man 'of whom he would say nothing'.[24]

Grey's powerful and wide ranging speech filled fourteen columns of *Hansard* but the result of the debate showed that the new opposition's hopes were wildly optimistic. They mustered only 155 votes against 350, a majority convincing enough to condemn Grey to many years of opposition. He stayed for the rest of the session, speaking frequently in debates against the government's measures and

[23] Lauderdale to Grenville [May 1807], Rosslyn to Grenville, 26 May, Lady Stafford to Grenville, 21 May, Holland to Grenville, 24 May, T. Grenville to Grenville, 28 May, BL Dropmore MSS Ser. 2, B7 (i); Grey to Holland, 20 May, BL Add. MS 51550, fos. 32–7. Grey gave up the seat at Appleby at the end of July and chose to be returned by Bedford for Tavistock, a seat he held, without ever sitting in the Commons for the borough, until he went to the Lords in November.

[24] Grenville to Auckland, 1, 10 June, BL Add. MS 34457, fos. 301, 303. Tierney had calculated an opposition strength of 210 during the elections: to Grey, 11, 18 May, G. 55; to Grenville, 19 May, BL Dropmore MSS, Ser. 2, B7 (i); *Parl. Deb.* ix. 614–27 (26 June).

in defence of those of the Talents. He took the opportunity on 30 June to declare his pride in being a 'party man',

first, because he thought a party connection was the most effectual way to promote any public object; and secondly, because, to say the least of it, he could not think from what he had seen in that House, or heard out of it, that men who disclaimed party, were the most remarkable for independence and purity.

He also made it clear that the Whig party wished to distance itself from Burdett and the radicals. Although he supported Burdett's nomination to the Finance Committee, he went out of his way in doing so to remark that 'there was no gentleman on the other side more averse to the general conduct of that person than he was ... Notwithstanding the attempts always made to connect us with this person's party, there was no party in the country more obnoxious to them than that with which I have the honour to act.' He was equally uncompromising on Ireland, pledging himself on 6 July to 'a general system of conciliation and kindness' to that country; nevertheless, his last speech of the session was on the Irish Insurrection Bill, in which he professed his support for the general principle of the Bill, objecting only to some of its details.[25]

That was to be Grey's last speech in the Commons. The session closed on 14 August and the Houses did not meet again until the following January. By that time Grey had become a member of the Lords in succession to his father, who died on 14 November. The threat that had hung over Grey's head for the past six years was now a reality. Had the eighteenth-century constitution allowed for the renunciation of peerages, there can be no doubt that he would have done so, but he had to resign himself for the rest of his lifetime to absence from the chamber where his political reputation had been made and where his heart always lay. The year 1807 closed the first half of Grey's political career.

[25] Ibid. 710, 714, 741, 924.

Part II

1807–1845

4 The Lessons of Experience, 1807–1815

Grey's resignation in the spring of 1807 and his succession to the peerage in November ended the first phase of his career. During the next 23 years, he frequently expressed reluctance to return to public life or to shoulder political responsibility. This was to some extent a purposeful political strategy, for if his suggestions that he was ready to retire from the leadership of the Whigs were ever taken seriously he quickly let it be understood that he had no such intention. His attitude, however, also reflected a growing sense of political frustration and impotence and the strong counter-attraction of his domestic life at Howick where his family was established after 1801.

Grey's character was a strange blend of headstrong ambition and of moody despondency. In his middle years, he was a man of striking appearance. He was tall (at Eton he was nicknamed 'Lanky'), slender, with a stately bearing. Byron remarked that 'He has the patrician thoroughbred look...which I dote upon', and Melbourne commented on 'his commanding figure, his lofty yet gracious deportment'.[1] His expression was thoughtful, detached, and often tinged with melancholy. A high forehead and small, intelligent, but cold eyes gave him a disdainful air and reflected an aristocratic and imperious temper. Women thought him handsome, and were often attracted by his looks and his manner in society, though they sometimes found him vain, moody and inconsiderate. His treatment of Georgiana during her exile when she bore his child and after her return to England showed that there was a good deal of selfishness and even petulance in his character. Many considered him cold and aloof, especially in contrast to Fox. Hobhouse related how when, in Grey's middle life, he occasionally went into Brooks's Club, the conversation would stumble and flag, whereas Fox's arrival had always brightened the room. He described Grey as 'peevish and wayward...always desponding, always out of spirits unless he thinks he is riding the winning horse', and 'always thinking of himself and his failures in life'.[2]

The decade after 1792 marked a low point in Grey's career, and his mood was restless and irritable as a result. His disastrous affair with Georgiana and the blunder he committed in rushing into the Friends of the People combined to depress his spirits. His marriage to Mary Ponsonby offered the prospect of a more settled life, but for the first six and a half years they lacked a permanent home, being forced to rent houses near to London or to stay at Howick as Sir Henry's

[1] P. Ziegler, *Melbourne* (1976), 59.

[2] Ibid. 71; Broughton, *Recollections of a Long Life*, ed. Lady Dorchester, iii. 21, 95; iv. 31, 55.

guests. Grey expressed a romantic nostalgia for country life and pursuits, away from the distractions of London society. In the spring of 1801 he thought

it would be a good plan, if I could borrow the money, to buy some small place with a few acres of ground... [which] would assist very much in our housekeeping, and being our own it might furnish us with some occupation.... I really am quite tired of this uncertain and unsettled life, without any home and without any occupation.

Howick itself was inconveniently far from London, and the four or five day journey made it impossible to reside there during parliamentary sessions. 'I wish I could divest myself of all partiality for it', Grey wrote in 1800:

The distance will certainly not only be a great inconvenience on account of the education of our dear children but will make it almost impossible to have any society which is pleasant; which, God knows, the County itself cannot afford.

By this time, the arrival of the first three children made it difficult for Mary to accompany him to London or to the round of country house visits which kept the Whigs together, during the secession, as a social and political body. Grey wrote from Woburn in the summer of 1800 of the pleasure and good companionship of these gatherings, but added

they do not make up to me for the absence of my Mary, and my sweet children. They are so necessary to me, that I cannot enjoy as I ought to society anywhere from home.... Indeed if I were at liberty to make my way of living conform to my situation I feel confident that I should have no regrets to disturb my happiness. A small comfortable house, a little land to afford me an occupation out of doors, my Mary and my children are all that are necessary to me, but if we were only rich enough to entertain occasionally at home a small society with comfort, I should not have a wish ungratified.[3]

In the summer of 1801, Sir Henry announced his intention of retiring to a smaller house and 'in the handsomest way possible' offered his nephew the full use of Howick 'on our *own bottoms*.... You must begin soon to make your preparations,' Grey wrote to Mary, 'and above all prepare yourself to become a very notable farmer's wife. For we shall be very poor, but I hope too very comfortable.' They occupied Howick as master and mistress on 17 July 1801—44 years to the day before Grey's death there.[4]

The house at Howick was a plain, classical building erected by Sir Henry in 1782. After his uncle's death in 1808 Grey set about making it more comfortable as a family home, and carried out many internal alterations as well as embarking on an ambitious planting scheme in the gardens to protect the house from the keen winds blowing from the North Sea, only a mile distant. His son Charles remarked in the biography of his father in 1861 that apart from one area near the house there was hardly one tree then standing that was not of Grey's planting.[5] He laid out extensive walks, amounting in all to seven miles in length, which

[3] Grey to Mary [*c.* 13 Apr.] 1801, 22, 23 July [1800], G. 27.
[4] To Mary [June] 1801, ibid.
[5] Grey, *Life and Opinions*, 401–4.

became the regular Sunday exercise for the whole family. Grey's life at Howick appealed to a side of his temperament which was repelled by the bustle of London society and politics. Howick offered the possibility of constructive achievement which politics seemed to deny him.

A succession of children soon confirmed his commitment to his country home. The first, Louisa, born in April 1797, was a close and affectionate favourite with both her parents. She later cemented the family friendship with the Lambtons of County Durham by marrying John, 'radical Jack', son of Grey's old associate in the Friends of the People and later first Earl of Durham. His proud and imperious temper surpassed that of his father-in-law and provided the Reform Ministry of 1830–4 with one of its most radical and troublesome members. The Greys' second child was Elizabeth, born in July 1798, the third, Caroline, arrived in August 1799, and a fourth daughter, Georgiana, Grey's own favourite, in February 1801. Elizabeth married in 1826 John Croker Bulteel, a Devonshire gentleman,[6] and Caroline in 1827 the Hon. George Barrington. Georgiana never married, and in later years became the archetypal maiden aunt to a large brood of Grey's grandchildren. After eleven years of marriage there was still no son: the longed-for heir arrived, to Grey's intense delight, three days after Christmas in 1802. He was christened Henry after Grey's uncle, and grew up to succeed his father as third Earl and to become one of the leading Whig politicians of the next generation, serving as Colonial Secretary in Russell's government of 1846–52. Like his father he was a man of strong personality, and impatient temperament; an 'advanced' Whig for his time, in the 1830s and 40s he often distressed his father by his enthusiastic support of liberal causes, such as free trade and the abolition of the death penalty. He was a dutiful son none the less, even though both Grey and Mary found him less appealing than their second son. This was Charles, named after his father and born in March 1804. He entered the army, rose to the rank of General, and became equerry and private secretary to the Prince Consort and then to Queen Victoria. It was he who produced his father's first biography in 1861.

The birth of Charles was followed 17 months later by another son, Frederick William, who made his career in the navy and rose to the rank of Admiral. In May 1807 a fifth daughter, Mary, was born. She later married Charles Wood, a member of a rising Yorkshire family with landed estates and colliery interests. He became the first Viscount Halifax in 1866. Almost exactly a year later came a fourth son, William. He was the only one of the Greys' fifteen surviving children not to live beyond childhood, dying of scarlet fever in 1815. By then he had five more brothers—George (b. 1809), who like Frederick was to become an Admiral, Thomas (b. 1810) who died at the age of sixteen, John (b. 1812) who entered the Church and became a canon of Durham, Francis Richard (b. 1813), another future clergyman, later rector of Morpeth, and husband of a daughter of the sixth Earl of Carlisle, and Henry Cavendish (b. 1814) who went into the army. The family was still not complete: the last child was born in February 1819, when his mother

---

[6] By this marriage she became an ancestress of the present Princess of Wales.

was almost 43. He was William George, who entered the diplomatic service and became secretary of the legation at Paris.

So Howick rapidly filled up with a group of lively and active children, in whom their mother and father delighted. The family atmosphere was unusually relaxed in an age when aristocratic parents normally saw little of their offspring and expected to be addressed by them in formal and respectful terms. Grey romped with his children when they were young, encouraged them in their games and pursuits, allowed them to roam freely over the countryside around Howick and, to the consternation of visitors, to wander at will over the cliffs by the sea. He even permitted them to use his christian name, or its abbreviation 'Car', as they also spoke to their mother as 'Mary'. In their letters to their children they often referred to each other in these terms. Grey also took an active interest in his family's education. He refused to send his boys to public schools, remembering his own unhappy years at Marylebone and at Eton, but a succession of private tutors and governesses educated them at home until the boys were old enough for university. That did not mean that they received a casual or deficient education. Grey himself supervised their progress and tried to implant in them his own fondness for literature by the family custom of reading aloud in the evenings—as he did to Mary when they were alone. General Charles Grey later remarked that:[7]

Of all the recollections connected with our Howick life, I do not know that there is any that comes back to me more vividly, or revives more pleasant thoughts, than that of our evening readings. From the earliest period I can remember, to within three years of his death, this was a practice never dropped, scarcely even intermitted, for a single day: and any unfortunate stray visitor who might occasion its interruption got, I fear, but a cold reception and black looks from the family.

And how beautifully my father read! Those who still remember his speaking in the House of Lords need not be told that there was a rich melody in his voice, a modulation of tone that without strain or affectation adapted itself to the varying interest of his subjects—and, in any touching passage, a pathos of expression that sent a thrill to the hearts of his hearers.

The readings were taken from a wide variety of sources:

Whatever amongst the publications of the day provided amusement as well as instruction, was eagerly watched for. Memoirs, travels, novels,—and notwithstanding what my father says of good novels being rare—these were the days of the 'Waverley novels', of Cowper, Washington Irvine [*sic*] etc.—of the poems of Byron, Scott, Crabbe, Rogers, etc., etc.

Much care was also taken over the formal education of the children, in the choice of tutors and governesses and, later, of universities. Grey's feeling that his own education had been defective was perhaps responsible for the careful eye he kept on his sons' industry, or, as he often feared, their idleness. He stressed the importance of acquiring the habit of constant occupation, and during his absences from home wrote frequently to enquire after their reading and other studies.

[7] Grey MSS D2, copy of *Life and Opinions* with MS additions by Gen. Charles Grey at p. 419.

Charles remarked in 1861 that his father could not bear idleness, and that the hours for study were strictly regulated. Grey set the example, for, Charles wrote,

no one, perhaps, ever possessed a greater power of occupying himself at almost all times. Even those broken minutes, those odd quarters of an hour, ... were seldom thrown away.

Waiting for others to be ready to walk or ride, he would take up a book 'and had the power of giving it at once his undivided attention'.[8] He expected the same from his sons.

Henry was his particular concern, for he was intended to follow his father into public life and to be a future statesman. Henry, however, was a difficult and obstinate boy. Grey worried about his lack of interest in literature, the classics, and history, all of which he regarded as important for the lessons they taught to public men. On Henry's coming of age in 1818 his father warned him against slothful habits—'there is no pleasure in idleness' he wrote—and recommended a diet of biographies of 'eminent persons, both ancient and modern', particularly Plutarch, and Middleton's *Life of Cicero*, which he described as

the book which almost above any other I should recommend ... From this book you will learn the true road to real distinction and true glory; the glory of a virtuous and honourable life, passed, as I trust yours will be in supporting the Constitution and Liberty of your Country, even at the expense, if it should be required, of every private interest.

Modern literature was also prescribed. Grey himself was a fervent admirer of Scott and of Byron's poetry, but he urged his son to be critical and discriminating. Hearing that he was reading *Rob Roy*, he remarked that it was not 'near so good as *Old Mortality*; not perhaps equal to any of the others ... It is, however, I think, a book of great merit.' In *Childe Harold* too Grey found fault; of the fourth Canto, he wrote, 'It is very obscure and the versification very inharmonious, though it contains, as everything of Lord Byron must, occasional passages of great beauty.' He nevertheless admitted that he preferred Byron's poetry to Scott's: 'I cannot bring myself to admire the style of poem which W. Scott has made so fashionable', he wrote in 1813. 'How much better the stanza of Childe Harold: Lord Byron has genius enough to be above trick and I wish he would adhere to the stanza of Spencer [*sic*], or the verse of Dryden and Pope.'[9] Spenser was a particular favourite of both Grey and Mary; but though Grey liked to read the latest novels, with a particular fondness for Maria Edgeworth, he allowed his opinion of Jane Austen to be influenced by Lady Holland, who disliked her books and, when *Emma* appeared, wrote that she could not recommend Grey to go to the trouble of reading it.

Grey tried to make a friend of his eldest son as well as supervising his education, but like many ambitious fathers he sometimes went about it heavy-handedly. He wrote in 1818 that he 'should have the greatest pleasure in having you with me; in taking you with me frequently to places where I visit; in making little excursions

---

[8] Grey, *Life and Opinions*, 412–13.   [9] Letters to Henry, G. 25.

of pleasure with you; and in partaking both in your business and your amusements'. Yet he could never refrain from trying to correct his faults: even as late as 1820 he warned him about his careless handwriting and spelling:

I hate to be obliged to find fault, but if you were to write to a stranger a letter with such faults, and so smeared, as that which I have received from you it really would be discreditable to you.

When Henry went up to Trinity College, Cambridge, he was exhorted to work hard and to qualify himself for the role his father had marked out for him:

... I am ambitious for you. You owe it to yourself, to your family, to me to occupy that station worthily, to which birth and fortune have destined you. Whether the country is to be extricated from the coils and dangers which a course of bad government has brought upon it, or whether it is doomed to experience convulsions which may produce a new revolution in society, it is equally necessary that you should qualify yourself to sustain a conspicuous and an honourable part.... If to these highest of all motives could be added anything of a personal character, I would appeal to your affection for me, to which, I trust, I shall never appeal in vain, and to your sense of the comfort and the pleasure I must feel, as I am retiring from the world, to see you advancing into it.

Grey's disillusionment and frustration with his own career fed his ambition to see his son achieve what he felt he himself had been unable to do; during the 1820s he frequently expressed a conviction that his political career was over, and that he was too old to pick up the threads again. He consequently tried to live his political life again through his eldest son:

I have every reason to hope that you will not disappoint the expectations I have formed; if you should, I believe it would break my heart... All my ambition is now for you; and to see you rise to the distinction, which an honourable and independent exercise of your talents will command, and which may be attended with equal advantage to the publick, and credit to yourself, is the first wish of my heart. To assist you in so honourable a pursuit with all the means which my experience or my influence may afford will be equally my duty and my pride.

Henry's entry into political life was eagerly anticipated by his father. Even four months before his twenty-first birthday, in August 1823, Grey responded eagerly to a hint that there might shortly be a vacancy for one of the Northumberland seats, though he added that 'I could not, in justice to my family, embark in the expense of a contest.' When one of the county members, Thomas Beaumont, applied for the Chiltern Hundreds in February 1824 Grey let it be known that Henry might be available as a candidate, though repeating his warning about a contest and further stipulating that he would allow him to stand only as an independent, and not under the aegis of the Duke. When it became apparent however that Henry might be the Whig candidate, Beaumont, who was both a radical and a personal enemy of the Greys, decided to retain his seat. The episode established Henry's claim to consideration as Whig candidate when a vacancy should occur, and in September 1825 Grey declared that he had made up his mind to bring him forward at the next opportunity. This unexpectedly occurred in the spring of 1826 when the other member, Charles Brandling, died. Grey professed annoyance at what he suspected was a plot to bring in Sir Charles Monck as a second radical member, and announced that 'my intention is that, come what may, Henry shall be put in nomination, and if he receives the countenance which I have a right to hope and expect, that he shall stand a poll against any candidate that may offer.' This time Henry waited on the Duke and received his approval as 'a very proper person' and his promise of neutrality. Henry immediately opened a canvass, but found the Whig and radical gentry of Northumberland reluctant to support a son of Grey's—even the Bigges and the Swinburnes seemed hostile to the prospect of an aristocratic member for Northumberland. Henry persevered only to lay a foundation for a future candidature at the general election, which was due within a year.[10]

Grey encouraged Henry to gain experience and helped him draft his speeches, attempting to tone down his more liberal enthusiasms but counselling that 'Honesty is always the best policy' and that 'nothing is ever gained by ambiguity or concealment' on political topics. He nevertheless tried to influence Henry's platform in the direction of his own cautious and moderate Whiggism. When the general election was announced in the early summer of 1826, Grey advised, in a letter intended as a model for a speech,[11] the avoidance of

sudden, sweeping, and extreme changes, which often produce evils greater than the abuse which it is intended to correct—I would rather approach my object by more gradual and easier steps, which if they may be somewhat slower in reaching it, at least afford the security of not going beyond it, and in the attempt at change producing a convulsion which may shake the whole frame of society to its very foundation.

The platform of his radical rival, Beaumont, was deplored as an attempt at 'humbling in the dust the proud aristocracy which he denounces as hostile to the best interests of the county. It is not therefore change but revolution that he preaches.' Whiggism supported

the more popular parts of the constitution ... but it looks also to that graduation of ranks, and to the due influence of each of the branches of the constitution.... As a Whig I will resist with equal zeal and with equal firmness the corrupt influence of the Court, and the indiscriminate attacks on all the institutions which have been sanctioned by the wisdom of ages and the feelings of mankind.

Behind Grey's concern for his son's political principles there lay an even greater anxiety about the cost of winning the seat. Grey wrote in March 1826:

You must be aware of my situation. I have a large family for which I am bound to provide. From your younger brothers and sisters, whose portions will be scanty enough, I can take nothing. These will form a large addition to the very heavy burthens with which my estate

[10] Grey to Sir M. W. Ridley, 31 Aug. 1823, 16 Sept., 14 Nov. 1825, Ridley MSS, Northumberland Record Office ZRI/25/45, 48.
[11] 15 May 1826, G. 25.

is already charged, and if further increased by the expense of a severe contest, will leave you, considering the rank and situation you will have to sustain, subject to great difficulty and embarrassment. The decision therefore must rest chiefly with you, for it is on *you* that the burthen will chiefly fall. My comforts may be somewhat diminished for the short remainder of my life, but that is comparatively of little consequence.

The cost of the canvass in the spring of 1826 exceeded his worst fears. He was astounded, he wrote on 17 May, at the size of the bills, which offered 'a frightful prospect' in case of an actual contest, 'one indeed which I cannot face'. The expenses were already over four times what he expected: and, he wrote when the election occurred, 'to continue an expense of at least £1,000 a day, without a possible chance of success, would be the height of folly.' Howick therefore withdrew from the poll and took a seat provided for him by his father's friend Lord Darlington at Winchelsea. Henry blamed his own misjudgement for the catastrophe and his father's financial sacrifice; in February 1827 one of the estate properties had to be sold for £40,000 to cover the cost. At least Howick was now in the Commons, however, and Grey wrote in December 1826 to urge him to attend constantly, to 'serve a regular apprenticeship till you have made yourself thoroughly master of all the forms and proceedings of the House'. It was Fox's maxim, he advised him, for 'all the young ones' to listen carefully to every speaker in every debate

as the best rule for becoming a good debater. To listen well, is the first, and perhaps the most difficult thing to attain, and the power of fixing your attention, and keeping it fixed during a long discussion, is that which I should recommend to you next to study most and to acquire.

He continued for some time to advise Henry on the content and manner of his speeches as well as to demand accounts from him of the debates in general. In the close supervision of his son's political career he tried perhaps to compensate for what he thought the failure of his own.[12]

Henry's launching into the political world was only part of Grey's efforts to establish his sons in their careers. Charles's progress in the army was equally close to his father's heart, and no effort was spared to put him in the way of promotion. Grey rather regretted Charles's choice of the military profession. In 1820, writing of the 'Queen's trial', he mentioned to him the 'extraordinary display of talents' by Brougham and Denman, her Whig counsel: had Charles been present, it might have stimulated his ambition for a career at the bar,

for which nature has given you all the necessary qualifications, and which in this country affords the certain means not only of acquiring an independence, but a splendid fortune, and opens the way to the higher distinctions of the state.

Characteristically, he added:

[12] 14 Mar.; Henry to Grey, 14 May, Grey to Henry, 17 May and 'Monday evening' [1826], 2 Dec. 1826, 9 Mar. 1827, Henry to Grey, 22 Feb., 2 Mar. 1827, G. 25; Grey to Mary, 5 June, G. 29.

Industry and resolution alone are wanting, but I have said so much upon this subject on other occasions that I will not repeat it now, and can only regret your choice of a profession, which affords much less opportunity for distinction, and in which success will depend too much on accident and favour.

Nothing was lacking however on Grey's part to push his son's chances of promotion. In 1821 Charles secured a commission in a regiment which took him to Ireland, accompanied again by his father's admonitions as to diligence and the best use of his spare time. He could do no better, Grey wrote, than read and translate Demosthenes, and cultivate the habit of learning by heart Latin and English verse and especially Homer, who

as well as the most eloquent perhaps of the ancient historians and orators, is a most useful exercise for the memory, and besides stores the mind with quotations and images, which give a grace and a force to every species of composition. Though the army is your profession, and having chosen it I hope you will pursue it with steadiness and perseverance, you are not to consider yourself as precluded from other things.

An opportunity might arise for attachment to foreign embassies or even for entering Parliament, and he should neglect no opportunity to qualify himself for such possibilities. Grey especially recommended study of history as

most advantageous. . . . I should advise you to read history systematically, that is by regularly connecting it in your mind, according to the different periods, the ancient, the history of the Middle Ages, and the Modern, and connecting also the history of different countries, according to the different periods, with each other.

He concluded:

There is nothing that I will not do for you, whilst you continue to deserve it, as I am sure you always will, that I can do consistently with what I owe to the rest of a large family. But you must be sensible how many demands I have upon me, and of the difficulty which I sometimes have in meeting them.

In the summer of 1821 Charles was temporarily reduced to half pay, which led his father again to enquire whether he would not do better to choose a different career, and again to propose the law as the alternative. His objection to the army was that 'your success in it must in all ordinary cases depend on the favour of those whose conduct may be the most exposed to censure', and he declared he had not given up his hopes that Charles would enter politics, pointing out that the great Chatham was a cornet of dragoons when first elected to the Commons. No doubt the expense of promoting his son's progress in the army weighed as heavily with Grey as his wish to see him distinguish himself in public life; in 1823 and again in 1825 he was advancing money for the purchase of rank, hoping to establish him in a Guards regiment 'though it will go far to ruin me'; in 1825 he secured him a half-pay captaincy in the 17th Foot, recently returned from India and to be stationed at Edinburgh, where he would be within reach of Howick and of 'opportunities for improvement which I hope you will not neglect'. In the meantime he read him a lesson on the scale of his debts, but agreed to pay them, though 'I may perhaps be under the necessity of denying myself some comforts'. Two years later Charles was in Portugal with a new regiment, the 43rd Light Infantry, and in October 1827 he was appointed an ADC to the Lord-Lieutenant of Ireland, Lord Anglesey. When Wellington became Prime Minister Grey neglected no opportunity to bring his son's claims forward, and in January 1828 arranged a majority on half pay for him at a cost of £1,400. In the meantime Charles's position in Ireland made him a useful source of information on Irish affairs. In 1829 and 1830 Grey was trying to get him a Lieut-Colonelcy, and offered to spend £6,000 on such a rank in the 10th Foot, though

I am wretchedly poor, and John, by the most unpardonable extravagance... has added to my present difficulties, but I would do anything in my power, to effect what may be for your advantage.[13]

Grey's sons were seldom left in doubt as to the sacrifices their father made to advance them, but it was equally certain that he did use all the influence at his command on their behalf. When he became Prime Minister in 1830 they, and the rest of his family, were amongst the first beneficiaries of his position. Charles became his private secretary, and Henry was launched on his political career as Under-Secretary for the Colonies.

The other sons were equally the recipients of frequent fatherly advice, admonition and concern. John and William gave their father most trouble. He castigated both for their idleness: in 1836, when John was offered a living at Wooler in Northumberland, he was angry that he at first refused it on account of the labour it involved: 'He speaks of fatigue and the necessity of rest', Grey wrote angrily to Henry: 'What fatigue has he ever undergone: if he cannot undertake such a parish as Wooler, not large in superficial extent, and very thinly peopled, the majority being dissenters, what can he do?'[14] John had a relatively undistinguished clerical career, and rose no higher than a canonry at Durham, no doubt bearing out his father's low opinion of his industry.

There was all the more concern about William, the baby of the family, born in 1819. His tendency to idleness was sharply noted; Lady Grey appealed in 1835 to Creevey to help extricate him from the bad company he was keeping at his school at Greenwich, where he spent his time playing billiards. A plan was conceived to send him abroad to university, away from the temptations of Oxford and Cambridge. The first notion was the university of Utrecht, but as the teaching there was all in Dutch the scheme was abandoned. Leyden and Dresden were then

[13] Grey to Charles, 22 Aug. 1820, 5 June, 19 Aug., 3 Sept. 1821, 25 Mar., 23 Sept. 1823, 1 Feb., 31 Mar., 5 Apr., 1 July 1825, 2, 11 July, 12 Oct. 1827, 24 Jan. 1828, 30 July, 22 Dec. 1829, 10 Jan. 1830, ibid. In Gen. Charles Grey's papers at Durham there is an examination paper in history, in Grey's hand, with questions on the Saxon invasions and kingdoms, Alfred the Great, and the Norman Conquest (XV/I). Charles later became Lt.-Col. and commanding officer, 71st Highland Light Infantry (1833) and was promoted to General on half-pay in 1865. He was MP for High Wycombe 1831–7, private secretary to Prince Albert 1849–61 and in practice to Queen Victoria until his death in 1870.

[14] 25 Mar. 1836, G. 25.

considered, and advice was taken from friends about their merits as places of study. William preferred a cosy job as a clerk in the Foreign Office, which Palmerston was willing to offer, but Grey thought that a year or two's study abroad would be desirable: 'I cannot tell you how much his repugnance to anything that requires diligence and industry has vexed me', he wrote to Henry. Dresden, however, would be distant and expensive, and would expose William to temptations which would be countered in London by closer supervision. Weimar was next considered, while the Duke of Bedford recommended Berlin, and Lansdowne Königsberg—'I don't fancy it much', Grey commented. Another objection to a European university was the expense of sending out a private tutor. Grey referred to his own unfortunate experience of his Grand Tour, when his tutor and he quarrelled all the time and he was deserted during his stay at any destination: 'He was a notorious whoremonger, one of the greatest fools I ever met with, and who inspired me with nothing but dislike and contempt, tho' he had been a second Wrangler.'[15] In the end he thought William might be better under the closer eye of his father and his friends in the Foreign Office and he took up his position there.

Grey's relations with his daughters were more relaxed, but their education too was not neglected. Mrs Sheridan, staying at Howick in 1805, noted 'how very well his children are brought up' and commented on the excellence in particular of their musical training. From 1811 onwards Grey took a London house in Portman Square for the parliamentary sessions so that the family might accompany him to town, these visits, according to General Charles, being more for the benefit of his daughters' education and introduction into society than from any desire to be active in the House of Lords. Even after marriage they maintained close and frequent contact with their parents. Though when Louisa married Lambton in 1816 Grey wrote that 'I like him so much, that I am as happy as I can be in a prospect which is to separate us from a child whom we have had so much reason to love, and who is so interwoven in our domestic existence, that it is really like the separation of a limb.' In the event, as General Charles recollected, the distance from Howick to Lambton was so short that 'the interchange of visits—long comfortable visits—between the houses was constant—and the family circle may be said to have been rather extended than broken up.' It was Georgiana, however, who never married, who became the dearest to both her parents and the companion of their old age. 'What have I to make life desirable to me but you?', wrote Mary to Georgiana in 1829:

...almost from your birth you have been the object and delight of my life, the person to whom I have said every thing, even those things which ought scarcely to have been broached to myself.

[15] Mary to Creevey, 1 Nov. [1835], Gore, *Creevey*, 41; Grey to Henry, 10, 17, 22, 24 Jan., 6, 24 Feb. 1836, G. 25.

She confessed that, much as she loved her husband, life at Howick could be dull without her children around her:

Car reads while I knit . . . this does very well—but never hearing a note of music! and never seeing you or Caroline or Henry makes me feel deserted and if I allowed myself I *could* be melancholy, however I drive away all selfish regrets as much as I can, and succeed pretty well with the assistance of constant employment.

Grey's letters to Georgiana were also deeply affectionate, and show him as a fond father devoted to all his children. Charles recalled 'a childhood and youth of more than common happiness' and

the affectionate indulgence of him to whom they owed it . . . Rarely indeed, if ever, has the grown man or woman had reason to look back upon that early period of life with such fond recollection.

In later years, Howick became the centre for family reunions of children and grandchildren on a lavish scale: in October 1830 Grey mentioned a gathering of sons, sons-in-law, daughters and daughters-in-law, and grandchildren numbering twenty-three.[16]

The picture of Grey as a devoted husband and father presents a contrast to the reputation which he had acquired in London society. In his youth he had shared in the dissipations of Fox's circle, and been reputed a heavy drinker even in such company.[17] Though he broke off his affair with Georgiana after his engagement to Mary and though he showed an undeniable and deep affection for his wife—'I never saw anything so fond of her as he is or so attentive to her in every respect', Lady Elizabeth Cavendish wrote to Mary's mother shortly after the marriage— gossip sometimes linked his name with others during his absences from Mary in London. Lady Bessborough, Georgiana's sister, remarked in 1805 on his apparent 'friendship' with a Lady Asgill, and declared herself scandalized two years later by his conduct towards Sheridan's second wife. She was Esther Jane Ogle, nicknamed 'Hecca' by Sheridan, a cousin of Mary's and daughter of a Northumberland family. A frequenter of Devonshire house, she was a fashionable, capricious, and extravagant woman, flirtatious and irresponsible. She was evidently attracted to Grey, commenting at Howick in 1805 on 'the extreme charm' of his 'good looks'. In 1807 Lady Bessborough reproached him with 'from first to last abominable conduct' towards Mrs Sheridan, and the interview culminated in an extraordinary scene:

[16] Mrs Sheridan to Mrs Creevey [Nov. 1805], Creevey MSS; Grey MSS D2, copy of Grey, *Life and Opinions* with MS notes; Grey to Fitzwilliam, 14 Oct. 1816, Fitzwilliam MSS, Northampton; Mary to Georgiana Grey, 23 Apr., [Dec] 1829, Hickleton MSS A.1.8.3/5, 8; Letters from Grey to Georgiana Grey, ibid. A.18.2; Grey, *Life and Opinions*, 404; Grey to Princess Lieven, 14 Oct. 1830, *Correspondence of Princess Lieven and Earl Grey*, ed. G. Le Strange (1890), ii. 108–9.

[17] 'Fox drinks what I should call a great deal, . . . Sheridan excessively, and Grey more than any of them': Sir Gilbert Elliot to Lady Elliot, 12 Jan. 1788, *Elliot*, i. 189. Grey admitted to Mrs Ord in 1792 that 'Unfortunately for myself I have not been . . . uniformly abstemious with regard to wine': 8 Nov., Creevey MSS.

I never saw such violence: he beat his head, call'd himself by a thousand harsh names, cried out and threw himself at my feet...he clasp'd both my hands in his, press'd them to his forehead as he knelt before me quite sobbing aloud, and then at once when I least dreamt of it clasp'd me in his arms.

She was at a loss to know whether he created the scene deliberately out of 'resentment at my just indignation for his conduct to her' or for some more embarrassing reason. She concluded that 'whatever he is among men, he is anything but honourable among women or classes them low indeed in society.' Others remarked on his moral reputation: Farington confided to his diary in 1807 that Grey was notorious for 'improper conduct' in his private life.

A constant reminder of Grey's past indiscretions was the presence at Howick after his father's death in 1807 of Eliza, Georgiana's daughter. Whether Eliza knew the truth about her parentage is not clear, but her presence must have created awkwardness for everyone in the household. Lady Bessborough, Georgiana's sister, observed on a visit in 1808:

Eliza is a fine girl, and will, I think, be handsome; but tho' they are kind to her, it goes to my heart to see her—she is so evidently thrown into the background, and has such a look of mortification about her, that it is not pleasant, yet *he* seems very fond of her. Ld. B. has this moment asked me whether she is not the governess.

In his later years Grey was captivated by Dorothea Christopherovna Benckendorf, Princess Lieven, wife of the Russian ambassador in London, who set out not only to win a leading position in English society but also to influence men of importance in political life for the benefit of her country. Grey began to correspond with her in 1823, and their letters quickly became intimate. 'Why is there this difference between us', Grey wrote in January 1826, referring to their views on the late Emperor Alexander and his policies, 'when I believe our characters to be so well suited to one another in all other respects.... Will you feel as I do regret that so many years were lost before I found out how much I was formed to love and esteem you?' Again in 1829, when the Princess feared that she might have to return to St Petersburg, he wrote: 'I feel a sort of self-reproach for the many years that were suffered to lapse almost without my knowing you... I felt myself drawn to you by an almost irresistible attraction...' During his residence in London as Prime Minister he visited her almost daily in her house in Berkeley Square. After her return to Russia in 1834 he assured her that

You are constantly present to my thoughts, and I have never ceased to see you before me as at the melancholy moment when we parted.... How constantly I am reminded of you [he wrote two months later], even without the assistance of your ring, which never quits me, except when I take it off at night, and in taking it off, and putting it on again in the morning, you are always the first and last in my thoughts. But how much will my regrets be increased, when I return to Berkeley Square, in sight of your house, but no longer able to make you the almost daily visits, in which I found so much pleasure, before I went to Downing Street...

Mary, however, was fond enough of her husband to tolerate his infidelities, though Creevey found it 'droll' when she assured him vehemently how lucky she considered herself in her marriage.[18]

Isolated with his family in Northumberland, Grey appeared the model husband and father. His days followed a set routine. 'I love regularity', he wrote to Princess Lieven in 1834, 'I find plenty of occupation in the improvement and care of my place, I am happy in my family, and I can safely say that not an hour has hung heavy on my hands, or been embittered with regret for the loss of power.' After breakfast at ten, the rest of the morning was for reading and letter-writing. The afternoons were spent in riding, walking with the dogs, or inspecting the plantations which he had laid out near the house. In the evenings he read aloud, listened to his daughters making music, played cribbage, or passed the time in conversation. Creevey has left an appealing picture of the elder statesman in retirement:

Lord Grey spends a good part of every day with his book.... It would do you good to see me send Lord Grey to bed every night at half after eleven o'clock, which is half an hour beyond his usual time. This I do regularly, and it amuses him much. He looks about for his book, calls his dog Viper, and out they go, he having been all day as gay as possible, and not an atom of that *gall* he was subject to in earlier life. ... The same tranquillity and cheerfulness, amounting almost to playfulness, instead of subsiding have rather increased during my stay, and have never been interrupted by a single moment of thoughtfulness or gloom. He could not have felt more pleasure from carrying the Reform Bill, than he does apparently when he picks up half-a-crown from me at cribbage.

Romilly, who visited Howick in 1812, remarked that, to be properly known, his host 'must be seen, as we saw him, in his retirement, surrounded by his family, his servants, his tenants, and appearing to be an object of love and admiration to all who are about him'. Even Lady Holland, who had no time for any place in England outside London, was charmed by a visit to Howick in 1817. She found Grey

all the time in the most perfect health and spirits, his countenance exhibiting gaiety and smiles which never are seen on this side of Highgate Hill.... The House is made one of the most comfortable mansions I know and the grounds are as pretty as they can be in the ugliest district in the island.[19]

Howick, then, was a refuge from the hectic world of London politics and the tiresome people who filled it. Lady Holland remarked in 1815 that she wished the Greys to come to Osterley, where he would be nearer to 'society, which is ... necessary to his well being', but one of Creevey's friends noted in 1827 that

---

[18] Lady Elizabeth Cavendish to Lady Ponsonby, 15 Sept. 1795, Hickleton MSS A.1.2.20; Lady Bessborough to G. Leveson-Gower, 15 Mar. 1805, 19 Aug. [1807], *Leveson-Gower*, i. 40, 274–5; Mrs Sheridan to Mrs Creevey [Nov 1805], Creevey MSS; Farington, *Diary*, iv. 162; Grey to Princess Lieven, 5 Jan. 1826, 1 Feb. 1829, 7 Aug., 7 Oct. 1834, Sutherland MSS, Staffordshire Record Office.

[19] *Creevey Papers*, ii. 299, 301–2; Romilly, *Memoirs*, ii. 53; Lady Holland to Mrs Creevey, Sept. 1817, *Creevey Papers*, i. 265.

Grey had 'grown 20 years younger since he left London'. After his retirement in 1834 he visited town only rarely, and took even more pleasure in his domestic routine. Creevey observed that

he seems the happiest of men, without any, the least calculated division of his time ... If you had seen him walk with all us *young* things today, and the pleasure he had in making Creevey jump over a ditch.... I feel that I compromise *the dignity* of *my character* in making him laugh so much, and yet it is such a delight to see him so pleased and happy.

Creevey's own delight in his food was amply stimulated by a lunch at which

I can swear to two hot roast fowls, two hot roast partridges, a dish of hot beef steaks, a cold pheasant, partridge pie, etc.... We had only at dinner, two soups, and two fishes, a round of beef at one end, a leg of mutton at the other, a roast turkey at one side and I forget what at the other, with three entrées on each side; woodcocks, snipes, plovers in the *second* course; red herring devil, cream cheese, etc., de plus....

Grey, Creevey remarked, enjoyed both his own dinner and Creevey's approbation of it: 'the whole to conclude with shilling *cribbage* at night, in which he displays as much energy as he ever could have done as Prime Minister'.[20]

Grey's eating habits were not always lavish. During the middle part of his life he suffered from agonizing stomach pains, probably the result of an ulcer, which incapacitated him for long periods. The painter Henry Thomson who stayed at Howick in 1812 noticed that his host 'ate plain food and drank not more than 2 or 3 glasses of wine' at dinner: when the Hollands arrived on a visit they brought their own cook. Their host, Thomson reported, 'who lives in a plain way never had such a choice of eating before at Howick, it was a luxurious time'. In his later years Grey's stomach complaint seems to have been less troublesome, and the menus at Howick became more lavish.[21]

Mary, too, suffered from frequent bouts of ill-health, and in the 1820s these became so serious that it was decided that she should not face the rigours of the Northumberland winter. In 1823, Wellington offered the Greys the use of Government House at Devonport, which became their winter residence for the next three years. It, too, however was remote from London so that Grey found it equally difficult to attend the parliamentary sessions and complained of being in such a faraway part of the country. Mary's health was sufficiently improved by 1827 for them to return to Howick, where they stayed for the rest of Grey's life. With that short break, the family house was their permanent residence except for the years of Grey's Premiership between 1830 and 1834, when they took a house at East Sheen to be nearer to Downing Street. After 1834, Grey's absences from Howick were short and infrequent: apart from the normal round of family visits, and occasional journeys to London to attend the House of Lords, he was content with his books and his fireside in the winter, and riding and walking round

[20] Grey to Princess Lieven, 4 Nov. 1834, Sutherland MSS; Lady Holland to Creevey, 23 Sept. 1815, Creevey MSS; Mrs Taylor to Creevey, 12 Nov. [1827], Gore, *Creevey*, 251, 392–8.
[21] Farington, *Diary*, vii. 289. Grey told Tierney that the Hollands also brought their own cook in 1807: 8 Nov., Tierney MSS 31770/33c.

the estate to supervise the gardeners or to enjoy some shooting. 'I am all day in the fields', he wrote in August 1828, 'enjoying this beautiful weather, and superintending my harvest and the labourers on my farm... I am much happier in these occupations in which I am not liable to be thwarted by base passions, and little jealous and sordid interests, than if I were... risking my life and health only to reap, after all, the fruit of disappointment.'

Yet Howick was not always enough to fill Grey's life and satisfy his need for occupation. Only politics could do that. He was sometimes restless, lacking the stimulus of intellectual pursuits. Visitors to Howick often commented on the superficiality of his reading or conversation. James Losh, a Newcastle lawyer interested in educational and philosophical questions and a radical in politics, recorded his respect for Grey's honesty and ability in public life, but he remarked in 1818 after a visit to Howick that 'Lord Grey is no doubt a man of great vigour of mind and very considerable eloquence. He seems to me however to be deficient in reading and even in general information.... He is not a steady and systematic reader and he is too apt to take his information on all subjects from those about him.' So, although

the mode of living at Howick and the society I met there were, I have no doubt, far above the average of what is found in great men's houses, they seemed to me inferior, both in comfort and even in amusement and interest, to what one meets with in the families of well-educated and sensible persons in the middling ranks of life.

Hobhouse, too, commented in 1832 that although Grey was an amiable man, 'I cannot discover his capacity, except, to be sure, as a talker in Parliament.' His conversation was mainly about the latest novels. His interests in the arts remained, as in his youth, conventional. He patronized Lawrence, Turner, and Henry Thomson, the last of whom remarked to Farington on Grey's delight in pictures. Farington, however, thought Grey's taste was poor, and Thomson formed the opinion that though Grey was 'a most agreeable man in his domestic character', his mind lacked depth and natural authority. Lawrence painted both Grey and Mary, and some of the children. He thought Grey's weakness was 'a disposition to talk upon subjects which he does not well understand, with as much confidence and obstinacy as he could do upon matters with which he is better acquainted. This makes him appear to be a man of less power and judgement than he would be thought if he spoke with more discretion.' Grey was not comfortable in the company of intellectuals, who tended to bring out his natural self-assertiveness and wish to dominate in circumstances where he lacked the equipment to do so. In general, he succeeded in giving the impression of a genial host, rather fussy and over-anxious, but generous and sincerely kind, and hiding from his guests the frustration he felt at his exclusion and remoteness from the centre of power: but the apparent idyll of his retreat at Howick masked only thinly at times a still burning ambition which continued to break through even after 1807.[22]

[22] Grey to Princess Lieven, 31 Aug. 1828, Sutherland MSS; *Diaries & Correspondence of James Losh*, ed. E. Hughes, i. (1962), 82; Broughton, *Recollections*, iii. 21, iv. 31, 94–5, 263, vi. 152; *Creevey Papers*, ii. 301–2; Farington, *Diary*, iv. 162, vii. 143, ii. 247, viii. 12, 97.

THE WHIGS AND THE CATHOLICS, 1807–1814

1. The Question of Leadership

Grey's removal to the House of Lords dismayed all his friends and political associates. It was, wrote Holland, a private and public misfortune, and Tierney was cast into despondency:

> The hour that made you an Earl made the Power of the Crown, during the remainder of the present reign at least, absolute... I quite despair and look upon the Party... as split or soon about to be split into a thousand pieces.

Thomas Grenville too foretold that 'our troops will speedily disband themselves' without Grey to lead them in the Commons, and Lauderdale feared that the argument about his successor would break the opposition into its component factions. Holland even suggested that the leadership be put into the hands of a committee or 'small council of war',

> trusting that the natural necessity of a leader will at the end of the session place some one in those numbers in that situation without the invidiousness of an election or *promotion* which I am convinced will not in the present circumstances be *borne by the army.*

All agreed that only Grey could keep them together: 'there were circumstances of fitness in him for the situation he filled which cannot be found together in any other person', Windham wrote. Without him, the opposition in the Commons fell to bickering about the personal and political rivalries amongst the main groups. Even if Thomas Grenville had been willing and able, in health and talent, to fill the post the Foxites would refuse to serve under one of his family, while the Grenvilles were equally determined not to have Whitbread, the obvious candidate on the Foxite wing and almost the only man who coveted the position. As Grey modestly remarked

> God knows the difficulty is not to find a person who would fill the station I held, better than I did. The difficulty will be to procure a general concurrence.

The only solution was to appoint someone who was sufficient of a nonentity not to offend any of the abler men on either side. Grey's candidate for the role was George Ponsonby, Lord Chancellor of Ireland in the Talents Ministry, who was inoffensive in every sense. He had the additional advantage of being Mary's uncle and closely related to such Whig grandees as Devonshire and Fitzwilliam, who had also married into his family. He was not, however, even a member of Parliament, and had to be brought in for Tavistock by the Duke of Bedford.[1]

The choice was welcomed with varying degrees of enthusiasm, among the least

---

[1] Holland to Grey, 18 (misdated 20) and [30] Nov. 1807, BL Add. MS 51544, fos. 140, 146–55; Tierney to Grey, 26, 28 Nov., [Dec.] 1807, G. 55; Lauderdale to Grey, 4 Dec., G. 39; Grey to Holland, 14 Nov., BL Add. MS 51550, fos. 55–6.

of which was Ponsonby's own. He accepted on the grounds that his refusal would hurt the party more than his acceptance, and wrote that

I have really and truly no wish for the situation: that I am sincerely convinced that I am not qualified for it, and that if our friends can agree upon any other person, I will act under him, with as much zeal and more pleasure than I shall feel in taking the lead myself.

The Grenvilles were more pleased than any of the old Whigs at Ponsonby's appointment mainly because it averted the spectre of Whitbread's. Tierney reported that Grenville approved of Ponsonby as 'an atonement to you for the opposition which he felt it would be necessary to make to . . . Whitbread'. Grey declared that, had Whitbread been generally acceptable, he would have preferred him to any other candidate:

Whitbread is my oldest and nearest friend and of course my partialities would be most strongly on his side, but I fear there will be a great deal of prejudice against him.

The appointment however marked another breach between the brothers-in-law. Whitbread described himself as 'smarting with resignation and silence', and declared to Tierney that 'His [Grey's] manner to me I confess has hurt me very much.' He referred to 'the mysterious superiority with which he has at all times treated me when there has been a question of distinction to be conferred', which was hardly consistent with the warmth of friendship he outwardly professed: 'I cannot endure it', he exclaimed. His old feelings that he was looked down on because of his middle class origins surfaced again. Grey failed to handle his brother-in-law with sympathetic understanding. He told Tierney that 'Nothing could at any time hurt me so much as any uneasiness between him and me. I am bound to him not only by close family connections, and long affection and friendship, but by a sense of the great obligations which I have received from him.' As for Whitbread's ambitions, Grey wrote that 'God knows there is nothing nearer my heart than that he should enjoy all sorts of distinction . . . nothing could have given me so much pleasure as to see him succeed me, but I felt that it was impossible, from every communication I received on the subject.' He begged Tierney to send on these assurances. Whitbread, however, responded with a tirade. He declared to Tierney that

I have the greatest possible affection and regard for him, and so I am sure has he for me. What I complain of is that he does not understand my feelings upon subjects of this sort, and of course cannot enter into them. I want not to be the leader of his party—if he in the warmth of his heart, and an intimation of my fitness far different from what he has, had pressed upon me to take his place . . . I am so much aware of the sort of reasons which prevail against me, and of the difficulties attending upon the situation itself, that I declare to you I would not have accepted it . . . But I am satisfied in supposing that he, above all other persons questions my capacity; and I am disappointed because he does not show at any time (except on very particular emergencies) any belief that I could assist him . . . He imagines I want him to *push me forward*. I neither wish him to do it, nor has he the power. I shall find my level and have always found it without his assistance, and my estimation with the country I would not change for his: however I may, and do acknowledge his superiority in many respects to be very very great.

He went on to refer again to Grey's proposal of a peerage in 1806, which rankled still: 'He could have no opinion of me at all, or he would not have dreamt of disabling me, and of disgracing me.'[2]

The misunderstanding between the brothers-in-law was now complete. 'Whitbread's jealousy of my conduct towards him', Grey remarked, was 'quite unaccountable. It is most unjust, but that does not prevent it from making me very unhappy.' Their relationship never recovered its old warmth. Holland later commented that Grey, 'frank, artless, and impetuous, and conscious of the sincerity as well as purity of his affections, never measured his words nor restrained his warmth in his intercourse with a man with whom he had been so long and so intimately connected', but Whitbread's sensitivity needed more tactful handling than Grey was able to provide.[3]

The 1808–9 sessions exposed the disagreements among the Whigs in the House of Commons and Ponsonby's limitations as their leader and made Whitbread even more discontented. Grey felt that the party's obligations to Ponsonby in agreeing to take on the leadership had to outweigh their sense of his inadequacy for the post, while Grenville and Fitzwilliam, amongst others, still refused to throw him over for Whitbread. On his part, Whitbread naturally resented being sacrificed to the Grenvilles. He was therefore thrown more and more into the hands of the radical young Whigs, nicknamed 'the Mountain' in satirical allusion to the extremists in the French Convention during the Revolution, and he drifted further apart than ever from Grey and the aristocratic party leadership. Their political differences were accentuated by the societies in which each tended to move. When Grey was invited to dine in May 1809 Whitbread felt obliged to warn him that the company might prove uncongenial, and Grey took the hint: he had hoped, he wrote, that their public differences might not affect their private relationship, but 'Today ... as you give me the choice, I think it will upon the whole be better that I should not dine with you.' They met only rarely on social occasions henceforward. When Grey stayed overnight at Southill on his way to town in the following January their conversation was pleasant enough and, Grey hoped, constructive: but, as Whitbread remarked to Creevey, 'we could not have held it long'.[4]

Whitbread's breach with Grey made him less governable as a party member. He refused to attend the eve of session party conference at Ponsonby's in January

---

[2] Ponsonby to Grey, 23 Nov., 9 Dec., G. 47/11; Tierney to Grey, 7 Dec., G. 55; Grey to Holland, 6 Dec., BL Add. MS 51550, fos. 58–66; Fitzpatrick to Whitbread, 22 Dec., Whitbread to Tierney, 21 Dec., Tierney to Whitbread, 24 Dec., Whitbread MSS; Grey to Tierney, 20 Dec., Whitbread to Tierney, 25 Dec., Tierney MSS.

[3] Grey to Mary [10], 14 Jan. 1808, G. 27; Holland, *Memoirs*, ii. 241.

[4] Lauderdale to Grenville, 30 Aug. 1808, BL Add. MS 58942, fos. 55–60; Grenville to Fitzwilliam, 30 Mar. 1809, Fitzwilliam MSS, Sheffield; Whitbread to Grey and Grey to Whitbread, 14 May 1809, G. 59; Whitbread to Creevey, 7 Jan, 1810, Creevey to Mrs Creevey, 20 Jan., *Creevey Papers*, i. 117–18, 121; Grey to Mary, 2 Jan. 1810, G. 31.

1810, still smarting under the impression that, had Grey accepted office with Perceval in the previous September, he would not have designated him for a post, though he added that 'notwithstanding our political differences which have been excited by some and exaggerated by others, I have the fullest reliance on his undiminished personal regard.' Grey attempted to quash Grenville's renewed interest in an alliance with Canning after the latter's resignation in 1809, largely for Whitbread's sake, and he confessed to Fitzwilliam and others his uneasiness with Ponsonby's ineffective leadership, despite his strong sense of obligation to him. Grenville and Fitzwilliam, however, argued for Ponsonby, and even went so far as to suggest that Whitbread be no longer regarded as belonging to the party. After consulting his leading colleagues Grey told Whitbread that it was the general opinion that Ponsonby should continue as leader; Whitbread demanded to know who those colleagues were, and made ominous noises about the opposition's lack of decisiveness over the Address: 'If Ponsonby can take the lead', he wrote, 'no body can prevent it. Neither can any body confer it upon him.'[5]

Whitbread's disgruntlement with Grey lasted to the end of his life. He seemed to the cautious Grenville and old Whig lords to be ungovernable, and wishing to press opposition to dangerous lengths, while they seemed to him indolent and selfish, sacrificing the public interest to personal convenience. Grey, caught between the two, succeeded at least in keeping Whitbread in the party, but there were times when the link seemed tenuous. Grey confessed to Holland in October 1809 that he saw the party as broken up, and that he felt no strong disposition to try to re-form it. It was partly because of his despair and embarrassment over Whitbread that he became reluctant to assert his leadership, though others urged him to come to London precisely to do so. As Rosslyn wrote,

You must know that it is not in debate alone that the weight of your abilities and authority can be useful, and indeed if I were certain you would not utter a sentence in Parliament, I should not be the less persuaded of the importance of your coming. The truth is that you can do more real good to the country by management and direction than by any speeches.

Tierney too wrote frankly that Grey's reluctance would be interpreted by the party as

an abandonment of them, and by the world at large as the effect of spleen and disappointment... You must shew yourself in the field as the leader of a party or you must cease to be so. Do not flatter yourself that a residence in Northumberland is compatible with the situation you at present hold in the public estimation, or that you can put greatness on and off as may be most agreeable to you.[6]

[5] Whitbread to Tierney, 27 Sept. 1809, Creevey MSS; Grey to Tierney, 10 Oct., 17 Nov., Tierney MSS; Grey to Whitbread, 26 Sept., Whitbread to Grey, 29 Sept., 11, 14, 16 Jan. 1810, G. 59; Grey to Fitzwilliam, 6, 13 Jan. 1810, Grenville to Fitzwilliam, 30 May 1809, Fitzwilliam MSS, Sheffield; Fitzwilliam to Grey, 12 Jan. 1810, G. 14/11.

[6] Grey to Holland, 3 Oct. 1809, BL Add. MS 51551, fos. 52–63; Rosslyn to Grey, 24 Feb. 1809, G. 51. See also Holland to Grey, 11 Nov. 1812, BL Add. MS 51545, fos. 24–6; Tierney to Grey, 25 Sept. 1808, G. 55.

Grey, however, refused to budge, and Whitbread in turn drifted further towards an alliance with Burdett and the extra-parliamentary radicals from which a close relationship with Grey might have saved him. Events were to show that Whitbread's true feelings and politics were more Whiggish than radical; but by 1812 the party was no longer a united and determined opposition. Grey cannot be absolved from some of the responsibility. His natural despondency in face of difficulties sapped his energies, while his removal from the Commons left a gap in his life which the House of Lords could not fill. The stimulus of heated debate had drawn out Grey's talents as an orator, and had filled him with enthusiasm for politics. His maiden speech in the Lords in January 1808 left him in despair. 'What a place to speak in', he wrote to Mary: 'with just light enough to make darkness visible, it was like speaking in a vault by the glimmering of a sepulchral lamp to the dead. It is impossible I should ever do anything there worth thinking of.'[7]

Grey accordingly tried to push Grenville into active leadership. As he had deferred to Fox before 1806, after 1808 he was content to act as second to Grenville, encouraging from a distance and coming forward himself only on major questions. When Holland wrote in November 1807 to urge a conference on the great issues of the day, pointing out that 'a party must be held together by some great and distinct object, or by devotion and attachment to men', Grey responded with what was to become his habitual pessimism: Mary's approaching confinement made it impossible to leave Howick, and 'indeed I quite dread the thoughts of going. The state of politics generally is disheartening enough, but if we are to have jealousies and contentions amongst our friends and perhaps some separation of the party besides, it will be more than I can bear.' When, however, Grenville also proposed that the opposition's activity should be limited to speeches on the first day of the session, with attendance thereafter only on a few major questions, Grey tried to stir him into greater activity. Admitting that Grenville's attitude reflected his own inclinations, he argued that 'a more active duty is required of us, and more especially of you'. While disapproving of 'an opposition factiously conducted', he believed that they should show the country that there existed

a body of public men, steadily united by an honourable principle, determined to uphold the honour of the country, and actuated in their opposition ... by no enmity but that which honourable minds must feel to rashness and injustice.

Remembering the disastrous mistake of the Whig secession in 1797, he begged Grenville to lead 'a vigilant opposition', and threatened that otherwise 'my dislike of Parliamentary business will be so much increased, that I am afraid considerations of duty will have but little power over me'. Grenville's position, however, was not that which Fox had occupied in the 1790s. It was to Grey alone that the old Foxites looked for leadership, and his refusal to assume the mantle encouraged

---

[7] Grey to Mary, Jan. 1808, G. 27. Wellington said in 1818 that Grey was 'lost by being in the House of Lords. Nobody cares a damn for the House of Lords: the House of Commons is everything in England, and the House of Lords nothing': *Creevey Papers*, i. 286.

others to try to do so. Despite their underlying unity on great matters of principle, in practice the opposition after 1807 appeared quarrelsome and factious, unable to offer the public a distinctive and consistent alternative to the weak governments of Portland, Perceval, and Liverpool, and unable to agree sufficiently among themselves to replace them with one of their own. The major political issues of the next eight years were the war and the Catholic question, with reform beginning to reappear as a further public concern. On all these questions Grey took up positions that were consistent and honourable, but too little tempered by political reality, and all proved in the end to disunite rather than to consolidate the opposition and to stand in the way of their political ambitions.[8]

2. The Catholic Question

The Catholic question, as Michael Roberts has written, 'stood first in the political programme of the Whigs' between 1807 and 1813.[9] Despite Grey's resentment at the irresponsible way in which he considered the Irish Catholics had pushed the Talents Ministry into the crisis of 1807, he and the Whigs considered themselves pledged to emancipation thereafter. In that, their attitude may have owed more to a desire for political consistency and for revenge on George III than to a genuine concern for the Irish themselves. They looked on Ireland in the traditional English aristocratic way, not as a nation struggling to be free from alien domination, but as a section of the British peoples who were unjustly discriminated against on account of religious opinions. The Irish cause touched their tender spot, the old Foxite cry of 'civil and religious liberty all over the world'. It was to them an ideological rather than a political, social, or economic problem, and they showed no sympathy—rather hostility—towards the Irish 'patriots' whom they regarded as dangerous and ambitious demagogues. They looked on Irish affairs through English eyes not only in this lack of sympathy for the real problems of that island but also in that they believed, as Fitzwilliam had done in 1795, that all that was necessary to cement the unity of the two countries was for the Irish upper and middle classes to enjoy the same civil status and rights as their Protestant English counterparts. They would then exercise the same social and political restraint upon the dangerous 'lower orders' as the governing aristocracy and gentry of England on this side of the channel. The harmony they hoped to achieve through Catholic emancipation was a Whiggish and aristocratic harmony under a single governing class.

Ireland was also a pawn in British party politics. Grey viewed the Catholic question in an essentially parliamentary light. The question was to be raised in a manner and at a time that would be of most benefit to the Whigs as a party. Thus Grey deprecated the renewal of a Catholic petition in 1808 because there was no

[8] Holland to Grey [30 Nov.], BL Add. MS 51544, fos. 146–55, Grey to Lady Holland, 12 Dec., ibid. 51550, fos. 67–70; Grenville to Auckland, 29 Dec. 1807, ibid. 34457, fo. 392; Grey to Grenville, 3 Jan. 1808, G. 21/4; Jupp, *Grenville*, 413–20.
[9] Roberts, *The Whig Party, 1807–12*, 2.

political advantage in it. 'I do not see that it makes much difference to our hope of office', he wrote: 'I shall have the trouble of making a long speech and the mortification of voting in a small minority; the next day we shall be just as we are now.' He refused to leave Mary 'confined to her room, at the bottom of Northumberland, with nine children and nobody but servants to look after them'. Even though the debate was postponed for his benefit he did not come to London. If, he told Grenville, his absence was misconstrued, it could not be helped:

This ... experience has taught me to bear with some fortitude, tho' after all that passed last year, and all my previous conduct, I could not help feeling a little indignant at being told ... that I was suspected by the Catholics ... I feel much inclined to leave this suspicion to make what progress it may till those who entertain it, shall become ashamed of it.

In any case his attendance would have made no practical difference: 'I am afraid that those who think the question as good as carried, go a little too fast, they know little of the power of the King and the Church if they do not expect that a hard battle is still to be fought.' One unexpected result of this absence, however, was an apparent improvement in Grey's standing at Court. Lady Holland told him that some quarters attributed it to 'a little policy in your abstaining from doing what is so obnoxious in a quarter where *you* of all the late ministry are the most esteemed and personally liked', and Tierney wrote in June that

at Head quarters you are in higher favour than ever and *you may depend* upon it ... you having been absent ... the king is firmly persuaded was a political measure on your part, but setting this aside there is a marked general disposition towards you in the old man which has shown itself strongly within these few days ...

Grey was amused by the misunderstanding, and assured Lady Holland that there could be no question of the King's partiality towards him; 'If it is now the fashion to speak more favourably of me at Court, to what can it be attributed but their superior hatred of Lord Grenville ... and perhaps to some foolish hope of exciting jealousy between us.' There was no question in Grey's mind of his taking advantage of such stories.[10]

One result of the Catholic debate was the taking up by the Whigs of a scheme which originated as long ago as 1791 and had been revived in English Catholic circles in 1805, for some kind of concordat between the Catholic Church and the Crown for the granting of 'securities' for the Protestant establishment. This might be achieved by allowing the Crown some right of nomination or a negative veto on Papal appointments of bishops in Ireland. Lord Fingall, the moderate Catholic leader, drew up a scheme for discussion early in 1808, and it was subsequently taken up by Dr Milner, the agent in England of the Irish Catholics, who informed Grenville on 26 May of his opinion that the Roman Catholic bishops would

---

[10] Grey to Tierney, 8 Nov., Tierney to Grey, 8 June, G. 55; Grey to Petty, 5 Nov., Bowood MSS; Lady Holland to Grey [17 May], BL Add. MS 51549, fos. 26–8; Grey to Lady Holland, 22 May, 3 June, ibid. 51550, fos. 106–22; to Grenville, 7 May, ibid. 58947, fos. 97–9. Lauderdale reported that the Duke of Bedford suspected Grey to be 'lukewarm in their cause': *Fortescue MSS*, ix. 197 (2 May).

'cheerfully consent' to a royal veto. Such a scheme, it was hoped, would allay Protestant fears of the consequences of emancipation, and disarm some of the opposition at Court. Ponsonby, Milner, and Fingall met to discuss the scheme on 3 May, and Grattan and Ponsonby referred to it as agreed with the Catholics in the debate on the Catholic petition in the Commons on the 25th. The proposal attracted favourable attention among the Catholic hierarchy in Ireland during the summer. Lady Holland reported on 6 June that even some English bishops and courtiers were now favourably disposed, on the grounds that 'there will not be a body of men more devoted to the Crown than the Catholic subjects'.[11]

Grey adopted the proposal with enthusiasm. It seemed to him the only way in which the hostility not only of George III but of the British public, as shown in the 1807 election, might be overcome, and without the veto, he told Ponsonby, 'all hope of carrying the question ... must be abandoned'. Unfortunately, however, the Irish democrats turned fiercely against it as being 'an essentially Aristocratic scheme' to increase the influence of Lord Fingall and they declared that it would subject the Catholic Church in Ireland to the Royal Supremacy. A vigorous press and pamphlet campaign in Dublin frightened the Catholic bishops, and in September their synod condemned the veto as 'inexpedient'. The Whigs felt themselves betrayed by Milner, who, Grey wrote, had proved himself 'a man not to be trusted'. All they could now hope to do was 'to preserve our consistency and honour'. 'No man', Grey wrote, 'more readily assents to or more cordially cherishes' the abstract principle of 'not excluding men from civil rights on account of religious opinions', but

there are few circumstances in human life, I believe I may say none in politics that can be reduced to pure abstractions. Expediency must operate in all and he who pretends otherwise is either a hypocrite, or unfit for the affairs of this world.

The veto was essential in the present circumstances and the Whigs must 'make early declaration that this concession is indispensable to our future support of the cause'. He hoped that such a declaration would strengthen the 'moderate' Catholics and diminish the influence of the democrats.[12]

Michael Roberts considered the affair another 'characteristically Whig *sottise*', on the grounds that they overestimated Fingall's influence on the Irish people and Church, and persisted after 1808 in flogging an obviously dead horse, merely in order to keep up an undeserved reputation as 'friends of Ireland'. He blamed Grey for locking the party into this impasse. Certainly Grey did not waver in his determination, firstly never to come in without royal assurances on the Catholic question, and secondly to insist upon some security for the Protestant estab-

---

[11] Roberts, *The Whig Party*, 39–41, *Fortescue MSS*, ix. 202–4, *Parl. Deb.* xi. 556, 608–9; Lady Holland to Grey [6 June], BL Add. MS 51549, fos. 42–5.

[12] Grey to G. Ponsonby, 28 Oct., G. 47/11, G. Ponsonby to Grenville, 19 Oct., T. Grenville to Grenville, 19 Oct., Sir J. Newport to Grenville, 20 Oct., Grenville to G. Ponsonby, 3 Nov., Grey to Grenville, 29 Jan. 1809, *Fortescue MSS*, ix. 226–8, 230–2, 237–9, 275; Roberts, *The Whig Party*, 43–7, 57–61, 67, 100–1.

lishment. This, Roberts maintains, was unrealistic because the Irish people would never accept it: it was 'rigid adherence to an arbitrarily determined solution'. Yet, as Roberts admits, the Whigs had to look at the question from a parliamentary angle, and 'they believed in the half-loaf'. The veto might, from a tactical point of view, moderate the opposition in England to Catholic emancipation, and so make it possible for the Whigs to remove this bar to their prospects of office; if their mistake was to ignore its unacceptability in Ireland, they committed it because they thought the Irish 'democrats' were as uninfluential there as the political radicals were in England. Grey's response to the problem was a typically English one: the Irish must accept concessions on terms acceptable to Britain or do without; and in the latter case, they would have only themselves to blame. There is little evidence that the grant of emancipation in any case would have resolved the Irish question. By 1812, agrarian, financial, and political grievances were at least as prominent as religion in the minds of the Irish activists, amongst whom O'Connell was emerging into prominence: Grey's hope was that Whig insistence on the veto would in the end prevail, and that its consequence would be to re-establish the control of Fingall and the aristocratic or 'moderate' party in Ireland, who were prepared to work with the Whigs. If this showed a misunderstanding of the depth of feeling among the middle and lower orders in Ireland, it was consistent with Grey's general views. Just as he resisted the radical agitation for parliamentary reform in Britain as a threat to aristocratic dominance, so in Ireland his objective was not merely justice for the Irish Catholic majority, but the support and confirmation of aristocratic control which would cement the connection with the sister kingdom. Grey was not wrong or foolish in seeing the Catholic question in the period 1808–12 as hinging on the veto: but it was the viewpoint of a fundamentally aristocratic politician obsessed by regard for his own character and consistency and for the political interests of his party.[13]

The question nevertheless brought the Whigs into disarray. Grey found that many of his leading colleagues, including Holland, Fitzwilliam, Bedford, and Whitbread, spanning the whole width of the party, were less insistent on the veto or wished to see it dropped. Tierney urged that it was pointless to advocate a solution which would be unacceptable to the Irish themselves. Grey, however, was not to be moved. In the autumn of 1809, when the government seemed about to collapse and the prospect of office appeared, the Catholic issue was one of the main considerations in his mind. The Irish Catholics were about to renew their petition, and Lord Ponsonby thought that they might be persuaded to postpone it in view of the possible change of administration. He suggested that Grey might negotiate with the King on the lines that the Catholic question be deferred, and negotiations be carried on with the Irish in the meantime; if the Irish insisted

[13] Grey to Grenville, 31 Oct. 1808, BL Add. MS 58947, fos. 102–4; to Sir A. Piggott, 16 Nov., G. 47/4; to Viscount Ponsonby, 6 Nov., G. 48/1. He described the opposition to the veto as the work of 'a malignant party amongst the Catholics whose views are of the very worst description' and quoted Fox as the authority for the opinion that emancipation was never intended to be unconditional: to Petty, 18 Nov. 1808, Bowood MSS.

upon pressing the question, it should be understood that he would resign. Grey replied that at one time he might have considered such a course, but that now the Catholic leaders could not be relied upon to hold back the question: 'It has been seen in too many instances that to retain the name and character of Leaders they must themselves submit to be dictated to by those whom they are supposed to govern', and thus there would be no security that they would not give way to pressure from the democratic party, or even be replaced by them. It would put his place in the government at constant and unacceptable risk. If the King approached him, he must insist on emancipation with the veto: 'This requires no consideration, or consultation with my friends, for if they were all to be unanimously of opinion that we ought to undertake the government subject to such a condition, I would not agree to it.'[14]

Grey nevertheless contacted the Irish Catholic body through the intermediacy of J. J. Dillon, an Irish lawyer, to ask whether they would abstain from raising the question if a 'friendly Administration' were formed. Would they be content with general assurances of favourable dispositions? In any case, he warned, the bishops would have to reconsider their resolution against the veto, which was 'reasonable in itself'. Dillon sounded out Fingall and others, and replied that there were possibilities of a compromise. Fingall had said that the bishops might be willing to modify their position, provided the British government would consider some financial provision for the Catholic clergy. Grey and Lauderdale thought that this might offer a basis for discussions, while in Dublin at a meeting of Catholic representatives the anti-veto party was defeated by four votes. When the expected approach from Perceval was made, however, Grey was to reject it out of hand on the ground that the number of Cabinet places offered was too few and that it would be impossible to insist on emancipation. Grey recognized his dilemma: he declared to Grenville on 3 November that they could not take office under any engagement, express or implied, not to bring forward *any* measure of Catholic relief; but they, in turn, ought to propose it with

all such regulations as, without danger of defeating the end we have in view, may tend to give satisfaction, as the cant is, to the king's conscience, to obviate the public prejudice, and to provide real or even ostensible securities for the Church.

The general strategy, therefore, was that

we should declare that we never can consent to take office if a bar is to be put to all consideration of the Catholic question; but that we should feel an anxious desire to annex to any measure which we might propose upon it all such guards as could with any propriety be required, either for the ease of the king's mind or for the security of the Church.

[14] Roberts, *The Whig Party*, 72; Grey to Petty, 25 Nov., Bowood MSS; to Lady Holland, 28 Nov., BL Add. MS 51550, fos. 174–80; to Wyvill, 28 Sep. 1809, G. 60/9; to Tierney, 3 Oct., Tierney MSS; Tierney to Grey, 7 Dec. 1808, 26 Oct., 28 Nov. 1809, G. 55; Ponsonby to Grey, 19 Sept. 1809 and reply, 22 Sept., G. 48/1.

Grey accepted the implications of this position. 'If this resolution is to be considered as a positive bar during the king's life, I must submit to it, for there is no earthly inducement that can engage me to abandon it', he wrote.[15] Tierney pointed out that this attitude not only barred the Whigs from office during George III's lifetime, but made a vigorous opposition pointless, for if they drove the government from office there would be no basis on which to form an alternative one. Grey, however, denied that this was the consequence: 'all that we should have to require in the first instance, if the Government were offered to us, would be that this subject should be open to us, to propose upon it such measures as we might think necessary', and those measures would unquestionably be 'complete emancipation...subject to all reasonable conditions which do not interfere with private conscience, for the security of the Church, and emphatically the *veto*.... without this much I could not be satisfied.' He believed that the Catholics would accept such an arrangement: 'I believe the discontent, or rather the desire of erecting discontent upon it, would be confined to a very few...and I have never admitted the validity of the objection that the removal of these would not be sufficient to satisfy those who can never be satisfied.'[16]

The confirmation of Perceval's government in office and Grey's decision to remain in opposition returned the Catholic question to its former state. The Irish Catholics again organized a petition and asked Grenville to present it. Grey advised him to do so, but expressed caution as to the wisdom of following it by a motion for a Bill while circumstances were so unfavourable. Holland urged support for the petition on the grounds that, as the only bond of party unity, the Catholic question must be their rallying-point, and that 'the preserving of it as the badge and standard of the party seems to me the only means of keeping us permanently united—for on what other point do our friends all agree?'[17]

Grey replied that he deprecated the renewal of the question in view of the Catholics' intransigence, which could do nothing but harm to the Whigs and their prospects. He refused to accept the view that Grenville's election as Chancellor of Oxford University, the Protestant stronghold, indicated a change of public opinion on the question: rather the contrary, 'There never was a greater danger than at this moment...of a strong manifestation of the public opinion against it.' Nevertheless, he would

give not a cold and reluctant, but the most zealous support I can give to the principles I believe to be sound, upon the ground, and with the explanations by which as it appears to me those principles ought practically to be regulated...and I must beg leave to lay all considerations of popularity out of the question. If popularity follows me in doing what I

---

[15] Grey to Dillon, 4 Oct. and reply, 11 Oct., G. 11/11; to Wyvill, 17 Dec. 1809, Wyvill MSS; to Grenville [Oct 1809], BL Add. MS 58947, fo. 192; to Brougham, 22 Oct., *BLT*, i. 465–7; to Viscount Ponsonby, 25 Oct., G. 48/1; Lauderdale to Grey, 19 Oct., G. 39; Grey to Grenville, 3 Nov. 1809, *Fortescue MSS*, ix. 362–3.

[16] Grey to Tierney, 3 Oct., 17 Nov., Tierney MSS; Tierney to Grey, 26 Oct., G. 55.

[17] Grenville to Grey, 29 Nov., G. 21/2, Grey to Grenville, 12 Dec., *Fortescue MSS*, ix. 407–9; Holland to T. Grenville, 3 Jan. 1810, BL Add. MS 41858, fo. 7; to Grey [3 Jan], ibid. 51544, fo. 230.

believe to be right, I shall always be glad of it; but I never have and I never will sacrifice one atom of what I believe to be right to obtain it.

Grey's attitude was rigid, and to some extent, self-righteous: but he had convinced himself that political consistency was the only honourable conduct and he was not prepared to change once he had made up his mind. On the veto he was inflexible, and when Grenville drafted a pamphlet in the form of a *Letter to Lord Fingall* for publication in February 1810, Grey insisted on the inclusion of the veto as a condition for the settlement of the question. As Grey wrote to Mary, who, ignorant of his part in the pamphlet, had remarked that she disapproved of it, 'my advice had a material influence in its being written.' The purpose was to reassert the Whigs' conditions in the hope of countering the intransigence of the extremists and so to help restore Fingall's moderate influence. Grey wrote that it was hopeless to carry emancipation on the democrats' terms, and it was important to read them that lesson as well as to reassure the Protestant establishment. In pursuit of the same strategy, Grey opened negotiations with the English Catholics, suggesting that they issue a declaration in favour of securities in return for emancipation. He met a deputation on 31 January and drafted a clause for their petition which became known as the 'fifth resolution', in which they accepted the necessity of 'adequate provision for the maintenance of the civil and religious establishments of this kingdom'. In February he and Windham presented the petition, Grey making what one of the Catholic deputies called 'a most capital speech', in the course of which he declared his firm adherence 'to every sentiment and to every word' of Grenville's pamphlet.[18]

The petition was widely signed in England, but the English Catholics were a small and politically unimportant minority, and the main result was to create anger amongst the Irish who were now thoroughly aroused against any form of veto. They reorganized their agitation on a new representative system, and became embroiled in disputes as to whether their meetings infringed the Convention Act.[19] At the same time, agrarian disturbances began to increase in ferocity, arousing English fears that civil war might be the only alternative to emancipation. In these circumstances the Catholic question began to assume a different political character. Canning had already pledged himself to it, and even Tories now began to consider the need for concession, while the Prince Regent's assumption of office led to negotiations through his friend the pro-Catholic Moira with Canning and Welles-ley. By 1812, the Whigs were faced with the need to modify their insistence on the veto lest they lose the role of champion of the Catholics. In January 1812 Grey signalled his change of tactics by declaring in the Lords that the veto was not 'an

[18] Grey to Holland, 5 Jan., G. 35, to Whitbread, 12 Jan., G. 59, to Mary, 2 Feb., G. 27, to Grenville, 30 Jan., BL Add. MS 58947, fos. 223–4; Roberts, *The Whig Party*, 74; Silvertop to Wyvill, 6, 23 Feb., Wyvill MSS; *Parl. Deb.* xv. 503–5, xvii. 423–31; Jupp, *Grenville*, 426–7.

[19] Roberts, *The Whig Party*, 81–7. The purpose of the Act was to prohibit 'unlawful assemblies' of delegates on a national basis for the purpose of petitioning Parliament. Grey argued in 1812 that the new Catholic system of delegate meetings was not for an unlawful purpose and therefore did not fall under the prohibition: *Parl. Deb.* xxi. 467–74.

indispensable obligation', and Grenville described it as 'an arrangement to which he attached no great importance'. Ponsonby and Tierney made similar statements in the Commons. Three months later, at the end of April, Lord Donoughmore presented the Irish Catholic petition in the Lords, and Grey brought forward another from the English Catholics, signed by all the Catholic peers and by the most wealthy and respectable gentry. The following day Donoughmore moved for a committee to consider the Catholic disabilities but lost by 174 to 102.[20]

The negotiations of 1812 for an 'extended administration' to be led by Wellesley and Canning and to include Moira and the Whigs hinged to some extent on the Catholic question. Those three statesmen were favourable to the Catholic claims, and Wellesley declared in the Lords on 23 June that

in the powers entrusted to him by the Prince Regent with a view to the formation of an administration, it had been distinctly laid down as a basis of that administration, that the claims of the Catholics should be taken into early consideration, with a view to a final and conciliatory adjustment.

Grey expressed great satisfaction that the subject was now to be brought forward under new, and, he trusted, happier auspices. He recollected that it was exactly 5 years since the present parliament had met, recalling the 'No Popery' cry fostered at the general election by members of the administration, and expressing satisfaction that in the same parliament the House of Commons had agreed to the principle of Catholic relief, brought forward by a former member of that administration (Canning, on 22 June). 'This would teach him [Grey] still more forcibly to persevere in the line of duty, whatever obloquy might be cast upon him, satisfied that sooner or later his motives would be justified to the public, and his conduct shown in its true and proper light.' He went on to state that though he would support[21]

any securities that could be devised ... he must say, that in his opinion the stability of the Protestant establishment would be best secured by the repeal at once of all the disabilities under which the Catholics laboured, taking as the best security their oaths of allegiance and their acknowledged loyalty to the state.

On 1 July, however, Wellesley's motion for relief was lost by one vote, though Canning carried a motion in the Commons on 22 June by 235 votes to 106 that Parliament should consider the question in the next session. The negotiations with the Whigs had broken down in early June, but in November Grey wrote to Holland that whatever else divided the Whigs from Wellesley and Canning, they should co-operate on the Catholic question, and Grenville declared that it was now the crucial issue in politics. Grey, however, remained cautious. He was full of apprehension, he wrote on 3 January, lest the Catholics remain intransigent

---

[20] Ibid. xvi. 474–6; Roberts, *The Whig Party*, 98; *Parl. Deb.* xxii. 452–60, 509–74. Grey did not speak but he voted for the motion.

[21] Corr. in Wellesley MSS, BL Add. MSS 37296, fos. 405–23, 37297, fos. 1–142: extracts printed in *The Wellesley Papers* (1914), 633–711. *Parl. Deb.* xxiii. 711–13; Wellesley's memorandum to Grey and Grenville, 23 May, *Fortescue MSS*, x. 266–7. Grey to Holland, 8 Nov. 1812, G. 35.

about unconditional emancipation and the Protestant agitation against them triumph in consequence. He still thought that securities might moderate opposition, but he now declared himself ready for 'simple repeal' if it could be done. Tierney was pessimistic. The collapse of the negotiations with Wellesley and the Prince had resulted in the confirmation of Liverpool's administration, in which Catholic emancipation was now an 'open' question; the Whigs feared that this meant that the Court would continue to oppose it, and Tierney thought the question would be lost as a result.[22]

During the early months of 1813 petitions against emancipation flooded into both Houses, including those from Oxford and Cambridge Universities and the clergy and laity of several dioceses. In these circumstances the supporters of emancipation felt obliged to raise the question of 'securities' again. When Grattan rose to move for a committee on the Catholic claims on 25 February, he assured the Commons that though the Catholics wished emancipation to be unconditional, they were prepared to 'give you every security you think necessary, provided it does not derogate from the rights of their Church', and Ponsonby, on 2 March, stated that he did not know that it was impossible for the veto to be again proposed: the Catholics had not said that they would never concede it, only that, in the resolution of 1808, they had declared it to be inexpedient at that time. The motion was carried by 264 to 224, and in May a relief bill was introduced. At the committee stage, however, Canning, with the agreement of the Whigs, introduced 20 clauses incorporating 'further precautions' for the Protestant establishment. These amounted to a recurrence of the veto. Two commissions were to be established, one in England and one in Ireland, to scrutinize proposals for nominations to bishoprics and deaneries and refer them for approval to the Crown: and Papal bulls were also to be submitted for approval.[23]

Grey disapproved both of Canning's scheme and of the way in which Grattan had agreed to it. He declared that it represented 'a complete veto, in the most objectionable form that could be devised' and that it would leave

our friends again involved in all the odium which attended the original proposition of the veto.... I see so much danger of the Catholic question falling back from the near prospect that there was of carrying it, into even a more hopeless state than it was before, that I wish you to possess this record of my opinion, under the reluctant acquiescence which I have been induced to give.

He feared that 'the violent people' in Ireland would gain ascendancy as a result, and indeed the Catholics condemned the new proposals without hesitation and resolved to insist on complete emancipation or separation from England.[24]

Grey's worst fears were realized when on the 24th the first clause of the Bill

[22] Grey to Holland, 3 Jan. 1813, ibid., to Grenville, 13 Jan., *Fortescue MSS*, x. 326–7; Grenville to Holland, 11 Dec., BL Add. MS 51531, fos. 15–16; Tierney to Grey [Jan. 1813] G. 55.

[23] *Parl. Deb.* xxiv. 747–1078, *passim*, xxv. 1–171, *passim*, 246–9, 271–95.

[24] Grey to Holland [May 1813], 18, 25 May, G. 35; Earl of Suffolk to Sir Charles Hastings, 24 June 1813, *HMC, Hastings MSS*, iii. 301–2.

1. Grey addressing the House of Lords during the 'trial' of Queen Caroline, 1820
(*G. Hayter, National Portrait Gallery, London*)

2. Grey, *c.*1828, from the portrait by Sir Thomas Lawrence, 1828
(*National Portrait Gallery, London*)

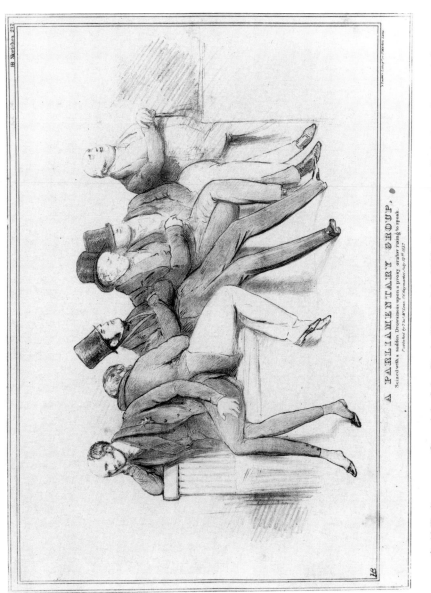

A PARLIAMENTARY GROUP.

Seized with a sudden Drowsiness upon a prosy orator rising to speak.

3. 'A Parliamentary Group', by John Doyle ('HB'), July 1832. Grey (on the left) sits in a characteristic attitude on the government front bench in the House of Lords. Beside him are five of his Cabinet colleagues: Lansdowne, Richmond, Melbourne, Goderich, and Holland

4. A sketch of Grey in 1834, by B. R. Haydon
(*National Portrait Gallery, London*)

proper, admitting Catholics to membership of Parliament, was lost by 4 votes. He unhesitatingly attributed it to 'the immediate exertions of Carlton House' and described the Regent as 'this anti-Catholic prince, who is a much more anti-Catholic than the king'. The Bill was immediately abandoned by its sponsors and though it was agreed that Grattan should give notice that it would be reintroduced next session the damage was done. Donoughmore presented another Irish petition in the Lords in June 1814 but, persuaded by Grey that the renewal of the question was 'highly inexpedient', announced that he had no intention of moving for legislation in that session. He renewed his motion for enquiry in June 1815 but lost the division by 26 votes.[25]

The Irish Catholics were now more frustrated than ever, and less disposed to look to any British politicians for a remedy. They became more uncompromising, and blamed the Whigs for selling out for their own political advantage. In fact the Whigs had not only failed to extract any advantage from the question, but rather the reverse. Tierney wrote in 1814 that 'the conduct of the Catholics has loosened the only tie by which for some time past we have even appeared to be kept together' and that consequently 'as a party there will in my judgement, be an end of us'. The existence of a minority group in the administration which supported emancipation under the 'open question' convention removed the distinctive Whig flavour from it, and it became in effect a non-party issue in Britain henceforward. At the same time the Prince's capitulation to the anti-Catholic lobby made emancipation, as before, a bar to the Whig prospects of office. Whether the result would have been different if Grey had been more flexible over the veto between 1808 and 1812 is highly doubtful, but his attitude might have contributed to the Catholics' refusal to accept the Whigs as their friends, and so to their decision to organize their agitation on non-parliamentary and populist lines. In 1808 Grey judged that English opposition to the Catholics could not be overcome without the veto; his change of mind in 1812 made no real difference because by that time Catholic opinion had hardened and Protestant resistance had been mobilized. With or without the veto, emancipation was not possible between 1807 and 1815 and all that the Whigs achieved by embracing the cause was to exclude themselves again from office.[26]

WAR AND PEACE, 1807–1815

Though the Whigs failed to make political capital out of the Catholic question, they were at least agreed amongst themselves on the principle involved. That could not be said of their attitudes to foreign affairs during the final 8 years of the

[25] *Parl. Deb.* xxv. 312–65, 405, xxxi. 666–86; Grey to Grenville, 27 May 1813, *Fortescue MSS*, x. 340–1, and 28 May [1814], BL Add. MS 58949, fos. 129–31.
[26] Grenville to Grey, 25 May, G. 21/2; Mrs Creevey to T. Creevey, Wed. [1813], Creevey MSS; Tierney to Grey, 3 Mar. 1814, G. 55.

struggle against Napoleon. The old divergences between Foxites and Grenvilles remained unresolved. Since 1803 Grey had believed that Britain had no alternative but to resist French aggression in Europe, and the breakdown of the peace negotiations in 1806 had confirmed his view that a satisfactory settlement was unattainable in present circumstances. A significant minority in the Whig party and amongst their supporters in the country believed, however, that victory over France was unlikely and that a negotiated settlement which left Napoleon in power was essential to the country's economic well-being. This attitude was reinforced by the ideological tradition associated with Fox and the 1790s. The peace party among the opposition consisted of much the same men who believed that the Whigs must continue to be the champions of domestic reform in alliance with extra-parliamentary radicalism. Peace and reform were still closely associated; but that association only stiffened the Grenvilles' resistance to both.

Grey's alignment with Grenville and the former Portland Whigs like Fitzwilliam and Windham could be interpreted as a move away from his old Foxite principles and laid him open to ideological criticism. His refusal to back a vigorous opposition to the war in principle seemed to accord ill with his former conduct against Pitt, and his record as the man who had brought to an end Fox's peace negotiations was not easily forgotten. It was even more unfortunate that Whitbread was the chief spokesman of the peace party. Grey found it difficult to forgive Whitbread's attack on him in the Commons after the end of the peace negotiations on 5 January 1807, and Whitbread seemed to delight in provoking him on every possible occasion by the sharpness of his dissent from the official party strategy. In the summer of 1807 there was a petitioning movement in the industrial districts of the North in favour of peace, which Fitzwilliam and his son Lord Milton, now MP for Yorkshire, attempted to suppress, with Grey's support. As the session of 1808 approached, however, Whitbread made it clear that he intended to move for peace in the Commons. Grey sounded a warning note:

I hope [he wrote in December] that nothing will be hazarded either in language or action, without the most serious consideration of the consequences it may produce. Above all, I hope that nothing will be done to encourage a clamour for peace, against which I must set my face decidedly and strenuously.

Shortly before he came up to London he repeated that though he was 'as desirous of peace as you . . . I deprecate measures which can have no possible effect but that of removing peace to a greater distance'. He believed that the only effect would be to stimulate counter-petitions which might encourage ministers to persevere in their policies, and also to encourage Napoleon by presenting a picture of war-weariness in England. Whitbread, however, was not to be deterred, and at the party dinner at Grenville's house on the eve of the session he took occasion to declare his dissent 'in so hot, and I must say, so wrong-headed a manner, that . . . Grenville seemed quite dumb foundered, and hardly spoke a word'. Grey, who was working to dissuade Grenville from abandoning regular opposition, feared

Whitbread's conduct would have the contrary effect, and was naturally angry at this threat to his strategy.[1]

On 26 January, Whitbread gave notice of three resolutions for peace, 'all in my opinion very badly drawn', Grey wrote to Mary, 'for one of which I certainly could not vote, and to another of which I should have considerable objection'. Grey used Lauderdale as a mediator: he drafted an Address for Lauderdale to propose, which played down the wish for peace. Whitbread was taken in by the stratagem and approved the Address, believing that Lauderdale was the sole author. Grey was amused to hear that Whitbread's only criticism was that it needed the translation of some of Lauderdale's 'Scotch' into English—though every word was Grey's. Grenville too consented, with some reluctance, in the interests of unity. The hope of compromise was dashed, however, at a meeting at George Ponsonby's, when Windham and some of the hard-liners in the Commons objected to the moderate tone of the Address, whereupon Whitbread reverted to his resolutions. He presented them in the Commons on 29 February, referring in his speech to Fox's name and declaring himself 'his true and genuine disciple. I am only feebly urging the sentiments which he would have forcibly uttered, if he had not been unhappily taken from us.'[2]

The debate was mismanaged by the opposition, who entered the chamber without a clear directive from their leaders as to how to vote. To the consternation of some members, Ponsonby, as agreed beforehand with Grey and Grenville, moved the previous question against resolutions from his own side of the House. A majority of the Whigs followed Whitbread into the lobby. 'I am afraid', wrote Grey, 'that the result in every view must be considered as fatal to the future union, and, at all events, to the power and consequence of the party.' On the following day he had recovered some of his spirits, but, he told Mary, the episode had 'left a considerably increased disgust on my mind with respect to politics'. He feared

that the encouragement Whitbread has received from his success on this occasion may increase his disposition to do things in future, acting upon his own separate views and opinions, which may again produce differences which, if repeated, must be fatal... Any chance of good, and God knows it is little enough, there yet remains consists in my opinion in the preservation of the union between Fox's friends and Lord Grenville's, and the discretion of the latter as the leader of the party.

He admitted that Whitbread had behaved in a 'moderate and conciliatory' manner and that 'a feeling very favourable to him has been created in the party'. He feared however that any efforts on his own part to reach a better understanding would be fruitless: 'feeling that he had a jealousy of me with respect to my opinions ... and

---

[1] T. Grenville to Grenville, 8 Dec. 1807, *Fortescue MSS*, ix. 157; Windham to Fitzwilliam, 24 Nov. and Grenville to Fitzwilliam, 26 Nov., Fitzwilliam MSS, Sheffield; Grey to Whitbread, 28 Dec. 1807, 8, [12] Jan. 1808, G. 59; Grey, *Life and Opinions*, 178–80.

[2] Grey to Mary, 23, [25] Feb., 1 Mar. 1808, G. 27; to Grenville, 23 Feb., BL Add. MS 58947, fos. 91–2; Grenville to Grey, 23 Feb., G. 21/2; Holland to Grenville, 28 Feb., BL Add. MS 58947, fos. 93–4; *Parl. Deb.* x. 801–53.

that we neither of us perhaps could discuss a subject on which we differ, with sufficient calmness'.[3]

With the question of immediate peace negotiations disposed of, the Whigs settled down to consider their opposition to the government's strategy and conduct of operations rather than to the war in principle. As Michael Roberts has written, the Whigs showed themselves 'barren of constructive ideas about the conduct of the war', and virtually confined themselves to criticisms of the government's military failures.[4] As in their own period of office, they failed to evolve a consistent policy with regard to the competing claims of diversionary expeditions or a full-scale continental campaign. The latter was, in any case, difficult to envisage in 1807 or 1808. The Treaty of Tilsit removed Russia, Britain's remaining continental ally, from the war and although the fleet protected Britain and Ireland from invasion there was no foothold on the Continent from which a campaign could be launched until the Spanish uprisings. The situation added some force to Whitbread's contention that the war had become a pointless stalemate, and the Milan and Berlin Decrees, by which Napoleon sought to defeat Britain by attacking her trade and economy, together with the counter-measure of the Orders in Council, created economic disorders which added to the unpopularity of the war in the country.

The Whigs' opposition was therefore marginal in its strategic and political effectiveness. The main effort in 1808 was the condemnation of the expedition to Copenhagen to seize the Danish fleet, which gave them a moral standpoint on which to condemn British policy as no more respectable than the French, but it had no effect on events. The year 1808 marked a low point in the Whigs' fortunes, and a severe attack of his stomach complaint meant that Grey was unfitted to raise their spirits by any political activity. As he had written to Petty in November 1807, they might attack the ministers on particular points such as Copenhagen, but

you will not suspect me of looking to any other success; and indeed hardly of wishing it, for unless power could be obtained with much more effectual means of exerting it for the public advantage, than there is under the present circumstances any hope of obtaining, our exclusion from office I cannot regard as a subject of regret.

His experiences as Foreign Secretary convinced him that the opposition would find it just as difficult to carry out an effective foreign policy should they return to office and confirmed his view that for the time being they were better where they were. In the circumstances, their conduct appeared captious and unconstructive. Sir Thomas Turton, one of their supporters, deplored Whitbread's attempts to infuse energy into their opposition as motivated by 'party spirit and personal enmity' and they seemed to spend their time criticizing the failures of the past rather than proposing alternative strategies for the future.[5]

[3] Grey to Mary, 1 and 2 Mar., G. 27; Grey, *Life and Opinions*, 182–3.
[4] Roberts, *The Whig Party*, 117.
[5] Ibid. 112–17; Grey to Piggott, 13 Jan. 1809, G. 47/4; to Petty, 5 Nov. 1807, Bowood MSS.

The Spanish risings against the French occupation in 1808 opened up new possibilities of a foothold on the Continent from which a military campaign might be launched. They also had an instant ideological appeal to the more liberal Whigs, who saw the Spanish people as heroic leaders of European resistance to tyranny: they filled the role played in the 1790s by the French revolutionaries against the *ancien régime*. The Hollands, whose extensive Spanish travels had brought them into contact with the liberals there, were foremost in pressing for British aid, and they transmitted their enthusiasm to Grey, Brougham, Sheridan, Horner, and indeed most of the Foxite Whigs. It was welcome too because it reduced support for Whitbread's peace policy: even the Grenvilles came to approve of a Spanish expedition, despite their reservations about assisting rebels and Grenville's conviction that Napoleon would rapidly crush the Spaniards.

Fitzwilliam sounded the rallying call in July 1808. 'I am like you, in heart about Spain', he assured Grey. 'These Spaniards are a fine people—by their own energy they will emancipate themselves.' Grey told Lady Holland that the Spanish news

really keeps me awake at night and in the day I can think of nothing else. I did not think it possible that anything could have made me regret being out of office, but I now wish I was in a situation, in which it might be possible for me to assist in this glorious cause.

He declared to Brougham in September that: 'To assist the Spaniards is morally and politically one of the highest duties a nation ever had to perform.'[6]

This euphoria soon gave way to a more habitual gloom when the news arrived of Sir John Moore's retreat and of the Convention of Cintra, which allowed the French to leave Spain with their arms and forces intact. Grey wrote that Moore had been scandalously treated and that 'on the Convention there can be but one sentiment. It is as bad as the business of Buenos Aires.' As Moore's retreat drew towards its disastrous climax at Corunna in January 1809 the Whigs' doubts about the Spanish campaign mounted. Grey and Grenville became pessimistic both as to the length of the campaign and as to its eventual outcome. Grey told Auckland that he still thought it right to send troops to Spain despite the government's 'gross mismanagement' but he declared himself 'full of grief and indignation about Spain . . . I really was sanguine to a degree that with your original opinions you would hardly believe possible.' Auckland and the Grenvilles were deeply shaken and Thomas Grenville thought Grey unaccountably 'giddy with all this wild Spanish dream'.

Grenville's inclination was to give up the parliamentary battle fearing that an opposition attack on the government would seem unpatriotic. 'I feel a strong reluctance to these wordy wars, at a moment when the country itself has not, perhaps, two years more of existence . . . I am sick of politics, and entertain a most melancholy picture of what is to come.'[7] He confessed that he had never thought

---

[6] Tierney to Grey, 12 July 1808, G. 55; Fitzwilliam to Grey, 22 July, G. 14/11; Grey to Brougham, 29 Sept., *BLT*, i. 410–14; to Lady Holland, 2 July, BL Add. MS 51550, fos. 139–42.
[7] Grey to Willoughby-Gordon, 25 Sept., 16 Nov. 1808, ibid. 49477, fos. 22, 26; to Auckland, 6 Jan.

that there was 'the smallest chance that an undisciplined nation so long crushed under the most degrading religious and civil tyranny, could with any aid we could bring to the contest defend themselves against such a military power as that of France now is'. He expressed his dislike of 'the cause of harrassing opposition pursued in the H. of C. last year', which he feared the 'young and ardent minds' in the party would be unable to resist again. He was inclined to confine his attendance to a few occasions for the discussion of 'great and broad lines of policy' rather than to 'the gratifying petty animosities, or pursuing inconsiderable triumphs on objects often scarcely worth the discussion they occasion'. He wrote to Ponsonby to ask him to make these views known at the eve of session party meeting. Grey, too, wrote to Sir Arthur Piggott of his own disapproval of 'a vexatious and harrassing opposition' and urged the overriding importance of maintaining the union with Grenville in 'a cordial and conciliatory spirit'. He regarded the opening debate as 'decisive as to the future' of the opposition.[8]

Whitbread disagreed. He contended that it would be improper not to move an amendment to the Address, and declared his intention to do so. Only Tierney's intervention averted a crisis, and he was able to report to Grey that the meeting 'went off without a single dissenting voice', and that Whitbread 'did not say one word'. The debate, however, exposed the opposition's disagreements and lack of general strategy. Grey was relieved that a semblance of unity had been maintained, but Whitbread wrote after the debate to say that he wished he had moved his amendment: he had refrained only out of respect for Grenville, who at least always said what he thought and in the hope that 'if there should at any time be a division' of the party, there would be no disagreement between Grenville and 'those in the House of Commons who are still attached to the memory and principles of Fox'. Grey responded by urging Tierney and his friends to be as conciliatory as possible towards Whitbread, and though Tierney remarked of him that 'there were many horses quiet enough in the stable, who kicked and plunged and played the devil when they got out with the hounds', he promised to do all he could to keep the party in good humour with each other.[9]

The news of Moore's death and the evacuation from Corunna arrived at Howick late in January. 'It deprives me of all power of expression, and almost of thought', Grey wrote to Grenville, 'I must confess that, as things have been managed, it is much to be regretted that your opinions, against sending troops to Spain at all, did not prevail.' Moore's connections with the Whigs determined them to paint him as a martyr to the government's incompetence. Ponsonby's speech on the campaign in the Commons on 24 February failed, however, to suggest how the disaster might have been averted. He censured the government both for its lack

1809, ibid. 34457, fo. 497; to T. Grenville, 16 Dec. 1808, ibid. 41857, fos. 106–7; corr. in *Fortescue MSS*, ix. 245–56, and *Court & Cabinets of George III*, iv. 288.

[8] T. Grenville to Grey, 31 Dec. 1808, *Fortescue MSS*, ix. 253; Grenville to Fitzwilliam, 9 Jan. 1809, Fitzwilliam MSS, Sheffield; Tierney to Grey, 16, [19] Jan., G. 55; Grey to Piggott, 21 Jan., G. 47/4.

[9] Roberts, *The Whig Party*, 125; Grey to Piggott, 23 Jan., G. 47/4; Whitbread to Grey, 29 Jan., G. 59; Tierney to Grey, 1 Feb., G. 55; T. Grenville to Grenville, 14 Jan., *Fortescue MSS*, ix. 269.

of caution and for undue delay in sending forces to Spain until the French had defeated Spanish resistance: he succeeded only in demonstrating the Whigs' complete lack of understanding of the campaign, and of the purposes and qualified success of Moore's expedition in drawing the French armies away from Badajoz and Portugal. Grey shared this failure: he wrote in November 1809 that Moore's diversionary strategy had ultimately only given the French a freer hand for operations against the Spaniards.[10]

In March 1809 Grey, having recovered from a stomach attack, left for London. He moved on 21 April for an Address to the throne expressing 'mortification and grief' at the disaster and laying it at the door of the government's 'rashness and mismanagement'. He spoke of the universal sensation at the first news of the Spanish risings:

One universal spirit broke forth, without distinction of rank or party.... all the generous sympathies of the nation, that love of liberty, hatred of oppression, a sense of the blessings we enjoyed, and a forecast of the struggles we might have to preserve them, all conspired to excite in the breasts of Englishmen, those feelings, which I trust we never shall want when the contest is between justice, freedom, and public independence on the one side, and the highest degree of atrocity and oppression on the other.

Under that spirit, Parliament had granted all that ministers had asked for, but their bungling and mismanagement had destroyed the nation's hopes. Grey concentrated his attack on two points: the failure to concentrate on the single objective, which he claimed had been the 'system which was steadily pursued and acted upon by the last administration', a system which 'the country will one day know how to appreciate', and the military tactics of the campaign. The blame rested squarely on the government's 'system of improvidence, imbecility, and impotence, which would be a disgrace to the government of every country'.[11]

Grey wrote to Holland, who was at Cadiz and had read only a garbled report of his speech in the newspapers, that his purpose was to show 'the excessive folly of the measures pursued by our Ministers'; but he had also abandoned 'reluctantly' his former opinion 'in favour of the spirit and resistance of the Spaniards' after hearing reports from military and diplomatic sources recently returned from Spain. His major source was Sir Robert Wilson, who had been with the Portuguese army and now installed himself as Grey's military adviser, where his main concern was to denigrate the valour of the Spaniards and the abilities of Wellesley, Moore's successor. The Whig attitude to subsequent events in the Peninsula was coloured by Wilson's opinions. They pilloried the Spaniards as apathetic and incompetent, and Wellesley as ambitious and careless of the lives of his troops. Even the Hollands, who returned from Spain in 1809, changed their earlier tune about the heroism of the Spaniards, and the Whigs descended into the depths of gloom.

[10] Grey to Grenville, 26 Jan., ibid. 274; to Brougham, 22 Nov., *BLT*, i. 477; Roberts, *The Whig Party*, 128–31.
[11] *Parl. Deb.* xiv. 121–50; Holland to Grey, 20 May and reply, 13 June, BL Add. MSS 51544, fos. 179–95, 51551, fos. 9–30.

Even if Wellesley reached the Ebro, Grey wrote, he would be pushed back again as soon as Napoleon returned to the Peninsula. Wellesley's strategy was not appreciated until he began to win lasting victories in 1811. His retreat behind the defences of Torres Vedras confirmed the Whig opinion that the war was lost, and when he emerged to win victories they asserted that they were disasters. Grey declared in the Lords in 1810 that he did not believe Wellington's despatch on Talavera, and criticized his tactics with what Roberts called 'incautious effrontery'. Milton suggested that he fought the battle only to get a peerage. The Whig attitude after 1809 cast discredit on themselves and did them no good in the country.[12]

The full effect of this strategy was brought home by the opposition's failure to capitalize on the disaster at Walcheren in 1809. The renewal of the war in central and northern Europe created the usual British dilemma between concentration on one theatre of war and the sending of diversionary expeditions to assist the allies. In the event it was decided to send a well-publicized expedition under Lord Chatham and Sir Richard Strachan to capture the island of Walcheren, the town of Flushing, and the Dutch fleet in the Scheldt.[13] It was an unqualified disaster, and its mismanagement led to bitter recriminations in the Cabinet which culminated in a duel between Canning and Castlereagh and the resignations of Canning and the Prime Minister, Portland. The government was reconstructed under Spencer Perceval, and in September he offered places to Grey and Grenville, which they peremptorily refused, partly because of the Catholic question but also because they scented the opportunity to destroy the government altogether and replace it with their own. Grey declared himself opposed, as always, to diversionary expeditions: 'There is no greater fault in military, as well as in most other affairs, than to attempt too many things at once', he wrote: if those troops had been sent to Portugal, Wellesley might have conquered Spain. On these grounds as well as on the usual theme of governmental and military incompetence, the Whigs prepared a full-scale attack for the session of 1810.[14]

On 26 January they carried a motion in the Commons for an enquiry into the Walcheren expedition and followed it up with other victories over the demoralized ministerialists in February and March. On 26 March Lord Porchester moved fifteen resolutions censuring the government. Despite the opposition's widespread support in the country, they failed to win over the independent members and so paid the price for the distrust they had created by their own record of disunity and untrustworthiness on foreign affairs. They lost all the crucial divisions by majorities of between 51 and 23. The truth was, wrote J. W. Ward, 'that the country is outrageously against them, and that it prefers anything to the Grenvilles'. 'I don't believe that any Ministers could have existed after such a career of

[12] Grey to Tierney, 25 Aug., Tierney MSS; Roberts, *The Whig Party*, 135–40; Creevey to Whitbread, 3 Jan. 1810, Whitbread MSS.

[13] The details of the expedition were common knowledge in London before it even set out. Rosslyn sent Grey frequent bulletins about the preparations: G. 51.

[14] Grey to Willoughby-Gordon, 9 Sept. 1809, BL Add. MS 49477, fo. 38; to Grenville, 10 July, ibid. 58947, fos. 160–4; to Tierney, 24 July, Tierney MSS.

wickedness and folly,' Grey remarked, 'if it had not been for the disgusting scenes of the last session.'[15]

Grey came up for the debates in the Lords, and rounded off the session with a motion on the State of the Nation on 13 June. It was one of his full-dress speeches, attacking the government both in detail and in general. Reviewing the whole of foreign and domestic policies, he attacked the enormous increase in public expenditure, which had risen from £16m. to £85m. in 17 years, the mis-management of the war which offered no chance of an honourable peace in the foreseeable future, the offence given to neutral powers and in particular the USA by the Orders in Council, incompetence in the management of the country's finances, the denial of Catholic emancipation, with the consequent danger of a French invasion of Ireland, and the increase in civil and military establishments and in the influence of the Crown. He concluded with a long justification of his consistency in supporting parliamentary reform since 1792. He proposed an Address supporting the continuance of the war but censuring ministers for their general incompetence.[16]

Grey's motion marked a watershed in Whig opposition to the government's foreign policy. After 1810, their criticisms of the war were muted. The 1810 session was the last in which they mounted a full-scale attack on foreign policy. For the next two years they were preoccupied with the revival of radical agitations in the country, stimulated by the Duke of York case and the distress attributed to the Orders in Council, which brought to the fore their fears of associating them-selves with extra-parliamentary radicalism. The King's illness and the consequent necessity for regency arrangements also concentrated their attention on domestic issues. The fleeting prospect of a return to office under the Regent seemed more pressing than the long-drawn-out stalemate in the Peninsula.

During these two years, however, Grey's attitude to the war slowly changed. He began to appreciate Wellington's military skill, and Wilson's depressing influ-ence was countered by a deeper understanding of the Spanish campaigns, perhaps stimulated by the publication of Captain Pasley's *Military Policy of the British Empire*. Grey found in this pamphlet a confirmation of his long-held view that the war effort should concentrate on a single aim and theatre, and it led him to take a more positive view of Wellington. On 19 March Grey was writing in his old tone of despondency about Portugal, fearing that Wellington behind Torres Vedras was keeping too many British troops in a hazardous defensive position, and pointing to the financial burden involved; but he also admitted that he supported the continuance of the war on the grounds that it tied up large French forces and strained their resources. The news of Wellington's break-out and Masséna's retreat, however, aroused him, and, speaking on the vote of thanks to Wellington in the Lords on 26 April, he confessed his complete recantation: he paid generous

[15] Roberts, *The Whig Party*, 144–7; *Letters to 'Ivy'*, 99; Grey to Lady Holland, 3 Sept., BL Add. MS 51551, fos. 33–6.
[16] *Parl. Deb.* xvii. 533–78.

tribute to Wellington, 'that distinguished general and his brave army', and though admitting his doubts of ultimate success he declared that he believed Portugal to be secure. He admitted that at the outset, he had expected a different issue: 'they were at the time his conscientious opinions... taken up from no illiberal or invidious feeling. He had now no hesitation to qualify and retract them.'[17]

In August 1811 he confessed himself in two minds, for Wilson's pessimism about French reinforcements and the sickness in the British army was countered by information from other sources. It was suggested that Napoleon's intended Eastern campaign might offer the British a better opportunity of success. The victories of 1812 gradually swung him round, and though doubts still broke through at times the news of Salamanca in August aroused his enthusiasm. 'This is indeed a great event in whatever view you may take of it', he declared to Holland; and if Napoleon's Russian campaign were to fail, 'its consequences may be incalculable'. For the first time he expressed doubts as to Napoleon's ultimate success, though he characteristically added that 'new disappointments' might yet arise, and that the Spanish and Italian allies might yet fail us. Surely, he wrote to Lady Holland, 'your friends the Spaniards shall at last make only a moderate exertion in their own cause: and surely such an event as this would animate even stones'.[18]

By December, his mercurial temperament was back in the depths: the Spaniards seemed as ineffective as ever, and he criticized Wellington's tactics after Salamanca. The mood was only temporary, and Wilson's departure to Russia removed a depressing influence on his mind. Grey now saw, more clearly than Grenville, the interdependence between British operations in Spain and the Russian campaign, and the vital contribution made by the former to the ultimate outcome. If Napoleon were obliged to winter in the East, he wrote, it would be possible to advance across the Ebro, and though Wellington's difficulties were not over the prospects were bright. 'I cannot agree with you', he wrote to Grenville on 27 October 1813,

... that the money spent in Spain has been ineffectual in producing the better hope which now exists... I still think that our opinions at the beginning and in the progress of the Spanish contest were well warranted by such data as we then had to reason upon... But I cannot say that as things have turned out, contrary certainly to my expectations, the event of the Spanish war has not been both honourable and advantageous to this country.[19]

Grey's analysis was that France's difficulties made 1813 a suitable year to seek a negotiated peace. He was fully aware of Napoleon's military genius, of the disunity of the continental allies, and of the possibility of French reverses stimulating a revival of patriotic energy in France. 'With all the uncertainty of the success of

[17] Roberts, *The Whig Party*, 149–53; Grey to Holland, 19 Mar., G. 35; *Parl. Deb.* xix. 766–8; Grey, *Life and Opinions*, 317–19.

[18] Grey to Lord Holland, 12 Aug., to Lady Holland 29 Aug., 1812, G. 35; to Fitzwilliam, 25 Aug., Fitzwilliam MSS, Northampton.

[19] Grey to Auckland, 10 Dec., BL Add. MS 34458, fo. 431; to Grenville, 29 Aug., 1 Nov. 1812, 27 Oct. 1813, *Fortescue MSS*, x. 294, 300, 354; to Holland, 24 Oct., 13 Dec., G. 35; Roberts, *The Whig Party*, 160; Grey, *Life and Opinions*, 319–22.

the next campaign, and with the absolute certainty that we are now making our last effort... I should be willing to conclude a peace, which compared with our situation a year ago would be most advantageous, though it may be one to which, with our resources entire, I should not have been willing to submit.' He agreed with Holland that even if peace were not concluded, a demonstration of British willingness to negotiate would have a good effect on the French people. He suggested in October that Britain 'should, *with the Allies*, offer a joint negotiation on moderate principles... a *sincere* proposal, mind, and with a real anxious wish for its success'.[20]

Grenville, on the contrary, was for persisting in the war in hope of a more conclusive victory. In two long and carefully reasoned letters Grey argued against that position. It was better to seize the opportunity of a satisfactory peace than to go on fighting in the doubtful hope of a complete victory: 'moderation in success is still my motto'. He concluded with a protest against the report of Grenville's recent speech in the Lords in which he mentioned 'the original policy' of the war in 1793 and spoke of the present alliance against France as the continuation of Pitt's policy at its outset. Grey regarded the present alliance as defensive against France and that of 1793 as offensive. He wrote:

There cannot now be, I think, a discussion more useless in itself, or to me more unpleasant, than who was in the right and who in the wrong in 1793. I am sure this must be equally your feeling, and that you must therefore be most unwilling to place me in the situation of being compelled either to vindicate my former opinions, or by my silence to seem to acknowledge that they were wrong.

Grenville sent a conciliatory reply. He believed that a few minutes' discussion would remove all major differences and misunderstandings. As regards the principles they should follow, he asserted his conviction that the war ought to be supported 'to the utmost', and he remarked that his agreement with Fox in 1804 was made with 'a most distinct reserve... on both sides as to former opinions to which we still adhered respecting past transactions'. However, his 'esteem and respect' for Fox's character and 'since his death the cordial friendship which I hope I may say has been established between yourself and me, has ever made me desirous of avoiding to the utmost of my power every subject or topic on which it was probable we might differ'. Though he could not give up his opinions as to the original purpose of the war, therefore, he assured Grey that his speech had not been intended to arouse past differences and that if it seemed to do so it had been misreported.[21]

Grey laid down in a letter to Robert Adair in November 1813 his view of the principles on which peace might be negotiated. There must be security for the European allies against a recurrence of French aggression, but to insist on the

[20] Grey to Fitzwilliam, 9 Apr. 1813, Fitzwilliam MSS, Northampton; to Willoughby-Gordon, 3 Oct., BL Add. MS 49478, fos. 19–20; to Holland, 24 Oct., G. 35.
[21] Grey to Grenville, 27 Oct., 12 Nov., Grenville to Grey, 24 Nov., *Fortescue MSS*, x. 351–8, 360–3. Grenville's speech, *Parl. Deb.* xxvii. 11–20 (4 Nov.).

reduction of France to her ancient frontiers would merely provoke a French reaction, the renewal of war, and the probable collapse of the alliance. The first object must be to balance the power of France; but it would be unwise to insist on the terms thought necessary a century before at Utrecht. He wished for independence for Holland, Italy, Switzerland, and the Austrian Netherlands, but thought these conditions might be too severe. He insisted, however, on the principle of national self-determination. In Holland the Orange party succeeded in November 1813 in restoring their Prince, not as formerly with the limited powers of Stadtholder, but as a hereditary monarch: a new monarchical constitution was proclaimed on 6 December. Grenville approved, but Grey expressed reservations about the protection of Dutch liberties. He regarded the episode as 'a manifest usurpation on the rights of a free people'. He also objected to the treaty with Sweden in which, in return for a Swedish alliance against France, Britain agreed to the transfer of Norway from Denmark to the Swedish empire. He moved an Address of protest in the Lords on the grounds that the rights of kings over their subjects were not rights of property and that they ought not to be transferred to another 'like cattle attached to the soil':[22]

His majesty sits on the throne in virtue of the recognition of this fundamental principle; we stand here, and enjoy freedom of speech, upon its basis, that a prince using his power to the injury of his people, or, in the words of our ancestors, having been guilty of violating the original compact between the sovereign and his people, forfeits his right to the crown.

The approach of victory therefore brought to the fore the old differences between Grey and Grenville on the nature and purposes of the war and the terms on which it might be ended. If Grenville was eager for the victory which Pitt had sought in the 1790s, Grey was as anxious as he had been then that the victory should not be one against the liberties of European peoples. Indeed, he could hardly believe that Napoleon could be finally defeated. 'It is impossible', he wrote in September 1813, '...not to admire his ability, resource, and fortitude, in presenting himself everywhere to repel the dangers which assail him.' Holland spoke Grey's language in the Lords on 20 December when he declared that peace would best be served by leaving France with some of her new possessions, which would give her an interest in maintaining it.[23]

The French Emperor's last hours had come, however. His defeat at Leipzig in October 1813 and his retreat across the Rhine proved to be the virtual end. As Napoleon retreated on Paris, Wellington was pushing into France from the Pyrenees, while Blucher and the combined Prussian and Russian armies advanced from the north-east. In November 1813 the allied sovereigns assembled at Frankfurt, with Castlereagh representing the Regent, and on 1 December they issued a declaration offering the French independence within their existing frontiers. The negotiations failed, however, and fighting resumed. The last battles were fought

---

[22] Grey to Adair, 14 Nov., G. 1/3; Grey, *Life and Opinions*, 330–3; Grey to Holland, 22 Dec., G. 35; *Parl. Deb.* xxvii. 768–84 (10 May).
[23] Grey to Holland, 24 Sept., 8, [24] Dec., G. 35; *Parl. Deb.* xxvii. 295–6.

on the outskirts of Paris in March 1814 and the allied sovereigns entered the city on the 31st. Napoleon abdicated at Fontainebleau on the 4th April and on the 11th the allies signed the Treaty of Paris, banishing him to Elba. The convention ending hostilities was ratified in Paris on the 23rd and on the following day Louis XVIII sailed from Dover with a British escort to reclaim the throne of his ancestors. The Peace of Paris, concluded on 30 May, restored France to her boundaries of 1 January 1792, with a few small exceptions, recognized the sovereignty of the House of Orange in Holland, the independence of Switzerland, the German and Italian states, and restored most of the French colonies overseas. The thirty-second article bound the signatories to send representatives to a general Congress in Vienna within two months. As the *Annual Register* remarked, no treaty was ever so generally approved in England.[24]

Grey had watched the negotiations of 1813–14 among the allies and then with the French with trepidation. He feared that Castlereagh might give way too much to the extremism of the absolutist powers and of the British Court, and he suspected that the ministers would be too feeble to resist those pressures. Almost to the end he still feared a French revival and a check to the allies which would disappoint hopes of peace altogether. A 'moderate check', he wrote in February 1814, might be desirable in order to bring the allies to accept a negotiated peace, but he feared that any victory by Napoleon would be too triumphant, and 'I look to a most disastrous retreat'. He persuaded Holland at the end of 1814 not to speak in praise of the government's role in the peace negotiations though Holland believed that ministers deserved more credit than Grey was ready to allow, and declared that no Whig government could have got better terms. He warned Grey that the public mood was strongly in favour of a Bourbon restoration, but Grey's reaction to the Bourbons' return was vigorous: 'the iniquity of such a measure at such a moment could only be exceeded by the baseness of attempting to screen ourselves from blame by alleging that we had not encouraged it', he wrote. He applied to France the principle that peoples should be free to choose their own form of government and not have one forced upon them by foreign intervention; and he foretold 'an immediate explosion, which would sweep them for ever from the throne of France'. He thought the conduct of negotiation since Chatillon 'most impolitic and unwise' but he found his colleagues in the party did not share his views, and as he was kept at Howick by the serious illness of his son he was unable to state them in the House of Lords as he would have wished.[25]

Napoleon's escape from Elba and his return to France, where he arrived on 1 March, deepened the rift between Grey and the right wing of the Whig party. Grenville stated bluntly at the end of March his opinion that 'real peace with Bonaparte on the French throne, is absolutely unattainable... War he must have,

[24] 1814, pp. 163–4.
[25] Grey to Holland, 8, 15, 22 Dec. 1813, 2 Jan., 6 Feb. 1814, to Lady Holland, 26 Dec., 27 Feb., G. 35; to Holland, 2, 25 Feb., Holland to Grey, 4, 11, 13, 18 Dec., BL Add. MS 51545, fos. 122–5, 136, 106–7, 110–21; Grey to Willoughby-Gordon, 7 Nov. 1813, 28 Jan. 1814, ibid. 49478, fos. 38, 56; to Adair, 19 Jan. 1815, G. 1/3.

and above all, war with England.' He supported the government's engagement with the allies to resume fighting to depose Napoleon again. Grey took a directly contrary view. The news of the allies' declaration dismayed him completely. He contended that the Treaty of Paris of 1814 was a treaty between the countries, and not the rulers, of Britain and France, and that it was 'not necessarily abrogated by any internal change in the government of either.' We should 'maintain the relations of peace with the Sovereign of France who now possesses de facto, the whole authority of the state; and consequently that we should not engage anew in hostilities without such a cause as would, in other circumstances, justify that melancholy extremity . . .'. He would not 'go to war with France, merely because Bonaparte is Emperor'. He formed his opinion partly on the principle of non-interference in the internal arrangements of other states, but also on expediency, for he regarded it as unlikely that the allies could co-operate effectively to the extent necessary to defeat Napoleon again.

Grey recognized that this division with Grenville was too great to be easily bridged, and that it might lead to the end of their co-operation.

Since Fox's death [he wrote], I have looked to you as the person best qualified to take the chief direction of the party in which we have acted together. *You* know how little I have sought for myself any such distinction. Separated from you I must abandon all hope of being useful, and I probably shall withdraw myself from all further interference in politics, except upon occasions, if any such should arise, when my duty as an individual Peer may require that I should state my opinion.

Grenville admitted that there was 'much difference' between them on principles, but suggested that they might be able to agree on tactics by supporting 'immediate and vigorous preparation' and a close union with the continental allies. Grey was willing to go this far in the hope of preserving the party from dissolution, a step which, he wrote, would destroy 'our best hope, in the event of a new war, of averting a revolution'. He particularly regretted that Fitzwilliam and Elliot had shown even greater warlike zeal than Grenville, had adopted language 'exactly that of Burke at the beginning of the Revolution', and had been foremost in encouraging Grenville to take the stand he had done. The split became public on 23 May, when Grey moved an amendment to Liverpool's Address to the Regent, deploring the principle of war on the grounds of personal objection to Napoleon.[26]

Grenville showed restraint in attempting to avert a quarrel. The Marquess of Buckingham declared a month after Waterloo that Grey's conduct and language had demonstrated 'a vital distinction upon public principles, and consequently a disunion of political party'. He could not act again in concert with those who professed Grey's views. Grenville, however, refused to follow his brother's lead, and the victory at Waterloo enabled both leaders to put the question behind them. Grey wrote to express the hope that 'our concert may be renewed with the same

[26] Grenville to Grey, 28, 31 Mar. 1815 and replies, 30 Mar., 1 Apr., G. 21; Grey to Wellesley, 2, 6 Apr., 18 May, BL Add. MS 37297, fos. 236–40; to Holland, 26 June, G. 35; Grenville to Fitzwilliam, 30 Mar., BL Add. MS 58955, fos. 135–40; Grey, *Life and Opinions*, 351–9.

cordiality as before this interruption', though he continued to deplore the way in which the old despotic and absolutist regimes in Europe had been re-established by the peace. He particularly regretted the fate of Poland, and told Lady Holland that the treaties had indeed proved, as he and Fox had argued twenty years ago, that the war had been fought to suppress liberalism throughout Europe. The domestic events of the next four years raised fears in his mind that this might apply to Britain herself: and in that period the alliance with Grenville was to be shattered by the re-emergence of the fundamental issue of the 1790s, whether peace at home was to be preserved at the cost of constitutional liberties. The stresses of the last years of European war were continued into the early years of peace: Waterloo proved to be only a temporary respite to the strains of a political alliance that was becoming too unrealistic to be maintained.[27]

WHIGS AND RADICALS, 1807–1812

In the 1790s Grey had seen parliamentary reform as a means to avert violent revolution on the French model. He had attempted to provide the movement with moderate and respectable leadership in the hope that by so doing Britain's liberal constitution and aristocratic institutions might be preserved, under the control of the Whig party. That strategy had failed because the French Revolution and the war had created a strong spirit of conservatism amongst the middling classes, and the majority of his own party had preferred to resist change rather than risk its dangers. The experience convinced him that any future commitment to reform must be even more moderate and gradual in tone, to preserve the fragile reunion of the Whigs after 1801 and their alliance with the Grenvilles, without whom there could be no realistic hope of power. After 1807 his task was to retain the liberal image he had created for the Whigs without again sacrificing his prospects of positive achievement by hurrying faster than his party would follow.

Between 1807 and 1815, Grey sought to concentrate the party's efforts and attention on issues on which there was broad agreement amongst them, particularly the Catholic question and opposition to governmental incompetence in waging the war. His views on the ultimate necessity of reform remained unchanged, but it now became a question to be postponed until opinion in the country turned in its favour. To many at the time and since, it seemed as though the caution and apprehension of middle age had turned Grey into a conservative. That view neglects the fact that, to Grey, reform had always been fundamentally a conservative, or at least conserving, measure directed as much against democratic radicalism as against reactionary Toryism, and that he always viewed it, as all other political questions, in the light of expediency and party interests. Grey's reputation has

[27] Buckingham to Grenville, 16 July, BL Dropmore MSS Ser. 2; Grey to Lady Holland, 22 Oct. 1815, G. 35.

suffered from the very 'Whig interpretation' of English history which painted him as an ideological hero, crusading for the principle of reform. The years after 1807 do not mark a break in Grey's reforming commitment: rather they help us to understand its true character.

The Whig party, as a recent writer has remarked, was 'an alliance between aristocratic landowners and professional men', whose liberalism sprang from different roots.[1] For the former, to which section Grey belonged by instinct and conviction, it derived from a long tradition of paternalistic responsibility exercised through great estates and territorial political influence, which was in general used to provide parliamentary seats for men of congenial principles and liberal views, who were held within safe bounds by the deference they had to pay to their patrons. The aristocrats regarded public opinion from the standpoint of territorial magnates, living in the countryside and accustomed to the deference of bucolic society. For the middle-class lawyers and businessmen who made up the rank and file in the Commons alongside the sons of the aristocracy and the Whig gentry, however, liberalism was an expression of political principle and it reflected their wish for social advancement. The professional and businessmen were largely metropolitan or Scottish, and had achieved social position through education, talent, and industry. Their liberalism was of a more utilitarian kind, fostered by the Scottish universities, the new 'science' of political economy, and radical protestantism. They were interested in philosophical debate, in journalism, in the awakening of the country at large to the ideals of progressive, bourgeois self-improvement. Where the aristocratic Whigs looked increasingly to the past, living on the glorious memory of Fox and his friendships, or gathering in the great country houses for hunting, shooting, and political reminiscence, the new Whigs looked to the future when Britain would be governed by an aspiring, intelligent, and wealth-accumulating middle class, relegating the aristocracy to the status of exhibits in a museum of historic curiosities.

After 1807, it was a party composed of these divergent elements that Grey had to try to lead and to satisfy. It was still the party of the Russells, the Cavendishes, and the Fitzwilliams: but it was also the party of Whitbread, of Brougham, of Horner, of Lambton, and of Romilly. Its ideology was a compound of old Whiggery and of new Benthamism. It is not strange that before it could be welded into an effective instrument of political reform it had to undergo stresses and strains that might have broken it apart. That it did not do so was as much due to Grey's leadership, much criticized though it was and has been, as to anything else. The triumph of 1832 was not only the triumph of reform: it was a vindication of Grey's political strategy. In this respect he is still 'Lord Grey of the Reform Bill'.

For twenty-three years before Grey took up reform as Prime Minister, however, the question was fraught with danger for the Whig party. Grey was sensitive to the divergencies of opinion within its ranks and he put its survival as a broadly-based coalition before a commitment to a cause which experience convinced him

[1] W. Thomas, *The Philosophic Radicals* (Oxford, 1979), 47.

was hopeless in the existing state of public opinion. He hoped by occasional expressions of general approval to maintain his own consistency as a reformer, but he shrank from any positive step which would alienate the right wing of the party and throw the remainder into alliance with the radicals. He saw the radicals as a threat to his own leadership and control of the party. Thus he promoted Ponsonby to the Commons leadership rather than Whitbread, and tried to restrain the efforts of the left wing to form an alliance with radical agitators like Burdett or Cartwright. When the latter tried again to organize a meeting in Middlesex to petition for reform at the end of 1808 Grey did his best to prevent the Whigs from involving themselves in it. Cartwright and Creevey urged Whitbread to associate the party with the rising swell of reformist opinion, reminding him that the Whigs needed to maintain their image as leaders of liberal opinion if they were to distinguish themselves from the Tories in the public eye. A Whig administration could not have the support of the Crown, so it needed the affection of the people. Whitbread was not yet ready to move against Grey's restraint, and told Cartwright that he considered it premature. Grey himself refused an invitation to be a steward at Cartwright's proposed reform dinner in Middlesex on the same grounds.[2]

The Whigs were prepared to support renewed demands for economical reform, but even this was done in a somewhat faint-hearted manner. A Finance Committee was set up in 1807 while the Talents were in office to examine the present number of sinecure offices and pensions and to see if any further reform was needed, but the initiative came from a private member, and Petty, the government's spokesman in the Commons, secured an amendment which limited its scope. Grey opposed Burdett's being made a member of the committee, in almost his last speech in the Commons, to avert the widening of its activity to reform in general. The Committee produced a number of reports in 1808 and 1809 which revealed the extent of the place system, showing that 76 MPs held offices, of which 28 were sinecures: but in 1810 the House rejected by six votes a motion, supported by Whitbread and Milton, for the abolition of all sinecure places. It was an embarrassing question in that the Grenvilles were amongst the leading beneficiaries of the system; Grenville's Auditorship of the Exchequer was only the most prominent of a number of offices held by his family, who, like the Greys, were not holders of large and profitable estates and who, Grenville argued, needed these resources to perform their public duty. Grenville suspected, with good reason, that Whitbread and his friends in 'the Mountain' supported the campaign as much out of dislike for their Grenville allies as for public reasons. The Whigs thus made little attempt to press the question with any force, and nothing was achieved. A Bill to prevent the giving of offices in reversion was more popular in Parliament, and this Grey

[2] Grey wrote to Sir A.Piggott on 21 Jan. 1809 that 'There is nothing that I have more at heart . . . than to preserve the connection which was formed . . . between the friends of Fox and Lord Grenville': G. 47/4; Cartwright to Bedford, 19 Nov. 1808, Bedford to Whitbread, 17, 23 Nov., Creevey to Whitbread, 11 Dec., Cartwright to Whitbread, 26 Jan., 17 Mar. 1809, Whitbread to Cartwright [Mar. 1809], Whitbread to Bedford, 15 Mar., Whitbread MSS; Cartwright to Grey, 26 Jan. and reply, 1 Feb. 1809, G. 9A/12.

supported, but though the Commons passed it three times it was twice rejected by the Lords and the third time converted into a temporary Act for one year only. The Whig attitude, as expressed by Grey in May 1810, was that this measure would be a useful gesture of goodwill to the public, but in truth they saw it as only a minor question, and an opportunity to express their general sentiments without doing anything positive.[3]

The real stimulus to the revival of a reform movement in the country came in 1809, when the activities of Mrs Mary Ann Clarke, the Duke of York's mistress, in trafficking in army commissions created a scandal. The question was raised in Parliament in January by a disreputable back-bencher named Gwyllm Lloyd Wardle, an ally of Burdett, and it attracted support from 'the Mountain'. Whit-bread moved an Address for the Duke's dismissal from the command of the army, and 125 Whigs voted for it. In April the younger members of the party elected Wardle to the Whig Club. Grey was horrified. He regarded the affair as dangerous to the public reputation of the whole political system. He had written to Piggott in January that the debates in the Commons during the last session had lowered Parliament in the estimation of respectable people, and he saw Wardle's attack on the Duke of York as a further step in this direction. He declared to Tierney his 'wish that opposition should appear to have had nothing to do with it' and agreed with Lauderdale that the affair would bring the whole royal family into disrepute. Whitbread, Bedford, Folkestone, and 'the Mountain' were for leading the public outcry, lest it turn against the interests of the party and create difficulties for members representing popular constituencies. Grey, however, was infected by Grenville's alarm. 'It is not by such means', he wrote, 'that I shall ever wish to see the influence of the Crown reduced. It is in truth fighting with poisoned weapons.' Wardle's relations with Mrs Clarke and the unsavoury characters of both were revealed in the subsequent enquiry. The public, however, was enthusiastically behind the exposure of these scandals and the radicals hastened to make capital out of the affair. In April Folkestone and Whitbread moved for an enquiry into corrupt practices in regard to the disposal of all public offices, and in the summer Madocks revealed Castlereagh's action in demanding the resignation of a member elected for a Treasury borough who had voted against the government. Whitbread, Romilly, and 83 other Whigs voted for the motion.[4]

Meanwhile, Burdett and his allies in the metropolitan area seized the opportunity to call for parliamentary reform. A meeting in Westminster in March, called to vote thanks to those who had assisted Wardle, and attended by Burdett and Whitbread, turned into a revivalist crusade. Burdett attacked the unrepresentative

---

[3] *Parl. Deb.* x. 1048–52, 1087 (10, 14 Mar. 1809), xvi. 1071–5 (17 May 1810). 'If it was little to do', said Grey, 'let it be done, and give some proof that the House was not inattentive to the general wishes and opinion of the country.'

[4] Grey to Piggott, 21 Jan. 1809, G. 47/4; to Tierney, 17 Feb., Tierney MSS; Lauderdale to Grey [3], 10 Mar., G. 39; Rosslyn to Grey, 24 Feb., G. 51; Grey to Holland, 5 Jan. 1810, G. 35; to Brougham, 17 Dec. 1809, G. 8/3; to Whitbread, 8 Mar. 1809, G. 59. Some constituencies, including Southwark, called their members to account over the Duke of York affair.

character of the House of Commons and declared that it was contemptuous towards the people. Whitbread spoke in favour of arousing a national campaign for reform, thus publicly differentiating himself from Grey, whose approach was based on the view that the Whigs should only take it up when the people demanded it. Whitbread advocated action by the Whigs to stir up the demand. He repeated his views at a City Livery Dinner in April, which was also attended by Wardle. Grey reacted strongly, calling in the Duke of Bedford to remonstrate, and seems to have convinced the Duke that Whitbread was playing Burdett's game. Petty saw Whitbread himself, and their conversation ended, as Grey reported, 'in an understanding that all party connection between him and us is, for the present at least, at an end'; but Grey expressed the wish that it might be only a temporary separation, not precluding co-operation on other matters. The Grenvilles were hoping that the episode would drive Whitbread out of the party, but Grey strove to prevent an open breach even at that stage. In November Whitbread and Grenville met for a discussion of the position. Whitbread professed the old Foxite principle that 'a difference of opinion on any particular subject did not in former times dissolve a Party, and was not considered by Fox as a direliction [sic] of him' and indicated his wish to continue to operate with the party.[5]

Though a formal separation, which would have thrown Grey even more into Grenville's camp, was avoided, the reform question was now launched. Grey took the opportunity to define his attitude in his speech on the Peninsular War on 21 April. He professed his continued support for 'a temperate, intelligible and definite reform', but his assertion that 'to promote that desirable object was ... the study of the last administration: and I can answer for it, that no man is more friendly to such an object than my noble friend near me' [Lord Grenville] sounded disingenuous.[6]

Grey's caution infuriated Burdett's allies, prominent amongst whom was Alderman Robert Waithman, leader of the City of London radicals. They planned a reform dinner at the Crown and Anchor Tavern on 1 May, with Burdett in the chair. Waithman spoke of the pusillanimity of 'Friends of the People', who, he declared, supported reform only when it suited their own political interests. Six weeks later Burdett revealed his plan of reform in the Commons, asking for it to be considered in the next session. It bore a remarkable resemblance to Grey's last motion in 1797, calling for the franchise to be extended to payers of direct taxes, for equal single-member constituencies, and voting by parishes. The object, Lauderdale suggested, was to test Grey. Grey refused to be drawn away from his cautious middle position. He refused in May to present Cartwright's Middlesex petition for reform, declaring that[7]

[5] T. Grenville to Grenville, 30 Mar., 1 Apr., Grey to Grenville and Auckland to Grenville, 31 Mar., Grey to Grenville, 28 Mar., *Fortescue MSS*, ix. 284–8; Bedford to Whitbread, 13 Apr., Whitbread MSS; Whitbread to Tierney, 13 Nov. 1809, Tierney MSS.

[6] *Parl. Deb.* xiv. 149.

[7] Ibid. 1041–70; Lauderdale to Grey, 19 June 1809, G. 39; Grey to Cartwright, 15 May, G. 9A/12; Roberts, *The Whig Party*, 246–59.

tho' I am, as I ever have been, sincerely attached to the principle of temperate and constitutional reformation, I must be allowed generally to decline all participation in measures which have been adopted without my concurrence, the character and tendency of which appear to me to be extremely doubtful, and which may possibly be influenced by views materially different from those which I entertain with respect to this important question.

Whitbread was alienated from Burdett by the latter's action in springing his reform motion on the House at such short notice that he was unable to travel from Bedfordshire in time to support it, as he declared he would have done. Whitbread was not a Burdettite; he wanted popularity for the Whigs, and, as he told Creevey, 'fair fame' for himself, which Creevey and his flatterers urged him to secure by standing forth as leader of both the Commons and the country: but he was no more prepared to be second fiddle to Burdett than he was to Ponsonby or Thomas Grenville, and he distrusted speculative radicalism as much as Grey did. He remained a House of Commons man and shared the Whig view that it should not be the tool of the masses of the people. In the end, his aspirations to acceptance in aristocratic society were stronger than his populism.[8]

Waithman repeated his attack on Grey at a Common Council meeting in November 1809, referring in contemptuous terms to Grey's speech in April. Grey responded with his famous remark that 'I was just as much at war with the patriots of this class in 1792 as I am now', and he remarked that, although he would stand alongside the people to combat any 'dangerous attack' aimed at their 'liberty and safety', he expected in return only 'great professions of gratitude at the time, and another denunciation at the first opportunity'. It was clear that, as J. W. Ward wrote, it would be foolish to expect co-operation between the Whigs and the jacobins, both of whom were competing for popular allegiance and neither of whom would submit to be led by the other. Grey's attitude was characteristically Whig: the radicals aimed at the destruction of the Whig party and its aristocratic foundations. They were therefore to be seen as allies of the Court, if not indeed outright Tories themselves, who would do away with the necessary buffer between arbitrary government and popular democracy, destroy the balance of the old constitution and inaugurate a system as tyrannical as that of Napoleonic France. When Holland begged him not to be too concerned about Burdett and the radicals because they could achieve nothing by themselves, Grey responded with a tirade almost worthy of Edmund Burke. Wardle's proceedings had done the greatest mischief by weakening the people's attachment to the Crown: 'it has perhaps laid the foundation for such measures as followed the accusation of the Queen of France'. Nevertheless, the radicals were 'the best friends of the Court' and by diverting public attention from the real issues

---

[8] Whitbread to Creevey, 14 Jan., 14 June, Creevey MSS, Creevey to Whitbread, 15 Nov., Whitbread MSS; *Parl. Deb.* xvii. 146–55.

they provide the best means of escape for the Ministers from the difficulties in which their folly and wickedness have involved them... They aim at nothing but the degradation of all public character, their watchword being that all Ministers are alike, and that no advantage is to be derived from any change, thus co-operating most effectually with the Court in withdrawing all public confidence from their opponents... there is in my opinion a degree of meanness in appearing to court them in the slightest degree to which I can never submit. In short I must be quite plain on this subject in declaring that they are men with whom I cannot consent to endeavour to keep any terms, and if that policy should be adopted I can hardly look to any other consequence than my separation from those who pursue it.

He added that he thought his friends ought to 'mark strongly their reprobation' of Waithman's personal attacks upon him. His irritation was no doubt partly explained by a conversation with Whitbread at Southill a few days earlier on his way to London, in which Whitbread had declared his view that Ponsonby ought to give up the Commons leadership to Petty. Grey now saw Ponsonby as a safeguard against Whitbread's reformist influence in the party, and flatly refused to throw him over, despite his ineffective leadership. After consulting Grenville and others who might be sure to share this view, he expressed it strongly again in a letter to Whitbread on 12 January and begged him to reconsider. He added (though with ostensible reference to the Catholic question) that he would not seek popularity, though he would be glad of it when it came: but 'I never will sacrifice one atom of what I believe to be right to obtain it; any more than I would for court favour... I must trust that eventually my conduct will satisfy the public.'[9]

Grey's attitude was thus an amalgam of intense personal resentment against attacks on his character with a shrewd, if somewhat over-coloured, appreciation of the damage that would be done to the Whig party if the radicals were allowed to steal their liberal clothes. Whitbread was not insensitive to this political consideration and when Cartwright urged him to co-operate with Burdett, offering to prepare for their edification some notes on the constitution, Whitbread fobbed him off with courtesies. He was sufficiently aware that he needed the Whig party as much as they needed him, and he agreed with Grey and Grenville that the party's reforming efforts should be concentrated for the time being on economical reform and financial retrenchment. The possibility of a successful attack against the ministry on Walcheren aroused Whitbread's ambition for office as much as Grey's.[10]

Burdett made himself an even greater popular idol in April 1810 when he was committed to the Tower on a charge of breach of privilege of the House of Commons after his defence of the publisher John Gale Jones, who had been committed for contempt in February. Burdett's removal to the Tower triggered off a violent popular demonstration in London that awoke in some minds memories of the Gordon Riots. Grey and Grenville had no sympathy with him, and indeed

[9] Grey to Brougham, 9 Dec. 1809, G. 8/3; to Holland, 5 Jan. 1810, G. 35; to Whitbread, 12 Jan., G. 59; *Letters to 'Ivy'*, 93.
[10] Cartwright to Whitbread, 25 Mar. 1810, Whitbread MSS; Grenville to Grey, 18 Jan., G. 21.

expressed satisfaction that he had gone where he belonged, but the episode caught less prejudiced Whigs in a dilemma. Holland was inclined, while throwing in the necessary condemnation of Burdett himself, to support his cause to the extent that the privileges of Parliament were being misused against the liberties of the people, as Whitbread and Creevey also argued. The London radicals exploited the incident for all they were worth. Waithman arranged a dinner to protest against Burdett's imprisonment, and a flood of petitions in his support poured into the Commons. That from Worcester incorporated the words of Grey's motion for reform in 1793, and Cartwright sent in one of his own which Whitbread had previously approved and for which he voted—though the House refused to accept it. Grenville demanded that Whitbread support the official party line, which he laid down as support for the House's privileges. It was, he wrote, 'a most pernicious experiment to encourage the People to any form of contest with Parliament', whatever the folly of the particular case, and he protested against Whitbread's connivance at the words uttered in his presence at Waithman's dinner. He threatened to sever their connection. Whitbread had to reply with assurances that he had not sanctioned Waithman's praises of Wardle, nor been present when he launched his attack on the Whigs. Grenville let him off with a caution not to attend such public meetings in future.[11]

Grenville's heavy artillery was followed by a fusillade from Grey in the Lords in June, when he again took the opportunity to state his views on reform at length at the end of his speech on the State of the Nation. The question

has long engaged my most serious contemplation. At an early period of my life, I certainly took up strong opinions upon this subject, and pursued them with all that eager hope and sanguine expectation, so natural to the ardour of youth. I will not say that there may not have arisen some difference between my present sentiments and former impressions; still I beg leave to assure your Lordships that the general opinions I then formed, I have not in my maturer age seen cause to change.

He confessed that 'perhaps, I do not see in the same high colouring the evil sought to be redressed' but declared 'I am now, as I was formerly, the advocate of a temperate, gradual, judicious correction of those defects which time has introduced.' He referred to the days of 1792 when 'we were...held up to obloquy by the same description of persons, who now describe us as no real advocates for the rights of the people, because we were not prepared to support, what was then as it is now called, and most falsely called, a radical reform.' He read out the Friends of the People's letter to Cartwright of 12 May 1792 disavowing any future co-operation with the Society for Constitutional Information: 'Those were the opinions arraigned by a description of persons with whom I then disclaimed all intercourse. They are the opinions now censured and misrepresented by the very

[11] Roberts, *The Whig Party*, 265–70; *Parl. Deb.* xvii. 119; Cartwright to Whitbread, 8, 12, 22 May, Whitbread MSS; Whitbread to Cartwright, 15 May, *Cartwright*, i. 400–2; Grenville to Grey and encl to Whitbread, 23 Apr., Grenville to Whitbread, 1 May, G. 21.

same men, with whom I still decline all intercourse or association.' He declared that

Whenever this great question shall be taken up by the people of this country seriously and affectionately—(for, notwithstanding all we every day hear, I doubt much whether there exists a very general disposition in favour of this measure) there will then be a fair prospect of accomplishing it, in a manner consistent with the security of the constitution. But until the country shall have expressed its opinion upon this subject the examples of the other nations of Europe should deter us from any precipitate attempt to hurry on to premature or violent operation, a measure on which the best interests of the nation so essentially depend.

Grey then went on to speak of the Burdett case. He gave strong support to Grenville's view of the necessity of parliamentary privilege, and declared that it was as legitimate to use it against those who 'excite against Parliament a popular indignation' as it was against the influence of the Crown. He launched into a personal attack on Burdett, 'holding himself forth as a martyr in the same good old cause for which Hampden died in the field, and Sydney and Russell on the scaffold!... A more unfortunate allusion than this in my opinion, could not possibly be made.' It would have been easy for himself to take up[12]

the popular side of the question, and meanly to have courted popular applause at the expense of sincerity and principles. But such a line is little suited to the habits of my life, still less consistent with the feelings and principles by which my public conduct has been governed. I am not, however, ignorant of the degrading artifices by which this applause is acquired—artifices with which neither virtue nor talents have any connection—arts which men possessed of neither are best fitted to practise—men such as we have lived to see in the present day, who, renouncing the obligations of faith and honour, breaking through all the bonds and engagements that hold society together in their career of foul slander and dirty calumny, entirely set themselves above all the decencies of private life... For such arts and for those who have recourse to them, I shall ever feel a sovereign contempt.

Grey's abuse of Burdett was considered somewhat excessive even by Lord John Russell, though Holland excused him on the grounds that it was a natural response to the provocation he had received from the radicals. However, the Whig leaders' fears that Burdett was about to lead a popular revolution were relieved by the fiasco of his release from the Tower at the end of the session. Preparations had been made for a triumphal progress back to his house, but Sir Francis had no wish to be another Lord George Gordon. He slipped away by river and avoided the welcome, no doubt fearing that the demonstration would get out of hand in the same way as in 1780. His supporters were disgusted at what they considered a cowardly act, and his popular reputation was so severely damaged that he no

---

[12] *Parl. Deb.* xvii. 560–73.

longer seemed a threat to the Whigs. There was much relief among the leaders, particularly since Whitbread and 'the Mountain' had returned to their obedience.[13]

On 21 May Thomas Brand, a moderate amongst the mountaineers, put forward in the Commons a comprehensive scheme of reform which was moderate enough to attract the assent of Ponsonby and Tierney as well as Whitbread. He stressed the importance of property as the basis of representation, even to the point of reviving a scheme like Pitt's in 1785 to compensate borough proprietors for the loss of their rights of nomination, and proposed the extension of the franchise only to copyholders in the counties and borough householders paying taxes. There was no mention of the more radical proposal of Grey in 1797 for equal electoral districts, and the duration of Parliament was to be three years and not annual. The Bill attracted 115 votes, though 234 were cast against it, and Fitzwilliam's son, Lord Milton, reflecting his father's conservative views, spoke strongly against it; the main body of the Whigs supported Brand.[14]

From this point, the Whigs sought to establish a moderate reformist programme which distinguished them from the radicals while maintaining their claim to be the true champions of reform. Their basis was the old Whig constitutional argument that the House of Commons should be not an assembly of the delegates of the people which would wield the power of the state, but a check upon the power of Crown and executive and a guardian of the people's rights. It was a shrewd amalgam of abstract principles and political tactics, and it marked the final breach between the Whig reformers, including Whitbread, and the popular radicals. The latter, indeed, condemned it. Cartwright produced yet another reforming tract, entitled *The Comparison*, in which he remarked that Grey's views on reform were 'so delicate, so faint, so evanescent, so equivocal, a man must have good eyes and close attention to find them out'. Leigh Hunt, founder of the *Examiner*, advocated a Whig-radical alliance and also attacked Grey's sincerity. But the steam had gone out of the question, and the King's illness in late 1810 focused attention instead on the Regency and reawakened Whig hopes of office. An attempt by Cartwright and Brand to form a joint body to agitate for reform in the spring of 1811 collapsed for lack of Whig support. Cartwright's Society of the Friends to Parliamentary Reform, and the Hampden Club, had more than a tinge of the old Friends of the People about them, but the impetus had been lost. Once the Whigs had given up hope of office in 1812, Brand renewed his motion in the Commons but it attracted only 88 votes. Waithman made a last attempt at co-operation with the Whigs by sending Grey a copy of the proposed City of London petition for reform in March 1812, but it was returned without comment.[15]

It was to be five years before reform was again proposed in the House, and by

---

[13] *Early Correspondence of Lord John Russell*, ed. Rollo Russell (1913), 131–9. In Jan. 1811 Whitbread refused to sign a requisition for a protest meeting in Westminster and in May he refused to present the reformers' petition to the Commons: Cartwright to Whitbread, 28 Jan., 3, 25 May, Whitbread to Cartwright, 29 Jan., Whitbread MSS.

[14] *Parl. Deb.* xvii. 123–64.

[15] Waithman to Creevey, 28 Mar. 1812, Creevey MSS.

that time Whitbread was dead and the situation in the country was quite different. After 1812, popular reformism was associated with the economic distress of the working classes, with Luddism, Cobbett, and the crusade of men like Bamford in Lancashire, or Spence and his extreme 'Philanthropists', while at the intellectual level the movement was permeated by Benthamite Utilitarianism and the aspirations of the middle class. Its Whig advocate was to be Henry Brougham, its organizing genius at Westminster Francis Place. The events of 1808–12 had failed to break the unity of the Whigs, and Grey's strategy was, from that point of view at least, vindicated. As the Catholic question and the war had shown, their prospects of office were minimal in that period, and neither from opposition nor from government could they have hoped to secure a Reform Bill. Grey was politically right in refusing to allow the party to commit itself to a radical programme that would have damned their prospects still further. That they emerged intact as a party, and with a restated commitment to moderate reform on constitutional grounds when the time should ripen, was in the end a more substantial achievement than the acquisition of a popularity which, as Grey pointed out, would not survive the disappointment of their inevitable failure to carry radical reform.

In the years after 1807 the politics of faction were beginning to give way to the development of a two-party division as the distinctions between Whig and Tory slowly hardened. In the political negotiations of 1809–12, differences of principle and policy on the Catholic question and the war stood in the way of coalitions between the government and any section of the opposition. Grey had instantly repudiated Perceval's advances in 1809 on precisely those grounds, and the negotiations for a new Regency administration in 1811 and 1812 similarly foundered on the incompatibility of policies. Yet these years also showed that the Whigs were not themselves a fully coherent party united on principles. The Whig party was still an alliance rather than a single group, and it was held together more by the trust and friendship between Grey and Grenville and by political expediency than by common convictions. Only the Catholic question was a secure bond between the two sections; on most other matters compromise remained necessary if they were to work together, but such compromises tended to break down if the major issues of reform and foreign policy came to the fore. The advent of the Regency issue in 1810 provided further evidence of their differences. Both Grey and Grenville believed in the importance of consistency, and the ghosts of Pitt and Fox in 1788–9 now returned to haunt them.

George III relapsed into mental illness in the autumn of 1810. Grey still hoped that the Prince of Wales would honour his old connections with the Whigs and that he would use his prerogative as Regent to bring them into office, as they had hoped in 1788. Before that could happen, however, the Regency had to be established and the question of procedure immediately presented itself. Grenville remarked that it was impossible to act on the Regency 'without some references to past times', and told Auckland that 'we are now in the same state as in 1788'. Grey in turn declared his opposition to a Regency Bill on the lines of Pitt's old measure and urged that, in view of the King's age and the need for a strong government to wage the war, the best course would be to proceed as Fox had proposed, to declare the Prince of Wales in possession of the unrestricted prerogatives of the Crown by joint Address of the two Houses. Grenville however regarded Pitt's precedent as authoritative and appealed for agreement on it to avoid 'the divisions and animosities which must follow a renewed discussion of the questions then agitated'. Grey's hackles rose at once. He replied that this 'forces us to enter on the most embarrassing question, that I ever was placed under the necessity of discussing'. Even under a sense of his 'most cordial attachment' to Grenville, he could not admit that Pitt's proposals had been anything but improper. In any case, the position was materially different from that of 1788:[1]

If I could not consent to them when the king was in the vigour of his life, had not been subject to previous attacks of the same nature, and might be expected to resume his functions with a full capacity to discharge them, how can I yield an assent to them now when all these considerations are reversed, and when the powers reserved would, to a moral certainty, be employed to cripple the government of the Regent ... to enable some of the worst men in the country to secure the government in their own hands.

During the later part of November and early December discussions proceeded between the Whig leaders, while the Prince, now represented chiefly by Moira but with Sheridan, as Grey believed, intriguing in the background once again, held ominously aloof for the time being from any indication of his attitude. The discussions failed to result in an agreed strategy, for when Parliament met on 15 November Grenville supported the government's motion to adjourn, quoting with approval the similar procedure of 1788, while Grey, though not opposing the adjournment, spoke strongly against following the precedent. Grey feared that the Prince's 'prudent reserve' in instructing his friends not to interfere or vote in any measures proposed for the present would isolate him from the Whig leaders and make their activity ineffectual—in which case he would simply act as his duty prescribed and return to Howick. Grenville thought that the ministers might not propose restrictions, in which case a conflict on that issue would be averted, but posed the question whether they should encourage the Prince immediately to change his ministers or wait to see if the King recovered in a short time. Holland pressed the procedural question of an Address rather than a Regency Bill, hoping that the Grenvilles could be brought to agree to it on the grounds that it would avert a long period of uncertainty: but he confessed that the likelihood was of a division between them.[2]

Grey returned to Howick in early December to be with Mary at her confinement. Colonel MacMahon, the Prince's secretary, alleged that he departed in high dudgeon because the Prince had not sent for him to ask his advice, but his mood was rather one of foreboding. He feared an alliance between Grenville and the ministers, and suggested to Holland a set of resolutions for the Lords in which he hoped Grenville might be persuaded to concur, which would avert discussion of the Prince's rights, and which urged the form of an Address of the two Houses. The draft resolutions he enclosed were carefully framed to avoid any opinion as to the expediency of limitations on the Regent, and left it open for restrictions to be incorporated in the Address. He hoped that this compromise would reconcile Grenville to the procedure: but when Holland introduced Grey's resolutions in

---

[1] Grenville to Fitzwilliam, 10 Nov., Fitzwilliam MSS, Northampton; to Auckland, 30 Oct., BL Add. MS 34458, fo. 140; Grey to Holland [31 Oct.], ibid. 51550, fos. 41–4; Grenville to Grey, 1 Nov. *Fortescue MSS*, x. 61–2, and reply 5 Nov., BL Add. MS 58948, fos. 5–7.

[2] Grey to Mary, 14, 16, 28 Nov., G. 27; to Adam [Nov. 1810], Blair Adam MSS; Grenville to Grey, 20 Nov., G. 21/2; Holland to Grey, 14 Dec., BL Add. MS 51544, fos. 247–50.

the House they were heavily defeated and Grenville voted in the majority, after speaking in favour of the 1789 precedent favoured by ministers. A hope that Grenville would after all come round to Grey's proposal was aroused when he supported Lansdowne's amendment on 4 January to omit all reference to restrictions in the resolutions, but he turned round on the second resolution and voted for a restriction on the creation of peers: his volte-face was crucial in giving the ministers a narrow majority. The consequence was the adoption by Parliament of a set of resolutions basically similar to those of 1789, which were submitted to the Prince for approval in January.[3]

Mary's safe delivery of a son on 29 December allowed Grey to return to London in time for the last debate on the resolutions. His friends had repeatedly urged him to come earlier, but, as he told Lord Ponsonby, his presence at Howick was essential:

I really believe Mary's life depended on it... You know how unwilling she is to send for assistance till the last moment; it has happened two or three times when I have been absent that the person sent for has not arrived till every thing was over.

If his motives were misrepresented it could not be helped: 'If my whole life cannot after an occasion of this sort protect me from a false construction of my motives, why let it take its course.' As soon as he was satisfied with Mary's recovery, he set out for London. William Adam had been called to Carlton House for consultations on 5 January and reported that the Prince then expressed 'his fixed opinion as to an Administration to be formed by Lords Grenville and Grey being the only Administration that could be really useful to the country'. He pointed out, however, that if the King were to recover in a short time he would be under 'great difficulties' in changing the ministers. Adam assured him that in such a case Grey and Grenville would not object, but that Grey 'thought the result must be entirely withdrawing from Parliament'. The Prince desired to see Grenville on the next day, and Grey as soon as he returned to London, and observed that 'if it was decided to change the Ministers, they must be prepared to give him complete support and to form a strong and efficient Government such as would justify him and satisfy the country as far as circumstances would admit.' Adam immediately wrote to Grey to inform him that the Prince wished to see him, and Grey received the summons on the 7th at Barnby Moor on his way to town. In the meantime the Prince conferred with Grenville and, Holland later wrote, reached general agreement on the whole question, though the Prince hinted at the need to consider a coalition with Canning, despite his own personal objections to the latter's old intimacy with the Princess of Wales. His sentiments on political and foreign affairs seemed however satisfactory to Grenville; and Adam was pleased to learn afterwards that the Prince had firmly told Moira that only Grey and Grenville

---

[3] MacMahon to Northumberland, 14 Dec., *CGPW*, vii. 104–5; Grey to Holland, 17 Dec., G. 35; Grey, *Life and Opinions*, 257–63; *Parl. Deb.* xviii. 406–66, 687–751, 804–7, 813–14, 1001, 1008–16, 1026, 1051–64, 1074–6, 1099–1100.

could form an adequate administration and that he would have to serve under them.

Sheridan and Moira almost upset the applecart by intervening at this stage. Sheridan threw doubt into the Prince's mind about the propriety of accepting the Regency immediately, in case the King should recover. Though Moira agreed with Adam in squashing this suggestion, he showed an ominous unwillingness to talk to Adam about the proposed Whig administration under Grenville, while the Prince was upset by Grenville's conduct in the Lords. Grey's arrival was therefore timely: he immediately went to Carlton House and had a 'most cordial and satisfactory' interview in which these difficulties were removed. To the Prince's suggestion about Canning he replied firmly that it would be wrong to weaken 'the attachment of old friends by a precarious connection with new or doubtful ones'; the Prince in reply expressed doubts about Grenville's retaining the Auditorship of the Exchequer with the Treasury. Grey left with the impression that the Prince would do all that the Whigs wished, and that possibly he would prefer him to Grenville as Prime Minister.[4]

The Whig leaders had now to consider how to advise the Prince to reply to the Regency resolutions agreed by Parliament in early January. They had some difficulty in reconciling their opinions. Grey's first draft referred to 'the possible practical inconvenience, and to the dangerous principle of the limitations ... however short their duration' and made no reference to any agreement to them. Grenville, however, refused to accept this wording and a passage was added signifying the Prince's willingness to accede 'to the arrangements ... which your wisdom shall ultimately deem best suited to such an occasion'. Grey read the letter to the Prince on the evening of 10 January and said that he would be at Holland's residence in Pall Mall if he wished to consult him about any alterations. The Prince could not forbear from consulting Sheridan again and, Grey wrote, 'instead of taking this course, he set to work with Sheridan and Adam, after dinner, to examine it; and the former, after pulling it to pieces, paragraph by paragraph, finally persuaded the Prince to reject it, and to substitute one of his own', in which the Prince gave full assent to the proposed restrictions, though reserving his opinion of their necessity. Sheridan and Adam then called at Holland's house with the amended letter. Grey flatly refused to approve it, as 'in its whole tenour and character, utterly objectionable'. He had difficulty in keeping his temper with Sheridan: his 'lying and baseness have been beyond all description', he wrote. He declared that if this was to be the Prince's procedure he could not consent to offer any further political advice to him. The Whig leaders protested to the Prince in as dignified a manner as they could muster against his deference to an 'inferior council', as being opposed to those 'principles of constitutional responsibility, the maintenance of which they deem essential to any hope of a successful administration of the public interests'. The Prince called on Holland the next day to try

---

[4] Grey to Ponsonby, 31 Dec., Blair Adam MSS; W. Adam's memorandum, *CGPW*, vii. 139–46; Grey to Mary, 7 Jan., G. 31; T. Grenville to Grey, 2 Jan., G. 21/1; Holland, *Further Memoirs*, 80–2.

to smooth over the quarrel, but could not resist pointing out that although he had consulted Grey and Grenville, they were not yet 'in a situation when his advisers would become strictly and constitutionally responsible' and that they were mistaken in seeing themselves in that light.[5]

It was not an auspicious start to the negotiations which Grey and Grenville now hoped would take place for the formation of a Whig government. MacMahon, the Duke of Northumberland, and probably Sheridan were poisoning the Prince's mind against Grey. Nevertheless, he asked Grey and Grenville to advise him as to the propriety and the means of forming a new administration, and they set about the attempt in a mood of some ill-humour which spilled over into their own relationship. Grey was driven almost to despair by the difficulties which were enough, he said, 'to drive more people mad than the King'. Apart from the Grenvilles' advocacy of an office for Canning, which Grey firmly squashed in mid-January, there were the vexed questions of Whitbread's pretensions to office and of Grenville's sinecure. Buckingham protested on 9 January against the first proposals sketched out by Grenville, which gave seven of the ten Cabinet posts to Whigs and included Whitbread at the Admiralty in, as he pointed out, 'an office of the greatest patronage and power' from which he would dominate the front bench in the Commons. 'I could not be brought to enrol my family and friends under Mr Whitbread's standard', he declared. He would prefer to have Canning or even Perceval and Sidmouth in the Cabinet to such an imbalance against the Grenville group. His protest was overruled, again by Grey's firmness.[6]

The question of Grenville's Auditorship was more difficult. Grenville displayed great reluctance towards giving it up, partly because it might seem an admission of impropriety not to have done so in 1806, and he pleaded his poverty without it in a way, said Holland, 'more becoming a merchant than a statesman aspiring to power and fame'. He proposed instead to hold the Home Office and serve under Lansdowne or Grey as Prime Minister. He insisted, however, that he should retain control of Treasury patronage. Grey flatly refused to hold the Treasury under such conditions. He was drafting a difficult but uncompromising reply to Grenville's fifteen page letter when Auckland arrived to say that Grenville wished to withdraw it. Whitbread was equally intransigent, and wrote that, though he had the highest personal esteem for Grenville, and believed it was the general wish to see him as Prime Minister, it was his settled conviction that he could not properly do so unless he gave up his sinecure, or at least the salary. Otherwise, Whitbread could not serve in the administration. Grey's reaction was that this intractability simply

[5] Grey, *Life and Opinions*, 266–70, 431–41; Adam's memorandum, 11 Jan., *CGPW*, vii. 160–4; Grey to Mary, 12 Jan., G. 27; Lauderdale to Grey, 11 Jan., G. 39; Draft for Prince's answer to the Address of Lords and Commons, 9 Jan., Grey to Grenville [10 Jan.], Grey and Grenville to Prince of Wales, 11 Jan., *Fortescue MSS*, x. 97, 100–1, 103–4, *CGPW*, vii. 158–9. For Sheridan's self-justification (to Holland) see ibid. 171–4.

[6] Northumberland to Prince of Wales, 8 Jan., and to MacMahon, 11 and 18 Jan. *CGPW*, vii. 148, 165–6, 182–4; Grey to Mary [10 Jan.], G. 27; Buckingham to Grenville, 9 Jan., *Fortescue MSS*, x. 97–9.

put an end to all hopes of forming a government, and even of the continued existence of the Whig party: and he said, with considerable irritation, it was all Whitbread's doing. However, Grenville reluctantly agreed to give up the salary and broke the deadlock.[7]

Two days later Grey told Mary that the negotiations were resumed, and that he and Grenville had seen the Prince that morning. On the 22nd a list of offices was ready whenever the Prince should call for it. Grey was enthusiastic that 'indeed almost the whole Administration is formed out of our division of the party; at least in the most important offices; for which in truth Lord Grenville has hardly any body to bring forward'. Of the ten places, eight were held by Whigs, with Grey nominated as Foreign Secretary and Whitbread at the Admiralty. The arrangements below Cabinet rank were still troublesome, however, with many competing claims to be settled, Grey being anxious to find places for as many old friends of Fox as possible and having to argue for them against supporters of Grenville. The Prince, too, was anxious to have offices for his friends, including Sheridan, who was suggested as Chief Secretary in Ireland. Grey was aghast—it would be, he wrote, 'sending a man with a lighted torch into a magazine of gunpowder', and the proposal was firmly rebuffed. The negotiations were at least as difficult as those of 1806, and their ultimate breakdown was more of a relief than a disappointment to him.[8]

At this point, with the Whigs poised for office as in 1789, the royal doctors once more claimed to discover signs of the King's recovery, and, as it was alleged, after a conversation with his mother, the Prince drew back. Grey and Grenville attempted to make the best of it and on 21 January advised the Prince, in what Roberts agrees was a 'frank and honourable' letter, that he should not change the government if there seemed a prospect of his father's early recovery. On 26 and 29 January Perceval was allowed to see the King and inform him of the whole course of events. The Prince then summoned Grey to Carlton House to be told, by Lord Hutchinson, that in the circumstances he had decided that it would be wrong to make any changes in the government, and he granted him a personal interview to the same effect on 3 February. Grey was convinced that the Queen and Perceval, abetted by 'that greatest of villains the D. of Cumberland', had thought up the scheme. The Prince's feelings, he thought, had been worked on by Sir Henry Halford, the chief physician, and he gave him credit for honourable and decent feelings in the circumstances. The Prince had been particularly kind in his manner towards him, he wrote, and assured him that his genuine wish was for a change, but that his feelings towards his father forbade it. His letter to Perceval confirming him in office had ascribed his action solely to 'filial duty'.[9]

[7] Grenville to T. Grenville [10 Jan.], ibid. 101–2, *CGPW*, vii. 129; Grey's memorandum to Grenville (marked 'not sent'), G. 21/3; Whitbread to Grey, 19 Jan., Whitbread MSS.

[8] Grey to Mary, 19, 29 Jan., G. 31; 16, 21, 22 Jan., G. 27; to Holland, 29 Jan., G. 35; Grey, *Life and Opinions*, 273–4; *CGPW*, vii. 130–5.

[9] Roberts, *The Whig Party*, 365; Grey and Grenville to Prince of Wales, 21 Jan., Queen to Prince of Wales, 29 Jan., Prince to Wales to Perceval, 4 Feb., *CGPW*, vii. 184–6, 200–1, 208–9.

Grey affected relief: 'What has passed has given me such an insight into the probable state of things under a new Government, that I much doubt whether any circumstances could ever induce me to take a share in it.' The Regency Bill was formally assented to on 5 February and the Prince was sworn in as Regent on the 6th. Perceval's government was confirmed in office, and the Whigs remained in opposition. The Prince's calculated rudeness to his ministers at the Privy Council on the 6th did little to sugar the pill, and despite his evident unwillingness to show them his confidence their parliamentary position seemed secure enough. Grey's reaction was characteristic:

After all, he has only relieved us from a situation of great difficulty and danger, and as I have neither to complain of him nor to reproach myself I am better pleased with this event, regarding my own personal interest, than with any other that could have happened.

He hoped that Perceval's government would survive through the session, for 'I have much to get over before I can again consent to accept office.'[10]

The danger was, however, that the Prince might gradually accustom himself to his ministers and that his natural indecisiveness would lead him to continue the status quo indefinitely. This would be increased if the opposition showed themselves too vigorous in criticizing the government's policies, as Fitzwilliam warned Grenville. In the summer of 1811 the Whig leaders were gravely concerned at the indiscretion of Lord Milton and some of the more outspoken members in the Commons in attacking the Duke of York, whom the Prince wished to see reinstated as commander-in-chief after his resignation over the Mrs Clarke scandal in 1809. Such conduct could only alienate the Prince from the Whigs, and Thomas Grenville regretted that 'since Fox and Grey are gone, there is no man in the House who can give it the tone of dignity which is necessary' and restrain the hotheads on the back benches.[11]

During the summer there were repeated rumours about the weakness of the government and supposed disagreements between Perceval and Wellesley and Canning. Moira continued to work for his own interests in a possible new administration with the latter two. He approached Grey in May 1811 to give a warning that, although there was little cordiality between the Prince and his ministers, he was 'daily accustoming himself more and more to these Ministers, that they had found out the way of managing him', and that as affairs went on smoothly enough the Prince's natural dislike of exertion increased his indisposition to change'. This was reinforced by the influence of Cumberland and Lord Yarmouth, particularly against the Catholics. Thus, suggested Moira, when the Prince assumed the full powers of the prerogative, 'he thought it probable that he might wish to introduce some of his friends, and to patch up an administration consisting in part of them, and partly of the present Ministers.' If such a proposition were made to him

[10] Grey to Mary, 30 Jan., 4 Feb., G. 27; 2, 6 Feb., G. 31; W. Elliot to Fitzwilliam, 2 Feb., Fitzwilliam MSS, Northampton; Grey to Whitbread [Feb. 1811], Whitbread MSS.

[11] Fitzwilliam to Grenville, 3 Feb., BL Add. MS 58955, fos. 123–4; Auckland to Grenville, 30 May, T. Grenville to Grenville, 1 June, *Fortescue MSS*, x. 140–3.

(Moira), he would find it impossible to refuse taking part. Grey brusquely terminated the conversation by remarking that if such a proposal were made to him he would unhesitatingly refuse it. Thomas Grenville's reaction was that such a blank refusal was more unjustifiable than in 1809: he told his brother that 'if the Prince proposes to frame a new government, I know not what right Lord Grey or you have to say to him that you will belong to no government that is not formed by yourselves upon a principle of exclusion.' Lord Grenville too thought that Grey went too far: he declared that 'the best interests of our Parliamentary constitution' required that leading men should always be ready to sink their differences in the public interest, as he pointed out he had done in 1804. If asked to join on these grounds he would place his concern for a strong government above his personal dislikes.[12]

Grey, however, still believed in the Prince's good intentions. In June 1811 he gave a great dinner at his London residence which the Prince himself attended, a gesture interpreted by the public in general as 'one of the strongest marks possible of H.R.H's predilection for his Lordship', and Grey expressed his hope that the government would eventually be offered on the same terms as in January. He suggested that they should settle their future policies towards the war, Ireland, public finance, and economical reform. Grenville did not consider that 'the Prince Regent has the smallest disposition towards what are called his old friends', but although Grey was ready to agree that 'we cannot look with any reasonable expectation of being allowed to act usefully for the public', he could not believe that the Prince would take any decisive step without at least consulting them first. If, as suggested in his conversation with Moira in May, the Prince might attempt to arrange a coalition, he held to his opinion that they should refuse to join it, grounding their attitude on the Catholic question and the war. At any rate, if any proposition was made to them the Whigs should be ready with an answer which would justify them to the public.[13]

Grey prepared to come to town for the new session in expectation of a final settlement of the administration when the Regency restrictions expired. His belief in the Prince's good intentions was tempered by scepticism of his ability to execute them. He declared to Holland, however, that the question must be resolved and that by the end of February the Whigs must either be 'in declared opposition, or Ministers with the confidence of Parliament and the Regent . . . Indeed,' he added, 'I have very little doubt that the Prince really entertains the intention which he voluntarily professed both to Lord Grenville and me last winter, and which I am not conscious that anything has been done by either of us to alter.' He would respond to any proposal for a coalition in good faith:

---

[12] Grey to Grenville, 23 May 1811, T. Grenville to Grenville, 25 May, ibid. 136–9; Grenville to Grey, 24 May, G. 21/3.

[13] Northumberland to MacMahon, 13 July 1811, *CGPW*, viii. 44–5; *Letters to 'Ivy'*, 142; Grey to Adam, 16 Aug., Blair Adam MSS; to Grenville, 4 June, [– June] and 1 Sept., *Fortescue MSS*, x. 144–5, 151–2, 167–9; to Holland, 4 Aug., G. 35; to Auckland, 23 Nov., BL Add. MS 34458, fo. 296.

To coalitions where circumstances have occurred to render them useful to the public and honourable to the parties concerned in them, I am, as you know, no enemy. I feel strongly and warmly in the moment of contest, but perhaps no man less cherishes permanent resentments either political or personal, than I do.

However, such coalitions were only honourable where there was agreement on major policies, 'and nothing of this kind can be said to exist with respect to the present Ministers', especially Perceval. Wellesley was too much committed to the present policies, especially in Ireland, for it to be possible for him to unite with the Whigs. A coalition would therefore seem impractical; indeed he went so far as to declare that he would reject such an overture as he had done in 1809.[14]

The Catholic question was the major, but not the only, obstacle to agreement; Grey heard in early December that Perceval's friends were openly boasting that the Prince was committed to them on the Catholic question, on the issue of the currency, and on the Peninsular War, and the longer a change was delayed the more difficult it became to make one. As the parliamentary session approached, Grey tried to restrain the opposition from any indiscreet activity that would risk alienating the Prince, but the omens were discouraging. Grenville and Fitzwilliam were anxious to raise the Catholic question, as necessary for the Whigs' public reputation, but the Prince could hardly avoid feeling that they were trying to force his hand. It was Wellesley, however, who brought on the crisis by informing the Prince on 16 January of his wish to retire from his office of Foreign Secretary. He gained the (mistaken) impression that the Regent was prepared to offer him the Premiership on the expiry of the restrictions. At any rate he felt that he could no longer act with Perceval, of whose abilities he had a poor opinion and who differed from him on the Catholic question and the conduct of the Peninsular War.[15]

Wellesley's action made some reconstruction of the ministry inevitable: the question was, would the Prince allow Perceval to remodel it on Tory lines by taking in Sidmouth and Castlereagh, or would he submit to a Whig government that would demand Catholic emancipation and other changes of policy, and probably expect him to be a mere figurehead? Neither possibility commended itself to the Prince, who was forced into an attempt to construct a broader coalition: but he insisted that any government would have to respect his scruples on the Catholic question. He was now arguing that, since he was merely a trustee for his father, he must respect the King's interpretation of the coronation oath, so that, although he was not himself opposed to emancipation, it could not be carried during the King's lifetime. Grey and Grenville regarded this as a disgraceful evasion: it confirmed Grey's insistence that they could not take office without a pledge that they should carry a Relief Bill, and Grenville's conviction that as

[14] Auckland to Grenville, 22 Nov., Grey to Grenville, 2 Dec., *Fortescue MSS*, x. 181, 183; to Holland, 27 Oct., G. 35; T. Grenville to Grenville, 28 Dec., BL Add. MS 58887, fos. 211–12.
[15] Grey to Willoughby-Gordon, 2, 11, 15 Dec., BL Add. MS 49477, fos. 155–9; Holland to Grey, 1 Aug. 1811, ibid. 51544, fos. 275–9; *CGPW*, viii. 302.

ministers they would never be able to rely on the Prince's 'steadiness and good faith'.

Both the Prince and the Whigs now thought it impossible for them to reach an understanding, but the Prince decided to sound out Grey and Grenville before reaching a decision. He used the Duke of York as his messenger, sending him on 13 February with a letter to Grey, who requested that they should go together to Grenville's house the next day so that the Whig leaders could receive it together. The Prince's letter declared his 'satisfaction' with 'the events which have distinguished the short period of my restricted Regency', particularly the success of the campaigns in Europe, and remarked that in view of the situation in the Peninsula

I shall be most anxious to avoid any measure which can lead my allies to suppose that I mean to depart from the present system. . . . I cannot withhold my approbation from those who have honourably distinguished themselves in support of it. I have no predilections to indulge, no resentments to gratify, no objects to attain, but such as are common to the whole Empire.

He concluded by expressing 'the gratification I should feel if some of the persons with whom the early habits of my public life were formed, would strengthen my hands and constitute a part of my Government'. He looked for 'a vigorous and united Administration formed on the most liberal basis'.

William Adam drew up a memorandum of the conversation between the Duke and the Whig leaders on 15 February. Grey and Grenville immediately said that they could not respond to the Prince's invitation. They 'disclaimed all personal exclusions' but pointed out that coalitions 'could not be honourable where there was not agreement on public measures'. The Duke explained that it was not the Prince's meaning that they should join the existing government, but that he wished 'to form an administration upon a broad basis, by a union of different parties, of which he should consider himself as the key stone, and as a centre round which their Lordships and others might rally'. Grey replied that this could not be regarded as a fair interpretation of the Regent's letter. He referred to the expressions in it approving the management of the war and 'entered warmly into his and his friend's feelings' on the Catholic question, which ought to be no longer postponed. The Duke asked whether the obstacle to a junction was only the Catholic question, but Grey and Grenville replied 'that they differed with the present Administration upon almost every political subject—many of them of the highest importance and only secondary to the Catholic question, so that they saw no hope or possibility of any favourable termination to a negotiation for a union with them'.[16]

The Prince's communication in fact provided Grey and Grenville with the excuse they needed to break off negotiations on public grounds of policy, rather

---

[16] T. Grenville to Grenville [1812], BL Add. MS 58887, fos. 218–19; *CGPW*, viii. 370–1; Adam's memorandum, Blair Adam MSS; *Fortescue MSS*, x. 217–20.

than on personalities. Fitzwilliam approved the outcome; though he warned Grey that 'we shall hear of nothing but your overbearing principles and conduct—the patriotic views of the P——', he agreed that a coalition would be 'disgraceful to the Parties, mischievous to the public', and he declared his eagerness to give his first vote against 'the P's *own* Administration'. He proposed an immediate attack on the Orders in Council as a popular measure with the country, and Grey urged Grenville to agree. Grenville, who wrote that he found the Prince's letter 'highly offensive', was even more bitter than Grey, despite his earlier conviction that the Whigs had nothing to hope for from the Regent. He considered, not unjustly, that the Prince's tactics had been all along to divide him from Grey and to construct a patchwork administration of his old Whig friends and the present ministers.

The answer sent by Grey and Grenville to the Prince on 15 February, as Roberts remarks, showed the Whigs at their best. They were frank but dignified:

We beg leave most earnestly to assure his Royal Highness that no sacrifices except those of honour and duty could appear to us too great to be made for the purpose of healing the divisions of our country and of uniting both its Government and its people. All personal exclusions we entirely disclaim: we rest on public measures, and it is on this ground alone that we must express without reserve the impossibility of our uniting with the present Government. Our differences of opinion are too many and too important to admit of such an union ... Into the detail of these differences we are unwilling to enter; they embrace almost all the leading features of the present policy of the empire ...

They referred especially to the necessity of an immediate solution of the Irish problem and of

a total change in the present system of government in that country and of the immediate repeal of those civil disabilities under which so large a portion of his Majesty's subjects still labour on account of their religious opinions. To recommend to Parliament this repeal is the first advice which it would be our duty to offer to his Royal Highness.

Even Buckingham approved of this answer, but the Prince declared to the Archbishop of York that 'he had been used most cruelly and most unkindly by his friends...he had *opened the door* for his old political friends, meaning and hoping that they would rally round him, instead of which they had most cruelly stood on punctilios and not permitted him, if he had been misconceived, to explain himself'; and he referred to the shameful abuse he had been subjected to by 'the under-strappers and even by the second-rates of the opposition', unchecked by their leaders. Grey responded that 'the agitation at Carlton House is extreme, and I am not without apprehensions that we may hear something more from thence'; but the Prince was smarting so much under what he considered the insult offered to him that he fell into abuse of Grey. Joseph Farington remarked that he was told by Sir Thomas Lawrence that the Prince hated Grey, 'whose mind and manners are not suited to the habits of the Regent', and that at a dinner at Carlton

House in March the Prince 'expressed his strong and habitual dislike of Lord Grey' to Lauderdale, who refused to listen and shut him up.[17]

Grey's political and personal relationship with the Prince, such as it ever was, was now at an end. Their mutual dislike was no longer papered over by political expediency or insincere professions of attachment. The causes lay deep in the early days of their acquaintance, in Grey's relationship with Georgiana, his refusal to disavow the Prince's marriage with Mrs Fitzherbert in 1787, his conduct during the 1788–9 Regency crisis, and above all in an insuperable incompatibility of temperament. Grey's honesty, stubbornness on political principles, and dictatorial manner contrasted with the weakness, vacillation, and shiftiness of the Prince. Even in his younger and more feckless days, Grey's personality did not accord with the Prince's. Neither ever trusted the other. In later years, Grey's support of Princess Charlotte against her father and his attitude over the 'Queen's trial' in 1820 confirmed the Prince Regent's dislike. If the Catholic question remained a bar to Grey's acceptance of office until 1829, George IV's personal hostility meant a veto on its being offered even as late as 1830. Yet there was more to it than personal antipathy. J. W. Ward was not far wrong when he wrote in July 1812 that the Whigs could only force their way into office:[18]

If they serve the Crown it must be always *against* the inclination of him that wears it. Every king *must* hate them in his heart, and only wait for a fair opportunity to capsize them and bring in the Tories, who are the natural allies of the monarch.

It was one thing for the Prince to take up opposition politics to embarrass his father, but when he took his father's place he was bound to look to a wider view of the national interest and to the maintenance of the royal authority. A party so openly dedicated as the Whigs had been since Rockingham's time to the reduction of the influence of the Crown was hardly equipped to be its servants. The point was made when another political crisis brought them to the brink in the summer of 1812.

On 11 May 1812, Spencer Perceval was assassinated in the lobby of the House of Commons by the madman John Bellingham. A reconstruction of the ministry seemed inevitable. The Cabinet, under Liverpool's 'acting-captaincy', opened negotiations with Wellesley and Canning. Grenville expected that 'they will easily form such a Government as may stand' with Perceval out of the way, and, though offering to come to town if Grey wished it, thought it probably unnecessary to do so. Grey expected that Wellesley would approach the Whigs, probably offering a concession on the Catholic question. He objected however to any offer which did not place him or Grenville at the head of the government, as being an indication

---

[17] Fitzwilliam to Grey, 16 Feb., G. 14/11; Grey to Grenville [17] (misdated 25) Feb., Grenville to Grey, 28 Jan., Grenville's memorandum, 6 Feb., T. Grenville to Grenville [13 Feb.], Grey and Grenville to Duke of York, 15 Feb., Buckingham to Grenville, 16 Feb., memorandum by Abp. of York, 19 Feb., *Fortescue MSS*, x. 233–4, 197–200, 205–6, 211–17, 220–2; Grenville to Hardwicke, 14 Feb., BL Add. MS 35424, fo. 92; Roberts, *The Whig Party*, 379; Farington, *Diary*, vii. 75–6; *Creevey Papers*, i. 159.

[18] *Letters to 'Ivy'* [6 July 1812], 165.

of the Prince's 'want of confidence, or rather of his dislike'. He conceded that it would be embarrassing and 'most of our friends would think us in the wrong', but thought that the most they could do would be to 'support an Administration that should be formed on principles that we can approve', while declining office for themselves.

Canning's refusal to join the ministry without agreement on emancipation, or to serve under Castlereagh in the Commons, wrecked the scheme to patch up the existing Cabinet and on 22 May the government resigned after being beaten in the House of Commons on J. S. Wortley's motion for an Address asking the Regent to form 'an efficient Administration'. Grey summoned Grenville to town in expectation of an approach from Wellesley, which the Prince immediately authorized and which was made in a letter on the 23rd. Wellesley made it clear that he was merely requested to explore the possibility of an arrangement, and that he had not been designated as Premier. He asked whether Grey and Grenville would negotiate on two conditions; the immediate consideration of the Catholic question and the vigorous prosecution of the war in Spain. Auckland thought the second condition 'a wild absurdity', and advised that the Whigs should avow no more than a willingness to support the war 'in whatever manner and to whatever extent a competent knowledge and consideration of our means and a due regard to the various interests of the empire may allow' and without 'improvident expense'. Grey and Grenville replied to Wellesley in writing in these terms on the 24th, expressing agreement on the Catholic question but remarking that the prosecution of the war was a matter of policy and not of principle, and would need to be judged in the light of circumstances and available resources. They added that they doubted whether the present state of the finances would allow any increase in expenditure for that purpose.[19]

The reply was conciliatory enough for Wellesley to take it to the Prince, who was expecting a refusal. He was disconcerted and, Grey reported, fell into 'such a state of irritation that he cannot be spoken to'. Liverpool consulted the Duke of York, who annoyed his brother still further by advising him to send for Grey and Grenville. For three days the Prince brooded on his predicament. He was determined not to send for the Whigs, particularly since Grey had offended him by remarks in his speech on the Catholic question in March. Moira did his best to smooth over this difficulty and persuaded Grey to offer an explanation of the speech; but the Prince was determined to escape a Whig administration. On 1 June, he gave Wellesley full powers to form a government and authority to approach Grey and Grenville once more. This time, new conditions were added: Wellesley was to be Prime Minister, Canning and Moira were to be in the Cabinet, and the Whigs were to have four out of twelve, or five out of thirteen, Cabinet posts. There

[19] D. Gray, *Spencer Perceval, the Evangelical Prime Minister* (Manchester, 1963), 455–8; Roberts, *The Whig Party*, 383–4; Grenville to Grey, 12 May 1812, G. 21/3; Grey to Grenville, 15 May, Auckland to Grenville, 23 May, Grey and Grenville to Wellesley, 24 May, *Fortescue MSS*, x. 250–2, 267–9, 271–2; Wellesley to Grey, 23 May, *Memoirs and Correspondence of Marquess Wellesley* (1846), iii. 243–4, 247–9.

were to be no exclusions on personal grounds. In an interview with Grey on the same day, Wellesley also hinted that the Prince wished to keep Eldon and Melville in the Cabinet, to which Grey coldly replied that he 'did not see any advantage to be derived from uniting with either of the persons he had mentioned'. He did not give a full answer on the spot, but indicated that 'I had conceived that it would be impossible for me to treat for the formation of a Government in the manner in which it had been proposed to me.'[20]

On 3 June the Whig leaders replied to Wellesley with a flat refusal, on the grounds that this was no way to set about forming an efficient administration: the criterion should not be the balancing of different parties, or, as Moira put it on 3 June, 'a principle of counteraction', but a cordial union and agreement amongst all members of the government on national policies and interests together with the full confidence of the Crown. It was perhaps slightly disingenuous: their objection was really that they were given too few places for their own party. In particular, Grey still felt insuperable objections to Canning. As Creevey put it, it seemed to the Whig aristocracy somewhat insolent that 'two fellows without an acre of land between them, the one an actual beggar, both bankrupt in character, one entirely without Parliamentary followers, the other with scarce a dozen' should 'condescend to offer to Earl Grey of spotless character, followed by the Russells and the Cavendishes, by all the ancient nobility and all the great property of the realm' a mere four seats in the Cabinet. It was particularly galling when the Whigs were now the strongest single party in the Commons, and might reasonably have expected to be directly approached.[21]

Doubtless the offer was intended by the Prince as a trap, for when Wellesley told him that the Whigs' refusal might be based on a misunderstanding, the Prince simply replied that 'he considered the matter at an end with the opposition', dismissed Wellesley's commission and turned to the more congenial Moira. Wellesley concluded that it was all 'previously arranged'. Moira too began by approaching Grey and Grenville, but neither side was prepared to give an inch. The Whig leaders refused to speak to Moira unless he produced a direct authority from the Prince. When he did so on 6 June, Grey immediately demanded that the offices in the Prince's Household be placed at their disposal as a public mark of confidence. Moira replied that this would not be possible and the negotiation ended. The Whigs were accused of making unreasonable demands and of breaking off on a mere question of patronage: but neither side was prepared to trust the other, and the demand for the control of Household appointments was intended to show the public that the Prince was not sincere. Peel felt obliged to make a similar demand of Queen Victoria in 1839. In that case it was the young Queen who was generally thought to have been unreasonable: her uncle was even more

[20] Grey to Grenville [30], 31 May, 1 June, *Fortescue MSS*, x. 275–9; Wellesley to Grey and Grenville, 1 June, *Wellesley*, iii. 260–1.

[21] Ibid. 262–4; *Fortescue MSS*, x. 279–80; Moira to Grey, 3 June, ibid. 280–1; Creevey to Mrs Creevey, 3 June, Gore, *Creevey*, 55.

so in the circumstances of 1812. As Roberts has shown, there can be little doubt that Moira and the Prince intended that the new administration should not include Grey and Grenville.

Moira immediately turned to their opponents, only to fail through lack of decisiveness, and perhaps courage, at the last moment. On 8 June Liverpool accepted the Premiership. This, suggests Roberts, was the Prince's intention all along: though Grey and Grenville might have stormed the closet by taking Moira at his face value and presented the Prince with a *fait accompli*, they knew almost in their bones that he could not be trusted to give them his confidence; and in demanding the resignation of the Household they put him to the test. Not all their followers understood their reasons. Grey found that Whitbread thought he ought not to have insisted on the Household, and despaired of setting him right as 'no good can result from any conversation between him and me'. The Prince had not only out-manoeuvred Grey and Grenville on taking office, but had sowed dissension in their ranks. Grey, however, was comforted by Holland's assurance that 'your conduct is clearly the true Whig line and that at which in common times no man who calls himself a Whig or a Foxite could depart from', and he returned to Howick satisfied in his own mind that no other outcome had been possible.[22]

IN SEARCH OF A POLICY, 1812–1820

By the summer of 1812 the Whigs' hopes of achieving office under the Prince Regent had been dashed. Though a strong party in numbers, their cohesion was too weak to enable them to act as an energetic opposition, even had Grenville been willing to engage in one. The general election in the autumn resulted in the loss of several leading speakers in the Commons, including Brougham, Romilly, Horner, and even Tierney, and although Grey did his best to find openings for them in close boroughs he found the party's electoral patrons unresponsive. He confessed to Holland that the party's difficulties seemed 'such as no plan that we can lay down can remedy' and that 'it is better that I should remain where I am' rather than come to town to engage in a fruitless contest. He wrote to Fitzwilliam that

After so long a warfare in which I have drawn upon myself the implacable enmity of the court, I feel that I have no support from the people. Can I be accused under such circumstances of any desertion of public duty, if I begin at last to wish to withdraw myself from a service in which I meet with such a return?

Tierney too was despondent. 'We can do nothing', he wrote in October, 'and

[22] Roberts, *The Whig Party*, 391–3; M. S. Grant to Prendergast, 4 June, Grey and Grenville to Wellesley, 3 June, BL Add. MS 37297, fos. 81–2, 90–3, 114; Grey and Grenville to Moira, 5 June, *Fortescue MSS*, x. 285–7; Moira to Wellesley, 1 June, *Wellesley papers*, ii. 109–10; Grey to Holland, 7 June, G. 35, reply [7 June], BL Add. MS 51545, fos. 5–6; Gen. C. Grey to C. Wood, 20 Nov. 1858, Hickleton MSS A.4.64.54.

my opinion is that the less we attempt the better.' He forecast the breakup of the opposition, with Whitbread and Canning drawing off members from each wing, leaving the centre of the party and its 'weight of talent, property and character' to follow Grey and Grenville. 'At any rate', he wrote, 'you would be more efficient with fifty adherents heartily united than with all the shew of numbers which the motley crew we have for some years mixed with has occasionally displayed.' In any case, 'we must come to a distinct understanding as to what we all mean' before the new parliament met. Grey agreed to come to town for discussions, but Grenville wrote in November to say that he thought it would be pointless to do so before Christmas; 'In the present state of our ranks in the House of Commons it would be better to avoid even the appearance of an effort.'[1]

Grenville now declared his own wish to retire and leave to Grey the 'full lead and conduct of what is called the opposition party', and the future Premiership. Grey tried to pass on the poisoned chalice to Holland, writing on 14 November that the breach between himself and Whitbread made it impossible for him to unite the party, and that his personal unacceptability at Carlton House would prevent an offer from the Prince: both difficulties would be solved if Holland were to take his place. Holland told him bluntly that he was talking nonsense:

The situation you hold is in the first place not transferable at pleasure—and in the second if it was that person who could consent to your sacrificing it to the unjust clamour of the court or the yet more unjust dissatisfaction or jealousy of persons who should be your friends, would not only be unfit to be the head of a party but unworthy to have any trust or confidence shown him among men.

Again in 1815, when Grenville once more indicated his wish to hand over the leadership of the opposition, Grey declared his unwillingness to assume the task. This time it was Rosslyn who read him a lecture on his responsibilities:

With respect to the transfer into other hands of the lead of the party who now follow you, do not flatter yourself that it is possible. No other man of the present day can undertake it—no other will carry with him the same share of public confidence, or the same respect from all persons of whatever party; no other person can keep your own friends together— the choice is between keeping the command, and an absolute dissolution of the whole thing ... Don't imagine that you can withdraw yourself or make any arrangement by which any political party conducted upon your principles can now subsist without you are at the head ...

Grey's attempted renunciation of the leadership was in truth half-hearted. His ambition still burned intermittently, despite the frustrations of seemingly perpetual and fruitless opposition and the troubles amongst the party. Though his own ill-health, or that of Mary or various of the children, kept him often at Howick, he attended some part of every parliamentary session during these years and spoke on his major policies of retrenchment, Catholic relief, reform and foreign non-

[1] Grey to Holland, 25 Oct., 14 Nov., G. 35, to Fitzwilliam, 22 Nov., Fitzwilliam MSS, Northampton; Tierney to Grey, 19 Oct., G. 55; Grenville to Grey, 10 Nov., BL Add. MS 58949, fo. 2; Smith, *Whig Principles*, 327–8.

intervention, and in defence of constitutional liberties. He nevertheless failed to energize his colleagues and followers or to lay down a decisive strategy for opposition. His temperament was either in the skies or in the depths: lack of success became almost an habitual expectation, so that any effort he was inclined to make quickly petered out.[2]

The opposition's failures were not all to be laid at Grey's own door. Holland put his finger on the crucial problem of the leadership in the Commons:

...no party can be well led that is not in a great measure really governed as well as nominally led by a member of the House of Commons and till we have some friend there who does not only inspire full confidence but who really has acquired some degree of ascendancy over our minds, we shall never prosper completely.

Ponsonby could be no more than a stop-gap until that moment arrived; Grey was forced into a waiting game, the danger of which was that the party would disintegrate before it came. A desultory negotiation with Wellesley and Canning in the autumn of 1812 failed largely because of Grey's prejudices against the latter and his unacceptability to 'the Mountain', and the result was to leave the situation unchanged in the Commons until Ponsonby's death in 1817. During these five years it was Tierney who corresponded most frequently with Grey on political questions and who, in effect, managed the party on Ponsonby's behalf. In 1818 Tierney was elected by the party members in the Commons to the vacant leadership, but even Grey, who regarded him as his closest friend in the party, confessed that he had little confidence in his success. As he told Lady Holland:[3]

...he must learn to consider constitutional questions as of more importance than the growing surplus of the consolidated fund and the baldness of comparative questions; and above all he must learn to press forward, without looking behind him except for the purpose of putting by those lessons which past events may afford.

Tierney proved no more successful than Ponsonby and no more able to control the left wing, led since Whitbread's suicide in 1815 by Brougham, whose willingness to speak in the House at every possible opportunity irritated his more cautious colleagues as much as it plagued the ministers. Grey admired Brougham's obvious talents and genius for hard work, but neither he nor the other party leaders altogether trusted him. Brougham's succession to the role of gadfly to the Whig leadership, and his attempt to bridge the gap between them and the radical wing of the party, made him suspect in their eyes.

All these circumstances confirmed Grey's view that his party was best led from behind, and that it would be broken up by a too energetic strategy. He was prepared to be uncompromising on the Catholic question and in 1815 on the peace

[2] Grey to Holland, 14 Nov., G. 35, and reply 17 Nov., BL Add. MS 51545, fos. 30–4; Rosslyn to Grey, 25 Dec. 1815, G. 51; *Parl. Deb.* xxxv. 48–52, 424–8, xxxviii. 1107–9.

[3] R. Adair to Grey, 22 Oct., 8 Nov., Grey to Adair 28 Oct., G.1/3; Grenville to Grey, 10 Nov., loc. cit.; Grey to Holland, 25 Oct., 8 Nov., G. 35; to Lady Holland, 30 Aug. 1818, BL Add. MS 51549, fos. 146–7.

treaties, but on other issues the opposition tended to hang back and wait for a lead from others. On the Corn Bill of 1815 Grey was cautious and open-minded He told Grenville in October 1814 that 'something must be done, not to raise the price of agricultural produce, but to insure it against very great and embarrassing fluctuations, and to secure to the people their subsistence upon the whole at a steadier and a cheaper rate', by preventing dependence on foreign supplies. At the same time, he thought it reasonable that the agricultural interest should be able to keep up their rental incomes in times of general inflation. The question was a difficult one for a party still largely composed of landed proprietors who also tried to present themselves as the champions of the people. Grey's own views on political economy were in line with old Whiggish principles, as he had expressed them in 1800 when the Commons had debated the distress caused by harvest failures and high corn prices. The best way, he had then declared, to obtain an adequate supply was 'to leave the commerce in that article completely unfettered, and to protect from all violence the grower and the dealer. The fixing of a maximum price would prove the ruin of the country.' He believed that the only cure for the general distress would be by 'the slow operation of remedies which could not be applied on the spur of the occasion'.[4]

He trusted, that no attempts would be made to regulate commerce by penal statutes, to fetter its course by narrow restrictions, to subject its operations to partial limitations. He hoped that the utmost freedom would be given to speculation and enterprise,... ensuring to everyone the fruits of his labours.

In 1800, Grey had looked to the coming of peace as a solution to the economic troubles of the country. In 1815, when they intensified, he linked the problems of the post-war depression to excessive governmental expenditure, and called for economy and retrenchment, both to reduce military establishments which might be dangerous to the constitution, and because such expenditure contributed to high taxation and inflation. He doubted whether the Corn Bill would help the agriculturalists, and feared that it would arouse popular discontent: 'Nothing can be more imprudent than to press a subject of this nature in opposition to the expressed sense of four fifths of the population of the country.' To Tierney's disappointment, however, the Whigs in the Commons failed to make any capital out of the Bill. After all the party's professions of attention to the people, he complained, no more than 40 of their number ever voted in the minority, even to delay the Bill until petitions could be received and considered against it: and 'the rest, and I am sorry to add our best Whig names amongst them, sided with Ministers and constituted a large proportion of their strength'. The party was damaged in popular opinion by this failure to defend the people's interest, and

---

[4] Grey to Grenville, 30 Oct. 1814, BL Add. MS 58949, fos. 139–46; to Willoughby-Gordon, 13 Nov. 1814, 16 Jan. 1815, ibid. 49478, fos. 83–4, 93–4; *Parl. Hist.* xxxv. 534–6, 791–2 (11, 16 Nov. 1800).

the radicals were not slow to point out that, by condoning the new Corn Law, they had shown themselves to be no better than the Tories.[5]

Relations between the Whigs and the radicals continued to deteriorate after 1815, when post-war conditions aroused a new popular agitation for reform, spreading once more to the lower classes in society in the manufacturing districts.[6] The new reform movement of the post-Waterloo years was fuelled by unemployment, low wages, high prices, and the deteriorating living conditions in the industrial areas, and it was fanned by popular demagogues such as Hunt and journalists like Cobbett, Hone, and Wooler. Luddism after 1812 was primarily a protest against conditions of labour and the erosion of craft skills, but there were signs that it masked an underground revolutionary movement amongst a minority of activists who preached that a change in the political structure was the only sure and permanent remedy for working-class discontents. Skilled and semi-skilled workers were developing forms of trade-union organization, despite the Combination Acts, and these readily adapted themselves to political agitation.

Alarmist magistrates and lord-lieutenants sent reports to London of secret meetings, drillings, and the purchase of arms, while the Home Office's own agents ferreted out every instance they could find, or sometimes stimulate, of popular disloyalty and conspiracy. The government's response was firm. The militia and some regular troops were stationed in large numbers in the 'disturbed districts' to reinforce the civil authorities, who were relatively weak and thinly-spread in the manufacturing areas, giving rise to Whig suspicions that military rule was being extended to the point where constitutional liberties would be endangered. Episodes such as the 'Pentridge Rising' and March of the 'Blanketeers' in the north Midlands, the Spa Fields riots in London, and strikes and labour unrest in many parts of the kingdom provided justification for a return to the repressive policies of the 1790s which Grey and Fox had then condemned as provocative and unnecessary.

In February 1816 Grey expressed his fears that governmental policies for the past 25 years had operated on the middle classes 'to break down all public spirit' and inculcate 'habits of submission' so that the opposition could not hope to arouse them to effective protest. To Sir James Willoughby-Gordon, an old friend and frequent correspondent who had served in the army under his father, and as secretary to the Duke of York as commander-in-chief, Grey confided his fear that the universal distress would end in military government and the loss of civil liberties. The only solution, he felt, was a total change of financial policy to economy and retrenchment. He accused ministers of working up local riots into a

[5] Grey to Fitzwilliam, 11 Mar. 1815, Fitzwilliam MSS, Northampton; to Holland [27 Mar. 1815], BL Add. MS 51584, fos. 52–4.
[6] For the popular protest movements of the post-1815 period see R. J. White, *Waterloo to Peterloo* (1957), E. P. Thompson, *The Making of the English Working Class*, F. K. Darvall, *Popular Disturbances and Public Order in Regency England* (1934), *The Early English Trade Unions*, ed. A. Aspinall (1949), M. I. Thomis, *The Luddites* (Newton Abbot, 1970), M. I. Thomis and P. Holt, *Threats of Revolution in England, 1789–1848* (1977).

dangerous jacobinical plot, which should give the opposition their opportunity to discredit them:[7]

I once feared that Cobbett, Hunt and Co. had done just enough to answer the purpose of Government in this view: but I begin to think it won't do, and that if the opposition play well the game that is now in their hands, it will be impossible to resist measures effectively useful and beneficial to the country.... This is not 1793, nor is Pitt the Minister.

Unfortunately, nor was the opposition of 1816–17 that of 1794–7. The Grenvilles supported the government's alarmist policies and, until the break in 1817, restrained the Whig section from taking a popular line, while even after their defection over the suspension of Habeas Corpus, Grey found it was necessary to soft-pedal the question of reform in order to prevent Whig conservatives like Fitzwilliam from following them. He was left with the unhappy compromise of opposing repressive legislation, while condemning the respectable radicals, like Burdett, Folkestone, and Hobhouse as well as Cobbett and Hunt for raising the people's expectations of reform. 'I see no symptoms of a true spirit of Liberty' he wrote to Lady Holland in October:[8]

Everything seems to me to be tending, and is pushed by Burdett and his adherents, to a contest between the crown and the mob; in which those who ought to be the leaders of the people, and would be so if they could, will be driven from a sense of their own security to support the Crown; the success of which, with the assistance of the Duke of Wellington, and the worst army in spirit and principle that I believe ever existed in the world, will be probably the utter extinction of all Liberty.

He resolved to try to identify the Whigs with respectable and moderate reformist opinion, and proposed an amendment to the Address in the next session 'conformable to that of the Address which I moved in 1810' which had advocated moderate reform. He agreed however with Holland that the party should steer clear of 'what is called a complete and radical change in our representation' and set out the party's creed in four points, the first three of which he bracketed as '*sine qua non*':

1. Reduction of establishments
2. Change of foreign policy
3. Catholic emancipation
4. A moderate and gradual Reform of Parliament, not a sine qua non, but to be supported.

He raised the reform question more tentatively with Fitzwilliam admitting that 'I cannot hope for the same concurrence of opinion' as on the first three points. Reform nevertheless would be 'forced upon us' and he declared his sentiments,

which certainly are a good deal tempered by the experience of the last 25 years, and most adverse to the sweeping and radical reforms which are the only ones that seem now to be tolerated.

If put to a choice between keeping things as they were or a system of 'annual

[7] Grey to Fitzwilliam, 25 Feb. 1816, Fitzwilliam MSS, Northampton; to Willoughby-Gordon, 21 Sept., 13 Dec. 1816, BL Add. MS 49478, fos. 156–7, 166–7.
[8] Grey to Lady Holland, 6 Oct. 1816, G. 33.

parliaments, universal suffrage and ballot' he would prefer the former: 'Nay . . . I would resist the latter with all my power, and chiefly because I think it would render the influence of the Crown in all ordinary times quite uncontrollable; but liable to be disturbed occasionally by popular violence.' He confessed that he would not now go so far as he had been prepared to do in 1797. 'The only reform I could now support, . . . would be one of a much more limited and gradual operation.' Even that was not to be an essential condition, or seen as a panacea for all the present distress of the country. 'You will see', he concluded, 'that I am moderate enough to be denounced by Cobbett, Hunt and Co. as a traitor, though not moderate enough to reconcile your opinion to mine.'[9]

Grey's letter exposed his dilemma. Anxious, as in 1792, to thwart extremism by harnessing reformist sentiment to moderate Whig leadership, he could not pledge the party as a whole even to such a half-measure without dividing it and so defeating the primary objective, a liberal Whig administration. He was left to appear indecisive, unable to offer a convincing alternative to the radicalism which he saw as the major threat to the future of the Whigs. Fitzwilliam's dismissive response on reform drove him back on to equivocation or avoidance of the question altogether. The northern radicals had already commented on his absence from the annual Fox commemorative dinner at Newcastle in September 1813, despite his excuse of family illness, and also his guarded language in the following year, when as James Losh noted, he 'never in direct terms mentioned parliamentary reform, tho' both Mr Lambton and Dr Fenwick gave him fair opportunities for doing so'. He did not attend again until 1817. In June 1816 he declined an invitation to chair a meeting of the Hampden Club at the Freemason's Tavern, and in December refused Cartwright's request to support the Club. He continued to attack the popular radicals, referring in August 1815 to Cobbett's 'black heart'.

Nevertheless, by the winter of 1816 Grey was seeking to re-establish his claim to be the leader of moderate reform, and he authorized his son-in-law Lambton to assure the Newcastle reformers of his attachment to the cause. Their leader, Dr Fenwick, confessed that he had begun to doubt it, but professed to be reassured. Sir John Swinburne also reported to Wyvill that Grey had pledged himself, but that 'he fears that were he to make that the first object of his efforts at this juncture, many hitherto steady friends of economy and retrenchment that act with him would be alarmed, and quit the party'; and he pointed out that the 'ultra-reformers . . . have so long and cruelly misrepresented his conduct and treated him with such evident contempt, that you cannot wonder he should hesitate to confide in them.' Grey's view was that the opposition had the opportunity to do good on other important issues, but that the question of reform would divide them and prevent it: he would support moderate reform if it were brought up, but not step forward himself to take the lead. Wyvill was disappointed, for he had been hoping for support from Northumberland for his proposed meetings in Yorkshire and

[9] Grey to Holland, 23 Nov., 8 Dec. 1816, G. 34, to Fitzwilliam, 13 Dec., Fitzwilliam MSS, Northampton.

Durham, but he expressed his continued faith in Grey's ultimate intentions. In the event neither of the two north-eastern counties could muster enough support for a meeting and Wyvill abandoned his plans, while Grey repeated in a conversation with Fenwick his intention to do no more than support an initiative if it came from elsewhere, accompanying his words with a positive disclaimer of the views of Hunt, Cobbett, and the Hampden Club.[10]

Grey's discouraging attitude ended the reformers' hopes of activity in the North. Lambton despaired of 'our supineness and want of union' and deplored that 'The Grenvilles! The Grenvilles! has always been the watchword to prevent our taking any step that could identify our cause with that of the People.' In the South, however, there were indications that a group of the Westminster reformers were prepared to look to the Whigs. Tierney reported to Grey in December that he had been approached by 'a large body of Westminster tradesmen who profess to have seen their error in countenancing Burdett and Lord Cochrane's party, and are very desirous of placing themselves under you'. They proposed to hold 'a grand dinner' before the meeting of Parliament and to invite Grey and Tierney 'to the exclusion of the violent men'. It would however be dependent upon the Whigs

satisfying the disinterested Patriots as to what we should do if we were in, and convincing the interested ones of our anxiety to get in. The doubts that prevail on these two points I am convinced keep many aloof from our standard, and in fact contribute to enable Ministers to pursue their present system.

He urged Grey to stop writing to Holland and others of his despondency and lack of spirits; if he did not mean to be active in the cause he should say so. He assured him that the feeling in favour of parliamentary reform was mounting, and that his Westminster contacts believed it would be impossible for the Whigs to recruit popular support without a declaration in its favour.[11]

With Grey's approval, Tierney fended off the proposal of a reform dinner, but suggested that the Westminster moderates should prepare resolutions against sinecures, a standing army, and in favour of economy and reform. In the meantime, the Whigs considered how far they could go in Parliament towards the popular demands. They found it difficult to agree on the terms of an amendment to the Address which would satisfy the country. Grenville was opposed to an amendment merely for the sake of opposing the Address, while Tierney suggested an alternative motion for a committee on the state of the nation. Lambton, admitting that the position was delicate, thought reform should be mentioned and asked Grey to draft the amendment. Tierney reported that the right-wingers like Elliot, representing Fitzwilliam's views, were not prepared to support any mention of

[10] Losh, *Diary*, 23 Aug., 19 Sept., i. 27, 40; Bennet to Creevey, 24 Sept. 1813, *Creevey Papers*, i. 187; Grey to T. T. Clarks, 4 June [1816], G. 10/8; Cartwright to Grey, 19 Dec. and reply, 26 Dec., G. 9A; Grey to Miss Wyvill, 19 Nov. 1816, Swinburne to Wyvill, 25 Dec., Wyvill to Swinburne, 11 Dec., to Sir G. Cayley, 27 Dec., Fenwick to Wyvill, 28 Dec., T. Monson to Wyvill, 30 Dec., Wyvill MSS 248–9.

[11] Lambton to Grey, 17 Dec. 1816, G. letter-book 4, A3; Tierney to Grey, 19, 26 Dec., G. 55.

reform in the troubled state of the country. Grey, visiting Fitzwilliam at Milton on his way to town, wrote despairingly to Holland about the state of the party. 'The party principle which distinguishes us as Whigs', he wrote, 'is a principle of moderation and liberality both in religion and government'; there should be no difficulty in agreeing on the Catholic question, the reduction of military establishments and of sinecure offices, and the consequent reduction of crown influence. But

as to reform of Parliament, agreement upon that question is hopeless. It must be left, as it hitherto has been for individuals to act upon, according to their respective opinions ... for the present it must be set aside in any consideration of our party politics. To get any declaration in favour of it assented to by the party is obviously out of the question.

Even so, he doubted whether Grenville would take any active part in opposition in the present state of the country: but it was important to keep Fitzwilliam and the conservative Whigs in the party and to respect their consistency of views since the period of the French Revolution. He proposed a declaration in favour of the reduction of establishments, retrenchment, a change of foreign policy, and complete religious toleration as the most that could be agreed on. On 29 January 1817 he moved an amendment to the Address in a long speech which set forth these as the party's aims.[12]

Grey was right in thinking that the alliance with the Grenvilles was about to break up. Affairs came to a crisis when the Prince Regent was attacked on his way back from opening Parliament on 28 January, and the two Houses agreed to appoint secret committees to investigate the state of the country. The committees assembled evidence for the existence of a widespread revolutionary conspiracy involving the followers of the extremist Thomas Spence and directed against the political and religious establishment of the country. Grey, now in London, wrote to Bedford that 'a person not more likely to be alarmed than either you or I' had told him of strong evidence of a large and dangerous conspiracy and plan of insurrection. Nevertheless the Whigs regarded the committees' proceedings with well-founded suspicion, believing that, as in Pitt's time, they were intended to provide justification for new repressive measures, and Grey advised Bedford not to take part in the deliberations of the Lords' committee. Unfortunately this left Grenville and Fitzwilliam as the two representatives of the opposition. Predictably, the committees reported in alarmist tones on 18 and 19 February, and Sidmouth proposed the suspension of Habeas Corpus. Grey opposed the suspension on the second reading, declaring that it was 'the most unnecessary and uncalled for attack upon their liberties which any Minister of the Crown, in any period of our history, had ever attempted'. He wrote to Wellesley that he found nothing in the evidence to justify the suspension, and to Grenville to express the hope that it 'may not produce any permanent interruption of an agreement and co-operation from which

[12] Tierney to Grey, 26 Dec., 4, 20, 22 Jan., ibid.; Grenville to Holland, 14 Jan., BL Add. MS 51531, fos. 104–7; to Grey, 14 Jan., G. 21/3, Lambton to Grey, 15 [Jan. 1817], loc. cit. A6, Grey to Holland, 11 Jan., G. 35; Smith, *Whig Principles*, 333–5; *Parl. Deb.* xxxv. 42–58.

I have derived so much advantage and satisfaction'. Grenville, however, was adamant, and the episode ended their thirteen years of political alliance. At the end of the session in July Grey wrote what was in effect his farewell letter, expressing his 'grateful remembrance of the kindness I have experienced from you during the whole time that I have had the benefit of your co-operation and direction', and his 'assurance that no political difference can ever alter or diminish the sincere affection and esteem' which he continued to feel.[13]

The breach over the suspension of Habeas Corpus proved to be permanent in Grenville's case, but only temporary in Fitzwilliam's. The latter's son, Lord Milton, was amongst the great majority of Whigs in the Commons who met at Grey's London house to agree on opposition to the Bill, and within a year he had persuaded his father, whose heart was still with Grey as Fox's successor, to change his view. His continued presence, however, with others of his way of thinking, continued to inhibit the party's support of reform, so that the departure of the Grenvilles did not resolve Grey's difficulties. He wrote to Holland in March that he was 'no longer fit for active and constant service either in or out of office: and all you must look for is a speech now and then, which, whatever my own opinion of their utility may be, I will endeavour to furnish when I am able'. In August he wrote to Willoughby-Gordon that 'I feel that I have no longer any personal interest in politics—I am politically dead.'[14]

Yet by the autumn of 1817 he had made up his mind to declare himself more explicitly on reform. He chose the annual Fox dinner at Newcastle for the occasion, much though he hated public speaking of that kind. James Losh, who attended the dinner, thought Grey looked ill but in good spirits, and reported that he spoke with 'much eloquence and good sense'. His speech, reported in the *Newcastle Chronicle*, ranged over the betrayal of the hopes of European freedom in 1815, the causes of distress in Britain, the burden of debt, and need for economy. Coming to the subject on which all waited to hear him, he spoke of the suspension of Habeas Corpus as a threat to 'our free constitution, the work of a thousand years, the envy and admiration of the world' and advocated public meetings and petitions against it; and he professed, to '*loud and continued applause*' that

I am still a reformer, but with some modification of my former opinions: with more fear of the effect of sudden and inconsiderate changes; with a most complete conviction that to be successful, reform must be gradual and must be carefully limited to that necessity which has proved it wanting. It is upon this ground only that I can support any measure of reform, and I cannot deprecate too strongly any indulgence in an extravagant spirit of innovation which would embarrass and confound us amongst extensive and erroneous theories.

Losh thought the speech would operate, 'if not to remove all doubt as to his

---

[13] Grey to Bedford, 11 Feb. 1817, *Early Corr. of Lord John Russell*, 189–90; 7 Feb., Bedford to Grey, 6, 9 Feb., G. 6/17; *Parl. Deb.* xxxv. 578–82 (24 Feb.); Grey to Wellesley, 19 Feb. 1817, BL Add. MS 37297, fos. 248–9; to Grenville [20], 22 Feb., 7 July, ibid. 58949, fos. 188–9, 191, 198–9; Grenville to Grey, 23 Feb., G.21/3.

[14] Smith, *Whig Principles*, 336–9; Grey to Holland, 20 Mar. 1817, G. 35; to Willoughby-Gordon, 1 Aug., 10 Sep., BL Add. MS 49478, fos. 171–2, 178–81.

sincerity and consistency, at least to lessen the suspicions which have been entertained against him very considerably'.[15]

Grey's attempt to reinvigorate the Whigs on reform was blocked by Tierney's
pessimism and yet another crisis in the House of Commons. Tierney wrote in
November that a good attendance was not to be expected after the previous
session's experience, and the sudden death of George Ponsonby left the party
leaderless throughout the session. Grey encouraged Holland once more to lead the
party in the Lords and to move for the repeal of the suspension of Habeas Corpus,
but declined to come up himself.

Do not imagine, [he wrote] that it is either indifference to the wishes of my friends, or to
the public interest, that detains me in the country. What I said last year, though the
moment at which it was said, was in some degree accidental, was the result of much previous
meditation, and of the conviction, produced by various considerations ... of the necessity
[of] withdrawing myself from the situation which I have hitherto, tho' most insufficiently
occupied.

He did not mean that he had entirely given up politics, but his family duties and
his health no longer allowed him to reside for long in London or take an active
part in Parliament. Grey's stomach attacks had been frequent and painful over
the past few years, and he was also suffering from rheumatism, so that his energies
were sapped and his spirits, after ten more years of opposition, were weak. Holland
urged in vain that he should come to raise the party's morale, but when his own
was so low it may be doubted whether he was capable of it.[16]

The Grenvilles were now sitting on the cross-benches and maintained themselves as a 'third party' in Parliament until they joined Liverpool in 1821. Their
defection made little difference to the numbers of the opposition, and it reduced
their disunion to some extent, but while Fitzwilliam and others still opposed
reform, there was no hope of a more vigorous party. Fitzwilliam even objected to
the terms in which the members in the Commons offered the lead to Tierney in
the summer because their letter referred to the prospect of 'carrying into effect
our views of the Constitution'. He urged that the party should confine itself 'to
the single object of resistance to those measures of Government ... which has been
the cause of that popularity which has been experienced by the opposition during
the present elections'.

Grey echoed these views in writing to congratulate Tierney on his election,
suggesting that the party concentrate on the defence of constitutional liberties and
the reduction of public expenditure; he failed to mention reform, and suggested
that a respectable and disinterested opposition was all that could be hoped for: to
displace the ministers was hopeless. Meanwhile, 'I am living here [at Howick] in
the way I always wish to live, and have upon the whole enjoyed much better health
than I have for some years.' He assured Lady Holland that 'If I were to indulge
my own inclination, I believe I should never quit this place again'; and as for

[15] Losh, *Diary*, i. 71 (27 Sept. 1817).
[16] Tierney to Grey, 1 Nov., G. 55; Grey to Holland, 28 Jan. 1818, BL Add. MS 51549, fos. 205–6.

politics, 'do not imagine that I any longer trouble my head about such matters, except so far as advantage and the credit of my friends, and the triumph of good principles may be concerned.' Tierney was understandably vexed, and wrote to Holland that he would say no more about the party's tactics: 'My orders from Grey are to defend the constitution, and to enforce economy, a line of conduct which will, he does not mention at what period, do wonders.'[17]

In November another blow fell, when Romilly committed suicide. Grey forecast that it 'must prove fatal to us in the House of Commons'; and he deprecated Tierney's attempt to invigorate the party by a public declaration of 'some acknowledged head of the party' in the Lords. 'Such an attempt can only have the effect of obliging me to withdraw myself more decidedly than I have yet done, though what I said 2 years ago I intended to have that effect, from all pretensions to that situation.' Nevertheless, in November 1818 Holland was again urging Grey to come to London in terms reminiscent of Fox in 1804–6:

... you cannot withdraw the influence you have over men's affections and opinions—something my dear Grey is due to those men and me among them.... If a season were to arrive in which a Government could be formed with you at the head and your friends in the body of it—what a silly reason it would be to forego such an advantage because some time before you had said you would not avail yourself of it ...

Grey replied in December that the most he looked for was the replacement of the present ministers by 'a middle Administration' rather than a purely Whig one: the latter would merely shift on to the Whigs 'all the embarrassment and confusion' of the moment and the responsibility for the difficulties and distress of the country, while the measures they would be obliged to adopt would make them unpopular, 'and the Court would again be able to turn them out injured in public opinion and reduced in power and influence, before the expiration of a year'. He again declined to come for the beginning of the session on account of Mary's health and yet another confinement, and he advised Holland that the opposition should limit themselves to general criticism of the government and advocacy of economy, retrenchment, and a non-interventionist foreign policy, support of criminal law reform, and the Catholic question. As to reform, if the subject were forced upon them, they might declare in favour of a 'moderate and gradual' policy and decidedly against annual parliaments and universal suffrage: but 'I must not be understood as binding myself by my declaration in favour of that reform, to my support of it as a *sine qua non*.'[18]

This caution again brought upon his head the censure of the Westminster radicals. Burdett secured J. C. Hobhouse's nomination for the by-election caused

[17] Grey to Fitzwilliam, 29 Jan., Fitzwilliam MSS, Northampton; Holland to Grey, 8 Mar., BL Add. MS 51545, fos. 215–16; Fitzwilliam to Grey, 18 July [1818], G. 14/11; Grey to Tierney, 30 Aug., Tierney MSS; to Lady Holland, 30 Aug., BL Add. MS 51549, fos. 146–7; Tierney to Holland, 6 Sept., ibid. 51584, fos. 72–3. Grey did attend in Apr. 1818 to oppose the Alien Bill and to support Erskine's Bill on procedure in cases of libel: *Parl. Deb.* xxxviii. 1033–1309 *passim*.

[18] Grey to Holland, 9 Nov. 1818, G. 35; Holland to Grey, 13 Nov., reply 13 Dec., BL Add. MS 51545, fos. 233–5, 240–1.

by Romilly's death, and though Hobhouse attempted to win Whig support he was driven by Place and the Westminster committee into a censure of Grey's 'apostacy' since 1806. Grey reacted with his accustomed annoyance:

It is a little hard, to be sure, after a Parliamentary life of three and thirty years, such as mine has been, to be held up to the country as an apostate and a traitor, and I do not say that I do not feel it deeply... We must consider Burdett and his party as our worst enemies... I only hope, now war is declared, that it will be open and vigorous war.

Holland tried to defuse the situation by counselling forbearance against 'every little impertinence of absurd partizans' but Grey was determined to take offence. At the Fox dinner held at Newcastle Grey had spoken cautiously on reform, one observer remarking that 'it was evidently his object to avoid pledging himself to any specific plan or specific time for bringing it forward' but Lambton had attacked the Westminster radicals as 'brawling, ignorant but mischievous quacks'. Lambton's vigorous defence of his father-in-law and the Whigs' resentment at Place's language led to the decision to put George Lamb in nomination at Westminster and Grey regarded Lamb's election as a personal vindication. He was even offended when Sir Robert Wilson urged him to make up the quarrel:

I must say that even to speak of the possibility of a reconciliation with them who have so conducted themselves, would betray so light an estimation of what is due to my character and honour, that it would have given me more pain than I can express, if I did not consider it as the hasty expression of that general good nature which makes you always anxious to allay or to obliterate enmities by every means in your power... I beg you to understand that nothing can ever make me forget or forgive the conduct of Burdett and his associates: that not only is the possibility of any public reconciliation cut off for ever, but that I must avoid even the intercourse of private society with men, whom I consider as having degraded themselves from the character of gentlemen.

His resentment was implacable from this time onwards: in October he made his famous remark to Wilson

Is there one among them with whom you would trust yourself in the dark?... Look at the men, at their characters, at their conduct. What is there more base, more detestable, more at variance with all taste and decency, as well as all morality, truth, and honour?

He declared to Lambton his gratitude for 'the affectionate zeal with which you have resented the insulting and injurious attack that was made upon me'.[19]

Nevertheless the reawakening of the reform agitation in the winter of 1818–19 forced the Whigs into the open lest the radicals steal their clothes altogether. Holland urged that the party should adopt some 'intelligible measure which we could agree upon' and should wage a press campaign to put themselves before the public as champions of reform. Perhaps they might support Russell's plan to take

[19] R. E. Zegger, *John Cam Hobhouse: a Political Life, 1819–52* (Columbia, 1973), 64–72; Grey to Holland 16 Feb., reply, 19 Feb., BL Add. MS 51546, fos. 14–15, 17–18; Losh *Diary*, i. 85–6; *Morning Chronicle*, 13 Jan. 1819; S. Reid, *Life and Letters of the first Earl of Durham* (1906), i. 45; C. W. New, *Lord Durham* (Oxford, 1929), 47; Grey to Sir R. Wilson, 7 Mar. and – Oct. 1819, BL Add. MS 30109, fos. 9–10, 56–8.

up the question of disfranchisement of individual corrupt constituencies such as Grampound and Barnstaple, where the 1818 elections had exposed widespread bribery among the electors. Grey agreed that a press campaign was essential, and that on the corrupt boroughs they were bound to try to satisfy the public outcry: but, he wrote,

I should be very much afraid of the effect of an attempt to engraft upon measures of this nature any more general measure of reform . . . Everything tending to general reform has been rendered so odious to some of the best men in the country by the proceedings of the Ultras.

He admitted that there was a good deal in Burdett's contention that it was wrong to punish 'a poor devil of a voter who is proved to have taken ten pounds whilst they tolerate the notorious practice of selling seats for 4 or £5,000'. But he was nervous of a general measure and preferred to wait for a more decisive lead from respectable public opinion:

Perhaps you will say a burnt child dreads the fire; and I am not sure that my experience of what happened in 1792 does not make me more timid than I ought to be on this subject.

It was also important not to pledge themselves in opposition to anything 'we should not have the means of carrying if we were in office'.[20]

Grey's animosity towards the radicals reinforced his determination to keep the Whig party to a line which clearly separated them from Burdett, Hobhouse, and the Westminster group, even at the expense of the Whigs' image as the party of reform. The events of the summer of 1819, however, forced him to declare himself. On 16 August a crowd of men, women, and children, assembled in St Peter's Field in Manchester to listen to a speech by Henry Hunt, was ridden down by a troop of the Manchester Yeomanry under orders from the magistrates to arrest Hunt. The Yeomanry became trapped in the hostile crowd and had to be rescued by the Hussars. At the end of ten minutes 11 of the crowd lay dead and over 400 were wounded, either by sabre blows or from trampling by the panic-stricken spectators. The 'Peterloo massacre' as it quickly became known demanded some positive reaction if the Whigs were to retain any credibility as the defenders of the people's liberties. Grey seized upon it as an opportunity to discredit both the government and the radicals. The conduct of the magistrates seemed 'unjustifiable', he wrote to Brougham on the 25th. If the country did not protest it would be the end of liberty, and it would be the fault of both sides:

this indeed is one of the most mischievous effects of the proceedings of the Radicals, that by abusing popular privileges they establish precedents for abridging them. My views of the state of the country are more and more gloomy. Everything is tending, and has for some time been tending, to a complete separation between the higher and lower orders of society; a state of things which can only end in the destruction of liberty . . .

He suggested that 'by placing ourselves on the middle ground' the Whigs might use the incident both to condemn the provocative conduct of Hunt and his

[20] Holland to Grey, 11 Mar. 1819, reply 15 Mar., ibid. 51546, fos. 21–3, 24–7.

associates and also to 'rally to our standard all moderate and reasonable men (and a great portion of the property of the country)', so that the people might again look to the Whigs 'as their natural leaders and protectors'. Even so, however, he confessed his lack of real hope of success in the present state of the country, and suggested that nothing should be done until the meeting of Parliament, 'unless sooner called forth by some strong manifestation of public feeling to take the part which, upon a full review of all the circumstances, our principles and our duty may dictate'. In the meantime he called for detailed reports from Lord Derby, the Whig Lord-Lieutenant of Lancashire, of the events at and before the 'massacre'.[21]

Grey's caution was overridden by the precipitate action of the Prince Regent in sending a message of support to the Manchester magistrates without waiting for a full enquiry into the event, and by the demands of Tierney and Holland that the Whigs must act immediately. 'Can it be right that we should continue to take no part whatever at the present moment, but wait quietly and in the background till it suits the convenience of Ministers to call Parliament together?' demanded Tierney on 6 September. He declared it to be both the Whigs' duty and their interest to arouse the public to petition and address the Regent and both Houses, and to forestall the radicals who had begun to organize meetings at Westminster and in Middlesex. Otherwise, the Whigs would be open to the reproach that 'we do not feel sufficiently for the rights of the people'. Holland too argued that if the Whigs stood aside, the country would be 'left to two outrageous parties, the legitimate Tories on one side and the violent reformers on the other, the rich and the poor, the governors and the governed'. Grey doubted at first whether such conduct would not merely alienate men like Derby and Fitzwilliam, Lord-Lieutenants of the principal 'disturbed districts', but he was eventually persuaded that 'this was the precise occasion on which we might take the game out of the hands of such people as Hunt and Wooler, and place ourselves where we ought to be.' The crucial factor, however, was the attitude of Fitzwilliam, whose liberal principles were outraged by the event of Peterloo, despite his 'horror of reform'. In his capacity of Lord-Lieutenant of the West Riding, he announced his intention to promote and attend a county meeting in Yorkshire to press for an enquiry. 'This puts an end to all my doubts and difficulties', Grey wrote from Doncaster, 'and I can no longer have any hesitation in saying that we ought to do all we can to give effect to the example . . . and to promote similar measures in other counties.' Brougham too urged the Whigs to take the lead in organizing meetings, to keep them moderate in tone, and busied himself with preparations in Cumberland and Westmorland. Grey now attempted to stimulate one in Northumberland, with the approval of the 80-year-old Wyvill who saw Grey's leadership as essential if the country were to be aroused. The plan failed however, owing to the lack of enthusiasm among the gentry.[22]

---

[21] For Peterloo, see D. Read, *Peterloo: the 'Massacre' and its Background* (Manchester, 1958). Reid, *Earl of Durham*, 139–40; Grey to Brougham, 25 Aug., *BLT* ii. 342–3; and corr. with Derby, G. 11/7.

[22] Tierney to Grey, 6 Sept., G. 55; Holland to Grey, 6 Sept, BL Add. MS 51546, fos. 38–40; Grey

The Whigs had mixed success in their campaign for county meetings. The Middlesex plan fell through, largely because of inability to agree with the radicals over reform, and the local grandees in the North and in Hampshire proved reluctant. By 10 October Grey was writing that 'there is unfortunately too much backwardness amongst our friends' because of their fear of providing an opportunity for the reformers. The Yorkshire meeting, however, was a triumph. Fitzwilliam and Milton attended and secured the passage of resolutions condemning the magistrates and calling for an enquiry. As a consequence, Fitzwilliam was dismissed from his Lord-Lieutenancy. His martyrdom, deliberate though it was, aroused Whig enthusiasm everywhere, not least because his well-known hostility to reform enabled them to focus attention away from that question and on to the issue of popular rights and liberties. Yet, as Grey quickly realized, it bound the party even more strongly to Fitzwilliam's anti-reformist views, and limited its options to either 'a distinct line' on reform or its dissolution. They could not 'support the government in putting down reform', nor could they 'assist the Radicals in putting down the government'; the most probable result would be 'the dissolution of the party or at least my relinquishing for ever the part I have hitherto had in conducting it'. First, however, they should attempt to define a strategy 'founded upon Whig principles' and incorporating 'economy, retrenchment, enquiry into the abuses of power, a salutary principle of reform applied to the corruptions of the Government and the Parliament, and a resistance to wild and impracticable theories'. It would, he admitted, be very difficult; and once again despondency overcame him, increased by an attack of his illness, which made him thin and feeble and obliged him to take laudanum.[23]

Grey attended the first weeks of the parliamentary session in November and early December, with results which depressed him still further. He spoke against the Address, declaring firmly against 'plans of innovation, leading to the subversion of the constitution and the state of society' but declaring that instead of merely suppressing popular discontents the government should be dealing with their economic causes. He also maintained that the existing laws were adequate to deal with any crisis that might arise and that 'the safety of the state could only be found in the protection of the liberties of the people'. Those liberties included the rights of free speech and assembly for lawful purposes, which had not been breached by the meeting at Peterloo: that meeting, he declared, and its outcome were 'by far the most important event that had occurred in the course of his political life'. There was a prima-facie case against the Manchester magistrates for hasty and

to Holland, 10, 11, 21 Sept., G. 35; Tierney to Holland, 14, 15, 16, 21, 28 Sept., BL Add. MS 51584, fos. 76–82, 86–7; Smith, *Whig Principles*, 346–50; Lord Milton to Sir F. Wood, 17, 21 Sept., Hickleton MSS A.4/10; Brougham to Grey, 18, 19 Sept., *BLT*, ii. 345–7; Wyvill to Fenwick, 28 Sept., Wyvill MSS 257/12; Sir M. W. Ridley to Grey, 8, 19 Oct., G. 49/12; C. W. Bigge to Grey, 27 Oct., G. 7/9; Sir C. Monck to Grey, 11 Oct., G. 41/8.

[23] Grey to Holland, 10 Oct., BL Add. MS 51546, fos. 55–6; 24 Oct., G. 35; Fitzwilliam to Grey, 15, 22 Oct., G. 14/11; to Lady Fitzwilliam [1819], Fitzwilliam MSS, Northampton; Smith, *Whig Principles*, 349–52.

unlawful action, and he also condemned the Prince Regent's letter to the magistrates for approving their action before all the facts could have been known. He demanded a full enquiry and moved an amendment to the Address, but lost the division by 34 to 159.[24]

The government then introduced six Bills laying further restrictions on the popular press, public meetings, and the training of persons in arms or military exercises. Three of the Bills were introduced in the Lords, and Grey opposed them vigorously, on the grounds that 'the system of force, coercion, and terror, which was now attempted to be established in this once free and happy country, was calculated rather to irritate and inflame the discontents that existed, than to allay or repress them.' He found, however, that even his own friends were less than unanimous on the subject; some of the Whig peers and commoners supported some of the Bills on the ground of the public danger, and Grey's protests against the Blasphemous Libels Bill and the Seizure of Arms Bill were poorly supported: only fifteen others signed the former and eleven the latter.

When Lansdowne presented a motion for a committee of enquiry into the state of the manufacturing districts it was lost by 47 to 178 despite a powerful speech from Grey, rising, as he said, 'perhaps for the last time, to fight once more for the liberties of his country'. Grenville and Wellesley spoke on the other side. Grenville's speech was one of his best and, Grey told Mary, was 'exactly in the tone of his speeches at the beginning of the French Revolution, and dwelling on the same topics, violent to a degree that quite shocked me'. These first two weeks of the session proved, he wrote,

that I have not influence enough to keep the opposition united in a firm and vigorous resistance to a course of conduct, so directly at variance with all my principles ... I never felt quite broken-hearted about politics till now; but everything now shows that our hopes with respect to the public interest are entirely blasted, and that the party, if it can be said to have an existence, can no longer exist for any useful purpose.

His health, too, was breaking down and he retired to Howick in early December without staying for the debates on the remaining repressive acts.[25]

Grey blamed the radicals as well as the government for the events of 1819, and in his speeches he took every opportunity to distance himself from their aims and activities. This no doubt helped to keep Fitzwilliam and the conservatives loyal to the party, but it cast further doubts on the Whigs' devotion to reform and weakened their hold on the public. Fenwick reported on 24 December that the radicals in the north-east were split, some supporting the moderate line but others staunchly pursuing annual parliaments and universal suffrage; there was little hope of the reformers all agreeing to follow the Whigs, though they might be rallied by a plan of reform being 'taken up in earnest and pursued with vigour'. He admitted, however, that Fitzwilliam's public services and high character 'entitle him to the

---

[24] *Hansard*, xli. 4–21, 50 (23 Nov.).
[25] Ibid. 349–53, 748, 755; Grey to Mary, 25 Nov., 3, 4 Dec., G. 28; *Eng. Hist. Docs.* xi. 335–41.

utmost consideration and it would be peculiarly ungracious to bring forward a question as one of the Party to which he cannot accede'. His conclusion was that 'there is not the slightest chance of a Reform of Parliament being obtained at present' and to bring it forward would weaken the party without attracting solid support in the country. He did not doubt Grey's continued personal attachment to the cause but agreed that it should not be brought forward at present. C. W. Bigge, another Northumberland correspondent, also placed the unity of the Whigs before the need of immediate reform, and advised that members of the party should not associate themselves for the present with the steps he was taking to revive a reform association in the county, though he pointed out that they would eventually have to declare themselves in favour of reform if they were to retain the support of the public.

Grey remained hopeful that the Whigs' resistance to the repressive Bills would maintain their standing in the country, and he remained sceptical about reports of impending insurrection amongst the Durham colliers. He hoped that when the present alarms subsided the Whigs would be better able to take up the reform question again: 'It will be impossible for any party, looking to the support of public opinion, to succeed, without taking some more direct measure with that view, than Lord John Russell's.' Lambton indeed had given notice in the Commons on 6 December of a motion after the Christmas recess for the repeal of the Septennial Act, the extension of the franchise to copyholders and ratepaying householders, and the abolition of rotten boroughs. Grey warned him on 3 January that reform must continue to be an 'open' question and not a party commitment, and that he deprecated 'the certain evil of the dissolution of such a body for any speculative or doubtful good, more especially when the attainment of that good is itself so problematical'. He thought that reform might well not come 'during my life or even yours'; his strategy was to 'have that object pursued individually by those who are favourable to it, in such a manner as may neither divide the Whig party, nor pledge them to it in such a way as may make their acceptance of office...a reproach to them without it'. Holland went even further, and at a conversation with Grey and Lambton had spoken so strongly against Lambton's plan that the latter was mortally offended and threatened to secede from the party. He also remonstrated at what he considered the excessive deference Grey was paying to Fitzwilliam's opinions, and distressed his father-in-law by attacking Fitzwilliam's record of support for repression since 1794. It was in this state that Grey and the Whig party stood when the death of George III on 29 January opened another era in British politics and brought to the fore new questions affecting the Whigs and their political prospects.[26]

[26] Fenwick to Grey, 24 Dec., G. 14/6; Bigge to Grey, 26 Dec., G. 7/9; Grey to Brougham, 18 Dec., G. 8, to Holland, 26 Dec., G. 35; *Hansard* xli. 757; Grey to Lambton, 3 Jan., Lambton to Grey, 3, 10 Jan., Reid, *Earl of Durham*, i. 129–33.

CROWN AND PEOPLE, 1812–1820

Grey's failure to achieve office under the Prince Regent convinced him that the Whigs could no longer rely on the 'reversionary interest,' the traditional hope of party oppositions. For the future, whether from inclination or from necessity, they must look to public opinion as the alternative to royal favour. The Regent's personal dislike of Grey and his increasing commitment to Liverpool's government and its policies suggested that no change was to be expected on his accession to the throne. The only hope lay in the mounting pressure of outside opinion and the unpopularity of the present ministers. George's quarrels with his wife and his only legitimate daughter, Princess Charlotte, were seen not as the prelude to a court revolution but as an opportunity to mobilize public opinion against the ministry, who were bound to side with the Prince. It was in this spirit that Grey attempted to exploit these domestic differences, while restraining the hot-heads in the party from rushing into alliance with those elements in the country who might attempt to discredit the throne and the political establishment in general. During the years 1812–20 Grey had to tread the middle path between old court Whiggery and radical popularism in dealing with the affairs of the two Princesses. Though feeling that the time was not ripe for radical reform, he sought to win the approval of moderate men by demonstrating the party's responsible attitude towards both the royal family and the public interest.

Princess Charlotte, born in 1796, had from her earliest years been the centre of an acrimonious war between her parents, who had separated immediately after her birth. The Prince's attempt to discredit his wife in the 'delicate investigation' of 1806, his own uninterrupted succession of mistresses, and his 'shameful' neglect of Charlotte helped to turn his daughter's affections towards her mother. The Prince feared his wife's influence over Charlotte and insisted on controlling her education and the appointment of her companions. By 1810 Charlotte had grown into a high-spirited girl, with more than a trace of her mother's headstrong and volatile temperament as well as her grandfather's obstinacy. Chafing at the seclusion of her life at Carlton House and at Windsor, she began in true Hanoverian fashion to seek help from those politicians who would take up her cause against the Prince. At the end of 1810 she began to consult Henry Brougham and Whitbread, who had supported her mother after the change of administration in 1807 deprived Caroline of her former advisers Perceval and Canning. Charlotte professed Whiggish principles, and in 1811 expressed her regret that Grey and Grenville were not to form a government. In the summer of 1812 Brougham began to consult Grey about the two Princesses. Caroline was protesting about the barriers raised by the Prince between her and Charlotte, and in particular her exclusion from her daughter's confirmation. Charlotte herself was becoming more restive about her own seclusion and the treatment of her mother. Brougham sent Grey copies of the correspondence between the two Princesses and the Court, but Grey was cautious. He condemned the Prince's attitude towards his wife and daughter, and praised Caroline's temperate and judicious conduct: Caroline and her companion Lady Charlotte Lindsay authorized Brougham to keep Grey informed of their affairs.[1]

Grey nevertheless tried to avoid direct involvement in the quarrels in the royal family. 'To court the young Princess, or to enourage her opposition to her father,' he wrote to Holland, would be 'foolish and . . . disgraceful.' He favoured support for Burdett's proposed amendment to the Regency Act, intended to provide for Charlotte's immediate assumption of 'full powers of the sovereignty without restriction or limitation' in case of the Regent's death in his father's lifetime, but he laid down that this support must be on public and not personal grounds. Acutely conscious of the dangers of seeming to be motivated purely by personal resentment, he wrote that though he had been ill-used by the Prince, 'and I will not deny that I have the feeling of it which may be supposed to belong to a heart not naturally very cold', such personal feelings ought not to be seen to govern the opposition's conduct. He repudiated the idea that 'any hope from the young Princess' should influence his public duty. He was too well aware of the views of many of his party colleagues, who feared to offend the Regent too openly while there was still the least hope that he might change his ministers.[2]

The Princess however was irrepressible. At the end of 1812 the Prince threatened again to expose his wife's supposed immoral conduct, and in 1813 the unsavoury details of the 1806 investigation were made public knowledge.[3] Rumours flew around London that he was preparing the ground for a divorce, with the attendant prospect of remarriage and possibly the birth of a son who might exclude Charlotte from the position of heir apparent. Charlotte was furious at the insinuations against her mother and worried about her own prospects; she feared her father was about to marry her off to the Hereditary Prince of Orange and send her away to live in Holland. She proposed to Brougham a scheme to escape from Windsor after her eighteenth birthday and to set up her own establishment, if necessary by appeal to Parliament. Brougham dissuaded her, pointing out that she would not be independent until she was twenty-one, and he toned down a letter of remonstrance which she wanted to send to her father. Grey prudently ignored his offer to send the letter to him for approval, despite Brougham's assurance that Charlotte was 'disposed towards popular principles'—in token of which she had acquired a cast of Brougham's bust. Grey remained detached, and denied rumours that he intended to bring the Princess of Wales's affairs before the House of Lords. He did not want to be found backing the wrong horse in case the Prince lost confidence in his present ministers, and he knew from bitter experience how unreliable an association with any member of the royal family could be.[4]

---

[1] *Letters of Princess Charlotte, 1811–17*, ed. A. Aspinall (1949), pp. xv, xvi, 8, 76; *BLT*, ii. 141–5, 148–50.   [2] Grey to Holland, 3 Jan. 1813, G. 35; Tierney to Grey [Jan. 1813], G. 55.

[3] *'The Book', Complete: being the whole of the depositions on the Investigation of the conduct of the Princess of Wales . . . in the year 1806; prepared for publication by the late Rt. Hon. Spencer Perceval . . .*, C. V. Williams (1813).

[4] *BLT*, ii. 163–75; Grey to Holland, 12 Feb. 1813, G. 35; Adair to Grey, 21 Nov. 1813, G. 1/3.

He repeated his temperate advice directly to Charlotte when she approached him, on her friend Mercer Elphinstone's suggestion, in October 1813. He wrote kindly but with some diplomacy that she owed the Prince her duty 'as a sovereign and as a father', and that she should as far as possible avoid opposition to his wishes. However, he pointed out that neither the parental nor the royal authority was absolute: the Prince had the right and duty to advise her, but his only constitutional power as Regent was to veto any proposal of marriage before the age of twenty-one. He counselled her to play for time and to be patient: 'The hardship of marrying you at once, from such a state [of seclusion], against your inclination . . . is, I think, too apparent to be persevered in.' He expressed the wish that she should 'at the commencement of your public life (which God grant may be long and glorious)' gain 'that general confidence and affection which is not more essential to the security and strength of the throne you are to inherit than to your own personal happiness and comfort'.[5]

Charlotte was delighted with Grey's 'dignified, candid, liberal and impartial' letter and professed herself 'quite *enchanted* with him'. It confirmed her own feeling that she wanted more experience of the world before marrying, and encouraged her to insist on the abandonment of the engagement to the Prince of Orange and upon a promise from her father not to force her against her inclinations. She declared herself in December to be 'as much attached to the Whig principles as ever' but wrote that she would not make any exhibition of her political views until 'a future period' when it might be possible to do so; when that occurred, she looked forward to 'personal intimacy and friendship' with Grey, a phrase which pre-echoes the relationship between Grey's successor Melbourne and the young Queen Victoria. For the time being, however, she settled down to wait on events.

At the same time she became reconciled to seeing less of her mother. Mercer Elphinstone, who was also Grey's confidante, used her influence to persuade her to remain on better terms with the Regent, who, in hopes of her turning more kindly towards the Orange match, put himself out to win her affection. When the Prince of Orange was brought back to London in December 1813, however, the Regent pressed his daughter for an immediate decision. Charlotte allowed herself to be persuaded by her suitor's considerate and lively manner, and gave the required promise, only to discover afterwards that she would be expected after the marriage to live half of every year in Holland. She believed that she had been tricked, but she allowed the arrangement to hang fire for a time until her eighteenth birthday early in 1814, when she still hoped her father would grant her an independent establishment in England. The Whigs suspected that the Regent's enthusiasm for the 'Dutch expedition' had something to do with ensuring that his daughter would not become a political focus for the opposition, and Grey again offered his advice. She should not, he wrote, be required to leave the country against her inclination. She should seek an assurance from her father that she

[5] Grey to Charlotte, 19 Oct. 1813, *Letters of Princess Charlotte*, 80–2.

would not be forced to do so, but he counselled against any attempt to raise the issue in Parliament, and particularly against any appearance of political involvement with the Whigs. He reminded her that from the outset she had sought his advice in a manner 'entirely remote from politics or political views' and declared that it was on this understanding that he had consented to advise her: though he would gladly offer his services if required as a mediator, he thought it would be damaging to her and to the Whigs if he were seen to be too closely involved. It would arouse the Prince's 'deepest resentment' if Grey were known to have visited her at Warwick House: and if the matter reached the extremity of an appeal to be public, it should not appear to do so as a party question.[6]

Grey's prudent caution could not restrain Charlotte from forcing the issue. She approached her father as Grey advised, but his response was an ultimatum. The terms of the marriage contract were of no concern to her or her fiancé: she would be expected to live mainly in Holland, and her first son would be brought to England when three years of age to be educated as a future king of England. Charlotte bridled: she was determined not to be forced to live abroad and turned again to Brougham for advice. Aware of the perils for the Whigs if, while Charlotte was abroad, the Regent were to divorce his wife and remarry, he encouraged her to be firm. Charlotte's obstinacy was confirmed when, during the victory celebrations in 1814 and the visit of the Tsar to London, the Queen refused to allow Caroline to attend the official functions in his honour. Her resistance was strengthened by her fiancé's undignified conduct at the balls and parties during the celebrations, when he was several times seen to be drunk, and by a sudden infatuation which she conceived for another royal visitor, Prince August of Prussia. In June she sent for the Prince of Orange and told him that she must stay in England with her mother, who had been so shabbily treated; and she insisted that after her marriage she should expect always to be allowed to invite her to her house. The Prince naturally jibbed, and Charlotte at once broke off the engagement.[7]

Grey disapproved of this precipitate act, even more so when the Princess of Wales cut the ground from under her daughter's feet by announcing her intention to leave the country. He warned Miss Elphinstone that this could only encourage the Regent's hankering for a divorce, and he advised Charlotte that 'patience and submission . . . are, I am persuaded, your best, perhaps your only arms. This is a hard lesson for a person of your Royal Highness's age, and born to such prospects', but 'resistance would be even less effectual.' He reminded her that the public would not support a rebellious daughter against legitimate parental authority, and suggested that she should use the excuse of her health to request the Prince's permission to spend the summer at Weymouth to reduce the tension between

---

[6] Charlotte to Mercer Elphinstone [24 Oct.], [20 Dec.], ibid. 85, 95–6. Mercer Elphinstone later married the Comte de Flahault, the son of Talleyrand and Mme de Flahault, whom she first met at the Greys' house. They became close friends of the Greys. Grey to Charlotte, 7 Feb. 1814, 'Earl Grey's hints to Princess Charlotte', 10 Apr., ibid. 109–12, 114–15.

[7] Ibid., pp. xvii, and Charlotte to Prince of Orange, 16 June, 117–18.

them. The Regent, however, threatened that Charlotte's disobedience would be punished by the dismissal of her present ladies and her virtual imprisonment at her residence at Warwick House with others of his own choice. Grey intervened to try to stave off such extreme measures, which he believed were intended to force Charlotte into the Orange match. On 27 July he had a private conversation with the Prime Minister, in which Liverpool agreed that it would be impolitic to force her consent. The Prince, however, lost patience and carried out his threats.[8]

Charlotte panicked. She fled from Warwick House one evening in a hackney carriage and went to her mother's house in Connaught Place, where she summoned Brougham to come to advise her and declared she would not marry the Prince of Orange. Brougham immediately called Grey to town, and in the meantime persuaded Charlotte to return to her father to avert a popular riot in her favour. He also arranged for her favourite uncle the Duke of Sussex, a friend of the Whigs, to raise the question in the House of Lords. Grey set off at once for London, where he found his friends in disarray, and, he wrote when he arrived, so timid or so adverse that there would be no hope of any success. He persuaded Sussex to drop his motion, and returned at once to Howick to be with his son, who was dying. He expressed his indignation at the Prince's cruelty towards his daughter, as 'not an unnatural accompaniment of base and unmanly conduct to a wife', but wrote to Mary that it was hopeless to try to do anything in Parliament. He spoke in support of Sussex's withdrawal,

stating the strength of my own feelings on the subject . . . asserting it to be a matter of public interest upon which it was both the right and the duty of Parliament to interfere . . . I executed this ill, my head being confused with the eternal whirl and rattle of the chaise for three days; but Rosslyn . . . assures me that I did not let down either the Duke of Sussex or the Princess. So ends the history of the famous expedition of the renowned Knight Carlos for the relief of a Captive Princess!

Grey had succeeded in pouring oil on the troubled waters, and Charlotte settled down quietly for a time. Grey on his part managed to prevent the opposition from raising the question of her independent establishment in the winter of 1814. The Princess of Wales's departure for Europe in the summer of 1814 also removed a major irritant. Charlotte spent the summer at Windsor and at Weymouth, where she recovered from her infatuation with the Prussian Prince, and after her return to London she fixed upon a new suitor, Prince Leopold of Saxe-Coburg. The Regent gradually came round to his daughter's wishes, and in 1816 they were married.[9]

The Princess's affairs had been resolved in a way which averted the threat to the Whigs of losing 'their' future Queen: but if they were complacent at the

[8] Grey to Mercer Elphinstone [20 June 1814], to Charlotte, 7, 15 July, ibid. 120, 122–4, 129–31, and p. xviii.

[9] Ibid. pp. xix–xxi, *BLT*, ii. 226–46, 271–3; Tierney to Grey, 14 July, G. 55; Grey to Holland, 18 July, G. 35; to Mary, 26 July, G. 28. H. G. Bennet told Creevey that Grey's speech and his coming to town 'had great effect': 26 July, Creevey MSS.

outcome, their hopes were cruelly shattered in 1817 when she died in childbed. Romilly noted in his diary:

Whether there was much chance if she had lived, of a Whig Administration again being the government of the country, I do not know: but that there is no prospect of such an event taking place in a long series of years, cannot be doubted.

In Newcastle, James Losh also recorded the event: 'as far as we short sighted creatures can judge', he wrote, 'a heavier calamity could scarcely have fallen upon my beloved country.' Grey's reaction was less despondent and perhaps more cynical. Princess Charlotte, he wrote to Willoughby-Gordon, could not have died at a better moment. Her quiet domesticity and her quarrel with her father had made her popular, but if she had lived the country's expectations might have been disappointed. She was a Hanoverian after all, and he thought 'she was not more remarkable for sincerity or steadiness of attachment than her father.' He was disillusioned with the idea of a 'reversionary interest': the Prince of Wales, 'till he was Regent, had less real influence upon the government of the country, than any considerable man in either House of Parliament', and there was nothing for the Whigs to hope for from any of the Regent's brothers, who were too unpopular to acquire followers and as lacking in ability as the Prince himself.[10] Grey had again learnt from experience. The Whigs' political prospects had never been advanced one jot by their alliance with the heir to the throne, and their future would depend, as he realized, upon their ability to appeal to and satisfy the public at large rather than on favour at Court. Princess Charlotte's death was more of a boon than a curse to the party, who were freed at last, as the 'reversionary interest' finally faded from British politics, from the court faction of the eighteenth century.

Grey was not done, however, with Charlotte's mother. When the Regent became King in January 1820 he at once took steps to rid himself of his wife and demanded in the meantime that the Cabinet agree to erase her name from the Anglican liturgy. He pressed for a divorce on the grounds of his wife's infidelity. Brougham immediately summoned Caroline back to England to claim her rights as Queen, hoping that he could use the affair for his personal advantage and as a political tool against the unpopular Court and ministry. The ministers were anxious to avoid the public scandal of a royal divorce when the new King was so unpopular in the country, but responded to Brougham's threats with one of their own. If the Queen set foot in England they would introduce a Bill of Pains and Penalties against her, containing a divorce clause. The Queen arrived in London on 6 June, and a committee of the House of Lords was appointed to examine the papers laid before the House by the government. The affair monopolized the attention of the press and public for the next five months, and gave rise to a degree of popular tumult which aroused fears of revolution. The mob came out on the Queen's arrival, 'breaking windows in all parts of the town', and there were reports of

---

[10] *Memoirs of the Life of Sir Samuel Romilly, ed. by his sons* (1840), iii. 318, Losh, *Diary*, i. 73; Grey to Willoughby-Gordon, 23 Nov. 1817, BL Add. MS 49478, fos. 184–5.

incipient mutiny amongst the troops. Processions of working men were organized throughout the capital with bands playing and banners flying, addresses and deputations arrived at her residence, Brandenburg House, and the Common Council of London addressed the Crown in terms not known since 1795. Cartwright, the city radicals, and the electors of Westminster linked the Queen's misfortunes with the cause of radical reform, and a torrent of lampoons, caricatures, and popular literature poured from the press. The collapse of the government seemed inevitable, and there were fears for the throne itself. The radical *John Bull* described the Queen as 'the pole to hoist the revolutionary cap of Liberty on'.[11]

Grey could not neglect the political possibilities of the affair for the Whigs, but he shrank from putting the party's weight behind the popular agitation. He had warned Brougham in August 1819 that 'we, as a party, have nothing to do but to observe the most perfect neutrality, and to decide upon the evidence, as we should do in any other case.' He was aware, as was Mackintosh, that the Queen's business could split the party. His first public intervention was cautious—too cautious for party hotheads like Creevey, who sneered that Grey was 'a rigid lover of justice; he did not care a damn about the [party] cause; he was come up to do his duty and should act accordingly. He is more provoking in all he does than these villains of Ministers themselves.' Before the Queen's arrival Grey laid down his view of the matter to Lambton:

When it comes before parliament, a public duty must be discharged, and can only be satisfactorily discharged by doing what appears to be strictly right without looking either to the right or left. I do not think it ought to be taken up as a party question.

Grey's stand was approved by Lambton on the radical wing as much as by Holland and Fitzwilliam on the right. To Holland he wrote in April that the Queen's business

is a question on which I think we may not only act individually without reference to our party connection, but on which perhaps it may be advantageous that we should do so. There could be nothing, I think, more prejudicial to us, than the appearance of making use of such a question . . . for party purposes.

Holland wrote that he considered the whole business as 'degrading . . . to all concerned, and disgusting and tiresome I think to the bystanders', and Fitzwilliam feared that 'the House of Lords is to be rolled in the kennel for the preservation of Ministers.' Apart from the repulsiveness of the Queen's indiscretions, the Whig lords feared that she would inflame the populace to a dangerous extent against the political establishment in general, for the King was no better than his wife.

[11] A. Aspinall, *Lord Brougham and the Whig Party* (Manchester, 1927), 101, 106–10; Smith, *Whig Principles*, 357–8; C. G. F. Greville, *Journal of the Reigns of King George IV and King William IV*, ed. H. Reeve (1874), i. 28–32; R. Fulford, *The Trial of Queen Caroline* (1967), 39–41; Rosslyn to Grey [July/Aug.] 1820, G. 51; J. Stevenson, 'The Queen Caroline Affair', in *London in the Age of Reform*, ed. J. Stevenson (Oxford, 1977), 117–29.

We are to dethrone a queen [wrote Fitzwilliam in July] and dissolve her marriage with the king, for the crime of disgusting intimacy with a menial servant ... but if these be crimes in a queen, that call down upon her the vengeance of the nation, what is the nation to do in the case of a king, guilty of similar crimes ... ?

Yet the Whigs could not ignore the political possibilities of the affair. The public outcry shook the government, and it was rumoured that the King was wavering in his attachment to his ministers and might call on the Whigs to replace them. Tierney reported on 12 June that he, Lansdowne, and Holland had been approached by Lord Donoughmore who had assured him 'that the ministers would be immediately dismissed if I would say that I advised him to press the king to do so. He offered to return to Carlton House and to finish the business in an hour.' He further asserted 'that the king was perfectly ready to forget all that had ever passed between you and him and that his inclination was to look to Holland, Lansdowne and yourself.' He added, 'I am sure Grey may be Minister if he chooses.' There would be no prior restrictions on the new ministry's policy, and 'on the Catholic question there was a disposition to give way.' Tierney thought that it would be inadvisable to precipitate a change of ministers in the middle of the negotiations now going on with the Queen's advisers, but urged Grey to come to town to discuss the matter with his colleagues.[12]

Grey set out immediately, but his old doubts and fears still remained. 'The more I think of the business that takes me to town', he wrote to Mary from Ferrybridge on the 17th, 'the more I am convinced that it can end in nothing, and that I shall be very probably laughed at, for having gone on a fool's errand. However I think I could not have done otherwise, unless I had declared my intention to have nothing more to do with politics, and that would have been neither right, nor handsome to my friends at such a moment.' His fears were confirmed by his conversations on arrival in London. He became convinced of 'our utter inability to make such an arrangement as would be necessary in the House of Commons', mainly because of Brougham's position. He had remarked a month earlier that 'everything I observe in his conduct puts me much more in mind of Sheridan with some mixture of Whitbread.' Brougham's commitment to the Queen, combined with his ambition to lead the Commons in a Whig administration, made him suspect, and on 20 June Grey wrote again to Mary to express his despair at the difficulties of a satisfactory arrangement in the lower House. 'In the whole of this business', he wrote on the 23rd, 'he [Brougham] has shown himself to be a man who cannot be trusted. ... I shall feel it to be a great misfortune, as well as a great danger, to be obliged to act with him in any confidential and responsible situation.'[13]

[12] Sir James Mackintosh to Lord John Russell, 12 Jan. 1820, *Early Corr. of Lord John Russell*, i. 210–12; Creevey to Miss Ord, 25 Aug., 23 Oct., *Creevey Papers*, i. 313, 331; Grey to Lambton, 29 May 1820, New, *Durham*, 64; to Holland, 12 Apr., G. 35; Aspinall, *Brougham*, 111; Fitzwilliam to Milton [23 Oct. 1820], Fitzwilliam MSS, Sheffield; Smith, *Whig Principles*, 359; Greville, *Journal*, i. 29, 32; Tierney to Grey, 12 June, G. 55.

[13] Grey to Mary, 17, 19, 20 May, 20, 23 June, G. 28.

Nevertheless Grey spoke in the Lords on the 19th, censuring the Ministry's conduct in postponing the meeting of the secret committee and demanding that they act positively to resolve the crisis. He was dissatisfied with his performance, feeling himself unprepared, so that 'I did either too much or too little'. To his surprise, however, a message arrived from the King on the 23rd to express approval of his words and saying 'that all former grievances were obliterated from his mind'. He spoke again in the Lords on the 27th after Brougham had appeared at the bar to plead the Queen's case, and the speech, Greville reported, was a powerful one against the Queen—'a speech for office'. The ministry's conduct, Grey declared, had been throughout extraordinary, weak, and unjustifiable: they had brought the honour of the Crown and the interests of the country into peril. They were a 'loose, disjointed, and feeble Administration'. Liverpool responded angrily, asserting that the speech was 'one of the most inflammatory party attacks that was ever made within the walls of Parliament'. When Grey went to the levee afterwards, he told Mary, he had a 'most gracious' reception but nothing more than courtesies and generalities passed with the King. He remained convinced that there was no possibility of his being asked to take office at least until after the Queen's business was settled one way or another, and he again expressed his fears at the alarming state of public opinion.[14]

The Lords Committee reported on 4 July, declaring that the evidence against the Queen was sufficient to merit a 'solemn enquiry', on the following day the Bill of Pains and Penalties was introduced. 'The Ministers ought to be hanged for the situation into which they have brought this unfortunate business,' Grey wrote, 'and I am by no means sure that this will not happen before its conclusion.' He feared that the Queen would be ruined by the evidence against her and that she would pull down the throne and the government with her. It was 'the most unpleasant business in which any public man was ever before engaged, and in which it is hardly possible for any man to act honestly without drawing upon himself the reproaches of a prejudiced and unjust public. I must, however, on this, as on other occasions do my duty to the best of my judgement and leave the consequences to God.' He left town on the 11th after the first reading of the Bill, to await the summons to the second reading on 17 August.[15]

Grey's judgement of the political situation was a realistic one. The weakness of the opposition in the House of Commons made it unlikely that the Whigs could form a government which could deal with the crisis without dangerously inflaming public opinion still further, or, perhaps worse, throwing themselves into Brougham's hands. Grey decided that his role should be that of an independent and impartial judge on the evidence of the case, and that he should not allow himself to act from party motives. This was to be his great strength in the coming trial, and it greatly enhanced his reputation as an honourable man. It was not only that he put reputation before party interest; in any case he saw that it would be

[14] Grey to Mary, 24, 29 June, ibid.; *Hansard* NS i. 1137–9, ii. 1–15; Greville, *Journal*, i. 32.
[15] Grey to Mary, 4, 7 July, G. 28.

ultimately counter-productive to try to ride into office on a wave of public agitation and then have to contend with the difficulties of continuing the government in such a situation. His ambition for office had long been tempered with a prudent recognition of the problems which a Whig administration would face, and if this disappointed the few party activists it preserved the party from the breakup which he foresaw if office were achieved on such terms.

The House of Lords reassembled in mid-August for the most theatrical event of the age. London presented scenes which to one of Grey's generation were all too reminiscent of Paris thirty years before, and Addresses expressing support of the Queen poured in from all over the country. Her progresses to and from the Lords were attended by cheering crowds, and the debates and evidence were assiduously reported and read throughout the land. Grey, on his way to London on the 15th, wrote to Holland that he feared 'a Jacobin Revolution more bloody and more atrocious than that of France'. His first moves on the opening of the Lords proceedings were designed even at that stage to try to avert the public scandal that the 'trial' would bring. The Duke of Leinster moved to rescind the order for the second reading of the Bill but Grey voted in the majority against the motion, on the grounds, as he later explained, that the serious charges presented against the Queen on the basis of the secret committee report should not be dismissed without thorough investigation and an opportunity for the Queen to present her defence. He spoke again to argue that a procedure by impeachment would be more proper than the Bill. Clear and certain evidence of adultery would then be required for a conviction, and the Queen would have a fairer trial. He moved that the judges be consulted as to whether her conduct, if proven, amounted to high treason, suggesting that if so, the House should amend the statute of Edward III to substitute divorce and degradation for the present barbaric penalty. If the judges decided to the contrary, he would submit to the procedure of a Bill. At this stage he offered no opinion as to the Queen's guilt or innocence:[16]

He came to do his duty as a peer of parliament, without any earthly consideration to warp or bias his mind. He neither came to support the cause of the king nor of the queen, but he entered that house with a strong desire and firm determination to do justice.

The judges determined that in the circumstances there would be no grounds for a charge of high treason, but Grey repeated two days later his conviction that an impeachment would be the preferable course, and moved to drop the Bill. He was defeated by 64 votes to 179, and the Bill began its course. Creevey criticized Grey's tactics, describing his first speech as 'as weak a speech as I ever heard', and he scoffed at Grey's wager at Brooks's that the Bill would not proceed. Grey, however, was following a consistent line. While disavowing party motives, he aimed to demonstrate the weakness and vacillation of the ministry and to point out the damage which was being done to the reputation of the Crown and government by their conduct. These accusations provided a basis from which Grey could build

[16] Grey to Holland, 15 Aug., G. 35; *Hansard*, NS ii. 612–25.

his strategy, as an impartial judge of an unsavoury affair, and it was in this light that he presented himself during the following weeks, taking a part in the examination of witnesses and speaking frequently to preserve the tone of judicial enquiry. In this way, he felt, the reputation of the Lords would be preserved from the consequences of involvement in an unpopular affair, and the Whigs in particular would appear as moderate and unprejudiced.

Grey's almost daily letters to Mary during the trial show him at his best, attentive to the evidence as a basis for his conclusions. As late as 2 October he declared 'I have not made up my mind' and two days later he was moving to a conviction that

this must end in a change of administration, at least if it does not, these Ministers will retain power, with a weight of public opinion against them which no others were ever able to withstand. Their removal I should look to as the means, I believe the only means, of saving the country, if the share I might be called upon to take in replacing them did not terrify and oppress me.

On the 6th, he wrote that he had still not decided what to do but that he could not shrink from the task of undertaking the government if the crash should come: 'I must trust... to Providence to direct me.' By the 26th, the day after Denman's closing speech for the Queen, he had decided to vote against the Bill, whatever the consequences: 'I should never have another happy hour if I did otherwise.' On the 30th he retired to Holland House to read over all the evidence before preparing his speech on the second reading.[17]

The speech was one of Grey's finest. It was, wrote Creevey, 'beautiful— magnificent—all honour and right feeling, with the most powerful argument into the bargain. There is nothing approaching this damned fellow in the kingdom, when he mounts his best horse.' Holland told Mary that it was 'the most perfect speech I ever heard in Parliament... This... has convinced delighted and affected us all.' Grey himself wrote that 'I think I never made a speech that was so generally commended. It certainly cost me a sleepless night... but upon the whole I believe it was useful as some of the passages which had the greatest effect were the fruits of my wakeful meditations.'[18]

The speech maintained to the end the tone of judicious impartiality which Grey had assumed throughout the Lords proceedings. He regretted that ministers had not adopted his suggested procedure of an impeachment, but forebore from making a party issue of the case. He reviewed the evidence in a 'detached and broad-minded' way, damning the vital prosecution witness Majocci, whose evasive replies of 'non mi ricordo'—I do not remember—had created a new catch-phrase in London, and expressed his disgust at the nature of some of the evidence brought forward. Nevertheless, positive proof of the Queen's adultery had not been

---

[17] *Creevey Papers*, i. 308–10; 17 Aug.: Grey to Mary, G. 28, 31.

[18] *Creevey Papers*, i. 336, Holland to Mary, 3 Nov., Hickleton MSS A.1.4.12; Grey to Mary, 3 Nov., G. 31. For Grey's speech, *Hansard*, NS iii. 1573–4. See plate I for Hayter's picture of Grey addressing the Lords on the Queen's 'trial'.

produced, and though her conduct had been reprehensible it would be unjust to exact the drastic penalties proposed in the Bill. His final peroration summed up the principles which had guided his conduct:

I should hold myself to be indeed acting unworthily if I were to make the present a subject of party feeling. I trust that I have not pressed into the present argument any unfair or unworthy topic. I trust I have treated it as a legislator and a judge. I trust that the motives which induce me to urge your lordships not to leave a brand on her majesty, of which she is, in my opinion, undeserving, are of a pure and honourable description. My lords, a great part of my political life has been spent in storms and convulsions. As far as human infirmity would permit me, I have endeavoured to pursue a direct and steady course. I have never courted power. In consequence of my adherence to principle I have been excluded from power. In the course of my life I have also been the object of much popular reproach. These, I trust, are proofs of the determination which I have invariably evinced to resist the undue encroachments of the Crown, and at the same time to defend from the attacks of the people those rights and prerogatives which are not more necessary for the dignity and splendor of the monarch, than they are for the protection and the happiness of the people. In the case before your lordships, I have not made up my opinion without much anxiety and much consideration. I fairly acknowledge that my prejudices and impulses were quite unfavourable to my present conviction.I hardly conceived it possible that a case would be made out which would not compel me to vote for this bill; but, such a case has been made out; and, my lords, first on the ground of justice, and secondly on the ground of expediency, I feel, that if I were to vote for this bill, I should never again lay my head down upon my pillow in peace. The only vote which, under the deepest sense of my responsibility I can conscientiously give on the present question is—Not content.

The Prime Minister followed Grey. Influenced perhaps by the reception of Grey's speech, Liverpool was studiously fair and moderate, declaring that no peer should vote for the Bill unless he was satisfied by the evidence of adultery. Other speeches followed, and at 3 p.m. on 6 November the House divided, 123 for the Bill and 95 against. The Whigs voted solidly against, together with many Tories who believed the Queen guilty but who were opposed to proceeding with the divorce clause. A government motion to drop that clause was defeated by 129 to 62, and the third reading on 10 November passed by only 9. Clearly the Bill would not pass the Commons, and its introduction there would be accompanied by civil tumult on a massive scale. Brougham was throwing out dark hints that he was prepared to disclose the King's marriage to Mrs Fitzherbert and challenge his right to the throne under the Act of Settlement. Liverpool announced that the Bill was shelved.[19]

The Queen's triumph was spectacular. Within half an hour of Liverpool's statement there was rejoicing throughout London. 'Guns were firing in all directions, bells ringing, and illuminations in every street and suburb.' Processions marched 'with bands of music, carrying busts of the Queen with the crown on her head covered with laurel, playing God Save the Queen and carrying torches'. The vessels in the river were illuminated, as were the streets throughout the capital,

[19] Fulford, *Queen Caroline*, 230; C. New, *Life of Henry Brougham to 1830* (Oxford, 1961), 259–60.

and the Common Council presented an address of congratulation. 'The greatest triumph has been gained by the People of England', wrote Anne Cobbett. On 29 November the Queen attended a thanksgiving ceremony in St Paul's, accompanied by a thousand gentlemen on horseback and the members of the Common Council. It was estimated that almost half a million people thronged the streets. Grey wrote to Wilson that the proceedings 'may be taken as a genuine and avowed expression of the feeling which at this moment animates a very great majority of the people of England, but', he added, 'I am afraid that this is still too much confined to the middle and lower ranks of society.... Such a state of things if pushed to extremity can only produce one of two results, either a democratic revolution or the destruction of our constitution.'[20]

Grey's words reflected the Whigs' dilemma. The collapse of the ministry under this degree of popular pressure would bring them into office as the champions of the people: but could they sustain this role in office, when many of their more aristocratic members remained hostile to the reform which the people's voice demanded? Could they, indeed, control the House of Commons? Would the independent country members, distrustful of metropolitan radicalism, give their confidence to a party which had risen on the back of such a movement? And how would they deal with the unresolved problem of the Queen's presence? The King might well insist that they support his determination not to allow her to be crowned or her name to be restored to the liturgy. All depended on whether the ministry would resign or be dismissed. Grey delayed his return to Howick, after receiving a message from Lord Donoughmore suggesting that the ministry was about to fall, but he was sceptical: he wrote that he did not expect any major change, and that 'the King can no more get rid of his Ministers, than he can of his wife, however bitterly he may hate both.' The summons did not come, and on the 14th he resumed his journey north, after a final tirade against the ministry on the 10th.[21]

He complained of the whole course which ministers had pursued... He charged the servants of the Crown with the grossest neglect of duty, in the first instance, in listening only to *ex-parte* evidence, and giving a willing credence to the most exaggerated and unfounded calumnies. They had thus for many months agitated the nation—they had produced a general stagnation of public and private business—and they had given a most favourable opportunity, were it desired, to the enemies of internal peace and tranquillity. They had betrayed their King, insulted their Queen, and had given a shock to the morals of society by the promulgation of the detestable and disgusting evidence, in the hearing of which, the House had been so long occupied...

The Queen was now a wasting asset to the Whigs. The withdrawal of the Bill of Pains and Penalties left her no better off than before, and deprived her supporters of a popular issue. The radicals were beginning to fall out with each other again, and the Queen was not clearly identified with any positive policy. During the

[20] Letters from Anne Cobbett to J.P. Cobbett, Stevenson, 'The Queen Caroline Affair', 131–3; Grey to Wilson, 5 Dec., BL Add. MS 30109, fos. 140–2.

[21] Grey to Mary, 11, 12, 13 Nov., G. 31; *Hansard*, NS iii. 1746–7.

winter the Whigs embarked on a campaign to stimulate county meetings to try to keep up the impetus gained during the progress of the trial, but the dropping of the Bill removed the prospect of all-party agreement. It was felt that the country Tories would revert to support of the ministers if the attempt was made to petition for their removal. Holland pointed out that if the Whigs wished to take advantage of respectable public opinion they would have to restrict their petitions to the restoration of the Queen's name to the liturgy and a deprecation of any further steps which would damage the honour of the Crown. Lambton was enthusiastic for meetings which would demonstrate the Whigs' commitment to popular causes, but Grey was more cautious. He was gratified by his reception at Alnwick and other places on his way back to Howick, and felt that 'here, at this moment, I could carry anything, with the middling and lower classes of freeholders, [but] with the Gentry, who are in general a proud, half-bred, narrow-minded and bigoted race of Tories, it would be otherwise.' Fitzwilliam, who had shown enthusiasm for a county meeting in Yorkshire, now backed away, fearing that it might raise the issue of reform. There was total failure in the South of England, to Grey's disgust. 'I doubted, as you know,' he wrote, 'originally of the policy of the measure, but being embarked in it, every effort should have been made to give it effect.' Grey attempted to energize his friends in Northumberland, and though the High Sheriff refused the requisition, an unofficial meeting was held in the town hall at Morpeth, the upper floor of which had to be strengthened to hold the crowd. The meeting resolved in favour of the restoration of the Queen's name to the liturgy, the dropping of further proceedings against her, and the provision of an establishment. Grey disapproved, however, when Lambton proposed to ask the County Durham meeting to congratulate the Queen and demand the removal of the ministers. Lambton agreed to restrict the proceedings to those approved in Northumberland. Grey felt the outcome 'satisfactory in every respect' as showing that in the North at any rate the government was opposed by the great weight of public opinion. However, he complained that even there 'everything . . . that did not depend on me was neglected . . . everything, I have no doubt, will subside into the usual torpidity.' There was no longer the same groundswell of public opinion and the Whigs were left to fight their own parliamentary battle. Without public support their cause was doomed. A motion on 26 January deploring the removal of the Queen's name from the liturgy was defeated in the Commons by 209 to 310, and a further vote on 5 February was also unsuccessful. The independents were not prepared to desert the ministry to that extent. The Queen's affairs no longer monopolized public attention, and her popular support melted away: the crowds who had cheered her in the autumn of 1820 mocked her pathetic attempt to gain admission to the coronation in July 1821, and a few weeks later she was dead.[22]

[22] D. Sykes to C. Wood, 14 Oct., Fitzwilliam to Wood, 9, 22, 30 Nov., 6 Dec., Wood to Fitzwilliam, 30 Nov., Hickleton MSS A.4.19.9; Holland to Grey, 19 Nov., BL Add. MS 51546, fos. 114–15; Lambton to Grey, 21 Nov., G. B4; Grey to Holland, 21 Nov., 6 Dec., 1 Jan. 1821, G.35; to Monck,

The Queen Caroline affair thus created a blaze of popularity which died away as quickly as it had arisen, leaving the Whigs no better off than before. It was apparent from the reactions of their own conservative wing that the party was not yet equipped to seize the leadership of reformist opinion, without which they remained dependent on the royal favour if they were to achieve office. A desultory negotiation through Lord Donoughmore and Tierney in November and December 1820 came to nothing. The communication, wrote Grey to Fitzwilliam, was like those which took place before he left London: 'equally inconclusive and equally insincere'. The King was, in his opinion, merely seeking to discover 'whether we would bid more for him than his present ministers, and probably to increase their bidding by threatening them with ours'. He expected that the meeting of Parliament would put an end to all speculations of change.

It is quite clear that the King will never have recourse to us but in the last extremity... It is equally clear that he will only watch his opportunity, if he should be compelled to take us, to betray and sacrifice an administration which he will detest. The security against this must be popular confidence: and can that confidence *now* be obtained and preserved without some concession of the principle of Reform? This is a question which occupies me sleeping and waking; and I have not nerve to encounter the responsibility of deciding it either way.

Writing on the same day to Holland, Grey summed up his feelings on the question which the Whigs had now to determine, 'the great preliminary difficulty whether we ought to make Reform a sine qua non, and if any, what'. In the first place, a large and influential group in the party objected to reform in principle. Secondly, there was no agreement as to the extent to which reform should be carried. Thirdly, would any moderate plan attract the degree of public support necessary to their establishment in office? Recognizing that

our Administration, if we should form one, could only stand upon public confidence and opinion, and that confidence and opinion I am strongly inclined to believe, in the present circumstances of the country could not be acquired and certainly not retained, if we were to put aside the question of a Reform of Parliament,

he confessed himself unable to decide how to proceed. He was sure that a half measure would satisfy no one: nothing less than an extensive scheme would serve the purpose:

Shortening the duration of Parliament to at least five years: admitting copy holders to vote for counties, and adding 100 members to be divided between the large towns, and the most extensive and populous counties; taking away the same number from the representation of the most obnoxious boroughs. Less than this I feel quite convinced would do little to conciliate public opinion...

Yet so much would be unacceptable to the grandees of the party. Fitzwilliam

15 Dec., G.41/8; to Ridley, 27 Nov., Ridley MSS ZRI 25/45; Fitzwilliam to Grey, 6 Dec., G. 14/11; Grey to Fitzwilliam, 6, 19 Dec., Fitzwilliam MSS, Northampton; to Lansdowne, 13 Jan., Bowood MSS; to Mary, 29 Jan., G. 28; Stevenson, 'The Queen Caroline Affair', 134.

wrote to reassert his total opposition to reform of any degree, and his opinion was to be decisive. Grey would not contemplate splitting the party again as in 1792, and as the Whigs moved into the third decade of the nineteenth century their old divisions remained. Yet Grey had recognized the central issue that now faced the party, and the strategy of 1830–2 was already formed in his mind. The Whigs were now free from the toils of the reversionary interest, and they looked to public opinion rather than to the Court for the basis of their political support. As long as George IV lived, his implacable resentment against Grey would bar the way to office, but the day would surely come when governments would stand upon public confidence rather than royal favour. William IV, ten years hence, was to see the dawning of that day, and Grey was to be prepared for it.[23]

THE WAITING GAME, 1820–1829

The decade which followed the Whigs' failure to exploit the Queen Caroline affair was one of frustration for Grey. His habitual pessimism reasserted itself. 'For my own part', he wrote in November 1820, 'I wish for nothing so much as a peaceable retirement for my declining years.' The continued division in the party over reform hampered any attempt to pursue a clear policy. Edward Ellice pressed the need for an understanding on the question, pointing out that neither the public nor the majority of the opposition in the Commons would be satisfied with less than a commitment to a substantial measure. If that risked the defection of the con-servative wing of the party, its omission would alienate many more. Grey confessed that reform was 'our great difficulty'. 'If I had nothing to consider [but] my own feelings I should not hesitate', but the division in the party made him reluctant to adopt the extensive proposals which he believed to be necessary for a lasting solution. 'My reflections upon this subject always end in an earnest prayer that it may not be proposed to me to undertake the Government; and I hope and believe it will not.' Fitzwilliam's reiterated hostility to any plan of reform yet proposed confirmed the view that the question must be laid aside for the foreseeable future, and in his speech at the County Durham meeting in December Grey made no reference to it. Madame de Flahault warned Mary that the omission had been noted by 'some less moderate Whigs in London' and that it had 'made an alteration in the popular feeling [previously] in his favour'.[1]

Grey's reserve created difficulties with the more radical Whigs. Both Holland and Fitzwilliam urged him to come to town for the new session in January 1821,

[23] Tierney to Grey, 21, 25 Nov., G. 55; Grey to Fitzwilliam, 6 Dec., Fitzwilliam MSS, Northampton; to Holland, 6 Dec., G. 35; Fitzwilliam to Grey, 10 Dec., G. 14/11; Smith, *Whig Principles*, 360–2.

[1] Grey to Willoughby-Gordon, 21 Nov. 1820, BL Add. MS 49479, fos. 24–5; Ellice to Grey, 7 Dec., G. 13a; Grey to Ellice, 4 Dec., Ellice MSS, National Library of Scotland, 15020 fos. 10–11; to Holland, 6 Dec., G. 35; Fitzwilliam to Grey, 10 Dec., G.14/11; Mme de Flahault to Mary, 28 Dec., Bowood MSS.

'were it only to keep in check ultra-eager heads', as Fitzwilliam put it. Holland wrote that 'You have not perhaps so much direct authority in [the] Commons as you ought to have but you may depend on it, our friends there are more reasonable and manageable when you are in London than when you are in Northumberland.' Grey asked Lansdowne for advice. Public opinion, especially in the North, seemed so hostile to the ministry that it could hardly stand against it: but the Whigs could not take office without a clear policy. A commitment to the repeal of the Aliens Act and the Six Acts, Catholic emancipation, and 'every practicable reduction in our various establishments' was an essential preliminary to the formation of any Whig administration: but such an administration would not last twelve months without also doing something to meet the public demand for reform. At the Morpeth meeting in December he had decided to make a general statement of his views, 'on the principles explained in my speech on the State of the Nation in 1810', and though this would not satisfy 'the eager reformers' it might provide a basis for 'a more precise declaration, whenever we may be in a condition, and it shall be deemed expedient to make one'. He urged Fitzwilliam to consider 'the danger and distress of the country... and the increasing alienation of the people from the Government, and the separation of the higher from the lower orders of the community'. The only hope lay in a change of ministry, but only the concession of reform could give a new ministry the security of public support against the hostility of the Court. Fitzwilliam confessed that the House of Commons could no longer be said to represent public opinion, but still considered parliamentary reform as 'a dangerous experiment—certain destruction in the hands of the vain and presumptuous fabricators of constitutions'. Within three weeks of his arrival in London, Grey was writing that the state of the party was hopeless, that Tierney was incapable of effective leadership in the Commons, and that nothing could be done. 'Car is remarkably well', wrote Mary in May 1821, 'I believe one reason is his having washed his hands of politics... Car laments that he has lost the confidence of almost all his other old friends—particularly the old Foxites.'[2]

Grey resigned himself to the waiting game which was to last until 1830. Holland's urgings in November 1821 that he should come to town to take advantage of the ministerial crisis which resulted in Canning, Wellesley, and the Grenvilles joining the government did not alter his mood. 'There can be no change of any consequence', he wrote to Lady Holland, 'till there is a general breaking-up, and that I hope will not take place before I am dust and ashes... I am no longer fit for anything but a quiet fireside.' He told Holland that 'I can now consider myself as little more than a bystander... In truth, I am grown stupid and useless; the effect, I believe, of living so much alone, and not being very well.' Mary, too, was alarmingly ill in the autumn of 1821, and Grey himself was suffering from a

---

[2] Fitzwilliam to Grey, 10 Jan. 1821, G. 14/11; Holland to Grey, 4 Jan., BL Add. MS 51546, fos. 120–3; Grey to Lansdowne, 13 Jan., Bowood MSS; to Fitzwilliam, 15 Jan., Fitzwilliam MSS, Northampton; Fitzwilliam to C. Wood, 12 Feb., Hickleton MSS A.4.19.9; Grey to Mary, 10 Feb., G. 28; Mary to Lord Ponsonby, 10 May, Ponsonby MSS.

recurrence of his old stomach disorder. 'Things are coming to the point which I have long foreseen', he wrote to Fitzwilliam in January, 'the only wonder being that it has been kept off for so long, and in which I feel that I can no longer be of any use. I am not equal to the exertion which must be required of any man who takes a leading part in opposition; much less should I be equal to the fatigue of the Government.'[3]

When Grey travelled to town for the session in February 1822, he found the younger Whigs in the House of Commons anxious to press the question of reform. Lambton and Lord John Russell had proposed Bills in 1821, the former including triennial parliaments, the enfranchisement of householders, and equal electoral districts—based on Grey's 1797 proposals—and the latter concentrating on a more gradual approach, disfranchising corrupt boroughs and transferring their seats to the growing manufacturing districts. Grampound had been punished for gross corruption by total disfranchisement in 1821. In 1822 Russell proposed to disfranchise 100 small boroughs, basing his calculations on an analysis drawn up by Lord Milton which demonstrated that the smaller boroughs provided an overwhelmingly large proportion of seats on the government side of the House, whereas the larger boroughs were predominantly Whig. Milton announced his conversion to reform and his intention to support Russell's motion. Grey told Holland that 'any nibbling at Reform will not now do' but agreed that it would be better to avoid any commitment to a specific plan until an offer of the Premiership should be made: until then, as Holland wrote, the issue could only be divisive. Russell himself was pessimistic, writing that 'the country is flat and dispirited, the country gentlemen base and servile', and Grey commented that 'nothing is to be done until the country gentlemen have suffered a little more, or till the country speaks to them in a language to which they must attend.' The Duke of Bedford declared his conviction that the support for reform in the country was growing, and that 'no set of men could come into power with the slightest hope of doing any good, unless they made a reform of the House of Commons a sine qua non of their Administration', but he agreed that the prospect was remote.[4]

Castlereagh's death in the summer of 1822 briefly kindled Whig hopes, and Grey assured Holland that if he were approached he would stipulate for 'nothing short of John Russell's plan'. Canning's appointment, however, frustrated what little hope he may have had. Discussions as to what conditions Grey might make on accepting office were futile, since to serve with Canning was impossible. In November Grey informed Holland again of his wish to retire. With their leader

[3] Grey to Lambton, 3 Jan. 1820, Reid, *Earl of Durham*, i. 129–30; to Holland, 26 Nov., 7, [?9] Dec., 30 Dec. 1821, 18 Jan. 1822, G. 35; to Lady Holland, 16 Nov. 1821, G. 33; to Fitzwilliam, 13 Jan. 1822, Fitzwilliam MSS, Northampton.

[4] Reid, *Earl of Durham*, i. 146–7; *Hansard* NS v. 359–453, 604–5, vii. 51–141; document headed 'Parliamentary Reform', addressed to Lord Milton, [Feb./Mar. 1823], Fitzwilliam MSS, Northampton X515; Fitzwilliam to Grey, 24 Mar., 4 Apr. 1822, G. 14/11; Grey to Holland, 9 Feb., G. 35; Holland to Grey, 11 Feb., 26 Aug. 1822, BL Add. MS 51546, fos. 160–3, 176–7; Russell to T. Moore, 26 Feb. 1822, *Early Corr. of Lord John Russell*, i. 223; Grey to Fitzwilliam, 23 Feb., Fitzwilliam MSS, Northampton; Bedford to Grey [19 Apr.], G. 6/17.

in this mood, the Whigs made little headway in Parliament, Grey confining himself to private expressions of disgust at Canning's foreign policy and Wellesley's conduct in Ireland. J. C. Hobhouse reported that Grey 'talked very despondingly of politics at home and abroad, wished that he had never set foot in the House of Lords again, and said "we were in the old age of our country: everything rotten, corrupt, and worn out."'[5]

Grey's spirits were further depressed by Mary's continued ill health, which made it necessary for them to seek a warmer climate in the winter of 1823–4. He was bored during a stay at Torquay, 'this detestable place', and gladly accepted Wellington's offer of the tenancy of Government House at Devonport, where he and Mary were to spend the next two winters. 'This excellent house' as he described it was, however, almost as far from the political world of London as Howick, and Grey was soon grumbling about his isolation. His temper was not improved by the abortive and expensive attempt to get Henry elected for Northumberland early in 1824. In May he wrote to Mary to say that he felt unequal to any political exertion, and that, having reached the age of 60 and having had only one year's experience in office, he could not expect to be qualified for any post except the Admiralty: 'Looking at all these circumstances surely a scene is exhibited, which may well excuse a person long past the vigour of his life, for wishing he pass the remainder of it in peace and retirement.' He came up to speak on the Catholic question in 1824 and 1825, but found 'the glare, the noise, the heat and the nothingness of large Assemblies quite overpowers me', and returned to Devonport as pessimistic as ever.[6]

The Catholic debates, however, showed that there was common ground between Canning and other pro-Catholics in the Cabinet and the opposition Whigs, some of whom were prepared to consider a junction to form a 'Catholic' administration—particularly since Canning's recognition of the independence of Spain's South American colonies had been generally approved by the Whigs, despite some grumbling reservations by Grey. Holland urged Grey to consult Lansdowne on the subject, remarking that the Catholic question, South America, and the Corn Laws were 'in truth the *only* questions now at issue, and the great parties in Parliament must ultimately be distinguished by their respective and opposite opinions on one or most of these topics'. In that case, there must be 'a jumble of men' into new alliances: 'a liberal Ministry with an intolerant Court opposition, or an intolerant Court Ministry with a liberal opposition'. He asked whether Grey wished to encourage, retard, or leave to chance this development; if his inclination was to do nothing, he should say so and leave others free to determine their course

[5] Grey to Holland, 21 Aug., 29 Nov. 1822, 2, 22 Jan., 2, 12, 23 Feb. 1823, G. 35; to Lady Holland, 18 Sept., G. 33; Holland to Grey, 26 Aug., 3 Sept., BL Add. MS 51546, fos. 176–9; Grey to Brougham, 30 Aug., 5 Sept., Brougham to Grey, 3, 16, 19 Sept., *BLT* ii. 442–58; Grey to Charles, 19 Feb., G. 22; *Journal of Mrs Arbuthnot, 1820–32*, ed. F. Bamford and Duke of Wellington (1950), i. 235–6; Broughton, *Recollections*, iii. 21, 81.

[6] Grey to Holland, 2 Dec. 1823, 2 Jan., 10 Mar. 1824, G. 35; to Mary, 28 May 1824, G. 31; 10 May 1825, G. 29.

of action. Grey replied that he did not believe that the party in general any longer paid attention to his opinions, and that if Lansdowne wanted advice he should ask him directly for it.[7]

On arrival in London in February 1826 for the session, Grey approached Lansdowne and told him 'that I wish him decidedly to understand that I stand out of the way, and look to him as the person the best qualified to undertake the chief direction of the party'.[8] Grey thus cleared the way for what was to happen in the following year, when, after Liverpool's retirement, Canning approached Lansdowne and the Whigs to form a government of the centre. Though Grey had in effect given up his position to Lansdowne, his hatred of Canning was too strong for him to acquiesce in a favourable response. The result was almost the destruction of what remained of the Whig party, which only Canning's early death averted.

Liverpool suffered a paralytic stroke on 17 February. At first, the King hoped that he would recover, and Peel and Canning advised him to await events. The ministry stumbled on until the end of March, when it became clear that Liverpool would not be capable of returning to office. During this interval, the Irish crisis was developing: the elections of 1826 had returned more Irish MPs committed to emancipation, while in England popular prejudice had slightly strengthened the Protestant party. On 5 March Burdett moved a resolution in the Commons in support of the Catholic claims, which was lost by only four votes; the debate demonstrated the disharmony on the ministerial benches and made it clear that there must be a change, one way or the other. Canning stood out as the obvious candidate to lead a pro-Catholic administration, but it was equally clear that the Tory die-hards would not support him. A number of Protestant peers set about undermining Canning's position, while the Whigs waited in the wings. On 28 March the King saw Wellington and Canning separately, Canning's interview ending in 'a polite deadlock', Canning insisting that he must either have the 'substantive power of First Minister' or resign. The impasse lasted until April 9th, despite Tierney's attempt on 30 March in the Commons to force the issue by proposing the withholding of supplies until a new ministry was formed. George IV then commissioned Canning to form a government on the same principles as Liverpool's. Peel and Wellington resigned, followed by 39 other office-holders. The King was furious at their desertion and assured Canning of his wholehearted support, even if it meant bringing in Whigs, rather than submit to Tory dictation.

Canning's first appointments were mainly of his own friends—the 'Canningites' who were to remain independent of the Tories until finally absorbed into Grey's Ministry in 1830—but it was clear that he needed reinforcement, which could only come from the moderate Whigs. They had much in common with the liberal Tories, and there was a long history of flirtation between them and Canning going back to the days of Grenville's Premiership in 1806. The looseness of party ties in the 1820s meant that party did not stand in the way of adjustments to political

---

[7] Holland to Grey, 2 Sept. 1825, BL Add. MS 51547, fos. 128–31; reply 4 Sept., G. 35.
[8] Grey to Holland, 10 Feb. 1826, G. 35.

principle to the extent that it had done ten years before, and in any case many Whigs believed that a junction with Canning was the only way to prevent continued Tory dominance. When Canning approached Lansdowne as *de facto* leader of the Whigs, the Marquess replied that he would consent to his friends taking office as individuals, even without a commitment to immediate emancipation. The Whigs were accordingly offered three Cabinet posts, though Lansdowne himself, despite his impression of Canning's 'candid and honourable . . . exposé and deportment', declined to accept office unless the Irish government was placed in the hands of pro-Catholics. The King's refusal terminated the negotiations.[9]

Grey was delighted. He was mortified at having been taken at his word when he offered to give up the leadership of the party to Lansdowne and consequently at not having been consulted. Lansdowne excused himself on the grounds that he understood Grey to have declared that he would never take office again 'under any circumstances', and that he was therefore free to form 'some political connexions to which I might not otherwise have looked'. Grey retorted that his remarks did not mean 'a positive determination . . . in any case', but only an unwillingness 'unless it was felt to be necessary to give strength to an Administration formed on right principles'. Not for the first time, Grey's expression of weariness with public life was shown to be something of a pose, to be thrown aside when the chance of office and power came along.

Grey's pleasure at the apparent breakdown of the negotiations between the Whigs and Canning was chiefly the result of his personal detestation of Canning himself. 'His conduct in 1807, and 1809, in 1812, and indeed on every public occasion down to the present', he wrote, 'has inspired me with the most rooted distrust of his character, his principles, his temper and his discretion.' He detested Canning above all other men he had known: even his early hostility to Pitt had been tempered by admiration for his talents, but for Canning he could find no expiation. 'My objections to him are of a nature which a cessation of political differences cannot remove', Grey wrote in 1809. He regarded him as an unprincipled upstart, and was disgusted by the belief that Canning had had an affair with Princess Caroline after her marriage to the Prince of Wales. Above all, he never forgave Canning's action in 1807, when, after protracted negotiations with Grenville to join the Whigs and bring about Catholic emancipation, he had taken Grey's own position at the Foreign Office in Portland's administration which was formed expressly to resist the Catholic claims. Canning's subsequent professions of support for the Catholics were, to Grey, blatantly insincere when Canning consented to serve in Cabinet with and under men who were pledged against them. Canning, therefore, was an unprincipled adventurer, ready to sacrifice principles for office, and ambitious beyond his station in life. Grey disdainfully declared that 'the son of an actress is, *ipso facto*, disqualified from becoming Prime Minister of England.' When, he wrote, Canning 'secured to

[9] Wendy Hinde, *George Canning* (1973), 435–43, 447.

himself the office of Prime Minister, there could have been no negotiation with *me*: . . . I could not be safe with *him* in that situation.'

Grey's attitude went deeper than rational explanation. He was incapable of doing justice to Canning's abilities or his conduct. If his Whig friends wished to negotiate with Canning, they were at liberty to do so, but Grey warned them that they should not accept any offers without full and explicit agreement to 'the principles to which they are pledged'. If, as he told Holland on 13 March, Canning formed an administration with 'a firm assurance of carrying the Catholic question', he would be 'disposed to give him a fair support, and even not to press him prematurely on that subject'. But if Canning merely patched up the old administration 'he remains the disgraced supporter of a divided Government, merely for the sake of office, [and] I can see no motive for forbearance.'[10]

Grey did not convince his colleagues. Holland argued that the only alternative to Canning was a recourse to the anti-Catholics, and that emancipation could only be achieved with Whig help. Brougham organized a breakaway meeting of thirty to forty members of the party at Brooks's on 20 April, which agreed to negotiate for a junction with Canning, and other more moderate Whigs wrote privately to Lansdowne to make the same proposal. Devonshire persuaded Lansdowne to drop his stipulation for a pro-Catholic Irish government, and on the 26th the two peers met Canning to reach an agreement. Devonshire accepted the office of Lord Chamberlain and Lansdowne undertook to enter the Cabinet and advise his friends to support the administration. On 16 May Lansdowne became Minister without portfolio, and two months later Home Secretary. Carlisle and Tierney also accepted Cabinet posts, and Holland declared his adhesion to the government. Even Fitzwilliam delighted in the dismissal of 'that proud oligarchical faction' and reproached Grey for being influenced by resentment at what happened twenty years ago.[11]

The events of April and May deeply divided both the old parties and created bitterness within them. Grey was especially angered, feeling that his friends had deserted him, broken up the party, and yet secured no firm commitment to the Catholics. He remained sure that Canning would betray the cause of emancipation. When Parliament reassembled at the beginning of May he came to town to speak in the Lords debate on the Corn Bill. In this debate, less attention was paid to the Bill supposedly under discussion than to the circumstances and character of the new administration, and Grey himself did not mention the Bill in a long speech designed to define his political position.[12] He began by stating that

nothing can be so truly painful to me, as to find myself in a situation in which I must explain those differences of opinion that have separated me from noble friends, with whom

---

[10] Lansdowne to Grey [29 Apr.] and reply 29 Apr., G. 38/10; Grey to Lansdowne, 17 Apr., Bowood MSS; to Fitzwilliam, 18 Apr., G. 14/11; to Holland, 7, 13 Mar., G. 35.

[11] Holland to Grey, 16 Mar., 13, 14 Apr., BL Add. MS 51547, fos. 176–8, 180–7; Tierney to Holland [29 Apr.], ibid. 51554, fos. 128–31; Hinde, *Canning*, 449; Fitzwilliam to Grey, 17 Apr., G.14/11.

[12] *Hansard* NS xvii. 720–33.

I have acted throughout the whole of my political life and for whom, at this moment, I entertain the most sincere and ardent affection.

He declared that although he would continue to sit on the opposition benches, he was not 'to be classed as one of those [ultra-Tories] who are now forming an Opposition to his Majesty's Government'. He disclaimed all notion of regular opposition: but he could not give any pledge of general support to a government in which he could feel no personal confidence:

If I see that the person who influences and directs the administration is one to whom I cannot safely commit myself, I am bound to decline engaging in the service... In that sense of the word, a personal objection may be the soundest and best objection that can be entertained.

On the other hand, 'if there be any persons in this House to whom my principles are more decidedly opposed than to any other, they are those whom I have lately heard professing themselves to be the opposition to the government.' He went on to detail his objection to the principle upon which he believed Canning's government was formed,

the exclusion of the Catholic Question as a measure of government. To that principle I have always been and always shall be, steadily opposed... It is nothing less than that which, in 1807, I rejected; and to which nothing shall ever induce me to agree.

Whether there were more pro-Catholic ministers in the Cabinet than under Liverpool was irrelevant: the important question was whether there was a positive engagement to the King not to make emancipation an official measure. Quoting his conduct in 1807, 1809 and 1812, he declared it to be impossible to support any administration formed on that basis.

Grey then reviewed Canning's record in foreign and domestic affairs.

During the whole course of the right honourable gentleman's public career, there is not any man who has less approved of his conduct than myself... I think still, that the right honourable gentleman deserved no exclusive praise for any liberal act of the late administration.

His recognition of the independence of the South American republics was to be approved of, but the basis on which he announced it was unacceptable. It was designed solely for Britain's commercial advantage, and did nothing to help Spain to resist French occupation—an act 'more base and oppressive than any committed even by Napoleon himself'. Canning's claim that he called the republics into existence was 'an idle and an empty boast'. His domestic record was no better. Admitting him to be a sincere friend to religious liberty, he asserted that Canning had in fact 'done more to injure that [Catholic] question, than has been done for a long time by any individual'. As for the assertion that Canning was a friend to civil liberty, he was astonished: For the past thirty years, 'there has not been an invasion of civil liberty... of which the right honourable gentleman has not been the prominent supporter'. If he wished to be considered a friend to liberty, he should set about repealing these oppressive Acts, particularly that which made a second conviction for political libel a transportable offence—'the most flagrant violation of the liberty of the press which has been attempted in modern times'. As to parliamentary reform, he would not criticize Canning's consistent opposition, since many of Grey's own former colleagues were not pledged to it, nor was the Whig party agreed on it. Lansdowne had never spoken for it in Parliament: if he was a reformer, 'he is the most moderate of all moderate reformers'. Grey admitted that it was 'not . . . so uniformly supported, nor has it at present the public opinion so strongly in its favour, as that it should be made a *sine qua non* in forming an administration'. He nevertheless adhered to the view that 'reform ought to keep pace with the march of human intellect—that its progression should be gradual', and referred to his own long and unwavering commitment to it, but he did not criticize the administration for not taking it up at the present time.

Grey concluded with a statement of his current position: 'The sentiments I now utter are my own. I speak only for myself, for I regret to say, that I am now almost without political connections of any kind.' He referred to his regret at the separation from old friends, whom he continued to respect, but

I now feel myself almost a solitary individual . . . The only course left to me is to adhere to those principles which I have professed throughout life . . . Those who have done me the honour to attach any importance to my opinions are aware, that I have, for some years, been withdrawing myself more and more from a direct interference in the politics of the country . . . To take a more active part in public business, is quite out of my intention.

He would be glad to support Lansdowne whenever he could, but he would not shrink from opposition on measures which he could not conscientiously approve.

I shall not, however, again embark upon the troubled sea of politics, upon which, all my life, till now, I have navigated—God knows, with how little success; but, at the same time, with the consolation of knowing that I have done so with an honest and approving conscience.

He sat down 'amidst loud cheers'.

Grey's speech was one of his finest, in the opinion of those who heard it, though little of its quality appears in the bald words of the parliamentary reporter. A correspondent informed Mary that it was 'one of the most impressive speeches, I remember to have been made in Parliament'. Greville remarked that it was a 'brilliant success' and Wellington was reported as saying that 'he never heard him speak so well and quite unanswerable'. Lord John Russell only read the speech, but wrote that 'the effect is more touching than the tenderest scene of any novel that I have for many years perused . . . Every sympathy of my heart was touched . . . You stand almost alone, my lord, but never in my humble opinion more gloriously so, in your political career. Your principles are a tower of strength.' The sustained attack on Canning created a sensation. It was said that Canning even contemplated taking a peerage in order to answer it personally. Even in his years of opposition to Pitt, Grey had rarely dissected the career of a political opponent so thoroughly and to such effect. His reputation, not merely as an orator, but as a statesman of principle, was confirmed and re-established.[13]

A week later Holland, who had crossed the House to support Canning, declared his own position in a way which gave Grey deep offence. Remarking that 'it had been greatly the fashion to enter into discussions totally irrelevant to any motions before the House, and, instead of standing upon general principles, to make professions of political faith'—intended as a reference to those formerly on the government side, but capable of interpretation as one to Grey—he justified his support of the government on the grounds that it was not, as Grey had claimed, formed on the same principle as Liverpool's, since the Premier was a pro-Catholic and that this was the reason why the ultra-Tories had resigned. He declared his conviction that without Whig support, the government would fall into the hands of anti-Catholics. He had also credited Canning with a more liberal foreign policy, and the establishment of the independence of the South American republics, contrary to Grey's speech. And he remarked that 'he considered it derogatory from the dignity of the House, and injurious to the service of the country, for public men to be flinging dirt at each other, and speculating as to what might be the principles of this or that man.'

Holland's remarks were certainly intended to apply to the Tory opponents of the administration, but they could be interpreted as referring to Grey, who took deep offence. He wrote two days later that it

> gave me the greatest pain... you marked the difference between us so strongly, that it was impossible to suppose it should not attract general attention; and that this should have been done without... a single expression of kindness or regret did, I again acknowledge, give me very great pain.

Holland tried to smooth over the difficulty, replying that he did not refer to his separation from Grey precisely in order to avoid giving the impression that he was replying to Grey's speech, and that he was not 'insensible to the pain of seeing and hearing you on an opposite side of the House—I am perhaps unwilling to consider it so much of a political separation as your anxiety about it occasionally implies.' Nevertheless, Grey's relations with Holland were seriously strained, and their correspondence was interrupted for several months. Adair reported that Holland was deeply distressed, and 'most truly regrets his having done anything to hurt Lord Grey. He said repeatedly that (except his uncle) there is no man living he ever loved so much or loves so still.'[14]

The support of so many of his friends and colleagues for Canning's ministry left Grey, as he told Lansdowne in April, 'an individual, almost totally without political connections of any sort'. 'I stand aloof from all parties', he wrote to Charles in July, 'acting upon my own principles, and anxious only to maintain

[13] A. Hope to Mary, C. Greville to Grey, unknown correspondent to Grey, Lord John Russell to Grey, 11 May, Hickleton MSS A.1.5.2, 7, 10, 12.

[14] *Hansard* NS xvii. 857–66; Grey to Holland, 19 May and reply dated 18 (?20) May, BL Add. MS 51547, fos. 188–9, 231–2; Adair to Mary, n.d., Hickleton MSS A.1.5.

my consistency and honour.' Even Holland and Tierney had deserted him, and he felt it keenly. Yet his political ambition still smouldered. He did not intend to retire into private life, and waited to seize an opportunity to recover his political leadership. Canning's death in August, hastened, some said, by his distress at Grey's attack on him, did not immediately restore the status quo, but the King's appointment of Goderich as his successor and the appointment of the Tory Herries to the Cabinet enabled Grey to reconstitute his old party. Burdett thought that Canning's death might revive the possibility of Grey being brought into office, while Lambton assured him that he had only supported Canning in the hope that it might open the way for Grey to the Foreign Office. Grey's objections, however, were strengthened by the new ministerial arrangements. 'There is not in any one of the appointments which I have heard mentioned any tendency to the support of good principles', he wrote to Ellenborough, and he would continue to support or oppose the government as his own principles directed. As to the re-forming of the old opposition, it would be a matter of time and experience. Lord John Russell thought that Goderich would be more dependent on the Whigs than Canning, and that this would enable them to 'get more out of them than by opposition', but he accepted Grey's view that it would be best 'to stand aloof from either party'.[15]

Goderich's tenure of the Premiership was too short-lived to have any great significance. His resignation in January, without ever having met Parliament, resulted in the appointment of Wellington and Peel and the return of the Tories to office, strengthened by the temporary adhesion of Huskisson and the other leading Canningites. It was widely expected that Wellington would offer a place to Grey. Lambton repeated in December his hope that Grey would join the government, and that in the meantime he would 'say and do nothing which he might hereafter find of such a binding nature as to preclude the possibility of a junction, when the "highest powers" may be brought to agree to it'. Grey held aloof, uncertain, as he wrote to Creevey, whether the King would put the government 'fairly into the hands of Lansdowne, allowing him to bring in some of the old Whigs, or will he take it as the head of a Tory administration? Or will Huskisson be the man . . . or will the whole concern break up, and Peel and the Beau [Wellington] be called upon?' In January he declared that he knew nothing of what was happening, but that he thought it would be 'a most fatal mistake' for Wellington to take the Premiership, especially in view of his uncertain relations with Huskisson. As for himself, 'No communication or proposition of any kind has been made to me . . . I certainly shall remain in my old position, and act as I may find right, without any consideration of either party.' Wellington was certainly well-disposed towards Grey personally, but when he received the King's commission to form a government on 9 January he was told that 'he has no objection

[15] Grey to Lansdowne, 29 Apr., G. 38/10; to Charles, 2 July, G. 22. Grey's 'isolation' did not prevent his soliciting from Anglesey, the Irish Viceroy, a position as ADC for Charles; he was appointed in October. Burdett to Ellice [8 Aug.], Ellice MSS 15007; Lambton to Grey, 15 Aug., G. B5; Grey to Brougham, 19 Aug., G. 8/3; to Ellenborough, 24 Aug., G. 12/16, Russell to Grey, 8 Sept., G. 50A/6; ?Tavistock to Grey, 7 Sept., G. 16/15; Grey to Holland, 16 Sept., G. 35.

to any of his late or former servants, or to anybody excepting one person whom he named . . . He gave me carte blanche in respect to everything and everybody excepting that one person, who is *Lord Grey!*'[16]

The King's veto tied the Duke's hands, and though Mrs Arbuthnot noted in March that he was anxious to give Grey the Foreign Office no proposal came. Grey remarked to Princess Lieven that 'I wish personally well to the Duke of Wellington, and I should be glad to see a Government established by him that might rescue us from all the disgrace of the last eight months' and as time went on his feelings grew warmer. In August he repeated his goodwill and general support, but he assured Mary that he could not take office 'without my party' and that he could not join the Cabinet 'without a general arrangement which would show that I had such a share in government, as is necessary to my character and station in the world'. Hobhouse thought Grey's attitude was explained by his fear that vigorous opposition would only strengthen the government but there is no reason to doubt that Grey respected Wellington's pragmatism and sense of public duty. He certainly thought him preferable to Canning or Goderich, and no doubt expected that Ellenborough would show the Duke—as he did—his letter of 24 January in which he remarked that 'so far from feeling any hostility to the duke's Government, it will give him great pleasure if he should be enabled to support it.' Ellenborough, who had joined the Whigs in 1822, had assured Grey that the Duke's object had been 'to reconstruct Lord Liverpool's government with such omissions as he might be able to make for the purpose of infusing new and healthy blood into it' and that he had consequently omitted old Tories like Eldon and Westmorland. The Cabinet was to include eight pro-Catholic members out of fourteen. Rosslyn, another of Grey's friends, was offered the Ordnance, though he declined it and instead was made Lord-Lieutenant of Fife. At the same time, Wellington made Mary's brother an Irish bishop—'which, as *his two first acts*', wrote Creevey, 'is not amiss'.

Wellington had written to Lauderdale to ask him to persuade Rosslyn to accept the Ordnance and directed the letter to Howick. Grey forwarded it, but seeing Wellington's signature on the cover, told Lauderdale that 'it had been a severe trial to his virtue to resist opening it'; Lauderdale sent the letter back to him, and Grey read the Duke's remark that 'he wishes his Government to be anything but an *exclusive* one, . . . but he finds considerable difficulties from preconceived prejudices'—which Grey correctly interpreted as a reference to himself, though, according to Creevey, he considered the prejudices as coming from Peel rather than the King. Rosslyn too assured Grey that Wellington's wish was to form an administration 'combining the talents and powers of the best of all parties' to deal with the impending prospect of an Irish crisis. Grey approved of the Duke's moderate and patriotic attitude. He told Ellenborough that he approved of all his

[16] Lambton to Ellice, 15 Dec., Ellice MSS 15032; Grey to Creevey, 15 Dec. 1827, 25 Jan. 1828, *Creevey Papers*, ii. 141, 144–5; Wellington to Mrs Arbuthnot, 9 Jan., *The Duke of Wellington and his Friends*, ed. Duke of Wellington (1965), 80–1.

measures, and differed from him only on the Catholic question. He instructed Henry to refrain from any hostility in the Commons. As Lambton (now Lord Durham) wrote in January, the King's life was not good, and the Duke of Clarence, his successor, was reported to have said 'Lord Grey is the only real statesman in the country.' Durham urged Grey not to give up his prospects: 'You . . . are now in the prime of life, and in the full possession of powers and talents unequalled and unapproachable', and 'there is a powerful body of persons ready and able to form a Government, if called upon, under your auspices.'[17]

The first months of Wellington's administration were marked by quarrels with the Canningites over the Corn Laws and the Bills to disfranchise Penryn and East Retford. The 'mutiny' of Huskisson, Palmerston, and Lamb on the last measure led to their removal from office when Wellington unexpectedly accepted Huskisson's offer of resignation. Grey was pleased, for he regarded Huskisson as inept and untrustworthy, and agreed with Creevey that Wellington had behaved well and honestly. The success of Russell's motion to repeal the Test and Corporation Acts in 1828 was a further sign of the government's vulnerability to parliamentary action. Wellington's lack of a secure majority seemed ominous as the Irish crisis began to loom early in 1829. The recall of Lord Anglesey from the Viceroyalty because of his pro-Catholic attitude alarmed Grey, who felt that it would increase the tensions in Parliament. He foresaw the development of a powerful opposition, which he declared he would not join: he was 'painfully embarrassed' at the threat to his strategy of waiting for events to force Wellington to concede emancipation. To Grey, as to Peel and Wellington, it was merely a matter of time and opportunity. Grey thus deplored the prospect of Anglesey's cause becoming a party question:

the quarrels of Ministers amongst themselves, their resignations, or their dismissals, can never afford advantageous grounds for parliamentary discussions. I have seen many discussions of this nature; I have been personally engaged in some: and I can safely say that I do not remember one, in which both parties did not sustain some damage, and which did not tend to lower all public men in the general estimation.

He expressed a similar view to Holland, adding that Wellington had more chance than anyone else of carrying emancipation and that he must not be pushed into opposing it. Reviewing the published correspondence between Wellington and Anglesey, he could see no reason to blame Wellington. Both he and Anglesey were 'men of high character and honour', and the Whigs should not say anything to inflame the situation. Northumberland, Anglesey's replacement, was a man of moderate opinions and would conduct his government in a spirit of fairness and

---

[17] *Journal of Mrs Arbuthnot*, ii. 178; Grey to Princess Lieven, 25 Jan., 24 Aug. 1828, *Lieven–Grey Correspondence*, i. 102–3, 135; to Mary, [27 Aug.], G. 29; Broughton, *Recollections*, iii. 275; Grey to Ellenborough, 23 Jan., *Lord Ellenborough, a Political Diary, 1828–30.*, ed. Lord Colchester (1881), i. 6, 108; Ellenborough to Grey, 18 Nov. 1822, 19 Jan. 1828, G. 12/16; *Creevey Papers*, ii. 151–3; Rosslyn to Grey, 18 Jan., G. 51; Grey to Henry, 1 Feb., G. 25; Durham to Grey, 21, 25 Jan., G. B6.

conciliation. Nothing should be done to diminish the chances of a peaceful solution.[18]

That solution was to arrive sooner than anyone expected. O'Connell was elected for County Clare in the by-election necessitated by Vesey-Fitzgerald's appointment in Wellington's administration in July 1828. If O'Connell were refused his seat as a Catholic, all Ireland would be in a flame: and the precedent of Wilkes and Middlesex in 1769 was sufficient to demonstrate the futility of such a course. Wellington made up his mind to the inevitable, and forced the King to submit. The speech opening the session at the beginning of February announced that a Bill would be introduced to satisfy the Catholic claims. The accompanying condemnation of the Catholic Association and the proposed measures to suppress violence and raise the qualification for the Irish county franchise were merely 'to save honour and pacify prejudice'. Grey agreed: 'There may be some things attending it, which you might wish otherwise,' he told Holland, 'but you must consider all the rogues and fools that are to be dealt with, and how necessary it is to do something really to satisfy them.' Grey's opinion of O'Connell as a violent demagogue no doubt influenced his view that firm action against him was compatible with the concession—though Holland remarked that 'If ever one man achieved a great object he is the man.'[19]

Grey also made a significant contribution to the 'great object'. During February and March, as the Catholic Relief Bill was passing through the Commons, the Lords received a flood of petitions for and against the measure. Grey spoke on several occasions, declaring that emancipation would strengthen and not weaken the Protestant established Church and constitution, that the Commons majorities for the Bill were a true reflection of public opinion despite the inadequacies of the representation, that the English Roman Catholics were loyal, respectable, and reliable subjects of the crown, and that the coronation oath was not an obstacle to the royal assent to such a Bill. He even paid a tribute to Peel which brought a cry of 'Hear, hear' from Wellington: though unconnected with the government, he was

ready to bear his testimony to the enlightened view which they had taken of their situation . . . There was one of them, too, who had made as great a sacrifice as any minister had ever made for the good of his country.

He advocated a fully liberal measure, not 'clogged' by those 'securities' which he had advocated twenty years before, asserting that the granting of equal civil rights under the constitution would provide all the 'security' necessary for Church and state.[20]

[18] *Creevey Papers*, ii. 159; Grey to Willoughby-Gordon, 5, 25 Jan. 1829, BL Add. MS 49479, fos. 57–60, 67–72; N. Gash, *Aristocracy and People, 1815–65* (1979), 135–7, 140; Grey to Holland, 9, 10, 13, 25 Jan., G. 35.
[19] *Hansard* NS xx. 4–5 (5 Feb.); Holland to Grey [5], [6], 7 Feb., Grey to Holland, 8 Feb., BL Add. MS 51547, fos. 223–30.
[20] Grey spoke eight times between 13 Feb. and 2 Apr.: *Hansard* xx., xxi.

The Bill received its second reading in the Lords in early April. Grey spoke on the third day of the debate, ranging widely over the question. Declaring his sincere attachment to the Church of England and the Protestant constitution, he reviewed the history of the anti-Catholic laws since the reign of Elizabeth to show that they were not fundamental or immutable, but always a matter of expediency and circumstance. Nor did the Bill violate the terms of the Bill of Rights, Act of Settlement, or Acts of Union with Scotland and Ireland. The coronation oath was never designed to limit the King's legislative discretion and was no obstacle to the royal assent. He pointed out that Irish Catholics were already qualified for offices in the armed forces, for the elective franchise, and able to inherit and purchase property freely. All that they lacked were the remaining civil rights of free subjects, and the grant of those rights would cement their affection for the Union and constitution. In practice, he suggested, it was unlikely that more than six or seven Catholic peers would take seats in the Lords, and possibly fifty MPs in the Commons: it was inconceivable that the King would appoint hordes of Catholics to offices, or that the English people would embrace the Catholic religion. The Church of England was secure in the affections of the people. The Church of Ireland was probably less so: but even it could scarcely benefit from the continued hostility of the majority of the Irish people. If the Protestant establishment in Ireland were superseded by a Catholic one it would be deplorable, but the political connection with Britain would still remain and the danger of separation in a future war with the Catholic powers of Europe would be averted. He ended with a tribute to Wellington, to whom the nation would owe a debt of gratitude 'not inferior to that which they already owe him for his more splendid perhaps, and more dazzling, but not more useful or more glorious services, in another field'.[21]

Grey's speech impressed both sides of the House, bearing out Adair's words when urging him to attend the debates in February: 'You do not do yourself justice, that you are not aware of your own means—I do not mean as a leader of party but as a statesman standing on your own individual character.' Grey had told both Adair and Ellice that he deprecated treating the Bill as a party question, and his conduct was widely praised for its impartiality. Mary told Henry that his speech on the second reading was one of his best, and Ellenborough, who commented that 'he ... fights the whole battle for us', thought it would have a greater public effect than any yet delivered on the question. Even Mrs Arbuthnot thought the speech was very splendid, and commented that Grey was 'a strange mixture of great talent and gross vanity'.[22]

Wellington's gratitude for Grey's services on the Emancipation Bill was tempered by his knowledge of the King's implacable hostility to his admission into the Cabinet, and by his own reservations about Grey's character. Mrs Arbuthnot

---

[21] Ibid. xxi. 308–48.

[22] Adair to Grey, 5 Feb., Grey to Adair, 3 Feb., G. 1/3; to Ellice 28 Jan., Ellice MSS 15020; Lord Howick's Journal, 8 Apr., G.C2/4; *Ellenborough Diary*, i. 358, ii. 6; *Journal of Mrs Arbuthnot*, ii. 264. Only Hobhouse dissented, finding Grey's speech 'commonplace, as all his usually are': Broughton, *Recollections*, iii. 318.

recorded in June that the Duke had spoken of him as 'a very violent, arrogant and very obstinate man' who would wish to dictate, 'besides which he has all kinds of fantastic notions about reform in Parliament, *triennial* parliaments and our foreign policy'. He wished to strengthen the government with Whig support but Grey 'would not suit him'. 'Nothing will win Lord Grey but a place for Lord Grey himself', Ellenborough noted, 'and *that*, in the present state of the king's mind, the duke is not in a condition to offer'. Wellington nevertheless hoped to recruit others from the opposition, and in the summer he offered Rosslyn the Privy Seal. Princess Lieven thought the Duke's strategy was to keep the Whigs quiet with the hope of further offers, and that it was a bait for Grey. Rosslyn consulted Grey before accepting and he did so, Grey wrote,

with my entire concurrence and approbation. The whole Whig party was entirely and irrecoverably broken up by the unfortunate and ill-advised junction with Mr Canning in 1827. Nobody therefore had any claim upon him personally except myself; and wishing to keep myself at perfect liberty to take a more or less active part in public affairs as might suit my own views and convenience, I should have deprecated his refusing, on my account, a situation which was honourable to himself...

At the same time, Grey felt that 'this way of picking off people one by one, is not right'. He would be willing to help promote a more extensive arrangement 'which might bear on its face an evident security for the principles and opinions which have governed my political life', the more willingly if he himself were not included: but he would not consider any other kind of offer. 'The result then is that I stand precisely as before, well disposed towards the Government which has carried the Catholic question, but entirely unconnected with it, and at liberty to act upon particular measures that may arise, according to my sense of public duty.'[23]

Grey nevertheless began in the autumn of 1829 to take a less supportive role and to begin the move into opposition to Wellington, which culminated in the overthrow of the government in November 1830. He was motivated partly by impatience at the Duke's continued refusal to approach him, despite the personal cordiality which was shown when he dined with him at Wynyard and at Alnwick on Wellington's northern tour in the late autumn. The major consideration, however, was his opposition to the government's foreign policy. The Greek revolt of 1821–7 against Turkish dominion had created a dilemma for British statesmen, who approved on ideological and religious grounds of Greek independence, but feared to weaken the Ottoman Empire as a barrier against Russian expansion to the Mediterranean. Whigs like Holland were enthusiastic for the cause of Greek liberty, but Castlereagh and Canning had followed a policy of *realpolitik*, seeking to mediate between the combatants and secure a settlement in British interests. In 1825 Canning had proposed joint action with Russia to force the Turks to a compromise, allowing Greece to become autonomous under Turkish suzerainty.

[23] *Journal of Mrs Arbuthnot*, ii. 291, 293; *Ellenborough Diary*, ii. 63; Princess Lieven to Grey, 27 July, *Lieven–Grey Corr.*, i. 254; Rosslyn to Grey, 2 June 1829, G. 51; Grey to Fitzwilliam, 30 June, Fitzwilliam MSS, Northampton.

The Treaty of London of 1827 between Britain, Russia, and France was designed to bring this about, but the Turks refused the terms and their fleet was sunk by the British navy at Navarino in October 1827. Wellington's government referred to the incident as an 'untoward event' in the King's Speech in 1828: in fact it destroyed British hopes of securing a settlement on her terms, and the Treaty of Adrianople of 1829 was directly negotiated by Russia and Turkey, arousing British fears that Greece would become a Russian satellite.[24]

Grey had condemned the action at Navarino, and he had reservations about associating France with the Treaty of 1827, fearing French rather than Russian ambitions in the Near East. Though a friend to Greek independence, he did not wish to see the immediate dissolution of the Turkish Empire in Europe. The 1829 settlement, he felt, left Greece too weak and insecure, and did not stabilize the area. He also disapproved of the change of government in France which brought a more absolutist regime into existence, and suspected that Wellington was too friendly to it. He had been anxious about French intervention in the Iberian peninsula, and had condemned Canning's 'new world' speech on the grounds that it did nothing to avert the threat of French domination. At first he had blamed Canning rather than Wellington for the ineffectiveness of British policy in Europe, but he was beginning to suspect Wellington's weakness towards both France and Russia. He believed that the government had grossly mismanaged the Eastern question.

By the winter of 1829 therefore Grey's independent attitude towards Wellington's government was beginning to change into one of hostility. He was less certain of the Duke's good intentions, and becoming convinced that the government must either become more Tory, or collapse. Princess Lieven, who was now a frequent correspondent and intimate friend, foresaw that he would sooner or later make a move against Wellington: 'My belief is that he is only waiting for an opposition to ripen to come forward and upset the duke', she wrote in February 1830. In October 1829 she had told her brother that 'it is not without importance to know Lord Grey's way of looking at things.' The most sensitive weathercock in Europe was beginning to turn in Grey's direction. The following year was to see her prophecy fulfilled.[25]

---

[24] Grey to Willoughby-Gordon, 4 Oct., BL Add. MS 49479, fos. 78–81; Gash, *Aristocracy and People*, 290–2.

[25] Grey to Holland, 21 Sept., 29 Dec. 1829, G. 35; to Fitzwilliam, 30 June, Fitzwilliam MSS, Northampton; to Ellice, 25 Aug., 15, 27 Sept., Ellice MSS 15020; Princess Lieven to Alexander Lieven, 10 Feb. 1830 and 10 Oct., 1829, *Letters of Dorothea, Princess Lieven during her residence in London*, ed. L. G. Robinson (1902), 215, 201.

THE GREAT REFORM

Despite Grey's changing attitude towards Wellington's government, the year 1830 opened with little sign of improvement in the morale of the Whig party. Rosslyn's visit to Howick in early January confirmed Grey's view that the Duke was unlikely to offer him anything. Though, as he wrote to Henry, he was well disposed towards the government in general because of Catholic emancipation, he had no confidence in Wellington's ability to survive and would be no more than a friendly neutral. He was angry that the Duke was using the King's veto on him as an excuse while professing a wish to bring him into office. He told Ellice on 24 January that he saw no point in going to town and could see nothing useful that he could do. Brougham thought that Wellington relied on the continued disunity of the opposition, now consisting of Ultras and Canningites as well as Whigs. The last were divided into the small group round Althorp who wished to press for parliamentary reform and the remainder who, like Grey, remained adverse to bringing it forward in the immediate future. Grey warned Henry in February not to pledge himself too far on the question, for, despite 'the appearance of a stronger [public] feeling in favour of that measure', it would subside as quickly if the prevalent distress diminished. He repeated his long-held opinion that there was no value in taking up a question 'which will always be opposed by the crown, and on which you cannot rely on the support of the people', so that if he were to enter the government he would be reproached, as Grey was after 1807, for not achieving it. Howick voted in the House of Commons, with his father's approval, for an amendment to the Address which declared the distress of the country to be 'universal' rather than local, but he did not mention reform. Grey thought that the early debates of the session showed that there was little prospect of a united opposition despite the government's incompetence. The harrassing tactics of Althorp and Brougham, he wrote, had nothing to do with him and when he set out for London in April he declared that he had no intention of political activity.[1]

The younger members of the Whig party in the Commons were less despondent. Though Althorp declared that he and his friends would not support any government in which Grey was not included, he resolved to harrass Wellington on the questions of retrenchment and reduction of taxes, and announced in March that he had formed a group, about forty strong, who would meet regularly at his

---

[1] Grey to Henry, 8 Jan., 10 Feb., G. 25; to Cleveland, 16 Jan., G. 10; to Ellice, 24 Jan., Ellice MSS 15021 fos. 3–6; and 18 Feb., G. 13; to Durham, 5 Feb., G. B6; Brougham to Grey, 10 Jan., *BLT*, iii. 17–19; Grey to Princess Lieven, 12, 24, 28 Feb., 2 Apr., *Lieven–Grey Corr.* i. 436, 452–3, 459, 473–4; to Adair, 14 Feb., G. 1/3; Howick Journal 4 Feb.

chambers in Albany to discuss tactics. Grey approved of Howick's joining the group but warned him that the result might be the defeat of the government without any prospect of being able to form a new one. As for himself, he repeated on the day after his sixty-sixth birthday, he was too old, and unequal to the exertions of office.[2]

As Grey set out for London at the beginning of April the political crisis began to gather. The trade depression, unemployment, and unrest among the agricultural labourers in the south-east created a mood of apprehension among the public as well as at Westminster, and Grey feared the outcome. He wrote in February of his apprehensions about the state of the country: 'All respect for station and authority entirely lost—the character of all public men held up to derision—and Parliament itself, no longer looked up to with respect or interest, but loudly arraigned as the cause of all the evils which its efforts ought to be directed to cure. . . . If I could see anything to encourage a belief that I could be of any public service, such exertions as I am now capable of should not be wanting.' Others too were concerned at the apparent weakness of Wellington's government in face of the crisis in the country: 'a weaker and more incapable ministry never sat in a Cabinet', wrote the Ultra-Tory Duke of Newcastle.[3]

Whig hopes were raised in mid-April by the news that George IV was ill, and at the end of the month by reports that he was dying. Howick wrote that the Duke of Clarence, the heir to the throne, wanted Grey to be brought in to strengthen the government and that if the King died Wellington would make an offer. In the meanwhile, his father was 'getting . . . inclined to oppose the duke . . .'. This inclination was no doubt encouraged by the fact that George IV's death would remove the royal veto on Grey's admission to office. It was manifested in Grey's speech in the Lords opposing the government's policy towards Greece, which Princess Lieven noted had rallied all the opposition groups to him. Ellenborough declared that the speech marked him as decidedly in opposition. As the King's death approached in June, Grey confessed his fears at the prospect of becoming Prime Minister, but his speeches on the Galway Franchise Bill, designed to remove a local anomaly in Catholic emancipation, showed that the fire of ambition was beginning to burn again. Mary asserted that the main reason for Grey's decision to oppose Wellington was the government's action in making the Galway Franchise Bill a government question in order to force him into opposition and exclude him from any new administration. The King's death on 26 June left the way clear: the only question seemed to be whether William IV would continue with Wellington but propose Grey's inclusion, or whether the government would collapse and Grey become Prime Minister. Grey declared in the Lords that the existing administration could not last five months; but Wellington declared privately that

---

[2] Grey to Durham, 20 Feb., G. B6; Althorp to Grey, 6 Mar., G. 52; Grey to Henry, 14, 28 Mar., G. 25.

[3] Grey to Adair, 14 Feb. 1830, G. 1/3; Diary of 4th Duke of Newcastle, 12 July, Nottingham University Library, Newcastle MSS NeC 2F/1.

he would sooner resign than bring Grey into office. Grey signalled the end of that possibility by telling Lord Jersey in July that his acceptance of the office of Chamberlain must mean the end of their political connection. Grey was also determined not to be set aside by his party as in 1827, and sealed his claim to the Premiership by a speech on 30 June opposing the immediate dissolution of Parliament. He declared that while he 'entertained a strong disposition of goodwill towards the noble duke', he had no confidence in the administration, which was incompetent to manage the country's affairs. He later described his speech as 'a declaration of war on the Administration'. 'The die is now cast and we are in complete hostility to the Govt' Mary wrote on 1 July.[4]

Parliament was dissolved, in consequence of George IV's death, on 23 July. The elections were held in an atmosphere of mounting excitement which reached a climax with the news of a revolution in Paris. Although the news was too late to influence the voting in most constituencies, members elected for many counties and popular boroughs were likely to be affected by the public enthusiasm. The return of Brougham for Yorkshire, where he owned no property, was particularly sensational. He claimed to have been elected solely on his liberal political principles—though he had support from the West Riding merchants and the Fitzwilliam interest under Milton, a committed reformer. More significant still were the results in constituencies where the control of old-established interests was broken, or where they survived at unacceptable cost. J. N. Fazakerley, a moderate Whig, made a significant confession that he had become a reformer because of his fear that the 40s. freeholders were breaking away from 'the old influence of aristocracy and property' and might at a later election return 'members of extreme popular opinions'. The desire to re-establish what in contemporary thinking was the 'legitimate' influence of property in elections was to be one of the chief principles behind the Whig Reform Bill, and it was indeed pointed out as such in Russell's first speech introducing the Bill in 1831. The establishment of Political Unions in the large towns to press for reform—Grey's papers include a note of the proceedings of the meeting of the Birmingham Union in July—also indicated the rise of middle-class demands for a more equal representation of new interests and was seen as heralding their eventual supremacy.[5]

Yet it would not be strictly accurate to say that Wellington's government 'lost' the 1830 election. In the first place, Treasury influence remained strong in the close boroughs, and returned its usual quota of office-holders and others committed to the government. Nor can it be said that the elections were fought to any

---

[4] Howick Journal, 25, 27, 29 June, 29 Apr., 5, 13 May; Lieven, *Letters in London*, 16 May, 218–21; Grey to Princess Lieven, 11, 25 June, 2 July, *Lieven–Grey Corr.*, ii. 4–7, 11–13, 16–21; to Jersey, 13 July, G. 37/5; *Ellenborough Diary*, 26 May, 30 June, ii. 257, 292–4; *Mrs Arbuthnot's Journal*, June–July, 366; Lady B. Cavendish to W. Cavendish, 4 July, Chatsworth MSS; *Hansard* NS xxv. 690–4, 726–33, 762–5; *Mirror of Parliament* (1830), iii. 2571–2, 2605–7; Mary to Lord Ponsonby, 1, [24] July 1830, Ponsonby MSS.

[5] J. N. Fazakerley to Milton, 3 Dec. 1830, Fitzwilliam MSS, Sheffield; *Hansard* 3 Ser. ii. 1086–7; Report of meeting of Birmingham Political Union, 26 July 1830, G. 47/9/2A.

considerable extent on the government's record or on the opposition's pro-gramme—indeed, it hardly had one. Though Greville remarked that the new House would be 'full of boys and all sorts of strange men' it was not markedly different from the old. The difference lay not in membership but in the fact that old parties were in disorder, new alignments had yet to emerge, and above all in the mounting concern on all sides that Wellington with what Greville called his 'awkward squad' was too weak to deal with the consequences of social discontent, especially in the rural counties, the heartland of the old system.

As the partisans tried to calculate party strengths, it became clear that Wellington could not go on without winning over some of the opposition, nor could the Whigs form a government on their own. The crucial question became, what would the Canningites do? Government supporters had attacked a number of their former seats in the smaller boroughs, and after their clash with Wellington over the disfranchisement of East Retford they were drifting into support for reform. Huskisson's death in September left Melbourne as their leader, and he assured Brougham that they were all inclined to refuse any offers from Wellington, for Huskisson's loss would reduce their strength in a coalition with the present Cabinet. Holland reported to Grey, who had asked him to sound Melbourne and Palmerston, that they were more favourable to a junction with the Whigs and would serve under Grey. Wellington himself began a secret negotiation with Palmerston, following, as Grey believed, his old tactics of trying to pick off individuals, but was repulsed. By late October Grey had made up his mind to try to bring the government down, and to stipulate for reform if he were offered the Premiership. His only anxiety was lest Wellington should propose a measure of parliamentary reform to forestall the Whigs, in which case his pledges would oblige him to support it, as they had done over Catholic emancipation.[6]

Grey's speech on the Address at the opening of the new Parliament ranged over the whole spectrum of politics, showing a statesmanlike grasp of domestic, Irish and foreign affairs. He warned that the best defence of the country against dangers was to secure the affections of the people by timely and moderate reform:

I have been a reformer all my life—in my younger days, with all the warmth, perhaps I may add, with all the rashness of youth, I pressed the matter of reform further than I might now be disposed to do. But . . . I have never urged the question of reform on the principle of abstract right . . . nor with a view to universal suffrage. . . . In my opinion the right of the people is to have a good government, one calculated to secure their happiness, liberties, and privileges: and if that be incompatible with a universal . . . suffrage, then, I say, that the limitation, and not the extension of the right of suffrage, is the true right of the people.

[6] Greville, *Journal*, ii. 29; *BLT*, iii. 55; Brougham to Devonshire [8 Sept.], Chatsworth MSS; *Annual Register*, 147; Melbourne to Brougham, 19 Sept., Grey to Brougham, n.d., *BLT*, iii. 66–9; Holland to Grey, 19, 25 Sept., 10, 14 Oct.; Grey to Holland, 8, 17 Oct., G. 35; BL Add. MS 51547, fos. 5–10, 72–3; Howick Journal, 27 Sept., 15 Oct.; Grey to Princess Lieven, 14 Oct., *Lieven–Grey Corr.*, ii. 103–4, 108–9.

Grey's speech ended all prospect of his joining Wellington and raised his standard as the alternative Prime Minister. Althorp's group met to agree to turn out the government and propose reform and retrenchment. Even Burdett declared his pleasure at the speech and his approval of Grey, who was now the only major political figure with a long record of commitment to reform and who commanded the respect of all parties. But it was Wellington's insensitivity to the importance of the question which brought Grey into office. His famous declaration against any reform on the night of 2 November in reply to Grey's speech may have been intended merely to scotch rumours that he intended to bring in a mild measure himself in order to retain office—a tactic which he almost certainly knew Peel would not support after his experience over Catholic emancipation. But it was the worst possible moment to nail those colours to the mast—an act, as Greville wrote, of 'egregious folly'. The uproar over the declaration led to another mistake when the new King's projected visit to dine with the Lord Mayor at the Guildhall was cancelled because of reports of threats to the safety of the Prime Minister, not of the King. On the night of 15 November, the government was defeated in the Commons on the civil list, the Ultras voting with the opposition despite Wellington's declaration against reform.[7] On the 16th Grey was summoned to the Palace and commissioned to form a government and to pass reform. Forty-four years of opposition, but for a few months in 1806–7, many of them years of hopeless despondency, had led to the Premiership at the age of 66, and to the Premiership on Grey's terms.

Yet Grey did not face his destiny with enthusiasm. Althorp noted that he was 'deeply dejected' by the prospect of becoming Prime Minister. For many years he had repeated, often tiresomely and to the distraction of his family and colleagues, that he was too old, tired, and worn out to face the pressures and burdens of office or even of public life. It is sometimes difficult to assess how genuine those feelings were, for underneath them the ambition which he had so recklessly displayed in his younger days never quite disappeared. The answer perhaps lies in Grey's nature. He had been wounded by the failure of others at many times in his life to appreciate him at his own high valuation and chastened by experience of his mistakes and failures when he committed himself too rashly to causes which were unripe. He desired above all the good opinion of his fellow-men, to be called on by them to do great things, to be encouraged and praised. He was miserable and indolent when his career was frustrated, yet his temperament soared to the heights when he made a good speech. A man of high principle and political rectitude, he was vain and demanding, a perfectionist in many ways, judging himself and others, resentful at the frustrations of what often seemed a life of failure. 'Had my object been exclusively personal emolument and power,' he wrote in 1828, 'the life of no person has been more unsuccessful: but I had what, I think, were higher and

---

[7] *Mirror of Parliament* (1831), 11–16; Howick Journal, 8 Nov. The Duke of Newcastle wrote in his journal that 'it is impossible to conceive a more ill-advised and injudicious measure' than the cancellation of the visit to Guildhall: 8 Nov., loc. cit.

better views, and in these I do not think I have altogether failed.' In a time of national crisis no one could respond with a deeper sense of public duty to himself, his party and the aristocratic order to which he was committed. Those feelings were now put to the test.[8]

It is important to realize that, though the Premiership gave Grey the opportunity to redeem his longstanding pledge to reform, both the occasion for doing so and the nature of the Bill arose from the immediate concern he felt at the dangerous state of the country and the need to preserve the aristocratic system of government through tried and tested institutions. Reform was merely a part of this major purpose. Grey had taken up the question in 1792 because he wanted to give his party a new impetus and stronger power base in growing liberal opinion, but he had done so in opposition to, not in concert with, popular radicalism, which he saw as a threat to traditional institutions and the distribution of property which they embodied. In 1830 his first concern was to reconcile the country as a whole to those institutions, and to prevent the wave of enthusiasm and disorder aroused by the new French Revolution and the economic and social distress of the country from overturning them. Princess Lieven assured her brother that 'There is no need to take alarm at the word "Whig": there are no greater aristocrats', and 'we shall have in his very monarchical, aristocratic principles ample guarantee that revolution will never receive from him protection or support, and that the maintenance of peace and order will be the aim of his wishes and his efforts.' His task was to restore order and confidence in authority, to prevent excess, and to maintain social distinctions. As he wrote in September, comparing France and England, 'a larger infusion of aristocracy' would be beneficial in France to moderate the republican spirit, but it should be an aristocracy 'which can reconcile and adapt itself to political liberty . . . If ours will revive its old spirit and learn to adapt itself to the alterations which time, improvement and knowledge effect in the community it not only may last, but be a benefit to the country.'[9]

Grey's government reflected these aims. There was no question of including in it radicals like Burdett or Hume; even within the Whig party itself, extremists like Radnor or Brougham were to be excluded or muzzled. The Cabinet was, indeed, formed on aristocratic principles. Grey told Princess Lieven on 9 November that

In the composition of my Ministry I have had two essential objects in view: the first, to show that in these times of democracy and Jacobinism it is possible to find real capacity in the high Aristocracy—not that I wish to exclude merit if I should meet with it in the commonalty; but, given an equal merit, I admit that I should select the aristocrat, for that class is a guarantee for the safety of the state and of the throne.

Of the thirteen members of the Cabinet, nine were members of the House of

[8] D. Le Marchant, *Memoir of John Charles, Viscount Althorp* (1876), 259; *HHD* 24 Aug. 1831, 39.
[9] Lieven, *Letters in London*, 25 Sept., 4 Nov., 255, 272; Grey to Darnley, 13 Sept. [1830], Darnley MSS, Duke University, NC. Grey wrote to Flahault on 7 Nov. of his anxiety lest the French Revolution spread to England: Bowood MSS.

Lords (Brougham became a peer on becoming Lord Chancellor), one was an Irish peer, one was heir to a peerage and of the two remaining commoners one was a baronet. This was perhaps not surprising when it is remembered that the Whigs had always been an aristocratic party, and that young professional men seeking careers in politics had long been accustomed to join the Tories where their prospects were better, but it is a significant confirmation of Grey's intentions. One Wiltshire Tory remarked that it was 'the most aristocratic administration that ever was formed'. Nor was the Cabinet a purely Whig party body. Grey took office with a House of Commons elected under his predecessor, whose supporters still occupied seats under Treasury influence, and at a time when parties were in turmoil. The Whigs could not have governed alone, and Cabinet places were found for four former Canningites—Melbourne, Palmerston, Goderich, and Grant— and Richmond, who was related to Holland, represented the Ultra-Tories. Within the Whig group in the Cabinet there was scarcely more unity. Grey, Holland, Lansdowne, and Carlisle represented mainstream aristocratic Whiggery, the last two being at best half-hearted reformers, while Althorp, Durham, and Brougham represented in varying degrees the radical side of the party and Graham, later to join Peel's Conservative party, was somewhere between the two groups. It was not to be an easy team to drive as the Reform coach began its troubled journey.[10]

There was, indeed, considerable difficulty in arranging the Cabinet offices. Grey himself professed horror at the prospect of the Treasury, for which he had no experience, though it took little persuasion to make him take it, Holland as usual filling the role of persuader. Lansdowne refused the Foreign Office, which was given somewhat unwillingly to Palmerston, but the major crisis arose over Brougham. He refused Grey's offer of the Attorney-Generalship as inadequate to his importance, tore up Grey's letter and danced on the pieces, and demanded to be Master of the Rolls. Althorp responded that he would not lead the Commons with Brougham in what was, in effect, a permanent and independent position. It was finally decided by the other new Cabinet ministers to make Brougham Lord Chancellor. He agreed under protest, because it would remove him from the Commons and deprive him of a far greater income at the Bar, after an ultimatum by Althorp that unless he accepted it Grey would resign. Grey's original proposal to keep Wellington's Lord Chancellor, Lyndhurst, in office was dropped after protests from Grey's colleagues—it was suspected that the idea had something to do with a supposed affair between Grey and Lady Lyndhurst. Another difficulty was to find an office for Holland, still the representative of the Foxite tradition, where he could do little harm by his indolence. He had refused the Foreign Office because of his gout, but was persuaded to accept the Chancellorship of the Duchy of Lancaster by Grey's assurance that the office carried 'some very nice patronage'.

---

[10] Grey to Lieven, 10 Nov., *Letters in London*, 278–9; Althorp to Milton, 22 Nov., Fitzwilliam MSS, Sheffield; C. Wood to Sir F. Wood, [18 Nov.], Hickleton MSS A.2.34; Burdett to Grey, 18 Nov., G. 8/11; *HHD*, pp. xxv–xxvii; New, *Durham*, 111–13. Grey's Cabinet and its diverse views on reform is discussed in J.Milton-Smith, 'Earl Grey's Cabinet and the objects of Parliamentary Reform', *Hist. Journal* xv. 1 (1972), 55–74.

Nevertheless, he managed to upset the King at the outset by suggesting financial reforms in the Duchy, which the King regarded as his private possession.[11]

The lower ranks of the administration were equally difficult to fill. Grey confessed at the outset that he was appalled at the difficulties of arranging the offices, for parties long out of power accumulate a tail of deserving relatives and long-serving supporters wishing for rewards. In the event the Grey family did rather well, Grey appointing six of his relatives, apart from Durham in the Cabinet, all seven having a total of about £16,000 a year in salaries. It was later alleged that altogether twenty relatives of Grey received during his ministry appointments, sinecures and pensions to the total value of £202,892. 6s. 2d. The 'Grey List' of these appointments was later published in the newspapers and provided an agreeable reek of scandal to critics of the ministry. Mrs Arbuthnot found it equally disgraceful that two places were given to men still in trade. Grey understandably remarked 'a little more of this work and I shall be dead'.[12]

So the great Reform Ministry of 1830–4 was conceived in confusion, born in tribulation, existed in disunity, and yet proved remarkably cohesive. Grey's skill at managing his troublesome infant was to be not the least of his achievements. He did it by a combination of willingness to allow his colleagues to express their variety of opinions, and a determination to have his own way, at times enforced by a threat of resignation that silenced dissidents. He remarked to Princess Lieven on 9 November

that I have no wish, like my predecessor, to shine at the expense and to the extinction of my colleagues. On the contrary, my Cabinet is composed of men who have all displayed high Parliamentary talents. I have chosen each of them with a view to his special aptitude for the post he occupies, and I leave to each full latitude to manage his department in accordance with his own judgement. Counsel of the Cabinet will then be a veritable counsel, and the dictatorship is abolished.

The reality was sometimes different. It may be true, as the editor of Lord Holland's diary argues, that 'Grey effectively guided the Cabinet... but he did not dominate it.' He allowed his colleagues full liberty to express their conflicting views, and on occasion allowed himself to be overruled by a majority, or the Cabinet to end without coming to any conclusion. In general, however, he managed to get his own way and until 1834 none of his colleagues resigned over a matter of policy. It was sometimes alleged that he was weak and allowed himself to be pushed along by one or other colleague who was more determined than he was, but these allegations are perhaps misconceived. There was no other way in which a

[11] Grey to Holland and Holland to Grey, 16 Nov., Grey to Holland, 18 Nov., G. 34; 2 Dec., BL Add. MS 51548, fo. 19; to Lansdowne 18 Nov., Bowood MSS; *BLT*, iii. 74–83; Greville, *Journal*, ii. 69–71; Le Marchant's Diary in *Three Early Nineteenth-Century Diaries*, ed. A. Aspinall (1952), 4–5; Brougham to Devonshire [18 Nov.], G. Lamb to Devonshire, 18 Nov., Chatsworth MSS; M. Brock, *The Great Reform Act* (1973), 130–3.

[12] Grey to Princess Lieven [16 Nov.], *Lieven–Grey Corr.*, ii. 121; *Ellenborough Diary*, 24 Nov., Aspinall, op. cit., 25; Losh, *Diary*, ii. 234–7; *Mrs Arbuthnot's Journal*, 405; Grey to Holland, 12 Dec., BL Add. MS 51548, fo. 23.

potentially disharmonious coalition could have been kept together. Grey's personal stature was generally recognized; the lack of any feasible alternative leader before 1834 gave Grey the major card in the pack, but also meant that it was rarely necessary to play it. His sincere and well-known dislike of office made it possible for him to contemplate with equanimity retirement into private life: more ambitious colleagues were therefore disinclined to push him to extremities. When Grey felt a particular interest in a question, he was more inclined to take a positive line. In foreign affairs especially, Palmerston, who quickly became an effective and hard working Foreign Secretary, complained of Grey's interference in his department, where he was made to feel like a clerk rather than a minister. Others found Grey dictatorial and insistent on getting his own way. He was to complain frequently of being harrassed to death with business, but it was the price he paid for being the real head of the ministry and keeping it coherent and consistent in purpose.[13]

The Cabinet was sworn in on 22 November, Althorp remarking on the King's graciousness towards his new ministers. On the same evening Grey set out in the Lords the principles on which they would govern. On reform, he repeated the views expressed at the opening of the session: his principle would be,

to stand as much as I can upon the fixed and settled institutions of the country....doing as much as is necessary to secure to the people a due influence in that great council in which they are more particularly represented.... guarding and limiting it, at the same time, by a prudent care not to disturb too violently, by any extensive changes, the established principles and practice of the Constitution.

He revealed that in his first interview with the King 'I had H.M.'s most gracious permission and sanction ... to submit a measure of this nature and this object, for the approbation of H.M.' He proposed the same mixture of concession and conservatism in relation to popular distress, the first object being to formulate measures to relieve it, but combined with a 'determined resolution' to suppress outrages with vigour. In the public service he promised every possible economy consistent with the maintenance of necessary establishments and in foreign affairs peace and non-interference in the internal affairs of other states. He concluded by saying that

I have undertaken an office, to which I have neither the affectation nor presumption to state that I am equal. I have arrived at a period of life when retirement is more to be desired than active employment.

He had taken office only from a conviction that otherwise no government could be formed on principles he could support; and if he could not 'execute the task which I have undertaken' he would have no hesitation in resigning his post. 'Very fair and explicit, so it seemed to me', commented Hobhouse, and the Tory Duke of Newcastle wrote that the speech was delivered 'in a very able, fair, manly and

[13] Lieven, *Letters in London*, 278–9; *HHD*, pp. l–liv, xlvii, 47; Grey to Althorp, 11 Mar. 1832, G. 52/25; *Mrs Arbuthnot's Journal*, 18 June 1831, ii. 425–6.

feeling manner: I differ with Lord Grey on the question of reform but [in] other respects his views and sentiments are quite what I can approve of.'[14]

The Cabinet's first meeting was concerned with the riots and disorders which had spread through the agricultural counties of the south and east, and it advised the King to issue a proclamation warning against violence and encouraging the magistrates to take firm action. Melbourne proved a vigorous Home Secretary in suppressing disorders, to the extent that the government seemed ruthless towards poor labourers driven by extreme deprivation. Special Commissions were appointed to try those arrested, and in the end 644 were gaoled, 481 transported, and 19 were executed. This severity might have seemed at odds with the liberal principles Grey professed, but it was designed to reassure those who feared that reform might encourage revolution and to emphasize his purpose to maintain the strength of government. In this setting the work of reform began.[15]

The story of the passage of the Great Reform Bills has often been told, and it is not the intention to repeat it in detail here. The emphasis will be on Grey's role in the framing of the Bills, in the prolonged crisis of their passage, and in the management of the King and Cabinet through a period when the country seemed at times on the verge of revolution. Grey's ability to keep his head in these circumstances contributed largely to the successful resolution of his task.[16]

One of Grey's first acts as Prime Minister was to appoint a sub-committee of four to draw up a scheme of parliamentary reform for the Cabinet. He asked Durham shortly after they took office to take the question in hand, and also appointed Duncannon, Graham, and Russell to form the sub-committee which began work on 11 December. On 14 January the sub-committee reported directly to Grey, submitting the drafts of three Bills, for England and Wales, Scotland, and Ireland, commenting that

In framing them we have been activated by the belief that it is not the wish nor the intention of His Majesty's Ministers to concede only as much as might for the moment evade or stifle the general demand for a complete alteration of the existing system, or to propose the adoption of such a measure as could merely be considered a bare redemption of their pledges to their sovereign and the country. We have been on the contrary convinced that it is their desire to effect such a permanent settlement of this great and important question, as will no longer render its agitation subservient to the designs of the factious and discontented—but by its wise and comprehensive provisions inspire all classes of the community with a conviction that their rights and privileges are at length duly secured and

[14] *Mirror of Parliament*, 22 Nov., 310–11; Althorp to Milton, 22 Nov., Fitzwilliam MSS, Sheffield; Broughton, *Recollections*, iv. 73; Newcastle Diary, 22 Nov.

[15] Cabinet minutes and Grey to William IV, 23 Nov., 4 Dec., *Correspondence of Earl Grey with King William IV*, ed. Henry, Earl Grey (1867), i. 1–3, 18; Grey to Holland, 24 Nov., BL Add. MS 51548, fo. 13; Ziegler, *Melbourne*, 130–7. For the riots see E. Hobsbawm and G. Rudé, *Captain Swing* (1969) and Rudé, 'English rural and urban disturbances, 1830–31', *Past and Present* 37, 1967, 87–102.

[16] For full accounts of the passage of the Reform Bills see J. A. Roebuck, *History of the Whig Ministry of 1830* (1852), J. R. M. Butler, *The Passing of the Great Reform Bill* (1914), E. Halevy, *The Triumph of Reform* (rev. edn. 1950), Brock, *The Great Reform Act*, Cannon, *Parliamentary Reform*, N. Gash, *Politics in the Age of Peel* (1953).

consolidated... We have therefore been of opinion, that the plan of reform proposed by His Majesty's Ministers ought to be of such a scope and description as to satisfy all reasonable demands, and remove at once, and for ever, all rational grounds of complaint from the minds of the intelligent and the independent portion of the community.

In detail, the scheme proposed the disfranchisement of all boroughs with a population of less than 2,000, as determined by the 1821 census, amounting to 60 boroughs returning a total of 119 MPs, and the reduction to single-member constituencies of those with a population under 4,000, providing a further 47 vacancies. The towns with populations over 10,000, of which there were estimated to be about 30 in England, were to receive representation, the franchise in all boroughs to be limited to householders whose property was rated at £20 per annum. Existing differential borough franchises were to be abolished either at once, or gradually. The counties were to receive an additional number of seats, roughly in accordance with population, and the 40s. freeholder franchise was to be supplemented by £10 copyholders and holders of leases for 21 years or more valued above £50. The expense and corruption of elections was to be reduced by the enforcement of residence for voting rights, the registration of voters, shortening the duration of the poll, providing additional polling places, and the secret ballot. Finally, the duration of Parliaments should be reduced to 5 years.[17]

The extent of Grey's involvement in the deliberations of the sub-committee is unknown. There is evidence that he discussed matters informally with individuals, and it was suggested that Durham and Althorp carried him towards a more sweeping measure than he might have originally intended. But it was Grey's own insistence that the Bill should be extensive enough to satisfy reasonable reformers and be a long-term solution that dictated its general character and shape. When he received the sub-committee's report he annotated it with his comments. The only item to which he noted an objection was the secret ballot, but he must have been aware that only Durham was strongly in its favour and that Althorp and Russell regarded its inclusion merely as a tactical step, so that its abandonment could be used to persuade the King and Cabinet to lower the borough franchise from £20 to £10—as indeed happened. Grey used it similarly to win Lansdowne's assent: it was useful to have some radical proposal that could be used as a bargaining counter and the tactics are strongly suggestive of Grey's own thinking.[18]

Grey carried the report, with those two amendments, through the Cabinet without much difficulty. On 13 January, the day before he received the report, he also wrote to Sir Herbert Taylor, who as William IV's private secretary was to play an important role in the later crisis, to prepare the King for the general nature of the scheme. He warned at the outset that not to go far enough to satisfy public

[17] Broughton, *Recollections*, iv. 178; E. J. Littleton's Diary, Hatherton MSS; Brock, *The Great Reform Act*, 136; Reid, *Earl of Durham*, i. 234–42; Minutes of sub-committee, G. 46; New, *Durham*, 114–24, 126–9.

[18] Ibid. 124–6, Trevelyan, *Lord Grey*, 263–4. Grey to Lansdowne, 14 Jan., Bowood MSS; Le Marchant, *Althorp*, 293, Reid, *Earl of Durham*, i. 243.

opinion would be worse than doing nothing, and that it was essential 'to make an arrangement on which we can stand, announcing our determination not to go beyond it'. He assured Taylor of his full confidence that, though it would not satisfy the radicals, the measure would be carried through Parliament provided it had the King's approval, and hinted at resignation if it failed. The evidence seems to indicate that Grey was fully aware of, and prepared to support, the general nature of the sub-committee's proposals before they were actually submitted to him.[19]

Having prepared the King to expect an extensive measure, Grey took the scheme to Brighton on 30 January. The King received him graciously. 'He has approved everything', he wrote to Mary, and he assured Brougham, the only member of the Cabinet, surprisingly, who had jibbed at the extent of the proposals, that 'the King entered into every part of the proposed plan of reform with great care, and, I must add, with great acuteness; and in the end, understood it completely. The result is, that it has his full and entire approbation.' In fact, the King asked for a few days to consider fully, and wrote to Grey on 4 February with detailed comments. He declared his insuperable objection to the ballot, and his relief that Grey had already excluded it, which made it possible for him to approve the rest of the scheme, including the £10 franchise. However, he laid down careful limits to his approval. These amounted to a stipulation that the influence of property, and particularly of the aristocracy, must be maintained, lest the House of Commons become too powerful in relation to the Crown and the Lords, and he expressed scepticism about the extent of public demand for extensive reform, which he believed could not be judged merely from meetings and petitions. He nevertheless approved both Grey's general principle that the Bills must go far enough to put an end to public agitation and the detailed proposals, expressing reservations only about shortening the duration of Parliaments to 5 years, but leaving it to the Cabinet to decide whether or not to do so. He would also have preferred to raise the county franchise from 40s. to £10 and he advised a new census so that the disfranchisement proposals would be based on more accurate figures. Grey assured the King in reply that the ballot would be deleted, and that the sub-committee had not insisted on it but proposed it as a consequence of the £20 borough franchise. Other ministers had also objected to the ballot, and the decision against it was taken by the full Cabinet with only one or two dissentients. Its removal would allow the borough franchise to be reduced to £10, a figure which would create a more satisfactory electorate in the smaller boroughs. The King assured Grey of his entire satisfaction with the proposals and with Grey's principles: he relied on him to uphold the monarchy and aristocracy, and declared that while he intended to be firm he would remain open to advice and persuasion. As a mark of his favour he allowed Grey to appoint a Lord of the Bedchamber instead of proposing a name himself.[20]

---

[19] *Grey–William IV Corr.*, 13, 15 Jan., i. 51–2, 65.
[20] Grey to Mary, 31 Jan., G. 29; to Brougham, 31 Jan., *BLT*, iii. 93; William IV to Grey, 4, 8

Grey's relief at the King's approval produced a temporary mood of euphoria which led him to overestimate the ministry's prospects of success in the Commons. He assured Princess Lieven on 28 February that he calculated a majority of 70 for the Bill, though admitting that the precise number was uncertain. He believed that the strength of public support once the details were disclosed would influence members from popular constituencies and that this, with the King's known support, would carry the measure. As Charles Wood, his private secretary, wrote, 'it will be hard if King and country do not beat the parliament.' He added, 'The main hope of carrying it, is by the voice of the country: thus operating by deciding all wavering votes.' But there were many MPs who objected to being forced by outside pressure, and many who had too much to lose themselves by the reform, to justify this confidence. Much depended on keeping secret the extensive nature of the Bill, and though Brougham leaked the outline through his brother to Burdett, who thought it too extreme to stand a chance, the secret was kept. This was crucial because it led the opposition to miscalculate their tactics. If they had realized how sweeping the Bill was to be they might have prepared themselves for an outright rejection on its introduction: as it was, they were so astounded by it that they allowed the initiative to be lost for long enough for the public enthusiasm to be felt and to make the second reading vote a nearer-run thing than Waterloo.

Nevertheless, Grey certainly miscalculated—probably, as has been argued, not in order deliberately to deceive the King, but because his knowledge of the House of Commons was sketchy and he was not told unpalatable truths by those around him who knew how discouraged and angry he was apt to become if they did so. Grey's tendency to isolate himself from his followers in the Commons was frequently remarked on, and his aloof and sometimes disdainful manner did not encourage confidences: his advisers were perhaps more concerned to keep him happy than to give him frank opinions. Grey himself expected to receive credit for his honest intentions, indifference to office for its own sake, and genuine sense of public duty. He had no patience with men who put self-interest above duty and perhaps failed to realize how those who had fewer natural advantages than he had needed to defend positions gained by financial or personal sacrifices. A long period of political isolation, from choice rather than necessity, had not equipped him to control the world he had to deal with and he responded with petulance rather than patience. Charles Wood echoed Grey's feelings when he wrote that[21]

The ministers have brought forward an honest and efficient plan, such as they believe ought to satisfy and will satisfy all reasonable men. This they have done neglecting all other considerations save that of doing their duty honestly: if the country think so, the country ought to support them; and on that support they now rely...

The government's precarious position in the Commons was brought home to

Feb., 3 Mar., Grey to William IV, 5 Feb., to Taylor, 8 Feb., Taylor to Grey, 8 Feb., 4 Mar., *Grey–William IV Corr.*, i. 94–107, 114–17, 135–6, 138–40.

[21] *Lieven–Grey Corr.*, ii. 176, 180; C. Wood to Sir F. Wood, 1 Feb., 3, 5 Mar., Hickleton MSS A.2.34; Lord John Russell, *Recollections and Suggestions*, 72–3; Brock, *The Great Reform Act*, 151–6.

ministers by their defeat on the timber duties on 18 March and on the following day Grey wrote to Taylor to sound his opinion as to the King's likely response to a request to dissolve. Unfortunately Taylor showed the letter to the King, who responded immediately by objecting strongly to such a step in the excited state of both Britain and Ireland. Taylor wrote that he thought the King's objections were 'insuperable'. The situation was made worse when rumours circulated about the royal attitude. Taylor assured Grey that the leak had not come from Windsor, but the damage was done. Grey alleged that the opposition to the second reading was strengthened by the rumours and when the second reading passed by only one vote on 22 March it was clear that the Bill could not go through the commitee stage in its existing form. Grey wrote on the 22nd to Taylor to emphasize the need for a new House since the seats under government control were occupied by friends of the previous ministry who were now in opposition, and he asserted that the public excitement dreaded by the King was in favour of a 'safe' Bill and would support the ministers in the elections. The King's reaction was to urge the Cabinet to take time to consider the possibility of modifications to the Bill to make it more acceptable to the present House. Grey forwarded to Taylor a letter he had received from Lord Durham, pointing out that refusal of a dissolution would arouse the public excitement to a more dangerous pitch, but the King continued to withhold his assent and forced the Cabinet to face the committee stage without a pledge.[22]

The first crucial amendment, to maintain the size of the House at its present numbers, was proposed by Gascoyne on 20 April and it was carried by 299 to 291 votes. Grey and the Cabinet, as he explained to Taylor on the 19th, had determined to resist the amendment, which they considered would effectually wreck the whole Bill. On the 20th the Cabinet met and advised the dissolution as essential to the continuance of the ministry. The King reluctantly gave way rather than face the alternative of its resignation, but repeated his hope that the Bill might be modified before resubmission in order to conciliate some of the opposition. The King showed his displeasure at being, as he thought, deceived by his ministers, by refusing to come to Parliament in person to announce the dissolution, but the opposition's attempt in the Lords to obstruct the measure aroused his irritation and he not only allowed himself to be persuaded but entered into the measure with some enthusiasm, reportedly saying that if the state coach was not ready he would go in a hansom cab. On the 21st, the Cabinet approved a fulsome minute of thanks for his confidence. However, the King made it plain that in return for his public demonstration of support he expected the Cabinet to modify the Bill, and to delay its reintroduction until the public was calmer. The episode had revived his fears that the country was set on course for revolution, and as the election returns came in during May the King stressed again the need for resistance to any further or consequent constitutional change. His action on 23 May in

[22] *Grey–William IV Corr.*, i. 154–207.

conferring the Garter, unsolicited, on Grey demonstrated his support but placed Grey under an obligation to try to meet his wishes.[23]

The elections greatly strengthened the government in the Commons and made the passage of the second Reform Bill there little more than a formality, but the House of Lords remained an obstacle. The King wrote on 28 May to repeat his concern at the prospect of a clash between the Houses unless the Cabinet offered sufficient modifications to conciliate the moderate opposition. Grey replied that nothing short of emasculation of the original measure was likely to suffice, and pointed out that, especially in view of the elections, anything less efficient than the first Bill would arouse public opinion. The elections had in fact placed the ministers in a cleft stick by showing the strength of public support for an extensive Bill but strengthening the Lords' determination to resist dictation by the people and the Commons.[24] Everything seemed to depend on the existence of a moderate group of peers who might dread the results of a collision between the Upper House and the Commons more than the effects of reform, and who might therefore support a modified Bill if the Cabinet could find an acceptable compromise. Grey and his colleagues examined the possibility of producing such a measure in Cabinet in early June, but found themselves unable to make sufficient concessions without damaging the principle that the Bill should be extensive enough to satisfy public opinion. Grey was determined that the measure should be sufficient to enable the reform to stand as a settlement for the foreseeable future and to put an end to further agitation. In the circumstances, rejection by the Lords on the second reading seemed inevitable, and Grey prepared to persuade the King to create enough new peers to pass it.[25]

The King's first reaction was decisive: 'no government could propose and no Sovereign consent' to such a step, he declared on 8 October after the second reading had been defeated by 41 votes, and he repeated his wish for a compromise. Though he expressed his continued confidence in his ministers, and gave it public expression by agreeing to dismiss Lord Howe from the office of Chamberlain to the Queen for voting in the majority, he refused to contemplate the creation of peers on the scale that would be required. Grey himself assured Sir Herbert Taylor that he could not advise the creation of a sufficient number in face of the unexpectedly large majority against the Bill: his own aristocratic principles made him reluctant to use the royal prerogative to such an extent in order to force the

---

[23] *Grey–William IV Corr.*, i. 162–3, 271; Durham to Grey [23] Feb., 22 Mar., Reid, *Earl of Durham*, i. 249–51, 254–6; Grey to Holland [25 May 1831], G. 34; to Princess Lieven, 28 May, *Lieven–Grey Corr.*, i. 227.

[24] C. Wood to Sir F. Wood, 27 May, calculated an increase in the majority of 35 from the counties and 72 from the boroughs: Hickleton MSS, A.2.34. Brougham to Ellice, 28 May, estimated a net gain of 90: Ellice MSS, 15006. For a modern estimate of party strengths during this period see the unpublished Ph.D. thesis by D. C. Newbould, 'The Politics of the Cabinets of Grey and Melbourne and ministerial relations with the House of Commons, 1830–41' (1971). William IV to Grey, 28 May, *Grey–William IV Corr.*, i. 276–81.

[25] Grey's speech on the second reading was described as 'one of the most memorable... ever delivered in that Assembly' (Reid, *Earl of Durham*, i. 264), and Brougham said that he exceeded himself (*BLT*, iii. 265).

Lords to accept the will of the people. Such a step would, in fact, be damaging to the main purpose of the Bill. In any case he now had to face opposition from some of the Cabinet to an extensive creation. Palmerston, on behalf of the ex-Canningites, deplored Grey's statement to the Lords, in accordance with the Cabinet minute of 11 October, that the ministers were determined to bring forward an equally extensive Bill or resign. Grey remonstrated, pointing out that nothing less would satisfy the public; the alternative was public disgrace for the ministry and possibly even revolution. Even in the old Whig ranks, however, there was dissension, Lansdowne joining the Canningites in urging moderation, while Durham on the other hand pressed strongly for no compromise.[26]

The King's continued insistence that the Cabinet should seek a means of satisfying the moderates among the Lords' majority led to Grey's negotiations with Lords Harrowby and Wharncliffe, leaders of an ill-defined group christened 'the Waverers'. The talks took place in the aftermath of widespread rioting, notably in Bristol and Nottingham, against the Lords' rejection of the Bill and the inflammatory declarations and activities of the Political Unions. Grey pointed out to the King that although the government would act firmly against violence, the best remedy for it was to pass the Bill, which would reconcile the middle-class leadership of the Unions. He asked that the King should use all the influence at his command to persuade the courtiers, the bishops, and the 'Waverers' to allow the Bill to pass. Grey's conversations with Wharncliffe were fruitless, despite his offer to restore the eleven largest boroughs in Schedule B to their membership provided the ten large towns which were to receive one MP should be given a second member, thus restoring the House of Commons to its present size. Wharncliffe declined to accept the proposal, and in the Cabinet Palmerston and Melbourne disliked it. Wharncliffe's rejection left Grey determined to press for the Bill unaltered, if necessary by the creation of peers.[27]

Ministers had discussed the possibility of creating peers since the end of May, when the elections of Scottish and Irish representative peers had disappointed their hopes of making substantial gains. Holland calculated the likely size of the opposition in the Lords and advised that a majority might be secured by persuasion of a number of doubtfuls and a creation of possibly 25 new peerages, about half of which might be eldest sons of existing peers whose promotion would not ultimately affect the total number of the House. Through the autumn Holland continued to press for a decision, drawing up lists of 'peerables' and appealing to Grey's vanity by declaring that 'Reform and peace is praise enough to fill the glory of one private man.' Grey resisted the pressure. 'I am afraid I shall not be able to screw my courage to the sticking place for so large a creation', he wrote. He hoped

[26] *Grey–William IV Corr.*, i. 360–8; Grey to Palmerston, 10, 14 Oct., G. 44; Althorp to Durham, 29 May, G. 12; Grey to Holland, 28 May, G. 34; Durham to Grey, 3 June, [25 Aug.], G.B6; Planta to Croker, 11 June, Croker MSS, Duke University, NC.

[27] For corr. between Harrowby and Wharncliffe and negotiations with Grey, see Wharncliffe MSS 516, Sheffield City Library and G. 46/2; *Grey–William IV Corr.*, i. 382–96, 435–79, ii. 1–11; Holland to Grey, 21 Apr., 31 May, 1 June, G. 34.

that the peerages traditionally given to mark the coronation in September would suffice. He complained of feeling nervous and distressed, harrassed by the conflicting pressures from his colleagues and by the intransigence of Durham, who reacted to Grey's refusal to promote him to an Earldom by declaring that all intercourse between them was at an end and that he would resign as soon as the Reform Bill was passed. The illness, and death at the end of September, of Durham's favourite son affected both Grey and his son-in-law deeply, and paralysed Grey's ability to take a decision. 'I suffer under a nervous irritation, which is distressing beyond anything I ever felt', he wrote to Holland.[28]

Grey's difficulties arose partly from his own reluctance to see a large creation of peers, partly from his knowledge of the King's extreme dislike of such a step, and partly from the fear that the Cabinet might disintegrate. Calculations suggested that a creation of even 80 to 100 peers might not be enough, bearing in mind the resentment such a step might create among the existing peers. Furthermore, the promotion of men who were sufficiently respectable and propertied would damage the status of the House of Commons. Grey resorted to delaying tactics, hoping that if the meeting of Parliament were postponed until the New Year the difficulty might somehow disappear: but the progressives in the Cabinet argued for an earlier meeting and the riots in October and November added cogency to their case that delay would cast doubt on the government's courage and inflame the country still further. On 19 November Grey, Palmerston, and Richmond were outvoted in the Cabinet in favour of calling Parliament together before Christmas, and he agreed to defer to the majority view. Stanley protested that the decision made it seem that the government was being driven on by its extremist supporters, and Grey himself wrote to Burdett that his friends were too impatient. He was now under pressure from all sides. Durham, still suffering mental agonies following the death of his son, created a dreadful scene at Althorp's Cabinet dinner in November, objecting to the changes that had been made in the Bill and even accusing Grey of causing the boy's death. Grey was close to tears but could not bring himself to discipline his son-in-law, though Melbourne remarked that in his place he would have knocked him down. The rest of Grey's family, including Mary and Henry, also urged him to force the Bill through with new peerages, and the breakdown of the negotiations with Wharncliffe left him little alternative. Writing to Lansdowne on 29 December, he declared that he agreed with his repugnance to the peerages but expressed his conviction that the Bill must be passed at all costs.[29]

[28] Grey to Sir John Dalrymple, 18 May 1831 and reply, 21 May, Stair MSS, GD 135/112, National Library of Scotland; Holland to Grey, 31 Aug., 17 Sept., Grey to Holland, 2, 31 Aug., 29 Sept., 30 Oct., G. 34; to Holland, 28 Sept., Lady Grey to Holland [15 Oct.], BL Add. MS 51548, fos. 44, 61–3; *HHD* 44–7; Grey to Brougham, 2, 3 Sept., *BLT*, iii. 125; Durham to Grey, 23, [25 Aug.], Grey to Durham, 28 Aug., 3 Sept., G. B6; Durham to Ellice, 16 Sept., Ellice MSS 15032; C. Wood to Sir F. Wood, 28 Sept., Hickleton MSS A.2.34.

[29] Grey to Holland, 1 Jan 1832, 15 Nov. 1831, G. 34; Duncannon to Grey [1831], G. 7/7; Fenwick to Grey, 18 Nov. and reply, 22 Nov., G. 14; *HHD*, 82, 88–9, 103, 107–10; Cabinet minute 19 Nov., *Grey–William IV Corr.*, i. 482–3; Stanley to Grey, 22 Nov., G. 11/8; Grey to Burdett, 24 Nov., G. 8/11; Grey to Althorp, 10 Jan. 1832, Le Marchant, *Althorp*, 386; to Lansdowne, 29 Dec., Bowood MSS; to

Grey had allowed himself to be persuaded, chiefly by Durham, Brougham, and Holland, and on 4 January he made a formal request to the King, detailed in a long memorandum prepared by Grey after the conversation. He submitted an estimate of a majority of 20 against the second reading, and declared his conviction that the loss of the Bill would have disastrous effects on the state of the country and threaten the existence of the House of Lords itself. Nothing was therefore left but the creation of additional peers, which it was deeply painful to him to propose but which was the lesser of the evils. He requested 'a partial addition' of 8 or 10 in order to dispel the notion that there would be no creations, and permission to create a further number if it should be necessary at a later stage. The King repeated his concern over the proposal but professed his willingness to listen to the advice of his ministers and requested it in writing. Grey assured him that the creations would be designed so as to avoid as far as possible any permanent addition to the size of the House and any substantial withdrawal of property from the Commons, and he agreed that after the passage of the Bill the ministers 'would make their stand against any further encroachments tending to a dangerous diminution of the necessary power of the Government'.

The King, writing in reply, declared that he would not add to the government's difficulties by hesitation, that 'he has no wish for any change of his Ministers' and that he doubted whether any other administration could be formed to carry on the government. His only condition was that, with two exceptions, the new peers must be exclusively eldest sons or collateral heirs of existing peers, and he urged that the measure should be 'effectual and conclusive and . . . not subject to contingencies which might defeat its object, to the risk of erroneous estimates of comparative strength, or to the possible necessity of a *second edition*, in consequence of the insufficiency of the first'. If Grey estimated that 21 were needed they should all be made at once, 'instead of feeling the pulse, and beating about the bush, by adding eight or ten, at the risk of failure, which would betray the absence of due calculation and discrimination'.

The King's native shrewdness identified the flaws in the proposal which derived from Grey's own half-heartedness about the measure, and his reply made the Cabinet ask for a delay before submitting specific advice. The Cabinet met on 7, 11, and 13 January and minuted their view that any addition to the peerage must be sufficient 'to the full extent which certain attainment of its object may eventually require'; they could not therefore propose any specific number until they had more certain knowledge of what would be necessary. Grey's covering letter emphasized the need for any creation to be 'to the full extent which may be required'. The King, not unreasonably, replied that Grey had given him to understand that the total number would not much exceed 21, and that there was a 'wide difference' between that and a blank cheque. However, he would give the pledge requested, subject only to conditions as to the categories of those to be ennobled. He ended

Brougham, 1 Jan., *BLT*, iii. 164; Greville, *Journal*, ii. 226; Durham to Grey, 29 Dec., Reid, *Earl of Durham*, i. 270–5.

by remarking that the creation of peers to force the Bill through the Lords might be thought inconsistent with the principle of the Bill and with the abolition of nominated seats, 'inasmuch as nomination votes are created and introduced into the House of Lords for the purpose of overpowering the independent voice of the House, and the character and integrity of the higher branch of the legislature are thus sacrificed to the reform of the lower'. Grey replied with a defence of his advice, stating that the proposal to make a definite number of peers was given up in consequence of the King's insistence that a sufficient number should be made at one time, and deferred until the last possible moment. This necessarily left the number indefinite but there was no inconsistency in principle. The possibility of a greater number being required also made it impossible to undertake to restrict creations to eldest sons, collateral heirs, or Scottish and Irish peers. Finally, he argued that there was a fundamental difference between members sitting for nomination boroughs in the Commons and peers appointed to the Lords, in that the latter would have as independent a tenure as other peers.[30]

In view of what was to follow, Grey's negotiations with the King can hardly be called successful or satisfactory to either. The ground had been laid for the King to believe, when the size of the Lords' majority against the second reading was revealed, that his ministers had again deceived either him or themselves; in either case it shook his confidence in them and aroused again all his fears that the Reform Bill was the beginning of a revolution that would sweep away the aristocracy and monarchy. It is difficult to resist the conclusion that Grey, buffeted on both sides by his radical or conservative colleagues, was gambling on an uncertain outcome. Probably he hoped that Wharncliffe, who had visited Brighton and had a long conversation with Taylor and one with the King on the 8 and 11 January, would be so impressed by the knowledge of the King's assent to the creation of peers that he and his friends would cease to oppose the Bill. The Cabinet had already agreed to amendments in the Bill to meet some of Wharncliffe's objections and possibly they hoped that it would suffice. Grey further indicated his willingness to accept defeat on any amendment in the committee which did not prejudice the principle. Nevertheless, it was a situation fraught with anxieties. There is no wonder that Grey confessed to Henry in February that he wished he had never introduced reform, and that Althorp thought it advisable, after reflection, to remove the pistols he kept in his bedroom. Grey wrote on 25 February that he was overwhelmed by the problem of deciding what to do. He doubted whether, even if Wharncliffe gave way, he was influential enough to deliver even the second reading, and some members of the Cabinet were still opposed to the creation of peers to pass it.

Nevertheless, Grey kept a cool head. On 11 March he wrote to Althorp, who was on the point of resigning in despair unless peers were made at once. He asserted his confidence that a majority for the second reading was 'nearly certain', to the extent that immediate creations were not justified. Defeats in the committee

[30] *Grey–William IV Corr.*, ii. 68–79, 96–102; the King's reply, 15 Jan., 108–15.

stage were more likely, but if the government refrained from making peers until that point it would show that they were reluctant to do so unless absolutely essential, and would counter the accusation that they did so irresponsibly. Besides, defeat in the committee was not certain, as the opposition was divided. In all this, Grey was hardly convincing. He admitted that the real reason for his opposition to peer-making was 'my extreme repugnance to the measure . . . I am conscious that my feeling is stronger than my reason. It is a measure of extreme violence . . . and . . . in my opinion very uncertain of success' because of the reaction it would create against the ministers.

The result then is, that all these considerations press on my mind with so irresistible a weight, that I really cannot bring myself to the adoption of a measure to which, as we now stand, there appear to me to be such insurmountable objections. I never had, I believe, at any time an overweening confidence in my own opinions. I am accused indeed sometimes of giving away too much to those of others. I do not wish to defend myself against this charge. I am not ashamed of abandoning an opinion when I am satisfied that it is wrong [but] . . . as at present advised, I do not think anything would induce me to be a consenting party to a large creation of peers.

Grey's letter averted Althorp's resignation, which Grey declared would be followed by his own, but it betrayed an agony of mind and spirit which contrasts painfully with the optimism he tried to show to others. Fatigue and despondency were ill-disguised by the façade which he tried to maintain.[31]

Grey had to call on his inner resources to the utmost during the next two months. He demanded the support of his colleagues in delaying the request for new peerages, while at the same time reassuring the King, whose letters in January and February did not attempt to conceal his apprehension. At length on 25 March the Cabinet agreed that if the second reading was defeated they would not resign, but demand the necessary additions to the Lords. On the following day a precautionary minute to the King warned him that there must be 'such an addition . . . as would afford a certainty of success'. The King replied that 'he cannot help considering the general interests of the country as being of superior importance to the maintenance of certain provisions of the Reform Bill' and repeated his wish that if the Bill were rejected the government would seek to frame a new one which would meet the principal objections of the moderate wing of the opposition.

Grey discussed the matter with the King at an audience on 1 April, emphasizing that such modifications would arouse public resentment and that such 'a mutilated measure' would reopen the cry for universal suffrage and vote by ballot. The Cabinet therefore stood by its demand. The King suggested that at least, in the

---

[31] 'Minute of conversation with Sir Herbert Taylor at Brighton, Jan. 1832', minute of conversation between Grey & Wharncliffe, and paper sent by Wharncliffe to Grey, 24 Nov. 1831, Wharncliffe MSS 516 f; Brock, *The Great Reform Act*, 271; Broughton, *Recollections*, 11 Feb., iv. 174–81; *HHD*, 146–9; Grey to Holland, 25 Feb., G. 35; memorandum, G. 46/2; Goderich to Grey, 4 Mar., G. 49/13; Grey to Althorp, 11 Mar., G. 52/25 and Le Marchant, *Althorp*, 407–13; Taylor to Grey 16 Mar., *Grey–William IV Corr.*, ii. 257–71; Grey to Burdett, 24 Nov., Patterson, *Burdett*, ii. 598; to Adam, 30 Mar., Blair Adam MSS.

event of defeat, there should be a delay in introducing a new Bill until the next session, to give time for consideration 'what should be done and the best way of doing it'. He then asked the crucial question 'what number of peers would be required' and Grey admitted that not less than 50 or 60 would probably be necessary. The King replied that this was 'a fearful number' and asked for time to consider. Grey emphasized that, in view of the fact that the party in the Lords which opposed the government had been in power for 70 years, a 'large creation' of peers was necessary in any case to correct the present balance of parties there, independent of the Reform Bill. Two days later the Cabinet minuted its unanimous advice that the rejection of the Bill should immediately be followed by the announcement that it would be reintroduced in such a manner as to afford a satisfactory assurance of its success, leaving the question of numbers to be decided according to the event. The King responded with a long review of all the proceedings and discussions since February 1831, stressing the way in which the requests for creations had steadily grown in number and pointing out that if the total of 50 or 60 had been mentioned at the outset he would have refused. He was prepared to consent to the addition of only 'a *reasonable* number' and refused to be committed to a step which was '*speculative, and . . . uncertain in its nature, its extent, and its issue*'.[32]

On 6 April Grey sent to the King lists of names of people to be considered for peerages, containing 38 eldest sons and collateral heirs, 2 others whose titles would expire with them and a further number of commoners whose promotions would constitute a permanent addition to the peerage, together with a supplementary or reserve list. The King offered no objection to the first 40 but repeated his refusal to go beyond the principle that no permanent addition should be made. If more were required, they should be additions in the first category: as he had made sacrifices to assist his ministers, peers who supported the Bill should waive their objections to having their heirs called up, to counter suspicion that their commitment to it was not sincere.

In this unsatisfactory position Grey and his colleagues had to face the second reading debate which began on 9 April. On the first reading, on 26 March, Grey had assured the House of his willingness to consider amendments to details which did not affect the principle or general extent of the measure, and Harrowby and Wharncliffe had given the assurance that they would not oppose the second reading, though warning that they had strong objections to the Bill in its present form. Introducing the second reading, Grey spoke in a similarly moderate and conciliatory tone, asserting that the three principles of the Bill were disfranchisement, enfranchisement, and the moderate extension of the franchise, and that these were unchanged from the first Bill. In detail, however, changes had been made in the hope of meeting criticisms then expressed in the Lords, and these were still open to discussion and final determination in the committee stage.

[32] Reid, *Earl of Durham*, i. 277–8; New, *Durham*, 163–8; *Grey–William IV Corr.*, ii. 254–62, 288–91, 299–300, 309, 311–27; *HHD*, 130 ff. (Cabinet discussion, 25–27 Mar., ibid. 160–8).

The general argument of the speech was that the Bill was supported by 'the great mass of the power, the opulence, the intelligence, the education, and all that is important in the community', that the Lords would damage their own House if they resisted that general and respectable public opinion, and that the Bill was fully constitutional in its intentions and by no means amounted to a revolution. Harrowby and Wharncliffe repeated the views they had expressed on 26 March, but Ellenborough, who moved the rejection of the Bill, Wellington, and several bishops and other lay peers spoke against a second reading.[33]

Grey wound up the debate on the morning of the 14 April in one of his finest speeches. He reviewed the origins and course of the agitation for reform since the autumn of 1830, repeated that, far from advancing a popular or democratic revolution, the Bill would reconcile the respectable public to the constitution, and he answered the various arguments advanced by those who opposed it. He concluded with a reference to the possibility of creating peers to secure the passage of the Bill, asserting that the power to do so was endorsed by all the major constitutional authorities as a means of preventing dangers which might arise from a collision between the Lords and a House of Commons which was backed by public opinion. He would be adverse to its use except in case of extreme necessity, but would be prepared to advise it if that case arose. The division, at 7.15 a.m. on 14 April, resulted in a majority for the government of 9 votes, 184 against 175.

Grey's speech was widely praised. Hobhouse remarked that 'he seemed to rise with the occasion' and reported that 'Lord Grey was extolled as the boldest and best of statesmen, and certain to hold office for life.' Holland wrote that it 'restored [him] entirely to the confidence of the whole party'.[34] Nevertheless, the ministry was clearly vulnerable, and when the King chose this moment to write a querulous letter expressing anxiety about the course of its foreign policy, particularly with respect to Poland and France, as 'a system . . . which appears to H.M. inconsistent with [the country's] real interests and its permanent prosperity, and calculated to alienate from it all Governments which are not disposed to encourage revolutionary projects and innovations destructive of existing power and authority', the implication was clear enough. Grey replied by expressing his 'deep sense of pain at the suggestion that there had been a great diminution of your Majesty's confidence in your Majesty's present Ministers'. The King's stipulation that all diplomatic instructions should be shown to him before being sent amounted to 'showing that your Majesty no longer reposes in your Majesty's Ministers the confidence by which alone they can be enabled to act . . . If that confidence is withdrawn, Earl Grey has no alternative left but of humbly rendering his resignation.' The King hastened to assure Grey that 'there is not the *slightest* ground' for any suggestion that his confidence in his ministers had diminished, but Grey complained to

---

[33] *Grey–William IV Corr.*, ii. 328–44; *Mirror of Parliament* (1831–2), ii. 1425–8, 1660–1783. Althorp thought Grey's speech 'very fine . . . clear, dignified, and eminently prudent and persuasive': Le Marchant, *Althorp*, 417–18.

[34] *Mirror of Parliament*, 1812–16. Macaulay called the speech 'almost unparalleled' (Le Marchant, *Althorp*, 417–18) and Holland 'almost miraculous' (*HHD*, 169–70); Broughton, *Recollections*, iv. 214.

Taylor that the King's manner in his interview on the subject had not removed his impression, and pointed out that rumours of his change of attitude were beginning to circulate, probably originating in the Court, to the detriment of the government's prospects. He repeated his sincere wish to reach agreement in the committee stage on the Reform Bill and his hope that Harrowby and Wharncliffe would show the same spirit, but pointed out that reports of their communications with Lyndhurst and Ellenborough cast doubt on this prospect.[35]

Doubts were resolved when the Lords committee stage began. On 28 April Ellice reported to Grey that Lyndhurst, Ellenborough, and the two 'Waverers', in Wellington's presence, had concocted an amendment to postpone the consideration of Schedules A and B until the enfranchisement proposals in Schedule C had been determined. The amendment was more than merely procedural; it would have opened the way to drastic remodelling of both the redistribution of seats and of the borough franchise, to whose uniformity Lyndhurst and the 'Waverers' were opposed but to which the Cabinet was firmly committed. Grey resented the part played by Harrowby and Wharncliffe in this secret plan, only a few days after another interview on the 28th with Grey, in which he formed the impression that they would resist postponement. He viewed it as rank treachery when they supported the amendment. It was carried on 7 May by 151 to 116, a majority of 35. After the division Ellenborough outlined the opposition's proposals which included the abolition of Schedules B and D and the continuation of the old scot-and-lot franchise in addition to the £10 borough householders. The only point left for the ministers to consider was whether they should request new peerages or resign. The Cabinet on 8 May resolved to present the King with these alternatives, specifying 'the expediency of advancing to the honour of the peerage such a number of persons as might insure the success of the Bill in all its essential principles, and as might give to your Majesty's servants the strength which is necessary for conducting with effect the business of the country'. The King replied on the 9th that he preferred to accept their resignations.[36]

The amendment had provided the Cabinet with the best issue on which to resign and forced Wellington, who was asked to form the new administration, to deal with the reform question. Brougham and Durham confidently expected him to fail, when they would return in triumph to force the King's hand. Grey's feelings were more ambivalent. He welcomed his release from the torments of office, and would have been relieved if Wellington had succeeded. At the same time, he must have regretted the prospective loss of the great achievement of his lifetime; but weariness and anxiety for the moment were uppermost. On 13 May the Whigs in the Commons held a party meeting at Brooks's and the majority, led by Althorp and Stanley, agreed to allow Wellington to pass a reform bill and to turn him out afterwards. Ebrington refused to accept this decision and persisted

[35] *Grey–William IV Corr.*, ii. 351–65, 372–5.
[36] Ellice to Grey, 28 Apr., G. 13; *Grey–William IV Corr.*, ii. 391–2, 394–6; Charles to Frederick, 29 May, G. D1; *Mirror of Parliament* (1831–2), iii. 1921–35; *HHD*, 177.

with the intention to propose a motion of no confidence in the new ministry when it should be formed. The issue was decided by Peel, whose refusal to repeat his conduct over Catholic emancipation by proposing a measure to which he had expressed repugnance in opposition, left Wellington without a leader in the Commons, and vulnerable to the accusation that he acted merely for the sake of office. Sir Robert Inglis, a leading Tory, declared that if a Reform Bill were to be carried it should be by those who had originally proposed it. This, as Hobhouse remarked, was the '*coup de grâce*' for Wellington.[37]

Meanwhile, the country took its own steps. London was placarded with the injunction 'To stop the Duke, go for gold', and the threat of a run on the banks and the fall of the stocks rallied the City to the Whigs. The 'days of May' revived fears of revolution. The *Morning Chronicle* declared 18 May to be 'the eve of the barricades'. On the 15th Wellington surrendered his commission and advised the King to recall Grey. The Whig ministers had not given up their seals of office, and when the Cabinet reassembled on the 16th they presented their ultimatum. Refusing the King's repeated request to Grey on the 15th that they would modify the Bill, they demanded that the whole Bill must be passed and that the King must agree to an unlimited creation of peers unless the opponents of the Bill ceased to obstruct its progress. The King pressed Wellington to make a declaration to that effect in the Lords, but in the debate the Duke, Lyndhurst, and others merely abused the ministry and repeated their refusal to accept the Bill, though privately assuring the King that they would individually withdraw from further proceedings on it. On the 18th the Cabinet nevertheless demanded an assurance that sufficient creations would be made if the necessity arose, and the King had no alternative but to give way. Grey announced in the Lords that the ministers had a confident expectation of being able to carry the Bill, though refusing to declare explicitly in public that they had the power to create sufficient peerages. The King and Taylor privately made strenuous efforts to persuade individual opponents of the Bill to stay away from the debates, Taylor assuring Grey that he had stated to a number of them that the King had given authority for any necessary number of creations. The result, as Taylor wrote on 28 May, was the 'rapid and almost unobstructed progress' of the Bill, 'wholly unaltered and *unimproved*'—a parting reference to the abandonment of modifications which the King had hoped Grey would have accepted.

Grey, who was anxious to be done with the whole question, was in no mood to accept reproof and retorted that if those who had opposed the Bill had behaved more responsibly, some changes might have been possible, but that the 'days of May' had made it essential to pass the Bill as it stood and with all speed in order to end the agitation. He would do as much as possible to meet the King's desire that the unhappy divisions which now existed in political life might be healed; but he pointed out that he had had to bear the brunt of 'a series of personal attacks,

[37] Grey to Holland, 14, 15 May, G. 35; Mary to Lady Holland [16 May], BL Add. Ms 51549, fos. 208–9; Russell, *Recollections and Suggestions*, 105–6; Broughton, *Recollections*, iv. 226.

such as, in times of the greatest political heat and animosity, have seldom been directed against any Minister'. He asserted his wish 'that the waters of bitterness may cease to flow' and concluded[38]

Much as I have been engaged, all my life, in political contention, there is no one to whom this kind of strife is more painful, and I should be too happy if, by withdrawing myself from the scene, I could see these angry passions allayed, and obtain for myself the repose which my age requires.

The royal assent was given to the Reform (England) Bill on 7 June and although the King refused to go to the Lords to do so in person it was an occasion of relief and rejoicing, tinged only with apprehension as to what its effects might be. Those effects turned out, in time, to be what Grey had hoped and forecast. The radicals did not win supremacy over the mainly middle-class and conservative electorate, most of whom were relieved that the question had been settled for the foreseeable future; the House of Lords was not threatened by a wave of democratic revulsion, and the great institutions of Church and State survived beyond Grey's lifetime, strenthened rather than weakened by the achievement of reform by, in the end, constitutional means. As Charles Wood, his private secretary, had forecast in March 1831, 'the reform is an efficient, substantial, anti-democratic, pro-property measure'. Indeed, Grey was almost too successful in restraining the forces of change, for in many respects it was Peel and the Conservative party who reaped the political benefits of the Act. The Tamworth Manifesto of 1834 was an ultimately successful appeal to those who valued order and good government above the contentions of parties to support moderate conservatism rather than radical change. The Whigs found themselves during the next generation fighting again the old battles, squeezed between a radicalism they continued to detest and a conservatism which was the ultimate beneficiary of their refusal to work with the radicals.[39]

The Reform Act, deservedly christened 'Great' by later commentators, remains Grey's supreme achievement. To its passage he had sacrificed the repose he had come to cherish after 15 years of enforced, but to some extent deliberate political isolation and exclusion. His succession to the Premiership in 1830 had shown that he still enjoyed general respect and authority as leader of the Whig party and of reformist opinion, and his handling of the long crisis of 1831–2, while not free from mistakes, miscalculations, and over-optimism, entitled him to the great reputation his name was to enjoy for the rest of the century and beyond. Britain came nearer to popular revolution during those years than at any others in modern times. Despite his relative inexperience, and that of his colleagues, he guided his country through a process of reform that strengthened those traditional values and institutions which he always respected and revered. As his colleagues recognized, only Grey's personal qualities kept the Cabinet together. He held the centre against

---

[38] *HHD*, 180, 182–4; memorandum [*c.* May–June 1832], General Charles Grey MSS XV/1; Broughton, *Recollections*, iv. 230; *Grey–William IV Corr.*, ii. 450–3, 455–7.

[39] C. Wood to Sir F. Wood, 3 Mar. 1831, Hickleton MSS A.2.34.

the centrifugal forces of its radical and conservative members, and his ability to manage the King which was crucial to the success of the Bill also derived from the reputation for political integrity which William IV recognized and relied on. It was, as Michael Brock has remarked, 'a great and beneficent piece of statesmanship',[40] and it was so recognized by Grey's contemporaries.

SECURITY ABROAD

Though the Reform Bill struggle almost monopolized public attention during the first eighteen months of Grey's administration, as Prime Minister he had to deal with all the other issues of government and policy that arose during that time and for two years after the Bill was passed. If his administration has been mainly celebrated for the achievement of reform, its breakup in 1834 followed from its less distinguished performance in other areas. The major problems it had to face lay in the fields of foreign policy and of Ireland.

Grey took office with a policy of peace, retrenchment, and reform, and the first was as important to him as the others, providing a secure framework within which they could be achieved. He took a particular interest in the details of foreign relations, sometimes to the annoyance of Palmerston, his Foreign Secretary. During the 1820s Grey had been a stern critic of Canning's and Wellington's foreign policies with respect to France, the Iberian peninsula, and the Near East. He consistently maintained the traditional Whig principle of non-interference by any state in the internal affairs of others, both as a means of preserving peace and, therefore, of enabling military and naval establishments to be reduced in the interests of economy and diminishing executive influence. He could rarely bring himself to approve of anything that Canning did, but he was sympathetic to Canning's attempts to restrain the intervention of Metternich and Talleyrand in the affairs of Spain and Portugal, and his criticisms of Canning's 'new world' policy were based more on its presentation than its substance. He was sympathetic on liberal grounds towards Greece's struggle for independence from Turkish rule, but anxious at the same time to prevent the extension of Russian influence in the eastern Mediterranean. In Spain and Portugal he followed Holland's long-expressed desire to see liberal constitutional regimes securely established and defended against Habsburg and Bourbon interference. Palmerston, a disciple of Canning, was in agreement on these issues and the two were able to work in harmony on policy. As Palmerston's latest biographer has written, Grey was probably more in sympathy with his Foreign Secretary's policies than anyone else in the Cabinet, so that despite occasional frictions they worked well together.[1]

In foreign affairs as in domestic ones, Grey was above all a pragmatist and

---

[40] Brock, *The Great Reform Act*, 335.

[1] K. Bourne, *Palmerston: The Early Years* (1982), 341 and, for the remainder of this chapter, 332–407, *passim*.

conservative. Even the cherished principle of non-interference in the internal affairs of other states was, as he wrote to Palmerston in October 1833, to be 'regulated by a just attention to our own safety' and to an overriding concern for national and commercial interests. Foreign policy too was related to party politics at home. Traditionally the Whigs—and in particular Holland as the self-appointed guardian of the Foxite legacy—favoured alliance with post-revolutionary France against the absolutist regimes of the Holy Alliance. During Palmerston's first period at the Foreign Office, despite his initial tendency to see France as a 'natural enemy', British policy did gradually move towards an *entente cordiale*, sealed in 1834 as the Quadruple Alliance with France, Portugal, and Spain, and designed to protect the constitutional regimes in the last two countries. Wellington and the Tories were identified, in Whig minds at least, with support for the reactionary Bourbon regime before the revolution of 1830, and with the military autocracies of central and eastern Europe. Whig foreign policy was designed not only to preserve British interests in vital strategic and economic theatres and to defend Britain against foreign enemies but also to prevent the domestic and international triumph of absolutist principles. To this extent it was ideological. Like his mentor Canning, Palmerston also had an acute appreciation of the importance of public opinion as a force to be engaged on the side of the government.[2]

Within these parameters, Grey and Palmerston conducted foreign affairs with, on the whole, cordial collaboration and reasonable success. Palmerston was an efficient and hardworking Foreign Secretary, and mastered the details of his office as few before or since have done. Grey quickly learned to respect his ability and to trust him, though always keeping a close eye on what was happening and occasionally trying to influence appointments in the diplomatic service in favour of old friends or relatives.[3] Their voluminous correspondence, almost daily at times when they were not meeting regularly, shows that Grey was kept informed of affairs in detail, and that he responded promptly with approval, advice, or occasionally disapproval. It was now conventional for the Prime Minister to assume particular overall authority for foreign policy. Like his predecessors, Grey preferred, rather than bring foreign affairs routinely before the Cabinet, to work with a small inner group, less formal than a sub-committee, and to consult the full Cabinet only when its authority was needed to endorse a major policy decision. His chosen associates were Lansdowne and Holland, the two colleagues whom he had originally approached to take the post of Foreign Secretary, together with Palmerston himself. These four operated as a confidential group; despatches were circulated as a matter of routine to them alone amongst the Cabinet, though Holland's notorious indiscretion led Palmerston on occasion to act alone or in consultation only with Grey. Of the four, Lansdowne was the least active and Holland the most insistent on pushing his own views, but both represented the Foxite Whig view and this tended to counter any Canningite tendencies that

[2] Grey to Palmerston, 9 Oct. 1833, G. 44.
[3] See for example, Grey to Palmerston, 17 Jan. 1831, ibid.

Palmerston might retain. This enabled Grey to reach a balanced view though at times it suggested a tendency to be influenced by the opinions of others and to listen to advice and argument rather than to give decisive leadership. It was unjust, however, for Princess Lieven to remark that he was weak, changeable, and easily governed. These criticisms, of course, referred to occasions when Grey's decisions did not suit her, and since she believed Grey to be much more susceptible to her own influence than he really was, any conduct to the contrary must be explained by Grey's inability to stand up to some other adviser. 'He is liberal and vain, [but] he is flexible and his opinion can be easily changed. Palmerston is a mule', she once wrote in vexation. In fact Grey, though subject as ever to fluctuating moods, suffered more from an anxiety to take all factors into account and to come up with the ideal solution, so rarely attainable in practical politics. The perfectionism which lay at the root of Grey's moody character sometimes operated to his disadvantage here as in other spheres of life: but he was capable of decision when he was convinced.[4]

The conduct of foreign affairs was not, of course, merely a matter of drafting despatches and instructions to ministers abroad or reading the intercepted despatches of foreign governments to their representatives in Britain. Social contact with foreign ambassadors and plenipotentiaries (or in the case of Russia, their wives) was equally important. This was particularly so in London in the early 1830s, for the London Conference which had been set up to settle the problem of the Netherlands by international concert was in frequent session and it involved the presence of envoys as well as ambassadors with whom personal contact was essential. Parties and social occasions in town and, during parliamentary recesses, in country houses often became pretexts for intense negotiation and discussion. Lady Cowper complained from Panshanger in January 1831 during a weekend at which Grey, Palmerston, Leopold of Saxe-Coburg, and the foreign ambassadors were present that 'there was no going into any room without disturbing a conference'. Personal relationships were an important dimension of foreign policy.[5]

The relationship most notorious in Grey's case was that with Dorothea Christopherovna Benkendorf, Princess Lieven. She was devoted to the social position she had established for herself during her husband's residence in London as Russian ambassador and tried to use her personal charms in the service of her country's diplomatic interests. Indeed, Prince Lieven's position appeared to be that of Mme de Lieven's husband rather than ambassador in his own right. She set herself to fascinate the leading British ministers and politicians of the time, and set her cap in succession at Castlereagh, Canning, Wellington, and Grey, though usually with results that fell far short of her imagination. Grey, who as Greville unkindly remarked, was 'all his life ... the fool of women', almost certainly at some time in the later 1820s became her lover. 'He is one of my most intimate

---

[4] *HHD*, p. xl; Bourne, *Palmerston*, 359,

[5] Lady Cowper to the Duke of Devonshire [8 Jan. 1831], Chatsworth MSS, Bourne, *Palmerston*, 334.

acquaintances in England', she wrote in November 1829. She was capable of shrewd judgement of Grey's feelings and correctly judged his aristocratic attitudes. Yet her claim to have persuaded Grey to give Palmerston the Foreign Office in 1830 in the hope that he would be more pro-Russian than the Whigs, has been generally disbelieved, though more on the grounds of the unlikelihood that Palmerston would connive at her activities than from any lack of evidence that she put considerable pressure on Grey. However, as Palmerston's biographer remarks, Grey 'was not as great a fool as that'.

Her attempts to influence her lover's domestic and foreign policies were likewise exercises in self-deception, and her outbursts of impatience at Grey's supposed spinelessness usually represented her annoyance that he failed to do what she wanted. 'He listens when I am speaking', she wrote on 24 June 1831, 'but it only lasts 24 hours, for then his accursed son-in-law Lord Durham comes along, and carries him off, and he becomes either a Jacobin or a child, as it suits the other.' By March 1833, she had despaired of him. 'Lord Grey has become such a thorough old woman that it is scarcely worth while mentioning him.' 'He bores me not a little', she declared in May 1832. Grey on his part used his correspondence with her to warn her and her government of British concern about intervention against popular revolutions: 'I have never yet known a popular revolution that might not be ascribed to provocation on the part of the Goverment', he wrote in September 1830. The best security against revolutions was not armies and Holy Alliances, but judicious internal reform—a process he was himself about to initiate in Britain. He was well aware of her calculated indiscretions and rebuked her in January 1831 for saying that he wished for the suppression of the Polish revolt. 'Really, if I have not a complete assurance that my name is not to be mentioned, my mouth must be shut as to everything but the mere gossip of the day.' Perhaps indeed Grey should have followed this rule in any case. His association with her does suggest a degree of indiscretion and misjudgement, fostering suspicion, however unjustified, of the nature of the relationship and its political significance. It provides some confirmation of the view that Grey was capable of being influenced by personal vanity, but the evidence does not suggest that it affected his political judgement.[6]

Other old friendships occasionally intruded into the consideration of foreign policy. The Comte de Flahault, who had married Mercer Elphinstone, Grey's friend and confidante in the Princess Charlotte affair, was the reputed son of Talleyrand and was employed as French ambassador to Berlin in 1831, and later to Vienna and, in 1860, to London. He and his wife were frequent correspondents and visitors to the Greys, providing Grey with opportunities to supplement official communications with the French government by private and informal means. There were 'few friends whom he valued so highly', Mary assured the Flahaults after Grey's death in 1845. Holland too, with his extensive circle of correspondents

[6] Greville, *Journal*, ii. 85; Lieven, *Letters in London*, 204, 272, 273, 278–9, 303, 321–3, 327, 337; Bourne, *Palmerston*, 330–1; *Lieven–Grey Corr.*, ii. 74–6, 80–3, 131–2.

and social contacts at Holland House, was on intimate terms with many foreign personalities, especially with Talleyrand and with Palmella, the representative of Don Pedro in the Portuguese crisis of the early 1830s. Despite the reputation of Holland House as a source of leaks and indiscretions, it provided a useful service in supplementing formal diplomacy, and sometimes the leaks operated in the reverse direction to Palmerston's benefit. Holland's strong Francophilia and simplistic Whig constitutionalism sometimes led him to argue against Grey and Palmerston's more cautious and pragmatic approach, but the drift of British policy towards the French entente by 1834 satisfied his general feelings.[7]

When Grey took office in November 1830, Europe was in a state of turmoil. The French revolution in the summer had been followed by the Belgian revolt against the forced unification with Holland under the Vienna Settlement, while in Spain, Portugal, and the eastern Mediterranean problems remained to be solved which might threaten European peace or British interests. Despite Grey's dislike of the principles behind the Vienna Settlement, he and Palmerston wished to maintain its essentials, particularly against French expansion. The Netherlands had always been regarded as a crucial theatre for British trade and security, and so Grey and Palmerston were anxious to prevent the French from exploiting the Belgian revolt to extend their influence in that direction. At the same time, the newly established Orléans monarchy needed to consolidate itself at home by success abroad and Belgium seemed a natural opportunity. Despite Grey's initial welcome of the new French regime therefore, he and Palmerston saw it as their first task to prevent an independent Belgium from falling under French influence. The fact that the Dutch had historically been regarded as Britain's ally also meant that they were reluctant to take coercive measures against Holland. Their strategy therefore was to use the London five-power Conference in order to achieve Belgian independence without either alienating the Dutch or enabling the French to take the credit. Palmerston's skilful and arduous work as chairman of the Conference was successful in achieving these ends, but much hard negotiation was necessary. On 20 December the Conference agreed to Belgian independence, and a month later Talleyrand was induced to agree to a self-denying ordinance in which France gave up any claim to compensation in territory or otherwise at Belgium's expense. The legitimist powers, Austria, Prussia, and Russia, were persuaded to accept this revision of the Vienna Settlement and to agree to the nomination of Leopold of Saxe-Coburg, formerly husband of Princess Charlotte, as King of the Belgians, so averting the accession of a French dynasty.

The task of reconciling the Dutch to the terms of a settlement was, however, a long-drawn-out one. The King of Holland did not finally agree to the terms until 1838, but the Convention of 1833 which established the basis of the final settlement was largely Palmerston's triumph. He achieved it by taking a firm line with all the other interested parties and being prepared to threaten war if necessary, but he

---

[7] Corr. with Comte and Mme de Flahault, Bowood MSS, copies G. 15/1, esp. 20 Jan. and 16 Feb. 1831, 26 Mar. and 24 June 1832; Lady Grey to Flahault, 20 Mar. 1845, ibid.; *HHD*, pp. xl–xli.

had also to contend with the nerves of other members of the British Cabinet and the reluctance of William I V to envisage a rift with the Holy Alliance powers. Grey too at times hesitated to back Palmerston's decisive line, and, though he did not share the full extent of Holland's Whiggishly pro-French inclinations he blocked Palmerston's wish in the late summer of 1831 to force France to terms over the barrier fortresses. Grey had a more sensitive understanding of the Cabinet's reluctance to back Palmerston's hard line, and of the need to secure its approval of major decisions. He did not wish to find Britain forced into co-operation with the Holy Alliance powers against France. The consequence of Cabinet discussions in September 1831 was to lead Palmerston towards a closer co-operation with France and the establishment of an *entente* against the eastern powers. As late as October 1833 Grey lectured Palmerston on the need for flexibility: 'This is indeed a maxim of general application... Nations cannot be governed by the obligations of friendship which prevail among individuals in private life... There can be, in the eyes of a philosophical statesman neither national enmities, nor national friendships.'

In October the Cabinet endorsed a new plan for a joint Anglo-French naval and military demonstration against the Dutch occupation of the Antwerp citadel and to open the Scheldt. The result was the suspension of the London Conference, which enabled Britain and France together to set the terms of the settlement and so protect vital British interests in the balance of power in north-western Europe.[8]

The successful resolution of the prolonged Belgian crisis owed much to Palmerston's skill and tenacity, and to Grey's support and guidance at crucial moments in the negotiations. After the spring of 1832 European diplomacy tended to fall into the pattern of confrontation between Britain and France on the one hand, representing liberal constitutionalism, and the three Holy Alliance powers on the other. This was a posture both satisfying to Whig attitudes and also compatible with the Canningite tradition, and it helped to consolidate the political alliance on which Grey's Cabinet was founded. Nevertheless Grey remained anxious that Britain should maintain her non-interventionist attitude. He had no wish to be seen acting on the side of insurgents against legitimate governments or conniving at the destruction of the European system established in 1815. The example of Ireland, as he pointed out to Palmerston in December 1830, was an uncomfortable reminder that Britain herself might be vulnerable to such policies on the part of other powers.

Princess Lieven remarked in December 1830 that 'notwithstanding the indiscreet words he may have uttered before becoming Prime Minister, since he has come into office he has been the most pronounced enemy of revolutions, revolutionists and of disturbances in general.' While therefore Whig sympathy would always be extended to peoples striving for free constitutional government

---

[8]   Grey to Holland, 9 Oct. 1830, BL Add. MS 51548, fo. 4; to Flahault, 4 Oct. 1830, Bowood MSS; to Palmerston, 12 Apr., 25 Dec. 1831, 8 Sept. 1832, 18 Sept., 9 Oct. 1833, G. 44.

on the Foxite principle of 'civil and religious liberty all over the world', practical and domestic considerations demanded that Britain should not be on the side of rebellion against established authority. When the Poles rose against Russian occupation, British sympathy was not followed by active help, which, as Grey remarked, it was not practicable in any case to give. He insisted that the appeal which Palmerston wished to address to the Tsar should contain no offensive expressions, though he was also prepared to welcome the Polish patriot Czartoryski in London to dinner, to the reproachful fury of the Lievens.[9]

Grey's caution in embarking on any adventurous policy in Europe was partly the result of his own anxiety to avoid embarrassments at home. His wish was to damp down the demand for further reform and to have a period of order and stability, which the Reform Act had been primarily intended to achieve. He was also aware of the views of the King, who hated the French as much as English radicalism and who as King of Hanover opposed the forces of German liberalism. There were also those members of the Cabinet who were less liberally inclined or, as in the case of Althorp, the Chancellor of the Exchequer, reluctant to embark on policies which involved seeking additional revenues to increase naval or military forces. British attitudes to liberal movements in Germany and Italy were friendly in spirit, but distant in terms of possible involvement.

The two major theatres after the Netherlands in which vital British interests were involved were the Near East and the Iberian peninsula, and in both she faced the possibility of counter-intervention by the absolutist bloc. In the East, the crucial question was the survival of the decadent Turkish Empire in face of the restlessness of the subject peoples in the Balkans, Egypt, and the Levant, and the prospect of a Russian advance towards the Bosphorus and the Mediterranean. The War of Greek Independence had raised the issue whether Britain would support the cause of freedom for Greece from alien and Muslim rule and whether the success of the Greeks would result in Russia gaining influence in that quarter. Grey had taken an intense interest in Wellington's policy towards Greece and had chosen the issue to make the speech in May 1830 which revealed his decision to move into opposition. He also had some unexpected influence on the question of Greece's territorial boundaries. He had suggested in September 1829 to Sir Robert Adair, the veteran Foxite diplomat then in Paris, a compromise between the wider boundaries proposed by France and Russia and the much narrower frontier supported by Wellington which confined Greece to the Morea. Adair's disclosure of Grey's suggestion to the Russian ambassador to France led to its being adopted as the compromise solution. 'Lord Grey's boundaries' as they were nicknamed, to Grey's amusement, were however enlarged, at Grey's own suggestion when he became Prime Minister, to the extent favoured by France and Russia and in principle by Grey himself in 1829. 'I really am of more consequence than I thought, if, from the bottom of Northumberland, I can prescribe the limits of new

[9] 9 Dec. 1830; Lieven, *Letters in London*, 285, 288–9, 298.

kingdoms', he had written to Henry in February 1830. As Prime Minister ten months later he was instrumental in settling the question more permanently.[10]

The Greek question, however, was only one part of the wider issue of the survival or partition of the Turkish Empire as a whole. Palmerston was at first inclined to Canning's view, that a number of independent successor states might be a better barrier to Russian expansion than the decrepit Empire, but the example of Greece where the new King Otto of Bavaria set up a despotic regime sympathetic to Russia, drew him round to the view that it was better to prop up the Sultan, and to hope that he might be induced to grant constitutional reforms in return for protection. Grey told Holland in February 1830 that, in view of the internal state of Greece after independence, ridden with faction and corruption, as was inevitable after the people had been so long 'degraded by a cruel and unsparing tyranny, . . . no Government can exist, even for their own advantage, which does not, for a time at least, possess powers almost despotic'. Otto's rule however was an ominous foretaste of what the Turkish Empire might become if Balkanized, or, as Palmerston put it, 'Polandised'. Grey and Palmerston therefore reverted to the old policy of bolstering up Turkey to block what Grey believed to be the consistent policy of Russia since Catherine the Great. The renewal in late 1831 of Mehemet Ali's campaign to carve out a Near Eastern empire from Egypt to Asia Minor, and perhaps to take over Constantinople itself, provided a possible alternative to the Sultan. Mehemet Ali was thought to be more influenced by Western ideas, and to be a better prospect for internal reform. When Palmerston suggested that Britain should support the Sultan, Grey wrote: 'I confess I feel a strong disposition to be on good terms with Mehemet Ali.' The result was to delay positive action until Stratford Canning could report from Constantinople. His advice was to back the Sultan, but the Egyptian victory at Koniek in January 1833 made him look like the wrong horse.

In face of Althorp's refusal to raise extra money to equip a fleet, the existing forces being committed to the Tagus and the Scheldt, Grey was ready to abandon plans to help the Sultan, but was then persuaded by Palmerston to agree to sending two battleships to put pressure on Mehemet Ali. British vacilliation offered little prospect of success, and despite Palmerston's efforts to repeat the Belgian strategy and convene an international conference in London, the Turks were compelled to cede Syria to Mehemet and in the Treaty of Unkiar Skelessi to agree to Russian terms for the neutralization of the Straits and Russian rights of access to the Mediterranean. The treaty, even with its secret articles in favour of Russia (which the British government received from Ponsonby, their ambassador in Constantinople, with the copy of the public treaty) in fact made little difference to the situation. Grey gloomily predicted the inevitable collapse of the Turkish Empire and suggested that Britain's best hope was to co-operate in 'propping up this falling power as long as it can be done'. In fact the Eastern Question was to

[10]   16 May 1830, ibid. 219; *Ellenborough Diary*, 26 May 1830, ii. 257; Grey to Henry, 13 Feb. 1830, G. 25; to Adair, 14 Feb., G.1/3.

dribble on for another half century and more, to trouble Gladstone and Disraeli, and indeed Churchill and Lloyd George, as it had done Grey and Palmerston.[11]

One result of the Turkish events was to accentuate Grey's and Palmerston's moves towards alliance with France and the division of the five powers into opposing Western and Eastern groups. Spain and Portugal completed the process.[12] The tortuous dynastic problems in both countries were resolved by 1834 in favour of Britain and France, and sealed by the Quadruple Alliance of the four nations. At the outset, however, British policy was hampered by lack of naval and military forces sufficient to ensure decisive intervention, by Grey's scruples about over-throwing even the anti-British tyrant Dom Miguel of Portugal while his regime appeared to be tacitly acceptable to the people, and by the untrustworthiness and incompetence of Don Pedro, the rival contender in Portugal and father of Donna Maria, who ultimately gained the throne on Miguel's downfall. As in Belgium, Palmerston was anxious to prevent a dynastic alliance between the French and Portuguese ruling houses. The Duc de Nemours, son of Louis Philippe, whose candidature for the Belgian throne had been successfully blocked, was suggested as a husband for Donna Maria, and Palmerston used this prospect to put pressure on his colleagues for more active British intervention. Nevertheless the Cabinet split over the Portuguese question in November 1831, the majority being against Grey and Palmerston, who had to resort to secret encouragement of Don Pedro's forces and connivance at the sending of ships, arms, and volunteers. Pedro's cause nevertheless did not prosper, until Sir Charles Napier, thinly diguised as 'Admiral Carlos de Ponza', took charge of the naval forces supporting Pedro and sank Miguel's fleet in July 1833.

By that time Spain had become involved. The death of King Ferdinand, the succession of his daughter Isabella under her mother's regency, and the revolt of Don Carlos in the autumn of 1833 drew the Spanish and Portuguese questions together. Carlos and Miguel represented the absolutist principle, against Pedro, Maria, and Isabella who were backed by the constitutionalists, and Palmerston advocated more active support of the latter. Again, however, the political situation at Westminster intruded. In the summer, the government had been defeated in the Lords on Wellington's motion on the Portuguese question. Only a defiant reversal of the position by the House of Commons saved the government, but it showed that its position on the Portuguese issue was shaky. In January 1834, the Cabinet again split, Althorp, Grant, Stanley, Melbourne, and Richmond leading the opposition to the proposal for active British intervention.

Grey, who by this time was weary of his responsibilities, took it as an opportunity to declare his intention to resign and despite an appeal, signed by all the Cabinet, to remain, stormed off to Windsor and had to be talked out of it by the King. In

[11] Grey to Holland, 9 Feb. 1830, G. 35; to Viscount Ponsonby, 7 Aug., 22 May, 3 Dec. 1833, G. 48/3 and Ponsonby MSS; Palmerston to Grey, 6 Sept. 1832 and reply 8 Sept., Grey to Palmerston 26 Sept., G. 44.

[12] Grey to Holland, 25 Jan. 1833, G. 35.

consenting to stay, however, he declared that he had 'acted for the first time in his life contrary to what he considered right, and as having consented to remain in office knowing himself to be unable to regulate his foreign policy according to his own views of what was safe and expedient'. Though, as Holland remarked, the episode confirmed 'the personal attachment of the whole cabinet to Lord Grey', it revealed Grey's fundamental inability to unite or dominate it on crucial matters of policy, and it foreshadowed the collapse which came over five months later.[13]

In the Iberian peninsula, as Holland noted in his journal, 'the English had better luck than they deserved.'[14] The right-wing Spanish government collapsed, the new one sought British assistance and proposed a treaty, which Palmerston converted into a triple alliance with Portugal and then, after overcoming French objections to being left out of the drafting of the terms, into the Quadruple Alliance of April 1834. The following month the forces of Miguel and Carlos surrendered. The Alliance marked the triumph of Palmerston's and Grey's foreign policy. If the Eastern Question remained unresolved, British interests in the Netherlands and in the Western Mediterranean and Atlantic had been secured. France was now, if only temporarily, a committed ally, and the Metternich system was excluded from Europe west of the Rhine.

IRELAND: THE BEGINNING OF THE END

Success in foreign policy was gained at a price. Grey's nerves were stretched by the intensity of repeated crises both in diplomacy and within the Cabinet. His frustrated resignations in the summer of 1833 and at the beginning of 1834 were a portent. Ellice told Henry in January 1834 that the administration showed 'every symptom of a *commencement de la fin*' and that Grey 'has no longer energy to control [such] a set of men ... and that the Government is consequently utterly without unity of purpose, and the sport of every wind that blows'. Nothing had contributed more to this mood than the affairs of Ireland, a country whose troubled shadow brooded over British politics for the whole of the nineteenth century, and it was Ireland that produced the final crisis of the administration.

Grey placed the conduct of Irish affairs in the hands of Lord Anglesey as Viceroy, with E. G. Stanley, later fourteenth Earl of Derby, as Chief Secretary linking the Irish administration with the Cabinet in London. It was an uneasy team. Anglesey, despite his previous 'Tory' associations, had long taken a liberal view on Catholic emancipation as a means of reconciling Ireland to the Union, while resisting the notion of Catholic ascendancy. As Lord-Lieutenant of Ireland in Wellington's

[13] Grey to Wellesley, 4 June 1833, *Wellesley Papers*, ii. 233–4; Russell to Grey, 8 June, G. 50A/6; Howick Journal, 13–30 Jan.; *BLT*, iii. 329–35; *HHD*, 249; note by Ellice on Mary to Ellice, 17 Jan., Ellice MSS 15026; Grey to Ellice, 15 Jan., [14 Feb.] 1834, ibid. 15022; Holland to Grey, 14 Jan., G. 34.
[14] *HHD*, 250.

administration he had professed impartiality between Catholics and Protestants and a wish to govern Ireland on sensible and moderate liberal principles. On these grounds O'Connell himself had welcomed the appointment.[1] Anglesey sought to meet Irish grievances by promoting British investment in the economy and by sympathetic but firm administration of government, but like a procession of Lord-Lieutenants since the eighteenth century he found it difficult to move or even win the attention of British Cabinets, whose consistent view was that Ireland was a nuisance and a distraction from more important matters and that if the Irish had grievances they were being unreasonable.

The concession of emancipation in 1829 was typical: the British government gave way to necessity, and rather than follow emancipation with further measures of conciliation, accompanied it with measures to restrict the electoral franchise and to exclude O'Connell himself from taking his seat at Westminster unless he stood for re-election. Even on emancipation itself Wellington and Peel had not consulted the Lord-Lieutenant or informed him of their intention to concede, and had waited to be forced on the question rather than follow Anglesey's earlier advice to concede it freely. Relations between the Viceroy and the Prime Minister deteriorated and Anglesey was dismissed at the end of 1828. He was, however, publicly identified with the Catholic cause, and widely seen as an advocate of 'wise, firm, good-tempered and impartial administration' in Ireland. He was therefore a natural choice for Grey, who on the day after his commission to form a new government, offered him the Viceroyalty a second time.[2]

Anglesey's conduct in Ireland was consistent with his former policy. He attempted to strike a balance among the different factions and interests by his appointments and his administrative measures. He wrote before departing from London:

The cruel fact in regard to all Irish affairs is, that it is almost, if not quite, impossible to find a man who . . . has not some strong bias, or personal attachment or dislike. I positively have none. I collect my information from a great variety of sources, and I endeavour to strike a fair balance, and to advise and act accordingly.

Anglesey took a firm line with O'Connell's agitation against the Union while advocating conciliation of the Catholics through some scheme for paying their clergy by the State. 'I would clearly prefer this to gibbeting O'Connell', he drily remarked, and promised to work out a practicable scheme. 'We want money', he wrote. 'Money for the Priests—Money for the People . . . or there will be no tranquillity in Ireland.' 'The payment of the clergy plus a million of public works would set us going, and defy O'Connell and all his Satellites.' The real villains were the landlords and the tithe-proctors: 'If they [the Irish people] were

---

[1] Howick Journal, 29–30 Jan. 1834.

[2] *One-Leg: The Life & Letters of Henry William Paget, first Marquess of Anglesey*, ed. Marquess of Anglesey (1961), 179–86, 209–10, 218; Grey to Anglesey, 16 Nov. 1830, Anglesey MSS, Northern Ireland Record Office, Belfast.

not the most enduring upon earth, they would not bear their hardships as they do.'[3]

From the outset, in such letters as these, Anglesey marked what was intended to be the character of his Irish administration, and it fitted well enough with what would have been expected of Grey. In Stanley, however, Anglesey had a Chief Secretary who did not share his chief's liberal instincts and who was committed to the Protestant establishment and inclined more towards firmness and authority. This attitude was shared by Melbourne at the Home Office and since Stanley developed a close relationship with Grey, founded on mutual respect and similar political instincts, he gained a strong influence with the Prime Minister.

Grey's paranoia about O'Connell was so strong that he was inclined to see him as the instigator of all violence and trouble between Britain and Ireland, and to favour stern measures against what he considered to be his wicked and disruptive attempts to dissolve the connection between the two countries. Writing on 25 December 1830, Grey declared his willingness to seek additional powers from Parliament 'to check the popular violence, which he is urging on to rebellion and revolution', while assuring Anglesey at the same time of his agreement with the need for measures 'to improve the situation of Ireland', which he asked Anglesey to consider with Stanley. The difficulties involved in such a dual approach proved insoluble yet again, and Grey's reaction was to single out O'Connell as responsible for blocking the good intentions of the government.

In truth the government itself was so divided on the question that British policy continued to fluctuate almost irrationally, and to expect a rational and co-operative response from the Irish was perhaps too much. Grey himself was schizophrenic on Irish matters, ready to take a fright at the prospect of rebellion and revolution in Ireland and to authorize draconian preventive measures, yet also wishing to find a means of removing legitimate Irish grievances so far as British public opinion would allow. Ireland therefore continued to suffer from the inability of her British masters to decide between coercion and conciliation. Once again, as in 1806–7, the good intentions of the British were limited by their inability to look at Ireland from any but a British point of view, or to understand that a just settlement from that point of view might not look the same on the other side of St George's Channel.[4]

Grey's attitude to O'Connell was the product of this dual thinking. It was not only that O'Connell led the Irish demand for the repeal of the Union and sought to achieve it by arousing popular agitation. He was also convinced that O'Connell was devoted to universal suffrage, annual Parliaments, and the ballot, and so identified him with those dangerous radicals in Britain whose designs threatened the constitutional settlement represented by the Reform Bills. In Ireland, his

[3] Anglesey to Grey, 25 Nov., 27, 29 Dec. 1830, 7, 8, 10, 13, 15 Jan. 1831. Grey replied to Anglesey's request for a million pounds with the hope that half a million might do: 18 Jan., ibid.

[4] Lieven, *Letters in London*, 273, 8 Nov. 1830; Grey to Anglesey, 25 Dec., Anglesey MSS; A. D. Kriegel, 'The Irish Policy of Lord Grey's Government', *Eng. Hist. Rev.* lxxxvi. Jan. 1971, 22–45.

programme would 'place the whole representation of Ireland in the hands of the priests' and result in the creation of a Catholic rebellion against the Union. O'Connell's agitation for repeal of the Union threatened the 'total eclipse of the power and glory of the British Empire' and determined Grey to break his power in Ireland. 'The question is becoming one of Union or separation' Grey wrote to Holland, and the latter 'we must resist *toto corpore regni*'.

O'Connell had initially welcomed the new government at Westminster and at Dublin, and there were discussions about offering him a legal appointment but Grey and Melbourne felt unable to trust him. He now reversed his attitude and organized demonstrations against Anglesey's government and a run on the Irish banks. With Grey's approval, Anglesey ordered O'Connell's arrest. Legal proceedings were delayed by various devices on the part of O'Connell's lawyers until March, when the publication of the Reform Bill changed the situation. O'Connell declared his surprise and pleasure at the real reform the government proposed, and in conversation with Duncannon promised to give it his support and suspend all other agitation. In return the Cabinet agreed to drop proceedings against him on the somewhat specious grounds that the dissolution of Parliament precluded further action. Burdett also intervened on O'Connell's behalf but Grey was unable to shed his suspicion of the Irish Liberator:

I acknowledge that he has rendered good service on the reform bill; and that on many previous occasions his conduct in the H. of C. has been such as to encourage a hope that he would abstain from the pernicious courses in which he has been engaged. But these expectations have been as constantly followed by disappointment... Under these circumstances it is quite impossible for us as a government to have any communication with him either directly or indirectly.

'We know too certainly from experience that he is not to be trusted', he wrote to Anglesey. Grey's insurmountable prejudice prevented an alliance with the only man who might have been able to preserve the peace and deliver an acceptable solution to the problem, and whatever goodwill the Whigs might profess towards Ireland would henceforward be received with that same scepticism with which Grey had received O'Connell's approach.[5]

Stanley, meanwhile, urged immediate measures to suppress disturbances in Ireland and advised martial law. Anglesey on the other hand urged 'a few popular Bills... and finally, pay the Priests; and I promise you shall never hear more of O'Connell or any such fellow.' He believed that the hostility of the peasantry was against the landlords, not the government. The British Cabinet, however, was now engrossed in the struggle for reform, and resorted to the usual expedients for

[5] Grey to Anglesey, 18, 25, 29 Jan., 31 Mar., Anglesey to Grey, 22, 29 Jan., Anglesey MSS; Grey to Anglesey 21 Apr., Anglesey in *Dublin Morning Register*, 13 Nov.; *One-Leg*, 250, 243; Grey to Brougham, 30 Dec., *BLT*, iii. 89; to Grant, 3 Jan. 1831, G. 15/14; to Holland, 5 Jan., G. 35; Melbourne to Anglesey, 18 Dec., 4 Apr., Anglesey to Melbourne, 21 Dec., *Lord Melbourne's Papers*, ed. L. C. Sanders (1890), 167–70, 180–1; Duncannon to Grey, 29 Mar., G. 7/7; Graham to Croker, 23 Aug. 1843, Croker MSS, Duke University, NC; Brougham to Grey [31 Mar.], 12, 20 Apr., Grey to Brougham, 3 Apr., G. 8/11.

delaying any effective measures for Ireland, which by their very nature must be controversial, until the Reform Acts were passed. The Irish Reform Act was generally welcomed across St George's Channel, but it was seen as irrelevant to Ireland's economic and religious grievances. For the remainder of Grey's Premiership those grievances were represented by the associated questions of tithe and church reform.[6]

Anglesey's position as Lord-Lieutenant was weakened in June 1831 when Grey decided to bring Stanley, together with Russell, into the Cabinet, on the grounds of their personal importance in the government and the House of Commons. Grey wrote to Anglesey to say that he had considered whether he, too, should be appointed to the Cabinet, but that there were practical difficulties in doing so, and that in Irish affairs Stanley would remain subordinate to him. Anglesey good-humouredly replied that 'I am perfectly satisfied with the decision.' Nevertheless, Stanley's new position gave him greater weight with Grey, and in the following months it was the Chief Secretary's opinions that tended to prevail.[7]

Stanley's tendency to act without consulting his colleagues was a further irritant. As early as mid-July Anglesey wrote directly to Grey to complain about Stanley's Arms Bill, designed to subject to transportation any person found guilty of possessing unregistered arms in a proclaimed district. Stanley had omitted to submit the terms of the Bill to the Cabinet, let alone to the Lord-Lieutenant. When it was presented to the Commons, Grey, Althorp and Holland were appalled: it was 'one of the most tyrannical measures ever proposed', wrote Althorp and it naturally aroused fierce opposition from the O'Connellites.

I like Stanley much [wrote Anglesey], and I am sure he has the best intentions; but, surely he was ill-advised, (and where he got his advice I cannot conceive) in bringing forward a measure, which the whole world must suppose, had my concurrence, and which involves me, but with which I had nothing to do, and one feature of which, when *I read it in the Newspapers*, perfectly astounded me.

The Cabinet insisted on amendments to the Bill but the alarm bells were ringing in Dublin Castle. Within another month Anglesey was writing to Grey complaining of Stanley's dilatoriness in preparing measures for the relief of Ireland, whereas

by a strange fatality, every thing that has yet been announced has had the character of coercion, or of restriction, or of taxation ... I know his difficulties—I know yours—I know the overwhelming business of the Cabinet—but conscious as I am that the fate of Ireland hangs upon a thread—that a false movement may involve us in insurrection—and that the only chance of averting it, is legislating rapidly for her improvement and that principally by the employment of the population—I do again strenuously urge the adoption of Poor Laws—of Rates for general employment—of a satisfactory adjustment of the education grant ...

---

[6] Stanley to Grey, 20 Apr., 18 May, G. 11/8; Anglesey to Grey, 10 Mar., 15 Apr., 23 May, Grey to Anglesey, 16 Aug., Anglesey MSS; *One-Leg*, 251.

[7] Grey to Anglesey, 13 June, Anglesey to Grey, 15, 16 June, Anglesey MSS.

These and other measures 'are our only chance of salvation' in face of growing agitation for repeal of the Union and abolition of tithes. The initiative was passing back to O'Connell. Anglesey declared that he was sending Lord Cloncurry to talk to Grey on these matters: 'Depend upon it, we are approaching a severe crisis.'[8] Grey's reply stressed the difficulties of doing anything controversial during the reform crisis but reassured Anglesey that Ireland was much in his thoughts and would be attended to as soon as practicable. The lack of any major Irish legislation before the close of the session however led to a resumption of agitation by O'Connell.[9]

In late November Grey wrote to ask what measures Anglesey had in preparation for the coming session. Anglesey's reply stressed the importance of doing something about tithes, on which he found Stanley co-operative, but he lamented that the Chief Secretary differed from him on the importance of a Poor Law and a labour rate which Anglesey thought were equally essential.[10] The tithe question was indeed the most pressing. The longstanding grievance of the Irish Catholic peasantry of having to pay tithe to the established Protestant Church had become critical by 1830. The great increase in population and the subdivision of holdings over the past 70 years had made the burden of tithe payments increasingly heavy for the peasants living already on the margin of subsistence, and by 1830 organized and often violent resistance to payment and distraint was widespread. The result was that tithes inflamed opposition to the church establishment without providing the clergy with the support intended. Yet the Protestant Church in Ireland enjoyed revenues disproportionate to the duties which it had to fulfil towards the small minority who attended its services, and like its sister Church in England it suffered from the abuses of clerical neglect, pluralism, and vast inequalities in incomes. Church reform and the tithe question were inextricably linked.

By the same token, powerful vested interests were involved in any solution. If Church reform were conceded in Ireland, it might be demanded in England. The High Church party in England, the bishops in the Lords, and Tories in both Houses resisted any secular interference with the churches in either country, and the Cabinet itself was divided. Stanley's sympathies were firmly with the Church, and he was utterly opposed to the principle of appropriation of surplus ecclesiastical revenues to secular purposes. Anglesey and a section of the Cabinet were prepared to accept some redistribution of ecclesiastical benefices and revenues and the principle of lay appropriation at least to educational purposes.

The King's Speech in December 1831 promised some unspecified action on tithes, and a Select Committee of Enquiry was appointed in each House. Stanley's chairmanship of the Commons Committee and the rule that only Protestants should be members ensured that it would reflect the Chief Secretary's views, and

---

[8] *HHD*, pp. xliv–xlv; Charles to Frederick, 4 Dec. 1831, G./D1; Anglesey to Grey, 16 July, 14 Aug. 1831, Anglesey MSS.

[9] Grey to Anglesey, 16 Aug., ibid.; Sir H. Parnell to Brougham, 29 Sept., *BLT*, iii. 130–2.

[10] Grey to Anglesey, 23 Nov., reply, 28 Nov., Anglesey MSS.

its proceedings were long drawn out. In the meantime, in January 1832, Anglesey brought forward a comprehensive scheme, under which tithe composition should be compulsory, the State should take over church revenues, pay Protestant clergy their present incomes less 4 or 5 per cent for collection of the commuted tithes, and use the calculated annual surplus of £350,000 for other purposes. Those might include £120,000 in payments to Catholic clergy and provision for the poor and unemployed. Stanley, however, insisted that any reform of tithe must be accompanied by stringent measures to collect arrears, which Anglesey considered provocative and impossible to enforce, and on 1 June the Tithe Recovery Act was passed.

Grey, preoccupied with the fate of the Reform Bill in the Lords during these months, stalled on any further action, using the excuse of the complicated investigations of the Committees of Enquiry and the hostility of the Irish members and the High Church party in Parliament. Ellice warned him on 1 July that no tithe bill could pass the House of Commons without the support of a large number of Irish members. The truth was that Grey was concerned at the support given to Stanley by several members of the Cabinet, and was himself impressed by Stanley's arguments. When Anglesey asserted that the measures needed to be introduced in the next session should be 'General Church and Tithe Bills' followed by eight further measures including a Poor Law Bill, Labour Rate Bill, and payment of Catholic priests, Stanley exploded:

Lord Anglesey's views are so extensive, so much at variance with mine on many important points, that our intercourse... is likely to be productive not only of personal annoyance, but, I fear, of considerable embarrassment to Government... [Anglesey's] plans are so wild, so destructive of the rights of lay, as well as ecclesiastical property, and founded on principles from which I entirely dissent, that if they *are* to be acted upon... it would be impossible for me to retain any situation which should make me responsible for them.

He asked permission to resign at the end of the session. He repeated that though he would be ready to reduce the number of Irish bishoprics and ecclesiastical sinecures, abolish church cess, suspend preferments without clerical duties, and other measures, 'I am *not* prepared, and I cannot agree, to admit the doctrine of a surplus, disposable for lay, or Roman Catholic purposes.' Stanley had convinced himself that the Irish Catholic priesthood was determined on 'the extirpation of the Protestant Church and the abolition of the Establishment' and that no mere reform of the Irish Church would satisfy them. He would like to be relieved of his own post, and suggested that the office of Lord-Lieutenant might conveniently be abolished, to mark the British determination to uphold the Union. It was clearly impossible for Anglesey and Stanley to work together. Grey told Melbourne he wished Anglesey would 'restrain the expression of his feelings of discontent in consequence of our not having taken all the measures which he thought necessary' and that 'as to the comprehensive measure which he talks of, he must know we had not the power of carrying it, even if there had been no difference of opinion upon it.'[11]

Grey gave a more measured response to Anglesey's confidante Lord Cloncurry. If he had the power to do as he wished, he wrote, perhaps there would be little difference from what Anglesey proposed, but there were so many conflicting opinions and hostile interests, not least that powerful party 'which has been nourished by a system of abuse and which clings to what it believes to be the necessary support of their influence and power'. He admitted that commutation of tithe as proposed by the Committee was the first essential in the next session, but hoped that, if it did not go to the lengths Anglesey wished, it would be seen as a substantial reform, 'not undeserving the support of those, who wish to maintain Government in its proper authority, and see the necessity of quelling a spirit of agitation, kept up with the worst purposes of selfish ambition and absolutely incompatible with the peace and good order of Society'.

Grey's inability to accept that O'Connell might be inspired other than by personal ambition and that the agitation in Ireland might spring from genuine hardship still clouded his vision. Typical also was his fear that the introduction of a poor law would merely spread to Ireland the pauperization experienced under the old English system. Subject to these limitations, he expressed his 'earnest and sincere desire, to meet as far as it might be in my powers, the liberal and disinterested views, which an enlightened zeal for the true interests of your country, and a spirit of real patriotism have induced you to entertain'. It was clear that Grey's support for Irish reforms would be moderated by his fear of difficulties in getting them through Parliament. It was natural that he should shrink from repeating his experiences over the Reform Bills, but his lack of enthusiasm was also the consequence of the depressed mood he had fallen into since their passage. 'I have no complaint', he wrote to Ellice, 'but I feel wearied and oppressed from the moment I get up till I go to bed, and I think it will be impossible for me to go through the work of another session, and particularly such a session as we are likely to have.'[12]

The session of 1833 did not open until February after the first reformed general election. Irish affairs dominated the business. During September Grey, catching up with his boxes at Howick, wrote at some length to Anglesey to say that he wished Stanley's tithe reform measure to be enacted quickly in the new Parliament and that, although Anglesey considered it to be inadequate, it ought to be a satisfactory solution for the time being to that particular problem. The further question of the reduction of the church establishment and its income was, however, one 'of great difficulty and great nicety'. Some reform was indispensable, but the

---

[11] Grey to Anglesey, 5 Feb., 2, 21, 29 Mar., 5 July, Anglesey to Grey, 1 Aug., ibid.; Anglesey to the Cabinet, 18 Jan., Anglesey MSS and *One-Leg*, 263–4; Russell, *Recollections and Suggestions*, 114; Ellice to Grey, 1 July, G. 13; Stanley to Grey, 4 Aug., 24 Sept., G. 11/8; Grey to Melbourne, 17 Sept., G. 41.

[12] Grey to Cloncurry, 13 Sept., G. 10/10; to Ellice, 3 Sept., Ellice MSS 15021.

issue of lay appropriation would arouse such an outcry that he believed Parliament would not pass it. What might be achieved would be a redistribution of surplus revenues to 'a very liberal construction of Church purposes'. He favoured extensive reform of the Irish Church, and 'the payment of the Catholic Clergy I consider as altogether indispensable to the peace of Ireland. But this will be a work of great difficulty.' He used the same expression with regard to the introduction of a poor law but he promised that the Cabinet would consider carefully any proposals on these two matters which Anglesey might send over. He ended with another tirade against O'Connell and his 'base and vulgar . . . attacks, like nothing that has ever been seen except in the worst times of the French Revolution', and stressed that reforms would be accompanied by firm and vigorous repression of 'the spirit which it is his constant endeavour to excite'.[13]

Grey's letter was hardly an encouraging one, but Anglesey set to work and on 9 October sent over a paper for the Cabinet in which he stressed the urgency of positive action. The campaign against tithes, he wrote, was merely symptomatic of a 'deep-rooted and widespread conviction in the minds of the Irish community, that the continuance of this [Protestant] Establishment, in its present extent and splendour, is no longer justified' and that its surplus funds should be applied to 'necessary national purposes'. He referred again to the plan previously submitted for extensive reform of the Church, but warned that it would now be necessary to go further, for example by reducing the number of bishops and clergy. Second in importance to the reform of the Church was a system of state provision for the Catholic clergy, and 'an extensive reform in the establishment of Maynooth', a seminary for training Catholic priests in Ireland. He repeated his conviction of the necessity of the other secular reforms he had advocated in the previous session and ended by opposing the imposition of any extraordinary powers of coercion.[14]

The Cabinet discussed Irish affairs at length on 10 October. Holland reported that while the majority of the Cabinet did not support Stanley and Richmond in arguing for the principle that church revenues should not be applied to secular purposes, and that 'our House of Commons colleagues' led by Althorp and Russell thought Stanley's plan did not go far enough, yet 'after some discussion . . . and more reflection, it was felt that Stanley's plan, if neither perfect nor complete, was yet a great improvement and might satisfy the reformers. Above all it was attainable', Stanley having won the agreement of 'large masses of Churchmen and dignitaries' to it. A 'larger and better plan' would be opposed by the bishops, House of Lords, and many of the public. So the Cabinet decided that an attainable half-loaf was better than 'to risk losing all by trying to get more'.

There was little else that they could do, given Stanley's threat to resign on the principle of lay appropriation and the likelihood that he would be followed by Richmond and possibly Lansdowne. As it was, Stanley complained of the way in which Anglesey openly advocated more extensive measures and declared that he

[13] Grey to Anglesey, 12 Sept., Anglesey MSS.
[14] Anglesey to Grey, 9 Oct., ibid.

could not continue in the Irish office if he remained as Lord-Lieutenant. Grey agreed that Anglesey had been indiscreet and hoped that he might be induced to resign because of his ill-health: he suggested to Holland that he might sound Anglesey as to his feelings and perhaps take the opportunity of throwing in a word to encourage this solution to the problem.[15]

Anglesey's first reaction to Holland's letter was less than co-operative. 'I do not like the tone of your letter', he wrote on 21 October; '. . . . there are expressions respecting my propositions . . . that appall me.' He warned that 'if *all* is not conceded, and very speedily too, you will have to submit to very different terms next year.' He blamed Stanley for emasculating his proposals, 'and a pretty mess he is making of it'. He roundly declared that

If you cannot screw up your courage to the sticking place, and force the timid of the Cabinet to adopt the whole Church scheme, and then, to force it upon the King and the Lords, it were better, at once, to throw up the reins of Government, for to attempt to keep peace in Ireland whilst Stanley's Church prejudices are acted upon, is utterly hopeless.

Holland, however, persevered, and wrote two letters in reply which soothed Anglesey's ruffled feelings. Holland, indeed, shared Anglesey's views and this made him an ideal mediator. Six days after his first letter, Anglesey wrote again to Holland in a quite different tone, agreeing to postpone the poor law and labour rate until the church and tithe questions were settled, and accepting the assurance 'that *some strong and extensive measure of Church Reform the whole of your colleagues, and even Stanley himself, are fully convinced of the necessity of*'. He conceded that the Cabinet 'must be better judges than I can be of what it is in their power to accomplish' and disavowed any intention of making their task more difficult by obstructing their policies. He even expressed friendly feelings about Stanley:

You must have greatly mistaken me, if you thought I had an unkind feeling towards him. Far, very far indeed, is this from the truth. I admire and like him—but I think he has strong *Church* prejudices.

As for Grey, 'I really venerate him. I think he is our Sheet Anchor. He is all kindness and candour, and attention to me . . . I would do anything for him.' Holland paid tribute in his diary to Anglesey's 'noble, disinterested, and friendly' response and his willingness to sacrifice personal feelings to public duty: 'never was there a more manifest disregard of all considerations of self.' Anglesey's self-restraint continued when Stanley arrived in Dublin towards the end of October: he reported that Anglesey seemed perfectly satisfied with the government's policy, and promised that he would keep his own views to himself and not allow anyone to discuss the matter with him. Stanley was sensitive enough to feel uncomfortable in thus writing behind his chief's back to Grey, and asked to be relieved of his post as soon as possible. Grey too was surprised by the altered tone of Anglesey's letters, which made it impossible to suggest his resignation: Stanley's retirement

[15] Grey to Anglesey, 24–25 Oct., ibid.; to Holland, 29 Oct., G. 35; *HHD*, 204–5.

also would have fatal political consequences, and so Grey begged him 'for my sake especially' to remain.[16]

Russell and Althorp were also on the verge of resignation and Grey had to write an emotional appeal to the latter on 21 October not to force the breakup of the government and 'destroy the Whig party forever', for if Althorp resigned he too must do so. He repeated the arguments he had already put to Anglesey, that reform of the Church of Ireland had implications for the Church in England and that whatever is done for one will be a precedent for those who wish for changes in the other. Any attack on the Protestant establishment in Ireland would therefore unite all English churchmen against the government. On the other hand, resignation would hand Ireland over to those who would abandon reform and govern by coercion. Furthermore, Stanley's plan was *not* founded on High Church principles—'Tho' attached to the church, I certainly do not consider myself as a *high churchman.*' Althorp and Russell gave way and the Cabinet tottered on.[17]

The episode showed Grey's strengths and weaknesses as a political leader. On the one hand, his personal qualities and the respect and affection of his colleagues enabled him to hold together a team whose views on crucial matters of policy were far apart; on the other, his wish for practical compromise saddled the government with a policy of half-measures whose effect was to give it a distinctly hesitant tone.

Anglesey's self-sacrifice and Grey's instinct for compromise held the Irish government and the Cabinet's Irish policy together, but they only papered over the cracks. Edward Ellice, who had resigned as government Chief Whip, warned Grey in November that 'the Cabinet are utterly unaware of the state of public feeling' and that they should realize that the first essential on matters like the Irish Church was not 'whether you can come to some compromise of opinion amongst yourselves, and act in concert upon it, but whether your decision... and the proceedings to grow out of it, will be satisfactory to a majority of the popular party in the House of Commons'. He predicted that in the next House the tone of the government's supporters would be more radical and the Cabinet might find it difficult to resist a demand for outright lay appropriation. Grey was firm. He denied that he or the Cabinet had been concerned 'to retain office by a compromise of opinions'. Stanley's plan 'accords entirely both with my principles and opinions ...[and] I believe it will satisfy most reasonable men'.[18]

One of the chief advocates of the radical solution in Ireland was Durham. He was in a disgruntled mood. He rarely attended Cabinets and considered himself not on speaking terms with Grey on public affairs. On 5 December he announced his intention to 'reluctantly withdraw myself from a connection which can ... only be a source of misery to us both'. His outburst stemmed from continued dissension between liberals and conservatives in the government. Althorp, Durham, and

---

[16] Anglesey to Holland, 21, 27 Oct., Anglesey MSS; Stanley to Grey, 29 Oct., reply 3 Nov., G. 11/8.
[17] Grey to Althorp, 21 Oct., G. 52/25, part only in Le Marchant, *Althorp*, 446; Grey to Holland, 21 Oct., G. 35.
[18] Ellice to Grey, 5 Nov., reply 9 Nov., G. 13.

Russell, and Duncannon outside the Cabinet, favoured lay appropriation for educational purposes, and the first three had refused Stanley's demand in October for a pledge from the whole Cabinet to resist any amendment which would widen his scheme in such a way. In November Durham circulated a paper to the Cabinet asserting that Stanley's plan implied agreement to the principle of 'inalienability' of church revenues, and that the Cabinet had not so pledged itself. Stanley demanded that the Cabinet must choose between him and Durham. Grey, knowing that Stanley would be followed by Graham and Richmond, and possibly Goderich, appealed to him to stay, excusing Durham's extravagance on the grounds of his family troubles—his daughter was dying, the third child to do so in just over a year. Grey made a distinction between the Cabinet's unanimity in support of Stanley's plan and their differences over the principle of lay appropriation, maintaining that the latter was not relevant, but he gave Stanley his full support and agreed that Durham's intervention was distressing. He appealed to Stanley to drop the matter, which could not be reopened in this way on the eve of the dissolution of Parliament.[19]

Stanley remained dissatisfied, particularly with his fraught relationship with Anglesey, who had not maintained full confidentiality on the Church Bill. The deterioration of law and order in Ireland was also causing increased concern. Anglesey wished to deal with it without emergency powers, but Melbourne and Stanley believed in the necessity for coercion. Grey was impressed by their case. He had already attempted to move Anglesey from Ireland in the autumn, but had been unable to find a suitable vacancy and also to gratify Stanley's wish to move to a more senior post. Brougham now suggested that Melbourne or Goderich replace Anglesey, and Stanley take whichever Secretaryship of State would be vacated. Althorp supported him and they had a long discussion with Grey at the beginning of December. Grey reproached them for raising such a matter at the very moment of the dissolution of Parliament, and threatened to resign himself if either of them did so, following up the threat with an appeal to Brougham's better nature. He (Grey) had, he said, perhaps shown weakness in not acting more decisively to change the Irish government earlier, but he could not bring himself to be unjust to anyone who 'has acted kindly and honourably towards me' as Anglesey had done. In any case, it was now too late to do anything because of the elections. Brougham remonstrated, but gave way when Grey refused to budge. Althorp also caved in, grumbling to Ellice that 'I have only one wish upon earth and that is to get out of office and I care little how this is effected or what may be the consequences of it.' Durham too was pacified by Ellice though he continued to exorcise his personal distress by making life uncomfortable for those around him.

'Here we are with all the support we could desire both from the King and

---

[19] Durham to Grey, 5 Dec., G.B6, Grey to Stanley, 12, 17, 27 Nov., 2, 7 Dec., Stanley to Grey, 15, 18, 23, 29 Nov., 5 Dec., G. 11/8.

People, but on the point of breaking up amongst ourselves', Grey wrote to Holland:

Really these things, coming upon me at the moment when I ought to be able to give an undivided and undisturbed attention to the neccesary preparations for meeting Parliament will go near either to kill me or drive me mad. The disgrace to ourselves and the injury to the country of breaking up the Government, at such a moment, is not to be borne—yet it seems inevitable.

Yet, when Ellice warned him a few days later that rumours of a split in the Cabinet were getting about, he replied tartly that 'It is a little hard that our friends will be imagining and propagating statements of divisions in the Cabinet which do not exist.' Having carried the Reform Bill, he wrote, the supporters of government should 'promote and . . . encourage a quiet and moderate course of conduct' and not be too rash or impatient in pursuing further reforms which were attainable by calm and temperate means. As long as he was head of the government its policy would be to avoid 'extreme and violent changes, and putting a drag-chain on the wheels, which if impelled with too rapid a motion, it may be impossible to stop, till we are precipitated into ruin.'[20]

As Grey again tried to slow down the Reform coach, he had to contend with continuing dissension among his passengers. Clearly relations between Anglesey and Stanley were on the point of complete breakdown and as the ministers at home became more convinced of the need for emergency powers in Ireland, the pressure for Anglesey's removal increased. On 2 January Grey even wrote to Lansdowne that 'I believe the iron hand of the Duke of Wellington would be the most effectual government for Ireland.' Wellington not being available, however, a week later Grey offered the Lord-Lieutenancy to Melbourne, only to meet with a refusal. It was decided to struggle on with the present team at least until Easter and Stanley gave what Holland called 'a somewhat ungracious consent' on condition that his resignation would then be accepted. Anglesey too was making ominous noises about his disagreements with Stanley and his own position as, in effect, subordinate to him rather than real Governor of Ireland, but he agreed to return to his post, remarking to Holland that 'I do not know what to make of you all.'[21]

The session opened with a pledge from the government to introduce 'extensive and useful reforms' accompanied by a Coercion Bill to deal with disorder fomented, Grey believed, by 'those who aim at the separation of the two countries'. Grey did not look forward to the session. He was again low-spirited and depressed.

I have seen nobody but Ministers and people on business (he wrote to Mary). How sick I

[20] Stanley to Grey, 6 Jan. 1834, ibid.; Grey to Anglesey, 3, 12 Nov. 1832, Anglesey to Grey, 6, 18 Nov., Anglesey MSS; Grey to Brougham, 4 Dec. (2 letters), 5 Dec., *BLT*, iii. 235–51; Althorp to Ellice, 30 Dec., Ellice MSS 15053; Grey to Althorp, 1, 4 Dec., G. 52/25, Ellice to Grey, 15 Dec., Ellice MSS 15021; [9 Jan.], G. 13; Grey to Ellice, 11 Jan., Ellice MSS 15022; to Holland, 6 Jan., G. 35.

[21] Grey to Anglesey, 31 Dec. 1832, 13, 20, 21 Jan., 3 Feb. 1833, Anglesey to Grey, 28 Nov., 18 Dec. 1832, 15, 18, 23 Jan. 1833, Anglesey to Holland, 12 Jan., Anglesey MSS; Grey to Lansdowne, 2 Jan., Bowood MSS; to Melbourne, 9 Jan., reply 11 Jan., G. 41/2; *HHD*, 206.

am of it and of them . . . I really feel so depressed and totally deprived of all energy and power, both physical and mental . . . that I sometimes think it will be impossible for me to meet Parliament.

And a week later, 'You cannot imagine with what difficulty I now do my work,' and

My plagues multiply to such a degree as almost to distract me. It is too hard at such a moment to be tormented by internal divisions and the selfish and interested feelings of individuals. I wonder whether I shall ever again have a night of real rest.

Even a more friendly letter from Durham, with assurances of support on the Irish Church Bill and 'my earnest co-operation in all the measures of your government' could not lift his spirits. 'I would give my right hand to be able to resign with honour' he told Holland on the morning of the eve of session Cabinet.[22]

The legislative programme for Ireland was successfully steered through Parliament, Stanley making a considerable reputation in the Commons for decisive and vigorous speaking. He declared the essential interrelationship of coercion and Church reform, pledging the government's resignation if either was blocked. The Coercion Bill passed despite O'Connell's opposition and, more seriously, some grumbling from the government's supporters in the Commons, which was only appeased by the understanding that it would be Anglesey who implemented it. The Church Bill, however, ran into the expected difficulties in both Houses. The debate centred on the question of appropriation, which clause 147 of the Bill appeared, despite ministerial denials, to leave open for future application—the result of Grey's and Althorp's attempt to fudge the question in order to appease its supporters in the Cabinet. Grey then decided, however, without consulting all his colleagues, that the clause must be dropped altogether in order to ease its passage through the Lords—to the disgust of those Whig members of the Commons who had supported the Coercion Bill on the tacit understanding that the appropriation clause would be part of the Church Reform Bill. Even so, the Lords forced a number of other amendments which again caused disagreement in the Cabinet in July, leading its more liberal members to the brink of resignation. The Bill passed the Lords on 30 July, but the prolonged and at times confused struggle over the two Irish Bills paralleled the confusion of the government's Irish policy and the internal stresses which it produced in the Cabinet.[23]

In the middle of the session Grey had also to redeem his pledge to Stanley that he would be relieved of his Irish post by Easter. It proved impossible to move Anglesey from Dublin, largely because of the insistence of many ministerial MPs that he should operate the Coercion Act, but a vacancy for Stanley appeared when Durham decided at last to resign from the government, so opening the office of Privy Seal. Stanley would not accept an office without important administrative duties, so Grey tried to persuade the ineffective Goderich to take Durham's place

[22] Grey to Tavistock, 17 Jan., G. 6/15, to Lord Ponsonby, 18 Jan., G. 48/3, to Mary, 24 Jan. [2], 3 Feb., G. 29; Durham to Grey, 30 Jan., G./B6; Grey to Holland, 3 Feb., G. 35.
[23] Kriegel, 'Irish Policy', 40–4; Durham to Grey, 30 July, G./B6.

and to vacate the Colonial Secretaryship for Stanley. Goderich resisted the move but was brought to heel when Grey threatened to take the Privy Seal himself and move Althorp to the Premiership in his place. Goderich demanded a return for the sacrifice he considered himself to have made, suggesting that the Garter might be suitable compensation, but after 'a most painful scene' was fobbed off with an Earldom.[24]

One consequence of the reshuffle was Howick's resignation from the Colonial Office, a step which hurt his father considerably. Henry had been working vigorously since his appointment as Under-Secretary to Goderich in 1830 to produce a scheme for the emancipation of the slaves in the West Indies—'slaved his life out for the last two years on the question of the niggers', as his brother Charles indelicately put it. His resignation was primarily due to the frustration he felt at the Cabinet's reluctance to go as far or fast as he proposed on emancipation, but the timing of it, and his suspicion of Stanley's less liberal views, made it seem like personal pique. Grey, wrote Mary, was 'seriously hurt at Henry's conduct', especially when some gossip reached him that Henry was 'active in organizing a regular opposition' to the government's plan for the slaves which might force its resignation. 'I cannot bear to see your father wounded, and disappointed in a person he loves so much', Mary wrote to Charles: 'Do my dear Charles see him as soon as you can.' Howick did reply to Stanley's speech on slavery towards the end of May, and showed a much greater grasp of the subject than the Colonial Secretary, as was natural after he had spent over two years working on it, but the House was not with him and the government's scheme went through with some amendment.[25]

The ministerial reshuffle, by removing Stanley from the Irish Office, restored the supervision of Irish affairs to Melbourne as Home Secretary, though Stanley continued to pilot Irish legislation through the Commons. Stanley's successors, Hobhouse for only a month and then E. J. Littleton, described by Grey to Anglesey, with some lack of warmth, as 'a thorough gentleman, a good man of business, [and] not a bad speaker', were not men of Stanley's stature and, to Anglesey's relief, were not in the Cabinet. Grey also corresponded with Littleton on the details of Irish affairs and seems to have kept a close eye on them himself. The main problem to be tackled was tithe commutation, an extension of the law already passed for general composition of tithes. Littleton found the business difficult, and in November 1833 Grey was becoming impatient for the measure to be completed for the Cabinet's consideration. The draft Bill was eventually ready early in January 1834, but it ran into heavy crossfire from Stanley when it reached the committee stage in June and it was to play a part in the government's downfall in July.

[24] *HHD*, 206; Grey to Anglesey, 27 Mar., Anglesey MSS; Grey's corr. with Goderich, 5–29 Mar., G. 49/13; Grey to Holland, 21, 25, 27 Mar., G. 35.
[25] Charles to Frederick, 2 Apr. 1833, G./D1; Howick Journal 16 Mar.–10 June; Mary to Charles [12 May 1833], G./VII; Grey to Frederick, 22 May, G./D1.

In September 1833 Anglesey was replaced by Wellesley. Anglesey had asked to resign at the end of August because of his ill-health, and declared his conviction that the time was suitable because Ireland had entered a state of 'singular tranquillity', due to the 'wise, vigorous and salutary measures' of Grey's administration. It was an over-optimistic assessment. Grey was exhausted by the Parliamentary session and the unruliness of his colleagues. In July 1833 he declared his intention of resigning at the end of the session and though his speech of two and a half hours on the Irish Church Bill in the Lords on the 17th was praised as one of his best, it was remarked that he seemed fatigued. On 7 August he called Henry in to talk about the future. He felt unequal to carrying on the government further, and would resign at the end of the session. He hoped that Althorp would agree to succeed him.

His colleagues however again rushed to dissuade him and Howick noted that 'his manner betrayed a consciousness that he is unlikely to succeed in doing so.' He was worn out, he wrote to Durham in September, but his colleagues would not let him go. 'He is the keystone that keeps the whole edifice together', Holland wrote. If Ireland was to provide Grey with his excuse for resignation the following summer, it was only the pretext for what he had been wishing to do for almost a year. 'I go like a boy to school, and with very little expectation of finding myself equal to the discharge of any duties', he told Lansdowne. Apart from Ireland, the dissensions in the Cabinet over foreign policy were taxing Grey's strength and patience and by the New Year he was again talking about resignation. 'How I wish he could have been allowed to resign last summer', wrote Mary after the King and Cabinet had again persuaded him to carry on, presiding over a ministry which seemed liable to split in any one of a number of ways according to the prevailing issue. His physical strength was no longer adequate for the task. 'I am very unhappy', he told Mary. 'For the first time I am placed in a situation of supporting what I think is wrong.'[26]

So Grey's administration limped towards its inglorious end. On almost every issue of policy there was disagreement among ministers, and Grey's only object was to keep things going until the end of the session when he was determined to resign at last. 'My father has no longer energy to control a set of men each of whom is in this manner pursuing his separate objects.... the Government is consequently utterly without unity of purpose, and the sport of every wind that blows', Howick wrote in his journal. The disunity of the Cabinet was paralleled by confusion in the House of Commons where ministers and office holders disagreed publicly because of the lack of a clear view of general policy.

The situation became public knowledge on 6 May when the Commons debated the second reading of the Tithe Bill. More O'Ferrall, an Irish member, had given

[26] Grey to Anglesey, 18 May, Anglesey to Grey, 29 Mar., Anglesey MSS; Russell, *Recollections and Suggestions*, 114; Grey to Littleton, 21 Apr. 1833–8 July 1834, G. 32/7; Howick Journal, 18 Aug.; Viscount Ponsonby to Grey, 26 Aug., G. 48/3; Grey to Durham, 8 Sept., G. 12/11; Holland to Ellice, 22 Oct., Ellice MSS 15016; Grey to Lansdowne, 24 Oct., Bowood MSS; to Ellice, 17 Jan. 1834, Ellice MSS 15022; to Mary, 26 Jan., G. 29.

notice that he intended then to move eight resolutions, the last of which endorsed the principle of lay appropriation. Four days before the debate Russell announced to Grey his intention to vote for the resolutions. Grey warned that it would mean 'the immediate breaking up of the administration' if he did so. O'Ferrall was unable to move the resolutions because the Bill had been designated a money bill, but he read out their text to the House. Four days later, on the adjourned debate, O'Connell and Stanley both made conciliatory speeches, the latter declaring that he would not argue on the point of lay appropriation since it was not part of the Bill, but saying that it would be open to any future Parliament to do whatever it wished in that respect. It was then that Russell, under the impression that Stanley's speech, if unanswered, would mark the commitment of all the ministers against lay appropriation, 'upset the Coach' by declaring that although lay appropriation was not relevant to the Bill, he wished to repeat his opinion

that the revenues of the Church of Ireland were larger than necessary for the religious and moral instruction of the persons belonging to that Church.... if, when the revenue was once secured, the assertion of that opinion should lead him to differ and separate from those with whom he was united by political connection, and for whom he entertained the deepest private affection, he should feel much regret.

Shiel, another Irish member, demanded an explanation of the differences thus disclosed in the Cabinet, and Althorp had to admit that there was a difference on this point, but he asserted that all the Cabinet were agreed on the necessity to secure the revenues of the Church first by this measure. When that was done the separate issue of lay appropriation might be discussed, but it was not part of the immediate question.[27]

Russell's speech nevertheless deeply wounded Grey: it was 'very unkind to me', and Holland thought Russell spoke 'unnecessarily warmly and prematurely'. Stanley was furious, especially as Russell's words had been cheered on the government side of the House. Matters were made worse by the action of H. G. Ward, a Radical, in giving notice of a resolution 'directly approving of the appropriation of Church revenues' and announcing that he spoke on Durham's behalf. The Cabinet was thrown into disarray. The majority in fact supported lay appropriation in principle: they had agreed, as Grey had written to Stanley in November 1832, to support Stanley's plan for church reform which did not contain provision for it, and on that point collective responsibility operated; it was brought forward as a measure of government, and any member who opposed or dissented would have to resign. The question of principle was, however, still open— which is indeed what Durham had argued in his Cabinet paper in November 1832. The Cabinet thus kept its unity only so long as the question of principle was not raised, and Russell had now done just that.[28]

[27] Howick Journal, 30 Jan., 25 Apr., 1834; Grey to Ellice [14 Feb.], Ellice MSS 15022; *Hansard*, 23, 622–74, Russell, *Recollections and Suggestions*, 114, 120.
[28] Grey to Russell, 7 May, G. 50A/6; *HHD*, 252; Holland to Grey, 24 May, G. 34; *Hansard*, 23, 426–30; Russell, *Recollections and Suggestions*, 121.

After a difficult discussion, in order to prevent the resignations of those ministers who opposed appropriation, the Cabinet agreed that Althorp should oppose Ward's motion. He was about to rise in the House to do so when he was handed a note from Grey to say that Graham, Stanley, Ripon (Goderich), and Richmond had resigned in protest against the Cabinet's decision to appoint a Commission to enquire into the revenues of the Irish Church. Grey at once determined to resign as well, and had to be urged strongly by Brougham that he would not be justified on such a question. Grey replied that 'I feel my moral and physical energies much impaired' and that 'if the Cabinet is to break up, as I think it must. . . . my public life is closed.' He would concede only that if the vacancies could be filled up now and another Prime Minister designated to succeed him, he would remain until the end of the session. Brougham was backed up by the Whigs in the Commons. On 28 May at the instance of Lord Ebrington a letter signed by 169 members of the Lower House was sent to Grey, expressing 'confidence in the wisdom with which you have held the reins of Government' and urging him to remain. Grey assured Ebrington that it was 'one of the most gratifying testimonials of confidence and good opinion ever received by any public man'. He promised to try to carry on, but warned that

I feel it is indispensable that we should be allowed to proceed with deliberation and caution, and above all that we should not be urged by a constant and active pressure from without to the adoption of any measures, the necessity of which has not been fully proved, and which are not strictly regulated by a careful attention to the settled Institutions of the Country both in Church and State.[29]

The King also pressed Grey to continue. On the 28th Grey wrote to Wellesley to say that he had determined to do so and to fill the vacant offices in the Cabinet. 'Our Billy has forced him to go on, whether he will or no' wrote Creevey. One of the new ministers, Abercromby, who had succeeded Stanley at the Colonial Office, made a stipulation that the martial law clauses in the Coercion Act should be omitted if it were renewed for a further year, and Wellesley and Littleton made the same recommendation. There followed a complicated series of misunderstandings typical of a government now at sixes and sevens with itself, and all the more tortuous for Brougham's attempt to manipulate the situation. Wellesley was given the impression that the Coercion Act would pass more easily if further clauses regarding public meetings were omitted. Althorp authorized Littleton to sound O'Connell's opinion, which the Chief Secretary did in such a way as to suggest that if O'Connell did not oppose the Bill, the clauses to which he objected would be dropped. At the Cabinet, however, Grey opposed any changes in the Act and it was introduced with the controversial clauses included. O'Connell then disclosed to the Commons Littleton's assurances. Althorp refused to accept the Cabinet's decision which 'goes against all my feelings and principles', and said he would

[29] Grey to Brougham, 25 May, *BLT*, iii. 382–4; Letter from members of House of Commons, Grey to Ebrington, 30 May, G. 15/6; *HHD*, 253; Sefton to Grey [26 May], G. 52/2.

resign. He withdrew his resignation on 30 June after an appeal from Grey but after the debate in the Commons, in which Stanley made a bitter attack on the Bill, and Althorp declared he was 'dragged through the dirt night after night', and attacked by both O'Connell and Peel, he refused to go on. Althorp's resignation was the last straw and Grey sent his own resignation with Althorp's to the King on 8 July. 'My political life is at an end', he declared.[30]

Grey's statement to the Lords on 9 July was, according to Hobhouse, 'most powerful and affecting'. The House and the galleries were so crowded that Howick was unable to get in. When Grey rose, he was so affected by his emotion and by the cheers of the House that he was unable to begin for some minutes, and he began, the reporter noted, 'feebly and tremulously as if he were still overpowered by his feelings'.[31] Grey began by stating that he had no knowledge of Littleton's contacts with O'Connell, that he disapproved entirely, and that he was firmly convinced of the need to renew the whole Act. It was, however, painful to disclose that there was disagreement in the Cabinet on this question. This morning he had received Althorp's resignation, and it was impossible to go on without 'the individual on whom my chief confidence rested, whom I considered as my right arm'. He was 70 years of age, and his strength inadequate to his duties. He had therefore sent the King his own resignation.

He then embarked on a review of his four years' administration:

On the first night I appeared here as a Minister, I stated the principles on which my Government should be conducted. I declared, that the three great and leading objects of my Administration should be a Reform of Parliament, peace, and economical Reform. I appeal with confidence to the House and the people to say, whether those principles have not been faithfully maintained? ... No one in this House, or elsewhere, will say that Reform of Parliament is a pledge which I have not fully redeemed. Peace was the next principle of my Government—how has it been maintained? When we came into office, we found the country in a most difficult position as to foreign policy—many of those difficulties have been removed ... We have not only maintained tranquillity, but ... we now leave the Government, having secured a greater probability of the peace of Europe being continued than when we took office ... We have reduced the expense of all the establishments in the country; we have taken off £4,500,000 of taxation ... Places have been abolished, and the patronage of the Crown has been diminished to a degree which your Lordships may, perhaps, consider inexpedient; and with regard to which, being now divested of any further interest in the question as a Minister of the Crown, I feel bound in justice, to admit that my only doubt is, whether we have not done rather too much. With respect to the internal state of the country, let your Lordships recollect what it was when we took office, and let it be borne in mind, that we now leave it in improved circumstances—trade in a sound and healthy state, the manufacturers generally employed, public credit improved, the revenue greatly increasing, and all interests in a better condition, with one single excep-

[30] *HHD*, 253–6; Howick Journal, 7–26 May, 9 July; *Creevey Papers*, ii. 276; Althorp to Grey [29 June], 30 June, 6, 7 July, Grey to Althorp, 7 July, G. 52/2; Le Marchant, *Althorp*, 493–512; Grey to Holland, 8 July, BL Add. MS 51548, fo. 101.
[31] Broughton, *Recollections*, iv. 353; *Hansard* 3rd Ser. xvi, 1313–15.

tion—agriculture; and even the depression of that interest rather affects the landlord ... than the tenant who chiefly suffers from the bad administration of the Poor-laws, and who will be relieved by the improvement of them. Political and Trades' Unions, my Lords, have disappeared and without the application for any extraordinary powers on the part of the Government ... I look with satisfaction upon the state in which I now leave the affairs of the country. It has been frequently indeed said, that we have done nothing. Was Reform of Parliament nothing? Was the passing of that delicate and difficult measure, the abolition of Colonial Slavery, nothing? Was the settlement of the East-India Charter, and the opening of the trade of our extensive dominions in India, nothing? Was the arrangement of the question as to the Bank Charter nothing? Are the various improvements in the Law, of which the whole credit is due to my noble and learned friend on the Woolsack, nothing? Were those reforms in the Irish Church, on account of which we have been reproved on one side that we have done too much—were they, and can they with truth be said to be, nothing? ... I leave the Government with the satisfaction, at least, that in having used my best endeavours to carry into effect those measures of Reform that the country required, I have not shrunk from any obstacles, nor from meeting and grappling with the many difficulties that I have encountered in the performance of my duty.

He concluded with a reference to the accusations that he had used his position to provide too generously for members of his family and friends. All those so appointed had been given 'situations which have been laborious', and had justified their appointments by their activity. As to himself,

I leave office with a fortune not more than sufficient to support my rank and station in society, charged as I am with the maintenance of a numerous family, and certainly with a fortune not improved by the emoluments of place. I leave office, not retaining one shilling of the public money, either for myself or any of my connexions.

He ended with reference to arrangements for outstanding parliamentary business and a promise that

I shall continue to attend in my place in Parliament as an individual peer, and to assist in promoting those views which I conceive to be the best for the general interests of the country.

The speech was loudly applauded. 'When he did get under way', Creevey wrote, 'he almost affected others as much as he had been affected himself. All agree that it was the most beautiful speech ever delivered by man.' Grey retired covered with praise and honour for the integrity and ability which all agreed had distinguished his public life. 'You have honourably crowned a long political life of consistent honour and integrity', wrote Stanley: 'in these labours it was my pride and pleasure to serve under you.' Few Prime Ministers have retired to such a chorus of tributes.[32]

[32] *Creevey Papers*, ii. 282–3; Stanley to Grey, 10 July, G. 11/8.

7 Return to Howick, 1834–1845

UNQUIET RETIREMENT

Although Grey had declared that his retirement meant 'the end of my public life' he did not retreat into isolation from political affairs. There was a suspicion that he was hurt by the King's ready agreement to his resignation and his failure to offer 'any little favour or mark of honour' or to request a copy of his bust. Grey was also rather annoyed, as Mary told Henry, 'at the facility with which his colleagues had acquiesced in his retirement', and she wondered why they had not all pressed him to stay. He certainly expected them to continue to defer to his wishes. He made it clear that his resignation was personal and did not involve the dissolution of the ministry. He tried to persuade the King to continue the administration under an alternative head, though his recommendation of Althorp, who remained in office, for that position was somewhat inept in view of Althorp's having precipitated the situation by his own threat of resignation. No one, indeed, really wished Grey to be taken at his word and it was thought that he might be talked out of it as on previous occasions. Holland noted that 'private conversations, court communications, club discussions, and parliamentary debates, management, manœuvres, persuasion and contrivance' were all directed to persuading Grey to resume his office.

The King flirted with his favourite notion that this would be a good opportunity to remodel the government as an all-party coalition, but he lacked the political skill, energy, or advice to achieve it. Having sent for Melbourne, not as a Premier-designate but specifically as Home Secretary, he suggested that he open discussions with Peel and Wellington. Melbourne replied, firmly, that the present time was not appropriate for such a step, and the opposition leaders were equally embarrassed by the suggestion. Gradually and without overt enthusiasm William came round to Grey's earlier advice that Melbourne should be Prime Minister, though not before his conversations had reassured him that he would not be disposed to press reform. The King, recorded Holland, 'after cautioning him against the admission of persons with visionary, fanatical or republican principles, gave him full assurances of support in continuing, replenishing, or supplying his Cabinet'.[1]

From Grey's point of view, and even more so that of his family, Melbourne was little more than his understudy. Melbourne seemed to accept that role, and seems at first to have submitted all his proposed appointments and measures to

---

[1] Howick Journal, 18 July; Mary to Lord Ponsonby, 20 Aug. [1834], Ponsonby MSS; Grey to Lansdowne, 14 July, Bowood MSS; *HHD*, 256–9. The King offered Grey the Order of the Bath or a Marquessate a week later, but he declined both: Howick Journal, 18, 20 July.

Grey for approval, appearing, as one of his recent biographers has remarked, as 'an inadequate deutero-Grey shuffling nervously in shoes that were patently several sizes too big for him'. Melbourne's confidence was not helped by Grey's tendency to scrutinize his actions in detail and to offer advice and criticism at every turn. Holland hit it exactly when he noted that

Lord Grey's family ... expressed and I believe felt a strong conviction that a continuation of a Ministry founded on his principles and chiefly composed of his friends, supporters, and colleagues was necessary to complete his glory and consolidate his domestic policy.

Among the steps seen as necessary to ensure this was the appointment of Henry to Melbourne's vacated Home Secretaryship, but Melbourne showed that there were limits beyond which he could not be pushed by giving the post to Duncannon, urging Henry to stay where he was. Henry indignantly refused to serve under Duncannon. Melbourne cannot be blamed for wishing to establish his own control in the Cabinet, free from the visible and no doubt audible presence of the eldest son to whom Grey had entrusted the legacy of his own career and principles, but it fed the suspicion in the minds of Henry's parents that Melbourne intended to slip the leash which they had fastened on him. Grey's intended role as an elder statesman was nevertheless much in evidence during Melbourne's first four-month tenure of the Premiership. During his second ministry, however, from April 1835 to 1841, that influence visibly declined and Grey became increasingly alienated from an administration whose measures and principles seemed to be deviating more and more from his own convictions.[2]

For the present, however, such ominous portents were forgotten in the blaze of honours which flared up around Grey and his achievements. A subscription was opened for a statue to be erected at Howick, and there began a round of 'visits, dinners of individuals and clubs, addresses and resolutions from private societies and public corporations ... and subsequently yet larger meetings and celebrations to his honour throughout the country'. Most notable among these was his Scottish tour in the autumn, culminating in the great Edinburgh dinner in September. Significantly, Grey took the opportunity in his speeches on these occasions to stress the need to rest upon the Reform Act and to consolidate rather than develop what had been done. This not only drew attention to the nature of his achievement but it was designed to set a barrier against the open or incipient radicalism of men like O'Connell, and those who had become to Grey a major threat to the stability he believed he had created by the Reform Act. He was pleased, he told Princess Lieven, that the disposition of the people who attended the Edinburgh dinner was 'uniformly and strongly conservative, in the true sense of the word', and disposed

to assist the government in maintaining its necessary authority, against the violence of democratic faction. Will the present Administration so conduct itself as to ensure this result? I must fairly say *j'en doute* ... I am not without the most serious apprehensions that the next session of Parliament may produce a conflict of the most dangerous nature. Will

[2] Ziegler, *Melbourne*, 171–5; HHD, 250.

you think me quite overcome by vanity, if I say that I believe I had the means, more than any person, of preventing such a collision, and that the Tories will live to repent the difficulties which they threw in my way. I may still be called upon to interpose, and I shall do so, if necessary, fearlessly and decisively, but I never will return to office.[3]

Melbourne, therefore, was to be Grey's surrogate in restraining the hotheads in the government as well as blocking the road to further reform, but Grey did not in his heart believe that he was capable of doing it. He was alarmed by the evident willingness of Durham and even Russell to flirt with the radicals, and annoyed at Brougham's indiscretion and tendency to intrigue. Brougham was indeed suspected in Whig circles of bearing the chief responsibility for the debacle over the Coercion Bill that had led to Grey's resignation. The allegations were printed in *The Times* in August. Although Grey assured Brougham that he 'disclaimed all suspicion and belief' on this score, and indeed 'entirely acquitted' him of any such intention, Durham and other members of Grey's family were furious. The news that Brougham was to attend the Edinburgh 'Grey Festival' and, furthermore, to be one of the chief speakers, incensed them further, and *The Times* continued to taunt Brougham with its allegations. Brougham's speech at the dinner did nothing to conciliate the family since he used it chiefly to eulogise his own services to the people and the country and deplore the haste and impatience of those who would drive reform at a faster pace. Durham, speaking after him, seemed to interpret this as an attack on himself and made an appropriate reply.

Though he afterwards denied attacking Brougham personally, the episode led to a quarrel between the two men which was carried on by Brougham during what Holland called 'an indecorous exhibition of itinerant oratory', in a speaking tour of the North and Midlands and a speech at Salisbury in October. Durham fired his answering shots in speeches at Dundee, Gateshead, and Glasgow, where he received the acclaim of the people for his radical services. Brougham meanwhile wrote or inspired an article for the October number of the *Edinburgh Review* which attacked Durham's record on parliamentary reform since 1817 and accused him of compromising his principles over the ballot and the £10 franchise in 1830–1. The attack was unfair in several respects, but Grey's advice to Durham to let the matter drop was sound. 'Nothing can be more prejudicial to the character of all public men, than these attacks and recriminations at public meetings', he told Henry. There was however, a further issue involved. Brougham's disclosures violated the principle of Cabinet secrecy, as Durham wrote in a letter to the publisher of the *Edinburgh Review* protesting against the printing of the article. Russell now took up the cudgels on this issue and there followed an exchange of

[3] Ziegler, *Melbourne*, 261. Duchess of Sutherland to Mary, 10 Nov. 1834 and letters from Duke of Sutherland in Hickleton MSS, A.1.4.20 and 19; list of subscribers to Grey's statue, Sutherland MSS, D593/P/22/4/3: £2,622. 10s. was raised from 318 individuals. Grey to Lansdowne, 30 Oct., Bowood MSS; to Willoughby-Gordon, 8 Sept., BL Add. MS 49479, fos. 114–15; to Princess Lieven, 23 Sept., Sutherland MSS.

private letters in which Russell and Durham compared their versions of the discussions in the sub-committee on the drafting of the first Reform Bill.

Grey tried to restrain all parties. Brougham's and Russell's versions of events were substantially true, but he deplored Russell's threat to raise the matter in Parliament. Writing, 'as your sincere friend', he urged him 'not [to] involve yourself... most unnecessarily in a controversy which can bring no credit to the parties more immediately concerned in it, and which cannot fail to be productive of great public mischief'. Russell agreed to drop the matter, but deplored the extreme radical tone of Durham's speech at Glasgow at the end of October in which he supported household suffrage, triennial parliaments, and the ballot. Grey could not but agree. After his promise to Grey to be moderate when he called at Howick on his way to Glasgow, his speech appalled his father-in-law. 'I was astounded at Lambton's having pledged himself to the three points', Grey wrote. He had plunged into 'the depths of Radicalism'. He advised Henry and his friends among the Whig gentry of the county to refuse an invitation to a dinner for Durham at Newcastle in mid-November, and wrote to Durham deploring his speech and declaring his opposition to the 'three points' should they ever come before Parliament.[4]

Grey's chief concern was the effect this public demonstration of disunity would have on the government's prospects. Brougham, he wrote, 'seems to me to be determined to make it impossible for the government to go on. You cannot conceive the degree to which he has injured both the Administration generally and himself personally, by his conduct.' Durham, too, had exceeded sensible bounds in pledging himself to a more radical platform than any Whig government was likely to endorse. It was no surprise to Grey therefore when Melbourne's government collapsed in mid-November. 'Thanks to Brougham, and Lambton and others', he wrote, 'circumstances are now more favourable to the formation of a Tory government than could have been expected.' The only consolation—and a not inconsiderable one—was that under Wellington's iron hand 'Radicals, O'Connellites, and the whole tribe of complainers will be found much more manageable than they were by those who were too much disposed to yield to them'.[5]

The political crisis broke when Althorp's father died in early November. The new session had not begun, and the Cabinet, delayed by the absences of some of its members, had not yet met to discuss its legislative programme. Althorp's removal to the Lords and hence from the Chancellorship of the Exchequer and leadership of the Commons might involve a major reshuffle. Brougham, Holland,

---

[4] Brougham to 'P', 22 Sept., Grey to Brougham, 4 Nov. 1834, 15 Sept. 1835, G. 8/3, and *BLT*, iii. 432, 434; Howick Journal, 6 Oct.; *HHD*, 264; Grey to Ellice, 15, 24 Oct., 8 Nov., Ellice MSS 15022; to Holland, 19, 25 Oct., G. 35; to Henry, 22 Oct., G. 25; to Durham, 25, 31 Oct., G. 12/11; Durham to Russell (copy), 21 Oct., G. B7/C3, C5; New, *Durham*, 252–69; Grey to Russell, 31 Oct., reply 3 Nov., G. 50A/6; to Willoughby-Gordon, 9 Nov., BL Add. MS 49479, fos. 116–17; to Durham, 7 Nov., New, *Durham*, 268; Reid, *Earl of Durham*, i. 264–6; Howick Journal, 29 Oct., 7 Nov.; Mary to Ellice, 4 Nov., Ellice MSS 15026.

[5] Grey to Holland, 25 Oct., G. 35; to Ellice, 16 Nov., Ellice MSS 15022.

and Melbourne agreed that Russell was the obvious choice for the last-mentioned office, though Grey considered him unequal to the task. Melbourne disliked Brougham's suggestion of Howick as Chancellor of the Exchequer, despite its 'advantage of gratifying Grey and indeed the deference due to his wishes'. Ellice, who knew Henry better than most, agreed that 'a Cabinet office for Lord Howick would propitiate Lord Grey and soften the irritation of his family', but against that one reason for offering it there were 'at least 99 strong reasons against it'. Melbourne 'laughingly observed' that 'the Greys... in or out were always dissatisfied. When *in* they wanted to be *out*, when *out* they wanted to be *in*, and while he was ready to acquiesce in any thing devised to gratify or honour them, he doubted any device answering that purpose.' He noted Holland's plea that 'the position of many and mine especially [would be] most irksome, if the Ministry should cease either in substance or appearance to enjoy the sanction of Lord Grey and the character of a continuance of his *Government*', though he cannot have found it particularly gratifying. Grey was told by Ellice and by Holland of the possibility that Henry might be offered a Cabinet post, and passed on their letters, saying that he did not wish to influence his decision. Perhaps a little hurt that everyone seemed to regard the suggestion as a compliment to his father rather than a testimonial to himself, Henry remarked that he did not much like the look of the ministry, but would be guided by his father, since his acceptance would be interpreted as a mark of Grey's approval of it.[6]

Henry's decision became irrelevant on the following day when the King told Melbourne that since the present ministry was so weak in the Commons he had considered it expedient to form a new one and had sent for Wellington. Melbourne admitted that the King had some justification: 'His great distrust of the majority of the members of the present Cabinet, his particular dislike to John Russell ... the recent conduct of the Chancellor and the absolute disgust and alienation, which it has created in the King's mind, his lively apprehension of the measures, which he expected to be proposed to him with respect to the Church...', were all valid enough reasons for his wanting to look about him. Melbourne's, and Grey's, past insistence on the essential role of Althorp in the Commons no doubt also had weight. 'All now depends upon which party is really the strongest in the country', Melbourne remarked, with a burst of that practical common sense that he possessed in full measure. Grey replied that he was 'not much surprised' at the news and that he was sure the King's conduct was 'fair and honourable' in the circumstances. He considered that in the light of recent events, the present government would have difficulty in going on: better that it should end at once than drift into collapse during the session. Brougham's 'strange conduct' and Durham's Glasgow speech, 'as if nothing had been obtained by the Reform Bill', would no doubt affect the elections which were bound to follow. As for himself, his determination to take no further part in public affairs was absolute: 'my only remaining wish is to see a Government established which may give us peace and security', the first essential

[6] *HHD*, 269–72; Howick Journal, 13 Nov.; Grey to Princess Lieven, 17 Nov., Sutherland MSS.

condition being 'maintaining the just authority of the government against the Radicals and O'Connell'.

Grey's last remark betrayed the root of his thinking. As Mary told Henry, the King's action seemed to Grey to be 'the natural result of truckling to O'Connell and the Radicals at the end of the last session'. His inclination, Henry guessed, would be to support any government 'disposed to act upon moderate principles and to resist the radicals'; his only reservation about Peel was whether he had sufficient moral courage to do so. Holland deplored Grey's attitude: 'It tends to show that he, his family, and immediate followers would have held language if not pursued a course of conduct on the meeting of Parliament which would have been very distressing', he wrote.[7]

Wellington advised the King to make Peel his Prime Minister and offered to hold the seals only until Peel could return from Italy. Grey, while professing respect for the Duke, feared the construction of a ministry 'composed of men who to the last moment have acted in opposition to the general opinion and to the spirit of the age, on all questions of Reform', which would lead to 'a fierce collision between extreme principles, in which the moderate party will be overwhelmed'. He would 'remain at my moorings' and await events. Peel was 'the only person who seems now to be acknowledged as possessing the qualities necessary to a leader of the House of Commons. I ... look forward with more satisfaction than ever to ... passing my few remaining years in quiet retirement: though my best assistance, if my duty should call upon me to give it [he inserted the words 'out of office' above the line] will never be wanting ... to my friends and to my country.'[8]

The new ministry made no approach to Grey or other Whigs. It was 'a purely Tory administration', Grey wrote, and 'it remains to be seen whether the country will bear it.' The dissolution of Parliament put the government to the test of the electorate, and the elections not only failed to give it a majority but, as Grey feared, increased the strength as well as the violence of the Radicals. Charles Wood calculated the party strengths as Whigs 258, Tories 235, Radicals 74, Doubtfuls 66. Grey told Holland that 'the *Whigs* are a small minority in the House of Commons and ... there is no hope of success against the Ministers, but by acting in concert with those whose opinions are of a more decided character. The result of this seems to me to be absolute despair.' His view of public affairs at the opening of the session was 'very gloomy'. If only the Tories had 'suffered me to carry the measures, which they now declare themselves convinced are necessary', and if he had not been compelled to resign by those who by their 'impatience and unreasonableness' broke up his Cabinet, none of this would have happened.[9]

[7] Melbourne to Grey, 14 Nov., reply 16 Nov., G. 41/3; Howick Journal 14–22 Nov.; *HHD*, 278.

[8] Wellington to Wharncliffe, 21 Nov., Wharncliffe MSS 576h; Grey to Willoughby-Gordon, 8 Sept., 23 Nov., 19 Dec., BL Add. MS 49479, fos. 114–15, 122, 131–2; to Charles, 7 Dec., G. 22; to Holland, 16 Nov., G. 35.

[9] Grey to Willoughby-Gordon, 17 Dec. 1834, 13 Jan. 1835, BL Add. MS 49479, fos. 129–30, 133–6; to Charles, 16, 29 Jan., G. 22; to Princess Lieven, 13 Jan., Sutherland MSS; to Holland, 10 Feb., G. 35; to Lady Holland, 16 Jan., BL Add. MS 51549, fos. 186–9; to Ellice, 21 Dec., Ellice MSS 15022;

He advised his correspondents that moderation should be the keynote of their politics and that they should avoid raising issues of principle, but wait for the government to bring forward its specific measures and oppose them individually. 'Premature declarations' he warned Henry, might confirm the Tories in power. His chief anxiety was not to drive Stanley further into the arms of Peel. 'With all his faults he is the only man to whom I think it possible to look as an efficient leader', he told Charles, and to Henry he confided that despite his 'great personal affection' for Russell he had 'no opinion of his power to conduct a great party in the House of Commons, and still less confidence in his discretion'. He was alarmed by Duncannon's disposition to oppose the Address and carry on outright opposition in conjunction with the Radicals, but reassured by Melbourne, who consulted him at the end of January. Grey said that he believed the elections had proved that 'the feeling of the country is decidedly in favour of the principle of Reform, in other words, of the principles on which we acted.' Peel's Tamworth Manifesto had shown that even the Tories were compelled to countenance it to some degree. 'There now appears to be little difference between him and me', Grey wrote. His advice was that the party should adhere in opposition to the conduct it followed in office, supporting necessary reform 'upon safe and moderate principles, in accordance with the constitution of our mixed government and with the spirit of the age'. As to men, Stanley would be 'a necessary card in the formation of a new administration', and discussion of the Irish Church should therefore be avoided, lest he be alienated further. He agreed with Melbourne that Durham and O'Connell, 'both to be considered as Radicals', could not be included in any new Whig administration, but put in a plea for Brougham with whom Melbourne had also declared he would have nothing to do. He looked to the early collapse of Peel's government, but wished to see 'a junction which might enable you to form an administration standing equally clear of the extremes of both parties'. 'My part will be to soften asperities, to prevent violence, and ultimately to bring about if possible a junction between those whose difference consists rather in position, than in principle or opinion; but to take no office myself', he wrote to Princess Lieven.[10]

As Melbourne warned him, however, there were many in the Whig ranks who wanted a vigorous campaign to turn out the Tories. Despite Grey's advice the opposition put up, and by a majority of 10 elected their own nominee as Speaker. The Stanleyites voted in the minority. An amendment to the Address, regretting that the dismissal of the former administration had interrupted the progress of reform, was carried by only 7 votes. Peel nevertheless remained in office. Grey was alarmed not only by the attitude of Stanley but even more by the contacts established between the Whigs and O'Connell, who was invited to the party

to Wellesley, 9 Dec. 1834, *Wellesley Papers*, ii. 253; Duncannon to Melbourne, 18 Dec., Sanders, *Melbourne's Papers*, 230. Duncannon calculated the outcome of the elections as: for Government 264, against 363, doubtful 31: G. 7/7.

[10] Grey to Henry, 26 Jan., 3 Feb. G. 25; to Holland, 10 Feb., G. 35; to Charles, 22 Feb., G. 22; Duncannon to Grey, 5 Feb., G. 7/7; Grey to Melbourne, 1 Feb., Sanders, *Melbourne's Papers*, 239–43, to Princess Lieven, 5 May, 11 June, Sutherland MSS.

meeting before the session, a step which convinced him that there was a design to co-operate with the Radicals. His own preference was inferred from Henry's speech on the Address, in which he expressed the hope that the amendment would lead to a reconstruction of the Cabinet. John Allen, Holland's secretary, was convinced that 'some scheme is in agitation to bring in Stanley and his friends and get rid of some or all of the ultra-Tories.' He commented, 'That family are full of rage at what they conceive to have been the forced resignation of their father.' He speculated on the possible intention of the Greys 'to break with the opposition unless the opposition break with O'Connell', and noted on 19 March that Grey's language was

unsatisfactory, doubts whether he is to consider himself in opposition to the present Government, cannot find that he differs on any point from Stanley, averse to the discussion of any abstract question on the appropriation of any surplus from the Irish Church . . .[11]

Grey was drifting away from the prevalent mood of the Whig party, or, rather he considered that the party was departing from the principles it had followed under his leadership. He was chiefly alarmed at what he considered their tendency to consort with the Radicals. Grey's apparent hope that it would be possible to bring the Stanleyites back and form a moderate, centre coalition was also unrealistic in that it depended on being able to avoid further discussion of lay appropriation, a question which Russell for one was determined to bring up. On 7 April his resolutions in favour of that measure were passed by a majority of 25, and on the following day Peel's Cabinet resigned.[12]

The King now sent for Grey to give him advice. He began by saying that he had done so because of the satisfaction he had felt in having him as Prime Minister for four years and because 'he thought his weight and authority and his having been aloof from the recent contentions of parties . . . might render [it] more easy for him to unite persons of different shades of opinion without giving a triumph to any.' He spoke very firmly against any participation of O'Connell or the Radicals and described the main object as 'stemming the tide of revolution'. He did not offer the Premiership, though saying that 'he wished it'. Grey replied that 'he considered his official life as closed' and that the only circumstance that would induce him to return would be the hope of a coalition 'of the leaders of all parties'. That, however, was impossible in present conditions, and 'he did not feel the energy and strength' necessary to conduct the only government which was practicable.

He advised the King to send for Melbourne, or Melbourne and Lansdowne together. The King asked Grey to see Stanley, but Stanley insisted that, though he agreed with Grey on every other question, he could not accept lay appropriation. Grey conferred with Holland, Lansdowne, and Melbourne, who agreed to inform the King that they would not propose the inclusion of O'Connell or any English

---

[11] Melbourne to Grey, 11 Feb., Sanders, *Melbourne's Papers*, 253–4; *HHD*, 280–2 (John Allen's diary); Grey to Holland, 22 Feb., G. 35; to Charles, 21 Feb., G. 22; to Henry, 9, 10 Mar., G. 25; Russell to Grey, 28 Feb., G. 50A/6.
[12] Ibid. 9 Mar.

Radicals. On 11 April the three Whig leaders together with Palmerston and Spring Rice wrote to Grey to say that no stable administration commanding public confidence could be constructed without him, preferably at the Head of the Treasury or at least as Foreign Secretary. Grey, Lansdowne, and Holland had further discussions and audiences with the King, who expressed his concurrence in the views expressed in the joint letter to Grey, but Grey repeated his unwillingness to return to office, not from any indifference to the wishes of the King and his colleagues but 'from a consciousness forced upon me and confirmed after the most careful and anxious reflection, that I am altogether incapable of acting efficiently for HM's service, under all the accumulated difficulties of the present crisis'. After a great deal of further discussion Melbourne reluctantly agreed to resume the Premiership, having insisted that the King should give his prior consent to the principle of appropriation.

The new Cabinet was sworn in on 18 April, the King displaying considerable discomfiture. Howick was brought into the Cabinet as Secretary at War, but Holland thought Grey was 'not particularly pleased' with that office or with some of the other appointments. 'He does not take a very cheerful prospect of things', Holland remarked. Only by praising Henry's talents and application to business could he be induced to give any favourable opinion of the ministry.[13]

Grey's reluctance to return to the Premiership in 1835 was partly the result of a genuine repugnance to put on again the chains from which he had escaped so thankfully in 1834, and especially to have to contend once more with the disagreements amongst his colleagues which had so often driven him to distraction. It also, however, reflected his annoyance that the circumstance which created the opportunity was once again the Irish Church and lay appropriation. His distrust of O'Connell and the Radicals had now become almost paranoid: 'It is not church feeling, but timidity and hatred of O'Connell that moves him—and added to this a little wounded vanity and not a little jealousy of his successors', wrote Hatherton (the former E. J. Littleton) in June 1836. Grey was indeed convinced that the Church reform would not settle the Irish problem nor put an end to O'Connell's agitation against the Union and, he believed, the Protestant establishment in Ireland and the constitutional settlement of the Reform Act. Lay appropriation was associated in his mind with the radical programme; and it was also the insuperable bar to a reunion with Stanley, which he regarded as the only sound basis for a moderate Whig administration. There was no ministry that could practicably be formed that he could agree to lead, or take part in. He took refuge in a fretful and grumbling retreat to Howick, leaving Henry as his agent and watchdog in the Cabinet and responding promptly to any report from him of doings of which he disapproved. Henry's wife, writing in her husband's Journal,

[13] *HHD*, 285–93; Howick Journal, 9 Apr., Melbourne *et al* to Grey, 11 Apr., G. 41/3, and Sanders, *Melbourne's Papers*, 267; Russell to Grey, 12 Apr., G.50A/6; Grey to Melbourne, 12 Apr., G. 41/3; Howick Journal 10, 12 Apr.; Melbourne to the King, 15 Apr., Sanders, op. cit., 273–4; Ziegler, *Melbourne*, 192–9, 222.

recorded with natural irritation that Mary kept saying that she had not the slightest interest in the administration, despite her eldest son's being in the Cabinet. Grey 'has a prejudice against everything the Government does', Henry added, and Mary remarked that 'I have a misgiving that he [Henry] will not belong to them long.'[14]

Grey's prejudice was overwhelmingly due to his increasing conviction that Melbourne had fallen into the arms of O'Connell. Ignoring the government's dependence on Irish and Radical support or concurrence in the House of Commons, he attributed every measure he did not like to O'Connell's malign influence. When Henry tried to convince him in March 1836 that matters had changed, and 'Ireland is now governed on very different principles from what it was when Stanley was in office', he received a blast of reproof; and in December there was a violent tirade, in Lady Howick's words, 'on the eternal subject of the union with the Radicals' as well as what he conceived to be 'the government's countenancing all the abuse of him and allowing itself to be praised at his expense'. Hobhouse attended a dinner at Chiswick at which Grey was present in June 1836 and found him 'in high dudgeon' and very unsociable. 'He does nothing but grumble and growl . . . I am surprised how, by mere fluency of speech and arrogance of manner, this really inferior man has contrived to lead a great party, and to connect his name imperishably with the most splendid triumphs of British legislation.' Hobhouse was one of the Radicals in the Cabinet of whom Grey so much disapproved, and his remarks were uncharitable if not unfair: but Grey's irritable moods and his apparent desire, if he could not govern from behind the scenes, to dissociate himself from the administration did create a bad impression. 'Lord Grey's anger at the name of O'Connell, or the mention of any of his doings deprives him almost of reason and warps completely his judgement on Irish matters', wrote Hatherton in his journal. Charles assured his elder brother that Grey was not really hostile to the government, but he seemed to be on the lookout for any possible personal slight, and consequently was too apt to resort to self-justification at every opportunity. 'He was always fretful . . . when at the Head of the Ministry himself', wrote Lord Granville in May, 'and it was not to be expected that he would take a more cheeful view of things . . . when the direction of the Government is in other hands.' Hatherton, writing of Grey after his death in 1845, noted that

After he quitted the Government, he gradually dropped all intimacy with the Political associates of his Administration. Lord John Russell he declined even to acknowledge if he met him . . . of Lord Spencer, Lord Palmerston, Lord Melbourne he saw nothing—In short he seemed to resent the conduct of all those who assisted Melbourne in reconstructing a Liberal Government.[15]

[14] Hatherton Diary, 30 June 1836, Staffordshire Record Office; Grey to Henry, 20 Aug., G. 25; to Holland, 22 Sept., 2 Nov., G. 35; to Ellice, 26 Nov., Ellice MSS 15022; to Melbourne, 29 Jan. 1836, G. 41/3; Howick Journal 25 Apr., 18 May.

[15] Ibid. 7–14 Mar. 1836, 2 Jan. 1837, Grey to Henry, 11 Mar. 1836, 10 Jan. 1837, G. 25; to Charles, 13, 22 Feb., 17 Nov. 1836, G. 22; to Willoughby-Gordon, 25 Sept. 1835, BL Add. MS 49479, fos. 154–7;

Grey's mood was darkened by his disappointment that Henry seemed to side with the liberal men and measures he himself disliked. Far from guiding the Cabinet along his father's lines, he seemed either powerless to prevent deviation or actively to participate in it. 'I seldom enter [with him] upon subjects on which I deeply regret, there being so little agreement in our opinions', Grey told Charles in 1838. At the same time, Grey blamed Melbourne and others for holding Henry back—he wanted him to be leader of the House of Commons, with a more prestigious office than Secretary at War. Others, however, disliked Henry's petulant and disagreeable manner and his tendency to extreme liberal views on capital punishment, flogging in the army, and other matters which Melbourne preferred to leave alone. He was a hard-working administrator and was developing a talent for speaking in the House, but he was a difficult colleague with a testy manner, though Holland believed that he had really 'an open, generous and amiable character'. Grey continued to grumble at his powerlessness and to suggest that matters would not have fallen into their present state if he had been allowed to continue as Prime Minister. 'I was forced out', he wrote to Ponsonby in September 1836, 'by the indiscretion, to give it the mildest name, of my own friends', and 'all the difficulties which I had foreseen as likely to arise from the wrongheadedness which first forced Stanley out of office, and was so soon succeeded by the necessity of my resignation, are daily increasing . . .'

He was nevertheless prepared to help his old colleagues on occasion. He attended the House of Lords a few times and showed that he still possessed the power to impress his audience. His speeches helped to take off the impression that he had become hostile. In September 1836 he spoke on the Irish Corporations Bill on which the Tory majority in the Lords was obstructing the government and, wrote Holland, 'did us great service'. Holland admitted that Grey had at times 'indulged in censures more freely than was quite reconcilable with the part he took in the formation of Melbourne's Ministry' and that his 'invariable but surely childish resentment at O'Connell's scurrilities' created a bad impression, but these 'are in him little venial infirmities' and Grey's relations with the leading ministers were not generally abrasive.[16]

In January 1837 Russell wrote to ask his advice on the proposal to drop the appropriation clause from the Irish Tithes Bill. 'It appears to me, after all that has passed, not a little extraordinary that such a reference should be made to me', Grey remarked to Charles. He replied that his opinion had not changed:

If it had been listened to in time, all the mischief that has followed, might have been prevented—*Now* all that I can say is, that having objected to the unnecessary assertion of an abstract principle from the beginning, I should be very glad to see the difficulty . . . got rid of. It never was worth one farthing . . . to the Irish. . . . Whether *you* can now give it up

Broughton, *Recollections*, v. 55; Hatherton Diary, 14 Apr. 1835, 25 June 1845; Charles to Henry, 10, 11, 13 Mar., G. D3; Lord Granville to H. R. Fox, 27 May 1836, Holland MSS, Duke University, NC.

[16] Grey to Willoughby-Gordon, 20 Mar. 1836, BL Add. MS 49479, fos. 173–4; to Charles, 14 June 1838, G. 22; *HHD*, 342, 357; Grey to Ponsonby, 13 Sept., 1836, Ponsonby MSS.

is ... a question depending ... on what you may think necessary for your personal character and honour.

Grey's reply was not intemperate in the circumstances. 'To be sure it required all his moderation not to triumph a little ... asking his advice at all is rather ridiculous', Mary wrote to her daughter. 'If it was not for Henry', he wrote to Charles, 'I should not care one farthing how they decided.' He censured the ministers' reluctance to come to 'a collision with the Radicals', which only helped the latter to gain strength. He had warned Russell of the necessity to oppose further parliamentary reform, on which point he thought the government had been insufficiently firm while the Radicals were 'opening the flood gates of unbounded change, and threatening to sweep away all the settled institutions of the state'.

The letter may have influenced Russell's decision in November 1837 to make his famous 'finality' speech on reform but if that pleased Grey it offended Russell's more radical colleagues and it was possibly in order to placate them in the winter of 1837 that the Cabinet, whose support had been weakened further in the Commons by the general election following Queen Victoria's accession, decided to reduce the civil list and to set up an enquiry into pensions. Both were seen by Grey as 'a mean submission to a vulgar and unjust popular cry', particularly since he suspected an intended slight on his own Premiership.

At the same time he become concerned at the state of affairs in Canada where the French Canadians were in rebellion against British control. The English Radicals supported the rebel cause, drawing parallels with the American Revolution. Melbourne decided to draw the sting of the Radical campaign by appointing Durham to go to Canada to investigate and make recommendations as to the future of the colony. The Cabinet disagreed, however, on the terms of Durham's appointment and the measures to be adopted for Canada during the meantime, with Howick arguing for conciliatory measures and at loggerheads with Glenelg, formerly Grant, the Colonial Secretary. The problem was resolved when Howick gave way to the views of his colleagues, but he remained unhappy throughout the following year with 'the desultory do-nothing way' into which Melbourne had lapsed. Grey had to send a sympathetic, but firm letter in October 1838 urging him not to resign. 'Above all', he wrote, 'this is required of you to prevent the danger of further influence and power being obtained by that party ... which exists only by applying to the worst passions of the people ... I do hope therefore, whether in or out of Government, that you will feel this obligation ... by connecting yourself with such persons whoever they may be, as will afford you the best assistance in giving them effect.' Both Grey and Howick became increasingly dissatisfied with the Cabinet's colonial policy, and at the beginning of 1839 Howick and Russell had to be persuaded not to resign. In truth, Howick's position in the Cabinet had become almost untenable. He was offensive to Spring Rice, the Chancellor of the Exchequer, impervious to Melbourne's avuncular reproofs, and with Russell's help bullied the Prime Minister into dismissing Glenelg.

Disagreement widened to include almost every question of policy—army reform, the Corn Laws, and inevitably Ireland.[17]

In May the government collapsed over a Commons vote on suspending the constitution of Jamaica, and the Queen, in great distress, sent for Wellington, and on the Duke's advice, for Peel. The ensuing imbroglio over Peel's demand for changes amongst the Queen's Whig Ladies of the Bedchamber led Melbourne again to consult Grey. Recollecting his own difficulties with the Queen Consort's Household over the Reform Bill, but perhaps forgetting the time when he and Grenville had made a similar demand on the Prince Regent, Grey advised that it was not unreasonable for ministers to wish 'to strengthen themselves both in public opinion, and with their adherents, by the change which they have required', but that Peel's attitude had been 'rather harsh and peremptory'. He suggested that Melbourne should support the Queen, on the grounds that Peel ought to follow the precedent of 1830–2, when the government had not insisted on changes in the Royal Households until Lord Howe had actually voted against it. An 'appeal to the public' on the grounds of the Queen's personal feelings might not be unsuccessful: 'I think the Queen has the strongest claims upon you to support her, even at the hazard of these difficulties, in the line which she has taken.' Only Howick suggested the precaution that, before advising her to stand firm, they should find out exactly how far Peel wished to press his demand. The Cabinet decided to follow Grey's counsel and to offer to remain in office, and with Radical support in the Commons they surmounted the crisis. The Radicals demanded, as the price for their support, a further instalment of parliamentary reform, but though Russell refused to concede this the Cabinet agreed to make the ballot an open question. Grey and Howick could not be expected to approve, and when at the end of the session Melbourne at last decided to reshuffle the administration it provided an opportunity to dissociate themselves altogether.[18]

The exchange of Home and Colonial offices between Russell and Normanby and the admission to the Cabinet of Labouchere left no opening for Howick to be promoted. He had hoped to replace Spring Rice at the Exchequer, but Baring was given the post instead. He therefore resigned, to his father's delight. Grey, though angry at the way Melbourne had treated Howick, was chiefly alarmed by the evident signs that, under pressure from its supporters in the Commons, the government was weakening over parliamentary reform. Russell in particular was culpable:

I know he was much discontented at not being placed in the Cabinet on the first formation of my Government; and it now appears that this old grievance is still rankling in his breast. The only cause for self-reproach which I now feel is for having put him too forward, and

[17] Russell to Grey, 27 Jan. 1837, G. 50A/6; Grey to Russell, 29 Jan., Lord John Russell MSS, Duke University, NC (copy G. 50A/6); Grey to Charles, 31 Jan., G. 22; Mary to Georgiana Grey [c.2 Feb. 1837], Hickleton MSS A.1.8; Grey to C. Wood, 10 Nov., 3, 10 Dec. 1837, ibid. A.2.73; to Henry, 15, 26 Dec. 1837, 25 Oct. 1838, G. 25; to Ellice, 22 Dec., Ellice MSS 15022; Howick Journal 13 July, Dec. 1838–5 Feb. 1839; Ziegler, *Melbourne*, 280–2.

[18] Grey to Melbourne, 10 May, G. 41/3, *HHD*, 399–400; Howick Journal, May 1839.

particularly for having given him the management of the Reform Bill. He is a little animal engrossed by an inordinate ambition, of the most narrow and selfish character.

Mary wrote in October that Russell had held Henry back and taken the credit himself for the measures Henry had prepared for him, out of jealousy of his talents. As to reform, Grey wrote a month later,

We must stop somewhere, unless we mean to keep the country in a state of continual agitation, equally incompatible with peace, good order and good government, and I think we have reached the point at which a stand ought to be made. I am completely convinced that the democratic power of the constitution is now as great, as is consistent with its fundamental principles, and with the security of the different orders of which it is composed; and above all with the happiness and welfare of the people themselves.[19]

Grey's liberalism had now become full-blown conservatism. Writing to Willoughby-Gordon on Howick's resignation, he asserted that Melbourne's administration had been

constantly deviating more and more from the course of policy . . . to which, after the passing of the Reform Bill, I felt myself no less strongly bound by a sense of public duty, and my conscientious opinion, than by the pledges I had given. I wished, therefore, to see Howick separated from men, in whom I could no longer place the slightest confidence.

On several recent occasions he had advised his resignation but he had persevered until he could stand no more. Grey concluded with a significant statement of his own political position:

With the leaders of opposition, I have no connection; with few of them more than a slight personal acquaintance; but I esteem many of them for their integrity and honour, the differences which previously separated us have gradually diminished, and I now am not aware of any essential points on which my opinions differ from those of the Duke of Wellington and Sir Robert Peel.

It was with this letter rather than with his resignation in 1834 that Grey closed his political career. The liberal 'Lord Grey of the Reform Bill', if he had ever existed, had become the conservative and aristocratic Earl Grey, who, in truth, he had always been. The full benefits of the Reform Bill, he had written in 1835, would have been that 'Property and Station would have regained their legitimate influence', through a union of moderate men of all parties and the exclusion of the Radicals. All sections and classes of the community would have lived harmoniously under a mixed constitution of monarchy, aristocracy, and people and a just execution of the law: 'regularity, order and power' would have been restored to the State. The Reform Bill was not a beginning, but an end:

I proposed the reform bill [and] . . . carried it . . . that the Government might rest upon it, in opposing any further organic changes. I looked indeed to many subordinate reforms, many of which have been proposed and carried, as its necessary consequences, but I

---

[19] Ziegler, *Melbourne*, 299–303; *HHD*, 409–10; Howick to Ellice, 30 Aug., 6 Sept. 1839, Ellice MSS 15025, fos. 43–8; Grey to Henry, 29, 31 Aug., 25 Sept., G. 25.

considered it as affording the best means of resisting a rash and inconsiderate spirit of continual innovation.

Grey's view may have been unrealistic, and out of touch with that public opinion in the towns which he had believed would be satisfied with the Reform Bill in 1832, but it was the view with which he had approached the task of his administration. 'If', he later remarked, with reference to O'Connell, 'I had thought that the result of the Reform Bill was to be the raising of a new Rienzi, and to make his dictatorship and the democracy of the towns paramount to all other interests of the state, I would have died before I would have proposed it.'[20] But at the same time, his belief in the necessity of wise and moderate concession to enlightened and respectable opinion could not stop at one moment in time. By its very pragmatic nature, Grey's achievement served the purpose of its own time. New times would need new advances. What Grey did, above all, was to ensure that those advances would proceed within the fundamental framework of a balanced and stable constitution. In that respect it still endures.

[20] Grey to Willoughby-Gordon, 3 Sept. 1839, 23 Feb. 1835, 27 Jan. 1837, BL Add. MS 49479, fos. 216–17, 142–4, 286–91; to Charles, 27 Sept. 1835, G. 22; to Ellice, 3 Sept. 1837, Ellice MSS 15022.

Epilogue

The last six years of Grey's life were mainly spent at his beloved Howick. Creevey's affectionate picture of him amongst his family, spending the days out of doors, riding, walking, and shooting, the evenings in light reading, conversation, and cribbage, give the impression of quiet domesticity typical of any not particularly distinguished upper-class household. Until 1839 that quiet domesticity was interrupted by the occasional calls of public duty and annoyance at the way the political world was turning. After Henry's resignation from the government Grey no longer felt the same degree of personal involvement, though he continued through newspapers and visitors to keep in touch and express his opinions. His family still came often to Howick, with their increasing number of grandchildren. Rarely were Grey and Mary alone, enjoying especially the companionship of their unmarried daughter Georgiana, their favourite child.

Grey's health remained good until the last three years of his life. Though in January 1841 he complained of failing eyesight and 'the loss of animal spirits' as 'amongst the worst consequences of old age', he was still riding and walking every day, supervising the work on the estate and 'staying out with the woodcutters as he used to'. An unusual accident in January 1839 might have been fatal, or permanently disabling. He was sitting reading in his nightcap on a sofa in the dining-room after Mary had gone to bed, when her portrait by Lawrence, in a heavy gilt frame, fell from the wall and made a deep gash in his head. 'It is really only wonderful that he was not killed on the spot', Mary wrote. His neck and shoulders were badly bruised. He was confined to bed, with Mary sleeping in his dressing-room, but he was a disobedient patient, insisting on talking to her through the open door, wanting something or other all day long, and provoked because she was trying to write letters. Mary was relieved at his escape but worried at his unusual manner—'so entirely free from all irritability, and contrary to his usual custom, without any anxiety about his own situation'. No permanent harm was done, and within a month he was up and about as usual, 'his eyes more than usually bright and vivacious... if you could see him standing with his unimpaired grace, laughing talking quoting and searching for words and passages in his books, as was his wont, you would be quite easy about him', while Mary, despite her distressing ordeal, was 'as acute and lively... as ever'.[1]

Grey's health began to decline in 1843. An illness in the summer, possibly a slight stroke, accompanied by deterioration in his speech and permanent damage to his eyesight, left him in low spirits. His enforced inactivity seems to have led

---

[1] Grey to C. Wood, 24 Jan. 1841, Mary to Lady Mary Wood, 3 Dec. 1840, 19 Feb. 1840, 1844, to Georgiana, ?30 Jan. 1839, Archdeacon Singleton to Georgiana, 23 Feb. 1839, Grey to Georgiana, 13 Feb. 1839, Hickleton MSS.

to problems with the circulation in his legs. His doctors at first diagnosed gout, but as time went on the flesh of his foot began to decay, exposing the bone and suggesting gangrene. For the last eighteen months of his life he suffered constant pain, but his mind remained acute. One of his last acts was to ask Mary to write to congratulate Brougham on his speech on the Factory Bill. On 17 July 1845 he had a sudden attack of erisypelas in his arm and began breathing fast and laboriously. Georgiana tried to feed him some toast soaked in tea. He revived for a few minutes, tried to speak to Henry, but could not. He lapsed into a coma and died peacefully at ten minutes past eight, with two deep sobs, as Mary knelt in prayer beside him and Georgiana wiped his face. He was buried in the church at Howick on 26 July, his funeral attended only by his family and close friends and labourers from the estate. After lunch, Frederick, Henry, and Charles Wood walked to the sea and sat a long time on the rocks talking.[2]

Grey was one of the great political figures of his age. His unbroken parliamentary career spanned nearly sixty years, and though he spent a total of only five years in office and occupied only three departments of state, those were the most important and efficient posts in government—the Admiralty and the Foreign Office in wartime, and the Treasury. Yet, though most of his life was spent in opposition, he was always a man of political consequence and, almost from the start, one marked out from his associates as a leader. He was an ambitious man. In 1788, at the age of 23, he had declared that he would be subordinate only to Fox, and not to 'those Norfolks, Windhams and Pelhams'. He despised mediocrity. In 1827 he watched with disgust his leading colleagues follow Lansdowne into office with Canning, but by 1830 he had made it clear that he was still the leader of the party and that, despite his show of reluctance to assume the Premiership, nothing else would satisfy him.

Grey was a man of extreme moods—in the depths of despair or at the heights of euphoria. He was a man of imperious temper and impatience; obstacles to his will quickly led him into despondency. Reckless and headstrong in his youth, in his middle and later years he was accused of excessive caution and indecision when his followers needed the stimulus of action. His often-repeated wish to retire into private life from the frustrations of an unrewarding political career, his complaints of ill-health, declining energy and advancing years exasperated his friends and colleagues, and provided grounds for criticism from those who wished for active opposition or radical reform. Grey was a man who needed the stimulus of praise. He had few inner resources, and lapsed easily into depression and pessimism when his career was checked. Howick was a refuge from political frustration, but it was always second best; though he loved the house where he spent so much of his life and though he hated the bustle and dirt of London, he never reconciled himself to retirement for long. Restless and nervous, unsure of

[2] Mary to Mme de Flahault, 3 July, 9 Oct. 1843, Bowood MSS; C. Wood to his wife, Jan.–Feb. 1845, Hickleton MSS; Howick Journal, 19–26 July 1845.

his course, he was led into dependence on others and hesitated before taking decisions, though he kept consistently to courses he was convinced were right or which involved his public reputation for honour and integrity, which he valued above all else. He often felt that his career before 1830 was a failure. 'I have struggled against the stream for six and twenty years', he wrote in 1812, against 'the implacable enmity of the Court', but with no support from the people. As Prime Minister at the age of 66, he was understandably apt to bemoan the trials and fatigues of his office, dealing with 'internal divisions and the selfish and interested feelings of individuals'.[3] Yet he handled his wayward team of diverse political views with some skill, blending a willingness to listen to their opinions with an inner assurance of the rightness of his own strategies, and, above all, keeping the support and respect of William IV through the desperate crisis of 1831–2 and so enabling the ministry and the Reform Bill to survive.

Grey was better suited to office than to opposition. His life would have been happier if he had always been at the centre of public affairs. Burdett spoke wisely when he remarked that: 'He should not have been a patriot; he should have been a Minister, that was his line.' Opposition rarely presented the opportunity to make a positive contribution to the well-being of the state or to build the political fame and reputation which Grey craved. When he served in Cabinet with the Talents, or later as Prime Minister, he showed energy, decisiveness, and persistence which were often absent from his time in opposition. Lord Sefton told Creevey that when Grey returned to the Premiership in 1832 he looked happier than he had ever done in his life.[4] He was proud of his achievements, and felt, rightly, that the Reform Act was a feat of statesmanship which outmatched almost all others of his time. Characteristically, however, he saw it as a personal triumph and resented any attempt to modify it or interpret it in any way that he had not intended. Grey was attracted to politics because it was the road to power, to public prominence, and to personal distinction. He was capable of constructive achievement and his talents in office were greatly respected by his colleagues. Had he spent more time in government, he would stand among the greatest of nineteenth-century Prime Ministers; yet without the culminating success of 1832, his career would have seemed sterile.

Whatever his deficiencies as a statesman, no one accused Grey of lacking in integrity. Few public men were ever listened to with greater or equal respect. The great speeches for which he was remembered were those that dealt with matters of moral and public principle—the Bill of Pains and Penalties against Queen Caroline, those on the Catholic question, on Canning's Premiership, and his great resignation speech in 1834. A great orator in the classical parliamentary tradition, Grey's reputation was largely built on his performance in the Commons and later in the Lords. He spoke also outside Parliament, particularly at the annual dinner at Newcastle to commemorate Fox, but he disliked the practice of speaking

[3] Grey to Mary, 3 Feb. 1833, G. 29.
[4] Broughton, *Recollections*, iii. 79, Gore, *Creevey*, 356–7.

directly to the people. 'The idea of being set up there as a sort of show to bring people to hear me speak', he wrote in 1818 '—this kind of meeting I always thought most odious, and this kind of speaking, which always appears to me to border on the ridiculous, is more irksome to me than any other.' His first instinct on receiving the invitation to the great dinner at Edinburgh after his retirement was to refuse. It has been said that 'Grey loved the people, but he loved them at a distance.'

Lord Grey's mien and carriage [wrote Hatherton in 1845] was aristocratic and lofty in the extreme; but still his Address—which could be most repulsive—was in its general character most winning and attractive. His style of speaking partook of his nature. It was a fine thing to see him with his erect stature and graceful figure—and bald elevated forehead—on the floor of the H. of Lords, delivering one of his great orations, which were always vigorously conceived, lucidly arranged, and given in fine classical language—in measured and stately phraseology. He was generally in his evening dress—black pantaloons (tight) and a white waistcoat, with Blue Ribbon and Garter. He was greatly beloved by his family and domestics.

All this suggests that Grey was, above all, a Whig aristocrat of the eighteenth century, who lived through but never entirely accepted an age of rapid political and social change.[5] At the outset of his career, Britain was governed by a landed elite whose attitude to government was that of a class of leisured amateurs. The executive's responsibilities, especially in time of peace, were small: the maintenance of order, the conduct of foreign relations, and the raising of revenue to maintain the Court and offices of government were almost all that fell within its sphere. Departments were run by political chieftains and staffed by their dependants through a system of patronage. Social and economic questions were the business of private enterprise and initiative. Parliament was still a gentleman's club, consisting of great lords and representatives of the country gentlemen who filled the offices of magistracy in which the conduct of local affairs was concentrated. Parliament met but for a few weeks in the year, and legislated very little, mostly at the initiative of local or private interests. Between 1760 and 1780, only about 166 bills were presented in each session. The public took little interest in its proceedings apart from the few 'great days' when matters of general concern were debated.

By 1830 the picture had changed radically. The responsibilities of the state had widened, the management of its finances had become a major task requiring professional expertise, foreign and imperial affairs, especially in time of war, had become more complex and the great expansion of the economy, with its attendant social consequences, required the increasing intervention of the government. Between 1780 and 1830 over 15,000 Acts were passed by Parliament covering a wide field of public and private matters, and countless committees of enquiry were set up to investigate and report on a multitude of questions, particularly social and economic. Government was becoming more professional, in terms both of the

---

[5] I am indebted to Dr P. J. Jupp for allowing me to see his unpublished paper on 'The landed élite and political authority in Britain, c.1760–c.1850' on which the following paragraph is based.

filling of offices of executive responsibility and of the growth of a subordinate bureaucracy no longer dominated by private patronage. 'Men of business' became essential to the functioning of the State.

Correspondingly, the public interest in political affairs greatly increased, as reflected in the growing number of newspapers and magazines and the space they devoted to them. Oligarchic was giving way to Parliamentary government. By the time that Grey became Prime Minister, that office had developed from the chief servant of the Crown, whose duty it was to blend in the Cabinet a group of the leading political interest-groups, to being the head of an administrative machine with wide public responsibilities.

Grey was not in sympathy with these changes, and in many respects he failed to understand them. He remained a man of the late eighteenth century, as against men like Peel who were to guide Britain into the new industrial era. He regarded the position of the native and financially independent aristocracy as vital to the protection of the people, at first from the threat of absolute monarchy and later the equally repulsive radical democracy. Reform, by re-establishing that aristocracy in control of the institutions of government, would ensure that the professionals—whom Grey identified with the detested 'Radicals'—were to be kept under control and prevented from extending the faceless power of a governmental machine whose criterion would be efficiency and not humanity. These ideas were simple and instinctive. They did not arise from intellectual speculation on the nature of government or society. They arose from Grey's natural feelings. Like his policies they were not derived from abstract principles but from a practical sense of the possible.

Of his administration, verdicts have in general been mixed. Parliamentary reform has been rightly seen as its greatest achievement, though it has not always been interpreted rightly. As this book has tried to show, it must be considered in the light of Grey's assessment of the state of the country in 1830 and the dangers, both internal and external, which threatened its security and tranquillity. Grey was no innovator, as his lifelong hostility to radicalism in all its manifestations clearly showed. His aim in 1830, as in 1792, was to reform in order to preserve the existing institutions of the country: law, monarchy, Church, aristocracy, and property. Only by making these institutions acceptable in a new age and to new and influential classes could they survive into the era of Britain's transformation into a great commercial and industrial country. Far from opening the road to democracy, reform was designed to preserve aristocratic governance and the rule of property by men of intelligence and respectability. The Reform Act opened a new era of aristocratic revival: the strength and durability of aristocracy was the unique legacy of Grey's Reform Act to the nineteenth century. To regard the Act, together with Catholic emancipation, as the ending of the age of aristocratic supremacy, a kind of '*ancien régime*', is a misconception. Rather, they refreshed and revived that supremacy, made it acceptable and relevant to the new age, and opened rather than closed an era in its history.

In other respects, Grey's administration deserves its reputation as a great reforming government. If the problem of Ireland was unsolved, Grey's Cabinet did not hesitate to tackle its immediate difficulties, and within the bounds of what was possible in view of its own differences and the attitude of the British public, it moved as far and as quickly as circumstances allowed. Grey's pragmatic approach and his attempt to do what was necessary without raising irreconcilable issues of principle was right in itself, and if the same approach had been followed by later administrations it might have resulted in greater progress towards a settlement between the two countries. Few administrations achieved more for Ireland, and many a good deal less. At home, beginnings were made in the extension of educational provision through the first Privy Council grant to the school societies, the Poor Law was reformed, on lines of which Grey approved, though more by the efforts of Benthamite radicals, the first effective Factory Act was passed, and, second only to the Reform Act as the great achievement of the ministry, slavery was abolished in the British Empire. The revision of the Bank Charter Act and the abolition of the East India Company's monopoly of trade with India stimulated the growth of the economy.

Grey's ministry was responsive to the needs of its time and if its response was conditioned by the ethos of its age no more could be expected. Abroad, Britain's influence in Europe was enhanced and her security established in an age of revolutions. All these achievements were temporary, but that is in the nature of political affairs. No government wisely attempts more than can be realistically achieved in its own time. By this criterion, Grey's was one of the great administrations of modern times and its achievements were peculiarly his own. Only he could have kept it together so long, in view of the differences of principle amongst its members on almost every subject and of the external crises which beset it throughout its existence. Its most important measures were largely due to Grey himself, and without him it would neither have endured as long nor achieved so much. Grey deserves a high place in the ranks of British statesmen and practical politicians.

Index

Note: Individuals are listed under the name or title under which they first appear in the text. Cross-references are provided only where they appear subsequently under a later title or description.

Abbot, Charles, 1st Baron Colchester, Speaker of the House of Commons (1757–1829) 121–2
Abercromby, Hon. James (1776–1858) 305
Acts and Bills of British Parliament (in alphabetical order)
  Aliens Act 57, 238
  American Intercourse Bill 130
  Arms Bill (Ireland) (1831) 292
  Bill of Rights (1689) 251
  Catholic Emancipation 250–1
  Catholic Relief Act (1793) 115, 120–3
  Catholic Relief Bill (1807) 108–9, 118–25
  Coercion Bills (Ireland) 78, 256, 263–79, 291, 293, 295, 299, 300–1, 305, 310
  Combination Act (1800) 208
  Convention Act 162
  Corn Laws 207, 240, 243, 249, 320
  Corporations Bill (Ireland) (1836) 318
  Factory Act (1833) 328
  Galway Franchise Bill (1830) 255
  India Bill (1783) 123
  Insurrection Bill (Ireland) (1807) 132
  Irish Church Bill (1832) 300–2
  Pains and Penalties (1820) 227–33, 325
  Reform Bills (1831–2) 256, 263–79, 291, 293, 295, 299, 311, 320, 321, 325
  Regency (1789) 26–8
  Regency (1810) 196, 223
  'Six Acts' (1819) 220, 238
  Test and Corporation Acts 36, 54, 249
  Tithe Commutation Bill (Ireland) (1833) 302–4
  'Two Acts' (1795) 59–60, 63, 65, 80
  Union (Ireland) 72–7, 118, 121, 251
  Union (Scotland) 251
Adair, Sir Robert, diplomat (1763–1855) 112, 175, 246, 251, 285
Adam, William, Whig politician (1751–1839) 192–3, 199
Addington, Henry, Viscount Sidmouth, Prime Minister (1757–1844) 7, 17, 24, 77, 78–81, 83, 88, 89, 90, 92, 93, 96, 98, 101, 102, 104, 105, 108, 112, 113, 114, 115, 117–18, 120–8, 194, 198, 212
Adelaide, Queen (1792–1849) 268, 320

Albemarle, William Charles Keppel, 4th Earl of (1772–1849) 58
Albert, Prince Consort (1819–61) 137
Alexander I, Tsar of Russia (1777–1825) 147, 225
Allen, John, Secretary to Lord Holland (1771–1843) 315
Alnwick 129–30, 235, 252
Althorp, John Charles Spencer, Viscount, 3rd Earl Spencer (1782–1845) 254, 258, 260, 262, 264, 270, 272–3, 276, 285, 286, 287, 292, 296–9, 301, 304–5, 308, 311–12
Amiens, Peace of (1802) 78, 86, 87
Anglesey, Sir Henry William Paget, 1st Marquess of (1768–1854) 144, 249, 288–302
Appleby 130, 131 n.
Arbuthnot, Harriet, Mrs (1793–1834) 248, 251–2, 261
Argyll, George William Campbell, 6th Duke of (1766–1839) 130
Asgill, Sophia Charlotte, Lady (d. 1824) 146
Auckland, William Eden, 1st Baron (1744–1814) 104, 126, 169, 190, 194, 202
August, Prince, of Prussia (1779–1843) 225
Austen, Jane (1775–1817) 139
Austerlitz, battle of (1805) 99

Badajos 171
Baker, William MP (1743–1824) 34
Bamford, Samuel, Lancashire reformer (1788–1872) 189
Baring, Sir Francis Thornhill MP (1796–1866) 320
Barnstaple 217
Barrington, Hon. George, Capt. RN (1794–1835) 137
Bathurst, Charles Bragge MP (c.1754–1831) 79
Batley, Jeremiah, reformer 41
Beaumont, Thomas Richard MP (1758–1829) 95, 130, 140–1
Bedford, Francis Russell, 5th Duke of (1765–1802) 58, 67, 69, 80, 85
Bedford, Lord John Russell, 6th Duke of (1766–1839) 101, 118–25, 130, 131 n., 145, 151, 159, 182–3, 212, 239
Bellingham, John, assassin (1771–1812) 201
Benckendorf, General Alexander 259

Beresford family 119

Bigge, Charles William (1773–1849) 141, 221

Bigge, Thomas, of Northumberland (1739–94) 51, 64–5, 71, 72, 141

Birmingham 62
Political Union 256
riots at (1791) 53, 56

'Blanketeers' 208

Blücher, Prince, Field Marshal of Prussia (1742–1819) 176

Bonaparte, Joseph, King of Naples (1768–1844) 111, 114

Bonaparte, Napoleon, Emperor of the French (1769–1821) 86–7, 97, 99, 111, 112, 114, 166, 168–9, 174, 176–8, 244

Brand, Thomas MP (1774–1851) 127, 188

Brand Hollis, Thomas (1719–1804) 41

Brandling, Charles MP (1769–1826) 141

Bristol riots (1831) 269

Brooks's Club 23, 26, 135, 231, 243, 276

Brougham, Henry Peter, Lord Brougham and Vaux (1778–1868) 111, 142, 169, 180, 189, 204, 206, 217–18, 222–3, 225–30, 233, 243, 254, 256, 257, 259–60, 265–6, 271, 276, 299, 304, 305, 320–12, 314, 324

Buchan, David Stewart, 11th Earl of (1742–1829) 40

Buckingham, George Nugent Temple Grenville, 1st Marquess of (1753–1813) 106, 110, 119, 178, 194, 200

Buckinghamshire, Robert Hobart, 4th Earl of (1760–1816) 101

Buenos Aires 113–15, 118, 169

Bulteel, John Croker MP (d. 1843) 137

Burdett, Sir Francis (1770–1844) 103, 132, 155, 181, 182–7, 209, 211, 215–17, 223, 241, 247, 258, 259, 266, 270, 325

Burgoyne, General John MP (1723–92) 22

Burke, Edmund (1729–97) 15, 20–3, 29, 36–8, 40, 41, 44, 54, 86, 131, 178

Bute, John Stuart, 4th Earl and 1st Marquess of (1744–1814) 86

Byron, George Gordon, 6th Baron (1788–1824) 135, 138–9

Cambridge University 9, 127, 140, 164

Canada 31, 319

Canning, George (1770–1827) 15, 16, 95–6, 97, 108–9, 110, 111, 112, 114, 122, 124, 125–6, 127–8, 154, 162–4, 172, 192–4, 196, 201–3, 205, 206, 222, 238, 239–40, 241–7, 248, 252–3, 279–80, 281, 324, 325

Canningites, the 247, 249, 257, 260, 269, 280, 284

Canning, Sir Stratford, diplomat (1786–1880) 286

Carlisle, Frederick Howard, 5th Earl of (1748–1825) 243, 260

Carlos, Don, Spanish pretender (1788–1855) 287–8

Caroline, Princess of Wales, Queen of England (1768–1821) 16, 60, 109, 115–16, 142, 201, 222–3, 225–37, 242

Cartwright, John, Major, parliamentary reformer (1740–1824) 39, 40, 41, 44–5, 58, 62, 67, 71, 95, 102, 103, 181, 183, 185–6, 188, 210, 228

Castlereagh, Robert Stewart, Viscount, 2nd Marquess of Londonderry (1769–1822) 172, 176–7, 182, 198, 202, 239, 252, 281

Catherine II, Empress of Russia (1729–96) 30, 31, 33, 286

Catholic Association 250

Catholic Committee (Dublin) 120, 121, 122, 160

Catholic Emancipation 22, 55, 61, 68, 72–4, 77, 88, 89, 90, 91, 96, 97, 103, 118, 122, 128, 156–65, 172–3, 179, 190, 197–202, 205, 206, 209, 211, 215, 229, 238, 240, 241–4, 249–52, 254, 257–8, 277, 289, 325, 327

Cavendish, Lady Elizabeth (d. 1835) 146

Cavendish, Lord John MP (1732–96) 25–6, 55

Charlotte, Princess (1796–1817) 201, 222–7, 282, 283

Charlotte, Queen (1744–1818) 195, 225

Chatham, John Pitt, 2nd Earl of (1756–1835) 172

Chatham, William Pitt, 1st Earl of (1708–78) 43, 143

Clarke, Mary Anne, Mrs, mistress of the Duke of York (1776–1852) 182, 196

Cloncurry, Valentine Browne, 2nd Baron (1773–1853) 292, 294

Cobbett, Anne 234

Cobbett, William, journalist (1763–1835) 189, 209–11

Cochrane, Sir Alexander Forrester Inglis, Rear-Admiral (1758–1832) 114

Cochrane, Thomas, Lord, Admiral (1775–1860) 211

Coke, Thomas William, 1st Earl of Leicester (1754–1842) 110

Combe, Harvey Christian MP (c.1752–1818) 64

Convention, British (1793) 57

Copenhagen expedition (1807) 168

Cork, city and county 119

Corunna 169–71

Courtenay, Eliza, natural dau. of Grey and Georgiana (1792–1859) 14, 147

Cowper, Amelia, Viscountess (1787–1869) 281

Crabbe, George, poet (1754–1832) 138

Creevey, Eleanor, Mrs (d. 1818) 85

Creevey, Thomas, Whig politician (1768–1838) 16–17, 111, 144, 148, 149, 153, 181, 184, 186, 203, 228, 231–2, 247, 248, 249, 305, 307, 323, 325

Cumberland, county 218

Cumberland, Ernest Augustus, Duke of (1771–1851) 195, 196
Cumberland, Henry Frederick, Duke of (1745–90) 9
Curwen, John Christian MP (*c*.1756–1828) 61
Czartoryski, Prince Adam, Polish leader (1773–1860) 285

Darlington, William Harry Vane, Earl of, 1st Duke of Cleveland (1766–1842) 142
Denman, Thomas, Baron Denman (1779–1854) 142, 232
Derby, Edward Smith Stanley, 12th Earl of (1752–1834) 58, 218
Derby, 14th Earl of, *see* Stanley, E. G. G. S.
Devonshire, William Cavendish, 5th Duke of (1748–1811) 11–14, 151
Devonshire, William George Spencer Cavendish, 6th Duke of (1790–1858) 12, 243
Devonshire, Duchesses of, *see* Foster, Lady Elizabeth *and* Georgiana
Devonshire House 10, 15, 20, 23, 106, 146
Devonport 149, 240
Dillon, John Joseph 160
Dissenters, Protestant 36–7, 40, 42, 63, 120
Donoughmore, Richard Hely-Hutchinson, 2nd Baron and 1st Earl of (1756–1825) 163, 165, 229, 234, 236
Dublin 73, 158
University 127
Duckworth, Sir John Thomas, Admiral (1748–1817) 114
Duncannon, John William Ponsonby, Viscount, 4th Earl of Bessborough (1781–1847) 263, 298, 309, 314
Dundas, Henry, Viscount Melville (1742–1811) 21, 88, 92, 94–7, 203
Durham, county 210, 235, 237
Durham, Earl of, *see* Lambton, J. G.

East Retford 249, 257
Ebrington, Hugh Fortescue, Viscount (1783–1861) 276, 304
Edgeworth, Maria, novelist (1767–1849) 139
Edinburgh, 'Grey Festival' at (1834) 1–3, 309–10, 326
reformers at 42
Edinburgh Review 310
Eldon, Sir John Scott, 1st Earl of (1751–1838) 116, 125, 203, 248
Ellenborough, Edward Law, 2nd Baron (1790–1871) 247, 248, 251–2, 255, 275, 276
Ellenborough, Edward Law, 1st Baron (1750–1818) 101, 105, 120, 122, 124
Ellice, Edward (1781–1863) 237, 251, 254, 288, 293, 295, 298–9, 312

Elliot, Sir Gilbert, 1st Earl of Minto (1751–1814) 17, 22, 44, 52, 54
Elliot, William MP (1766–1818) 94, 101, 120–1, 178, 211
Elphinstone, Margaret Mercer, Comtesse de Flahault (1788–1867) 224–5, 237, 282
Erskine, Thomas, 1st Baron Erskine (1750–1823) 40, 46, 50, 100, 122, 124, 127
Eton school 8, 135, 138

Fallodon 7, 8, 14
Farington, Joseph RA (1747–1821) 150, 200
Fazakerley, John Nicholas MP (1787–1852) 256
Fenwick, Dr J. R., of Durham (1761–1855) 210–11, 220
Ferdinand VII, King of Spain (1784–1833) 287
Fingall, Arthur James Plunkett, 8th Earl of (1759–1836) 120, 121, 157–60, 162
Letter to (pamphlet) 162
Fitzgerald, Lord Edward (1763–98) 41
Fitzherbert, Maria Anne, wife of George IV (1756–1837) 12, 18, 96, 201, 233
Fitzpatrick, Richard, General MP (1747–1813) 26, 67, 101
Fitzwilliam, William Wentworth, 2nd Earl (1748–1833) 38–9, 41, 47, 54–5, 64, 69, 72, 77, 78, 80, 92, 93, 100, 102, 108, 120, 124–5, 128, 151, 153, 154, 156, 159, 166, 169, 178, 196, 198, 200, 204, 209–14, 218–19, 220, 221, 228–9, 235, 236–9, 243
Flahault, Auguste-Charles-Joseph, Comte de (1785–1870) 282
Flood, Henry MP (1732–91) 39, 49
Folkestone, William Playdell Bouverie, Viscount, 3rd Earl of Radnor (1779–1869) 103, 182, 209, 259
Foster, Sir Augustus John (1780–1848) 110
Foster, Lady Elizabeth, Duchess of Devonshire (1758–1824) 12, 13, 26, 28, 29, 104, 110
Fox, Charles James (1749–1806)
character and political leadership 10, 12, 19, 34, 36, 37–8, 41, 47, 54, 55, 67, 68, 69, 70, 76–7, 80, 84–7, 91, 135, 155, 324
oratory 15, 16, 21, 142
and Regency crisis 25–9
relations with Prince of Wales 18, 88
relations with Grey 24, 68, 80–1, 83–7, 94, 105–6
and Whig party split (1792–4) 36, 42–4, 52, 54, 56–7
in opposition (1792–1806) 58–60, 67, 69, 72, 78, 79, 81–2, 88–94, 96, 98–100, 175, 208
views on foreign affairs 30, 32, 33–5, 54–5, 56, 60, 86–7, 97–8, 179
on parliamentary reform 39, 43–4, 46–8, 50, 55, 64, 77, 102–3
on Catholic question 55, 96

Fox, Charles James (*cont.*):
in Ministry of Talents 100–1, 104, 127
illness and death 106
political legacy 107, 109, 110, 111, 115, 117, 118, 127, 128, 131, 142, 166–7, 170, 180, 190, 196, 324
Francis, Sir Philip MP (1740–1818) 23, 38, 40–1, 47, 50, 63, 101
French Revolution (1789) 24, 35, 36–8, 43, 46, 48, 50, 54–5, 153, 179
French Revolution (1830) 256, 259, 283
Friends of the People, Society of 36, 38–53, 55, 58, 61–4, 66, 135, 186

Gascoyne, Isaac, General MP (*c.*1763–1841) 267
George III, King (1738–1820) 10, 21, 24–9, 38, 44, 63, 69, 77, 81, 84, 88, 92, 93, 96, 98, 100, 101, 102, 103, 104, 108, 112, 116, 121, 122–6, 127, 128, 156, 157, 158, 159–61, 165, 173, 188, 190, 192, 195, 198, 221
George, Prince of Wales, Prince Regent, George IV (1762–1830) 12, 18–19, 25–9, 60, 69, 79, 85, 86, 88–9, 92, 96, 102, 106–7, 109, 115–16, 127, 162–5, 178, 190–3, 195–204, 212, 218, 220, 222–30, 234, 236–7, 241, 244, 247–52, 254–5, 320
Georgiana, Duchess of Devonshire (1757–1806) 11–15, 25–6, 28, 95, 98, 135, 146, 147, 201
Glasgow 42, 311, 312
Glenelg, Baron, *see* Grant, Charles
'Glorious Revolution', English (1688–9) 75
Goderich, Frederick John Robinson, Viscount, Earl of Ripon (1782–1859) 247, 248, 260, 298–9, 301, 304
Gordon, Sir James Willoughby (1772–1851) 208, 213, 227, 321
Graham, Sir James Robert George MP (1792–1861) 260, 263, 298, 304
Grampound, Cornwall 217, 239
Grant, Charles, 1st Baron Glenelg (1778–1866) 260, 287, 319
Granville, 1st Earl, *see* Leveson-Gower, Granville
Grattan, Henry MP (1746–1820) 72, 90, 121, 125, 128, 158, 164–5
Grenville, Thomas MP (1755–1846) 96, 106–8, 114–15, 124, 130–1, 151, 169, 184, 196, 197
Grenville, William Wyndham, 1st Baron Grenville (1759–1834)
relations with Pitt 32, 78, 88, 89, 91, 93, 98–9
relations with Canning 122, 124, 125, 127, 154, 241
in negotiations with Whigs (1802–4) 78, 88–91, 93, 98–9
as Prime Minister (1806–7) 100–12, 116–17, 122–5, 127–8
as co-leader of opposition (1807–17) 126–8,

130–1, 152–6, 161, 166–7, 169–70, 182–3, 185–6, 190, 205, 207, 211–12
on Regency and negotiations with Prince (1810–12) 190–5, 197–200, 201–4, 320
ends alliance with Grey 212–14
support of Liverpool 220, 238
views on Catholic question 88, 90, 91, 96, 97, 98, 118, 127, 129, 157, 162–3, 172
views on foreign policy 78, 88, 111, 112–15, 128, 166, 169, 175–9
views on reform 91, 166, 181–5, 185–7, 211
Greville, Charles Cavendish Fulke, diarist (1794–1865) 230, 245, 257, 258, 281
Grey, Caroline (1799–1875) 137
Grey, Sir Charles, General, 1st Earl (1729–1807) 7–8, 9, 64, 71, 79, 81, 83, 89 n., 95, 105, 130, 132
Grey, Charles, 2nd Earl (1764–1845)
1. *Personal details*
birth and childhood 7–8
education 8–9, 138, 145
appearance 135, 326
personality, character, and qualities 7–8, 23–4, 25, 68, 81–4, 110–11, 135–6, 151, 155, 206, 237–9, 240, 242, 251–2, 258–9, 261–2, 266, 324–6
marriage and family life 14, 72, 83–4, 94, 130, 135–46, 192, 323–4
recreations 70, 136–9, 148–50
oratory 15–17, 42, 245–6, 325–6
elections to House of Commons 9–10, 65, 129–31
illness and death 323–4
assessment of 324–8
2. *Relationships*
friendships at Eton 8–9
parents 7–8, 71, 83, 89 n., 95
Sir Henry Grey 7–9, 136
Georgiana, Duchess of Devonshire 11–15, 146–7
Charles James Fox 10–12, 15, 20, 30, 55, 56, 57–8, 68, 81–2, 84–5, 106 n.
Prince of Wales (George IV) 18–19, 26, 60–1, 88–9, 106–7, 115–16, 191–204
Princess Charlotte 222–7
R. B. Sheridan 26, 29–30, 38, 76, 80, 88–9, 193, 195
Samuel Whitbread 101, 152–5, 166–8, 170, 185
Lord Grenville 89–91, 104, 109, 111–12, 155–6, 166, 174–9, 190–5, 205, 212–13
George Canning 95–6, 109, 154, 241–7
Daniel O'Connell 289–92, 295, 314–17
E. G. Stanley 291–2, 307, 314–16
Henry Brougham 229, 310–12
Princess Lieven 147, 281–2
J. G. Lambton, Earl of Durham 137, 270, 298, 300, 310–12

King William IV 264–5, 267–78, 305, 308, 315
attitude to Pitt 17–20, 52–3, 60, 93

3. *Political principles*
10, 11, 36, 42–3, 48–9, 56–8, 64, 128–9, 141,
159, 162, 166, 175–85, 205–6, 208–10, 213,
215–16, 259–60, 314, 321–2, 326–7

4. *Views on political questions*
Catholic emancipation and Ireland 72–5, 96–7,
118–28, 156–65, 240, 250–2, 288–305, 316–
19
Foreign affairs 30–5, 86–7, 111–15, 252–3, 279–
81, 283–8
French revolution and war 36, 56–7, 60, 64
Napoleonic war 86–7, 97, 99, 165–79
Parliamentary reform 2–3, 38–51, 53, 55, 61–
2, 64–7, 71–2, 74–5, 129, 179–89, 209–21,
237–9, 259, 264–5, 268–9, 275, 278, 309–11,
321–2

5. *Offices*
Leadership of whig party 110–12, 155–6, 205–
7, 237–43, 246–7
Leadership of House of Commons (1806–7)
110–11
First Lord of Admiralty (1806) 100, 104–5
Foreign Secretary (1806–7) 108, 111–15
Prime Minister (1830–4) 258–307, 315–16,
325

6. *Major speeches* (in chronological order)
French commercial treaty (1787) 17
impeachment of Warren Hastings (1788)
21–2
Ochakov crisis (1791) 34
parliamentary reform (1792) 43; (1793) 48–9;
(1797) 66; (1800) 74–5
proclamation against seditious writings (1792)
52–4
Irish Act of Union (1800) 73–5
state of public affairs (1805) 97
abolition of slave trade (1807) 117
Address (1807) 131
state of nation (1810) 173, 186–7
reform (1817) 213
Bill of Pains & Penalties (1820) 232–3
Canning's administration (1827) 243–5
Catholic emancipation (1829) 250–1
Address (1830) 257
policy of his government (1830) 262–3
Reform Bill (1832) 275
resignation (1834) 305–7
at Edinburgh (1834) 2, 309
Grey, Charles, General (1804–70) 92, 136, 137–
9, 142–4, 145, 246, 302, 314, 317–19
Grey, Elizabeth, Countess (c.1745–1822) 7–8
Grey (later Whitbread), Elizabeth (d. 1846) 8
Grey, Elizabeth (1798–1880) 137
Grey, Frances Richard, Rector of Morpeth
(1813–90) 137

Grey, Frederick William, Admiral (1805–78) 137,
324
Grey, George (1767–1828) 7, 105
Grey, George, Admiral (1809–91) 137
Grey, Georgiana (b. 1801) 137, 145–6, 323–4
Grey, (later Ellice), Hannah Althea (d. 1832) 8
Grey, Sir Henry, 2nd Bart (1722–1808) 7, 9, 130,
135–6, 137
Grey, Henry, Viscount Howick, 3rd Earl (1802–
94) 137, 139–42, 144, 145, 240, 249, 251,
254–5, 270, 272, 288, 301–3, 308–9, 310,
311–21, 323–4
Grey, Henry Cavendish (1814–80) 137
Grey, Henry George (1766–1845) 7, 105
Grey, John, Canon of Durham (1812–95) 137,
144
Grey, Louisa, later Countess of Durham (1797–
1841) 14, 137, 145
Grey, Maria (Copley), Lady Howick (d. 1879)
316–17
Grey, Mary Elizabeth (Ponsonby), Countess
(c.1774–1861) 1, 14, 59, 78, 81, 83, 87, 92,
94, 130, 135–6, 145–6, 149, 151, 155, 157,
162, 167, 191–2, 195, 205, 215, 220, 226,
229–30, 232, 238, 240, 245, 248, 251, 256,
265, 270, 282, 300, 301–2, 303, 308, 313, 317,
319, 321, 323–4
Grey, Mary, later Viscountess Halifax (1807–84)
137
Grey, Thomas (1810–26) 137
Grey, William (1808–15) 137
Grey, William George (1819–65) 137–8, 144–5
Guilford, George Augustus North, 3rd Earl
(1757–1802) 58, 67, 69

Habeas Corpus Act 59, 79, 209, 212–14
Halford, Sir Henry, royal physician (1766–1844)
195
Hampshire 219
Hanover 113, 285
Hardwicke, Philip Yorke, 3rd Earl (1757–1834)
97
Hardy, Thomas, secretary to London Cor-
responding Society (1752–1832) 58–9
Hare, James, friend of Fox (1749–1804) 41
Harrowby, Dudley Ryder, 1st Earl of (1762–1847)
269, 274–6
Hastings, Warren, Governor-General of India
(1732–1818) 21–3
Hatherton, Lord, see Littleton, E. J
Hawkesbury, Lord, see Jenkinson, R. B.
Heath, Revd Dr George, Headmaster of Eton
(c.1748–1822) 8
Herries, John Charles MP (1778–1855) 247
Hertford, Isabella Anne, Lady (d. 1836) 127

Hobhouse, John Cam, 1st Baron Broughton de Gyfford (1786–1869) 135, 150, 209, 215–17, 240, 248, 262, 275, 277, 302, 305, 317

Holland, Elizabeth Vassall Fox, Lady (1770–1845) 14, 15, 20, 70, 80, 139, 148, 149, 157, 158, 169, 174, 179, 206, 209, 214, 238

Holland, Henry Richard Fox, 3rd Baron (1773–1840)
  activities and views in domestic politics 83, 106–8, 123–4, 159, 161, 184, 186, 191, 193, 194, 206, 209, 214, 216, 218, 221, 228, 235, 239, 240, 243, 246–7, 250, 257, 292, 300, 304, 310, 311–12, 316
  on foreign affairs 111–15, 169, 171, 175, 176, 177, 252, 279–80, 282–4
  in Grey's Cabinet (1830–4) 260–1, 269, 279–80, 296–7
  on Grey, 16, 41–2, 128, 151, 153, 187, 204, 205, 215, 232, 237–8, 246, 260, 275, 288, 302, 308, 313, 318
  as correspondent and memorialist 64, 67, 94, 116, 117, 130, 154, 163, 174, 197, 211, 215, 223, 231, 236, 238, 249, 250, 299

Hone, William, journalist (1780–1842) 208

Horner, Francis MP (1778–1817) 110, 169, 180, 204

Howe, Richard William Penn Curzon, 1st Earl (1796–1870) 268, 320

Howick 7, 14, 65, 67, 70, 81, 83, 87, 90, 94, 98, 104, 130, 135–9, 145, 147, 148–50, 155, 170, 177, 191, 204, 205, 214, 220, 226, 234–5, 240, 248, 295, 309, 316, 323–4

Howick, Lord and Lady, *see* Grey, Henry, and Maria

Hume, Joseph MP (1777–1855) 259

Hunt, Henry, radical orator (1773–1835) 208–11, 217–18

Hunt, James Henry Leigh, journalist (1784–1859) 188

Huskisson, William (1770–1830) 247, 249, 257

Hutchinson, Sir John Hely, Baron, later 2nd Earl of Donoughmore, Major-General (1757–1832) 195

Inglis, Sir Robert MP, 2nd Bart (1786–1855) 277

Ireland, Pitt's commercial resolutions (1785) 24
  Union with Great Britain 72–6, 118, 251, 290
  and Ministry of the Talents 118–22, 156, 290
  under Grey's ministry (1830–4) 288–305
  Orangemen in 119, 128
  'Threshers' in 120
  Catholic question in, *see* Catholic emancipation

Isabella II, Queen of Spain (1830–1904) 287

Jenkinson, Robert Banks, Baron Hawkesbury, 2nd Earl of Liverpool, Prime Minister (1770–1828) 49–50, 100, 125, 156, 164, 178, 201–2, 214, 222, 226, 230, 233, 241, 244, 246, 248

Jersey, George Child Villiers, 5th Earl of (1773–1859) 256

Jervis, Sir John, Earl of St Vincent (1735–1823) 71 n., 79, 81, 88, 95–6

Jones, John Gale, radical journalist (1769–1838) 185

Keogh, John, Irish leader (1740–1817) 120, 121, 122, 128

Labouchère, Henry MP (1798–1869) 320

Lamb, Elizabeth (Milbanke) 1st Lady Melbourne (1752–1818) 12–13

Lamb, George MP (1784–1834) 216

Lambton, John George, 1st Earl of Durham (1792–1840) 8, 137, 145, 180, 210, 211, 216, 221, 228, 235, 239, 247, 249, 260–1, 263–4, 267, 269, 270–1, 276, 282, 298–9, 300–1, 302, 304, 310–12, 314, 319

Lambton, William Henry MP (1764–97) 8, 9, 40–1, 47, 137

Lansdowne, 1st Marquess, *see* Shelburne

Lansdowne, 2nd Marquess, *see* Petty

Lauderdale, James Maitland, 8th Earl of (1759–1839) 40–1, 58, 67, 84, 85, 101, 113, 130, 151, 160, 167, 182, 183, 201

Laurence, French MP (1757–1809) 69–70, 80, 94

Lawrence, Sir Thomas RA (1769–1830) 150, 200

Leeds 62

Leeds, Francis Osborne, 5th Duke of (1751–99) 33, 35

Leicester 40

Leinster, Augustus Frederick Fitzgerald, 3rd Duke of (1791–1874) 231

Leopold of Saxe-Coburg, King of the Belgians (1790–1865) 226, 281, 283

Leveson-Gower, Elizabeth, Countess of Stafford and Countess of Sutherland (1765–1839) 130

Leveson-Gower, Lord Granville, 1st Earl Granville (1773–1846) 127, 317

Lieven, Dorothea Christopherovna Benckendorf, Princess (1785–1857) 147–8, 248, 252–3, 254, 259, 261, 266, 281–2, 284–5, 309, 314

Lieven, Prince Christopher (1772–1839) 281

Lindsay, Lady Charlotte (1771–1849) 223

Littleton, Edward John, 1st Baron Hatherton (1791–1863) 302, 305, 316–17, 326

Liverpool, Earl of, *see* Jenkinson

London Corresponding Society 59, 63–4, 67

Losh, James, of Newcastle (1763–1833) 41, 150, 210, 213, 227

Loughborough, Alexander Wedderburn, Baron, 1st Earl of Rosslyn (1733–1805) 25, 54

Louis XVI, King of France (1754–93) 54

Louis XVIII, King of France (1755–1824) 177

Louis Philippe, King of France (1773–1850) 287
Luddism 208
Lyndhurst, John Singleton Copley, 1st Baron (1772–1863) 260, 276–7
Lyndhurst, Sarah, Lady (1795–1834) 260
Lyttelton, William Henry, 3rd Baron (1782–1837) 127

Mackintosh, Sir James MP (1764–1832) 41, 228
MacMahon, Sir John, Col., secretary to the Prince Regent (c.1754–1817) 110, 191, 194
Madocks, William Alexander MP (1773–1828) 182
Majocci, servant to Princess Caroline 232
Malmesbury, Sir James Harris, 1st Earl of (1746–1820) 54
Manchester 62
  Constitutional Society 45
Maria, Donna, Queen of Portugal (1819–53) 287
Maynooth, Irish Catholic seminary 296
Massena, André, Marshal of France (1758–1817) 173
Mehemet Ali, Pasha of Egypt (1769–1849) 286
Melbourne, William Lamb, 2nd Viscount (1779–1848) 135, 224, 249, 257, 260, 263, 269, 287, 290, 294, 299, 300, 302, 308–10, 311–12, 314–21
Melville, Lord, *see* Dundas
Metternich, Prince (1773–1858) 279, 288
Middlesex 72, 102, 181, 183, 218–19, 250
Middleton, Sir Charles, 1st Baron Barham (1726–1813) 96
Miguel, Dom, King of Portugal (1802–66) 287–8
Milner, Dr John, Bishop of Castabala (1752–1826) 157–8
Milton, Charles William Fitzwilliam, Viscount, 3rd Earl Fitzwilliam (1786–1857) 166, 181, 188, 196, 213, 219, 239, 256
Miranda, Francisco, Gen (c.1754–1816) 114
Moira, Francis Rawdon Hastings, 2nd Earl of, 1st Marquess of Hastings (1754–1826) 69, 79, 80, 86, 89, 92, 98, 115, 116, 124, 162–3, 191, 192–3, 196–7, 202–4
Monck, Sir Charles Miles Lambert (1779–1867) 141
Moore, Sir John, Lt.-Gen. (1761–1809) 169–71
Morpeth 42, 130, 235, 238
'Mountain', the 153, 181–2, 188, 206

Napier, Sir Charles, Admiral (1786–1860) 287
Napoleon, *see* Bonaparte
Navarino battle of 253
Nemours, Louis Charles Philippe, duc de (1814–96) 287
Newcastle, Henry Pelham Fiennes Pelham Clinton, 4th Duke of (1785–1851) 255, 262

Newcastle upon Tyne 42, 64, 210, 213, 216, 311, 325
Nootka Sound 30–2
Normanby, Constantine Henry Phipps, Marquess of (1797–1863) 320
North, Frederick, Lord, 2nd Earl of Guilford (1732–92) 10, 24, 39, 87, 91
Northumberland 7, 29, 42, 64–5, 71–2, 83, 95, 210, 218, 221, 235
  parliamentary elections in 9–10, 65, 105, 129–30, 140–2, 240
Northumberland, Sir Hugh Percy, 2nd Duke of (1742–1817) 7, 64–5, 69, 95, 97, 102, 105, 110, 116, 129–30, 141, 194
Norwich 40, 42
Nottingham 40, 269

Ochakov 30, 32–5
O'Connell, Daniel (1775–1847) 159, 250, 289–92, 295, 300, 303, 305, 309, 311–18, 322
O'Ferrall, Richard More MP (1797–1880) 303
Orange, William, Hereditary Prince of (1772–1843) 223–6
Ord, Elizabeth 8
Orders in Council 168, 173, 200
Otto, King of Greece (1815–67) 286
Oxford University 127, 161, 164

Paine, Thomas, radical journalist (1737–1809) 40, 44, 45, 56, 63
Palmella, Pedro de Souza, Duke of 283
Palmer, Revd Thomas Fysshe, reformer (1747–1802) 57
Palmerston, Henry John Temple, 3rd Viscount (1784–1865) 145, 249, 257, 260, 262, 269, 270, 279–88, 316, 317
Parliamentary reform 2–3, 10–11, 22, 24, 36–51, 53, 55, 61–2, 68, 71–2, 74–5, 78, 128–9, 179, 209–12, 215–21, 234, 236–9, 245, 252, 254, 256, 257, 259, 262, 306, 310–11
  see also Reform Bills
Pasley, Sir Charles William (1780–1861) 173
Payne, John Willett, friend of the Prince of Wales (c.1752–1803) 25
Pedro, Dom, King of Portugal (1798–1834) 283, 287
Peel, Sir Robert, 2nd Bart (1788–1850) 50, 203, 241, 247, 248, 249, 250, 260, 277, 278, 289, 305, 308, 313–15, 320–1, 327
Pelham, Thomas MP, 3rd Baron Pelham, 2nd Earl of Chichester (1756–1826) 44
Peninsular campaigns (1808–14) 169, 170–2, 173–4
Penryn, Cornwall 249
'Pentridge rising' (1817) 208

Perceval, Spencer, Prime Minister (1762–1812) 116, 121, 126, 129, 154, 156, 160–1, 172, 190, 194–6, 198, 201, 222

Percy, Hugh, Lord, 3rd Duke of Northumberland (1785–1847) 129–30, 249

'Peterloo' (1819) 217–19

Petty, Lord Henry, 3rd Marquess of Lansdowne (1780–1863) 100, 124, 168, 181, 183, 185, 192, 194, 220, 229, 238, 240–3, 245, 247, 260, 264, 269, 270, 280, 296, 300, 302, 315–16, 324

Piggott, Sir Arthur Leary MP (1749–1819) 170, 182

Pitt, William, Prime Minister (1759–1806) 9, 10, 15, 16, 19–20, 24, 27–8, 31–4, 36, 38, 41, 43, 47–8, 49, 50–62, 64, 66, 71–2, 77–8, 79, 88–100, 102, 111, 117, 118, 126, 131, 175, 188, 190–1, 212

Pittites (after 1806) 104, 107, 108–9

Place, Francis (1771–1854) 189, 216

Political Unions (1830–2) 256, 269, 306

Ponsonby, George MP (1755–1817) 90, 108, 120, 121, 124, 125, 126, 127, 128, 151–4, 158, 163–4, 167, 170–1, 181, 184–5, 188, 206, 214

Ponsonby, Sir John, 2nd Baron, 1st Viscount (c.1770–1855) 121, 159, 286, 318

Ponsonby, Louisa, later Countess Fitzwilliam (1749–1824) 72

Popham, Sir Home Riggs, Admiral (1760–1820) 113–14

Porchester, Henry George Herbert, Viscount, 2nd Earl of Carnarvon (1772–1833) 172

Porchester, Henry Herbert, Viscount, 1st Earl of Carnarvon (1741–1811) 40

Portland, William Henry Cavendish-Bentinck, 3rd Duke of (1738–1809) 25, 37–9, 52, 54–5, 64, 80, 109, 125, 126, 129, 156, 172, 242

Powys, Thomas MP, 1st Baron Lilford (1743–1800) 49–50

Priestley, Dr Joseph, nonconformist divine, scientist, and reformer (1733–1804) 39

Pulteney, Sir William MP (1729–1805) 69

Radnor, Earl of, *see* Folkestone

Reform Act (1832) 3, 36, 50, 256, 263–79, 285, 290–1, 309, 316, 321–2, 325, 327–8

Regency (1810–20) 173, 188, 190–204
  crisis (1788–9) 18, 23–9, 37, 38, 85, 201

Richmond, Charles Gordon Lennox, 5th Duke of (1791–1860) 260, 270, 287, 296, 298, 304

Rockingham, Charles Watson Wentworth, 2nd Marquess of (1730–82) 9, 39, 87, 201

Rogers, Samuel, poet (1763–1855) 138

Rolle, John MP, Baron Rolle (1756–1842) 29

Romilly, Sir Samuel (1757–1818) 105, 148, 180, 182, 204, 215–16, 227

Rosebery, Archibald John Primrose, 4th Earl of (1783–1868) 2

Rosslyn, Sir James Erskine, 2nd Earl of (1762–1837) 130, 154, 205, 226, 248, 252, 254

Russell, Lord John, 1st Earl Russell (1792–1878) 68, 137, 187, 216, 221, 239, 245, 247, 249, 256, 263–4, 291, 296–8, 303–4, 310–12, 314, 315, 317, 318–21

Ryan, James, Irish Catholic leader 118

St Vincent, Earl of, *see* Jervis

Salamanca, battle of 174

San Domingo 117

Scott, Sir Walter, novelist (1771–1832) 138–9

Sefton, William Philip Molyneux, 2nd Earl of (1772–1838) 325

Seymour, Lord Henry (1746–1830) 96

Sheffield 40, 62
  Constitutional Society 45, 47

Sheil, Richard Lalor MP (1791–1851) 303

Shelburne, William Petty, 2nd Earl of, 1st Marquess of Lansdowne (1737–1805) 9, 20, 43, 67, 87, 91

Sheridan, Esther Jane (Ogle) Mrs (c.1771–1817) 145, 146–7

Sheridan, Richard Brinsley (1751–1816) 10, 12, 15, 19, 22, 25–30, 37–8, 40–1, 45, 47, 50, 55, 58, 59, 60, 67, 69, 76, 80, 88–9, 92, 106, 109, 110, 169, 191, 193–5, 229

Sidmouth, Viscount, *see* Addington

Sinclair, Sir John, 1st Bart MP (1754–1834) 69

Slavery, abolition of (1833) 301–2, 306, 328

Slave trade, abolition of (1807) 61, 116–17

Smith, William MP (1756–1835) 63, 110

Society for Constitutional Information 40, 41, 44–5, 59, 63, 186

South America 112, 113–15, 128, 240, 244, 246

Southwark 64, 70

Spa Fields riots 208

Spence, Thomas, radical (1750–1814) 189, 212

Spencer, George John Spencer, 2nd Earl (1758–1834) 98, 100, 102, 107, 108, 119, 124–5, 311, 317

Spencer, Henrietta Frances ('Harriet'), Viscountess Duncannon, Countess of Bessborough, Georgiana's sister (1761–1821) 12–14, 91, 96, 99, 146–7

Spencer, 3rd Earl, *see* Althorp

Spenser, Edmund, poet (1552–99) 139

Spring Rice, Thomas, 3rd Baron Monteagle (1790–1866) 316, 319–20

Stanley, Edward George Geoffrey Smith, 14th Earl of Derby (1790–1869) 270, 276, 287, 288, 290–305, 307, 314–18

Strachan, Sir Richard John, Admiral (1760–1828) 172

Sussex, Augustus Frederick, Duke of (1773–1843) 226

Swinburne, Sir John Edward of Capheaton, Northumberland (1762–1860) 41, 65, 95, 141, 210

Talents, Ministry of All the (1806–7)
formation of 100–1
attitude to reform 102–3, 181
internal relationships 103–4, 109
measures on defence 104–5
reconstruction, (1806) 106–11
foreign policy 111–15
and Irish Catholic question 118–27
collapse of 124–6, 156
Talleyrand de Périgord, Charles Maurice (1754–1838) 279, 282–3
'Tamworth manifesto' (1834) 278, 314
Tankerville, Charles Bennet, 4th Earl of (1743–1822) 19
Tavistock 130, 131 n., 151
Taylor, Sir Herbert, private secretary to King William IV (1775–1839) 264–5, 267, 268, 272, 275–7
Thanet, Sackville Tufton, 9th Earl of (1769–1825) 130–1
Thelwall, John, lecturer and reformer (1764–1834) 58
Thomson, Henry RA (1773–1843) 149, 150
Thurlow, Edward, 1st Baron, Lord Chancellor (1731–1806) 25, 89
Tierney, George MP (1761–1830) 41, 45–7, 64, 67, 70, 78–81, 101, 103, 127, 151, 152, 154, 157, 159, 161, 163–5, 170, 182, 188, 204–7, 211, 214–15, 218, 229, 236, 238, 241, 243, 247
Times, The 310
Tooke, Revd John Horne, reformer (1736–1812) 58, 63–4
Torquay 240
Treaties and alliances (in chronological order)
French commercial treaty (1786) 17, 30
Triple alliance (1787) 33
Convention of Madrid (1790) 31–2
Tilsit (1807) 168
Convention of Cintra (1808) 169
Swedish (1813) 176
Paris (1814) 177–8
Holy Alliance (1815) 280
Vienna (1815) 178–9, 283
London (1827) 253
Convention of London (1833) 283
Unkiar Skelessi (1833) 286
Quadruple Alliance (1834) 280, 287–8
London (1838) 283
Turner, Joseph Mallord William RA (1775–1851) 150

Turton, Sir Thomas MP (1764–1844) 168

United States of America, relations with (1806–7) 112–13

Verona 9
Vesey-Fitzgerald, William, Baron Fitzgerald and Vesey (1783–1843) 250
Victoria, Queen (1819–1901) 137, 203, 319–20

Waithman, Robert, Alderman of London (1764–1833) 183–6, 188
Walcheren expedition (1809) 172, 185
Ward, Sir Henry George MP (1797–1860) 304
Ward, John William, 1st Earl of Dudley (1781–1833) 110, 172, 184, 201
Wardle, Gwyllm Lloyd MP (c.1762–1833) 182–4, 186
Waterloo, battle of 178
'Waverers', the 269, 276
Wellesley, Richard Colley, 2nd Earl of Mornington, 1st Marquess Wellesley (1760–1842) 8, 50, 98, 162–4, 196, 198, 201–3, 206, 212, 220, 238, 240, 305
Wellesley, Sir Arthur Wellesley, 1st Duke of (1769–1852) 16, 111, 144, 149, 171–4, 176, 209, 240, 241, 245, 247–8, 249–53, 254–8, 275–7, 279–80, 281, 285, 287, 288, 300, 305, 311, 312–13, 321
Westminster 39, 47, 64, 86, 189, 211, 218, 228
Association (1780) 39
Committee (1807) 216–17
Westmorland, county 218
Westmorland, John Fane, 10th Earl of (1759–1841) 248
Wharncliffe, James Archibald Stuart Wortley, 1st Earl (1776–1845) 202, 269, 270, 272, 274–6
Whig Club 46, 55, 56, 63, 65, 80, 182
Whig party
and reform 10–11, 38–42, 51, 64, 67, 87–8, 179–89, 209–12, 221, 237–9, 245, 254, 256, 260; *see also* Acts and Bills, Reform Bills
and French Revolution 36, 39–41, 44, 46–7, 51, 179
coalition with Pitt (1792–4) 52, 54–8
and French wars (1793–1815) 54–7, 60, 64, 88, 97–9, 111–15, 165–79
secession (1797–1801) 66–78
opposition to Addington (1801–4) 83, 87–93
alliance with Grenvilles 87–93, 97–9, 100–3, 109, 129, 166, 173, 179, 190, 209, 211–13
Foxites after 1806 106, 108–10, 112–13, 115, 127, 151, 155, 156, 166, 169–70, 183, 204, 238, 280
and Catholic question 156–62, 165
coalition with Canning (1827) 241–7, 252

Whig party (*cont.*):
  and Corn Laws (1815) 207–8
  foreign policy 279–80
Whitbread, Samuel MP (*c.*1764–1815) 8, 9, 40–
  1, 47, 50, 58, 70, 80, 81, 87, 90, 92, 93, 94,
  96, 100, 101, 102, 103, 108, 111, 151, 152–5,
  159, 166–70, 180–6, 188–9, 194–5, 204, 205–
  6, 222, 229
Wilberforce, William MP (1759–1833) 21, 60, 94,
  116–17
Wilkes, John MP (1727–97) 250
William IV, King (1765–1837) 237, 249, 255, 258,
  261, 262, 263, 264–79, 284–5, 287, 299, 303,
  305, 308, 312, 315–16, 325
Wilson, Sir Robert Thomas Gen (1777–1849)
  171, 173–4, 216, 234
Winchelsea 142
Windham, William MP (1750–1810) 41, 49–50,
  55, 88, 94, 96, 97, 99, 100, 104, 105, 107–8,
  113, 114, 115, 117, 123, 124, 151, 162, 166–
  7

Wood, Charles, 1st Viscount Halifax (1800–85)
  137, 266, 278, 313, 324
Wooler, Northumberland 144
Wooler, Thomas, journalist (1786–1853) 208,
  218
Woronzov, Count Simeon Romanovitch, Russian
  ambassador (1744–1832) 33
Wyvill, Revd Christopher, reformer (1740–1822)
  39, 62, 71, 77, 80, 91–2, 95, 102, 210, 218

Yarmouth, Francis Charles Seymour-Conway,
  Earl of, 3rd Marquess of Hertford (1777–
  1842) 127, 196
York, Archbishop of 200
York, Frederick Augustus, Duke of York and
  Albany (1763–1827) 63, 98, 173, 182, 196,
  199, 202, 208
Yorkshire 71–2, 77, 166, 210, 218–19, 235, 256
  Association for parliamentary reform (1779) 39,
  62